'Loyalty in me Lieth'

King Richard III and Francis Viscount Lovel

A Book by Richard Mark Hogg

Published by New Generation Publishing in 2013

Copyright © Richard Mark Hogg 2013

First Edition

www.newgeneration-publishing.com

New Generation **Publishing**

Dedicated to my darling wife Karen for all of her support over the years and to my mother Jean for all of her help in proof reading and checking my various texts and finally to the much maligned King Richard III, a medieval man who has had the misfortune to have been judged by 21st Century standards!

A note from the Author

Loyalty in me lieth (the motto of King Richard III) tells of the life and times of Francis Viscount Lovel, a lifelong friend and supporter of Richard throughout the Wars of the Roses and the various trials and tribulations of firstly being the foremost magnate of the realm and later through the burden of Kingship.

Throughout my life I have had a love of and fascination with all aspects of History and as such have read many books. Unfortunately it seems to me, that to date one has had only one choice, to read the factually correct academic books that I find somewhat 'stuffy' and 'hard going', or those Historical novels many of which are 'fanciful'and have limited factual basis and tell of 'Love' in an age when 'Love' was probably one of mans most unused emotions! (I apologise unreservebly to any authors out there whom I might have insulted or upset by my observations).

This Book is my attempt to bridge the gap between the aforementioned History Book and the Historical Novel. Yes, in the absence of proof positive I have had to make certain assumptons about what may or may not have happened, but I have done this with reference to all of the available evidence and as such I stand by them and am prepared to argue that they are valid interpretions of the events. Thus my book is in essence a History Book written in a novel style and as such I hope that it will bring to a larger readership the 'true' history of the times, often 'violent'and where the majority of men went about their business with a ruthlessness, which in the 21st Century is hard to either appreciate or to undestand.

And don't think for one minute that the History is not still out there for all to see! Each Chapter of this book is based at certain locations all over England. Yes, at the majority one doesn't find the excellent visitor facilities that one finds at say the site of the Battle of Bosworth (albeit that the location of the visitor centre no longer corresponds to where the battle actualy took place, Whoops!). But that said the lay of the land is very much as it was in the fifteenth century, the church where Francis Lovel was married still stands and Foulney Island where Francis's invasion fleet landed in the summer of 1487, is just as windswept and desolate now as it was then. Indeed imagine my suprise when I drove into Ravensworth, the village where Franics's wifes family lived, to be confronted by the ruin of a medieval castle, stuck in the middle of a farmer's field, that wasn't on any of the maps that I had! I strongly recommend anyone who has read this book to visit those sites, as I have done so on many occasions, and trust me with a little imagination you like me will be able to bring those events back to life. To see in your minds eye the battles, the pagaents the tournaments and the executions. To meet Francis as he was then, the lifelong supporter of Richard III, one who in contrast to so many other men 'of his age' loyally dedicated his life to another and after his friend Richard's death at Bosworth raised rebellion in the name of the House of York.

And finally before I bore you anymore, may I suggest a short walking holiday. To trace the route that Francis's small and inexperienced invasion force took once it had landed at Foulney Island on the banks of Morecombe bay, as far as Middleham where the army mustered and Francis and his colleagues finally realised that they had not gathered together anywhere near the number of troops required to defeat Henry VII. And as you go say a short prayer for Francis, very much a forgotten hero of the fifteenth century, one whose personal characteristics were so very different to his contempories.

Prelude
June 16th 1487. Stoke Field.

To the sound of pipe and drum the Rebel army finally began its advance towards the Royalist troops that were drawn up in Battle order at the base of Burham Furlong, the hill on which the rebels had gathered. Sadly, Henry Tudor's army seemed to Francis, Viscount Lovel, both limitless and invincible. As the various denominations within the rebel ranks gathered speed the orderliness of the advance slowly gave way to a headlong dash towards the mass of armed men that was the Royalist vanguard. The sounds of the 'cosmopolitan' rebel armies continental pipes and drums were soon replaced by the battle cries of the various components of the rebel host and the screams of those on both sides of the engagement, who were unfortunate enough to have been cut down whilst the battle was still in its infancy.

Francis who'd experienced many misgivings since the beginning of their present campaign, his disquiet increasing with each new disappointment, seemed in an instant to lose all of his nerves as the recklessness of his comrades impacted on his own consciousness.

The rebel army struck the Lancastrian battle line with such ferocity, that the opposition at once reeled backwards. Francis himself, deafened by the din and pressed in from each side, was not even able to exchange any blows with his first victim, a longbow man who bore the blue boar device of John De Vere, the Earl of Oxford and the commander of the Royalist van. The unfortunate man lost his footing on the uneven ground and on the incline that favoured the Rebels attack and, as a consequence, fell to his death, trodden beneath the weight of Francis and the advancing Yorkist infantry.

Unfortunately it now appeared as if the Earl of Oxford had chosen not to join their rebellion as expected, nor had he given any indication that he may do so at some point during the battle itself. As a result, both Francis and his fellow commanders had reluctantly conceded that without Oxford's assistance, and as a result of the difficulties that their men had experienced in protecting themselves against the English archers, they would have to take their destiny into their own hands. Thus, in an effort to force the issue, they had finally decided to sacrifice the advantage of the high ground and engage the enemy. Success was now solely dependant on the outcome of this daring yet dangerous assault.

Despite putting some 10,000 men into the field, the Rebel Yorkist army, which was intent on a Plantagenet restoration, was outnumbered by the 'Lancastrian' army of King Henry Tudor, by some three to one. Moreover, much of the ranks of the Yorkist army were comprised of ill equipped and inexperienced Gaelic Irish tribesman. The better equipped and more experienced English men at arms and German and Flemish mercenaries, being very much in the minority.

Francis, as always, had hoped that intrigue would obviate the need for arms. He had trusted that both his personal visit to Oxford's camp on the eve of battle and the persuasiveness of his cousin Thomas Lovel, who was the head of the Earl's household, would secure the Earl's support for their cause. This now seemed little more than fruitless fancy and De Vere had seemingly given his reply, when his archers had inflicted the Yorkist army to a withering fire that had wrought devastation within its ranks, especially amongst the poorly armoured Irish. Despite the fact that the Rebel army had many of its own archers and its continental mercenaries possessed the very latest firearms, the Yorkists had comprehensively lost these early exchanges. Thus, despite the fact that they'd chosen the battle site well and had initially planned to remain atop the hill on which they'd been drawn up, the Yorkist commanders, concerned that their men would buckle under this onslaught, had had no alternative but to order the attack. Unfortunately, although none said so, all knew that this manoeuvre would not only relinquish the advantage of the high ground, but would also bring their entire army down into the Trent flood plain and the meadows that surrounded the old Roman Road, the Fosse Way. This was flat and open land, where Tudor would be able to deploy the entirety of his larger army to the greatest effect. Francis knew that unless they were able to secure a speedy victory, their men would soon become prey to the Lancastrians, who would now be in a position to capitalise on their numerical superiority.

Prior to the commencement of the Battle, the Yorkists had amassed together on the summit of Burham Furlong. This escarpment, which stood to the East of Newark and the small village of Stoke, was high above the River Trent and the Fosse Way, both of which bisected the east midlands countryside from West to East. As such the Furlong was ideal for their purposes. It's plateau was just large enough to enable them to deploy all of their available troops in a single wedge shaped phalanx. Moreover its steep sides offered their army protection, in the event that the Lancastrians attempted to outflank them either to the East or to the West. This phalanx formation, very much continental in design, was deigned to be the only disposition that would offer both shelter and support to each contingent of their army in the forthcoming battle. Unfortunately, Martin Schwartz the captain of the German and Flemish mercenaries and the main exponent of this plan, had had only limited experience of the English Longbow in the field. Earlier the German had haughtily dismissed the Longbow as both 'outmoded' and 'inferior', when compared to his own men's firearms and crossbows. Francis had however remained unconvinced by Schwartz, who bragged that the English archers would be no match for his own men. In contrast to Schwartz, Francis who'd witnessed first hand just how destructive the longbow could be, had argued against the phalanx idea. He believed that such a formation would present the English archers with a perfect target. Sadly as Francis had gloomily predicted, Schwartz's weapons, despite their technological superiority, had turned out to be no match for the Longbow. Neither their crossbows nor the side arms had either the range, nor the rate of fire that was achieved by the English archers. Indeed, as if to add insult to injury, during the early exchanges, the firearms had probably caused more injuries amongst their own troops than the enemies as, with the gunpowder still wet from when they'd forded the River on the previous afternoon, they misfired and exploded into the faces of those who attempted to discharge them. As the Yorkist cross bowmen and the German gunners had fumbled with their own weapons, Oxford's longbow men had stepped forward and had fired a number of volleys, their arrows sent high into the sky, had arched above the Rebel phalanx and turning back towards the earth had rained down upon their men. Indeed it seemed as if each and every arrow had found an easy target, amongst the mass of men who had stood in open ground upon the apex of the hill.

Neither Francis nor his friend and fellow commander John De La Pole, the Earl of Lincoln, had previously had much experience in the marshalling of an entire army, especially one of these proportions. As they'd witnessed first hand the devastation that was wrought within their ranks during these early exchanges, they'd been dumfounded and had been stunned into inactivity. Dismayed, all Francis had been able to do was to watch in silence, as all of his earlier anxieties had materialised and their soldiers had been exposed to a maelstrom, which had all but decimated their army. Even now, in the din of Battle, Francis was able to picture in his minds eye how they'd all stood transfixed, observing the progress of the steel tipped projectiles, as they'd whistled through the still and quiet air. This exchange, the precursor to the commencement of hostilities, had also heralded a strange silence, that had separated the noise generated by those insults and abuse, which were exchanged between the opposing sides before the battle began and the bedlam that followed it, once the arrows had finally found there mark. Still ringing in Francis's ears were the sickening screams of the stricken men who, clutching at the bloodied shafts of willow that protruded from their bodies, had collapsed onto the turf to endure the inevitability of a slow and lingering death. The Crossbow men within the Rebel army had returned fire and a number of their bolts had reached those in the very front ranks of the Royalist battle line. Unfortunately their volley had had only a limited effect and the Lancastrian's slow yet deliberate advance towards the base of Burham Furlong, had merely been checked momentarily. It was perhaps macabre, but Francis never failed to be amazed to see how even that expensive and intricately worked plate armour which was worn by the better equipped amongst their troops, was no defence against the tempered steel of the bowmen's bolts and the archers arrows. Despite the armour, the missiles slid effortlessly through both breastplates and helmet to find their mark. Disappointingly, the Royalist advance had soon recommenced as those smitten were soon replaced by men from the rear of the vanguard who, keen to be involved in the battle at the earliest juncture, had earlier failed to secure a place within the forefront of the Lancastrian army. As Oxford's men had neared the base of the furlong, his archers had continued their ferocious and torturous rate of fire. Eventually, both Francis and his colleagues, knowing that their men could stand no more and conceding that their archers were no match for their counterparts in the Lancastrian army, had reluctantly ordered the advance.

The Yorkist army, angered and wounded by the Lancastrian archers, had taken no time at all to cover the short distance that had remained between the two battle lines. As the Rebels reached Oxford's men, the speed and ferocity of their advance had stunned the Lancastrian's, whose battle lines immediately buckled and gave way. Within seconds Francis had sufficient room to wield his mace.

Seizing the initiative both Francis and his men continued their advance, crushing and smashing at their enemies, as the 'madness' that was battle took control of their psyche. Despite their previous military experience, Oxford's retainers appeared to be no match for the rebels, whose momentum carried them far into the Lancastrian lines. The Scots-Irish gallow-glasses, with their fearful war cries, whooped with delight, as they wielded their double headed axes with remarkable dexterity. The continental mercenaries, well armed and well drilled, went about their task with a steely professionalism, using bill and pike and even, to the horror of the English, their firearms, weapons rarely seen in this theatre of war. Happily, as the two armies had closed upon each other, and had then combined and fought at close quarter, these weapons had come into their own. Even Francis, who'd had previous experience of the guns, was both amazed and horrified as he saw how a loud explosion and cloud of smoke, was immediately followed by one of their enemies head's disappearing in a red mist, or a hole, so large that one could place a man's hand in it, appearing in either a breast plate or a limb! One unfortunate Lancastrian, who'd foolishly chosen to stand firm against an armed mercenary, had had his leg blown clean off!

Both Francis and his companions delighted not only in the success of these new fang led inventions, but also in the fear and panic that these weapons generated amongst the enemy. This, in all honesty, far outweighed their practical usefulness as, once fired, frustratingly the gunners seemed to take an age to reload their weapons.

Even the poorly equipped Irish tribesmen met with success, as they were at long last able to exact their revenge upon the Lancastrian archers. Now, within the ranks of the King's army and no longer exposed to their arrows, they skipped here and there amongst the armoured English, jabbing and stabbing with their daggers and darts. Able now, in close contact and within the confines of the battle itself, to use their own shorter bows which, unlike the Longbows of their English counterparts, were still of use to them. Francis, despite being in the press of his enemies, could clearly see that the Yorkist left and right flanks had, like the centre which was commanded by De La Pole and himself, made significant inroads into the Lancastrian van guard. The banners of the Yorkist leaders fluttered proudly above the carnage that had once been the ordered lines of the Kings army. Francis prickled with pride as he saw his own device, that of the chained wolfhound, raised aloft by his friend Ned who, like his father before him, had accompanied his master the Baron Lovel into battle. Maybe, just maybe, this would be the battle that would finally bring an end to this conflict between the houses of York and Lancaster, a War that had preoccupied Francis's life to date. 'Goodness knows,' Francis felt that he, like so many of his friends and even his enemies, those who'd fought on both sides during this long civil war, was now so weary of this struggle, that all would be glad to see it come to an end. It had, in truth, brought nothing but misery and loss to their countries populace. Now it seemed as if it'd come down to this one last battle, the battle of Stoke Field, their final opportunity to wrest control of the Crown from the Lancastrian usurper, to replace Henry Tudor with a Plantagenet King. In Francis's opinion the only true royal line.

Smiling, Francis wondered how Henry Tudor now felt, as from his vantage point, the King saw his battle lines melting away under the ferocity of the Yorkist's attack. From the 'furlong,' Francis had earlier seen how Tudor had afforded himself, both a safe and excellent view of the forthcoming Battle, by retiring to the tower of the nearby church at Hawton. Francis and his companions had scorned the King for his cowardice, as they'd observed the progress of his standard, the red dragon, as it'd hastily retreated to that location, once the King had addressed his anxious troops prior to the commencement of the battle. Francis wondered what Tudor was thinking as he, just like King Richard before him at Bosworth, had witnessed first hand the destruction of his vanguard. Did Tudor now worry, as Richard had done so before him, if he could count upon the loyalty of both the main 'battle' and the 'rearguard' of his army. Those of limited experience who'd been forced to stand by, watching and waiting for orders, as the cream of their army, Oxford's vanguard had been slaughtered in front of their very eyes! Francis shuddered as he recalled how, not two years since, King Richard had vainly and with increasing desperation, repeatedly requested assurances from his commanders of their continuing support. Francis smiled, for here at 'Stoke Field' it appeared to him as if the boot was securely on the other foot. At Bosworth it'd been the Yorkist's most loyal and experienced commander, John Howard, Duke of Norfolk, who'd failed to carry the day. Now it was the Lancastrian's most senior commander, Oxford, whose men were wilting under the ferocity of their attackers onslaught. Was he to face a fate similar to that of the hapless late Duke of Norfolk? Francis smiled again, for without Oxford, Henry would be forced to rely upon the middle ranks of his army for victory and these consisted predominantly of inexperienced and uncommitted feudal levies and retainers. Men whose allegiance rested solely with their own Lords and not with the King. Stanley's Cheshire men and Percy's Northumbrians. Francis smiled laconically as he considered the irony of it all. It now seemed to him as if Tudor's fate rested with those whose treachery had earlier undone King Richard! Yes, in Hawton Tower, surrounded by his personal body guards, the Beefeaters, Tudor may for the time being be safe. But there, in contrast to Richard at Bosworth, he was in no position to exert any influence over the battle itself. Francis smiled again, Tudor would be forced to stand idly by and observe events as they unfolded before him, hoping, no doubt, that this time in contrast to Richard's at Bosworth, his army would stand firm.

Francis paused briefly as he recalled, with surprising clarity, his own experiences of the Battle of Bosworth. The exhilaration of that final fateful cavalry charge, an assault ordered by Richard that had so nearly brought them victory. Ultimately, and unfortunately however, it had been the intervention of the Stanleys, that had ensured that this manoeuvre, an action that had initially had such a promising and startling effect, had come to nought and had petered out. The Stanley's Cheshire men slaughtering both Richard and his Knights, Richard dying as a King should, *'fighting manfully within the press of his enemies.'* Indeed had Francis's own horse not stumbled and fallen, the stricken horse throwing Francis clear, then he to, like his friend, would now no doubt be mouldering in a roughly hewn unmarked grave in Greyfriars, Leicester. Francis sighed as he considered again, for the umpteenth time, that which might have been, had the King's mount, 'White Surrey,' shown such awkwardness as his own. Maybe in those circumstances it would have been Richard here now and not Francis, God knows, Francis would readily have sacrificed his own life for that of his friend.

Indeed, had Richard, survived that battle then he would, Francis felt, almost certainly have secured more support for their present cause, than had their present figurehead, the recently crowned Edward VI. Yes, Edward was a Plantagenet, a Prince of the Royal blood, the son of Richard's elder brother the late George Duke of Clarence, but could he, a mere lad, be a successful King? Moreover, there were many in England, who believed Tudor's propaganda that would have them believe that the boy was an impostor, a commoner, one Lambert Simnel, a native of Oxford and the son of a carpenter, a youth whom the Lancastrians maintained had been passed off as Prince Edward, by both Francis and his co-conspirators!

Francis was at once brought to his senses, as he encountered a particularly obstinate opponent. Trading blows with his adversary, a Lancastrian knight whose insignia of the white bear was not immediately identifiable to him, Francis was first to yield, as his adversary's poleaxe connected with Francis's right shoulder. The blow crushed both the plate armour and the bone and muscle that lay beneath it and Francis felt a searing pain spread throughout his frame and his now useless right hand dropped the mace, his favoured and his only weapon. Pessimism soon replaced optimism as Francis raised his left arm, to deflect yet another blow that was aimed directly towards his exposed face and was clearly designed to bring about his immediate death. Strangely, all now appeared to Francis as if it was in slow motion and the din of the battle receded, as Francis heard once again the voice of his long dead father, chiding him 'for going into a battle with his visor raised,' the late Baron Lovel dismissing Francis's argument that an open faced helmet was both 'less claustrophobic and afforded its wearer a better all round view.' Fortunately, the angle of Francis's arm and the fact that he'd sunk to one knee and was now well below his assailant, ensured that Francis was able to use his forearm to deflect the blow downwards and in contrast to the Lancastrians's earlier attack, it caused minimal injury.

It was Ned who, like his father before him saved his master's life. Dropping Francis's banner, Ned drew his sword and standing firm and resolute above his friend, he was able to fend off Francis's opponent. After trading a number of token blows with his new adversary, the Lancastrian, no doubt feeling that Ned was more than a match for him, trudged off to find easier pickings, amongst the Yorkist army that seemingly, having lost both its impetus and cohesion, had alarmingly begun to disintegrate.

Fatigue now enveloped Francis who, with Ned's help, reluctantly retired to the rear. With increasing alarm Francis noticed that, unlike many of the other battles in which he'd taken part, where there had always been a ready supply of eager comrades to take his place in the battle line, here at Stoke field none seemed either available or willing to replace him. Indeed, as both pain and exhaustion cleared from Francis's mind the last vestiges of the rage of battle, he noticed that, on all sides, their army was being forced back, up the hill from whence they'd come. Francis could no longer hear the jubilant battle cries of his comrades, for these had been replaced by the cries of both the dying and the demoralised.

As Francis made his way back towards the top of Burham furlong, he hoped that once back on high ground and in a position to survey the whole of the battlefield, he'd be able to ascertain what troops they still held in reserve. Their charge had so very nearly won the day. If they were able to reassemble and reinforce the phalanx and this time concentrate their attack on the main body of the Royalist army, they might still just carry the day.

Chapter 1
Minster Lovel Oxfordshire. September 1708.

1737: Letter from one William Cowper, clerk to Francis Peck esquire.

"In 1708 upon the occasion of laying a chimney at Minster Lovel, there was discovered a large vault or room underground, in which was the entire skeleton of a man, as having been sitting at a table, which was before him, with a book, paper, pen etc. etc., in another part of the room lay a cap; all much mouldered and decayed.... Which the family and others judged to be this Lord Lovel, whose exit has hitherto been so uncertain."

Robert Parker awoke late. The sun, which by that time was high in the sky, was streaming through the open window of the gamekeeper's cottage where he lived alone. As soon as Robert got out of bed and pulled on his waistcoat and breeches, he began to regret the celebrations of the previous evening. He'd had ale enough when Will Preston, the landlord of the Swan Inn, had brought out the rhubarb wine that he served free of charge each year to celebrate the harvest. The wine had completed Robert's intoxication. Even now he could taste it in his dry mouth, although it was now quite stale and no longer as sweet as it had been just a few hours earlier. Robert's head throbbed and he could hear his mothers protestations about how he was drinking himself into an early grave, just as his father had done so before him. Despite his discomfort Robert smiled to himself, living alone did have its advantages.

Master Robert Parker had fared well these past six months since he'd accepted the post of "Woodward, Wallreeve and Gamekeeper" and the cottage that came with it, from Mister Wheeler, who managed the Minster Lovel estate on behalf of its absentee owner, Sir Thomas Coke. Despite his hangover, Robert smiled to himself once again as, exiting his small bedroom and bidding farewell to his unusually empty bed, he considered that being able to get drunk whenever it took his fancy was not the only advantage of a good looking single man living alone!

That morning, on his way to the front door, Robert bypassed the kitchen. A breakfast of cheese and bread seemed even less palatable today than usual and anyway, he'd got much to do. He was late and should have been up at the hall some two hours earlier. Even Robert, who by nature was usually quite optimistic, seriously doubted that his master, the 'easy going' Mister Wheeler, would appreciate the excuse of a hangover and the associated lack of sleep, for his failing to keep their appointment.

Minster Lovel Hall was to be made ready for Sir Thomas, who was to spend the winter there with his new bride, and although it was still only September, the new chimney in the south tower had to be laid to allow the new rooms to be plastered and decorated in time for their arrival. Indeed, Sir Thomas himself was due at the hall later that day to inspect the progress of the work and, although a gamekeeper was his usual trade, today Robert was to be employed as a labourer. That is, of course, if he managed to keep his job!

Still feeling drunk and half asleep, Robert stumbled out of his door and onto the village main street. In contrast to Robert, the village of Minster Lovel was already wide awake. The Taylor and Buck boys, fishermen by trade, were on the river in their coracles, laying out the pots that would, they hoped, catch some of the River Windrush's plentiful supply of crayfish. Friendly as ever, they greeted Robert with a smile and a nod that obviated the need for any words. Robert's route to the Manor house took him over the medieval packhorse bridge that led from his cottage into the very heart of the village. That morning Robert shared the bridge with a large flock of sheep, who seemed to be making for 'wash meadow,' common land, situated beside the river, that was used by villagers and visitors alike to graze their livestock. The flock's two drovers, on seeing Robert, mumbled something to each other in their native tongue. Judging by their appearance, Robert fancied that the men had probably been on the road for some days. They'd probably have to stay awhile, allowing their hungry sheep to take their fill of the lush grass that the meadow had to offer, before the animals would be fit for sale at the nearby market at Burford. Robert smiled to himself, in the days to come he'd no doubt see quite a bit of these men in the Swan Inn. He chuckled, perhaps the Welshmen would be more convivial when their bellies were full of good old Cotswold ale!

Robert paused for a moment on the bridge to allow the flock to pass. Surveying his surroundings, he took in a deep breath of fresh clean air. As Robert took time to consider the sights, smells and sounds of the village and its environs, he concluded that this land was unequalled in it's beauty. The Welsh, who regularly passed through the village en route to Burford, were always boasting of the magnificence of their mountainous lands, but on this September morning, Robert could imagine no place on earth to rival Minster Lovel. Despite being pressed for time, Robert, who was apt to day dream from time to time, remained on the bridge long after the sheep and their shepherds had exited. Here, he took in the 'glory' of his surroundings. The clear and sparkling waters of the River Windrush that snaked throughout it's green and fertile valley; the surrounding forest of Wychwood, a dense and in places almost impenetrable mass of ancient trees and shrubs that Robert knew well; the village itself with it's buildings of soft yellow sandstone and ordered thatch, the cottages in which they lived and the Mill that cleverly utilised the power of the River to grind their cereals to produce the flour for their bread and the meal for their animals; And finally the church and the Great Hall, buildings that had been built in centuries past by the founders of the village, the Lovels, a family whose power and eminence was exemplified by the magnificence of these structures. It was said that men had lived here since time began and Robert could see the sense in it. The village was, as it had been then, completely enclosed by the forest, which, in addition to affording the village protection, provided both food and building materials for the populace, even down to the dry bracken that was collected as bedding for their animals. The river, whose meandering had first created the clearing in which the village now stood, in addition to supplying a plentiful supply of clean and fresh water, provided both fish and fowl and the reeds that were used in thatching. Gazing eastwards, Robert followed the line of the river that, bordered with high rushes, ran directly by the Hall, this before it finally disappeared once more into the dark forest beyond. Robert could easily appreciate why people described it as the 'winding est' river in all of England. Indeed, despite their relative proximity to the capital, it was said to take a full two weeks for the great barges to float stone down from the nearby quarry at Taynton to London, via the Windrush and the Thames, the river into which it flowed.

Admittedly, Robert had nothing to compare this land to. Never in his short life had he ventured outside the county of Oxfordshire, but he was sure that nothing could rival the rolling countryside, with its sheltered valleys and wooded hills, that was his home.

On that morning, Robert had no inclination to travel further afield although, as he started once again towards the Hall, he thought to himself that perhaps, one day, he may visit London, but as for the Welsh, they could keep their mountains!

On reaching the Mill, Robert turned right to continue on up the 'street' that led in the direction of the Hall. He turned back however as he heard a familiar voice, 'How yer feeling today Rob,' Ralph Allen was standing outside his Mill, grinning.

'I've felt better,' Robert replied truthfully.

'Will we be seeing yer tonight,' Ralph asked eagerly.

'It all depends on how we get on with this new chimney Ralph, the Lords expected later as well, so in truth I couldn't say. I'll be in if I can.' Ralph smiled as Robert, massaging his brow, added wryly,

'I'll be damned if that swine Preston'll get any of his wine into me tonight though, my head's as thick as your bloody millstones.'

Ralph laughed and went back into the Mill shouting after himself, to be heard over the crashing sound of the water that channelled underneath the mill house turned the great wheel, which then turned the millstones to grind the flour.

'I'll see yer if I see yer then.'

As was the case with most of the inhabitants of Minster Lovel, the Allen family had been in these parts for generations and presently Ralph leased the Mill from the Coke family. In fact the Allens had been the village millers ever since Ralph's great grandfather's time. In contrast, Robert's family were relative 'newcomers,' the Parkers having come to the village when Robert's father, a woodsman and charcoal burner, had sought permission from the Cokes to ply his trade in the surrounding forest. This he had done for only six years before his untimely death, some two years earlier. Robert still ached with the grief of it and time had not lessened the sense of loss that he felt, not only in losing his father, but also in losing his best friend and almost constant companion. Robert warmed as he remembered, as a child, those days that he had spent in the forest, watching as his father enthusiastically went about his work. How he would coppice and pollard the trees to ensure regular crops of brushwood, how he'd make the hurdles and gates which he'd then bartered with the villagers for food, or how he'd expertly stacked the wood in such a way to ensure that, when burnt, it would produce the optimum amount of charcoal. Robert recalled the sense of pride that he'd felt if, and when, his father had entrusted him with carrying out this skilled and intricate work on his behalf, or on those occasions when his father had occasionally sought Robert's advice on the maintenance and management of the ancient woodlands. Robert's father had taught him well and this had enabled Robert to gain his current employment, a job that would undoubtedly have gone to his father, had he not finally succumbed to the 'weakness of chest' that had plagued his final years.

Thoughts of work once again roused Robert from his daydream and he set off up the 'street' towards the Hall. The lack of rain that summer meant that the carriageway was thick with dust. As Robert passed and bid 'good day' to young Amy Blake, he chuckled to himself for she appeared most unladylike as she stumbled in the 'patten's' or clogs that she wore, large wooden shoes that were designed to keep her skirts out of the dirt. Robert smiled as he recalled how he'd often admired Amy from afar, most recently at the country fair. Together with the other village girls she'd danced and made merry, as they'd all coyly tried to attract the attentions of those single young men who were there looking for their future wives. Today, in her clogs and work clothes, Amy was not nearly so nimble nor as attractive as Robert remembered her to be!

On passing the bakery Robert, who was beginning to feel a bit better, was enticed in by the smell of freshly baked bread. He turned out his pockets and sighed, he'd spent more than he'd meant to on the previous evening. As a result, lunch that day would now have to consist of 'clangers,' a hard bread made from barley meal, that was a lot cheaper than its wheat counterpart. Clutching his meal, Robert turned right into the lane that led from the main street towards the Hall and the river beyond. On his right, an orchard of apple and pear trees stretched all the way down to the banks of the river. Come late autumn, the Lord would allow the villagers, as was the custom, to pick the ripened fruit that would fill the pies, or would make the wine and cider, that would hopefully cheer the long winter evenings that were coming. To Robert's left was the village common and as he passed it he chuckled as he noticed the old grey horse that, minding its own business, was contentedly grazing in its furthermost corner. If Mister Wheeler saw it there again, there would be trouble. Robert smiled as he remembered how earlier that year, the horses owner, Rob Rushe, had cursed as he'd recounted to the regulars at the Swan how he'd been fined 2s at the 'courts baron' for,

'keeping a mangy horse on the common at Minster Lovel to the great damage of his neighbours.'

As Robert entered the churchyard of St Kenhelm's, a building that was adjacent to the Hall, he crossed himself to ward off *'the evil spirits that possess wicked men and women.'* Sadly, this ritual had no discernible effect upon John Wheeler, who was sitting on the low stone wall that marked the northernmost boundary of Minster Lovel hall and divided it from the church. On seeing Robert walk from the lane and into the churchyard, Wheeler, who was clearly very angry shouted, 'And where might you been, you should have been here some two hours since.'

Robert, who thought it prudent not to offer his poor excuse, merely replied, 'Sorry sir, it'll not happen again.'

Wheeler, who no doubt needed Rob's help that day more than an argument, surprisingly let the matter lie.

'The lads need you over at the South West tower,' he said, as he jumped down from the wall and trotted through the Hall's entrance porch and into its inner courtyard. Robert hurried after him, and breathed a sigh of relief, it appeared as if his job was safe, for the time being at least!

John Wheeler had managed the Minster Lovel estate on behalf of its absentee landlord, Sir Thomas Coke, for the past twenty years. He was now fifty five years old and recently, as had Robert's own father in his declining years, he'd began to show his age. Wheeler's face was heavily wrinkled and had been stained a rusty brown colour by many hot summers and harsh winters. His hair, that until recently had been dark and tousled, was now both grey and thin. As Robert followed his employer, he noticed that Wheeler now walked with quite a protracted limp. The old man, who seemed unable to pick up his feet, stumbled and tripped on the uneven cobbles that adorned the Hall's courtyard. Mr Wheeler had neither a wife nor issue and Robert worried about who would look after things when he was gone, for, despite the odd burst of anger, John Wheeler was a fair and kindly man and Robert could think of none better than him to serve. As they reached the South West Tower, Robert was, however, startled as Mr Wheeler turned to him and exclaimed angrily, that he'd 'best get to work without further delay.'

Robert complied without complaint, now feeling extremely guilty, not only for being late for work, but also for having spent the last few minutes contemplating Mr Wheeler's inevitable demise!

At once, Robert rolled up his sleeves and entered the South West tower. Two of the estates farm hands, the Locke brothers, who'd already begun working, were digging out the foundations of the new chimney place. The South West tower, which overlooked the wall that divided the Hall from the River, was the last part of the Hall to be renovated and it seemed as if it would be the most difficult too! In contrast to the Hall's other rooms, which had all been updated and renovated in the preceding centuries, the Tower had apparently remained unaltered since the late 1400s, a time when the Lovel family had still been masters at the Hall. Sighing, Robert picked up a spade to commence work. Before he began however, he couldn't resist a small jibe, taunting the brothers as he said, 'Come on you two, I thought you'd have finished this little job by now.'

Neither Harry nor Bill Locke were impressed by Robert's attempt at humour and they both looked disdainfully towards him. Harry, the elder of the two and the pairs usual spokesman replied,

'We bloody well would've finished by now, if you'd have been here on time,' 'instead of whoring around again,' his brother Bill added words that seemed, to Robert, to be laced with more than a modicum of jealousy.

Robert was about to protest but thought better of it. They could think what they wanted and anyway, it was better to be thought of as one for the girls, than as one for the drink.

It was Mr Wheeler who interrupted the exchange, as he shouted at them, 'Stop your arguing in there and get on with it, the Lords due at any time and I want those foundations dug out by the time he arrives.'

Both Robert and the Lockes found it extremely hard going. Although it was mid September, the summer had been late that year and Robert was soon down to his breeches, as both he and the day warmed considerably. The sun baked ground was also unusually full of stones. Consequently it was well past midday before they'd managed to dig down just a couple of feet, the minimum depth that would be required for the fireplace's foundations. As Robert was about to call a halt to the proceedings, the spade with which he was digging hit yet another large stone. Unfortunately, unlike the others that they'd encountered, this slab of sandstone that, judging by its markings, was not at all natural, was too large to either undermine or to break up by using their picks alone. All three hurriedly scraped away at it's surface and soon discovered that it was huge, some three paces across in either direction.

'What's to be done now? ' exclaimed Harry. Bill sighed, 'We'll be here well into the bloody night shifting this.'

Robert tried to cheer his companions, 'I'll speak to Mr Wheeler, we may be deep enough as it is,' he said, more in hope than in truth. He too sighed as he gazed into what was quite a paltry hole, the sum total of their exertions that day. Robert sighed again for he knew what Mr Wheeler's reply would be. He left the Locke brothers, hands on their hips, staring quizzically at this unusual stone, which seemed so out of place. Robert, himself fatigued yet keen to be finished, walked briskly up to the main hall where he knew that he'd find Mr Wheeler, who would, no doubt, be fussing over the preparations for the banquet that was to be held that night, in honour of the lord's new bride.

Unfortunately, Mr Wheeler's solution to the problem was very much as Robert had anticipated and, as a result, it was some two hours before the stone was finally moved. A vexed John Wheeler had sent to the village for help. This finally, and ironically, arriving in the shape of Rob Rushe and his mangy horse, whose grazing, at the expense of the other villager's livestock, had been rudely interrupted. It was, therefore, well into the afternoon before the obstacle was finally, and with much effort by both man and beast, removed, to reveal, not as expected solid earth, but an old oak trapdoor. The wood, which was extremely rotten, proved to be far less of an obstacle and with just a modicum of effort, Robert's spade splintered it with ease. Once the door was removed, to the surprise of all present, a number of stone steps were exposed.

John Wheeler, appeared as puzzled as both Robert and the Locke brothers. He exclaimed that his plans of the manor house and its grounds made no mention of any cellar and to position one here, merely ten paces from the river itself, was, he said 'pure folly' and was bound to 'invite regular flooding.'

Robert had one of those brains which seemed to store up all manner of nonsense and useless information. He at once cast his mind back to evenings in the Swan when he'd listened to the ramblings of the older folk, those who told stories of times past, tales that had been passed on from one generation of villagers to another. Of secret passages that led to a host of different destinations. Of the plots and intrigues of the Augustan friars who used to frequent these parts. Of the Lovels, a family who were once masters at the Hall and whose fortunes had fluctuated with various dynasties. These stories had, no doubt, been embellished and bastardised with each new telling. All had been heard, at one time or another, by all of those present and now they served to create an impasse. Each man present looked at the other, none dared to chance the stairs that led to who knew where, or to goodness knew what!

After what seemed like an eternity, but in reality was merely a moment, Wheeler turned to Bill saying 'Get up to the hall, fetch a lantern and be quick about it.'
    Robert, noting the anxiety in his masters voice, wondered if it's cause was the imminent arrival of Sir Thomas, or the prospect of exploring the long forgotten cellar. Sadly his question was answered, when the newly acquired lantern, after being handed to Wheeler, was thrust into Robert's tentative grip. Wheeler's orders were final and Robert was left in no doubt that to protest or debate was futile. 'Check it

out and be quick, Sir Thomas'll be here at any time and he'll be none too pleased if these foundations aren't laid.'

The Locke brothers hurriedly cleared away the last vestiges, of what had once been the cellar door and smiling, stepped back as they made way for Robert. The way was now clear. Robert hesitated as he leaned over the cellar steps, he lowered the lantern into the opening, only to see the steps spiral away, stubbornly refusing to disclose their secrets.

'Go on then,' Wheeler sounded angry. Robert started on the steps, which were surprisingly unworn, in contrast to those other steps that in and around the hall, displayed the signs of centuries of use.

As Robert reached the base of the staircase, he noticed that it had doubled back on itself. It opened out into a large vault, that was positioned directly beneath the Halls inner courtyard. No longer able to hold his breath, Robert gagged, as he was forced to breathe in the chambers stagnant air. He shivered, the place reminded him very much of the crypt underneath St Kenhelm's, which contained the remains of the most prominent amongst the deceased villagers. Those who, for whatever reason, had been deemed worthy of the accolade of being buried within the confines of the church itself. Robert had helped the reverend James to re-render and whitewash the crypts walls in the previous spring. Once the job had been completed he'd vowed never to visit the place again, except possibly 'in Death', he'd said as he'd described the crypt to his friends in the Swan Inn. 'That was,' of course if he was 'deemed' to be 'one of the chosen few'. Robert smiled laconically as he recalled how, at the time, he'd been unimpressed by the fine and intricately carved and decorated monuments and caskets. These receptacles, in his opinion, did nothing to propel their inhabitants more speedily towards paradise and merely ensured that their heirs received less in life in the way of inheritance! Robert truly believed that regardless of what power 'people' wielded in life, or however great were their effigies, the truth was plain to see, in death, they were the same as everyone else, they were merely dead and decaying cadavers.

Robert held out the lantern in front of him, a dim and flickering light slowly filled the four corners of the vault.

Startled, Robert jumped as he saw the remains of what had once been a man. An entire skeleton, with the occasional piece of leathery skin and mouldered clothing stuck to it. The body was half collapsed over the great desk at which it had once sat. As Robert cautiously approached the desk, he trod on something. Picking it up he was surprised to see in the half light, that it was a cap of crushed velvet. The cap's badge, still intact, was of solid silver and depicted a chained dog with a crown for a collar. Robert had seen this crest many times before, for it was carved into the stone above the entry porch of the manor house. It was the coat of arms that belonged to the Lovel family, a family whose origins could be traced far back in history, but whose lineage had apparently been extinguished in medieval times.

Robert examined the vault in more detail, he guessed that the chamber was some twenty paces across in each direction. This would take it underneath the courtyard, but also meant that it extended as far as the river itself. Against the wall that was situated furthest from the river, was a rude wooden bed, on which were the remains of a straw mattress. Next to the bed, Robert could see the rounded shaft of the well, that he recalled was sunk from the centre of the inner courtyard. A small hole in the well's wall meant that, ingeniously, any occupant of the vault would have had a ready supply of fresh water. Towards the other side of the vault, Robert saw an open sewer that, cut into the vaults floor, ran out under the base of the wall, in the direction of the river. The wall around the sewer was starting to show signs of decay caused, no doubt, by water in times of flood backing up and entering the vault rather than leaving it.

Finally, Robert's inquisitiveness got the better of his apprehension and he approached the remains. Even if this man could have caused him hurt once, he could do him no harm now. The skeleton was shrouded in cobwebs, a testament to the fact that not all within this vault was dead. Around the table Robert saw a collection of papers and books, most of which were decaying, due no doubt to the dampness that, despite the dry conditions above ground, seemed to pervade into everything within the chamber. Robert noticed an old quill and a silver ink pot, whose contents had long since dried up. Underneath what had been the man's right hand, was an old leather bound bible. Robert could see that it was of the church of Rome, a faith now despised by the majority of Englishmen. A small strongbox stood on the desk in front of the skeleton and, to Robert's surprise, the key which was still in the lock, turned with ease. Robert opened the box, disappointed to find even more papers, albeit that they'd been saved from the vaults dampness by the sturdy chest.

    The writing contained within the papers was in long hand and, although neat, was in a style of English alien to Robert. Also contained within the box was a letter, again in long hand. Robert gently lifted the letter towards the lantern, so that he could read it more easily. The corners of the parchment crumbled in Roberts hand but, thankfully, the body of the letter remained intact.

Impatient as always, Roberts gaze went initially to the signature at the base of the letter. It was signed, 'Viscount Francis Lovel, constable of Wallingford castle, chamberlain of the Royal household and Chief Butler of England.' Robert had heard of this man before. He remembered how at Sunday school, as they'd all gathered around the effigy of William, the seventh baron Lovel, in St Kenhelm's church, the Rev. James who was a keen historian, had taught the children about the history of their village. Now Robert was confused, according to Bacon's history, a book that was often quoted by the Reverend, Francis, the last of the Lovels, had died in the rout that had taken place after the Yorkist defeat at the battle of East Stoke. This battle, which had been fought over two hundred years earlier in the later part of the fifteenth century, had brought to a conclusion a chapter in the History of England which was now known as 'The Wars of the Roses.' Robert remembered a line in Bacon's 'history' that had regularly been repeated by the Reverand, who'd been keen to instil in the children a fascination for the subject in which he himself was passionate. Robert smiled, it'd obviously worked with him, for he remembered the sentence verbatim.

'There was a report that he (Francis Lovel) fled, and swam over the Trent on horseback but could not recover the other side........and so was drowned.'

Robert was confused, who then was this man whose remains now faced him? Once again he examined both the letter and the manuscript, he guessed that the answer must lay somewhere within and he was determined to discover it. Robert carefully placed the items underneath his shirt and returned to the others, whom he found where he'd left them.

'Well,' both impatient and vexed Wheeler clearly wanted an explanation.

'There's a body down there,' replied Robert, 'I don't know who he is, but he's clearly been dead for some time.'

Wheeler snapped at the Locke brothers, 'Get the lantern and come with me.' As Mr Wheeler reached the first step, he turned to Robert, 'what have you got there,' he said, pointing to the barely concealed papers under Robert's shirt. 'It's just some papers that were down there' Robert replied truthfully, 'I'm taking them to the Reverend.'

Wheeler, who seemed satisfied with Roberts' explanation, turned to go down into the vault, followed closely by the Locke brothers.

Robert hurried up to the Hall and, after questioning various people, he eventually found the Reverend James in the chapel. The old man was busy laying out the altar in preparation for the private service that he was to conduct to celebrate and bless Sir Thomas's recent marriage. Robert smiled as he remembered how the Reverend had earlier proudly declared, that he was to be the first cleric to conduct a religious service at the hall since King Henry VII's visit in 1503. At which time the King's uncle, Jasper Tudor, Duke of Bedford, had been in residence.

Upon seeing the Reverend, Robert could hardly bring himself to speak, he couldn't remember, ever being so excited, 'Reverend'.

Reverend James turned to Robert and smiled. The Reverend was a kindly man, a bachelor who'd devoted his life, both to the service of God and to his study of Medieval History. Unlike many clergy of the time, the Reverend James was a local to his parish, having been born at the nearby village of Little Minster, some sixty five years earlier. The Reverend had no surviving relatives and his only wish in life was to make his mark in the world, not by leaving children, but by leaving his writings. Robert, who'd often thought what a good father the Reverend would have made, had recently spent much of his spare time doing various chores for the Reverend, this as he craved that paternal company, which had been denied him, by the death of his father. Indeed, Robert's mother had recently scolded him and told him not to 'bother' the clergyman, who was 'far too busy to act as a surrogate father to him.' As in most things Robert had chosen to ignore his mother, content in his own mind that the Reverend appreciated both his help and his companionship. Robert had even tried to tackle some of the many books that were held in the Rev. James's vast collection, but he was often chided by the old man for skipping whole chapters at a time, as he searched for the explicit accounts of the various Battles, the only things in the books that really interested him. On more than one occasion, the Reverend had reminded him that there was much more to history than this!

'What is it my son?' The Reverend appeared quite alarmed by Robert's demeanour.

Robert who could not reply, took the papers from underneath his shirt and thrust them towards the old man.

The Reverend James clearly recognised the Lovel family crest on the head of the letter, for he too began to tremble as he took the bundle of papers from Robert and started to read them............

It took the old man some minutes to read the letter that accompanied the manuscript and when he'd finished he turned to Robert. Robert couldn't ever remember seeing the Reverend, who was normally so calm and placid, so excited.

The Reverend stuttered, 'Do you....Do you know what this is?'

Robert apologised, 'The language is foreign to me.'

The Rev. James laughed nervously, 'It's medieval English, I wouldn't expect you to understand it, even I can only translate it with difficulty.' At once he became more serious, 'Who knows about this Robert?'

Robert explained to the Reverend what had happened that day and how he had come to be in possession of the contents of the box. Once Robert had recounted his tale, the Reverend hurried off to tell Mr Wheeler to 'seal up the vault until he'd had time to translate the manuscript.' As the Reverend left a confused and perplexed Robert, he added, 'For the time being, tell no one of this Robert, I think your 'body' is none other than the ninth baron.'

Robert made himself scarce at the hall that evening. He didn't want to be present when Sir Thomas was told that the completion of his new apartments was to be delayed because of an old corpse!

Robert, who was extremely truthful, worried what he would say, in response to any requests that he might receive, for information on the find. He need not have worried, for when he arrived at the Old Swan that night, nigh on all the village was present, stirred up by the stories and rumours, which the Locke brothers had already recounted, to any who were keen to hear and were willing to buy the teller a pint!

Apparently, the vault had been sealed on the orders of Sir Thomas and physicians had been sent for from Oxford, to examine the remains in an effort to identify them.

It was common knowledge that Sir Thomas had been trying to resurrect the title of Baron Lovel for himself. The discovery of the remains of the last in that line, a man who was known to have died without issue, would no doubt jeopardise these claims. Robert had a good idea about what would happen next. The discovery would be fobbed off as some kind of elaborate hoax and Sir Thomas, like most of the rich landed gentry of that time, would invent a genealogy to support his claim to a long dead title. Robert smiled, well at least the manuscript still existed and the Reverend James had promised him that he would be the first to read it, once of course it'd been translated into 'proper' English.

It was almost two weeks before Robert received the invitation that he'd so eagerly awaited. The Reverend James had completed his translation and, as promised, he wanted Robert to be the first to read it. It was then, with a feeling of growing excitement, that Robert made his way up to the Vicarage on the evening of the offer. On passing the Swan, despite a thirst brought on by a hard days toil in the forest and an offer from Ralph Allen, he did not digress from his path, arriving at the vicarage whilst some hours of daylight still remained. Upon being greeted at the door by the Reverend, Robert sensed that the older man was himself once again unusually excited.

'Come in my boy.' Robert accepted the invitation and soon found himself sitting in the Reverend's kitchen, a glass of French brandy in hand, an honour reserved for the Reverend's more familiar guests. Before Robert had managed to drain the contents of his glass, the Reverend had dropped a large manuscript in front of him and was in the process of lighting the large candles by which Robert was to read it. Robert looked up, his eyes met the older man's, who nodded encouragement to him, 'Go on my boy, you found it and you'll be the first to read it.'

Robert again noted that the manuscript began in the form of a letter, although, unusually, this was not addressed to anyone in particular. Prior to reading it, Robert once again scanned down to the signature at its base, it had been signed by a Viscount Lovel and it listed that man's various titles and honours. So this was it, he thought, the translated version of the manuscript, whose advent he had so eagerly awaited. Robert's thoughts were interrupted by the Reverend, 'If you want anything else I'll be in the drawing room,' 'help yourself to the brandy', he added, pointing to the opened bottle on the kitchen table, as he backed out of the kitchen and into the hall, closing the door behind him. Robert was left alone with the manuscript, he poured himself another drink and began to read, the letter began.

'I, Sir Francis Lovel, tell my story in the expectation that it will one day be read by this land's populace. My story is a true account of the history of King Richard and that of the House of York, with whose fortunes mine have been so closely tied and which have caused my life to end in such cheerless circumstances. I tell this story as I have recently met with one Polydore Vergil, late of Urbino and now of

Church Langton, who has been commissioned by Henry Tudor, Earl of Richmond, who now calls himself the sovereign of this land, to write a history of our peoples. In his 'history,' Vergil tells of the heinous crimes committed by Lord Richard and, on his behalf, by myself and others, many of whom are now long dead. He has dismissed my accounts of our actions and has based his stories on the recitals of Richmond's retainers, many of whom took no part in the actions or have given fanciful accounts, to cover up their own treachery or cowardice. For these last few years, I have had time to contemplate the actions of myself and others and I know that, on the day of reckoning, I will have to justify these to God, as have those others who have gone before me. But before I die I want to tell my story, so that the people can decide for themselves, whether or not our cause was 'just.' That what we did was for the benefit of our people, in an effort to bring a long and lasting peace to our troubled nation..

'My story begins and ends here, at my beloved Minster Lovel Hall where, whilst still a child, I received my first lesson in Politics, a lesson that I was to spend my life remembering. My story begins in the year 1461..

Robert turned the page, draining his glass of its contents, he read on and soon found himself beguiled and bewitched, transported into a world that was so very different from his own.

Chapter 2
Minster Lovel Oxfordshire. April 1461.

Sighing, Francis stared once again at the meal that was laid out in front of him. The baked venison, cooked in a pastry called 'coffynes' and served with roast baby pigeons, with it's exotic blend of herbs and spices was, usually, one of Francis's favourite meals, but today Francis had no appetite for it. It wasn't the fact that Francis, keen to keep his mind active, had for the first time ever assisted Ned, his friend the kitchen hand, in collecting and despatching those birds that would be used in the meal, that had made the dish so unappealing. Although the manner of the pigeons demise was, to Francis, less than palatable. The boys collecting the dozen young pigeons, or 'squabs,' from the Dovecote that adjoined the manor house and having carried the unfortunate creatures, still warm, soft and very much alive, into the kitchen they had watched mouths agape, as the birds were slowly bled to death around the venison. Francis, who wasn't normally squeamish, had been both surprised and upset, by the way in which the young pigeons were almost ritualistically slaughtered by the cook. Today, however, whichever dish was presented was of little consequence to Francis, who had no desire to be here, here in this crowded, smoky hall. Francis, whose thoughts were elsewhere, once again studied his meal, prodding the now lifeless bird with his knife. Francis sighed again, for this particular bird had died in vain for the food lay cold and untouched on Francis's platter. At that moment in time Francis ached, not with hunger, but with a need to be back once again, upon the manor houses battlements. A place where he'd spent most of his waking hours these past few days. Time spent desperately scanning the horizon, searching for anything that may give an indication of his father's return from Yorkshire, where the Baron had been campaigning on behalf of their King, Henry VI and his Queen, Margaret of Anjou.

Francis's father was none other than John, the eight Baron Lovel, Lord Holland and master forester of the surrounding Wychwood Forest. As a prominent Lancastrian, John was continuing a family tradition that had begun when his own father William, the seventh baron, had been chief amongst those who had supported the founder of the Lancastrian dynasty, Henry Bollingbroke. Bolingbroke, the eldest son of John of Gaunt, had become King Henry IV after he'd deposed his cousin, King Richard II. Henry had only been successful in wresting the crown from Richard, after he'd managed to secure the support of many from within the aristocracy, who'd tired of Richard's reign. This group of affected nobles had included Francis's grandfather.

Francis, despite his tender years, as with all of the first sons of the nobility, was expected to show a keen interest in the politics of the day. As these politics were inextricably linked to the Civil War that had raged in England for the past nine years, they were to Francis, one who normally shied away from the pursuit of learning, quite palatable and their study served to fire his already vivid imagination. Francis dreamed of the great battles in which he too would one day take part; To fight for his King; To champion his Sovereign's cause; To vanquish any who stood in his way; To seek and earn both fame and glory on the field of battle; To follow in the footsteps of his Lovel ancestors who'd fought on behalf of their King in centuries and decades past. Indeed, Lovels had fought and in some cases died for many Kings, for Edward I in Wales and Scotland. For both Henry IV and his son Henry V in France and most recently for Henry VI in France and latterly even in England itself. It was, however, fair to say that Francis's aspirations had been severely tempered by the news that they'd received from Yorkshire. News that told of the recent shocking reversal in Lancastrian fortunes. A report that had been all the more unexpected when one considered that in recent months, many amongst the Lancastran hierarchy had all confidently predicted that the Civil War was at long last reaching a conclusion. This in favour of the Lancastrians, whose armies had defeated the Yorkists at both the battles of St Albans and Wakefield. Moreover, through these victories the Lancastrians had also been successful in depriving the enemy of much of its leadership, with the battle of Wakefield resulting in the deaths of the then Yorkist leader, Richard Duke of York, his friend and ally the Earl of Salisbury and also that of York's second born son Edmund, Earl of Rutland.

Now however, if the accounts given of the latest battle were to be believed, at Towton on Palm Sunday, the Lancastrians had suffered a catastrophic defeat at the hands of a numerically inferior Yorkist army, which had been commanded by both Salisbury's son, Richard Neville, the Earl of Warwick and by the eldest son of Richard of York, Edward Plantagenet, the Earl of March, who, upon receiving news of his father's death at the battle of Wakefield, had even had the audacity to have himself crowned as King Edward IV!

News of the Lancastrian defeat, together with rumours of the atrocities committed on both sides, had all but soured Francis's perception of 'chivalry' and 'noblesse,' to such an extent that Francis now cared not, who won or lost. He wished only, above all else, for the safe return of his father, who was reputed to have fought for the

Lancastrian army that, under the command of the Duke od Somerset, had been assembled in Yorkshire by King Henry's Queen, Margaret. Since receiving news of the defeat, Francis had heard nothing of his father. Helpless, he could do no more than cry, but at the same time pray for his fathers safe return. He did this quietly and in solitude, for if his father was, as they all now feared, dead, Francis was potentially the ninth baron Lovel and as such, he could not allow his retainers to see him distressed. In addition to his fathers safe return, Francis prayed that King Edward would be merciful. It was said that the new King was intent upon avenging the murders of both his father and brother and Francis worried that Edward would frown upon his Lovel families Lancastrian pedigree. Stifling a sob, Francis pictured in his minds eye his father, stripped naked and dead, in a cold Yorkshire field, surrounded by so many of his friends and comrades. They'd already received word that many notables amongst the Lancastrian army, had either been killed on the field of battle, or had lost their lives in its aftermath. Lords Dacre and Clifford, Sir Henry Percy Earl of Northumberland, together with their 'great Captain' and 'soldier', Sir Andrew Trollope, who was said by many to have been 'undefeatable.' Even the 'gentle,' 'mild mannered' Lord de Maulay, a dear friend of Francis's father and a regular visitor to Minster Lovel, was now dead. Mortally wounded in the battle, Maulay had apparently been so badly injured, that he was even unfit to be executed alongside his comrades who, captured after the battle, were unfortunate enough to have fought for the losing side, at a time when the victors were in no mood for mercy.

The nature of warfare was changing and Francis was not alone in his assessment, that this present conflict was unlike any that had gone before. It seemed, to Francis, that revenge and slaughter had all but replaced the notions of chivalry and aristocratic etiquette. Formerly for those of rank, defeat invariably meant honourable captivity and eventual ransom. Now it seemed to Francis that all the vanquished could expect, was death, either at the hands of the 'chasing pack' or upon the 'block,' under the executioners bloody axe. Francis sighed, as he considered that prior to this Civil War, disputes had almost always been settled through 'honourable engagement's' and these were invariably conducted without the need for bloodshed, either by way of parley or through a fight to the point of submission, involving only those nominated as champions on each side. In the unlikely event that such negotiations failed and battles or skirmishes were felt necessary, and this wasn't very often, any engagements were fought according to a rigid and well defined code. If quarter were asked for it was given. Francis shuddered, it seemed to him that in recent years, warfare had degenerated into a series of 'bloody feuds.' Moreover, many men from within the higher echelons of the nobility, those who in the past had seemed content with their lot, were now happy to disregard the 'natural order of things,' as they attempted to seize power for themselves or for other family members. Unfortunately, those amongst the lesser aristocracy and the gentry, men who were normally immune from such considerations, were dragged into the conflict, either when called upon to support their Lord as feudal levies, or by having to provide sustenance for the men of those armies, who marched and fought upon their lands. Sadly, many wicked men had also taken the opportunity to use the war, and its associated lawlessness, as an excuse to settle local feuds and petty quarrels. Lawlessness was now the norm, Francis sighed, for presently it seemed to him as if no-one in England, from the King down to the poorest serf, was safe!

Even now it was difficult to trace the origins of the Civil War. Most still blamed King Edward's father, Richard Duke of York. It was fair to say that York had initially instigated the disorder, although he'd maintained that he'd only sought to question the suitability of King Henry's councillors whom, he said, were taking advantage of the King's 'weaknesses' and 'feebleness of mind.' The Duke of York and his supporters had blamed these men, not only for the state of the Kingdom, but also for the loss of the war with France. Unfortunately, the matter was further complicated when, on his return from exile in Ireland and immediately prior to his own death at the Battle of Wakefield, the Duke of York had finally laid claim to the throne in his own right. York had maintained that his own title to the throne was superior to that of his cousin King Henry VI, whose grandfather Henry IV had, he said, usurped the Crown from York's forbear Richard II. York had even gone so far as to accuse the Lancastrians of murdering the late King Richard in Pontefract Castle.

In spite of his present frame of mind, Francis allowed himself a small smile. York's ambition had been his undoing and now even he was dead, having been killed in the aftermath of his armies defeat at Wakefield by Queen Margaret's Lancastrians, this as recently as December 1460. Unfortunately, York was soon replaced as the Yorkist 'pretender' by his eldest son Edward, Earl of March, who, seeking to pursue his fathers claim, had had the audacity to have himself crowned as King.

Up until that point in time, one could have been forgiven for believing that each and every battle should have had the potential to end the conflict but, surprisingly, each engagement fought, only served to exacerbate the situation. With yet more deaths, additional 'blood feuds' were created as men became intent upon avenging the murders or the executions of their relations. Thus, Edward of March sought revenge for the 'murders' of both his father and brother. Richard Neville Earl of Warwick now sought recompense for the execution of his father the Earl of Salisbury. The Cliffords demanded retribution for the death of their patriarch Sir John, as did the Beauforts, who'd lost the head of their own family, Edmund, Duke of Somerset, when the unfortunate Duke was felled by an axe during the first battle of St Albans.

At the battle of Towton, it was said that two of the largest armies ever amassed on English soil, had fought it out to the death. According to all sources, the Yorkists had been the overwhelming victors and the Lancastrians had been virtually annihilated. But still the War continued, those who supported King Henry, who'd been fortunate enough to have survived the battle, had vowed to fight on. On the other hand the Yorkists, who for the time being at least were victorious, now hoped to establish the government of their King, Edward IV. Francis sighed again, it now seemed to him as if the wars would continue for ever! Especially when one considered that each faction now had its own King!

Francis, who had neither slept nor eaten for these past few days, could only imagine what a pitiful sight he was, his red and swollen eyes testament to his inner torment. As Francis looked up from his plate and his gaze met that of his grandmother Alice, he smiled weakly. Francis loved his grandmother and he really didn't want her to fret over him, especially when she was also clearly worried for her son. Alice returned Francis's smile, for she was a gentle and kindly soul. Francis warmed as he remembered how his father had often rebuked his grandmother, for 'moddy coddling' Francis, whom the old woman unashamedly admitted was the 'favourite' of all of her grand children. Alice had often likened Francis to her late husband, the seventh Baron, saying that Francis's 'gentleness of spirit' and his 'fierce sense of loyalty' reminded her very much of 'her William.' Francis smiled as he recalled those evenings which he'd spent in the solar, cradled in his grandmother's arms, in front of a roaring fire. Alice slowly and gently stroking Francis's hair as she proudly recounted to him the many stories of her late husbands exploits. Both as a great warrior in France and latterly, as the years of campaigning had taken their toll upon his health, as a farsighted philanthropist, who'd sought to secure his families future fortune. William had been a fair-minded Lord, who'd made the safety and welfare of both his family and his servants and retainers a priority, he'd secured his families future by both his loyalty to the Crown and by the numerous building works in and around Minster Lovel, which he'd commissioned. Projects that had seen the demolition of the old timber framed manor house, which had been replaced by the present stone built fortification, together with its associated farm buildings and the church, which William had himself dedicated to Saint Kenelm. Presently, Francis yearned for the comfort that his grandmother could offer and it hurt him to think that she too feared for the safety of her family in these uncertain times. In an effort to cheer her Francis once again smiled weakly, but as he gazed into her eyes he became even more troubled, for he could see only fear and pity. Francis shuddered, was his father now dead? Was his grandmother looking at the ninth Baron Lovel? That is, of course, if the family were fortunate enough to keep their titles! As a prominent Lancastrian Lord who'd fought against the Yorkists from the outset, Francis's father could expect little in the way of mercy from the new King and was, in Francis's opinion, sure to be attainted for treason. His lands and titles forfeit, seized by King Edward and given to some Yorkist noble, in return for their support. Francis sighed again as he wondered, would he ever be able to escape his Lancastrian pedigree? Even Alice herself was 'thoroughly Lancastrian' having been governess to King Henry's son and heir, the young Prince Edward. In fact when Francis's grandmother had heard of the Lancastrian defeat at Towton, she'd been distraught, not only from concern for her son and family but also at the thought that her charge, the young Prince, still only a child, was now a fugitive.

Francis needed no other encouragement other than the slight nod from his grandmother, this indicating that he could be excused from the table. He hopped down from his chair and running out into the courtyard, narrowly missed Ned, who, bringing out the next course of plover and snipe, skilfully side stepped Francis without spilling a thing! Recently Ned, Francis's dearest friend, who was himself only fifteen years old, had taken on much of the responsibility of the running of the manor house. This because Ned's father Thomas, the Barons Chief Butler, had been amongst the twenty men-at-arms, whom Francis's father had taken with him in answer to the King's call to arms.

Francis made short shrift of the staircase that led to the battlements. On reaching his vantage point, Francis perched himself high upon the buildings fortifications. Scrutinising the cold and wintry sky, Francis guessed that the sun still had almost an hour to go before it reached it's zenith. Would his father return that day? Francis could only sit and wait and wonder, as once again he began to scour the horizon for any sign of the men's return.

Francis remembered with fondness how, only six weeks earlier, he'd watched from this very spot, as his father had left with his small contingent of troops, all of whom were intent on avenging the Lancastrian defeat at the battle of Mortimers Cross. From his position atop the battlements, Francis had been able to follow the line of the men's march for quite sometime as the soldiers, on leaving the eastern gate, had made their slow yet deliberate progress, along the rough track that followed the line of the River Windrush as it made its way eastwards, towards the Great North Road. Those villagers and servants who had gathered at the hall to bid the men 'farewell,' had all excitedly and enthusiastically cheered and wished their neighbours and loved ones God's grace and good luck. Francis had remained upon the battlements long after the others had left, observing, as the men in good order, had followed their Lord. Well versed in drill, the small detachment marched alongside the river until eventually, after crossing it via the packhorse bridge, they'd turned southwards to be swallowed up by the great Forest of Wychwood, into which both they and the river ventured. The Baron and his men were to join the Queen's army at Northampton and from there, they were to accompany her on her march upon London. At that time both the capital and King Henry were held by the Yorkists and Margaret hoped to bring the Yorkist garrisons commander, the Earl of Warwick, to battle before he could be reinforced by the Earl of March, who was coming out of Wales with an army, having himeslef defeated a Lancastrian army at the Battle of Mortimers Cross. A victory would, it was hoped, secure for the Lancastrians both London and King Henry who'd been in 'honourable captivity,' since being captured by Warwick at the Battle of Northampton during the preceding summer. Francis knew the route, which his father would take well. When he'd been out riding with Ned (he had learnt to ride almost as soon as he could walk), to visit the old Roman Villa at North Leigh, he'd heard the instructions that had been given to the older boy by his father. 'Follow the river until it turns southwards, go into the Forest and where the track forks, head east and eventually you'll meet the old Roman road.' It was this road, Akeman Street, that Francis had hoped would lead his father to Northampton and onwards to London and to the great battle that was sure to follow.

Francis had bristled with pride as, together with all of the other inhabitants of Minster Lovel, he had gathered and had clapped and cheered as they'd all enthusiastically wished the men, 'good fortune' in their quest. When Francis had considered how well armed and provisioned the men were and how invincible his father had seemed astride his great white destrier war horse, in full armour with the Lovel banner of the leashed wolfhound unfurled above, Francis had doubted that there were any who could withstand them!

Initial news of the Lancastrians campaign had been excellent and, as expected, the Earl of Warwick had been soundly defeated, just north of London at what had become known as 'the second battle of St Albans.' Here, King Henry had been liberated. Francis had heard, not without a tinge of jealousy, that Prince Edward, who was only a year older than he, had been present at the battle and had been knighted by his father the King in it's aftermath. The young Lancastrian prince had even had a hand in the fate of two of the captured Yorkist Lords, Bonville and Kyriell. These knights, despite being promised safe conduct by the King, whom they'd safeguarded during the battle, were thrown to their knees in front of the young prince. Edward's mother, Queen Marageret, had reputedly asked the Prince, 'Fair son, by what means shall these knights die?' Apparently Edward, 'coldly and without emotion,' had replied to his mother, 'Let their heads be taken off.'

Before he'd met his death, Bonville had apparently addressed the Prince, telling him, 'May God destroy those who taught thee this manner of speech.' No doubt, Francis felt, the families of these two men would now do everything in their power to avenge their deaths and in doing so would attempt to ensure that Bonville's prophesy would come to pass.

Despite its rural location and the relative tranquility of Minster Lovel, neither it nor Francis remained completely untouched by the war. Sometime after the Baron's departure, it had become apparent to the villagers, that both the remnants of Warwick's defeated army and the Earl of March's troops, who were marching towards London from the site of their victory at Mortimers cross, were converging on that small corner of the Cotswolds. There had been some days of indecision, during which time both Francis's mother and grandmother had considered flight. For Francis, as the son of a prominent Lancastrian lord, would have been quite a catch for the Yorkists. Ultimately, the enemy had come no nearer than the town of Burford which, an hours ride from Minster Lovel, was the site at which the Earls of March and

Warwick were reunited. Wasting no time, the combined Yorkist armies had then raced towards London in an attempt to take the City before the Lancastrians reached it from the north. In a strange way, Francis had been doubly disappointed, firstly, as his capture had obviously been deemed not at all necessary by his enemies and secondly, after his mother had steadfastly refused to let both he and Ned visit Burford, obviously in disguise, to see their enemies at close hand. At long last it had been decided that those men who had been left behind by the Baron would gather together what arms they had, just in case any Yorkist foragers came across the village. Thankfully, as far as Francis's mother and grandmother were concerned, the enemies' troops, who had obviously been well victual led, hadn't needed to stray too far from their line of march in search of either food, woman or wine and Francis, together with the other inhabitants of Minster Lovel, had remained unmolested.

Gripped once again by the cold easterly wind Francis shivered and tightened his cloak around his neck. Despite it being April, the winter, that had been unusually long, still lingered and the past week alone had seen both snow and icy rain. Francis was moved yet again to tears, as he wondered 'how, if at all, his father would next appear to him.' Try as he might to remain optimistic, Francis's mind filled with dark thoughts. He cast his mind back to those stories of the recent hostilities, which had been recounted to him by his father. One such story, which had had quite an impact on Francis at the time, told of the cruel murder of Edmund Plantagenet, Earl of Rutland, in the aftermath of the Lancastrian victory at the Battle of Wakefield. The Yorkist Earl, who was little more than a child himself, had pleaded for his life to be spared, only to have a dagger plunged into his chest by the vengeful Lord Clifford. Edmund, a prince of the royal blood and the younger brother of Edward of March, had been left to bleed to death on Wakefield bridge, humiliated even in death, as his head was cast off and placed, together with that of his father, Richard Duke of York, on Micklegate Bar in York. Francis remembered how his father had laughed as he'd added, 'And our Queen has sworn that those heads will remain there, until they've been joined by those of the Earl's of March and Warwick.' Francis no longer saw any humour in this story and he could only imagine how gruesome the sight must have been. Duke Richard's head next to that of his son, the Duke's head ironically wearing a paper crown, a sign of his failed ambitions. Francis shivered again, as he remembered those stories of the Yorkist atrocities, which had taken place after the battle of Mortimers Cross. How Edward, Earl of March, before the battle, had apparently instructed his troops to, 'Kill the Lords and spare only the common soldiers.' Francis shuddered again, for his father in his ornate Italian armour, with the Lovel family crest emblazoned on his sur coat, would be easily identifiable on the field of battle. If Edward had given such orders prior to the engagement at Towton, Francis's father could have expected little in the way of mercy. Indeed, after the Battle of Mortimers Cross, Edward had even had the audacity to execute King Henry's stepfather, Owen Tudor. Apparently Tudor, who was very much 'old school', had expected 'honourable confinement' and 'eventual ransom,' this after he'd surrendered without a fight, when cornered in nearby Hereford after the battle. Unfortunately for Tudor, Edward had had very different plans for him and it was only when the old man was finally kneeling at the block, that the penny had dropped and he'd finally realised what his fate was to be. The messenger who'd been sent north to inform Queen Margaret of the execution, had stopped at Minster Lovel for a change of horse en route. There he'd recounted the execution's story for the benefit of both Francis and his family. Apparently Tudor, who'd been married to Henry Vs widow, Catherine of Valois, had only finally realised that he was going to die when the executioner had torn his collar from his doublet, to expose his neck. When he'd finally grasped what was going to happen to him, Tudor, who was said to have been quite a charmer in his time and who fancied himself as quite a poet, had said, *'That head which shall lie on the block, was wont to lie on Queen Catherines lap'* and then, according to the messenger, Tudor had theatrically thrown himself forward and, prostrate upon the scaffold, had given himself up to the *'headsman'*, and had, *'full meekly took his death.'* Apparently, the old man's head had been, *'set upon the highest grice of the market cross, and a mad woman had kemped his hair and washed away the blood from his face, and she'd got candles and set them about him burning, more than a hundred.'*

Intent on staying there for what remained of the day, Francis sat at his outpost. Cold and wet, he yearned for his creature comforts. From where he sat, Francis was able to look down into the Hall's Solar. This room, where the house's occupants spent much of their time, was located above the Great Hall, its large south facing window, which opened out onto the courtyard below, was designed to soak up what heat the sun had to offer. Although Francis hankered after it's comforts and for the company of his grandmother, from it's window he could not look eastwards, and it was from the east that his father would return, or so he hoped.

It was at around three o'clock that afternoon, that Francis first saw the signs of the return of his father's contingent. Francis was able to accurately estimate the time, as he'd only just begun to hear the commotion coming from the buttery and bake house, that was associated with the preparation of supper. The twenty or so men that had, so recently, eagerly left for battle had been reduced to a mere handful. Francis's heart sank as, try as he might, his straining eyes could not make out either his father's form or that of the Baron's great war-horse. It seemed to take an eternity for the ragged group of survivors to make their way back along the valley, to cross the river by the old packhorse bridge and to enter the Hall by the same gate by which they had previously left. By the time the men had reached the gate, Francis, having alerted the rest of the hall's occupants to the men's imminent arrival, had joined the others in the courtyard.

It was not the triumphal return that everyone had hoped and prayed for. The air was filled with the wailing of the wives and children, of those men who had failed to return. Francis too cried when he finally saw his father. The Baron's armour was dented and rusted and although a tall man he appeared , to Francis, as quite diminutive, slouched on a mule, his great horse, no doubt, long since dead. Francis noticed a large gash on his father's forehead, its ragged edges, having failed to knit together, were red and angry, indicative of the fact that infection had already set in to the wound. Francis, who had seen this type of injury before, immediately recognised it's cause, a mace or pole axe used to bludgeon, an effective, if not the most skilful means by which to put a man down.

The Baron was in no fit state to give Francis their customary greeting. A ritual reserved for father and son, which usually involved Francis coming off worse in a wrestling match. Once safely inside the courtyard, insensible, the Baron fell from the mule into the arms of Ned's father Thomas, who, although clearly very weary, appeared to be relatively unscathed. Both Ned and his father then proceeded to carry Francis's father up to his private apartments in the West wing. The physician was summoned for from the village. It was some time before Francis saw his father again.

Despite his mother's assurances to the contrary, Francis felt that the outlook was indeed bleak. Rumours in their small community abounded, of the Baron's death and of his attainder for treason. It was said that Francis's father was a fugitive and each day brought news that foretold of the arrival of Yorkist troops to arrest him. Since Towton, the

Yorkists had been rounding up and summarily executing all known Lancastrian sympathisers. On a number of occasions Ned's father Thomas, with Francis's mother at his side, had gathered everyone together, in an effort to quash these rumours. Thomas told them that Francis's father had in fact surrendered to the Yorkists and in doing so, had placed both he and his family at the mercy of King Edward. No doubt to add authenticity to this doubtful tale, Thomas had even added that Francis's father had pledged to support the Yorkists in any future campaigns and when well again had promised to host a hunting party for the benefit of King Edward, who was said to be a keen sportsman.

Francis was not misled. His family were and had always been staunch Lancastrians. Francis's father had always shared these sentiments and in stark contrast to some amongst the aristocracy, the Baron had been unwavering in his support for King Henry. Francis could never believe that his father would denounce his King for the Yorkist King Edward!

It was not until almost two weeks later, at Whitsun, that Francis finally got answers to the questions that he'd been so desperate to have answered. Francis, who'd been sitting in the nave of St Kenelm's receiving instruction from their priest, Father Bonde, was finally summoned to his father's presence. That morning, Francis had not been at his most attentive, nor, it was fair to say, had he been since his father's return, saving his moments of concentration for those times when he'd prayed for the return to good health of his father.

It was perhaps ironic, Francis thought that his grandfather had built this church and had dedicated it to Saint Kenhelm, in the hope that this ninth century Cotswold saint, whose tomb was said to have healing powers, would restore the old man's ailing health. It hadn't and Francis's grandfather had finally succumbed to his old wounds and had been interred within the alabaster tomb, which decorated the nave where Francis now sat.

That day, Francis's lessons were brought to a premature end by his mother who, hurrying into the church, told Francis that his father had asked that he join him in the solar. Francis didn't wait for the priest's blessing. Rushing by his mother in a headlong dash towards the Hall's north porch, Francis ignored her advice, that 'less haste meant more speed' and in doing so he tripped on the cobbled pathway that led from the church to the Hall. The skin on Francis's knees tore, almost as easily as the cloth of his tights, but he felt no pain. Seconds later he stood, out of breath and bleeding, in front of his father, blinking and temporarily blinded by the bright spring sunshine, which was streaming in through the solar's window. Francis's father was sitting on the window seat and it was not until Francis's eyes had become fully become accustomed to the brightness of the room, that he was able at last to examine his father in detail. By that time his father had beckoned for Francis to join him on the soft cushion of velvet that, sun bleached, softened the seat and gave warmth to the cold stone of the window's ledge.

The wound on the forehead of Francis's father, which was still open, had been scraped almost to the bone by the physician, in an effort to remove the infection that had set in during the Baron's journey from Towton to his manor house. Francis burst into a flood of tears as his father, who was apt to make light of many things, looked at his sons broken knees and said, 'Been in the wars again Francis?'

It took some moments for Francis to compose himself, then came the questions that Francis was so eager to have answered. His father quietened him, gently placing a rough hand over the boy's mouth, 'Francis, it is important that you listen to me now'.

What followed, took the form of the customary discourse between father and son that had, up to that point, followed each and every episode of the Civil Wars. The Baron using this means to describe to Francis recent events, its primary purpose being to instruct the boy in the ways of war, strategy and politics. Although the discussion itself lasted only a few hours, it contained within it a message, a message that Francis was to carry with him for the remainder of his life, counsel with which Francis, despite his love for his father, could never ever be reconciled.

Francis's father began by summarising the recent campaign. Throughout the ensuing discussion, it was only subtle differences in his fathers perspective, which slowly led Francis to appreciate the fact that, as he'd feared, his father's opinions and allegiances may, as a result of his recent trials and tribulations, have changed. Initially, Francis, blinded by love and respect for his father, whom he saw as virtue itself, listened intently, all too unaware of the revelations that his father was soon to disclose to him.

Francis eagerly listened to his father's account of the recent battles. This began with the Baron recounting those lessons to be learned from the second battle of St Alban's, a battle in which the Lancastrian forces under Andrew Trollope, who'd hoped to secure both the capital and the captive King Henry, had been victorious over the Yorkist's London garrison, which had been commanded by the Earl of Warwick. This success was achieved, Francis's father said, 'in spite' of the fact that prior to the encounter, the Earl had entrenched his numerically superior forces, in what had appeared to have been unassailable positions within the Towns environs.

'If the enemy appears too strong in one position, attack him in strength where he is weaker and least expects it,' Francis's father said.

'Yes, but surely at some point one needs to face the enemy at all points of the field,' Francis retorted,' 'and is it not better to attack his stronger positions when one's own troops are fresh?'

The Baron laughed, 'You have a lot to learn of men Francis. These men we command cannot be trusted to fight to the point of death, one has only to spread discord amongst the enemies ranks and he will flee the field in panic,' Francis father chortled as he added wryly, 'it is at this point that the slaughter truly begins.'

The Baron went on to describe to Francis how, on hearing of the strength of the Yorkist positions in front of the town, Andrew Trollope, the Lancastrian commander, had marshalled his troops in a complicated yet successful flanking movement, attacking the enemy from the North West, this being their weakest point and a direction from which the defenders had not expected an assault. 'Yet even this,' he said, 'had not finally won the day,' as Warwick's army were both 'well prepared' and 'well led.' Francis's father smiled again as he added, 'Trollope was a master tactician, he recognised the benefits of both good communication upon the field, together with an adaptable plan. Recognising weaknesses in the Yorkist battle line, Trollope had used those troops which he'd cleverly held in reserve to exploit his enemies vulnerabilities in the centre.' Becoming serious Francis's father added, 'It's important to engage as many of one's own troops on the field as possible.'

As always, Francis listened attentively as his father marvelled at how, with the use of superior tactics, Trollope had managed to overcome the larger Yorkist army. An army which the Baron explained was an 'extremely efficient fighting force,' having been made up of both the Earl of Warwick's 'experienced and battle hardened retainers' and 'seasoned Burgundian mercenaries.' This in contrast, the Baron said, to the Lancastrian army, which consisted for the most part of 'poorly paid' and, 'untrained Scottish levies.'

'Mark my words Francis,' his father added as he described the skill and steely professionalism of the mercenaries, 'I'd give a hundred of that normal rabble for just a dozen mercenaries or well paid retainers,' he laughed as he said, 'there's nothing that ensures loyalty on the field like the promise of money and riches.'

Francis thought it surprising however that, in spite of everything, ultimately it had been one man's treachery that had ultimately decided the matter in favour of the Lancastrians.

'Victory was ours' his father said, 'when one of Warwick's battle captains, at the crucial moment, deserted to our cause thereby creating a gap in the Yorkist's line,' the Baron laughed as he described how this breach in the Yorkist battle lines had been exploited by the Lancastrians' mounted knights, who in turn rolled up each of Warwick's flanks, causing both he and his men to flee the field in disorder.

The Baron went on to describe how Sir Henry Lovelace, an accomplished warrior, who was both steward to Warwick's household and the commander of his guns, had been captured by the Lancastrians at Wakefield and had only been spared the executioners axe after he'd sworn never again to take up arms against Queen Margaret. Lovelace had ridden south with the Lancastrian army only to give the impression that he'd changed sides yet again, when he'd seemingly deserted the Lancastrians and had joined his old master the Earl of Warwick in St Albans. There the Earl had foolishly placed Lovelace in command of a body of his Kentish retainers. Lovelace had not let his new Queen down and at a critical point in the battle he'd declared once again for King Henry. In doing so he created a gap within the Yorkist battle lines, which was exploited by Trollope's Men at arms. With obvious cynicism, Francis's father added somewhat grimly 'One can only wonder what Lovelace would've done if things hadn't at that point have been going our way.'

Francis was appalled that one man's treachery, together with a less than chivalrous flanking attack, had sealed the fate of the thousands of Yorkist troops who, fleeing the field, had been slaughtered in the rout that had followed, he protested to his father.

'But what of the rules of war?'

The Baron sighed, 'Francis, you still have much to learn. Forget what you've read in those books of yours and any notion that you may have of 'chivalry' and 'noblesse.' In this day and age the only rules that truly apply are these, firstly, one must win at all costs, secondly, that the end justifies the means, thirdly, trust no one and finally and perhaps most importantly, leave none alive who may in the future have the potential to do you any harm.'

Francis's father then went on to point out that with the advancements in technology and tactics, the age old principals of warfare were no longer applicable. He could obviously see the disquiet in his sons face as he added. 'And don't think for one minute that the Yorkists too wouldn't use any trick in the book' he said, as he went on to describe to Francis how, at St Albans, Warwick's Burgundian mercenaries and his 'professional' soldiers of the Calais garrison, had used a whole raft of modern equipment and tactics, which until very recently had been considered 'taboo'. New fang led 'handguns,' that had horrified the Lancastrian infantry as they'd fired steel tipped arrows and pellets which could puncture the finest plate armour with ease; 'caltraps,' steel devices that the Yorkist's had laid out before their lines, metal spikes that projected upwards to injure and maim both man and beast; large nets that were stretched across entire streets, structures made almost impenetrable with the addition of nails that, tied to every second knot, stood rigid when the nets were pulled tight and finally portable barricades, behind which the archers hid, hurdles that could be swung to the horizontal to enable the defenders to fire, before being raised once again to the vertical to prevent any form of reply.

'But our victory turned out to be worthless,' his father spoke with bitterness. 'The Queen ignored our counsel. She thought that if she had possession of the King she had the Kingdom; she was wrong. We begged and pleaded with her to push onto London, indeed the City's Lord Mayor himself had even written to her promising both his support and that of the city fathers.' Francis's father sighed as he added, 'But the Queen feared that our ill disciplined army would pillage the city and in doing so would further alienate its populace. At a time when we needed her to be positive she dithered and delayed, by the time she'd finally agreed to march upon London it was too late. The gates of the Capital had been closed to our army for the last time. We had no option but to retire to the North and leave the capital to the Earl of March, who, reinforced by the remnants of Warwick's defeated army, entered the city in triumph!'

Francis's father's account of the Lancastrians withdrawal to York, seemed to Francis to be more like the retreat of a defeated army, rather than the return of one that had been victorious. He described how the army, demoralised and desperate for food and victuals had cut a swathe of land either side of the Great North road, along which it had marched, pillaging and plundering both villages and towns as it went, much to the 'chagrin of the common people.' 'To make up for the booty that they hadn't taken from the Capital that had been ours for the taking,' his father added stiffly.

'Morale,' the Baron said, had suffered further when they'd received the news that Edward of March, who'd entered the Capital at the head of an army that was said to have numbered some 50,000 men, had been crowned 'King Edward IV'.

Francis's father said that at that point both he and his comrades had wondered if their misfortune was God's punishment, 'the Almighty seeking recompense for the murder and deposition of Edward's forbear King Richard II by King Hemry's grandfather'.

Much to Francis's disquiet Francis's father described how, after the decision had been made to retreat northwards, he'd 'shamefully' begun to regard his King, a person for whom both he and his family had risked so much, as 'a fool.' He described how, rather than deal with matters directly, as a 'King should do,' Henry left each and every decision, either to his wife or to the Duke of Somerset, who was rumoured to be the 'Queen's lover' and who, it was said, had even fathered Prince Edward! Looking directly at Francis the Baron asked him, 'Tell me Francis why did I risk everything in support of one who chooses to distance himself from his men, a religious zealot who spends his day's praying, one who is disinterested in what he calls his wordily concerns.' Francis's father sighed as he added, 'Henry's a puppet controlled by a French Queen, who seeks only to preserve the Lancastrian dynasty for her spoilt child.'

Francis, who loved his father, tried in his minds eye to excuse his disloyalty, sensing that it was born of disaffection with the King's advisors, who had clearly given Henry bad counsel.

Even here in this backwater of the Cotswolds they'd heard a variety of rumours and false stories, propaganda circulated by each side to weaken the morale of their enemy, tales that were born from the confusion that reigned in a land with two kings!

Francis smiled wryly as he remembered how one day he'd been joined on the battlements by Ned, who'd exclaimed to him that he'd heard it on 'good authority', that Henry had abdicated in favour of his son and that the Queen, who apparently despised the King, had given him poison and was purported to have said, 'At least he will know how to die, if he is incapable of doing anything else! '

Francis felt sick to his stomach for, in truth, he knew in his heart of hearts what was coming next. Francis listened, almost as if in a daze, as his father went on to describe how, even with such serious doubts about the Lancastrian leadership, he couldn't at that point in time bring himself to defect from a cause to which he was 'already heavily committed.' The Baron said that he'd owed it to his own father to at least give King Henry the opportunity of proving himself in battle. By that time, the Baron said, the Yorkist army had left London and was marching northwards to confront them and, as such, Henry had 'needed each and every man.' As Francis's father explained his rationale to him, Francis could appreciate that his father had been in quite a dilemma. That said, in spite of his obvious and understandable misgivings, the Baron added that they had had at least had some cause for optimism. The Lancastrian army had retired to York, a city that, despite it's name, was Lancastrian in it's sympathies and there, despite the desertion of many of their troops, especially amongst the Scottish, both the King and Queen, 'against all the odds,' had managed to gather together the 'greatest army ever amassed on English soil.' They did this, Francis's father said, by firstly appealing to the aristocracy, all of whom had in the past sworn allegiance to Henry, and secondly by drawing to their attention Edward's numerous alleged misdemeanours. Francis was amazed to hear that the Lancastrian army, swelled by these new recruits had at that point numbered in the region of some 50,000 or so fighting men.

'We were all there' the Baron said, as he proudly listed those who had answered the call to arms, 'Maulay, Dacre, Percy and even the Nevilles from Westmoreland, Warwick's own cousins,' Francis's father sighed and wiped a tear from his eye, before adding incredulously, 'I truly never believed that such a host could ever be defeated.'

The Baron, clearly still devastated by the outcome of the battle, went on to to describe to Francis, the circumstances that had led to the Lancastrian defeat at Towton field.

He sighed again as he said, 'King Henry, or should I say Queen Margaret, placed the Duke of Somerset in command of our army, damn etiquette, we all knew that Anthony Trollope was the man to lead us, he'd had too many tricks, even for Warwick at St Albans,' the Baron exclaimed, 'but a Duke, even if he is only twenty four and still wet behind the ears, outranks a mere knight.' Francis's father sighed again, 'this in spite of the fact that that knight Trollope, was probably the greatest military strategist of our age.'

Francis, who for once was completely lost for words, didn't know how to respond to his father, who, staring out of the window, continued his story, almost as if he was in a day dream, 'We knew King Edward would have to bring his army over the river Aire at Ferrybridge. It was here, Trollope told us, that we could beat him, with his back to the river. But the Duke of Somerset, who was still envious of Trollope's victory at St Albans, wanted to claim the victory for his own. He only sent a small force under Clifford which, in spite of early successes, was soon outnumbered and outflanked as the Yorkists crossed the river at Castleford and came upon Clifford's men from behind.'

The Baron sighed again, 'We lost many good men that day. Even Clifford himself was killed. After finally sounding the retreat, he was pursued all the way up the Dintingdale valley, almost as far as the main body of our army, which was camped between the villages of Saxton and Towton. I was told that, exhausted and having given up all hope of out running his pursuers, Clifford had loosened his gorget for a drink and a loose arrow had stuck him in the throat. Apparently, he'd died in great distress, as the Yorkists who'd run him to ground, refused to end his suffering and instead stood by and taunted him, as he slowly choked to death on his own blood. Some said the manner of his death was God's retribution for his murder of Edmund of Rutland on Wakefield bridge,' Francis's father tutted before he added, 'if nothing else it was clearly Yorkist vengeance.'

'I say it was Henry Beauforts arrogance that did for him,' the Baron added as he rose from the window seat, spitting out the Duke of Somerset's name with contempt. Clearly frustrated, Francis's father clenched his fist and struck the window's mullion as he confirmed that Trollope had indeed been right all along. As Trollope had predicted Clifford had caught the Yorkist's forerunners on poor ground with their backs to the river, where 'he'd routed them with ease.' Francis's father smiled sardonically as he described how 'many of the fleeing Yorkists' had been 'drowned in the River Aire,' he added, 'If at that point we'd brought all of our army forward, we could have caught them all and I've no doubt that we'd have been victorious.'

According to the Francis's father, the Duke of Somerset, who was inexperienced in such matters, hadn't had the confidence to commit all of his forces until forced to do so, unfortunately he'd chosen to disregard Trollope's advice, electing instead to array his army in open ground betwixt Towton and Saxton, in the traditional three battles.

'By that time we'd lost any advantage that we might have gained,' Francis's father said adding, 'the young fool even drew us up in positions on Towton Dale where we had a beck to our right and a river to our left,' his father sighed before he added, 'and if that wasn't bad enough both rivers were in flood and were nigh on impossible to cross.'

Even Francis understood that if one didn't give ones men an obvious and easy line of retreat, they were quick to panic and it was this panic that invariably led to defeat.

'We fought on Palm Sunday' Francis's father continued, 'many said that it was God's displeasure that we'd fought on such a holy day that led to the slaughter that followed.' Francis's father sighed as he paused, no doubt remembering those whom had died. Sitting down once again on the window seat, he continued in a faltering voice, 'It's said that those who lost their lives on that day will spend eternity in purgatory.'

The Baron crossed himself and lowered his head. Francis was surprised to see that his father, who wasn't normally the religious type, appeared to be whispering a prayer to himself. Francis wondered if he should say or do something to try to relieve his father's obvious discomfiture, but knowing how his father shied away from such personal contact, which the Baron had often described as 'over familiarity', he could do nothing, other than silently chide himself for remaining inactive. Eventually the older man regaining his composure, went on to describe the battle itself. 'It was as bloody an affair as I've ever seen,' he said.

'The battle began at around ten in the morning. Inexplicably, the wind, that at the outset had been at our backs, changed direction, as a result our arrows fell well short of the Yorkist lines, whilst theirs wrought havoc in our own. We were all forced to stand by as our men fell, their cries and the taunts and insults of the Yorkist archers ringing in our ears.' The Baron shook his head as he added incredulously, 'unscathed the Yorkist archers even had the audacity to retrieve our own arrows from the snow and fire them back at us!' Shaking his head again, Francis's father described how, 'Somerset dithered and it was only after we'd all been forced to stand by for what seemed like an age, whilst our men were slaughtered, that he finally listened to our advice and ordered the attack.' The Baron sighed as he described how by advancing into the valley bottom their troops had been forced to relinquish any advantage afforded by the high ground upon which they'd arrayed, he smiled though as he added, 'but at least our archers could pay the Yorkist's back in kind.'

Francis's father proudly described how their men had fought with bravery, 'I truly thought we'd won the day,' he said, 'when King Edward's cavalry were chased from the field.' The Baron shook his head again as he added, 'but their army seemed limitless and the Yorkist dead and wounded were soon replaced by others who were brought forward from their reserves.'

Francis could clearly see the tears that welled up in his fathers eyes as the Baron described the slaughter that followed.

'Our two armies were locked together in driving snow for the best part of the day. The only respite we had was when our comrades from behind pushed us, exhausted, to one side, so that they could get at the enemy, to hack and bludgeon him to the ground. I saw no-one killed with the thrust of a sword,' he said as he described how, 'Most were knocked to the ground with the blow of the pole axe or mace, to receive the inglorious death of a knife through the eye slit, or even worse, suffocation under the mass of dead and dying men.' By now the Baron's head was bowed low and he was staring at the floor, 'I fought with Trollope on the right flank and, although we were hard pressed, we were holding our own.'

As his father described how their army had fought with such strength and determination, refusing to give way to the Yorkists, Francis wondered what had happened to cause the Lancastrians' line to buckle and give way.

Sadly it was all to soon before his father answered this question. 'After about four hours of fighting, the Yorkist right was reinforced by the Duke of Norfolk's men, who'd only come to the field late in the day. Dacre's troops on our left slowly started to give ground. By that time, Somerset had stupidly used up all of our reserves and as we were all so hard pressed throughout the battlefield, Dacre's men couldn't be reinforced. Eventually, they could take no more and, as fear turned to panic, they broke from the field and made towards Tadcaster and the only bridge. With our line broken, Edward's troops turned on our centre and right. We fought on but the Yorkists, reinforced and refreshed by their successes, gradually rolled us up, pushing us back towards the beck, which, in flood, prevented our escape. I saw Trollope fall under the blow of a mace. His squire was unable to help him, as a pack of Yorkist men-at-arms fell upon him, hacking and slashing.' Francis's father shuddered as he said 'it was at this point that I went down. I was exhausted and I didn't see the pole axe that crushed my helmet. I felt my knees crumple beneath me and I fell to the floor unable to rise, the weight of dead and dying men pressing me down.' Surprisingly, the Baron allowed himself the slightest of smiles as he added, 'it was Thomas who saved me, he'd been at my side throughout the battle and when he saw me fall, he managed to haul me away from the battlefield and over the beck, he told me later that this was over a bridge of our own men's bodies. I don't know how, but he brought me to York and to Clifford's tower.' Francis's father sighed yet again as he added 'at least I was spared the torment of seeing our fleeing army virtually wiped out.'

Shaking his head, the Baron explained incredulously, 'At least at York of all places we hoped to receive the support of those sympathetic to our cause' he scoffed as he added, 'we were to be disappointed even in this, for its citizens who'd previously welcomed our army with open arms, now opened the gates to the City for their new King on Easter Monday, without even a struggle.'

Francis's father sighed yet again, 'And to cap it all I heard that King Henry, who'd chosen not to fight with us, had taken flight with the Queen and Prince Edward, running before they'd even received confirmation of our defeat.'

'How did you escape father?' Francis said, eager to hear stories of how the Baron had 'bravely' managed to elude the Yorkists after the Battle.

Disappointed yet again, Francis sat quietly by whilst his father recounted to him how he'd been captured by the Yorkists and had only managed to escape execution by paying homage to the new King. Francis's father said that even now he couldn't quite believe why the new King had chosen to be 'merciful towards him.' Especially when one considered that Edward's first task, after he'd arrived in York, was to recover the decaying heads of both his father and younger brother from where they'd been displayed upon Micklegate Bar. The Baron said that he'd truly believed that the King was going to 'burn the City and everything in it.' 'And he probably would have done so,' Francis's father added, 'but for the intervention of the Earl of Warwick who counselled caution.' The Baron smiled wryly as he added, 'Thankfully, Edward's desire for revenge was satiated by the summary execution of some forty Lancastrian knights who, captured during the battle, had refused to submit to him.' The Baron sighed and shook his head as he described how it was these knights' heads which had been used to replace those of their Yorkist counterparts on the City walls.

Francis's father did his best to justify his actions in capitulating to the new regime, 'And my head would be with them now, had I not thrown myself upon the mercy of the new King, kneeling before him and promising to support him and not King Henry in any future campaigns.'

The Baron added, 'I was spared only because I had not been at Wakefield and had not been party to the murder of Edward's father and brother'. Francis's father then described how the Earl of Devon, who'd shared his sanctuary in York's Clifford's tower and who had been present at Wakefield, despite being sick and wounded had been dragged from his hiding place and had met his end beneath the headsman's axe.

'We'd managed to barricade ourselves in the Tower, but we hadn't sufficient troops to defend our position and Edward's captains took us easily. Both Devon and I were brought before the King, who didn't even hesitate before ordering Devon's execution, even though the Earl fell to his knees and pleaded his innocence in the murder of Edward's brother.' Francis's father continued, desperate no doubt to justify his actions to Francis who, try as he might, found it very difficult to disguise his displeasure. 'The King is only a young man but he commands such great respect,' his father said, 'I could sense that even he'd had his fill of the carnage and as our cause was over.....,' After a brief pause, during which time Francis bowed his head and remained silent, he continued, 'Even King Henry clearly no longer had the stomach for it, did he not seek refuge from this conflict in both his prayer and his insanity?'

The Baron obviously sensed Francis's disappointment, for, as he continued his justification, his voice became quieter.

'I was thinking of you,' he said, 'Your inheritance would have died with me in York had I not sworn allegiance to Mar.....' he corrected himself, 'Sworn allegiance to the King.'

It angered Francis that his father had the audacity to blame him for his own submission!

Smarting, Francis chose to remain silent as the Baron continued, 'The old order is dead, these wars have changed things forever, one can no longer trust in people's loyalty, the commoners serve only those who pay the best, the Lords look only to the Prince who can advance their own ambitions.'

Francis had heard of this new doctrine. Ideologies which were beginning to emerge from the continent and in particular Italy, a country which was divided into a host of kingdoms, each trying to outdo the others, through both intrigue and war. These teachings argued that in Government, any act could be justified, if it were done in the interests of the 'greater good.'

The Baron continued, 'In truth, Edward has only claimed that which is rightfully his. His claim to the throne comes through his grandmother, Anne Mortimer, who was married to Lionel, Duke of Clarence, the older brother of John of Gaunt Duke of Lancaster, who is the forebear of King Henry's line.'

Francis suddenly felt a coldness spread throughout his body. Try as he might he could not disguise the disenchantment that he now felt, he edged away from his father, who at once became more authoritarian. 'Francis you must listen to what I have to say to you. It saddens me that you are disappointed by my capitulation and my new allegiances, but this is the way it must now be. These recent wars have shown us that dynasties come and go, the only thing that is constant is the power of the nobility. It is the likes of us who create Kings, not God. Edward, for all his qualities, without the support of the nobility would, like his father before him, have only worn a paper crown. Francis, listen to me, in future you must support only that cause which can benefit both you and your family. If it becomes politic to do so, you must abandon that party, because if you don't, when they fall you fall too. Like England's aristocracy, the qualities of loyalty and honour have been destroyed. Many from within the old nobility are now dead, the old families have been replaced by a new breed, men who are no longer willing to accept their position in society without question, men who are ambitious for riches and power, men who will stop at nothing and who are willing to support anyone for the furtherance of their own cause. Tell me Francis, how long do you believe Edward can survive on the throne without the support of the Earl of Warwick?' The Baron scoffed as he added, 'Even now they are calling Warwick the Kingmaker.'

It was with these words still ringing in his ears, that Francis was sent from his father.

Over the next few months Francis tried to come to terms with that which his father had told him. Indeed everyone else with whom he spoke, seemed to understand that this was the way it must now be. But try as he might, Francis could neither forgive, nor justify his father's actions, telling himself that if a man's word was worthless then surely so must be the man.

As Francis wrangled with his own conscience and tried to find ways to justify his father's capitulation, the occupants of the Manor house at Minster Lovel settled down to enjoy the relative peace and prosperity that the present respite from the wars afforded their small hamlet. Everyone, that is everyone except Francis, talked little of the recent struggles between the two houses of York and Lancaster, which many assumed were all but over. For it seemed as if England now had a young and powerful King who, in contrast to old king Henry, was both energetic and charismatic. At some point, Edward would have to take a wife and if, as expected, he was as prolific as his father had been before him, he would sire many heirs and would thereby ensure the continuance of his house. The 'Plantagenet's,' a dynasty that had ruled England for centuries yet whose rule had been 'cruelly interrupted' for three generations by the 'Usurping House of Lancaster'.

Francis, on the other hand, eagerly questioned any travellers that came to Minster Lovel, desperate to hear of any news of events in the north. Rumour had it that both King Henry and his Queen were still very much alive. At the Scottish court they'd been joined in their exile by the Duke of Somerset and many other Lancastrian nobles who, refusing to submit to the Yorkists, had been fortunate enough to escape their vengeance. It was said that Henry wished only to remain in Scotland, content to live out the remainder his life in safe seclusion.

The Queen, on the other hand, would not settle and it was she who chose to travel throughout both Scotland and France, taking each and every opportunity to make trouble for the new King of England. It was even said that Margaret was willing to sacrifice anything to restore her son to his 'birthright'. Apparently, she'd even offered the English town of Berwick to the Scots and the town of Calais to the French, in return for money and military aid from both countries. But, for the time being at least, or so it seemed, the new King was secure on his throne and the vast majority of his subjects rejoiced in him. England was at peace both at home and abroad. The Bishop of Exeter in one of his sermons had echoed these sentiments when he'd said that *'After so much sorrow and tribulation, I hope that grateful tranquillity and quiet will ensue, and that after so many clouds we shall have a clear sky.'*

Francis, who'd heard that Queen Margaret was planning to invade England from both France and Scotland, wondered how long it would be before the outlook changed yet again!

Chapter 3
January 1462. Castle Hedingham, Essex.

The Great Keep of Hedingham Castle perched, as it was, on the man made hill or 'motte' above the Colne Valley, dominated the surrounding East Anglian countryside just as its occupants and masters, the De Vere, Earl's of Oxford, had done so for many centuries past. The ancient fortress which had been built soon after the Norman conquest, its purpose primarily for defence in what was then a hostile and alien land, appeared to Francis both austere and Spartan, especially when compared to the Lovel's contemporary Manor house in Oxfordshire. That said when first sighted the stronghold had cheered Francis who, together with his companions, had been in the saddle now for almost a week. The party of horsemen, Lord Lovel's most faithful retainers, having departed Minster Lovel as soon as the festivities that had welcomed in the new year had come to an end. Francis had been surprised at his fathers desire to make such a long and dangerous journey during the winter months, especially as the purpose of their visit was ostensibly to deliver his cousin Thomas to the De Vere's, the family with whom the boy was to complete his education. This, Francis felt, was an undertaking that could easily have been put off until spring and the fine weather came. Moreover, any journey to Essex from Oxfordshire involved both the passage of the Chilterns, with its exposed ridges and poor thoroughfares, and the navigation of the great forest of Epping, full as it was with bands of villains, ex soldiers and mercenaries, men who were redundant, now that the Wars were over. Presently these men's subsistence relied heavily on that which travellers could be 'persuaded' to hand over to them. As such, Francis had speculated on the possibility that there was another, more pressing reason why his father had felt it necessary to hazard such an undertaking at this time of the year. Usually Francis wouldn't have thought twice about quizzing his father about the real purpose of the visit. However since the Baron's return from Towton and his subsequent revelations, neither Father nor Son had felt the need to communicate with each other. In fact when his father had announced his intention to personally convey Thomas to the De Vere's and had told Francis that he was to join them, 'To keep his cousin company on the long journey,' Francis had been extremely surprised that his father had felt it necessary to invite him at all!

Anticipating danger the Baron, as always, was well prepared and as such they were accompanied by a dozen heavily armed retainers. Since

Towton the new King Edward and his government had made great efforts to restore order to the shires and in an effort to deal with the lawlessness that was still commonplace, Edward had even gone on a 'progress' throughout his realm. Unfortunately, however, years of War both at home and abroad meant that it would be sometime before the English countryside would once again be safe for travellers. Consequently, each rider was well armoured and all had been advised by the Baron that if challenged, they were to 'strike first and ask questions later' and were to 'stop for no one.'

Francis need not have worried too much, for they had been extremely fortunate throughout the journey, making good time on roads and by ways that frozen were still passable. Moreover, they had met with only one party of poorly clad and ill equipped outlaws, this whilst deep within Epping forest. These 'unfortunates' were easily put to flight however, without any casualties on either side, with a volley of arrows despatched using the crossbows that the men had been instructed to 'always have to hand.' It was obvious that these 'naer do wells,' who hadn't even had the foresight to set an ambush, were merely testing the mettle of the Lovel retainers. Once they'd discovered that these travellers were willing to stand and fight rather than to yield, the brigands, who appeared even from a distance as if they hadn't eaten for sometime, backed away and made off, intent no doubt on seeking easier prey. Despite their strength of arms, Francis was still greatly relieved to leave the dark and gloomy Forest that, even without the seasonal coverage of leaves, still managed to shield out what meagre light the weak winter sunshine had to offer. As the men finally emerged out into the flat and open Essex countryside it was, to Francis, almost as if they'd travelled to a different country. This contrast was extenuated by the fact that earlier, their journey had brought them down into the lowlands that signalled the approach to the capital. It was here that they'd witnessed the devastation that the Wars had wrought upon the English countryside. On either side of the great North road there was a swathe of desolation, this having been cut by vast armies that had advanced and retreated over the same ground. The great burial mounds, which surrounded the town of St Albans were a testament to the thousands of men who had fought and died in the two battles fought there. But here, in the flatlands of Essex, where the land had remained untouched by the ravages of War, the countryside had flourished. En route to Hedingham they passed a great many manor houses, built by the new prosperous merchant classes, no doubt on the profits of the wool trade with Burgundy. Those poor village 'cots' of wattle and daub in which the majority of the population lived, in most cases alongside their livestock, structures that were commonplace elsewhere, were a rarity in this prosperous land. The countryside here consisted chiefly of sleepy hamlets, set upon open lush grasslands that were home, not to serfs and peasants who eked out a living on the small strips of land provided by their local lord in return for their feudal dues, but to vast herds of tamed sheep that grazed contentedly on lush green grass and seemed disinterested in the horseman as they cantered by.

Their ultimate destination, 'Castle Hedingham', was visible for many miles around and the riders had seen it in the distance for some time before they finally came upon it. The fortress had initially appeared quite inconsequential until, as the party got closer, they were able to appreciate its true nature and size. Francis had gasped as the Castle had loomed large before them, a massive keep towering above its surroundings, a huge fortified stone structure that sat atop a perfectly formed hill and almost appeared, Francis felt, as if it had been thrust upwards from the earth itself.

As they were almost upon the Castle, Francis twisted around in his saddle and turned to his cousin, anxious to see what Thomas's reaction would be to his new home. Thomas who was staring transfixed at the stronghold, failed to acknowledge Francis. In his cousin's deep blue eyes Francis saw none of the gaiety that was usually there and he was immediately worried for Thomas, who seemed overawed by the edifice and merely sat silently staring straight through Francis, scouring the dark battlements for any signs of life.

Unusually Thomas, who was a Lovel, a cousin from the Norfolk branch of the family, shared none of the family characteristics that were evident in Francis and his father, these evidence of their Norman ancestry. Whereas Francis was dark in both skin and hair colour, Thomas was fair and, as such, he'd earned himself the nickname of 'Saxon'. Normally so chirpy 'Saxon' remained silent and Francis feared that his cousin, coming from such a small village in Norfolk, would be overwhelmed and overcome by this colossal castle and the associated grandeur and power of its occupants the De Vere's, a family who were masters of East Anglia and who were also soon to be the masters of poor Saxon. Francis felt for his cousin and in an effort to reassure Thomas he patted him on the back saying, 'I'm sure the De Vere's are fine people.' Francis's words clearly did nothing to assuage Saxon's disquiet and, unusually, for one who was normally so gentle in nature, he snapped at Francis saying 'I'm not the one who'll be going home in two days time.'

Helpless Francis could think of nothing to say in reply. Thomas, the alleged reason for their journey, was to be squire to John De Vere the 12th Earl of Oxford. He was to remain at the Earl's Castle until he finally came of age, learning, as was the custom, the ways of chivalry and knighthood. Francis could understand why his companion was so apprehensive, to be parted, as he was, at such a tender age from his family and friends. The thought that his turn would soon come did little to cheer Francis, who wondered when he would see his cousin again. The realisation that his own childhood was coming to an end struck Francis, as day dreaming once again, he reflected on those long summers spent with Thomas, at both Minster Lovel and on the family estates in Norfolk, times that would never again be repeated.

Finally Francis's attention was drawn away from his cousin, as he studied the approach of the lone horseman, who rode out towards them from the direction of the Castle. The rider whose sur coat was emblazoned with both the 'Blue Boar' device and a star of silver, was immediately identifiable as a De Vere retainer. The Squire obviously recognised Francis's father, 'Greeting's Lord Lovel' he shouted, as he approached the Baron, who as always rode at the head of their small contingent. 'My Lord of Oxford has, these past day's, awaited your arrival with pleasure.'

The Baron nodded in acknowledgement to the rider, as the small band of Lovel retainers following De Vere's squire clattered over the small wooden bridge that spanned the dry moat, which in turn surrounded the Castle's outer battlements. Once inside the fortresses outer walls the men dismounted and handed their horses to waiting grooms, who led the animals off to be fed, watered and rested. The Baron stood his men down and, clearly both hungry and thirsty, they too scurried off in search of sustenance in the form of the bake house and buttery. Meanwhile the Squire led both Francis's father and the two boys into the keep via the external stone staircase that led to the stronghold's only door which, situated on the first floor, was designed to protect it from attack.

As they entered the garrison chamber they were greeted by an old man who must, Francis felt, judging by his father's reaction to him, be John De Vere, the Earl of Oxford. Oxford clapped Francis's father on the back and took hold of the Baron in a manly embrace. Nothing was said, but in that moment Francis could see that the two men relived many shared experiences.

De Vere was an old man, at least fifty years of age, Francis guessed. It was clear to Francis, that many years of campaigning on behalf of both his country and the house of Lancaster, had taken their toll on his well being. Ironically, it'd been the Earl's poor health that had ensured that he'd taken no part at the Battle of Towton. Francis smiled as he considered that this in all probability had saved both the Earl's life and his lands and titles. Francis was surprised to see that De Vere's grey and thinning hair was cut unfashionably short in the military style. Francis smiled as he noticed that in spite of his age and infirmities the old man was still very much a 'warrior' of the 'old school'. The old man who wore none of the extravagant clothes that were now becoming increasingly popular amongst the aristocracy, was clothed 'simply', in a plain woollen doublet and tights. After a moment Oxford released Francis's father and becoming more serious said 'John, we have important matters to discuss, a meal is prepared and at it's conclusion we must talk'.

A plain meal of salted mutton was taken by the party in the great hall which, situated on the keeps second floor, was sandwiched between the Garrisons quarters and the families private chambers above. Here, higher up in the fortress, the windows were slightly larger than those on the first floor, but they still afforded its occupants precious little light to cheer the austere surroundings. Francis pitied his cousin who'd said almost nothing since they'd first sighted the Castle earlier that day. Indeed, as they'd sat down to dinner Thomas had visibly winced as Francis's father, joking, had said that he'd brought the Earl someone 'to turn his meat and to hold his horse.'

Castle Hedingham had been built by a family of Norman warriors in what had then been a hostile land, as such it was designed not for pleasure, but for war. Indeed, as Francis took time to examine their surroundings, the only accoutrements which he could find that were given over to comfort, seemed to be the great fireplace and the 'minstrel's gallery'. The gallery that was situated at one end of the hall, was draped in tapestries that depicted the De Vere family history, a history, which stretched back in time to the day's of the conquest itself. The De Veres were one of the oldest noble families in the country, having accompanied William on his conquest of England in the eleventh century. Since that time they had earned their many Lands and Titles through years of unwavering Loyalty to the Crown.

During the meal the Lovel's were introduced to the Earl's two son's, Aubrey and John. Francis was astonished to see how two people, so closely related, could be so very different. The younger son, John, was nineteen and resembled his father in all things but the Earl's grey hair. In contrast the eldest Sir Aubrey, was one whom Francis, who frowned upon such 'fashionable types,' would describe merely as a 'fop'. Aubrey, who almost seemed to dance rather than to walk, was dressed in the finest of cloth. His doublet was of black satin and it's cuffs, as was the fashion, reached almost to the floor. Aubrey's shoes, which he'd proudly announced, were fashioned from the softest of calf leather, came to a point some distance from the ends of his toes and were, Francis hoped, the real reason for De Vere's feminine gait. Aubrey's hair, unkempt and uncut, fell about his shoulders and Francis smiled as he noted an alarming resemblance to the Earl's hunting hounds, which lay close by warming themselves in front of the roaring fire. Throughout the meal the Earl, who sat between his sons at the head of the table, could do little to disguise his obvious disaffection with his eldest son. Aubrey who seemed to enjoy the sound of his own voice above all others, spoke with a lisp and in rhymes that seemed to say everything, yet nothing. On the other hand it was obvious to Francis that the Earl clearly held his younger son and namesake John in high regard.

Once the final course of 'soteltie', sugar, eggs and pastry, that, presented in the shape of a chained hound in honour of the Lovels, had been finished, both Francis and Thomas were sent to their beds.

Being dismissed at such an early hour upset but did not surprise Francis, as both he and his father had been on the poorest of terms since his father return from Yorkshire. Whereas in the past, despite his tender years, Francis had been privy to much of his father's business, now he was excluded. It was also fair to say that Francis had not helped matters, as try as he might, he was unable to understand his father's capitulation to the Yorkist's. That Christmas Francis had only compounded matters, when on St Nicholas's day, having been voted 'boy bishop', as custom dictated he'd been asked to present a sermon to the congregation at St Kenelm's. Francis, who'd resisted all of his father's efforts to influence this address, had enthralled his audience with a well crafted speech. He'd spoken of 'Loyalty' and of 'Honour', of how mankind should please God by striving to be 'good shepherd's' and not by being 'mercenary people'. The congregation had not really appreciated the true meaning in Francis's words. One person had however and at the conclusion of his address, as Francis had graciously accepted the audiences applause, he'd looked down from the pulpit to see his father, who was seated at the very front of the church in the Lovel family pew, with his head bowed, not, Francis guessed, in prayer.

Neither Francis nor Thomas, both of whom were keen to hear the older men's discussion, went to their beds as instructed and once they'd been shown to their bed chambers, they crept down the stairs and secreted themselves in the gallery that overlooked the great hall.

The Hall was empty now, save that is for Francis's father, the Earl and Aubrey. The three men had all gathered around the fire, whose dying embers afforded the only light to be had in the growing gloom. Both Thomas and Francis who quietly hid themselves amongst the musty tapestries that adorned the gallery, were surprised to hear that those 'important matters' to which the Earl had earlier referred to, had no bearing whatsoever on Saxon's immediate future.

Francis's father's voice which was raised, failed to disguise the anger that he so obviously felt.

'Even if a Lancastrian restoration were still possible and even if you were able to raise an army, who would you find to support you? Much of those who were sympathetic to your cause died at Towton,' the Baron sneered as he added, 'Many whilst your beloved King and his French Queen were already escaping to Scotland.' Shaking his head Francis's father became more serious, 'Those who are still alive, who haven't already sworn allegiance to Edward are penniless exiles at foreign courts.'

In what appeared to be an attempt to reassure Francis's father, Aubrey interjected, 'We have the whole of Europe behind us. The Queen has been promised the support of the Duke of Brittany, the King of France and even the Queen of Scotland, all of whom are desperate to see King Henry restored to his throne.' Smiling Aubrey chortled as he added, 'Our plan is fool proof, it cannot fail.' Francis's father, who even then was still slowly shaking his head was clearly not convinced, undeterred Aubrey continued, 'The Duke of Somerset coming out of Scotland is to raise rebellion in the North. The Queen who is presently in France, intends to land in the North East with the French seneschal, Pierre De Breze. De Breze is to command an army of French troops who have been provided by his excellency King Louis'. Smiling knowingly Aubrey added, 'Edward will be forced to march north to meet this challenge. Our task, once we've recruited an army in the Southeast, is to follow him,' Aubrey chuckled as he added, 'Obviously we'll assure King Edward of our continuing support and good intent.' He laughed, as nodding towards his father, he added 'That is of course until we will catch him betwixt our army and that of Somerset and the French and then we'll crush them him once and for all.'

'Fool', the Baron's admonishment echoed around the Hall. 'Do you truly believe that you will get any Englishmen to join you, in an enterprise that will ultimately put a puppet of the French and Scots back on the throne. Who in England would fight for a Scottish French army? Especially when word gets out that our Queen has promised to surrender both Berwick and Calais to these foreigners, in return for their assistance?'

Oxford who'd remained silent throughout the conversation between Francis's father and his son Aubrey, rose slowly from his seat by the fire and placing an arm around the Baron's shoulders, he spoke calmly. 'John, we only wish to restore our King to his throne. Any enterprise designed to bring about that conclusion has my support.' The older man smiled as he added, 'Trust me friend, there are still a great many Lancastrians out there and I know that they'll not settle until Henry is restored.' Oxford who clearly felt that Francis's father wasn't convinced by their arguments, let go of the Baron, becoming more serious he frowned as he added, 'Do not think that we're alone in this venture,' he paused before he added 'and as your friend I'd rather that you're with us than against us.'

Francis's father's reply too was both calm and measured. 'De Vere you're one of my oldest and dearest friends, but I cannot join you in this undertaking. The Earl of Warwick is, as we speak, negotiating a marriage between the King and a French Princess. Should this match come to pass, then both you and your co-conspirators will be undone, you'll receive nothing from the Louis, other than his disclosing your designs to Edward. And that I fear will cost you your heads.'

Clearly agitated it was Aubrey and not his father who replied, as he did so his lisp became even more pronounced, 'Sir, every enterprise has it's risks; risks we believed that, as a true Lancastrian, you were prepared to chance. If we succeed think of the power and influence that you'll enjoy at Henry's court. Sir, if you support Edward you do so at your peril.'

Francis's father replied in a low sharp voice that did nothing to hide his anger at being threatened by one such as Aubrey, 'Sir, I'm satisfied with my lot as should you be. Are you not still masters of the South East, despite the fact that it was the Duke of Norfolk and not you who fought for Edward at Towton? Are you not all growing rich on the back of the wool trade with Burgundy and the Low Countries? Trust me, the French King won't buy your wool.' The Baron laughed as he added, 'And neither will the Dutch or the Burgundians, once your Queen concludes her alliance with their enemies the French.' Shaking his head again, Francis's father sighed as he added, 'Everyone is sick and tired of this war and I can tell you, with certainty, that no one will come out for either you or for Henry and his French Queen.' Even Francis was shocked when laughing contemptibly, the Baron insulted their hosts, 'Your so called friend's and allies will only come out long enough to tell you to go back to your homes.' Calmer Francis's father continued, 'I apologise for my harsh words but you risk everything.' Turning to Aubrey Francis's father added, 'Aubrey your father is an old man, he's one of my oldest and dearest friends, do not bring this down upon him I beg you.'

Aubrey who was clearly incensed, glowered at Francis father, as he was about to reply Oxford raising his hands quietened him and answered on his behalf, 'Many years ago I swore allegiance to Henry's father and I pledged my support for their lineage for as long as I lived. My family have prospered under Henry's government and I owe him a debt of gratitude. I am not prepared to accept Edward as our sovereign and I will do everything in my power to destroy him.' He sighed as he added, 'I beg you to reconsider your position.'

With that Francis's father turned away from their hosts and walking slowly away, he was soon enveloped by the Hall's darkness. As he went he said in a low voice that was barely audible, 'Sir's, I counsel caution.'

As he left the hall Francis's father did not stop nor did he turn around and Francis could only assume that he'd not heard Aubrey De Vere's reply, 'My Lord Lovel be very careful, for I now fear for your safe return.'

Both Francis and Thomas spent a restless night upon a rude wooden framed bed and straw mattress, which they shared in one of the Castle's cold dank bedrooms, a room which seemed to Francis, who was used to much more modern conveniences, to be no better than a cell. Throughout the night Francis, who could both feel and hear his cousin sobbing gently beside him, wondered if Thomas's fear was borne of homesickness or whether he, like Francis, had truly understood the implications of the conversation that they'd been unfortunate enough to overhear.

What would his father do next? The De Vere's had taken him into their confidence. Without his promise of support how could they allow them to leave this place? Francis shuddered as he recalled Aubrey's threat, 'You support Edward at your Peril.'

And even if they were able to get away from this place unscathed, was his father to say nothing? If he did, and as expected the enterprise failed, the authorities would surely see this visit to the De veres as proof positive that Francis's father was involved and he'd be arrested.

Alternatively, in spite of what he'd said, would his father join the scheme? But how could it possibly succeed without the support of the English nobility?

Or should he.....Francis shuddered as he thought of only other option open to his father. Should he report the conversation to Edward? But how could he? It was one thing to forsake ones friends, but to betray them? How could his father, Francis thought, expose these people who had, until recently, been his comrades, men who had fought with him side by side?'

It was not until well into the early hours that sleep finally took Francis, but it did not release him from his turmoil and he spent what remained of the night haunted by nightmares, a vision or was it a prophecy of a bloody execution. Upon waking, try as he might, Francis could not recall whose figure it was that he'd seen upon the scaffold, the unfortunate man crossing himself before laying upon the block, he'd given himself up to both God and the executioner.

At first light, despite previous plans to the contrary, the Lovel contingent rode away from Castle Hedingham. Impatient to be off, Francis's father had brushed aside his men's protestations that the horses needed further rest. Francis who'd told his father that which he'd overheard on the previous evening, had been surprised that the De Veres seemed content to let them go. Francis's father's explanation, that both he and Oxford 'were the oldest of friends' and that De Vere as an 'honourable' man who would never sanction any action that would compromise the safety of his guests, did nothing to assuage Francis's fears. Francis shivered as in his minds eye, he retraced the route that they'd taken to Castle Hedingham and considered all of those places where there was the potential to be ambushed or way laid.

Ultimately the only person who rose to bade them a safe journey was Thomas. As Francis bent down from his pony to take his cousin's hand, he felt extremely sorry for Thomas. He'd implored his father to take Thomas back with them to Minster Lovel, but his father had argued that as there visit had been made, ostensibly to deliver Thomas to the De Vere's then, in case any questions were to be asked later, they had no option but to leave him at Castle Heddingham. Worried Francis wondered what would become of his cousin. Was Thomas to be held as a hostage to ensure the Barons silence? And in the event that the De Veres fell, what would become of his young cousin? Francis wondered, would he ever see his cousin again?

As they turned their horses to the West, looking back towards the great Castle, Francis reckoned that the De Veres could be very dangerous enemies indeed.

If Francis had been unsure about his father's next move, his questions were seemingly answered when, reigning in his own horse and, turning his back on the fortress, his father whispered, 'Tis a pity, Oxford, you were a good friend to me.'

Neither Francis nor his father were surprised by the ambush, which was sprung upon them once they'd travelled some distance into the depths of Epping Forest. What did surprise them, however, was the level of sophistication by which 'these bandits' conducted their business. 'Ever careful', Francis's father had sent two men forward of the main body and it was these two unfortunates who, in triggering the trap that parted them from their horses, gave their companions sufficient warning of the impending attack. Sadly, neither man survived the skirmish to receive the Lovel's gratitude as both, stunned from the fall, were pounced upon by a number of outlaws who cut their throats where they lay. Francis's father an experienced soldier, was quick to marshal his men. Deciding that offence was the best form of defence and having ensured that Francis was safe guarded towards the rear, he spurred on both his mount and his men and fell upon their attackers with fury. The poorly equipped outlaws were no match for Lovel's men at arms and the matter was decided in minutes. At its conclusion half a dozen of the bandits lay dead on the forest floor, their knives and staves ineffective against the Lovel retainers plate armour and their leather jerkins affording the wearers little or no protection, against the Lovel's maces and poleaxe's. Two of the dead had however fought well and skilled in swordplay, these men had confronted Francis's father, who was only able to overcome them once he'd been joined by Ned's father Thomas. Intrigued, once the skirmish was over Francis's father had taken time to examine the men's bodies, although their faces were so disfigured that any positive identification would have been impossible. Both men's hands, which were smooth and clean, had seen little in the way of hardship. Moreover under their cloaks both men wore chain mail and their doublets were made of good quality cloth. Francis's father smiling wryly, said to Thomas 'I'd wager anything that these are De Vere's men.' Overhearing their conversation, for the first time in many months Francis agreed with his father.

Chapter 4
February 1462. London.

Francis's first visit to London was neither as he'd hoped nor imagined it would be. Instead of being at liberty to explore what was described as 'the wealthiest city in Christendom', both Francis and his father were to be 'Guests' of Sir John Tiptoft, Earl of Worcester, the person whom the King had recently created Constable of England and had thereby entrusted to administer his justice throughout the Kingdom. Rumour had it that Sir John took his duties extremely seriously and in doing so had already earned himself the title of 'Butcher of England'.

Francis's father had not been surprised to receive the Kings invitation to Court. An order that had arrived at Minster Lovel in the shape of a written summons, delivered by the hand of Sir Ralph Hastings, one who had recently been promoted to the post of 'Captain' of the 'Kings bodyguard'. Ralph had acquired advancement as a consequence of both his and his older brother William's support for Edward, throughout the recent conflicts. As such the King, on his coronation, had wasted no time in knighting Ralph and promoting his elder sibling, who was already a knight, to the peerage. William now Lord Hastings had been furnished with vast tracts of land and a large number of palatial residences that befitted both his new rank and his position within Yorkist society. William who was known as the 'King's favourite' was also created 'Lord Chamberlain of England'. Said to be closer to Edward than anyone else, William Hasting's was even reputed to share the King's bed!

Unfortunately the bulk of Hasting's recently acquired property, which consisted solely of land which had been seized by the crown from the estates of those Lancastrian Lord's who'd been attainted, was to be found in the midlands and it bordered that of the Lovel's. Worryingly, Hasting's desire for land and power had not been satiated by such unprecedented generosity on the part of the King and it was rumoured that William now hoped to extend his authority southwards, this at the expense of his new neighbour, Lord Lovel. Indeed, many said that Hasting's even coveted the Lovel's Manor House at Minster Lovel.

Upon his arrival at Minster Lovel Ralph Hasting's enjoyed none of the hospitality that his rank merited. Francis's father still considered the Hastings family as 'mere gentry', a genre not worthy of his esteem. In fact whenever and wherever possible, the Baron took each and every opportunity to vaunt his disdain for those of the middle classes, who having been fortunate enough to make their money through commerce, had greedily gobbled up those titles that lay vacant, as a result of the destruction of much of the old aristocracy in the Civil Wars. Lord Lovel hated these 'made men' who, through business success and not lineage, had secured their advancement into the aristocracy. Francis's father had often lamented to Francis how these men had only 'come to the fore', as both society and the King became increasingly reliant on their money. According to Lord Lovel, 'the ancient nobility of England', those who could trace their ancestry back to men who had accompanied the Conqueror to England in 1066, were being superseded by this new class. 'And', the Baron had added, this problem had been exacerbated by the fact that there presently were plenty of titles available for purchase, now that so many of the peerage had been killed or exiled in the recent wars. 'Sadly', Lord Lovel had said, 'these men were here to stay'. For in surrounding himself with these 'made men', the King benefited not only from having sufficient funds with which to secure his position on the throne, but he was also safe in the knowledge that those at court could be trusted implicitly, because they owed him everything and without his patronage they were nothing. Francis's father had bemoaned the fact that the only people who had suffered 'in all of this' were those of the old nobility who still remained.

As Ralph stood waiting in front of his father, Francis could clearly see that there was no love lost between the two men. A sardonic smile passed over Ralph's face as he served the summons on Lord Lovel, a man whom he had fought against at Towton and whom he still, so obviously, considered as a traitor to his cause. Ralph did little to hide the delight that he so plainly felt, as Francis's father was unable to hide his dismay as the Baron noted that the summons was not only for himself but also included Francis. Both were to appear 'without delay' before the Constable of England, at the Tower of London.

Francis's father's objections were futile, as was his request to be accompanied by his own retainers on the journey to the capital. Francis, who'd heard about Worcester's style of justice, was immediately thrown into a panic, for had he himself not been privy to the De Vere's conspiracy against the King, the cause of this present investigation? Through tears he looked towards Ralph Hastings who, smiling, seemed to delight in the Lovels discomfiture. Self-assured, unblinking, the King's captain stared back at Francis who, averting his eyes and noticing the Hastings device of the 'Man Lion' displayed on Ralph's doublet, immediately considered that both he and his father were soon to ride 'into the Lions den with the Lion himself.'

Circumstances had moved apace since the Lovels return from Essex. Francis had been made privy to the letters that his father had secured whilst at Castle Heddingham. This correspondence between Queen Margaret and the Earl of Oxford was, in itself, proof positive of the involvement of the De Veres and others, not only in the plans disclosed to the Baron, but also in a series of raids by Lancastrian privateers, operating out of French Ports, all along the East Anglian coast. Ironically, these raids had even impacted on the Lovels themselves, their lands in Norfolk suffering at the hands of these insurgents. At the time Francis's father had been unnerved to see the names of many of his old friends amongst the conspirators. Sir Thomas Tuddenham of Norfolk, Sir William Tyrell of Suffolk and John Montgomery of Faulkbourn in Essex. Tuddenham was a 'great friend of the family' and his previous position as treasurer to King Henry's household and keeper of the Kings wardrobe, were offices that had brought him into close contact with Francis's grandmother Alice, who had been governess to Prince Edward. Unfortunately for the plotters, as Francis's father had earlier gloomily predicted, other than the hapless Earl of Oxford, the list contained no one who could be deemed to be of the 'higher aristocracy' or who could expect to wield the power and influence that would be necessary to depose King Edward.

On his return to Minster Lovel Francis's father had reported the matter to the King forthwith. He excused his actions by arguing that he'd had no choice in the matter. He said that Oxford's enterprise had been doomed to failure from the start and that in the present climate, he must 'above all else,' 'protect the interests of his family,' regardless of past friendships and former loyalties. Francis's father had been supported in this point of view by both his Wife and his mother. The only person who'd objected to the Baron's actions was Francis who, when questioned further, could not explain why he felt so strongly about the issue. His fathers proposals were, of course, the only sensible ones open to him, but to Francis they seemed very wrong and only served to confirm his father's disloyalty towards the Lancastrian movement. A cause to which their family had, in the past, given so much.

Not surprisingly Lord Lovel had disregarded his sons protestations and had made his evidence available to King Edward by fast rider. Within the week their summons had arrived, as had the news that the conspirators had all been arrested and were at that time ensconced within the Tower of London, awaiting trial. They too were to be interrogated by the King's constable.

Their small company left Minster Lovel immediately after Hastings had served the summons. The thought of what lay ahead and the unusually tight embraces of both his mother and grandmother filled Francis with a strong sense of foreboding. At one of the infrequent stops en route to the capital, that were necessary to water the horses, Francis had managed to steal a word with his father, the conversation did little to cheer him.

Francis reminded his father that both he and Thomas had witnessed the conversation between his father and the De Veres at Heddingham. The Baron hissed his reply 'You say nothing, you know nothing of this matter, do you understand? If you follow my advice you may yet escape with your life.'

'But what will become of you?' Francis wondered, but he dared not voice his concerns to his father.

The dream that had haunted Francis's troubled sleep at Heddingham, came back to him in an instant and he wondered again, whose figure he had seen upon the scaffold?

London was unlike anything that Francis had imagined it to be. On entering the City, via the Northern gate from Watling street, he was immediately overcome with a sense of claustrophobia brought about by the cramped and crowded streets. It had been a bright winters day, but here in the Capitals dank and dark streets their was little sunlight to be found. Each thoroughfare was lined with numerous 'rickety' houses and shops, buildings whose upper stories overhung their ground floors and, reaching far into the road, practically embraced their counterpart on the other side of the street. It was astonishing that such buildings could be deemed safe and Francis feared that these precarious structures of wood and plaster, would topple over at any time! Francis's pony, usually quite sure footed, repeatedly slipped and tripped on the smooth and uneven cobbles of throughfares that had seen the passing of many feet. Gripping his mount hard, Francis wondered if he'd be able to stay in the saddle or if he'd be dumped unceremoniously onto the street in front of its other residents and passengers? Francis smiled wryly, he seriously doubted that in the event that he did fall, anyone would care, as the 'Londoners' too busy to take note of their fellow man in this anonymous place, would either ignore him completely or would merely side-step him as heads bowed they hurried about their business.

'Ribs of Beef', 'Pies Pies', 'Hot Sheep's Feet', 'Rushes fair and Green', the cries of the street traders deafened Francis. The smoke from their fires, together with the lack of light, meant that the City was enveloped in an almost constant twilight.

Overwhelmed by the City's stench Francis retched. The open sewers that ran alongside the edge of each street were home to a miscellany of repulsion. Human excrement and urine deposited from the dwellings upper storeys and animal carcasses in various states of decomposition. Francis gazed on in horror as a butcher deposited inedible offal in the street directly outside his shop, an open invitation, Francis thought, to disease and sickness.

Even the famous River Thames failed to escape the City's clutter. London bridge, with it's nineteen arches of white stone, was home to an innumerable amount of small houses and shops. Buildings perched so perilously upon it that Francis felt it may, at any moment, capsize into the River itself. One could hardly see the brown waters of the river as contained within it's shores was a heaving mass of boats of all shapes and sizes, descriptions and colours. Be they the small ferries by which the boatmen plied there trade ferrying passengers up and down and across the River in all directions; the great barges adorned in silk and velvet that carried their masters to the King's court; or the Venetian Galleys that docked on the river's many wharfs exchanged their cargo's of spice, velvet and other luxury goods for wool, the primary export of England.

The bridge itself was home to two great towers placed on each end. As Francis looked up at the northernmost tower he retched yet again as he was reminded in an instant of his purpose in that City. Adorning the towers battlements were the putrefying remains of what was left of the heads of traitors.

Looking Westwards Francis saw what appeared to be a fortress of stone, a great citadel housing three great arches or gates that opened directly out onto the River.

'Look Father, the Tower of London.'

In his excitement Francis had shouted and was heard not only by his father, but also by the rest of their company. On hearing him, the other riders burst into fits of uncontrollable laughter. Francis could not understand why he was the butt of their hilarity, until his father whispered

'That is the steelyard, the headquarters of the Hanse merchants' and, pointing to the East, the Baron identified the great fortress, the Tower of London, that dominated the capitals skyline.

'That is the Tower, where we are bound' his father said as Francis considering his own naiveté, coloured.

Embarrassed, Francis stayed silent as the men found stabling for their horses and then boarded one of the Kings barges that, with the aid of its master, obviously an experienced water man, successfully negotiated one of the centre most arches of London bridge and took them East along the river, before it finally deposited them safely on the quayside, which signalled the final approach to the Tower.

It had been Francis's first experience in a boat. He had, in the past, often marvelled at the fisherman on the Windrush at Minster Lovel, enviously watching them for hours from the Manor's Southeast tower, as they expertly guided their small coracles between the rushes and along the twists and turns of the river, as they laid out their pots to catch it's plentiful supply of Crayfish. He had often wondered what it had felt like to glide over the water, but his father had always forbidden such a venture, saying that he would not risk his only son on the River. Drownings were commonplace amongst the fisherman.

Now Francis knew how it felt, the sensation of almost weightlessness, as the boat slid over the surprisingly smooth surface of the river.

Once 'safely' back on dry land Francis stood on the quayside and took time to marvel at the great monument to the English monarchy, the 'Tower' that rose high above them. A host of turrets and battlements encircled the great white Norman keep that had been built over four hundred years earlier, by the Conqueror himself. 'Tower quay' signified the final approach to their destination and was, unlike the other City streets, surprisingly airy and uncluttered. Francis felt that it was almost as if the Capital, giving due deference to this mighty fortress, dared not encroach further upon its environs.

On entering the Tower of London, it soon became apparent to Francis that this fortress was, as his father had earlier described it, 'many things to many people.' Francis was amazed to see that amongst other things it was a Zoo, home to a vast menagerie of exotic animals of varying shapes and sizes. They passed cages that were home to both Lions and Leopards. Francis who had heard of the existence of such animals, had never before seen them in the flesh. Francis's father must have noticed the wonderment on Francis's face as he explained.

'They're presents from visiting monarchs and ambassadors from far off lands.'

Francis shuddered, in 'real life' these creatures were even more dreadful than the various depiction's of them that were incorporated into the shields, tapestries and standards of much of the Nobility.

Francis's father explained to him that 'The Tower, as well as a fortress, is also a residence, a prison, a court, the Royal armoury, Mint and the seat of government, the location at which the King's council meets to discuss policy, when of course the King is in his capital.'

Both Francis and his father were guided into one of the many rooms that comprised the keep or white tower.

On entering, Ralph Hastings, who was by this time the Lovel's only remaining attendant, spoke to the rooms only occupant introducing both Francis and his father.

'My Earl of Worcester, may I present to you the Baron Lovel and his only son.'

Francis now knew who this man was.

Sitting behind the great oak desk that dominated the small room in which Francis and his father were stood, Sir John Tiptoft, Earl of Worcester and Constable of England, was reading from a great leather bound illuminated manuscript. The Earl took some moments to acknowledge his visitors and even then, without having to look up and with the sweep of a hand, he was able to both excuse Hastings and indicate to Francis and his father to sit at the two chairs that had been placed in front of his desk.

John Tiptoft was a young man, his dark brown hair hung about his head in waves that were uncut as fashion dictated. His eyes, when he finally looked up and met Francis's gaze, seemed older than the rest of his body. These were, Francis thought the Earl's most unattractive feature. Pale grey in colour they protruded from the Earl's face and immediately drew Francis's attention to them. Francis's mother had always told him that if one stared into another man's eyes one could see his soul. Francis could see nothing in this man's unblinking eyes.

After the briefest of moments Francis, feeling extremely uncomfortable, looked away and began to study the room in more detail. The first thing that struck him was the large number of books that adorned the shelves that filled each of the chambers walls. As he examined those that were closest to him, Francis was unable to decipher any of the strange languages which appeared on their spines.

Surprisingly Francis's father spoke in a raised voice

'How dare you summon my son to this court?'

Tiptoft halted the Baron's protestations by raising his right hand, palm outstretched, to reveal smooth skin that had seen little hardship.

His voice was shrill and nasal and he was obviously in no mood to brook further dissent.

'I will decide who I interrogate, not you. You may think that by falling on your knees before the King at York you excused your past treason's, but I know you, like I know all of you 'Lancastrians.' If there had been the remotest chance of Oxford's venture succeeding, do you expect me to believe that you would have revealed his plans to me?' Tiptoft's voice had risen as he spoke and as he concluded his sentence he was shouting. Once the Earl had finished his tirade the room once again descended into an awkward silence. Francis disappointed that his father remained silent looked in his direction. But what could his father say? Had Tiptoft not spoken the truth?

Composed again, Tiptoft continued in a voice that was now barely audible.

'Do not think, Lovel, that you will come out of this lightly. The King may be content to forgive those who submit to his rule, but trust me there are powerful men who have the his ear, men who even now covet that which you have.'

Francis knew that this was a reference to William Hastings, he shuddered and could almost taste the hatred that Tiptoft obviously felt for their kind. This fact, and the knowledge that there seemed to be so many enemies ranged against his family, made Francis despair for his very life. Try as he might he could not prevent the tears that welled up in his eyes and started to roll down his face. Francis's father sensing his son's discomfort placed his hand on the boy's shoulder and gripped it gently. Despite the recent difficulties in their relationship, Francis was thankful for his fathers support and the warmth that seemed to emanate from it.

If his father was at all unnerved he did not show it, his voice was both stern and steady.

'I demand an audience with the King, as is my right as a Lord of the realm.'

Tiptoft who was clearly unused to being challenged in this way was plainly unsettled by the Baron's defiance.

'It is the King who wishes to see you' the Earl replied, recovering his composure he added 'But not until I have finished with you.'

Their interrogation lasted for the remainder of the day. The Baron was truthful in his replies, unlike Francis who denied any knowledge of the matter. Francis's father repeated many times his account of the conversation that had taken place at Castle Heddingham. Francis guessed that Tiptoft was looking for any anomaly or irregularity in the

73

Baron's explanation, anything that would give him the evidence that he clearly so desperately sought, to enable him to convince the King that Lovel was a co-conspirator and should therefore face the same fate as the others. Fortunately, as Francis's father had often repeated to him, 'The truth never changes and the truth will always out' and the Baron was consistent in his account. Francis, on the other hand, was wracked with guilt. Had his priest father bonde not taught him that 'To bear false witness was to risk eternal purgatory?' As he repeatedly lied and denied all knowledge of the affair, Francis silently resolved to confess his sins as soon as practicable, but not until he'd left this fearful place.

Finally, and only after many hours, both Francis and his father were dismissed by the Earl. They were accompanied to their quarters by a single guard who, wearing Worcester's livery, surprisingly, smiled warmly when he saw the Baron. Their room was situated within the Tower's West wall. On entering the Spartan room Francis was aghast as, fearing that they were now prisoners, he asked his father 'Is this the Beauchamp or the Wakefield Tower?' These being the only Towers that Francis had heard of, both of which were famed prisons.

His father replied 'No Francis, that accommodation is reserved for Oxford and his comrades.' The Baron smiled as he added 'Don't worry Francis, the Earl, much as it has pained him, has had to accept our account.' He laughed as he too surveyed their surroundings and added, 'Looking at it you wouldn't believe it, but this room is for guests not prisoners.'

Francis shuddered as he speculated on those conditions, that the Tower's prisoners must therefore be kept in. The walls of their chamber were plain and without plaster and Francis could clearly see the many marks on the stone, made by the masons who had chiselled and shaped the blocks. Their accommodation was devoid of any furniture, save that is for the crude wooden bed and the latrine or guarderobe that, built into the outside wall, drained directly into the Tower's moat. Francis craned his neck to peer out of the small arrow slit that served as a window and observing the moats filthy stagnant waters, he at once realised that it was this body of water that was responsible for the foul stench that seemed to pervade the fortresses outer quarters. Francis wondered how people could stand the smell, especially in the height of summer. He smiled, this must he felt, be a contributory factor as to why the King invariably embarked upon a 'progress' throughout his realm during the warmer months.

Looking Westwards Francis sighed as his thoughts turned to his beloved Minser Lovel, so very different from the capital. Here in the

City one could see few trees and there was almost no greenery within its boundaries.

Straining, with difficulty Francis was able to pick out just one field, which to the North West was encompassed within the City's walls and appeared as an 'oasis' of green in a desert of streets and structures. Pointing to the greenery, Francis asked his father to identify the unusual feature. The Baron smiled as he explained to Francis that the field which was known as 'Smiths Field', was used by the King to stage the many jousts and tournaments, which were commonplace in London and were designed to emphasise his 'majesty' to both his subjects and to foreign visitors and dignitaries.

Francis was bemused, 'Why build everywhere else in the City and leave this field? Surely any tournaments could easily be sited on land outside the City walls' he said.

His father who'd obviously not considered this before, clearly thinking out loud, replied thoughtfully 'Maybe the Lancastrian Kings wanted to preserve Smith field, as a reminder of the failings of the last Plantagenet King, Richard II. For that field was the scene of one of the most shameful actions of his reign and was used in part, as justification for his despotism.

Francis's father went on to explain. 'Towards the end of the last century, the peasants of Essex rebelled against Richard. The rebels grievances had begun with cries for bread but soon developed into an attack on the inequalities of feudal society. They were remarkably sophisticated.'

Francis's father smiled, as from memory he was able to quote from the manifesto which the peasants had circulated at that time. *'When Adam delv'd and Eve span, who then was the gentleman'.*

Interested Francis listened intently as his father continued, 'Eventually the peasant army was of sufficient strength to march on London. They chose a leader, Wat the Tyler, a veteran of the French wars. None had either the will nor the wherewithal to stand in their way. Save for the Tower, London soon fell to the rebels who sacked and burned a number of great houses,' Francis's father chuckled mischievously as he added, 'even the great Palace of Savoy, the London home of the Kings uncle, John of Gaunt was raised to the ground.'

Francis had heard of this John of Gaunt, he was the great grandfather of King Henry.

The subject clearly fascinated Francis's father, who smiling continued. 'Can you just picture it. King Richard and his council, trapped in this very Tower, prisoners in their own capital. They must have looked out from these very battlements, to see thousands and thousands of peasants, each demanding an end to their slavery.' As Francis tried to picture in his minds eye such a sight his father continued, 'The Towers Garrison was weak having been depleted by the Plague and Richard was therefore powerless to proceed against the peasants. Indeed, some of the rebels even forced entry into the Tower itself, dragging out the Kings Treasurer and the Archbishop of Canterbury, both of whom they blamed for the abuses of Richard's Government.' Francis's father chuckled again as he added, 'Both men were led out onto Tower Hill and were put to death.' Francis's father laughed as he described how, once parted from its body, the Archbishops head was returned to his parish, 'where it is still displayed to this day!' Francis's father continued, 'King Richard could do no more than negotiate with the rebels and it was there,' Francis's father said pointing to the greenery that Francis had earlier inquired about, 'on Smith field, where the King finally rode out to meet Wat the Tyler. The rebels, who were for the most part decent men, observed the King's flag of truce, but the King, who was without either honour or integrity, had Wat cruelly murdered. Struck down by the Mayor of London, stabbed through the heart.' Shaking his head Francis's father added, 'to save his own life Richard promised both bread and pardons to the rest of the peasants, this on the understanding that they would disband and return to their homes. Leaderless, the rebels complied.' Francis's father sighed as he added, 'but the King never kept his word and he had the rebels hunted down and tortured, put to death, many within these very walls.' Francis's father sighed again as he explained, 'In dealing with the rebellion in this way, Richard lost the trust and respect not only of the common people, but also of the Aristocracy and the Gentry who were angry that it had been the King and his favourites who had seemingly brought the wrath of the peasants down upon them.' Francis's father smiling patted Francis on the shoulder and added, 'and this is where our own family come into the story. The King's cousin, Henry of Bolingbroke, son of John of Gaunt and the grandfather of our own King Henry, at the behest of his subjects took up the crown of England and so commenced the rule of the House of Lancaster, our family were amongst those who first offered the crown to Henry and Lovels have supported the House of Lancaster ever since'.

Francis who was about to disagree with his father, for had he not abandoned King Henry, chose instead to remain silent. Frowning Francis scratched his head, astounded that one action that had taken place all those years ago between men long dead, could still impact upon the lives of people in the present. What if the King had acceded to the rebels demands? What if it had been King Richard and not Wat Tyler who'd been struck down on Smith field? How very different things could have been?

Francis's father interrupted his son's deliberations, 'Enough of History, we must apply our minds to the present, somehow we've got to get ourselves out of our predicament. Come with me, I know our guard, we fought together at St Albans, he'll allow us to pass. We need to speak with Oxford, for he can still be our undoing.'

Through a combination of bribery and the calling in of past favours, both Francis and his father managed to gain an audience, with the Earl of Oxford. As they'd made there way towards the Wakefield tower, where the Earl was reputed to be held, Francis had remarked on his surprise at the small number of guards who were stationed within the Tower. Laughing his father pointed to the thickness of the fortresses walls, the strength of its doors and the width of its moat, all of which ensured that a large garrison was not required. 'Indeed' his father said,

'If any prisoners did manage to escape from their cells where would they go'? Francis's father, clearly a font of knowledge when it came to History, went on to describe how a Welsh prince Gruffyd, a prisoner in the Tower, had tried to escape from his cell, only to fall to his death when the makeshift rope that he was using had snapped.

Wakefield Tower, where the Earl of Oxford was held, was situated in the Tower of Londons south wall. Here the stench of the moat had been replaced by another smell that was equally unpalatable, that of fear, of unwashed bodies and of blood and sweat.

Francis's father pressed some coins into the hand of the lone guard who stood at the door of the Towers middle chamber, furtive, the guard secreted the coins in his pocket as he said in a whisper.

'Please sire, a moment only.'

The guard unlocked the cell and using all of his weight he slowly pushed the heavy door aside. Francis and his father entered quickly. Francis was thankful for the lighted torch that his father had given him, for it's flickering light slowly filled the four corners of the darkened room. Sitting in the corner of the room on a straw mattress, that also served as a bed, was the Earl of Oxford. Oxford inspected the Lovels with blinking eyes that were clearly unaccustomed to the light. The old man was barely recognisable as the great Lord whom Francis had so recently admired. His tights and doublet were ripped and his face, no longer angular, was bruised and swollen, almost to the point of disfigurement.

Oxford did not rise to meet his guests as convention dictated. Francis, ashamed that the Earl's undoing was their fault, wondered if the reason for this was purely physical. Francis's father, plainly shocked to see his friend in such circumstances, went over to the Earl and stooping down gathered the old man up in a tight embrace. Francis could now see that they needn't have worried that Oxford may have informed on them, for the Earl clinging to the Baron wept openly.

Francis could hear his father whispering something to the Earl but, try as he might, he could not decipher the entirety of the conversation. He did, however, hear words such as 'forgiveness' and 'friendship' and 'loyalty' and as he crept silently closer to the older men he heard his father say,

'You are a Lord of the Realm, invoke your rights under the laws of chivalry, meet your end as befits a man of your rank and stature.'

Francis didn't understand what his father meant and he became even more perplexed when his father pressed some coins into the old mans hand and added,

'For your executioner my friend.'

No sooner had it begun than the hurried audience was over. Both Francis and his father returned to their room in silence. That night they shared both a bed and a night that brought little sleep.

The trial of John De Vere, his son Aubrey and the co-conspirators, which began on the following day, was held in the Great Hall of the Palace of Westminster. Both William Lord Hasting's and the Earl of Worcester who presided over proceedings, were accompanied by a number of councillors and officials, none of whom were known to Francis, who wasn't able to recognise them from their various coats of arms. King Edward was not present upon the stage, which had been erected along one side of the room to seat the Judges, the matter, no doubt, being judged too trivial to command the King of Englands presence.

When commanded to do so by Worcesters herald, both Francis and his father who were sitting towards the back of the court, rose together with the rest of the audience. As they stood up everyone turned around to see the prisoners escorted into the chamber.

Francis shuddered as he saw that the heavily armed guards who wore the Hastings device emblazoned on their tunics, were commanded by Ralph Hastings, who led the procession carrying before it the King's 'Axe of Justice.' Surprisingly Oxford, still a pitiful state dressed in rags, seemed to have regained his composure and once again, in spite of his physical appearance, he appeared to command the respect to which his rank and his reputation entitled him. Even Francis smiled as he noticed that some amongst the Kings council, even went so far as to touch their caps in a salute to the old man. That said it was fair to say that the majority of those present merely averted their eyes, fearful Francis felt, that at some point in the future they too may share Oxford's fate.

Unfortunately in contrast to his father Aubrey De Vere failed to maintain any semblance of dignity. Head bowed the Earl's eldest son shuffled into the courtroom, his shoulders dipped and his frame shuddering as he wept openly. Aubrey's fine clothes were now torn and soiled and his hair had been shorn almost to the scalp. Aubrey's lisp was even more apparent to Francis, who noticed that all he kept repeating over and over again were the words,

'Please, kind Sirs.'

Standing in front of his accusers, in deference to the court and in honour of the Trinity, Oxford bowed three times. Arrogant, Worcester failed to acknowledge Oxford's gesture of humility, rising to his feet he chose to ignore the prisoners and addressed the audience directly, as he read out the indictment.

'My Lords, these men stand before you charged with the gravest of Crimes, that of treason against our Lord and Sovereign Edward Plantagenet, King of both England and of France. They have conspired with others to meet our King in the field with armed levies, intent on destroying him and placing Henry of Lancaster on the throne in his stead.'

Tiptoft continued for some time, as triumphally, he read out those confessions which he'd exacted from the prisoners. Relieved Francis sat and listened, thankful that the prisoners admissions, had obviated the need for his father to give evidence against his old friends. Once he had finished, Worcester turned to the defendants and smiling he asked them if they were willing to acknowledge their guilt in the mater. 'So that judgement can be meted out according to the Law of the Land.'

All present, save that is for the De Veres, admitted their part in the scheme.

Worcester, who plainly wished to see the matter resolved without further delay, was constrained by both tradition and the rule of Law, irked, he was forced to invite each of the De Vere's to speak in turn.

It was the Earl of Oxford who spoke first in a firm and unfaltering voice. If he feels fear, Francis thought, he does well to hide it.

Oxford began, 'My Lords I stand before you accused of the crime of treason. And yes I do admit that I plotted the downfall of Edward of

March, a man whom some if not all of you presently recognise as your King. But I act in the name of my King, King Henry VI. Was he not crowned in this very City? Did we not all cheer together as we swore allegiance to him when he was but a child? 'God save King Harry', Oxford shouted. Francis was not the only member of the audience startled by the old mans outburst. Oxford, confident, continued, 'Were we not all comrades in arms? Did we not fight together in foreign lands to recover Henry's possessions?' Despite his piteous state Oxford stood defiantly before them as he concluded his speech by saying, 'Yes, I may be guilty of this crime, but if this is so then are you all not Guilty too? Answer me this, if a land has two sovereigns then are not all it's subjects guilty of Treason?'

For a brief moment those within the great hall were stunned into silence as they all considered Oxford's logic. Ultimately it was Worcester who replied in a voice laced with sarcasm.

'I thank my Lord of Oxford for his clever rhetoric, perhaps his son can also entertain us.' Tiptoft turned towards Aubrey who, with his head bowed, was still stuttering out his pleas for mercy.

It took Aubrey some moments to realise that it was his turn to speak.

'Please, kind sirs,' his lisp together with his bedraggled state meant that Aubrey, in contrast to his father and the other prisoners, appeared quite comical. Francis could hear others in the Hall who were trying unsuccessfully, to stifle laughter, disguising it for coughs and wheezes. The result of all of this, was that much of what Aubrey said was lost on his audience.

Aubrey, oblivious to his audiences prejudice head bowed, continued, 'It was not me, I....., I am not Guilty of this Crime. I was forced into this by my father.'

Francis noted that as he spoke Aubrey's head remained bowed, his eyes averted from his father, who in contrast stared at his son. Was it pity in the old mans eyes, Francis wondered, or anger?

Aubrey went on to say that at no point had he wished to be party to the scheme. 'But' he asked, 'how' was he expected to 'disobey his father?' Aubrey finished off his short speech by saying,

'Does the bible itself not say that we should obey our Father and follow him in everything'?

On hearing these words, the majority of the audience could no longer control themselves and as Tiptoft, with a smile, said 'Sir Aubrey, I think the book to which you refer asserts that God is our father, not this man stood beside you,' the Great Hall resounded to the sound of unfettered laughter.

Francis wondered if Tiptoft had planned it so, letting the old man speak first so his words would be lost in the hilarity that followed his son's.

The Captain of the guard, shouting for order, brought the proceedings back under control. William, Lord Hastings, spoke at last. Without consulting the other members of the Kings council he pronounced its sentence. A sentence that had patently been resolved long before the court had convened, Francis thought.

'By your own admission you are all Guilty of Treason and the Law demands but one sentence.' As Hasting's spoke, the prisoners stiffened and a small puddle which had appeared about the feet of Aubrey began to grow. As Lord Hasting's continued, Francis soon appreciated why Aubrey had lost control of his bladder.

'You shall be taken from this place to Tower Hill, there you will be hanged. Your hearts will be cut from your body and cast upon your faces, your bodies desecrated and your heads cast off and set upon London bridge, as a reminder to other would be traitors.'

Aubrey's legs appeared to give way from underneath him and it was only the firm grip of his guards that prevented him from falling to the floor. Francis now felt only pity for this man. Indeed this lamentable figure bore little resemblance to the arrogant young fop whom Francis had so recently disliked.

The Earl of Oxford spoke again. 'I beseech My Lords grant me but one request, that, as is the custom, as a Lord of the Realm, I may suffer the death of a nobleman'.

Hastings, in spite of his heritage, understood the laws of chivalry and knowing that he could not refuse De Vere's request he replied 'so be it.' He then drew the proceedings to an end by shouting 'God save King Edward.' The only people in the Great Hall who remained silent as everyone applauded the King were the prisoners, one of whom was John De Vere, the twelfth Earl of Oxford, of Castle Heddingham in the County of Essex.

Francis's father finally got his audience with the King on the following day. Francis, a minor, was not privy to the meeting. The Baron returned to Francis in a foul mood. The Lovels were not going to return to Minster Lovel that day as planned.

'We're to stay and witness the end result of our loyalty' he said before he continued to explain to Francis how the King had 'requested' that they both witness the executions of the De Vere's.

Francis had never witnessed an execution before. In fact he'd never actually seen another human at the point of death. He wondered if a man's death would resemble that of the boar or the stag, animals that he'd often hunted in the forest of Wychwood. He recalled the gargling sound that they made or, as his father described it, 'the Death rattle', as one drew the blade across their throat, to mercifully finish that which the arrow had started. Francis decided that a man's death must be different. For are we not better than animals? Do we not go on to a better place he thought? No, he decided, man is better than the animal and as such he must die with dignity.

It was then with a sense of trepidation that Francis awaited the executions. Sir Aubrey was to die first and as a mere Knight he was to suffer a traitors death.

Both Francis and his father accompanied the procession that drew Sir Aubrey, on a hurdle, the short distance from the Tower where he'd spent his last night on earth, to Tower Hill where he was to meet his end. Crowds of people, desperate for a glimpse of the prisoner, lined the route that took them from Tower wharf, alongside the West moat, along Thames street and Tower Street and finally up onto Tower Hill, where the execution was to take place. This itinerary, Francis's father pointed out, ensured that the cortege was seen by the maximum number of people, both as a warning to would be traitors and as 'the Londoners always enjoyed a good execution!' Francis also noticed that the route taken meant that the party was always in the shadow of the Tower, he grimaced as he considered that poor Aubrey couldn't even escape the fortress at the moment of his death.

More crowds awaited their arrival on Tower Hill. Francis saw that a scaffold, which he estimated was some eight feet high, had been erected especially for the executions.

'So everyone can have a good view,' his father noted cynically.

Sir Aubrey made no movement, nor uttered any words, as he was untied from the hurdle and, with his hands and feet still bound together, was lifted up onto the scaffold that had been prepared especially for the executions. Here Aubrey was held upright by the executioners assistants, as a rope was placed around his neck by the Executioner who, dressed all in white, could easily have been mistaken for the butcher whom Francis had seen when he'd first arrived in London. Francis wondered if Aubrey was in some way drugged or if he was, in fact, momentarily frozen with fear. As it turned out Francis needn't have worried, for as the noose was tightened around Aubrey's neck, he stiffened and then began to struggle violently, throwing his head from side to side as, restrained by both his executioners and his fastenings, he vainly attempted to cast off this foreign entity, the rope that was shortly to be his undoing.

Francis saw that Sir Aubrey De Vere was afforded none of the comforts that he'd heard were sometimes granted to prisoners, 'to ease their transition from this world into the next.' But why should he need a priest Francis thought? To pray for a soul that guilty of the greatest crime, was already doomed and destined to remain forever in purgatory, whilst its body lay for all of eternity in un-consecrated ground?

Using the rope that was now secured around Aubrey's neck, the executioner, with the help of his assistants, slowly hauled Aubrey up into the air for everyone to see. As he became increasingly starved of air Aubrey began to twitch and dance, as his bound feet sought the ground that was now some distance below him. The crowd jeered and threw rotten vegetables at Aubrey, everyone cheering when one of these struck their mark. Francis winced, but by now Aubrey was in no position to object as both the rope around his neck and his now swollen tongue prevented any speech. Francis could only imagine what Aubrey was going through, he felt sick as he saw that Aubrey's eyes which were protruding from his face, were staring wildly at his tormentors.

The Executioner, clearly an expert in his trade, removed a large dagger from the fire which, well fuelled, was burning furiously upon the scaffold. In one swift movement the fiery blade sliced open Aubrey's chest to reveal its contents, surprisingly unbloody as the hot metal of the knife cauterised the many vessels which it'd cut. The Executioner reaching into Aubrey's trunk ripped out his still beating heart and, turning from his quarry, he held it aloft for all to see. Ironically it was only now that he was finaly dead, that Aubrey's blood began to flow, spilling out onto the scaffold. Amazed, Francis couldn't quite believe how much blood was contained within one body. Finally the executioner returned Aubrey's heart to him, the crowd cheering as the now still organ was cast into Aubrey's dead face. Francis who had hoped that this was to be the end of both his and Aubrey's ordeal was disappointed. Once cut down, Aubrey's lifeless bluing cadaver was laid out by the side of the fire and the Executioner went about the grim ritual of castrating it, disembowelling it and burning it's bloody contents on the fire. As the smoke reached him and Francis smelt for the first time ever, the stench of burning human flesh and hair, he retched and in the process brought up the contents of his stomach. Francis who could bear no more averted his eyes. Unfortunately, and not for the first time, it wasn't too long before Francis's inquisitiveness got the better of him and as the crowd once again cheered enthusiastically, he looked up towards the scaffold, just as the Executioner, whose white apron was now a deep red, was proudly displaying his prize to the audience, Aubrey's lifeless head. A head frozen in the agony of that moment when death had finally relieved it of its suffering. Francis was appalled to see a large number of small children, urchins, who were busying themselves about the scaffold, collecting Sir Aubreys blood that was dripping from its edges, in whatever utensils they had to hand, before the plentiful supplies of straw that were liberally sprinkled about the floor were able to soak it up.

'They collect it and sell it as a trophy or souvenir,' his father said. Placing an arm around Francis's shoulder his father added, 'Don't worry Francis, next weeks affair will be nothing like this,' he sighed as he added, 'Mark my words you'll never see a worse death than this'.

Francis's father was correct, but only just. Six days later the Earl of Oxford met his end on the very same scaffold, but it was here that the similarity between his execution and that of his son ended. The Earl, washed, dressed and in clean clothes, walked to Tower Hill of his own accord. Meeting the Executioner at the top of the steps, he took off his cloak and carefully folding it he handed it to the priest, his close companion. Oxford then turned to the Executioner and kissing him on each cheek, he pressed a number of coins into his outstretched hand. Francis wondered if they were the very same coins that his father had given to the Earl during their meeting in Wakefield Tower.

Francis's father whispered to him 'Its to make ensure that he finishes it cleanly and in one blow.' Smiling his father added matter of factly, 'I've seen it take eight or nine strokes, if you've an inexperienced man with a blunt axe.'

Francis shuddered as he pictured in his minds eye the executioner hacking repeatedly at the unfortunate Earl's neck.

The crowd fell silent as Oxford addressed them, calling upon them, as was the custom, to hear his final words. Francis was surprised to see that the self same crowd who'd been so hostile to poor Aubrey, could display such reverence to his father who was convicted of the same Crime.

He turned to his father

'Why do they not heckle and throw, as they did last week?' he asked.

Smiling again Francis's father explained, 'The Earl is an aristocrat, a high noble. Whatever his Crime, God has placed him in a position of pre-eminence over these commoners and they dare not show him any incivility.' Francis's father sighed as he added, 'I'm afraid my old friend will answer for his Crimes before God and not these people who are assembled here today.'

Francis could not help thinking that it seemed unfair that Aubrey, the Earl's son and heir, guilty of the same crime, had not been afforded the same rights as his father.

At long last Oxford addressed the crowd. 'I was condemned to die as a traitor, to be hung and drawn, but Edward Plantagenet has been merciful and has granted me the death of a nobleman, I thank him for this clemency. I pray that God will show me such mercy when I stand before him, as I stand before you.' His voice strong and clear, Oxford bravely exclaimed, 'I still maintain that I am Guilty of no Crime, for I serve our true sovereign, King Harry.........'

Unfortunately what was left of the Earl's speech remained unheard, as the London crowd, pro Yorkist in their sympathies, clearly losing patience with Oxford's 'ranting' and ignoring etiquette, began to jeer and voice their dissent for 'this traitor'.

Turning his back on the now largely unsympathetic crowd, Oxford removed his collar to bare his neck and nodded towards his executioner. With difficulty the Earl who was an old man, knelt at the wooden block, the scaffolds only furnishing. Francis was able to see that both Oxford and his priest were reciting the creed in Latin. Once silent again Oxford clapped his hands together, an indication that he was now ready to meet his death. Refusing the blindfold that was offered to him, the Earl leaned forward and lowered his head onto the block.

Wasting no more time the executioner raised the heavy axe high above his head, before he brought it crashing down towards the Earl's exposed neck. Unfortunately the blow missed its intended target and, failing to detach the Earl's head, it merely crushed the back of the old mans skull. Disappointed, the crowd gasped and Francis who was standing close to the scaffold was horrified to see that, despite his horrific injuries, the Earl was still very much alive. Francis too gasped as he noticed that Oxford's lips were trembling in what must have been a silent prayer for a quick release. Alarmed, the executioner desperately parted his axe from the back of Oxford's head and, keen to see the matter finalised he raised it once again. The next blow found its mark, but now blunter the blade once again failed to decapitate the Earl. As defiant in death as he had been in life, Oxford's head stubbornly remained squarely upon his shoulders, albeit it was now only attached by a few sinews. Agitated, the executioner fumbled about his waist and, drawing a dagger, he gripped Oxford's short hair and pulling the head backwards he used the knife to finish the job. As the Executioner presented the Earl's head to the crowd, he was greeted not with cheers but with jeers, as the audience voiced their disapproval for what had clearly been a very sloppy job.

Francis's father sighed as he remarked dryly. 'A waste of a good tip, I could have done better myself.' 'He'll not find work again' he added, with an obvious reference to the Executioner.

Neither Francis nor his father remained to see the execution's aftermath. Returning to the Tower, they hurriedly collected what few belongings that they'd had with them, before they sought, and received, leave to depart. As both he and his father were spirited away along the river to where their horses were still stabled near to London Bridge, Francis resolved never to return to this place. It was here, at the bridge that they both paused for a brief moment to examine what was left of the head of Aubrey De Vere, which placed upon a pole had joined the heads of other traitors, which were displayed upon the North Tower. Despite it being dipped in pitch to prevent the birds from devouring it too quickly, Aubrey's head was still very much recognisable to Francis, not only by its shape but also by its bulging eyes and its gaping mouth, both testament to the fearful death that the unfortunate Aubrey had suffered.

Back at Minster Lovel Francis could not bring himself to discuss what he had seen with anyone. He felt somehow different, although he couldn't quite describe how. It was as if he'd been enveloped in a darkness from which he couldn't escape. Games and pursuits that in the past had pleased and entertained him, no longer did so and sombre, Francis now considered them both pointless and irrelevant. Not even Ned, Francis's dearest friend, could liberate him from this depression.

One afternoon soon after returning from London, Francis happened upon his parents in the Solar. They were both discussing his changed personality.

His mother who was clearly concerned by the change in Francis was silenced by his father who scalded her saying, 'You must leave him be, Francis has experienced things that many do not see in a lifetime. He's become a man, and yes I accept that he's been forced to do so before his time, but you must understand that your child has gone, Francis'll never be the same again.'

On hearing his fathers words Francis cried quietly, he cried for the innocence of childhood that had been taken from him so abruptly.

Oblivious to Francis's presence Francis's father continued, 'Mark my words, when he becomes the Ninth Baron Lovel, he'll be glad of these lessons learned.'

Casting his mind back to that which he'd witnessed in London, Francis shuddered and wondered if he ever would!

Chapter Five
May 1464. Lillingstone Lovell, Buckinghamshire.

The first day of May had broken with sunshine in a cloudless sky. Upon leaving the manor house at Lillingstone Lovell at first light, both Francis and Ned had ridden through the Forest of Whittlewood that completely surrounded the manor in which Francis's Buckinghamshire cousins lived.

Francis had been at Lillingstone for the past month, having been left there by his father who had once again journeyed North with his armed retainers. On this occasion the Baron's intention had been to rejoin the Lancastrian army of King Henry and the Duke of Somerset, which was in the process of assembling at Bamburgh, in Northumberland.

Since returning home from London, and having witnessed the trial and execution of the De Vere's, Francis's father had finally conceded to his son, that he could no longer support such a brutal regime as that of Edward. He had, however, waited until conditions appeared to favour them, before he'd secretly declared himself again for the House of Lancaster. Moreover Lord Lovel had been extremely careful in his dealings with the Lacastrian leadership, this as he hadn't wanted to openly join the rebellion, until he'd gone to Northumberland and was able to assess for himself the likelihood of a Lanastrian victory in the forthcoming campaign. Francis smiled to himself, for ironically those men who'd left Lillingstone with Francis's father, save that is for Ned's father, had had no idea whom they would end up fighting for in the end and could, Francis felt, even be forgiven for thinking that they were all still King Edward's men!

Up until that point in time, King Edward had relied upon both the Earl of Warwick and his brother John, to deal with the continuing Lancastrian threat in the North. Although both men had enjoyed a number of successes, neither had been able to crush all resistance to Edward's regime. As such, it was said that the King, who was becoming increasingly more frustrated by the Lancastrian's stubborn resistance, hoped to ride north to personally deal with Henry and his followers, 'once and for all.'

Perplexed, even Francis, one who prided himself on his knowledge of current affairs, had been frustrated and confused by the ever changing climate. Whilst spending time at Lillingstone with his cousins, he'd at least been able to take the opportunity to rationalise things for himself, as he considered the prospects for a Lancastrian restoration.

After both the Battle of Towton and the De Vere's failed rebellion, all had seemed lost to the Lancastrians. Admittedly both King Henry and his Queen Margaret, together with the Prince were all still at large, but militarily, there were few amongst the English Aristocracy who seemed either willing or able to come out and fight on their behalf. Events had taken a further turn for the worse for them when, on the eve of Christmas 1462 the Queen's champion, the Duke of Somerset who'd been holding Bamburgh castle on behalf of King Henry, surrendered having accepted Edward's offer of a pardon, a small pension and even friendship!

Despite the apparent hopelessness of their situation, Queen Margaret refusing to give up, had once again travelled throughout the courts of Europe, desperately seeking any offers of either financial or military support. Initially the Queen had met with little or no success, for at that time each and every one of the European powers, were all keen to cement an alliance with Edward's increasingly prosperous England. Moreover since he'd come to power the new King, despite his inexperience, had proven himself to be quite adept when it came to matters of foreign policy and in spite of meeting with both the French and Burgundian ambassadors, was yet to show any preference for an alliance with either country.

At this present time none knew with whom England would finally form an alliance with. Edward had always been pro Burgundian in his sympathies, however his mentor the Earl of Warwick, who was said to exercise significant influence over the young King, favoured an alliance with England's 'old enemies' France and Scotland. This latter prospect worried Francis, for both Scotland and France had in the past been safe havens for Lancastrian exiles. If Edward chose an alliance with the French, the Lancastrian cause would be irreconcilably damaged.

As ever, Queen Margaret had been determined and her resilience had paid off, when she'd finally managed to procure the assistance of the Duke of Brittany who, fearing isolation borne of an English alliance with either Burgundy or France, had provided her with both men and money. Using Brittany's promise of aid, Margaret had been successful in securing pledges of support from many amongst the 'Old Lancastrians.' Sir Ralph Percy in Northumberland, the Earl of Pembroke in Wales and even the Duke of Somerset, who'd changed sides yet again, had all recently declared for King Henry. In contrast Francis's father had been far more circumspect. He had written to both

Queen Margaret and to King Edward, assuring both of his intention to answer their 'call to arms', telling them that he would join them in the North with his retainers, 'arrayed for battle'. Francis's father had told him that if the Lancastrian army appeared capable of victory, he would join it. If, on the other hand, they appeared too weak to prevail, he could always proclaim his allegiance to the Yorkists and bide his time until another opportunity for a Lancastrian restoration presented itself. Francis, concerned by his father's duplicity and remembering quite vividly how the King repaid such treachery, had implored his father to remain at Minster Lovel where, in relative safety, he could, 'Wait and see how things went.' The Baron had however disagreed with his son, pointing out that the King had sent him a number of commissions of Array and if he didn't mobilise his men, Edward would consider this on its own to be an act of treachery. Moreover, Edward's proposed line of march northwards, would take him close to Minster Lovel and as the King had previously promised to visit their home to avail himself of the Lovel's hospitality, he would, Francis's father said, be bound to call upon them. The Baron had smiled as he'd added, that he didn't want to be present to welcome either Edward, Tiptoft nor either of the Hasting's brother's. Ultimately then, having deposited Francis with his cousins at Lillingstone his father had travelled north.

It was said that Warwick's brother, John Neville, Lord Montague, who was in command of the Yorkist's northern army, was to due meet with the Scottish envoys at Norham to conclude a treaty between the two countries. Such a treaty would effectively banish the Lancastrians from Scotland, it was vital therefore, that the Lancastrians intercept Montague and his men and prevent the alliance from being signed.

Francis understood why his father had left him in the care of his cousins at Lillingstone. If he remained at Minster Lovel and fell into Yorkist hands he would undoubtedly have been used as a hostage to ensure his father's continued loyalty. Frustratingly however, for Francis, Lillingstone Lovel was in his opinion, the 'back of beyond' and in contrast to Minster Lovel, accurate news of any of those events that were taking place in the north, was practically non existent. Rumour had it that the Lancastrians, under the Duke of Somerset, had intercepted Montague's men as planned at Hedgley Moor in Northumberland. Unfortunately however, things had not gone their way and Somerset's army had been, routed with Sir Ralph Percy himself being killed in the skirmish. More worryingly still the Scottish envoys had apparently reached York, where they were said to have agreed a fifteen year truce with Edward's government.

As time went by and Francis heard no news of his father, he began to worry. Had the Baron and his men been present at the Hedgeley Moor? If that had been so, what part they had played in the battle, be it on behalf of the Yorkist's or the Lancastrian's? Francis had heard tell that the Duke of Somerset's army had not been completely destroyed in the encounter and it was said that the Lancastrian commander hoped to regroup his forces and bring Montague to battle, before he could be reinforced by the King. Impatiently, and with increasing frustration, Francis had waited in vain for any news from the North.

It had been to take Francis's mind off recent events that Ned had arranged that days excursion, ostensibly to enjoy the exceptional hunting that the surrounding forest had to offer. As always, Francis had had very different ideas and much to Ned's angst he'd hoped to use the day as an opportunity to discover any news from the North. Riding in a North Easterly direction, Francis hoped to clear the Wittlewood forest and make for Watling street the great London to Shrewsbury thoroughfare. This old Roman Road carried many travellers who must, Francis felt, have word of recent events in Northumberland. Ned, as always, had counselled caution, telling Francis that they would have to be extremely careful as King Edward and his household men were also reputed to be in their vicinity at Stony Stratford, here the King was said to be enjoying the excellent hunting that this heavily forested area had to offer, before he to resumed his journey northwards.

Like Francis, Ned was also concerned for his own father's fate. But he had 'promised' the Baron that he would look after Francis and, as such, the older boy had had serious reservations about any plan to venture beyond the immediate vicinity of Lillingstone. Not surprisingly then, that morning Ned had been both angry and impatient. Keen to enjoy a days hunting, welcome relief from the tedium of life with Francis's cousins, Ned had protested strongly when, on saddling their horses, Francis had waved away the men who were to join them, telling them to put away their dogs for they, 'Wouldn't be needed that day'.

'What.............but I thought'.

Ned's protestations as always, had been futile and Francis had cut him off asking him, if he cared at all what had become of their father's. Francis had immediately regretted his words and Ned, hurt by Francis's insensitivity and unable to censure his charge, had turned instead on the men chiding them for their impetuousness, before he'd sent them home without any pay.

Consequently Ned had spent much of that morning, sulking in silence, seemingly disinterested as Francis had excitedly outlined his proposals for the day.

It was mid morning by the time the boys cleared the forest that surrounded Lillingstone Lovel. They rode out into open and rolling countryside which was bathed in bright summer sunshine. Both boys accelerating from a trot to a canter and onwards into a gallop, urged their mounts forward, now that they were no longer hindered by the low hanging branches that had, up until that point, impeded their progress.

It was Francis who first noticed the small body of horsemen that were some distance ahead of them. It appeared to him that these riders were also making for the Old Roman Road. With difficulty, Francis was able to make out that the men were carrying the King's own standard, 'The Sun in splendour,' Edward's personal device, which he'd adopted after the Battle of Mortimers Cross. Prior to that battle Edward had witnessed the phenomena, of a sky with three suns and considering how the outcome of the battle had been decided in his favour, Edward had decided that this had been a lucky omen and as such he'd adopted this as his own personal emblem.

Ned, who'd also studied the flags spoke out loud.

'Could it be the King himself.'

Francis doubted it, the riders were few and as such would be prey to those ruffians and villains who preyed upon travellers. He was, however, still intrigued to discover what the King's men were doing here so far from their line of march.

'Let's follow,' he urged.

Ned looked doubtful as Francis added,

'The Sun will soon be at our backs, they'll not see that we're following them, even if they take time to turn and look.'

Reluctantly the older boy agreed and Francis was left wondering if Ned's experiences of his younger charge, had convinced him that to raise any objections would be futile.

Soon, both boys and their mounts were enthusiastically galloping after the King's men.

Surprisingly upon reaching Watling street, the riders ignored the Roman Road and continued straight on up into a rough and overgrown thoroughfare, which itself soon entered into a thickly wooded valley. It was there that the Boys finally lost sight of their quarry.

Francis sighed as he considered that all of there efforts had been in vain.

'We'll never find them in there,' he bemoaned, as both he and Ned reigning in their charges dismounted, giving the horses who were both sweating profusely, a well deserved rest.

'They must be hunting,' Ned guessed.

'What, with no hounds,' Francis queried, 'And why would they ride so far from their line of march,' he asked.

Both he and Ned knew that the Whittlewood forest, through which they'd earlier ridden, would have provided much more fruitful hunting, than the countryside in which they now found themselves.

Ned examining the ancient forest into which the riders had disappeared, shrugged as he said,

'Well we're not going to find out what they're doing now.' Smiling he added, 'Besides which, it's getting late and we should really be turning back.' The older boy shuddered as he added, 'Come Francis even you don't want to cross Watling street or go back through that forest after dark.'

Francis keen to go on, tried to reassure his friend, 'Come on Ned.' He patted the older boy on the back as he added. 'We've still some hours to spare and we don't know how deep that wood is. Aren't you keen to find out what they're up to? We'll wonder for days if we don't.'

Ned shook his head as he replied truthfully, 'You might but I certainly won't.' The older boy sighed and Francis grinned, he'd got his way again.

Unfortunately for the boys and their mounts, the wood was, as expected, a deep and virtually impenetrable forest. The path upon which they'd entered it soon petered out and time and time again they were forced to dismount and follow any feint animal tracks that they were fortunate enough to happen across. Both boys cursed as cloth was both torn and pulled and skin was both stung and scratched. Still, neither willing nor in fact able to turn back, they 'soldiered' on, compelled to lead their reluctant horses through knee high nettles and brambles that, having taken advantage of the mild spring, had proliferated throughout the dimly lit forest floor.

Even Francis, recently so optimistic, was beginning to wonder if they'd find the King's men or if they'd even manage to find their way out of this Forest at all! Try as they might neither Ned nor Francis were able to peer through the thick canopy of trees that shielded them from the Sun, the only thing that could have given them an idea of the direction in which they were slowly and all too painfully travelling.

Ned could clearly see that Francis was beginning to worry.

'Don't worry,' he said, 'If we keep going in a straight line we're bound to reach the boundary of the wood.'

Thankfully the older boy was right and after what seemed like hours, the boy's were finally able to force their way through a thick hedge of hawthorn, which marked the outer perimeter of the forest. The hedge, both cultivated and maintained, had clearly been planted by villagers, to keep the wild forest animals away from their livestock.

The boys once again emerged into bright sunshine. Blinking Francis could see that they'd happened upon one of the many small hamlets, which were commonplace in this area of the Cotswolds. The fields in which they were now stood, were criss crossed with strips of land, each strip cultivated by a serf who worked the land for the benefit of their master, the Lord of the manor.

This Lord's not fighting in the north,' Francis spoke out loud, as he noticed the large number of peasants, most of whom were of fighting age, who were bent double, tilling the fields and tending to the crops that were just about beginning to grow.

Francis had always pitied the serfs, born as they were into a harsh and cheerless existence as a slave to another. In the past he'd often been scolded by his father for sentiments that were, the Baron said, borne not of compassion but of weakness.

'It's God's will,' his father had said, 'Everyone is born into a rank that is predetermined by the Almighty, be it the nobility or a lowly serf.' Frowning he'd added, 'This world may be an unhappy place for some, but we can all comfort ourselves with the certainty that we will all go on to a better place, once our time on Earth is at an end.'

Of course Francis appreciated that the peasants at Minster Lovel were treated better than most. For the Lovels could afford to be charitable, their lands remaining virtually untouched by both the ravages of the recent wars, or the pestilence and disease that commonplace, wreaked havoc elsewhere. Black death and famine, drought and disease. Crops stolen or destroyed by foraging armies. Manors neglected by absent landowners and their retainers who had either been away fighting or had been unfortunate enough not to return at all! Francis sighed, in England, what should have been both a modern and prosperous country, starvation was commonplace, for many still survived through 'subsistence' agriculture. They had but one opportunity to plant, cultivate and to harvest those crops that must sustain them through the long and cold winters.

'Who is your Lord and what is this manor?'

Addressing the serf who was closest to them, both tired and hungry Francis was sharper and more authoritarian than he'd intended to be.

It took some moments for the peasant to even acknowledge their presence, never mind answer them. Much to Francis's chagrin, the old man appeared at first to ignore him, continuing about his business, bent double, as he slowly pulled out the weeds, that proliferating were choking his intended crop. Finally, just as Francis was about to challenge him once again, the Peasant looked up and noticing that Francis was clearly one of rank, he nodded in deference.

The old man's hands and face of wrinkled and brown leathery skin were testament to the many years that he'd toiled in the fields. The white scar that ran down the side of his face and the two fingers that were missing from his right hand were indicative of his past soldiering.

'He may have fought with my Grandfather,' Francis thought as he eagerly asked the man, 'Did you fight for the king in France?'

The old man's smile revealed a pitifully few blackened and decaying teeth.

'Aye, I did young Sir,' he replied adding, 'I fought in France under Lord Talbot and his son De Lisle.' He sighed as he added, 'And I was at Castillon where they lost their lives and we lost the war.'

He shrugged and sighed again before adding ruefully, 'That's where I received this,' he said as he raised his mutilated hand for both boy's to see.

Surprisingly the old man chuckled, as nodding his head towards his lost fingers he said, 'We must have been good, for they went to quite some effort to make sure that we'd never flight arrows at them again.' Shaking his head the peasant added, 'Many amongst our army fought to the death, rather than allow themselves to be so disfigured,' he tutted as lowering his head he said, 'And many's the time I wish that I'd died with 'em.'

Francis's grandfather had also fought at Castillon. Badly injured, he'd escaped the battle with his life. Sadly his wounds, together with the sickness that had been brought on by many years of campaigning in France on behalf of the King, had taken their toll on his health. Sadly, Francis's grandfather had succumbed and died soon after returning to England and his beloved Minster Lovel. Francis who'd loved his grandfather had been distraught at his loss. When, however, he'd taken time to consider the old mans premature death, he'd felt strangely relieved. For it was perhaps merciful that his grandfather, who'd fought for many years on the continent, had not had been forced to witness England's final and humiliating defeat in France. A complete reversal in fortunes, that during the reign of King Henry had seen England lose all of her European possessions, save that is for the port of Calais!

Francis's father had often said, that had it not been for the incompetence of those men, who'd directed the War in France on behalf of Henry, they would still be masters in France. Francis on the other hand, and he was not alone in his opinion, doubted this. Yes, for decades the English longbow, supported by men at arms, had dominated the battlefields of Europe. English archers striking fear into the hearts of their adversaries. But the latter battles of the war with France had, however, ushered in a new era of warfare. Advances in the plate armour worn by the Knights and men at arms now meant that conventional archers had all but had their day. The bow and arrow had been superseded by both field artillery and the smaller handheld firearms. The culverines of the French had smashed their adversaries at Castillon, the English lines disintegrating under a hail of cannonballs, that obliterated a dozen or more men in one go! The English archers and men at arms, who were normally so resilient and dependable, had been scattered by this artillery barrage that had preceded the inevitable French cavalry attack. The French Knights, when they had charged, skittled aside those English who'd still remained on the field and slaughtered them. As always, the English had fought with stubborn determination and stories abounded of their bravery and chivalry. The English commander, John Talbot the Earl of Shrewsbury, had ridden into the battle un-armoured, carried upon a small white pony. Talbot, who'd previously been captured by the French, had been ransomed and released, only on condition that he'd sworn an oath never to bear arms against the French again. The brave English general was a man of his word and he'd kept his promise. It was perhaps fitting that Talbot had died on the battlefield, alongside so many of his brave men. Unhorsed by a cannonball, he'd been trapped beneath his mount and, helpless, had been disfigured by a Frenchman with a battle axe. So fearful were Talbot's injuries, that his body was only identified after the battle, due to a missing tooth. Many of the English archers, fearful of French retribution for their victories at Crecy and Agincourt, had fought on grimly to the death. They had been right to be terrified, for the French cavalry keen for revenge upon those who had up until that point, been their nemesis, gave no quarter. Many who attempted to surrender had their throats cut, the French mimicking the English's mistreatment of their prisoners during the battle of Agincourt. Even those who had been fortunate enough to evade the French horsemen died, drowned in the Dordogne River that had been at their backs throughout the engagement.

'This be Grafton Regis in the County of Northamptonshire.'
    Francis was startled, the old man's words woke him as his mind wandered.

The peasant continued, 'My master be Richard Woodville, Lord Rivers, husband to Lady Jacquettea, Duchess of Bedford.'

You'll find the manor house over there,' the old man said pointing towards a church tower, that nearby, rose above the small copse of trees, that signalled the eastern boundary of the cultivated clearing in which they stood.

'Near to the Church,' the Peasant added as he followed Francis's line of sight.

Both Ned Francis turned their horses towards the church. Almost as an afterthought, Francis reached into his tunic pocket and took out a newly minted groat, which he tossed towards the old man who in turn muttered his thanks for, 'Sir's kind generosity,' the peasant now no doubt congratulating himself on his good fortune in being approached by the two boys in the first place.

Francis, who was normally extremely careful when it came to money, satisfied himself with the consideration that the old archer, 'May have served with my grandfather in times past.'

As Francis dug his spurs into his horse's sides and urged it onwards towards Lord River's manor house at Grafton Regis he wondered, 'What do King Edward's men want in such a place and why the Woodville's.'

Noble society had been scandalised when the Duchess Jacquetta, widow to the Duke of Bedford, had married Richard Woodville who, at the time, had been little more than a Northamptonshire Squire. Jacquetta a French princess was the daughter of the Count of St Pol, in marrying the Duke of Bedford she had joined the elite of English society, Bedford being the King's Uncle, his regent in France and the one time governor of Normandy. Upon her first husbands death, unusually Jacquetta had married for the second time out of love, this a sentiment that rarely featured in noble society, that saw marriage as a 'means to an end'.

Francis knew that one day soon he too would be betrothed, no doubt to one whose only qualification was to bring the Lovel family more in the way of wealth and power. Francis shuddered as he considered those who, in similar circumstances to himself, had been married off to wealthy widows, some of whom were thirty to forty years their senior! In this Francis had always envied his friend Ned who, as a commoner, was not constrained by custom and could make his choice of wife from any amongst his own people. Francis smiled, Ned with his sturdy frame, good looks and excellent position within the Lovel's household, would no doubt have his pick of the village girls. Francis on the other hand, would have to console himself with the consideration that, as the Lord of the manor, in spite of his marriage vows, he would at least be able to satiate his desires with any of the woman folk, who were under his control. His wife on the other hand would be there to provide him with legitimate heirs.

Francis was a realist. He knew that even his own parents marriage was born of political expediency, rather than of love. He sighed, but this was the society in which they lived. On the surface a semblance of contented family life, yet in reality a thin veneer that concealed an undercurrent of baseness. Francis's mother as with all Noblewoman, was forced to overlook her husband's adultery. Those visits to the village, where the Baron was able to satiate those urges, that his wife was either unwilling or unable to countenance. Francis's father coupling with those women who were motivated only by their desire for money and would do anything for it! The Baron was reputed to pay well for these services, Francis's father rewarding handsomely, any who submitted to his brief struggling. Francis grimaced as he wondered how his father was able to lower himself so. To Francis still immature in both mind and body, these acts shamed his father and seemed both sordid and pointless.

Having tethered their horses to a slender willow tree in an adjacent copse of immature trees, both Francis and Ned approached the parish church of St Mary's at Grafton Regis on foot. Francis had decided, for the time being at least, to avoid the Woodville's manor house, which was situated in close proximity to the church. Both buildings were attractive, having been constructed of that soft light coloured Cotswold limestone for which the area was famous. Each structure was positioned atop each of the two hills, that were bisected by the small thoroughfare which ran through the hamlet. As such each of the buildings was ideally placed to command the approaches to the village. Crossing this road which was little more than a dirt track the Boys approached the church, which was itself surrounded by numerous rude dwellings of wattle and daub, that were clearly home to the majority of the villagers. Francis had surmised that it would be far more prudent to gather as much information as possible before considering any formal visit to the Woodville's manor house, especially now that they'd seen that the house was flying not only Edward's personal colours, but also the Royal Lions and fleur de lye. So King Edward must have been amongst the small group of riders. 'But Why?' Francis was intrigued. 'But where better,' he thought, 'To discover the real reason for the King's visit,' than in the church. For the church was the centrepiece of all rural communities, a place where people came not only to worship but also to gossip, share stories and news and even on occasions, when the Priest wasn't about, to conduct business.

Francis, closely followed by Ned, skipped up the rough path of cobbles that, via an avenue of ancient yew trees, led to the church's porch. Francis paused for some moments to breathe in the powerful fragrance exuded by the trees and to admire the beauty of their foliage, dark green and enduring regardless of the season. This in contrast to those commoner species of tree, whose transient beauty was confined only to the warmer months. Francis smiled as he considered his naivety, it was only very recently that he'd discovered why the yew, important for both its religious connotations and its practical uses in supplying the wood for the longbow, was confined to churchyards. Ned had laughed at Francis when he'd asked him why such a beautiful tree wasn't more commonplace throughout the countryside. Ned had sighed as he'd explained to Francis that the trees berries were extremely poisonous to livestock and, as such, the Yew was restricted to those locations where animals were not allowed, namely the churchyard. Francis smiled, he was fascinated that many religious customs seemed to have quite practical applications and he'd often wondered what had come first. Francis smiled again as he considered that both the Jewish and Islamic religions required that their people were buried within twenty four hours of death, ostensibly this was to facilitate the deceased's smooth progression to paradise. However, as these religions were generally centred in those countries were the enduring heat would putrefy a body very quickly, they were also extremely practical considerations! Unfortunately in this issue Christianity differed from those other religions. Chuckling to himself Francis remembered how his father had told him that, upon his death in France, King Henry III's body was delayed for some weeks in being brought back to England for burial. This due to storms and bad weather in the English channel. Apparently those monks who'd been enlisted to recite prayers and psalms over the King's corpse, had themselves soon succumbed to disease brought about by living in such close proximity to Henry's decomposing remains!

It took the combined strength of both Ned and Francis to open the great oak door that lined with iron plate, like the building which it secured, was no doubt centuries old. The creaking of the door echoed eerily within the hollowness of the ancient church. Followed closely by Ned, Francis was first to enter the nave. The air inside the church was cool. To the boy's right was an altar upon which a plain gold cross and chalice were displayed. Adjacent to this was a rood screen, which was decorated with the finely painted figures of Christ and his attendant saints. Turning to his left Francis shivered as he noticed at the back of the church that there was the alabaster tomb of an old knight. Interested, having hurried over to the monument, Francis ran his hand over the cold marble, tracing both the knights features and the old fashioned chain mail that indicated the tombs age. 'Preserved forever' Francis thought.

'He fought for the Holy father and the Plantagenet's in Palestine.'

Startled Francis jumped as a man's voice echoed throughout the church, that up until that point he'd assumed was empty. Francis turned to see that a young clergyman was approaching them from the direction of the altar and the vestry beyond.

Even though it was still sometime before evensong, the priest was clothed in both a surplus and cassock.

'And what do you two boy's seek here in the parish of Grafton Regis?' Direct, the young clergyman clearly wanted an explanation for their presence in 'his' Church.

Irritated that another so young could refer to him as a 'boy', Francis answered for them both, 'If you must know we saw the King's standard and were curious as to why he had chosen to visit your masters house.'

'The King does not visit my master in his house.' No doubt seeing the quizzical look on both Francis and Ned's faces, smiling triumphantly the priest explained, 'My master is God and this is His house, the King does not visit my master, he calls upon Lord River's at his manor house. My master he is not.'

Unimpressed by the priests rhetoric and keen for an argument, Francis was quick to reply, 'Was it not Lord River's forbears who built this church?' Is it not he who puts meat on your table and provides money for the upkeep of your fine church.'

The priest interjected, 'Be careful young sir for your blasphemies may be your downfall, Lord Rivers knows that which is required of him to guarantee his place in paradise,' he frowned before he added, 'Do you?'

Francis fell silent as he contemplated the cleric's words and conceded to himself that his immature and inexperienced mind was no match for that of the clergyman. One who had no doubt received his education at the hands of Jesuit priests, who themselves were trained and had studied in Rome. Men who dedicated their lives to the devotion of the Catholic Church and to its teachings.

Ned spoke for Francis, 'Please forgive our impudence, we are young and are intrigued to know why the King, who has pressing matters in the North, would deign to visit your small Parish.'

The Cleric smiled, 'The King is this day to be wed, to Lord Rivers daughter, the Lady Elizabeth Woodville.'

Astounded Francis blurted out his thoughts, 'But the King is to marry a French princess, the Earl of Warwick has these past few months been negotiating with King Louis's envoys....' The young priest smiling again interrupted, 'Wrong again. Edward has been charmed by the Lady Elizabeth who is beauty personified, he will have no other and they are to be married today in the chapel that adjoins Lord Rivers's manor house, this by the hand of my master, Father Bloxham.' The young man laughed as he added, 'it seems as if Lord Warwick's efforts with the French have been made in vain.'

Francis stifled a desire to scoff at his arrogant and condescending adversary, whom he'd now discovered wasn't even the parish's priest! He's probably the second or third son of some local squire, Francis thought, sent for a life in the church because his father had only sufficient funds to secure the future of his eldest offspring. Francis scoffed, if only he knew who he was talking to. But Francis chose not to take the opportunity to reveal his true identity merely to satisfy his vanity, this in spite of the fact that he felt as if he'd taken quite a pounding in the recent verbal exchange.

'Who is this Lady Elizabeth,' Francis enquired somewhat quizzically.

'You're not from these parts are you?' The Young man studying Francis, continued when no reply to his question was forthcoming, 'She is the Lady Elizabeth Woodville, the widow of Sir John Grey of Groby whose Manor at Bradgate adjoins the City of Leicester.'

Francis was astounded, he knew of this man. Grey was a Lancastrian battle captain, he had fought with his father and had been killed at the Second Battle of St Albans. Surely the King would not sully himself with the wife of a mere knight, he thought, especially one who'd been party to and had been implicated in the deaths of both his father and brother at Wakefield.

'You bear false witness,' Francis accused the prelate, he went on without giving the young man the opportunity to protest. 'The King would not, nay could not, marry such a woman, a commoner, the nobility will not stand for it. And anyway it is said that the Earl of Warwick has all but negotiated Edward's marriage to a French princess.'

As Francis took breath, the curate was able to interrupt him, haughtily saying, 'Young Sir, you are indeed misinformed, for I am to sing at their wedding today. The ceremony will take place in the hermitage, Lord Rivers's private chapel, which is close to his manor house,' The priest smiled as he added triumphantly, 'You may accompany me there if you wish, to see for yourselves that I speak the truth. Perhaps once you've seen how beautiful the Lady Elizabeth is you'll be able to appreciate why it is the King has become infatuated with her and must have her for his own.'

'Why should he be forced to marry her though,' Francis wondered, for King Edward was famed for taking any woman who took his fancy, this invariably done even with the blessing of their husbands! The prelate who must have been reading Francis's thoughts smiled again, 'The Lady Elizabeth would not allow herself to be shamed, she has said that she'd rather die than be taken by Edward out of wedlock,' he chuckled as he added, 'My Lady may only be a woman, a poor widow but she knows how to make the best use of her assets and she has many relatives who seek advancement at Edward's court.'

The Priest could no doubt see that neither Ned nor Francis were convinced. As he left the church the young prelate beckoning for them to follow shouted after himself, 'Seeing is believing my young sceptics.'

The 'Hermitage' differed greatly from those other private chapels that were usually incorporated within or were adjoined to the manor houses of many of the aristocracy. Unusually Lord Rivers chapel was situated in a small copse near to his house. Consequently both Ned and Francis were able to secrete themselves with ease, amongst the large number of willow saplings that surrounded it. From their position both boys enjoyed an uninterrupted view of the small building and its porch. A robed clergyman, whom Francis assumed was Father Bloxham, was standing upon the flagstone pathway that led to the chapel. Francis smiled as the Priest chided his assistant for his lateness. 'Not so clever now,' Francis mumbled to himself as the young cleric, humbled, was quickly ushered inside by the older man. After a few moments Francis heard and then saw a small party approach the chapel from the direction of the manor house. The procession was led by an elderly couple who, judging by both their rich clothing and their demeanour, were obviously people of substance. 'The Duchess Jacquetta and her husband' Francis whispered. The couple were followed by two gentlemen who bore no livery. Behind these, arm in arm were a young couple, whom Francis assumed must be the Bride and Groom.

Francis gasped, for the bride was, in his opinion the most beautiful creature that he had ever seen. The young woman's gown of crushed pale blue velvet, failed to conceal her slender, yet womanly figure, which curved gently both at her hips and at her full bosom. Her long blonde hair which was swept back from a small head dress, revealed a fashionably high forehead. Her eyes were large and, from were he was hidden, Francis could see that they were of a deep emerald green, her skin, milky white and pure, bore no blemishes.

'She's beauty itself' Francis whispered as he nudged Ned, for his friend appeared equally mesmerised.

However as he studied her further Francis became concerned. For this woman, whom he took to be the Lady Elizabeth, in spite of this being her wedding day, the occasion of her marriage to the King himself, was not smiling at all. Indeed her thin lips were pursed together and she appeared to be scowling!

As he examined the future Queen of England, Francis was filled with a sense of foreboding. 'What does the Lady Elizabeth want with the King?' 'What manner of witchcraft has beguiled the King to marry beneath himself? Contrary to the wishes of his cousin and mentor the Earl of Warwick.' Shuddering, Francis could only guess how society would react to such a scandal, the King marrying an older woman who was both a widow and a commoner.

Accompanying the Lady Elizabeth was one whom Francis could only describe as her male equivalent in beauty. Francis had not previously met the King, but to him this man was instantly recognisable. Edward was tall and of an extremely athletic build. His face, closely shaven, was slightly rounded, this softening those features that exuded both might and power, which in others may have been described as purely manly. Surprisingly the King's expression exuded kindness. This man was a Yorkist and an enemy, yet in spite of himself Francis couldn't help but admire him. Francis smiled as he noticed the darker skin beneath the King's eyes that alluded to the fact that presently, Edward didn't appear to sleep soundly without worries. The King's hair a dark chestnut in colour, was cut fashionably just above the collar of his tunic of black and gold. If one still doubted the man's provenance it was confirmed when one studied the Livery of England that was emblazoned on Edward's tunic, as was his personal badge, 'The Sun in Splendour'. As the small procession slowly made its way towards the chapel, the King held his head high. Edward smiling confidently was clearly relishing the prospect of his marriage. Upon being greeted at the porch by the Priest he clapped his hands together as he presented his bride to be.

'Naive and blissfully unaware,' Francis whispered to himself, as he considered the repercussions of such an impetuous and ill conceived marriage.

'Can he not see what he is doing.' Francis hissed. Before Ned had time to whisper any reply or indeed to tell Francis to quieten himself down for fear that they would be discovered, Francis added gleefully in a hushed voice, 'The nobility's sure to be scandalised, The Earl of Warwick'll be furious.' Smiling Francis's thoughts turned once again to their father's, 'Ned do you realise that this marriage might create a rift between Edward and his mentor and this might just tip the balance in favour of King Henry', he too clapped his hands together as he added, 'Our fathers may still yet prevail.'

Once the small group had all reached the porch and had been greeted and blessed by the priest, all present bowed their heads in what appeared to Francis to be a silent prayer. 'At least the Lady has respect for God, if not for the King,' Francis thought.

Marriages were always conducted at the entrance to the church, as the couple could only thereafter enter the church as man and wife. Father Bloxham began the service in a voice that was, to Francis, barely audible. 'It's as if he too is fearful of the consequences,' Francis whispered to Ned, who muttered in agreement as they continued to stare, transfixed by the strange and unexpected event upon which they'd happened.

Silent Francis could hardly breathe, as he tried desperately to listen to the proceedings.

Father Bloxham began, 'Edward Plantagenet, hast though will to have this woman, Lady Elizabeth Woodville, to thy wedded wife.'

The King replied in a soft voice, 'Yes Father.'

The priest went on, 'Edward Plantagenet will thou do thy best to love her and to hold her and no other to her life's end.'

Edward again replied, 'Yes Father.' Francis did his best to stifle a chuckle for he, like so many others, had heard of the King's reputation for whoring, which was well deserved. Ned, no doubt fearful of discovery, silenced Francis with a well aimed jab of his elbow to Francis's ribs. Suitably chastised, Francis fell silent.

Father Bloxham continued, unaware that the ceremony was being witnessed by the two uninvited boys.

'Edward Plantagenet, take this Lady by the hand and say after me.......'

The King then repeated those words, that tied him in the eyes of God to Lady Elizabeth Woodville. Incredulous, Francis gazed on in awe. Who would believe what they'd witnessed that day.

'I Edward Plantagenet take thee, Lady Elizabeth Woodville, in the form of Holy Church to be my wedded wife forsaking all others, in sickness and health in riches and in poverty till death us do part and there I do plight my troth.'

King Edward IV of England had married both a widow and a commoner!

Neither Francis nor Ned remained to witness the remainder of the service, which was to take place within the chapel itself. As the group were beckoned inside by Father Bloxham and his young assistant began to sing a thanksgiving to God, both boys recovered their horses and in the growing gloom, hastily made their way back to Lillingstone Lovel.

Francis felt that once back in the relative safety of his cousins manor house, he could take time to consider that which he'd witnessed and how best to act upon the knowledge that he'd acquired.

There was no disputing the fact, that in the hands of the Lancastrians this information would be invaluable. In marrying the Lady Elizabeth the King had not only insulted his mentor the Earl of Warwick, but he'd also thrown away his most valuable asset, his own marriage. Noble society would be scandalised. Would the aristocracy of England continue to support such a naive and impetuous King? One who was guided by that which was within his trousers, rather than by his councillors and that which was between his ears!

Whilst Francis remained at Lillingstone Lovel and prevaricated about how and to whom he should disclose this information, tragically circumstances beyond his control once again overtook him.

In the third week of May news came that the Lancastrian army that had assembled in Northumberland under the general ship of the Duke of Somerset, had been annihilated at Hexham, by the Yorkist army commanded by Warwick's brother, Lord Montague. Both Francis's and Ned's fathers were said to have been present at the rout. Since news of the defeat had arrived at Lillingstone, no information about their present whereabouts or situation was forthcoming and both were now assumed to be dead. According to the despatch rider who'd delivered the sad news, a significant proportion of the Lancastrian nobility present at the battle, had either been killed in the rout, or had been executed at Hexham, Newcastle and Middleham in the days that had followed it. Francis, despite his grief and worry, as always was keen to hear the details of the engagement and after much pressing the informant, who was keen to be on his way, reluctantly imparted what information he had. Apparently after the debacle at Hedgely Moor, the Duke of Somerset had managed to regroup his forces and, on being reinforced by fresh troops, he'd marched southwards intent on bringing Montague to battle, before he was reinforced by the King. The two armies had finally met outside Hexham where, Somerset discovered that he was outnumbered by some four to one. Moreover Somerset who'd failed to post any picket's, without spies, was effectively blind in what was hostile country. The Lancastrian army had been arrayed at the base of a ridge, in a small meadow which was situated in the loop of a small river, or beck to their rear. Apparently the Duke had maintained that this position was more easily defensible, this because there was only, 'one way in and one way out.'

As the despatch rider described the events to Francis, it was clear that the young soldier was clearly still exasperated and non plus sed by his commanders ineptitude.

'We tried to tell him it was a death trap,' he exclaimed. 'The Yorkists came upon us without warning, they swept down the hill and were upon us before we were even able to arm ourselves. We'd nowhere to go, those who stood and fought were cut down within minutes and most of those who chose to flee were drowned in the river.'

Francis shuddered as he remembered how his father had always maintained that a General should always ensure that the men under his command had an, 'open and obvious line of retreat,' 'to prevent panic and any consequent rout.'

Apparently Somerset who'd chosen not to fight, had been captured on the field of battle.

'The Duke can't have expected mercy,' Francis thought as he recalled how Somerset had already availed himself of the King's pardon at Bamburgh, he shuddered as he recalled how his father too had been reprieved after Towton.

Thankfully, King Henry was still reputed to be at large with a small number of his retainers.

'Please let God spare my father,' Francis prayed.

Neither for the first nor the last time, God was to disappoint Francis who never saw his father again.

Summoned back to Minster Lovel, Francis discovered that his father, who had been present at Hexham, was not in King Henry's party and was therefore assumed to have been killed in the Battle. On hearing this news Francis had objected, surely there must be news of his father's fate, for any person of rank, dead or alive, would be easily recognisable on the field. Francis was disappointed yet again. Apparently the Yorkist attack had been so swift and unexpected, that many amongst the Lancastrian army had been unable to don their armour and, as such, many Noblemen were taken for and were slain as commoners. This time Edward had been in no mood for mercy and his orders to Lord Montague had been explicit, spare no-one.

It was therefore now assumed that Francis was the Ninth Baron Lovel.

Fortunately, as the late Baron's body had not been found upon the field, the Yorkists could not prove his complicity in the rebellion. As a result the Lovels, in contrast to many others, were allowed to retain their lands and titles. Sadly as a minor, Francis was adjudged to be too young to inherit. The King therefore sold Francis's wardship to the highest bidder, who ironically happened to be none other than the Earl of Warwick. Francis's grandmother, mother and sisters were to remain at Minster Lovel at the 'Earl's pleasure.' Francis on the other hand was to travel to the Earl's Castle in Yorkshire, at Middleham, there to serve out the years of his wardship and minority, until Warwick determined that he was of an age to assume his rights and titles. Francis saw that this would present him with a number of problems. Firstly, he was a Lancastrian and as such would be much despised by both the Earl and his retainers. Secondly, and perhaps more importantly, whilst a minor the Earl would receive all of the moneys generated by the Lovel possessions. Why then would the Earl ever relinquish these by declaring Francis 'of age?' And thirdly, Francis like so many other 'Southerners', had a deep distrust of the 'northern people', those whom he adjudged to be uncivilised, uncouth and uncultured, he shuddered at the prospect of living amongst these people.

The prospect of leaving for Yorkshire and his new yet uncertain life, this coming so soon after receiving the crushing news that his father was dead, was almost too much for Francis to bear. But Francis was determined that none should witness any tears or emotion, for he was the Ninth Baron Lovel and, as such, he resolved that he would cry no more.

Chapter Six
July 1464. Middleham, North Yorkshire.

Francis, out of breath, collapsed onto the soft green grass that marked the high ground to the north of the great fortress that was Middleham Castle, the court and preferred residence of Richard Neville, Earl of Warwick, Francis's new patron. As he lay back on the small hill of springy turf, all that was left of the motte of the original Norman timber castle, Francis sighed and gazed up into the clear blue sky. This northern land, that was so very different from his beloved Oxfordshire, was to Francis both beautiful and enthralling. Smiling, Francis considered what a difference a few weeks had made.

It had been precisely three weeks since Francis had first arrived at Middleham in the 'far north' of England. The Earl's Castle, his new home, which was situated at the foot of Wensleydale, was ideally sited to secure this Pennine thoroughfare for its masters, the Yorkshire branch of the Neville family. Since arriving in Yorkshire, homesick Francis had spent much of his spare time sitting on this very spot, the site of the earthworks of the original castle of Middleham, built by Alan the Norman Lord of Richmond some four hundred years earlier. He had to admit, it was an ideal location from which to peruse their magnificent surroundings. To their west were the Pennine's, the 'backbone of England', a mountain range that divided the Kingdom in two, impassable for many travellers, save that is for the few passes that bisected it from East to West. One of these thoroughfares was Wensleydale, a route that was said to have been used by man since pre history. Looking to the North, West and even to the South, the traveller could easily appreciate that he was now in the 'wild and rugged northlands', a part of the country much maligned by the civilised South. For Middleham was all but surrounded by bleak and mountainous lands. Following the line of the River Ure to the West, one could see how over many years the river had carved a course for itself as it avoided the great outcrops of hard granite. Twisting and turning throughout the soft peat earth and rock of the Pennine landscape as it created Wensleydale and the pass which this Castle now protected. Here the landscape was for the most part un populated, save that is for the few hill farmers who struggled to eke out an existence in those small pockets of productive earth that had been created by the river. The steep valley sides were unlike anything that Francis had seen before in the heavily forested south and were practically devoid of any vegetation. The only plant that survived was the heather which in flower was a deep purple, the only colour to soften the wild terrain. North Yorkshire was, however, not the singularly inhospitable place that many Southerners would have you believe. From Middleham if you looked Eastwards you would see a land so very different, countryside that reminded Francis very much of his home. Here the river slowed to meet a wide plain. With its course no longer dictated by rock the Ure gradually meandered its way through a wide and lush valley as it passed through both thick woods, ideal for hunting, or through fields that had been cultivated over many years by the Monks who inhabited the magnificent Abbeys of Jervaulx and Fountains. Finally at Ripon the river met Dere Street, the Great North Road, from whence it maintained its easterly course to the sea beyond. This land, in spite of its proximity to the bleak Moors, was so very different. Here man had prospered and here resided some of the most influential men of the English nobility. Scropes, Fitzhughs, Greystokes, Dacres and the Neville's, a family who were by far the most influential and who had been masters here at Middleham since the latter half of the thirteenth century. Francis's patron Richard Neville, the Earl of Warwick, or as he was now known 'The Kingmaker', was arguably the greatest of all of his forbears. Moreover through his marriage Richard Neville had acquired the Beauchamp inheritance of the Midlands and hence his present title, the Earl of Warwick. He had added these acquisitions to those Neville possessions in the north which he'd inherited from his father the Earl of Salisbury who had died with Richard of York at the Battle of Wakefield. The Neville family now enjoyed a monopoly of power in the north. The Earl's brother John Lord Montague the commander of the King's forces who had been victorious at the Battle of Hexham, was even said to be in the process of receiving from a grateful King the Earldom of Northumberland, this honour seized from the Percy family after Sir Ralph Percy had been killed fighting for the Lancastrians at Hedgely Moor. Moreover, the Westmoreland branch of the Neville family controlled all of England's western borders with Scotland. Historically, the Percys had been the Neville's opponents in the north and had helped to counter the expansion of their power and influence. With them gone there was now noone to challenge Neville supremacy and as a consequence the Earl's family had become the most dominant faction in all of England. Many shrewd men said privately that it was the Earl and not the King who shaped the policies of the realm. Francis smiled as he recalled how the political situation in England had been summed up by the French Ambassador who had recently visited England and on his return to France had claimed that there were now two Kings in England. 'Monsieur de Warwick and another whose name escapes me.'

Presently the Earl was in the process of negotiating a marriage alliance between the King of England and a French princess. It was rumoured that the French King Louis, keen for the proposal to go ahead, had even promised Warwick his own European Duchy if the Earl was able to secure Edward's support for the union. Unfortunately for Warwick it was common knowledge that the King presently favoured an Alliance with the Burgundians. Francis smiled as he recalled the many conversations that he'd had with his fellow courtiers at Middleham. All were confidant that Warwicks 'will' would prevail in the matter as it did in most things. Francis knew better but dare not tell anyone that which he had witnessed at Grafton Regis. As a result it was with both dread and anticipation that he awaited his first meeting with the Earl, his benefactor, who was due to return to Yorkshire in the near future.

Sitting up, Francis looked down the hill towards the castle. Both as a stronghold and a palace Middleham rivalled anything that the south of England had to offer. Its light grey stone contrasted sharply with the green, yellow and purple of the surrounding fields and moors. The great citadel seemed to shine as the sun picked it out above all else. The original part of the castle, the stone keep, was the centre point of the stronghold. Incorporating both the Great Hall and its kitchens, it rose above and dwarfed the Castle's outer walls and chambers, these structures having been added in later centuries. As with Castle Hedingham, access to the Keep was restricted to a single external staircase. At Middleham however this staircase was protected by three gates and a guardroom, all of which ensured that the keep was practically impregnable to attack. Not surprisingly therefore, the keep also housed the private chambers of the Earl's immediate family. The outer fortifications of the castle were protected on all sides by a deep moat. These walls incorporated the living chambers of both the Earl's household servants and any guests or visitors. Francis was impressed, for the Neville's in their design and building, whilst managing to retain the Castle's defensible strength, had also incorporated into it many of the comforts of modern living. The Garderobe Tower positioned in the west wall contained the most sophisticated system of latrines that Francis had ever seen! Moreover, an intricate system of timber bridges and raised walkways ensured that Middleham's visitors and inhabitants rarely had to venture onto the ground floor, cluttered as it was with both servants and waste. The southern tower in the outer wall was home to both Francis and to his new friend, the Earl's 'most distinguished guest', Francis's companion that day, Richard Plantagenet the Duke of Gloucester. Richard was King Edward's youngest brother and was a 'Prince of Royal Blood'. Surprisingly despite his birthright, like Francis, the King's brother was also presently in the wardship of the Earl of Warwick.

Francis glanced side wards at the boy who had become both his companion and ally. Since his arrival at Middleham both Francis and Richard had become firm friends. Francis often wondered why Richard, two years his senior, had shown such an interest in him, he was after all a Lancastrian, an enemy to Richard's family. Francis theorised that it was in all probability because their current circumstances were so alike. Both of their young lives having been tinged with a deep sadness at the loss of their fathers in the recent wars. Again Francis scrutinised his friend who lay next to him. Richard was breathing heavily from his recent excursions and his eyes, half closed, were protected from the bright sunlight by the palm of his raised right hand. Richard, Francis felt, was in appearance much like himself. His dark straight hair and angular features testament to the fact his ancestry also stretched back to the Norman's, those who had built the castle on whose remains they now lay.

Richard seemed to sense that Francis was studying him, he turned to Francis and resting his head on his left elbow grinned saying, 'It's kitchen duty for you again today.'

Francis rankled at the thought of the hot and airless kitchens and wondered why he continued to bet with the older boy who was both stronger and cleverer than he. 'I'll never beat him' he thought as he recalled all of those races lost. How he'd vainly chased after Richard as they ran from the castle walls and up the steep hill to the spot where they now lay.

'You're only friends with me because I'm the only one you can beat in your little wagers,' he laughed.

Richard immediately became more serious, his forehead creased in a deep frown, as sitting up he confronted Francis. 'I can trounce them all' he said. 'Was it not me who thrashed the others when they started to bully and torment you...'

Alarmed at Richards sudden and unexpected change of mood, Francis interjected in an effort to placate the older boy. 'I know you can beat them all. I'm sorry, I was only joking, I'm grateful indeed for your help.'

Francis silently chided himself. Why didn't he think before he spoke? He recalled how, before Richard had intervened on his behalf, his first few days at the Castle had been miserable. Bullied by the other henchman and home sick, still grieving the loss of his father he'd often despaired of life itself.

Thankfully Richard's mood seemed to lighten again and he rose to his feet saying. 'It's time we returned to the Castle.' He grinned again and laughed. 'You've work to do in the kitchens.'

Before Francis had time to reply he found himself running as fast his legs would take him down the hill in pursuit of the older boy, Richard by now some distance ahead shouted. 'For the stables tomorrow.'

Francis, too tired to either answer or argue, out of breath and unbalanced by a speedy descent on uneven ground, fell face down as he contemplated the prospect that tomorrow would also be yet another busy day. As he considered his additional duties on the following day Francis smiled and thought to himself. 'Now that I'm on my own I'll have to chose my friends much more carefully.'

Other people's chores or not, Francis's time at Middleham as a 'henchman' to the Earl of Warwick, was to say the least extremely hectic. As a result once evening came, Francis was happy to take to the bed that he shared with Richard. Unfortunately despite his tiredness Francis enjoyed little sleep. Richard talked incessantly, often well into the night. Francis often wondered if his friend even continued long into the small hours, even after Francis had finally succumbed to the exhaustion that was induced by the rigorous training of his new life. Richard spoke of politics, of the power that he would enjoy when he finally came of age. He proudly announced that he would one day marry one of the Earl of Warwick's two daughters, Anne or Isabel, and how in doing so he would secure not only his own inheritance, but also that of the Neville's as well! Richard seemed to delight in the battles that he predicted would follow. Confused, Francis would question him further,

'But who would oppose your brother, is he not secure on his throne?'

Richard had alarmed Francis with his reply. 'He will never be secure, not whilst Henry, his son and that infernal Queen still live and anyway' he'd added 'How can a King ever be secure on his throne? To rule A King must be able to count upon the support of others.' As Francis had frowned, Richard had become impatient with his friends naiveté. 'Look around you, what do you think would become of my brother if the Earl of Warwick took up arms against him.'

Francis protested. 'But they're comrades and cousins, as their fathers were before them, they would never bear arms against each other.....surely not.'

Worryingly Richard had remained silent, choosing not to reply to Francis's question.

Francis knew that the system of education in which he now found himself in, was much reviled by England's 'civilised' European neighbours, who considered the English both 'course and vulgar'. Francis and his fellow 'henchman' however knew no different, although Francis had not been surprised when he'd recently discovered that the Venetian Ambassador who'd recently visited England had voiced his opinion on the matter!

'The want of affection in the English is strongly manifested towards their children; for after keeping them at home till they arrive at the age of seven or nine years at the utmost, they put them out, both males and females, to hard service in the houses of other people, binding them generally for another seven or nine years. All these are called apprentices or henchmen, and during that time they perform all the most menial offices. Few are born who are exempted from this fate, for everyone, however rich he may be, sends away his children into the houses of others, while he in return receives those strangers into his own. When I inquired their reason for this severity, they answered that they did it in order that their children might learn better manners. But I, for my part believe that they do it because they like to enjoy all of their comforts themselves, and they are better served by strangers than they would be by their own children. Besides which the English, being great epicures and very avaricious by nature, indulge in the most delicate fare themselves and give their household the coarsest bread and beer and cold meat baked on Sunday for the week, which however, they allow them in great abundance. Whereas if they had their own children at home, they would be obliged to give them the same food they made use of for themselves. If the parents sent their children away from home to learn virtue and good manners and took them back again when their apprenticeship was over, they might, perhaps, be excused; but they never return, for the girls are settled by their patrons, and the boys make the best marriages they can, and, assisted by their patrons, not by their fathers, they also open a house and strive diligently by this means to make some fortune for themselves.'

When Francis had discussed that which he'd heard with Richard, the older boy had done little to hide the contempt that he obviously felt for 'the foreigner' and 'his opinions', which Richard said were 'best kept to himself'. For 'We the English are breeding a race of warriors and not sops'.

Francis knew that this regimen was hardening and quickening him both physically and mentally. He also knew that these qualities would help him in later life, so his grumbles were infrequent and were confined to only a few stolen moments. Times when he was able to escape from the hustle and bustle of the Castle to enjoy his own company, usually when perched on 'his hill', as he contemplated both his present and his past life. Francis missed both Oxfordshire and his parents but he was a realist, he knew that he would need to make the most of his time at Middleham. At some point in the future he would he be declared 'of age' and then no longer a minor in the wardship of the Earl, he could return to his beloved Minster Lovel. But as the Baron Lovel he must be well versed in the intricacies and complexities of feudal Society. He must learn to fight, joust, and command a host of men, as well as developing an appreciation for the arts, to be accustomed to the literature of Gower, Chaucer and Hoccleve. Francis smiled as he pictured in his minds eye those other boys at Middleham. He laughed as he wondered how they would fare in modern society. that's if in fact they ever got there. The Boy's having to master the skills and graces required before they'd be accepted into 'proper society'. Francis smiled again as he considered the 'book of nurture', the 'hench man's' rule book, their 'bible', which if followed to the letter, would ensure that the reader would be able to make the transition from Boy to youth and from youth to a Man.

Even now Francis was surprised by works frankness, he laughed as he remembered a particularly graphic section which advised that the reader should under no circumstances.

'Slump against a post, fidget, stick your finger in your nose, put your hands in your hose to scratch your privy parts, spit over the table or too far, clean a dish by licking it with your tongue, pick your teeth, breathe stinking breath into the face of the Lord, blow on your food, stuff masses of bread into your mouth, scratch your head, loosen your girdle and belch, 'burnish' bones with your teeth or probe teeth with a knife, pick not your nose, nor that it be dropping with no pearls clear.....

And always beware of thy hinder part from guns blasting'.

If these were examples of the already brutish behaviour of some of the henchmen, Francis felt that he'd got quite a head start on them already!

Sharing a bed with the Kings youngest brother, also helped Francis to cope in this new environment. Much as it tried him, whenever possible Francis forced himself to stay awake as his friend rattled on! For as he listened to his friend, Francis was learning much of politics and of recent history, even if these observations were based upon a differing viewpoint, a Yorkist one! Francis slowly began to appreciate that acts of savagery and treachery were not the sole preserve of the Yorkists, nor was the House of Lancaster the only dynasty with legitimate claims to the thrones of both England and France.

Richard, two years Francis's senior, was the youngest son of the late Richard Duke of York. As the male heir to the house of Plantagenet, York had coveted the crown for himself and was in fact, the original Yorkist claimant to the throne. The pedigree of both the houses of Lancaster and York originated from lines of descent taken from Edward III's sons. Henry VI was the great grandson of John of Gaunt, Edwards third son. Richard's father, through the male line was grandson of Edward's fourth son Edmund Duke of York. However matters were complicated further when one considered that York was also descended from Edward's second son, Lionel Duke of Clarence, this through his mother Anne Mortimer, who was the great granddaughter of Lionel. Francis had been surprised to learn from Richard that in England there was no law that disbarred a claim to the throne that was made through the female line and as such the Duke of York's 'Plantagenet' claim was irrefutably senior to that of the House of Lancaster. Francis was also slowly beginning to appreciate Richard's concerns in respect of the stability of his brother's throne, especially when one considered how closely many amongst the upper echelons of the English aristocracy were interrelated. Francis's mind whirred as he tried to understand how all of the families were connected to one another by marriage. Practically speaking if one was a member of the higher nobility, one was effectively 'cousin' to those who called themselves King. Thus many amongst the aristocracy had some form of claim to the throne. Moreover the whole situation had been exacerbated when those amongst the lower nobility had latched onto one side or another. Men encouraging their patron to press his claim to the throne, in the hope that if successful their master would repay them for their support, conferring both power and influence upon them.

Since the Battle of Hexham Francis had erroneously assumed that the Lancastrian cause, like so many of its exponents, was now dead. Now he could see that Richard was right when he said, 'ambitious men will follow whatever cause from which they can gain the most.' Whilst either King Henry or his son still lived so did the House of Lancaster, for eventually men would rise up again on its behalf, for victory could bring them both rewards and high office.

Richard's knowledge was vast, he had opinions on almost everything and in contrast to Francis was very well travelled. Francis had marvelled as Richard had described to him his period of exile in Burgundy at the Court of Duke Philip at Bruges. How both Richard and his elder brother George Duke of Clarence had even had the honour of being escorted from the port of Sluys to the capital and to the Duke's court by the papal legate himself!

Richard had also played a prominent part in his brother's coronation. Francis pictured in his minds eye how his young companion must have looked, dressed in a blue velvet gown edged in white fur, as he rode before his brother the King, leading the procession that took Edward to the palace of Westminster for his coronation. Francis, who had no brothers himself, could not help but feel a tinge of jealousy as Richard spoke of his elder brother the King. How he described the great feats of arms that Edward had accomplished, Francis did not doubt his friend for one moment for the King was venerated as a the great warrior. Francis, who himself had only recently seen the King for the first time, could only imagine both the adoration and fear that Edward generated when, fully armoured and horsed upon on his great white destrier, he addressed his troops and personally led them into battle.

Richard had also known much sadness. He spoke with grief as he described how his other brother, Edmund Earl of Rutland, had been cruelly murdered on Wakefield bridge by the Lancastrian Lord Clifford. Tears had welled up in Francis's eyes as Richard had explained that all Edmund had wanted in life, 'Was to sing and to read his poetry.' Francis had been unable to answer his friend as Richard had repeated the same question, each time that he spoke of his dead father and brother. 'Why did they ride out of Sandal Castle to meet an army that outnumbered them? For both Edward and Warwick were riding north to Wakefield to relieve the garrison.' Francis couldn't understand why the Duke of York had left the comparative safety of the Castle to engage Queen Margaret's larger Lancastrian army. Rumours abounded, some alleged that the Lancastrians had disguised themselves in Warwick's livery to mislead the garrison into believing that they'd been relieved. Others said that the Lancastrians had concealed both their right and left flanks in woodland, to make it appear that there army was far smaller than it was. It was generally accepted however, that a truce had been agreed between the opposing factions. The understanding was said to have covered the period of the Christmas festivities and was to have lasted until at least after the feast of Epiphany on the sixth of January. The Battle had actually been fought on the penultimate day of December. Apparently Richard's father had maintained that as God himself recognised his right to the throne he was invincible, even with a lesser force. It was said that York, who was a proud man, could take no more of the daily goading of the Lancastrian heralds who, in clear breach of the truce, had called up to the Yorkists on the battlements of Sandal Castle taunting the Duke. The Lancastrianis had questioned York's. 'Want of courage in suffering himself to be tamely braved by a woman,' that is King Henry's French Queen, Margaret of Anjou. Ultimately it had became too much for Richard's father to bear. On the thirtieth of December 1460 a foraging party returning to the Castle had come under attack. The Duke used this skirmish as an opportunity to confront the Lancastrians. Assembling a small army from the men of the garrison York rode out of the Castle and into what was a trap. The battle cost Richard's father his life together with that of his son Edmund and the Earl of Warwick's father, the Earl of Salisbury. Richard, who also believed in his families divine right to rule, was however more practical than his father had been in his assessments, he grimly quipped, 'Beware Francis, for on the field of battle, the treachery of man far outweighs even the will of God.'

Throughout their long discussions Richard spoke little of his other brother George Duke of Clarence. Francis often wondered what had passed between the two as they'd both shared many experiences in their young lives. Indeed it had been George and not another of his siblings who had accompanied Richard to Burgundy. When Richard did speak of Clarence it was with disdain, as he described to Francis the older boy's petty jealousies and grasping nature. Ironically it seemed as if the King was blind to both George's failings and to Richard's admiration of Edward, for it was Clarence and not Richard whom the King showered with gifts of lands and titles. Francis was bemused and often wondered what had passed between the Brother's.

Francis was fascinated to hear of Richard's family, especially of his brothers. Francis's only siblings were sisters and although they were dear to his heart they were hardly the same! In the past Francis had found companionship and friendship with Ned, but Ned was a commoner and, as such, as time went by their relationship had become increasingly inappropriate. Richard obviously sensed Francis's envy. One evening in their chambers Richard said something that had a profound effect on Francis and gladdened his heart. At the time Richard had been explaining how his brother Edward, 'A great General', had engineered the Yorkist victories at Towton and Mortimers Cross. Richard had clearly appreciated Francis's longing, for as Francis was finally falling to sleep he was sure that he'd heard Richard say to him, 'Don't worry Francis, I'll be your brother.'

When Francis awoke early on the following morning he turned to see Richard next to him, still sleeping soundly. Smiling at his newest friend Francis wondered if he'd in fact dreamt the words.

Chapter 7
Middleham. August 1464.

Francis finally met his illustrious benefactor, the Earl of Warwick, towards the end of August. This after the Earl and his brother in law, Henry Lord Fitzhugh of Ravensworth who was the English ambassador to Scotland, had both returned home to Middleham. These two men who politically speaking were extremely important, both at home and abroad, had most recently been formalising the truce with Scotland, which had been signed by the Earl's brother at Norham. The Anglo Scottish alliance was designed to compliment the treaty that the Earl had agreed with the French, earlier that year in March, a settlement with Scotland's 'auld ally' that was due to be ratified and further extended in October. The Earl who had taken a personal interest in the matter, was due to attend a Conference with the French at St Omer on the 1st October. At that meeting Warwick hoped to conclude those negotiations which had been conducted throughout the summer on his behalf, by Lord Wenlock and his lieutenant at Guines, Richard Whetehill. Wenlock who was said to be one of the Earl's 'oldest and dearest friend's' was also due at Middleham, to brief Warwick in respect of these negotiations.

Francis had been excited for quite sometime, for he was to be present at the great feast that had been arranged to celebrate the Earl's homecoming.

Francis first set eyes upon his patron within the great hall, where the festivities were held on the evening of the Earl's return.

Surprisingly for once, both Francis and the other 'henchmen' were allowed to take part in both the banquet and the celebrations that followed. Usually at mealtimes the boy's had to wait upon the other guests and only once everyone else had been served, were they at last able to eat. This was purgatory for the growing boys who were constantly hungry and had to stand by and watch as the others enjoyed their food. Thankfully the Neville's were famous throughout England for their extravagant and generous banquets that consisted of numerous courses. This invariably meant that there were usually plenty of leftovers for Francis and his companions. Tonight for a change, the boys were able to join the other guests at the commencement of the feast. They were however, seated at the very southern end of the Hall, some distance from the head table, which was reserved for the Earl, his family and his closest friends.

As he studied his patron from the far side of the hall, Francis who'd always imagined the Earl to be both a great warrior and a chivalrous knight, was not at all disappointed. For Warwick, who was now known as 'the Kingmaker', was the embodiment of the 'might' of the Yorkist Cause. Upon seeing the Earl, Francis could easily appreciate how Warwick had almost single handedly secured the Crown for his cousin. Francis shuddered, if this were the true nature of his father's enemies, he could appreciate why, after the Battle of Towton, the Baron had been reticent to oppose the Yorkists again and why throughout the Civil Wars, both Henry and his commanders had been no match for their Yorkist counterparts. Still a relatively young man, the Earl appeared extremely strong and powerful. His fine clothes failed to disguise a taut and muscular frame. For a man, the Earl's face was, Francis felt, actually quite beautiful, if of course a man's features could ever be described as such! Francis coloured as he silently chided himself for such thoughts and considered the baiting that he'd receive, should the other henchmen have ever been able to read his mind. Homosexuality, although practised since ancient times and prevalent within the houses of many of the great Lords, was very still very much taboo. Francis had always considered himself to be heterosexual. However as he found himself being educated in such close proximity to others of his own gender and even sharing a bed with them, he'd often questioned his own sexuality. Had he not felt the stirrings of desire when, on occasions, he'd happened upon men and boy's engaged in licentiousness? As he remembered those occasions Francis coloured again.

Once he'd taken time to study the Earl in detail, Francis's attentions turned to those who were seated with Warwick. Thankfully their were those amongst Francis's group who were able to identify these noblemen for him. As they did so Francis slowly began to appreciate just how powerful the Neville faction was; Warwick's brother John, an accomplished soldier and leader of men, the 'victor at Hexham' who'd effectively secured the north for the King and was rumoured to be on the verge of being created the next Earl of Northumberland; the other Neville brother George, who in contrast to his siblings had devoted his life to the church. It was rumoured that Edward had promised him the Bishopric of York and many said that he was destined one day to become the Archbishop of Canterbury; Sir John Wenlock, the Earl's great friend and mentor, the treasurer of Calais and a royal councillor, reputed to be the Kings most trusted Ambassador and finally the Earl's brother in law Henry Lord Fitzhugh of Ravensworth, the King's envoy to the Scots.

Although in awe of those Nobles who were assembled at the Earl's table, throughout the evening Francis's attention was distracted by a pretty young girl, who laughing was sat with the Neville Womenfolk at the opposite end of the head table. Francis wondered who this girl could be, he recognised her companions as the Earl's daughters, Anne and Isabel, but he'd not seen this girl before.

The girl wore a gown of deep purple that was gathered in immediately below a chest that even now, despite her tender years, was beginning to fill out. The folds of crushed velvet failed to conceal a slim frame that was beginning to develop the curves of Womanhood. The girl wore her golden hair high upon her head, gathered in under a head-dress that matched her gown.

'Who is she?' Francis gasped in wonderment.

Richard was sitting next to him, this in spite of his earlier protestations that as the brother of the King and a 'Prince of Royal Blood', he should be sitting at the right hand of the Earl.

'Who is she?' impatient for an answer Francis nudged his friend who'd obviously forgotten his earlier disappointment and seemed engrossed in the scene. Richard took some time to answer, replying only after his friend had once again dug him playfully in the ribs.

'That's Anne the third daughter of Henry Lord Fitzhugh,' he replied, 'They say that she'll be quite a beauty when she comes of age.'

'I can see that,' Francis replied truthfully, 'but what's she doing here,' he shouted in an effort to make himself heard over the din for, as well as the good natured chattering of the guests, musicians had now entered the hall, adding to the commotion with their pans and pipes.

'She's to remain here with the Earl's daughters whilst her father accompanies the Earl to France.' Richard pointed to a rather clumsy looking youth, one who'd only recently joined their company, who was sat at the end of their table. 'That's her older brother', Richard said, laughing as he added, 'And it's clear that the unfortunate fellow's inherited none of his Sister's good looks.'

The feast, which Francis estimated as having consisted of at least fifteen courses, lasted long into the evening. Nothing was wasted though, for at its conclusion that which was left, was distributed amongst the poor of Middleham. After the final course, the Earl together with Fitzhugh, Wenlock and the Earl's Brother's, retired to the Earl's private apartments, which adjacent to the Great Hall, were used by Warwick to entertain his most eminent guests.

Sadly Francis who was amongst the last to be served, wasn't able to enjoy his 'flowers of violet', a dish that he loved, the violet flowers' delicate petals tempered with almond milk, rice flour and sugar. Worryingly it was Francis and not Richard who was summoned to see the Earl in his chambers.

As Francis sat outside the Earl's private apartments and waited to be admitted, he grew in nervousness. What could the Earl of Warwick possibly want with him? In an effort to take his mind off the impending meeting, Francis scrutinised his surroundings. In all of his time at Middleham, Francis had never before been admitted into these rooms. He gasped, his Solar at Minster Lovel, which up until that point he'd considered as quite elaborate, paled into insignificance when compared to these apartments. A vaulted roof; Ornate windows, which framed by intricately carved mullions, were testament to the skills of the stonemason's who'd produced them; Walls that were draped in a number of rich tapestries, one of a great Bear and Staff the Earl's personal emblem, others, pictorial histories of his Neville forbears, which recounted their many great victories over both the Scots and the Percies; Recesses carved into the stonework which cleverly afforded space to house the Earl's many and varied personal effects; A great fireplace, home to a fire that crackled and flickered as it burnt both apple and cherry wood, which, in addition to warming the chamber, filled it with a pungent yet sweet smelling smoke. Unfortunately none of these things comforted Francis nor did they take his mind off the imminent meeting, as he waited his fear intensified.

Eventually, Francis was summoned into the privy chamber by the Earl's personal valet. On entering the room, remembering those instructions that he'd been given in haste by the steward of the Castle, Sir John Conyers, Francis bowed low averting his gaze from his patron.

'You can look at me Lovel,' the Earl spoke with an authority borne of both power and influence, that which creates Kings! Francis thought. Laughing the Earl continued, 'Young Sir, does my ugliness offend you.'

Francis immediately looked up, 'No Sir......, sorry my Lord of Warwick,' Francis stammered as he corrected himself, silently cursing himself for forgetting to use the Earl's correct title.

Forthright Warwick asked, 'Do you blame me for your father's death?' Francis gasped, how was he expected to answer this? Thankfully before he had the opportunity to do so, the Earl added, 'Your father and I were great adversaries, I fought against him on many occasions,' Warwick sighed as he said 'he was a worthy opponent, but War is War and I know he'd have killed me as I would him.'

Francis, who still felt extremely awkward, decided that it was probably best not to answer at all.

It was Warwick who again broke the silence. 'What's the matter Lovel, has the cat got your tongue.'

Francis continued to stammer, 'No ....no, I cannot answer for fear of offending you......my Lord,' at least this time he'd remembered the Earl's correct title.

Warwick spoke with laughter, 'Don't worry lad you're amongst northern folk now, you may speak plainly, come tell me your thoughts.'

Smiling the Earl added, 'Richard of Gloucester tells me that you're both firm friends. He says that for a Lancastrian you're not at all bad. He even asks that I protect your interests and do my best to ensure that you retain your inheritance.' Shaking his head and tutting he added 'I sometimes wonder what he imagines of me. The Earl of Warwick, party to the theft of one's inheritance? The very thought of it.' Smiling at the irony of the Earl's comments, Francis considered how his patron was rumoured to have amassed his great fortune. He smiled again, for according to the Earl, Richard had described him as 'his friend'.

'I'll see what I can do,' Warwick added and becoming serious once more said, 'You've chosen your friends well Lovel. Richard of Gloucester knows his destiny, that path which he is to take in life, you'd do well to follow him.'

Francis eagerly nodded his agreement.

The Earl continued, 'Lovel, I do not hold your father's Lancastian sympathies against you. If you carry out your duties well, I'm sure that in time when you come of age, you'll be able to assume your rights and then maybe we may become friends. But now to business. I have arranged your betrothal and trust that you will take pleasure in my choice for you.'

Francis was horrified, since arriving at Middleham he'd not considered the matter of his own marriage. Was he, like so many others before him, to be married to some middle aged widow to secure her inheritance for the Earl?

Clapping Lord Fitzhugh on the back the Earl smiled again as he said, 'You're to marry my brother-in- law Henry's daughter, Anne.' Becoming serious the Earl added, 'Be assured Francis, this betrothal which welcomes you into my own family, gives me almost as much pleasure as the match that I've arranged for our King, who's to marry the French King's sister- in- law, Bona of Savoy.'

Francis did not know if it was the excitement of his impending betrothal to one so pretty as Anne, or the Earl's shock announcement that he'd arranged for the King to be married to a French Princess, when Edward was plainly already married, that caused him, to ignore Sir John's earlier instructions not to 'talk unnecessarily'. But he did and Francis spoke out of turn without any thought of the consequences.

'But Sire the King is already married. I saw it with my own eyes, he married the Lady Elizabeth Woodville, at her father Lord Rivers manor house at Grafton Regis this past Easter'.

At first, the Earl, who'd been quietly conversing with his brother John, did not seem to be listening to Francis, however, as Francis's words found their mark, his facial expression changed from one of merriment, to one of trembling anger.

All present turned to stare at Francis who, realising that he'd obviously spoken without thought, was desperately trying to think of words that would return the room to its earlier ambience.

It was John Neville who spoke at last. An invitation for Francis to make amends for what they all clearly hoped was a poor joke made in bad taste, 'If that was meant in jest, young sir, it was said in bad part.'

As always Francis could do no more than tell the truth. Fearful for the consequences of what he was going to say, not only for himself, but also for the country, he described to the Earl and his companions, that which both he and Ned had witnessed at Grafton Regis. At points during his discourse, Francis looked up, but quickly lowered his head once more, as he noticed that anger had not left the Earl's face, which was still twisted in fury. Francis realised that that which he had to say would have dire consequences, for both the Earl's relationship with the King and for England's relationship with both France and Scotland. Not only had Edward thrown away his greatest asset in foreign policy, his hand in marriage, but he'd also made a fool out of the Earl of Warwick, the greatest magnate in all of Christendom. How absurd, the Earl arranging the betrothal of a King, who unbeknown to both he and his subjects was already married!

Once he'd finally recounted those events that he'd seen at Grafton Regis, Francis was haughtily dismissed and ordered not to disclose the information of the King's secret marriage to anyone else. As he returned to his own chamber, Francis wondered why he'd not spoken of the matter earlier. He'd had many opportunities to do so, especially during his conversations with Richard. Ultimately, he concluded that since arriving at Middleham he'd had a great deal on his mind and not wanting to jeopardise both his new life nor his friendship with Richard, he'd unconsciously put it to the back of his mind. But now the cat was well and truly out of the bag. Francis sighed, 'What would his friend think of him when he discovered that he'd kept such a secret from him?'

Upon returning to their chambers Francis found his friend in bed wide awake, keen no doubt to hear the news of Francis's betrothal. In spite of the Earl's orders, Francis felt that his loyalty towards his friend was greater than that to the Earl and, as such, he felt that he must tell Richard now, regardless of the consequences.

'Well what happened then?'

Richard settled back on the bed, clearly expecting Francis to tell him, that thanks to him his inheritance seemed secure and that he was now betrothed to Anne Fitzhugh.

'Richard, your brothers already married. I've just told the Earl and he's less than pleased.'

Richard replied with a quizzical look on his face, 'Who, George? I thought the Earl wanted him for his own daughter Isabel and anyway he's much too young, Edward would never allow him to marry.....'

Francis interrupted, 'No, not Clarence, your brother Edward the King, he's married, I saw it with my own eyes.' Sighing Francis added, 'I'm sorry, I know I should've told you sooner.'

Richard smiled, but it was no joke. Francis's expression remained unchanged and Richard too began to frown as he demanded to know, 'To whom the King was married?' and 'When and where?'

For the second time that evening, Francis was forced to recount those events that he'd been privy to at Grafton Regis. Thankfully, when he'd finished Richard said that he wasn't at all concerned that his brother had married secretly, adding that in his opinion it'd do Warwick the world of good to see that Edward wasn't, 'after all', 'his puppet'. Richard even went so far as to forgive Francis for not telling him sooner. Richard was, however, uneasy, 'For the Lady Elizabeth, despite her lowly rank, has a reputation for having both an ambitious and scheming nature.' Apparently the new Queen had numerous relatives, all of whom would now have to be found spouses from within England's aristocracy, 'As befits the family of a Queen.' This, Richard said, was bound to arouse jealousy amongst those of the old nobility. In contrast to his friend, Francis who'd now had the opportunity of meeting the Earl, was extremely concerned about the effect that the revelation would have on The King's relationship with his cousin Warwick. For everyone knew that in recent months, the bond between the two allies had become quite strained. This as Warwick favoured a French alliance and was working tirelessly towards this end, whereas, Edward was said to prefer an alliance the Burgundians, who were at that time at war with the French. Having seen the Earl's reaction to the news of Edward's secret marriage, Francis feared that this latest development in the two men's worsening relationship, would, no doubt, create a rift between the two. Many said that Edward had Warwick alone to thank for his throne and without the Earl's continued support, Francis doubted if the King could keep it.

Ultimately all hoped that what Francis had seen was a sham ceremony, devised by Edward who was a renowned womaniser. A trick to bed the Lady Elizabeth, whose beauty was legendary. It was, Warwick said, quite conceivable, for Elizabeth had apparently repeatedly spurned Edward's advances and had even gone so far as to threaten suicide rather than to allow herself to be taken by him out of wedlock.

Francis chose to remain silent on the matter. It seemed to him that the Nevilles were merely grasping at straws. And anyway, they would all know the truth soon enough, for Edward would have to answer to the Earl.

Over the next week or so it became apparent that the Earl had been forced to change his immediate plans. Instead of going to France Warwick was to travel to Reading, to personally attend the meeting of the King's council that had been arranged for September. It was said that the Earl, who was furious at this potential slight, was to personally challenge the King as to the question of his marriage. Unfortunately Francis, who was witness to the marriage, was to accompany both the Earl and his prospective father in law Lord Fitzhugh. Francis's fiancee Anne was to remain at Middleham and Francis would have to wait until after he'd endured these latest trials and tribulations before he finally got to meet his future wife.

Chapter 8
September 1464.

In spite of that years favourable summer and as a consequence the dry and even roads, it took the Earl of Warwick and his large retinue the greater part of nine days to reach their destination, the town of Reading where the King was to hold his Royal Council.

Francis found the journey tedious in the extreme. Richard his friend, and since his arrival at Middleham his almost constant companion, had remained in Yorkshire, this despite the protestations of both he and Francis. Worryingly, in one of their quieter moments together Richard had wryly described himself as, 'A hostage to ensure my brother the Kings continued support for the Earl of Warwick.'

Unfortunately, for the entirety of the journey Francis's companion was to be Miles Dobson, one of the Earl's more lowly retainers. Dobson had, it was said, proven his courage and loyalty to the Earl on the field of battle, both at St Albans and later at Towton. But even Francis, who was normally quite charitable when it came to assessing a man's worth, found Dobson to be both slow-witted and ignorant. Miles was a clumsy youth of some twenty years whom Francis teased incessantly, that is until even he tired of this pastime, for Dobson had not even the intellect to appreciate when he was the butt of Francis's humour.

The Earl of Warwick's entourage was sizeable, especially to Francis who'd never seen such a great host of armed men. Unfortunately this meant that at the end of each days march, the men were forced to forage for their own food and lodgings. Thankfully as their journey was made in peacetime, they were all able to go their separate ways, until the march recommenced again at first light on the following day. When it came to arranging their accommodation, Francis generally left this onerous chore to Dobson. Francis, who was the first to admit that his life to date had seen little hardship, was embarrassed by the undertaking which he likened to 'begging'. As they sat down each evening to partake of their host's meagre offerings, Francis would feel wretched as he wondered how these common people, especially those in the less prosperous regions, could spare the travellers both food and wine.

As the sixth day of their gruelling march drew to a close, to relieve the boredom of yet another long hot day in the saddle, for once Francis agreed to join Miles and a number of their company, as once again they sought sustenance from the surrounding countryside. As the sun was setting the riders swung away from the long straight road along which they'd marched and rode the short distance towards the first sign of habitation that they'd seen for quite some miles.

As a result of the 'Black death', a plague that had periodically decimated the Country since the times of King Richard II, the countryside of England had become extremely depopulated. This had been exacerbated by the Civil War that had devastated both the land and its occupants. At no time was this desolation more apparent to Francis than now. As they'd ridden along the King's highway they'd passed vast tracts of land that, once cultivated, had now fallen into rack and ruin. Everywhere villages of thatched wattle and daub dwellings, that in the past had been home to many, were abandoned and uninhabited. Huddled together around small churches and manor houses, these villages were now in an accelerated state of decay and disrepair. Francis felt that it was ironic that a way of life that had flourished since Saxon times and had survived many centuries of hardship, was to be destroyed, amongst other things by a Civil War betwixt two rival Norman families! Francis worried as he wondered what would become of his own lands in Oxfordshire, especially if the Wars resumed, be it through King Edward fighting either the Earl of Warwick and the Neville faction or King Henry and his surviving Lancastrians.

As a member of the aristocracy, albeit a lowly one, Francis grimaced. In his opinion the ruling classes had a lot to answer for! Even in relatively peaceful times the Nobility still managed to have quite a negative impact, especially in these quiet rural areas. Lords exacting what they could from those who at the best of times struggled to feed themselves, never mind pay their feudal dues to their 'masters'. And King Edward was the worse offender of all! In contrast to his predecessor Henry, Edward had quite a penchant for hunting. Francis had recently heard that, as a consequence, the new King had recently extended the boundaries of the Royal Forest of Wychwood, one of his favourite hunting sites. This was bound to impinge upon Francis's neighbouring manor of Minster Lovel, as in the past the villagers had relied heavily upon these woodlands for their livelihood. Now the inhabitants of Francis's manor would be forbidden, on pain of death, from entering the Forest in search of food and firewood. Francis sighed, his people would be forced to look elsewhere for their sustenance, all for the sake of the King's sport! Francis smiled, his father had always criticised him for his 'weakness' in pitying the poor. But Francis knew that he'd never change, for he believed that his 'philanthropy' was one of only a few redeeming features that he possessed! As he'd studied the many rude dwellings of straw and mud which they'd passed on the march, Francis wondered what would become of these poor people and how they were able to cheer what was, in his opinion, both a meaningless and impoverished existence.

As Francis contemplated that evenings accommodation he sighed again. Usually those of rank would lodge with local Squires or Knights. These dignitaries, who were desperate to please such a great Lord as The Earl of Warwick, would go to great lengths and expense to entertain their visitors lavishly. Thus the Earl and his immediate entourage, would invariably be accommodated in substantial buildings, such as a manor house or castle, residences which enjoyed all of those modern conveniences that were denied Francis, who in spite of his title, was still deemed to be a 'minor' and was therefore considered no better than the common soldiers. And tonight, here in 'the back of beyond', it appeared as if their accommodation was going to be even cruder than normal.

Unfortunately Francis's gloomy predictions proved to be correct and after much 'twoing and froing', Francis and Miles were finally forced to settle for accommodation that could only really be described as 'impoverished'. Lodging with a family of peasants who lived beyond the far reaches of the village. Ironically Francis's hosts 'cottage', if one could call it that, was one of those residences that Francis had so recently pitied. A 'roundhouse' which, constructed of 'wattle and daub' with a reed roof, was in Francis's opinion, like something out of the 'dark ages'!

Francis had been quite surprised to discover that when one accompanied the Earl of Warwick, no form of words nor any negotiations were necessary to acquire both board and lodging. Standing at the cottages makeshift door, Miles had merely drawn back his cloak to reveal the Earl's device of the Bear and rugged staff that was emblazoned on the chest of his tunic. The 'master' of the house, despite his obvious ignorance, immediately recognising the Earl's badge, had immediately ushered them into his home.

Apparently as retainers of such great a Lord, both Francis and Dobson could 'request' the hospitality of strangers whenever and wherever they travelled. To refuse them was to incur the displeasure of the Earl himself. The Earl's device had both an immediate and humbling effect on their would be hosts who, bowing low, made way for the travellers, who then proceeded to help themselves to what little their hosts had to offer.

Upon entering the roundhouse, Francis was relieved to discover that both he and Miles were to sleep upon the wooden platform or mezzanine, which erected at one end of the building, was designed to accommodate the dwelling's human inhabitants. As he inspected their quarters, Francis, who'd slept in some crude places over the last couple of nights, was appalled. It was, however, a small comfort to him, to discover that at least he'd be sleeping apart from the livestock. Tonight that pleasure was reserved for their unfortunate hosts, who numbered a dozen or so of varying ages and sex. The family, making way for their guests, would now be forced to share the ground floor of compacted clay, with the few animals that they had.

Francis had no appetite, either for the food offered or for their unwelcome imposition. The stew that contained little in the way of meat and vegetables and its accompaniment of stale bread were less than palatable, as was the crude ale that did little to slake Francis's thirst and merely made his head ache. Francis retired early but enjoyed little sleep, tortured by itching brought on, he hoped, by the straw on which he lay. In contrast Dobson remained up, greedily helping himself to all that their hosts had to offer, he disgusted Francis, a bully who enjoyed exerting his authority over these poor people.

Francis awoke before first light and was anxious to discover that Miles had already left his side. Rising Francis stretched his aching back and, brushing himself down, examined his surroundings. Their hosts were all still sleeping soundly and when Francis considered the gloom, he guessed that it must still be quite early. Francis always hated this time of the day, as still half asleep, one wondered what night creatures lay in wait amongst the shadows. Startled, Francis jumped as he heard the sound of a muffled cry coming from the direction of the remotest part of the building. It was here, he recalled, that the hay pile was located. The forage stored as far away as possible from the fire that, always burning, could be found in the very centre of the dwelling. Hesitant Francis made his way towards the site of the noise which, in spite of its increasing volume, seemed not to disturb the dwellings other occupants.

On reaching the hay pile Francis discovered not only the cause of the commotion but also the whereabouts of his companion. Miles, naked from the waist down was struggling atop their hosts wife. The unfortunate woman, struggling violently, was clawing and biting at Dobson's clutch, which was forcing her head into the makeshift bed of hay. Dobson's 'embrace' was not only stifling the sound of the woman's screams, but also seemed to deprive her of her very breath. Miles, obviously experienced in such matters, used his spare hand to explore the woman's body, roughly rubbing and kneading her large breasts and the secret parts between her legs, legs which he forced wide apart before he finally took her. Francis, disgusted and ashamed, could only stand and stare as Miles took his pleasure with the woman. It seemed to Francis that his companion delighted, not only in the sexual act itself, but also in the power that he exercised over this poor woman. After some moments Francis could stand it no longer. With a strength born of both anger and disgust he grabbed Miles by the hair. With surprise on his side Francis was able to haul Dobson from the woman and throw the older and larger man to one side. In the growing light Francis could see the trembling rage upon Miles's face. Dobson spat out words of insult as his hand went immediately towards the hilt of the dagger which, in spite of his state of undress, he still wore in a scabbard about his waist. Fortunately Francis was able to forestall Miles's impending assault by reminding him of the consequences of such an action. For Francis was 'The Baron Lovel' who was currently enjoying, 'The protection of the Earl of Warwick himself'.

As her 'guests' argued the woman lay mute and motionless, staring wide eyed at Francis until with a wave of his arm, he gestured for her to return to her husband. For the second time that day Francis was revolted. As the woman scurried back to the other side of the cottage Francis saw that her husband who was wide awake, had clearly chosen to ignore his Wife's rape and was merely tending to the fire!

Neither Miles nor Francis spoke as they breakfasted on gruel. Leaving their lodgings soon after dawn they rejoined the Earl's company, which had assembled on the highway before continuing its journey southwards. As he'd ridden away from the cottage, ashamed, Francis had allowed himself a glance backwards. Shaking his head he'd sighed, for it'd appeared to him as if, surprisingly, there visit had had little impact upon the peasants, who, with heads bowed, had trudged off in the direction of the fields, where they would spend the hours of daylight.

Whereas in the past he'd considered his companion somewhat comical, now Francis was beginning to realise that Dobson and those like him were in fact very dangerous men. Men with power but no intellect. At least in his time with the 'northerners', Francis was learning some extremely valuable lessons. Firstly, never underestimate others, regardless of their lack of learning and manners and secondly, never appraise others using ones own morals or sense of honour. For all men are different and act according to their own personal principals, or lack of them! Francis feared these changing times. As always, those who wielded power could do as they pleased, but where in the past men's behaviour had been largely tempered by feudal etiquette, honour and chivalry, the 'moral code'. Now, those who should have known better, chose to ignore these principals and this was in Francis's opinion a very dangerous combination indeed. Francis shivered, it almost seemed as if Dobson could read his mind, for when his companion spoke at last, he said, 'You see how these people live, they're no better than animals and it's our duty to treat them as such,' the older man scoffed as he added, 'they neither expect nor deserve any better.'

Francis chose to remain silent. In his opinion Dobson had said nothing that could ever excuse or justify his actions, he was a rapist. But sadly, Francis felt that if he was to openly condemn his companion, he would be very much in the minority.

As the Earl's entourage approached Reading their surroundings, as Dobson had earlier predicted, changed quite dramatically. Here in the South a larger and healthier population guaranteed that land was much more valuable. As a consequence the countryside, no longer open moorland, was dissected into plots, each bounded by neat hedges of hawthorn and blackthorn or by ditches of rushes. Here travel was limited to the highway. Francis smiled, ironically the only land that remained wild and uncultivated, was that which was to be found within the large number of 'Royal parks' which they passed. Woodlands and grasslands that were filled with deer and game for the Kings pleasure. Francis noticed that both the houses of this region and its populace displayed a greater sophistication than their northern counterparts. Here the communities were home to the growing numbers of artisans and merchant classes. Those men of the emerging middle class, who chose to conduct their business in a number of small towns that were beginning to spring up all around the capital. Francis had heard tell that this new breed of man who seemed intent on personal advancement, was no longer content to work the fields on behalf of their Lord. Francis smiled, it seemed as if people in the South were at last beginning to appreciate their true worth. He cast his mind back to the incident that he'd witnessed earlier and wondered, why then didn't Miles and his kind?

In Francis's opinion Reading was very much like its bigger sister London. Originally a small town, it had grown in both size and stature as the capital's growing population had sought to escape its disease ridden streets, where the black death had flourished. Unfortunately it appeared as if those responsible for planning and erecting the new borough, had learnt nothing from their experiences in London, the towns builders merely recreating the capital, albeit on a slightly smaller scale. Poorly built timber houses and shops straddled narrow streets and alleyways that were despoiled with the waste of both man and beast. Moreover, presently Reading's population was swollen by both the

Kings court and by the retinues of some of England's greatest magnates, all of whom had gathered in the town for the impending Royal Council. A Council that many argued was, to date, the most important of Edward's short reign.

Not surprisingly, it was said that the Earl of Warwick's entourage outnumbered even that of the King! Indeed one had only to examine the tunics of the many armed retainers who roamed the City's streets, to see that those who wore the Earl's device, far outnumbered those who wore Edward's, Sun in splendour'. It didn't take a shrewd man, Francis reasoned, to understand why the Earl chose this meeting of the Royal Council to make such a show of force. In addition to safeguarding the Earl in any quarrel that he might have with the King, Warwick's private army would surely help him to persuade those who were uncommitted, when it came to the question of whose proposals to support.

In addition to approving the King's request for additional taxation, the Royal Councillors hoped to discuss and debate matters of both domestic and foreign policy. Apparently those members who were due to recommence negotiations with the French at St Omer, were desperate for instructions from Edward. For some months now the King had prevaricated both over the question of his marriage and in respect of whom he favoured in continental affairs, be it the Burgundians or the French.

For a host of different reasons, England, despite being an Island kingdom, could not remain independent of and aloof from affairs in Europe. English merchants were dependant upon continental markets to sell their goods, consequently the wealth of the nation relied heavily on England's European neighbours. Moreover, the other European powers were regularly 'interfering' in English affairs, either by giving exiles succour or by financing and supporting the various 'Pretenders' to the English throne. Thus, whether they liked it or not, Edward and his councillors would, have to resolve the question of a European alliance. It was common knowledge that the King, whose own family in exile had enjoyed the hospitality of the Burgundian Court, favoured a defensive alliance against France with both the Dukedoms of Burgundy and Brittany. This proposal would enable Edward, once secure upon his throne, to consider recovering those possessions in France that his predecessor had so 'in-gloriously' lost. It was said that privately, Edward dreamt of a resurgence of war with his French cousins, that would ultimately see him crowned King of France. A warrior through and through, Edward yearned for those glory days, to repeat the great victories of Henry V and before him the Black Prince, at Agincourt and Crecy. In contrast to Edward, the Earl of Warwick, who was supported in his proposals by many of his peers, favoured an alliance with the French and a war against the Burgundians. The population at large, as with England's ruling elite, were also divided on the subject. Many amongst the growing middle classes, especially those in the South who relied heavily upon Flanders and the low countries for their trade in wool and cloth, supported a Burgundian alliance. On the other hand, much of the nobility and those amongst the poorer classes who had an opinion, favoured an Anglo French alliance against the Burgundians and Bretons. England was also split geographically on the matter. The northerners who tired of the incessant raiding of the Scottish, the traditional allies of the French, saw an alliance with France as a means to ensure that England, who in recent times had been humiliated on the European stage, would once again be a great power. Many in the North were also jealous of the increasing wealth of their southern counterparts, whom they said were growing 'fat' and 'rich' on the back of the woollen trade. Moreover Burgundy had also recently angered many with their imposition of restrictions upon English imports. Others in the Yorkist government also pointed to the past pro-Lancastrian sympathies of both the duchies of Burgundy and Brittany. Most Englishmen believed that ultimately the King would be forced once again to accede to his cousin, the Earl of Warwicks wishes. Many had resigned themselves to the prospect of an alliance with the French and, as a consequence, the fact that they would in all probability, once again have to 'suffer' a French Queen. Happily though, Lord Wenlock who had met the proposed match, Bona of Savoy, was said to have described the French Princess as a 'comely and virtuous woman'. This in stark contrast to King Henry's 'controlling' wife, the 'arrogant and aggressive' Margaret of Anjou. But then again, Francis mused, why would Wenlock not describe her in such glowing terms? It was common knowledge that the French King Louis, had promised him a fortune if he was successful in securing the marriage. On the other hand, if the Earl of Warwick was to be embarrassed and his counsel disregarded, what, Francis worried, would follow, further civil war? The only thing that cheered Francis, was the consideration that any conflict would at least be limited to the House's of York and to that of the Nevilles. Surely Warwick would never countenance an alliance with the Lancastrians? For the Earl's hatred for Margaret of Anjou and hers for him was legendary.

It had been Margaret who'd ordered that the head of Warwick's father, Richard Earl of Salisbury, was to join that of Richard of York upon Micklegate Bar after the battle of Wakefield. The Earl had sworn vengeance upon the French Queen for his father's humiliation.

Moreover neither Margaret nor the Lancastrians, who blamed the Earl above all others for their present predicament, would ever, Francis felt, countenance any form of alliance with the Earl. But Francis had seen with his own eyes the Earl's fury when he'd discovered that the King may have secretly married. If that which Francis had witnessed was true and the King had married a commoner and if he confessed this to the Council, Francis couldn't guess what the reaction of both the Earl and England's other great magnates would be! Ultimately Francis hoped that the rest of Royal Council, who were said to be of a more even temperament than the impetuous Earl, would counsel caution in their dealings with the King and that somehow the matter could be resolved without resorting to arms.

Bored, Francis spent much of his time at Reading, billeted in one of the many inns that were to be found in the town's central quarter, businesses that were, due to the impending Council, enjoying an extremely busy period. As a minor Francis took no part in the Council proceedings. It had been impressed upon him, that he was only there in the unlikely event that he was called upon, should the need arise, to evidence Edward's apparent indiscretion at Grafton Regis.

The King had been in Reading for some days prior to the arrival of the Nevilles, having travelled the relatively short distance there, from his sumptuous palace at Windsor. Francis smiled, ironically, Windsor was reputed to have been the favourite residence of Edward's predecessor, Henry. Francis smiled again, presently Henry would have to content himself with far less lavish accommodation. As a result of the truce that had been signed with the Scots the Lancastrians had been deprived of their base within Scotland. Consequently the 'Ex King of England' was rumoured to be at large in the north. A renegade, reliant on the hospitality of those few northerners who still supported the Lancastrian cause and who had the nerve to shelter him.

Unfortunately, once the Earl of Warwick reached Reading, relations between himself and the King could not have got off to a worse start. Arriving at the town gates the Earl had been met by some of the more prominent townspeople, who dressed in the full regalia of their offices, had knelt before the Earl and had offered him gifts of money and goods. Edward was said to have been furious that an Earl had been honoured in such a way, a custom that he maintained should be reserved for the sovereign alone.

As he was not party to the council proceedings that took place within Reading Abbey, Francis was forced to rely upon the accounts of others, for any news arising from the meetings that took place within the 'secrecy' of the council chambers. As the days went by many rumours and stories circulated throughout the Town, amongst those servants and retainers, who had little more to do with their time than spend it in the alehouses. Those who took an interest in such matters discussed and debated these accounts, as they tried to second guess those decisions that were being made on their behalf, for the 'good governance' of the realm. It was rumoured that not all was going well for the King, who was heavily criticised for his extravagance, which had forced the council to debase the coinage in an attempt to control the countries rising inflation. The 'Golden Age', promised by the Yorkist Government in the propaganda that they'd circulated throughout the Civil Wars, had failed to materialise. Inflation and heavy taxation, together with the depopulation and lawlessness of the countryside, had placed a heavy burden upon the nobility, many of whom made up the King's Council. It was these men, most of whom who were already greatly angered, who led by the Earl of Warwick, repeatedly urged the King to once and for all decide upon the issue of his marriage.

It was said that the vast majority of the council now supported a French alliance and the match with Bona of Savoy.

Over a period of some weeks the Earl repeatedly asked Edward why he chose to disregard the question of his marriage. Apparently Lord Hastings was alone in supporting the King and favouring an alliance with the Burgundians. Throughout the council meetings Edward stubbornly refused to discuss the matter and soon many began to question why?

During the period of his confinement at Reading, Francis ventured out rarely. He was content instead to sit at the small window seat of the rudely decorated room which had been his home for almost three weeks and watch the world go by. Francis would spend many hours each day observing the various comings and goings in the streets below. This pastime, he felt, was much safer than to venture out into the hustle and bustle of the busy town with its associated dangers. To negotiate those swollen thoroughfares that were bursting with armed men who had little else to do but to make trouble for others.

Francis marvelled at those people who chose to follow the King's Court: the women of low morals who bedded those men who preferred to pay for such pleasures; the smiths who shod the horses and who cleaned and repaired the armour and arms of the various knights and squires; the merchants and artisans who depended on the King's progress for their prosperity and who had set up a vast array of stalls in the already cluttered streets. Francis was astounded by the skill of the street entertainers who juggled and balanced to the delight of the onlookers. He was amazed at the proficiency of the minstrels and players who, in their bright and elaborate costumes, acted out plays that told of the lives of Saints or of glorious past histories. Francis was stupefied by the size and strength of the wrestlers who fought and bloodied each other for the entertainment of others. The Reading Council was clearly a wonderful distraction for the common folk, who delighted in the change of scene and who, contrary to the orders of the Town Council, allowed themselves to be distracted, when they would no doubt be 'better employed' on the town common practising their archery!

As he sat at his window Francis was astonished at the mental capacity of the town crier, who on each and every hour throughout the day announced to the townsfolk the very latest proclamations that were issued from the King's Council. It was primarily from this source that both Francis and the people of Reading and latterly the entire population of the country, finally heard the news that shook their nation. News that until that point few people other than Francis, the Earl of Warwick and the King himself had been privy to. On the 28th September the announcement that Francis had been both expecting and fearing was finally made. An eerie and unusual silence descended upon the Town as the crier informed the gathered crowd that their King was in fact already married, to the 'Lady Elizabeth Woodville' and had been so for some four months. Rumour and speculation mingled with fact as the news was disseminated amongst the people. From his window Francis saw first hand the distress and the consternation on the faces of the townsfolk as they asked themselves, and each other, how 'their' King a 'Prince of the blood Royal', could marry a 'widow' and a 'commoner', 'in secret'. One whose father, brother and husband had all fought against the House of York!

Francis soon heard news of how the council meeting itself had gone. Of how the King, repeatedly pressed by his councillors for an answer, had finally lost control of his temper and had, to the 'great displeasure of many great Lords and especially to the larger part of all his council,' angrily told them, not only that he was already married, but to whom and when!

It was on the evening of the announcement that Francis, who'd been present at the Earl's lodgings, had overheard Warwick and his friend, Lord Wenlock discussing the matter.

The Earl, who'd obviously hoped that the King's marriage to Elizabeth had been some kind of elaborate hoax or that Francis had been mistaken in some way, had been infuriated. He had, he said, been

137

made to look a fool, not only in the eyes of England but also in the eyes of the entire civilised world. Warwick clearly either cared little or did not fear the King or his supporters, for he spoke his treasonous words so loudly that Francis feared that the whole town would hear him.

'I can no longer suffer myself to be ruled by a man who is willing to be led by blind affection at the expense of the rule of reason.'

Lord Wenlock, a shrewd and experienced diplomat, attempting to pacify his friends legendary temper, advised caution.

'My Lord, we must be patient in spite of ourselves. This Lady our Queen will soon turn the King's subjects against him. Mark my words the time to strike is not now but it will be soon, we need to busy ourselves with preparations,' after a short pause he added, 'But who will rule England for us in Edward's stead.'

The Earl had, in all probability, considered and solved this problem well in advance of the meeting of the Royal Council, for he replied without hesitation, 'George, Duke of Clarence will serve our purpose, my brother the Bishop is as we speak arranging the necessary dispensations from the Holy father in Rome. Clarence will marry my daughter Isabel. With the Nevilles and Plantagenets united by marriage it will be my grandchild and not my cousin who will ultimately rule England.'

Wenlock queried, 'But what of Edward, is he not the eldest male in York's line?'

Laughing Warwick replied, 'Have you not heard the rumours. Edward's mother the Lady Cecily was not quiet as pious as the King would have us all believe. Apparently Edward is the bastard son of one of the King's archers, conceived and born at Rouen whilst her husband the Duke was away campaigning.'

Now Francis was really scared. What would become of them all? Warwick was clearly plotting against the King and hoped to supplant Edward with his younger brother George. What would Richard make of this? Was George complicit in the Earl's plans? These were treasonous words and Francis had witnessed first hand the fate that befell those who plotted treason against the King? Fearful for his own safety, Francis managed to slip out of the room unnoticed. He returned to his own room and retired to bed early. He was to be present at the Abbey of Reading on the following day when the 'new' Queen was to be presented to her people. Now he could only wonder and worry. How would the Earl of Warwick and the rest of the aristocracy assembled there receive her?

Thankfully on the following day Francis found himself seated towards the rear of the ancient Abbey, that was full of the King's subjects, who, like him were all anxious to get a glimpse of the new Queen, of whom many knew little. As the Queen's entourage entered the Abbey Francis gasped, not at Queen Elizabeth's beauty, but at the audacity of the Earl. Elizabeth was escorted into the Abbey by both Warwick and the Duke of Clarence, both smiling as they each gently held their new Queen's hands. The Earl had clearly listened to Wenlock's advice and it appeared as if he now intended to wait and bide his time. Rubbing his forehead, Francis who'd slept little on the previous night, tried to weigh up all of the various possibilities. Would the King's subjects be won over by the Lady Elizabeth's exceptional beauty? Or would they all join the Earl in making both Edward and his Queen pay for their impetuousness?

Sadly for the King, his Queen did nothing to ingratiate herself with her new subjects. Francis was not at all surprised to discover that Elizabeth's physical appearance was not matched by a beauty of spirit. Indeed in a relatively short period of time the Queen succeeded in upsetting almost everyone with whom she had contact. Despite her lowly birth, Elizabeth would insist on being treated as a Queen and all men, regardless of rank or birth had to kneel before her, rising only when being given leave to do so.

It was perhaps ironic, Francis felt, that the magnificent Abbey at Reading, a great monument to the Norman King's and Queens of England who'd built it as the last resting place of both the Empress Matilda and of Henry I, had been forced to witness this low point in the monarchy of England. Francis had sensed the disquiet of all those present who'd whispered the questions that they'd all wanted answering. Why had Edward treated the crown of England with such contempt? Why had he ignored his Kingly obligations, merely to satiate his desire for a woman? Surprisingly the King, who was clearly still blinded by his affection for Elizabeth, seemed unaware that the assembled aristocracy had been scandalised by the marriage. In contrast to her husband, it appeared to Francis that Elizabeth herself was all too aware of public opinion and Francis could only guess what the new Queen was thinking, as she'd scowled and pursed her lips together, just as Francis had seen her do on the day of her wedding!

Even after Francis had returned to Middleham he continued to hear many stories of the unpopularity of both the new Queen and her family. Apparently Elizabeth had insisted that her family should be allowed to 'marry well', as 'befitted' those who was related to the 'Queen of England'. Unfortunately, as Elizabeth's forbears had been extremely prolific, there were many who had to be found a suitable match, this from within an aristocracy that was already much diminished through war and disease. Moreover the Queen's family all had to be provided for financially and many Woodville's were given 'high office' within Edward's government, this invariably at the expense of the old nobility. The Queen's brother Anthony, married the heiress of the late Lord Scales and thereby acquired his title. Her younger brothers, Lionel and Edward, were created Bishop of Salisbury and Admiral of the fleet respectively. Overnight the Queen's father, Lord Rivers, became a man of great importance at Edward's court. At Middleham, Edward's patronage of the Woodville's became a constant topic of conversation amongst the Neville affinity, all of whom were furious both at the King's slight to their Lord and at being deprived of suitable matches for their own heirs and wards or of posts and offices that were now the preserve of the King's new brethren.

The Earl did little to hide his disdain for the Queen's kind. He decried Edward for both his naivety and inexperience. At each and every opportunity Warwick would remind them all, that the King, 'for want of a woman' had' placed both himself and the Kingdom in peril.' The Earl said that it was incredulous that Edward should now be relying on those who recently had been his avowed enemies, to conduct the business of his Government. Disgusted Warwick would often recount the story of how in 1460, at the height of the Civil War, both he and his men had raided the Kent coast, capturing Lord Rivers and his son Anthony Woodville, whilst 'they'd slept in their beds'. Prisoners the Woodville's had been carried over the channel to Calais where they'd been met by Edward who, *'Before the Lords assembled with eight score torches, rated him (Lord Rivers), calling him a knaves son that he should be so rude to call him and these other Lords traitors, for they should be found to be the King's true liege men when he should be found traitor, and that his father was but a squire and brought up with Henry V, and since then he himself was made by marriage and that it was not his part to have the language of Lords'.*

Now Warwick raged that, *'the Queen could be allowed to introduce so many strangers to court and they alone should manage the public and private business of the Crown.....give or sell offices, and finally rule the very King himself'.*

When he listened to the Earl's tirade, Francis who chose to remain silent, would often allow himself a secret smile, for was that not what the Earl himself had intended, to rule England through his young, immature and impressionable cousin Edward!

Unfortunately for the Woodville's the Queen's introduction to her subjects, coincided with a further outbreak of the Black Death, especially in the south and east of England. Many aware of the growing rift between the 'King and his cousin of Warwick', said that this was a sign from God and a portent of things to come. A popular story that was circulating at the time told of a, *'A certain woman in the county of Huntingdon, who was with child and near the time of her delivery, who to her extreme horror felt the embryo in her womb weeping as it were and uttering a kind of sobbing noise.....we may suppose that even the children unborn deplored our impending calamities'.*

Francis's own betrothal to Anne Fitzhugh remained unaffected by events in the capital. Francis knew that the marriage would tie him to the Earl's immediate family and, as a consequence, may bring him into any confrontation with the King. He could only hope that with time the matter would blow over. As for the umpteenth time he considered all of the various possibilities Francis sighed, he preferred to deal in definite's and not in what might be's. Presently none could guess what would happen. Stubborn, Warwick remained at Middleham, alienated from his one time ally. The King remained in London, surrounded by his wife and his new family, seemingly oblivious to public opinion that was railed against him. In the North King Henry, friendless, remained at large, whilst his Queen scoured the courts of Europe seeking their support for yet another Lancastrian invasion.

Chapter 9
February 1466. Ravensworth, Yorkshire.

In spite of its implications for his future affiliations, it was fair to say that Francis was more than content with the betrothal that had arranged for him with Anne Fitzhugh, daughter of Henry, the 5th Baron Fitzhugh and the Earl of Warwick's brother in law. Besides the fact that Anne was of the nobility, a member of one of England's most influential families, she was, Francis thought, one of the most beautiful human beings that he had ever seen. Surprisingly, in contrast to most of those arranged marriages amongst the nobility, where negotiations would invariably become quite protracted, the arrangements in relation to Francis and Anne's union were progressing quite smoothly. The formalities of arranging a suitable dowry and allowing Anne's father time to consider whether or not Francis's family possessed the required rank and property to ensure the future advancement of his daughter, were dealt with expeditiously and without any complications. Happily, throughout the course of the negotiations the young couple, properly chaperoned, were allowed time with each other to get to know one another.

From the outset Francis had been left in no doubt that this match would please his patron the Earl and that any refusal on his part would have displeased his master and would therefore have been an act of pure folly on his part. Not that this was an issue for Francis, who in the short time that he'd got to know his future wife, was besotted with Anne and wouldn't have turned down the marriage, even if he had been given a choice in the matter! Francis couldn't still quite believe his good fortune, to have been found such an alluring fiancee, and from such a family as the Fitzhughs! Moreover as Francis got to know his would be bride, he was delighted to discover that Anne appeared to posses a sweetness of spirit that mirrored her physical appearance.

As with the Lovels, the FitzHugh's were of Norman Descent. It was, however, not until earlier in that century that their fortunes had improved significantly and they'd begun to enjoy a position of notability within the hierarchy of the realm. It was Anne's father's namesake, his grandfather the third Baron, who had served under Henry Bolingbroke, later Henry IV of England, who had thrust the Fitzhughs onto the national stage. Never one to boast, Francis smiled as he pictured in his minds eye Anne's slow witted brother Richard, who was also henchman at Middleham, if these boy's were going to be the families future, he wondered if by tying his family to Francis, Lord Fitzhugh hoped to prevent his families fortunes from waning too much in the future! For there was no denying the fact that Anne's father was also very much in favour of the match.

Francis did, however, puzzle as to why the Earl himself was so keen for him to marry. Presently as his patron the Earl enjoyed the proceeds of all of the Lovel estates. If the marriage went ahead, as Francis was still very much a minor, these revenues would go to instead to Lord Fitzhugh and annually, this income was not an inconsiderable sum. Francis wondered if the Earl's blessing had been given in return for some past service, or maybe even for the promise of support in some future enterprise. That said as far as Francis was concerned, the upshot was, that for the time being at least, his fortunes were tied inextricably to that of the Fitzhughes and by their association to the Nevilles. As he considered this, Francis's thoughts turned once more to the conversation that he'd overheard between the Earl and his friend Lord Wenlock at Reading, he sighed as he realised that once again he seemed powerless, as he was drawn into the disputes of others.

As custom dictated, Lord FitzHugh had spoken often with Francis throughout the previous months, since the proposed marriage had been suggested and later approved by the Earl and latterly by the King himself. Protocol dictating that the King, who'd originally granted Francis's wardship to the Earl, would have to consulted in the matter.

Henry FitzHugh was a kindly man of early middle age. Even if one disregarded his abilities as a diplomat and orator, skills that had ensured that he'd been chosen as the King's ambassador to Scotland, his physical presence alone would have commanded the respect of many men. A tall man of obvious strength, Francis had at first felt intimidated by the older man. Now, however, despite his age and inexperience, Francis counted his future father in law as a friend. As their relationship developed Francis found that he could speak openly to the older man, who in contrast to the Earl wasn't bound by etiquette and convention and seemed to value Francis's opinion. Yes, Francis was still a 'minor', but he was after all Henry's future son in law and according to Lord Fitzhugh had 'quite a future in front of him'. Francis and Lord Fitzhugh would talk for hours and when in the company of Anne's father Francis felt that he could really speak his mind. He spoke excitedly of his future life with Anne, of how when he finally attained his majority he hoped to return to Minster Lovel to manage his family's estates and how he would do his best to serve both his King and his family. In turn Francis received frank and honest replies. Throughout the course of these conversations Francis listened well and in doing so he'd learnt much, not only of the history of the FitzHugh family, but also of the intrigue and complicated nature of domestic and international politics. Lord Fitzhugh cautioned Francis to be very careful when it came to choosing his allies, the older man arguing that one must always think in the long term. He described how men's fortunes could rise and wane, how dynasties that had appeared 'all conquering' could fail for the silliest of reasons. Fitzhugh had smiled as he'd pointed out that his own families fortunes had seemed inextricably linked to those of the House of Lancaster, yet when that family had fallen from power his own had flourished. He'd described to Francis how his grandfather had gained prominence, through his service to Henry IV both at home and abroad. Grinning he'd pointed out that after Henry Vs victory over the French at Agincourt, 'the whole world' had been 'at their feet', for Henry was to be crowned both King of France and England! Yet how things could change in an instant. Whilst campaigning in France, the King, still very much a young man, had died prematurely, having contracted dysentery. Fitzhugh had smiled as he'd described how the Lancastrians, deprived of strong leadership had floundered, whilst the fortunes of his own family had flourished, not as their forbears had done through service to the crown, but by tying themselves to the power behind the throne. Lord FitzHugh who'd lived through the minority of Henry VI and had fought for both the Lancastians and the Yorkistss, had wisely judged that England's might in these times was wielded not by the monarch, but by great families who supported them. Having witnessed the decline of the House of Lancaster, he'd cleverly succeeded in transferring his allegiance to the Nevilles, by marrying the Earl of Warwicks sister. Presently he was, not only Warwick's brother in law, but also one of the Earl's most trusted friends and advisors. Francis could see parallels between his own family and that of the FitzHughs. Where in the past Lovel loyalties had rested solely with the

Lancastrians and his grandparents had attained power and influence through service to the crown. Now they rested solidly with the Nevilles at Middleham and he too now seemed destined to tie himself to this family, through marriage. Laughing and telling him not to worry, Lord Fitzhugh had clapped Francis on the back as Francis had said that he hoped that his marriage to Anne, would prove just as successful as his future father in laws had!

If their families enjoyed similarities, it was at this point that any comparison between Francis and his future wife ended. Where Francis was dark in skin and hair, Anne was fair. Where Francis was strongly built of heavy bone, she was tall and slender. In character too, Francis determined that he was the antithesis of Anne, she appearing to have few cares or worries as she skipped through what was an untroubled existence. Francis often wished that he too could adopt Anne's light-hearted indifference to life, rather than to suffer as he did, with a mind that worried and had to digest and interpret each and every piece of information, before he was at last able to decide on a given course of action. Francis knew that this trait in his character caused the impetuous Anne great annoyance, as she, eager to make a start, would have to wait whilst Francis prevaricated. Francis had often heard it said that opposites attracted and he hoped that Anne was in earnest when, during their times together at Middleham, she whispered in his ear that she loved him, as he did her. Unfortunately these moments were for the most part spent in the company of chaperones and it was rare for Francis to be able to spend any time alone with Anne. On those rare occasions that the young couple were able to steal away from the watchful gaze of Anne's family, Francis would take his future bride to his special place upon the earthworks of the old castle. Here he would tell her of his earlier life, spent in the company of his own family and friends at Minster Lovel. Using his limited vocabulary, Francis would try to describe to her his beloved manor house and its surroundings, the river, the rolling Oxfordshire countryside and the splendour of the ancient woodland of Wychwood. Francis, who missed his home, hoped that one day Anne would love these things as he did. When he described his home to Anne she would often appear transfixed, staring intently with eyes that unusually changed colour with each differing emotion. But then rising quickly to her feet, Anne would skip away over the springy turf, shouting after for him to follow and he would be left wondering if she'd even been listening to him at at all!

Surprisingly Richard, whom Francis understood to have been instrumental in suggesting the betrothal in the first place, now seemed to disapprove of Anne. His friend reasoning that a 'companion of the Duke of Gloucester' and a 'Lord and Baron in his own right', should make a better match, than to marry the third daughter of 'one who is merely a member of the lesser nobility of Richmondshire.' Francis who felt that his friend must be jealous now, that he'd had the opportunity of meeting Anne, chose to ignore Richard's warning, that the FitzHughs 'will have your inheritance.' Francis argued that he would soon be of age and then both he and Anne would be able to enjoy his wealth together, independently of the intrusions of the outside world. Francis was however, saddened by his friends attitude which deprived him of a much needed confidant when he needed it most, indeed at times he felt as if he would burst, unless he could speak to another of the intensity of emotion that he was feeling, a sentiment that was so unlike him. Regrettably, when it came to Richard, Anne was very much a persona non gratia and unfortunately Anne, who didn't seem to care what others thought of her, did nothing to ingratiate herself with Richard. Clearly sensing the older boy's disapproval, Anne would delight in irritating Richard, skipping and dancing around him in an attempt to embarrass and upset both he and Francis. These flirtations which did little to rankle Richard, merely upset Francis who would sulk for hours, until Anne would deliver him from his misery either with the slightest of kisses or the brush of her hand against his face.

Thankfully in spite of the presence of Anne and Francis's impending marriage, both Richard and Francis remained close. Choosing to avoid what was quite a thorny subject, their daily discussions had resumed in earnest on the very night of Francis's return from Reading, Richard having been desperate to hear news of the Kings council. It had, however, puzzled Francis that Richard had seemed disinterested as Francis had described the sorry state of the countryside, ravaged as it was by the effects of war and pestilence. Richard had been even less interested in the plight of the poor peasant woman, taken by force at the hands of Dobson. This had disappointed Francis who'd hoped that Richard, as brother to the King, would have taken the matter up with the Earl, ensuring that Dobson would have received a suitable punishment. It now seemed as if Miles was to go unpunished. In fact Richard had been more surprised that Miles had 'shown such restraint', when Francis 'had seen fit to interrupt him!' In truth Richard had been preoccupied with hearing only of the news of the rift between his brother and Warwick. When Francis had recounted the conversation that he'd overheard at Reading between the Earl and Wenlock, Richard had become deadly serious asking, 'And who Francis do you think I should support in this matter, Edward or the Earl and my brother

George?' It had however been clear to Francis where his friends true allegiance lay, for Richard hadn't given Francis time to reply, before sighing he'd added, 'I'm afraid Francis, that we may yet find ourselves on opposite sides in this conflict'.

Since this conversation Francis had spent many a sleepless night, wondering what the future had in store for them all. For he knew that Richard's wardship in the Earl's household was nearing it's end and soon his friend would be summoned to Court, whereas Francis was to enter the household of the Earl's brother in law. It was now clear to Francis that if the rift between Edward and the Earl widened, both he and Richard would, as his friend predicted, find themselves in opposing camps. Berating himself Francis asked himself how he could ever have believed any different, for Richard, who seemed to worship his older brother, could never have valued their friendship over his love for Edward. Although pessimistic about what lay in store for them, Francis did hope, perhaps somewhat naively, that somehow maybe both the King and the Earl would be able resolve their differences, or possibly, Richard may indeed choose his friendship with Francis and the Nevilles, over his obligations to the King!

Keen to discover his friends true position, before Richard was called to London, Francis had summoned up the courage and had asked him outright, 'but surely the King will never fight the Earl, they're cousins and Edward would never have been able to defeat the Lancastrianss without Warwicks help?'

Francis had been appalled, as shrugging, Richard had reaffirmed his support for Edward, before he'd added quite nonchalantly, 'Don't you see that they must, if my brother is ever to be King in his own right.'

Francis, much to his own and Richard's embarrassment, had immediately declared, 'May God strike me down if I ever raise a sword against you.'

Sadly Francis hadn't been comforted by his friends response to this outburst, Richard smiling wryly as he pointed out that in Civil Wars, 'the final blow is often delivered by ones family, or ones friend,' the older boy adding to Francis's discomfort, as sighing he'd added, 'Come Francis, since you've taken up with that FitzHugh girl you've become quite emotional.'

Although disappointed that his friend had said nothing to reassure him, Francis could see that Richard was right. Soon his friend would have to assume his rightful position at the Kings right hand, whilst Francis would enter the household of Lord Fitzhugh, to become one of Warwick's retainers. If it did come to war, an event that now seemed more and more likely, both he and his friend were bound to find themselves as adversaries.

Unfortunately, events in the aftermath of the King's Council, only served to confirm Richard's prophesies. Since Reading Edward had made an attempt at reconciliation, by creating the Earl's brother George, Bishop of York. However as time went by and both men stubbornly remained at either end of the country, the rift between Neville and Plantagenet widened further. The Earl, in spite of the King's marriage and opposition to an alliance with the French, still hoped to come to some form of agreement with the French King Louis, whereas Edward, urged on by the Queens relatives, favoured an alliance with the Burgundians.

Francis had heard the Earl on many occasions, angrily decry the Woodvilles for the influence they now held over Edward, but now it seemed that the Earl was joined in his condemnation by many others. Francis still found it somewhat ironic, that the Earl saw fit to criticise others, for attempting to do that which he'd been doing ever since the beginning of Edward's reign! That said, the politician in Francis which was determined to set himself within the victorious side, chose to keep these opinions to himself, he didn't want to anger his patron and anyway, as time progressed it seemed that Wenlock had been right all along when he'd advised patience. For the Earl was gaining much support, whilst clearly oblivious to the mood of the country, Edward was losing it! Many from within England's aristocracy were becoming greatly concerned in respect of the King's patronage of the Woodvilles, who until recently, they argued, had merely been members of the 'Northaptonshire Gentry'.

The Earl had become further incensed when his uncle was dismissed as the Treasurer of England, to be replaced in his post by none other the Queen's father, Lord Rivers!

Now it was rumoured that the Nevilles were even considering an alliance with the Lancastrians! Francis had hardly believed this, that is until one of King Henry's messengers, en route from France to the Lancastrian stronghold of Harlech in Wales, had been detained by the King Edward's men. The unfortunate man, who'd soon found himself dismembered on the King's orders, was found to have in his possession letters that'd been sent by Henry's Queen to Warwick. Francis had initially doubted that the story was true, discounting it as either fanciful speculation on the part of those Lancastrian Lords who could now see no prospect of a restoration without the assistance of Warwick, or as maliciousness spread by those who hoped to foment further discord between the Yorkists. That said Francis had witnessed first hand the

Earl's anger and presently anything seemed possible in this mad mad world. And what did the Lancastrians have left to lose? Yes, Queen Margaret had been directly responsible for the death of Warwick's father? And yes she hated the Earl whom she apparently blamed above all others for the loss of her sons inheritance. But now the French Queen was living in abject poverty in France, whilst her husband who'd been betrayed and captured in Lancashire, was presently ensconced within the Tower of London, having been humiliatingly paraded through the Capital, tied to a mule with a straw hat upon his head! Now her son and Henry's heir was almost of age and was said to be bragging to anyone who was willing to hear, how he, 'Edward of Lancaster, Prince of Wales' would recoup his kingdom from the 'usurper Edward of March'. As much as it pained him to say it, in Francis's opinion Margaret's only hope of a Lancastrian restoration, was if she somehow fell in with the Nevilles. And when one considered that both she and her son were at the French court and that the Earl was still involved in negotiations with the French King Louis, who saw himself as quite a schemer, one could only wonder what would happen next!

In spite of Francis's misgivings, he was at least happy to be reunited with both his mother and his sisters, who finally joined him at Middleham for that Christmas's festivities. Once the Lovels had welcomed in the new year, they had all made the short journey north, through the dense woodland of Richmond shire, to the FitzHugh's family seat at Ravensworth.

Although modest in comparison to Middleham, Ravensworth Castle was of sufficient magnitude to reflect the Fitzhughes eminent position within northern society. As with Middleham, the fortress was built of the light coloured sandstone that was common in that region. The castle, very Norman in design, consisted of four towers, each of which were placed upon a corner of the island upon which it was stood and all of which were joined by a thick 'curtain' wall. The fortress could only be entered via a large gated archway, that adjoined the North West tower, this being the largest of the towers, that, overlooking the small hamlet of Ravensworth, housed the guardroom. Francis was surprised to see that in contrast to many similar strongholds, the Castle, as with its larger counterpart at Middleham, was not built on high ground, but was sited within a valley, at the base of a ridge of higher ground to its South. Francis wondered if the Castle's position reflected the limitations of its builders, or if in fact the FitzHughs enjoyed such prominence within the local community, that they could afford to sacrifice defence at the expense of luxury. The Fitzhughes Castle was surrounded on three sides by a large lake and to it's north by a deep moat which, in addition to being one of the few concessions to thoughts of defence, was well stocked with salmon and trout, fish which were served in a variety of dishes at most mealtimes. The great hall and above it the 'solar' could be found within the Castle's courtyard. It was from the large window seat in the solar, so like that in his own home in Oxfordshire, that Francis gazed southwards, in the direction of the steep ridge of bracken and gorse, upon which a number of sheep managed to eke out an existence. Despite the paleness of the winter sun and the mist that clung about the hillside and settled within the Valley below, Francis could still easily pick out the Church of St Peter and St Felix that, positioned as it was almost on the apex of the high ground, overlooked the Castle and the surrounding hamlet of Ravensworth. Francis felt a tingling sensation of growing nervousness, for it was here, on the morrow, where he, would marry Anne.

Francis turned with a start as he sensed that someone else had entered the solar. He blinked as his eyes slowly adjusted to the darkness towards the back of the room. Before he was able to fully discern who the visitor was, Francis was grasped in a tight embrace. He smiled for he knew in an instant that it was Anne. His nervousness disappeared as he felt her soft kisses on his face and neck and smelt the scent of her that mingled with the faint aroma of lavender and rose waters.

'How is my love?' she whispered in his ear. Francis wondered if it were the words themselves or the feel of her soft breath about his ears and neck that seemed to make every hair on his body stand on end.

'Richard cannot know true love,', he thought, as he briefly cast his mind back to conversations held between himself and his friend at Middleham, when Richard had bewailed the fact that Francis, who was usually so rational, now at times seemed to be overly preoccupied with 'thoughts of love'.

But now his friend was gone, having left Middleham after it'd finally become clear that the Earl and King Edward were both embarked on a course that would ultimately lead to a resumption of the Wars. And Francis feared for his friend, for the Nevilles were no longer alone in their opposition to the King and his new Queen. The ancient families of England, proud of their heritage, smarted as their offspring were forced into disadvantageous marriages with the new Queen's brethren. Their 'noble blood' 'contaminated' by that of the lower classes. Thankful for his own impending marriage, Francis shuddered as he recalled how the Queen's nineteen year old brother Thomas, had been married to the Dowager Duchess of Norfolk, who was sixty seven years old! During this past month he'd heard that the Duke of

Buckingham, still a minor and in the wardship of the Queen, had been forced to marry Elizabeth's sister! Francis smiled, it was said, that the young Duke had been 'scorned to wed her on account of her humble origins.' Francis warmed as he appreciated just how lucky he'd been, to have had his betrothal arranged prior to the Woodville families rapid rise to power.

Unfortunately it seemed that neither Richard nor his brother George Duke of Clarence, would be as fortunate. It'd always been assumed that the Earl's daughters Isabel and her younger sister Ann would one day be married to the King's younger Brothers. But Edward had again insulted the Earl by refusing to countenance such a union. Unbeknown to the King, since the beginning of the previous year, George had become a regular visitor to Middleham, it was clear that both he and the Earl were actively plotting against the King. It was even said that George was going to marry Isabel without the Kings approval and then, with the Earl's support, he hoped to seize the crown for himself, thereby uniting the Nevilles and Plantagenets on the throne.

Francis, despite the warmth of Anne's embrace, shivered as he wondered when and who the 'kingmaker' would make use of his alternative King.

Anne no doubt sensing Francis's disquiet and perhaps worrying that Francis was having second thoughts about their forthcoming marriage asked, 'are you all right? You seem a little distant.'

'I'm nervous,' Francis lied, he didn't want to concern Anne with his fears for the future, besides, as always, she'd probably think that he was being over pessimistic, 'I worry that I'm not worthy of you'.

Anne smiled kindly, 'Don't worry Francis, for tomorrow we'll be man and wife.' Despite the winter chill and his fears for their future, Francis was warmed as he noticed, what he hoped, was excitement in Anne's voice.

'Yes, but did you not know that it's unlucky for a couple to meet on the eve of their wedding?'

Practical as ever, Francis had inadvertently ended the conversation, as Anne gathering up her gown scurried out of the chamber, leaving Francis alone once again, with only his thoughts to keep him company and these did little to cheer him, as he wondered how long it would be before he'd be 'called to arms' and thereby forced to leave his new wife.

Impatient, Francis stood at the small gate that marked the final approach to church, where he would soon be married. From where he was stood Francis could clearly see the progress of the wedding train, led by both Anne and her father, as it made it's way slowly up the track, that leaving Ravensworth, wound its way up the hill and along the ridge to the church.

Dressed in the purist white, her long golden hair swept back in a headress, Francis's bride looked radiant. As she joined him, Anne seemed to follow Francis's line of sight, as he looked in the direction of the entrance porch, where they were to exchange their vows. Above the doorway in a small alcove was a carved miniature of St Peter, the church's patron saint. Francis's shuddered and felt that it was quite eerie, for Anne must have been able to read his thoughts. Looking at the statue under which they would soon be married, for no apparent reason she said, 'Don't worry Francis, I'd never deny you as Peter did our Lord.'

Francis heard and remembered nothing of the marriage service itself, save that is for the joy that he felt, as married, together with his wife, he finally entered the church and heartily sang along with the other guests, celebrating the fact that he was now joined to Anne, 'Till Death do you part'.

The festivities held in the Castle's great Hall seemed to last an eternity. Until that is, Francis was at last able to find himself alone with Anne in their chambers. Francis silently berated himself for his clumsiness as he tried to undress Anne, wondering if his awkwardness was due to the quantities of wine and ale that he'd consumed, or due to his nervousness and his eagerness to be joined with her. Francis chided himself for his inexperience, as sighing Anne finally took hold of his fumbling hands and placed them upon her small firm breasts, which Francis had only just managed to unclothe. Anne disrobed in an instant and Francis held her tightly, instinctively pulling her slim waist into his as he grew in excitement. Looking up Francis's eyes met those of Anne's, before his lips met hers in a soft but lingering kiss.

Francis undressed as Anne watched, thankfully his anxiety evaporated until it was gone altogether, replaced by a base desire, as he stood in front of his young wife, each delighting in the others nakedness, the shape and curve of Anne's frame highlighted by the glow of the fire, the bedchambers only light.

No words were exchanged as Anne finally lay down upon the bed of down. Francis taking the briefest of moments to admire further the beauty of her surprisingly mature body, before he too lay down next to her. Soon Francis was joined to his wife in an act of love, an act so different to that which he'd witnessed on the road to Reading. As Anne clung to him Francis felt the warmth of her pervade throughout his whole body. This was not the brief struggle that Francis had been witness to in the past and had, until that moment been his only experience of the act of lovemaking. After what seemed like an eternity, Francis finally let himself go as he felt Anne's body tighten against his own, he looked deep into her eyes and wondered how it was possible to love another human being so much.

Sleep finally took the young couple late into the night. When Francis awoke the following morning to see his wife sleeping soundly by his side, he felt that he never wanted to rise again, snug as he was in this safest of environments. Reluctantly however he did, having to share his wife with the Castles other occupants at breakfast and throughout the entirety of the meal having to endure their bawdiness, as they questioned both he and Anne as to their activities of the previous evening. In contrast to Anne, Francis took no pleasure in the humour, feeling that it merely debased what had been for him, a truly wonderful experience. As Francis gazed at Anne, who together with everyone else was laughing, he hoped that she too felt the same.

Chapter 10
June 1467. London.

Surprisingly, in the sixteen months that had elapsed since Francis's marriage, the resumption of the Civil War that Francis had prophesied as imminent, had failed to materialise. Life should have been wonderful. Yet for some reason, Francis, who with age seemed to became even more serious as Anne became even sillier, was not able to forget either the past, or his fears for the future. Anne, who Francis felt had no understanding of such things, had often criticised Francis for his 'melancholy', which Francis preferred to call, 'A realism borne of experience'. Indeed this oft repeated phrase had been the cause of much hilarity amongst the Fitzhughes, who would always remind Francis that he was still very much a minor! This angered Francis, for clearly both Anne and her family failed to appreciate quite what Francis had experienced in his short life. In truth Francis often wondered if his wife truly understood him at all! For Francis married life was not all that he'd hoped it to be and when it came to decent conversation, Anne was a poor replacement for Richard, for she had no interest in current affairs. Francis, eager for anthers opinion, would often turn to his wife, to be met instead by an expressionless face and he would be left wondering if in fact she ever listened to anything that he said.

In spite of sharing his bed with another Francis still slept poorly, yet Anne, one who should care about his well-being, seemed all too easily satisfied with Francis's brief and inaccurate explanations for the nightmares that regularly interrupted their sleep. Nightly Francis was tormented by the tortured figure of Aubrey De Vere on the scaffold, a vision made more horrific, as the face of Aubrey was often replaced by that of Francis's father or latterly by that of Francis's benefactor the Earl of Warwick.

Francis liked to think that he was no different from many others, who in such dangerous and unpredictable times were desperate for answers. Like them, Francis had even risked incurring the wrath of his priest, as having vainly sought answers from a variety of other sources, he'd visited the village soothsayer. Ultimately Thomas Bent, who many said practised the 'Black Art', was yet another in a long line of disappointments and Francis's visit to him had proven to be both futile and expensive. It'd cost Francis a penny just to elicit any kind of response from the silly old man, who upon Francis's arrival, had completely ignored him and had sat there motionless, as if in some form of pathetic, self induced trance. It may have impressed others but it hadn't inspired any confidence in Francis, who hated himself for not getting up and leaving there and then! Indeed it was only upon payment of a further penny that Bent had recounted to Francis, what was clearly, a well rehearsed speech, that in Francis's opinion, could easily have been adapted to suit a variety of differing people and their situations. If Francis had been any older he'd have thrashed the man for his deceit, as it was he had to satisfy himself with Bent's suggestion that, 'Many great and wondrous things' would 'befall' him, 'in a long and prosperous life'. It was not only the loss of two pennies that had been the cause of bitter disappointment to Francis, but also the fact that he was no further forward in seeking an explanation for both his dreams and the increasing sense of foreboding that he felt. As always Francis chose to be hard on himself. In contrast, Anne who'd found the whole incident quite comical, said that Francis wasn't the first and certainly wouldn't be the last, to have been duped by Gypsy folk. And ultimately even Francis was forced to admit that on occasions these soothsayers could be quite accurate in their predictions. Francis smiled as he remembered how they'd all laughed when his father had told them that his friend, the Duke of Somerset, who'd been forewarned by a Gypsy to beware of castles, had point blank refused to go anywhere near them and had even refused to visit King Henry at his Castle at Windsor. No one had laughed however, when the prophesy had come true. During the first Battle of St Albans, the Duke had found himself hard pressed and engaged in the bitter hand to hand fighting that had taken place within the town centre and it was there that he'd met his end, struck down and killed, directly outside the Castle Inn! Yes, Francis had to admit that even in this modern world, many people still believed the 'soothsayer's' and stories abounded of their success in foretelling the future. Francis smiled again, for he'd got to admit that the concept did appeal to his dark sense of humour. A story that Francis had always enjoyed, was that which told of how the Duke of Suffolk, in the times of Henry Bolingbroke, was said to have been advised by a soothsayer that he'd be safe if he managed to escape the, 'Danger of the Tower'. The hapless Duke, who'd feared that he was going to be executed in the Tower of London, had only finally been convinced that he was safe once he'd boarded a ship that was to take him to France and exile. The unfortunate Suffolk had however been horrified to discover that the name of the ship that was to deliver him out of England, was the, 'Nicholas of the Tower'. Needless to say, the ships company chose not to deliver the Duke to France, but instead robbed and then murdered him, throwing his body overboard.

Nor was Francis's anxiety relieved when he heard numerous tales of the lawlessness and civil unrest that abounded in the shires, especially in the north of the country. Presently none could travel the highways in safety, especially once darkness had fallen, for fear of being robbed and murdered at the hands of the bands of vagabonds and villains who roamed the countryside, ex-soldiers, redundant now that the Civil Wars had ended. And this disorder was the cause of yet more disaffection between the King and his subjects, for Edward in the numerous manifestos that he'd circulated throughout the civil war, had promised an end to the 'Lawlessness that flourished throughout the realm.' For once, Francis was not alone in his assessment that the situation had worsened since the Yorkists had come to power. Sadly, many 'n'aer do wells', who always seemed to prosper at such times, took advantage of this anarchy to settle old scores and many good people were maimed and even murdered by old adversaries, who staged such deeds to make it appear to others as a simple, yet unfortunate, acts of criminality.

At times Anne did lighten Francis's life. And at least in refusing to listen to his gloomy predictions and by regularly admonishing him for, 'darkening their days together', she would force him out of his depressions. She told him that these days should be the 'happiest of their lives!' And in truth Francis could see that she was right. On the brightest of days both Francis and Anne would ride out together in the glorious countryside that surrounded Ravensworth. Sitting on the banks of the moat Anne would watch, smiling, as Francis fished or flew his hawks. Francis had to admit that these could and should have been idyllic times. Francis delighting in impressing Anne, with both his skills as a horseman and at arms as he jousted and engaged in mock combat with the other squires. Surprisingly, Anne's brother Richard proved to be the worthiest of Francis's opponents, the lad more than making up for his slowness of wit by the speed of his sword arm. Annoyingly, Anne would become helpless with laughter as she was witness, on a number of occasions, to the unceremonious dumping of Francis from his horse, this invariably at the hands of her brother. Francis would try to take these defeats in good grace, but unfortunately his competitive nature often got the better of him and he would often refuse to take his opponents hand, sulking as he retired to his chambers. There he would remain, sometimes for hours, until Anne would eventually join him and would restore his humour, using those means made available to members of the fairer sex.

Francis's and Anne's life at Ravensworth was both modest and unsophisticated. It was to Middleham that they ventured on those rare occasions that they felt the need for culture, refinement and for Francis, reports of events in London. They would find all of these things in plentiful supply at the Earl's Court, especially news from London, information that Francis constantly craved. Unfortunately, these trips were limited, for the most part, to those infrequent festivals and pageants that, commonplace elsewhere, at Middleham seemed to be restricted to those times when the Earl himself was in residence at the Castle. Whilst at the Earl's castle Francis and his young wife would take the opportunity to socialise with the other notaries of the northern nobility, who had all now wholly accepted Francis into their affinity. On these occasions both Francis and Anne would delight in the jugglers, jesters, pipers and players that cluttered the outer courtyard of the fortress, or they would marvel at the various wild animals that were exhibited. On one occasion a great bear, thankfully chained, actually danced! The great animal, to everyone's amusement, going about it's complex and well rehearsed routine at the instigation of it's master and 'bearward'. In the evenings the Earl's guests would retire to the comfort of the keep and their Lords private apartments, there to enjoy the Earl's legendary banquets and after to play chess or cards and drink, sometimes long into the dead of night.

Francis, despite his age and the fact that in theory he was still a minor, now considered himself as belonging to the Earl's inner circle of friends and retainers. As a result, both he and Anne together with Anne's parents, had been invited to accompany the Earl to London, to witness what many said was to be the 'greatest tournament of the age.'

The Queen's brother Anthony Woodville, Lord Scales was to meet Anthony the illegitimate son of Duke Philip of Burgundy, who was known as 'The Bastard of Burgundy', in the lists at Smiths field. Both were the respective champions of their countries and the event had been conceived to decide once and for all which of the two was to be declared, 'The greatest Knight in all of Christendom.' Francis knew that the Earl had no interest in the outcome of the match, for although the Earl, a great knight and soldier himself, enjoyed such 'Tournaments' and admired such skills in others, he hated each of the two combatants. Scales as the Queen's sibling and the 'Bastard' for being a Burgundian and an enemy to his friends the French. The Earl had agreed to attend, not to witness the event, but to introduce the latest in a long line of French envoys to the King. The Earl still hoped to persuade Edward to abandon his planned alliance with the Burgundians and instead, to conclude a treaty with the French King Louis. Thankfully in recent months the Earl had backed down from a direct confrontation with the King, ostensibly, Francis felt, as the Earl was beginning to realise that the Duke of Clarence, a petulant and arrogant youth, may not, after all, have been such an 'ideal replacement' for his brother Edward. Unfortunately Clarence was used to, 'Getting his own way' and as such, the Earl was concerned that by placing him on the throne, he would merely be replacing a 'like for like'. Keen therefore not to 'burn all of his bridges' by offending Edward further, the Earl had asked that the Lovels and the Fitzhughs represent him at the tournament. Francis, who'd never before witnessed such an event, in spite of his misgivings at having to revisit London, had keenly accepted the Earl's invitation.

Francis had been fortunate in securing them all lodgings in a comfortable house in Fleet Street, which was both adequately furnished and close to the centre of London. The Capital's already large population had been swelled considerably by those who had visited London, eager to witness what was going to be, the 'greatest event of their age'. In addition, many others had been summoned to the Capital by the King, for the forthcoming opening of Parliament, an event that was set to coincide with the tournament. Both Francis and Anne had been lucky enough to be present when the 'Bastard of Burgundy' had arrived in the City. The Burgundian and his entourage having sailed directly into the City via the Thames, in four magnificent caravels. Great ships that were bedecked in banners and tapestries with their standards and pennants unfurled. Ironically the 'Bastard', for the duration of his stay, was also to reside in Fleet Street, at the London residence of the Bishop of Salisbury. This happy coincidence added to the Lovel's excitement and enabled both Francis and his wife to meet with the Burgundian, to witness first hand the flamboyance and extravagance for which the great Knight was famous. After they'd met him, grudgingly, Francis was forced to acknowledge that Anthony of Burgundy, like his namesake Anthony Woodville, Lord Scales, was the embodiment of the chivalrous age in which they all lived. Apparently Woman throughout Europe fell at the two Knight's feet and many songs and poems were written, celebrating their prowess both as knights and as lovers. Keen to drum up interest in the event, Edward had presented the Burgundian to his adoring fans on the very night that he'd arrived in England. Jealous, Francis could not help but notice how, on being presented to the knight, Anne had flushed and fidgeted in a manner that was in his opinion quite unbecoming for a Lady of her position. That said Francis couldn't help but admire the Knight, who on being introduced to the crowd had spoken boldly and gracefully to them in perfect English. The 'Bastard' thanking his 'English friends' for their warm welcome, before he confidently, and in Francis's opinion arrogantly, predicted that he would easily defeat, 'their English champion.'

Ever since the King had received word that the Burgundian had accepted the challenge that had been laid down by Lord Scales, the lists in Smiths field had been prepared meticulously. On the day of the Tournament both Francis and the Fitzhughes, as the personal guests of the Earl of Warwick, who was conspicuous by his absence, were seated in the larger of the two grandstands, which had been erected predominantly to accommodate the King and his court. Francis was in the process of explaining the Earl's absence to Anne, this being that the French ambassador, whom the Earl was entertaining, would have seen it as a personal slight if Warwick were to attend an event staged on behalf of one of his nations bitterest enemies, when, to a blaze of trumpets, the King and his entourage finally arrived. It was not however the King, resplendent as he was in the finest cloth of purple, who attracted Francis's startled attention, nor was it Lord Hastings who was standing at the King's right hand. Neither was it the dozen or so Royal Councillors who were all dressed in the murray and blue of the House of York, it was in fact the person who preceded the King's host, upon whom Francis's attention was transfixed. As was the custom, the Constable of England strode forward before the King, proudly carrying aloft the sword of state.

Francis shivered as he was reacquainted with one whom he'd vowed to avoid in the future at all costs, John Tiptoft the Earl of Worcester. The passage of time had not altered the 'Butcher of England's' appearance, nor had it lessened the feelings of fear and horror that his presence elicited in Francis. In an instant Francis recalled that which he'd felt and witnessed when he'd last had cause to visit the capital. Francis was both disgusted and repulsed as he saw how Tiptoft seemed to delight in the hatred that his presence provoked in the gathered crowd. Francis silently cursed the constable and then chided himself for not daring to shout out his hatred for this man. Many others were not so fearful and these people booed and hissed as the Earl strode by. Eventually Francis turned his attention to the King who chose to ignore the hostility that his constable evoked amongst his subjects. After Edward had appeared to share a joke with Hastings, he raised his arms aloft to receive the clamorous applause of the crowd. It was obvious that the King still commanded the respect and loyalty from the majority of his subjects, for when he lowered his arms the crowd fell silent as they waited for him to address them. As Francis examined both the

King and Hastings he shuddered, for he still considered them to be potential enemies and seeing both men close up, he could easily understand why neither had ever lost a battle in which they'd fought! It was said that both men preferred to lead from the front and in the height of the fighting were, to be found in the very press of their enemies. The Queen, who was clearly heavily pregnant, together with the members of her immediate family, was sat on the King's left, not surprisingly neither she not the other Woodvilles received any of the rapturous applause that was reserved for the King.

Pregnancy, Francis thought, had done little to detract from the Queen's unquestioned beauty, Sighing Anne echoed Francis's thoughts as she said, 'If only the Queen would allow herself a smile, then she would easily be the most beautiful Lady in England'.

'Save that is for one', Francis smiled as he turned to kiss his wife softly on the lips.

Once the King had finally concluded his speech, in which he warmly welcomed both the competitors and the spectators, he assumed a position at the very top of the Grandstand. Edward was then attended upon by the Lord Mayor and Aldermen of London who, kneeling in his presence, bowed in deference to the King's authority over them. The excited crowd once again became silent as the King thanked the Lord Mayor and, raising his staff, signalled to each of the combatants, who were waiting at either end of the lists, to take to the field.

Francis was amazed at the quality of the tournament field, the like of which he'd never before seen. Apparently the ground had been levelled with vast amounts of gravel, before a top dressing of stripped bark and sand had been added. Francis sighed as, for a brief moment, he wished that he too was taking to the field, to receive the accolades and adulation of the cheering crowd. This thought, however, was short lived as Francis was deafened by the cheers which greeted the two adversaries, who astride their great destriers, galloped at full speed onto the field. The two Knights came to an abrupt halt in front of the King's stand, both briefly enveloped in clouds of dust, as the crowd clapped and cheered in admiration of this display of such great horsemanship. Scales and the Bastard were obviously highly skilled and although their actions didn't appear to overawe their opponent, they certainly intimidated Francis. Surprisingly, Scales was accompanied onto the field by the Duke of Clarence who, despite the rumoured animosity between himself and the Queen's family, held the English Knight's helmet, a modern Sallet of German design. Other nobles and squires followed the Duke onto the field, each bearing various weapons or additional items of armour. Agile, in one swift movement, Scales was able to dismount. The English champion bowed low in reverence to his monarch. Surprisingly the bow, rather than give the impression of submission, seemed to reinforce the sense of power, grace and agility that exuded from this handsome Knight. Scale's hand almost touched the floor as it swept down beneath his bowed head in a salute to both his King and his sister the Queen. Scales remained bowed and the crowd once again became silent as the King blessed his champion, before Scales once again mounted his horse and rode the short distance to his tent where he would prepare for the first joust. Scales obviously loved the occasion and showed no fear of what was to come as he waved to the spectators who were all cheering enthusiastically. Francis was amazed by the spectacle. In places the crowd was some three or four deep, as people clamoured to get a better view from each and every vantage point that the lists afforded. Apparently the second grandstand, which had been built for the use of the commoners, had been filled long before dawn by those who were desperate to see an event that was to be unique in their lifetime.

Lord Scale's opponent. Anthony, 'The Bastard of Burgundy' had entered the lists from Francis's right. The Burgundian's war horse, which was sweating profusely, had obviously been spooked by the crowd and Francis feared that the creature might take off at any moment. Despite his distance from the Knight, Francis was both reassured and impressed to see how the Burgundian's strong yet skilful hands and heels, strained successfully to control his unpredictable mount. The crowds welcome to the foreigner was almost as great as that which had been given to the English champion. The Burgundian, on reaching the King's grandstand, dismounted as he paid his respects to Edward. As he did so the Knight handed his reigns to his squire who now had the onerous task of controlling the beast, which by that time was covered in white foam. The animals flashing and unblinking eyes indicated the wildness of spirit for which the horse was bred. Francis recalled how his tutor at Middleham, Sir John Conyer's, had always described the 'Destrier' as a 'Weapon in it's own right,' one that, given leave to do so, could take off half of a man's face in one viscous bite. It was not surprising then, Francis thought, that archers, when charged by cavalry, would shoot first at the great horses, preferring first and foremost to bring them down rather than their riders!

Francis smiled, it was clear that the Burgundian Knight also had the greatest respect for his Destrier, for once he'd paid tribute to the King he remained unhorsed, choosing to walk back to his side of the lists. Much to the delight of the female spectators, the Burgundian then proceeded to arm and clothe himself in the open. Anne coloured as Francis turning to her said, 'Have these foreigners no shame?'

As each piece of highly polished Italian armour was brought forward, Francis marvelled at its intricacies and the obvious skill that the Milanese workmen had put into it's design and production. Francis hoped that one day he to would own his own suit of Italian armour, rather than the crude English equivalent that he presently had to satisfy himself with. Once fully armoured upon their horses, the men dipped their heavy lances in deference to the field, before they both returned to their starting positions within the Lists.

Once again as the King rose to his feet and held his staff aloft, a hush fell throughout the crowd. All present waited in nervous anticipation for the contest to begin. After what seemed like an age, the King signified the start of the tournament by lowering his staff. The two Knights needed no more encouragement and each spurred their mounts onwards as they thundered down the lists towards each other, their lances lowered and aimed at a point somewhere upon their opponents chest. The crowd squealed with delight as in a cloud of dust and flashing metal, the two men finally clashed. Unfortunately, the audience's cries of excitement soon turned to sighs of disappointment, as it became apparent that none had prevailed. Neither Knight scoring the direct hit that would have lifted their opponent backwards and out of his saddle, dumping him unceremoniously onto the ground. Francis, who felt that he was quite knowledgeable in such matters, explained to Anne that each of the men had skilfully swivelled around in their saddle at the very last second, thus ensuring that their opponents lance delivered only a glancing blow that was easily deflected harmlessly downwards.

Both Knights, unable to slow their horses, were forced to continue the charge to the opposite end of the field. Here they dismounted and discarded both their shattered lances and much of their heavier armour. Lighter, and consequently more agile, both men remounted and drew their broad swords before returning to the fray. The audience, who'd all keenly anticipated the fight and who all expected the combat to begin in earnest, were once again disappointed. All had looked forward to a great battle between two champions. Adversaries and worthy opponents who would repeatedly exchange blows, either mounted or on foot, before the vanquished finally fell, either injured, dead or exhausted. In an effort to unhorse the English champion, the Burgundian rode his horse headlong into that of Lord Scale's. Unfortunately rather than flinging the Englishman to the floor, as intended, the 'Bastard's' horse merely crumpled beneath him, it's neck broken in the collision. Nor was the Burgundian thrown clear, for the man who would have them all believe that he was, 'Greatest Knight in all of Christendom,' was humiliatingly pinned underneath his dead horse. Worse still, the 'Bastard' was forced to remain there for quite some time, until the men at arms, who surrounded the field ostensibly to keep back the crowd, finally realised what was going on and rushed over to the centre of the lists to assist him. With difficulty the soldiers were eventually able to extricate the Burgundian, who was clearly both shaken and injured. Scales, leaning on his sword and clearly mystified by the whole bizarre scene, could only stand by and watch. Bloodied, the Burgundian was only able to stand before the King with the assistance of his Squire. Apparently Tiptoft, as the Constable of England, was the arbiter in all matters of chivalry. At the insistence of the Burgundian Knight and much to the disgust of both Lord Scales and the crowd, Tiptoft was asked to examine the English champions saddle for any illegalities. As the crowd booed and hissed, Francis smiled, as he'd hoped the contest was definitely developing into quite a grudge match. Once Tiptoft had finally declared the matter a fair contest the King offered the Bastard a further mount. Not surprisingly the Burgundian, who was in no state to continue, declined the offer. Much to the disgust of the spectators he retired to his tent, this time choosing to disrobe in private! Francis, who by that time had made his way towards the front of the grandstand, smiled as heard the Bastard mutter bitterly to his squire as he limped from the field, 'Doubt not: He's fought a beast today, tomorrow he shall fight a man'.

The crowd assembled early on the following day, all looked forward to seeing what they hoped would be a decisive contest, as the Knights were expected to resume the match on foot. Instead, once again the spectators were forced to stand by as proceedings were held up once again, this time to enable Tiptoft to examine each of the rivals' spears and battle axes for any illegalities. Apparently the King, fearing the effect that the death or maiming of the Duke of Burgundy's son, albeit an illegitimate one, would have on their proposed alliance and likewise the effect that such an injury to the Queen's brother would have upon his marriage, had forbade the use of lethal weapons. Eventually, late into the morning, the combat finally began, both Knights using spears and battle axes that had been blunted by the King's blacksmith. Lord Scales having gained the admiration of the crowd when he'd insisted on fighting with his visor up. Unsurprisingly the Knights soon discarded their spears, weapons which were normally associated with poorer soldiers and with which both Knights were clearly unfamiliar. Both chose to fight on at closer quarters with the battle axe, the favoured weapon amongst the majority of the Knighthood. The spectators cheered and nodded approvingly as Scales soon gained the upper hand, his accurate and well timed blows repeatedly raining down upon the Burgundian. Backing off, with increasing desperation, the 'Bastard' tried to put his opponent off balance with a number of jabs, which using the point of his axe, were directed towards Scales' breastplate. These defensive strikes seemed to have no discernible effect on the Englishman who repeatedly raised his own axe above his head, before he delivered yet another strength sapping blow to the Burgundian's already crumpled and crushed helmet. Although Scales appeared to have the upper hand, Francis noticed that some of the Burgundian's jabs, despite the bluntness of his weapon, had succeeded in puncturing Scale's breast plate and smears of blood were beginning to appear on the English Knight's once bright armour. The contest continued as each man stubbornly refused to yield and as expected, both men's actions became slower and more deliberate as fatigue set in. Francis couldn't help but to admire the way in which each of the Knights equipped themselves, although it soon became apparent to him, that with the use of blunted weapons, neither man had either the skill nor the strength to prevail. Eventually once again much to the annoyance of the spectators, the King ended the stalemate by raising his staff and calling a halt to the proceedings. Francis couldn't tell whether it was angst, the intensity of the men's concentration, or the fact that they were so tired, that caused the Knights to initially disregard Edward's command. However, after exchanging a few more blows both men finally acknowledged the instruction and, casting their weapons aside, they took hold of each other in an embrace that lasted for some minutes. Francis smiled as he wondered if this was a sign of the genuine respect and admiration that the two adversaries had for each other or was borne of the fact that they each needed the others support to stop themselves from collapsing altogether!

Many arguments followed, for obviously the contest had failed to produce a clear victor. Who was the 'Greatest Knight in Christendom?' There was even talk of an immediate rematch, although when one considered the effort that had gone into organising the original contest this may have proven difficult to arrange, especially at such short notice. Initially, Francis felt that the Queen's brother had been victorious, for he'd had the upper hand for most of the fighting, but even he had to admit that it was unlikely that the Englishman could have bested the tenacious Burgundian. Anne, who seemed to have a particular soft spot for the foreigner, disagreed with her husband, pointing out that Lord Scales armour had been breached and that the

English Knight had reputedly received a number of deep lacerations to his chest. Despite her inexperience in such matters, Anne argued that in time these wounds would have sapped Scales' strength and eventually the Burgundian would have been able to overcome him. Her obvious favouritism and Francis's consequent jealousy ensured that Francis, despite his dislike for the Woodvilles, soon became convinced that Lord Scales would, had he been given the opportunity, have defeated the foreigner and thus proven that he was, 'The greatest Knight in Christendom.'

The Earl's entourage had been due to remain in the Capital for sometime after the conclusion of the tournament. Unfortunately, a number of events conspired to draw their stay to a premature and unexpected end.

It had all began when Archbishop Neville, Warwick's brother and the Lord Chancellor of England had failed to attend the opening of Parliament. The Archbishop had sent a message saying that he was ill, but all knew that he was expressing his displeasure in the proposed Burgundian alliance. The King, furious and suspecting the Earl of Warwick's interference, had immediately, and without any consultation, dismissed the Archbishop from his office. Irate, Edward had even gone so far as to personally visit the Lord Chancellor at his Inn at Charring Cross, further humiliating the Earl's brother, by there and then demanding that he return the great seal of office to him. To make matters worse the Archbishop was replaced as Lord Chancellor by the Pro-Woodville bishop of Bath and Wells, Robert Stillington.

The crisis was exacerbated when the Duke of Burgundy, Philip the Good, suddenly died. The 'Bastard of Burgundy's father', who'd been ill for sometime, was succeeded by his legitimate son Charles 'the Rash'. In addition to ensuring the Bastard's speedy return to the continent, thus dispelling once and for all any rumours of a rematch, this event ensured that the proposed marriage between Edward's favourite sister Margaret and the new Duke went ahead, as previously planned. Thus, the King was to become the brother in law of Charles, the new Duke of Burgundy. As a consequence, the likelihood of an English-Burgundian alliance was no longer a possibility, it was now, practically speaking, a certainty.

Whilst in London the Earl had declined to attend the tournament, preferring instead to entertain the French envoys who'd visited England in the hope of securing an Anglo-French alliance, against both the dukedoms of Burgundy and Brittany. The Earl, who had truly believed that he still held enough influence over his cousin the King to secure such an alliance, had sought an audience with Edward at Westminster. The King, who at the time had been in the company of Lord Herbert and the Queen's father Earl Rivers, men whom the Earl preferred to call the 'King's Cronies', was reported to have ignored the Earl, refusing even to acknowledge his cousin's presence at the Palace. This had embarrassed the Earl, who was said to have been incensed at the King's slight. Worse still, on the following day, in an effort to coerce the King, the Earl had taken the French envoys with him, no doubt assuming that Edward would not show such bad manners to the Ambassadors of the King of France. The Earl had been sorely disappointed. This time the King failed to acknowledge the presence of the either the Earl or his guests. Francis had been present on the quay side when the Earl's barge had returned from the ill fated trip and he had never seen his Lord so angered. White with rage the Earl's hand kept reaching for the short dagger that he carried in the belt of his tunic. The Earl was a proud man and Francis could only imagine his fury at being humiliated in front of the French Envoys, whom he had always been so keen to impress.

Francis who'd always believed that one day the Earl and Edward would come to blows, knew that it had only needed a catalyst to set it off. Now this catalyst had been provided by the King who was obviously either ignorant as to the effect that his actions would have upon his cousin, or no longer cared. In Francis's opinion Edward only had himself to blame. For it was his treatment of the Earl together with his patronage of his 'made men' that had finally brought the matter to a head. Francis was neither surprised by the Earl's reaction to the King's slight, nor by the remarks that the Earl made in the presence of the French envoys, a proclamation made so loudly that all in the vicinity could hear it, 'Have you not seen what traitors there are about the King's person.'

The French alarmed by the Earl's outburst had tried to calm him, 'My Lord, I pray you grow not hot, for some day you will be avenged.'

The Earl who would not be appeased shouted, 'Know that those very traitors were the men that had my brother displaced from the office of chancellor.'

Francis guessed that the Earl had finally, at last, acknowledged that the influence that the Woodvilles and there allies now had over the King could not be reversed. Politically speaking the Earl had lost. The Woodviles rise in power had been mirrored by the Earl's diminishing prestige. Francis, knowing his patron well, knew that the Earl could never accept such a curtailed role in the Politics of the realm.

It was then with an increasing sense of foreboding, that Francis once again turned his back on the capital and, returned north to his new home. He now knew felt sure that when they returned Southwards once again, it would be with an army.

Chapter 11
July 1469. Edgecote Field.

As dawn broke in the valley that was known locally as Danes Moor, the Northern Army, that was already arrayed in battle order on the high ground of Blackbird Hill, was finally revealed to those who were awake within the Royalist camp. As Francis stood patiently and waited for orders, despite the eager anticipation that he felt for what was to be his first taste of battle, his mind, as it was want to do on occasions, wandered. He pondered. This location, situated just a few miles to the north of the small hamlet of Middleton Cheney in the county of Northamptonshire, was not dissimilar to the gently rolling countryside that he'd been accustomed to in Oxfordshire, yet it was very different to the northern lands from whence the majority of his present comrades came. It was, he felt, quite beautiful and on any other day would have been an idyllic spot. Today however, Francis mused, it was more likely to be the scene of much slaughter that hopefully would see the Yorkshire men victorious. As Francis anticipated the battle, thankfully, he was able to focus once again on the task at hand. From his vantage point within the vanguard of the rebel Neville army, Francis could clearly see that the Welshmen who comprised the majority of the Royalist army, had been caught unprepared for battle. Francis smiled, no doubt the men, on waking up to discover there opponents amassed on the high ground, would have cursed their commander for his ineptitude both in selecting such an indefensible position and for posting insufficient pickets to raise the alarm. Francis was surprised, for King Edward's army was said to be commanded by one of the King's 'favourites', Sir William Herbert Earl of Pembroke and Herbert was said to be both a brave and knowledgeable general. Despite the distance between the two armies, Francis, fascinated by his first sight of an opposing army, was able to observe the enemy soldiers under Herbert's command as they desperately tried to ready themselves for the battle. Many of the Royalists were still within the confines of their own camp which was situated upon the lower ground, in a large meadow that was dissected by a tributary of the River Cherwell. Francis smiled again as he heard Pembroke's battle captains frantically barking out the orders that sent their soldiers, who were in varying states of undress, scurrying about in all directions. 'Like rats in a trap,' Francis joked with those young men who were standing with him and they all laughed nervously, relieved for the time being at least, to have had the atmosphere lightened. The Conyer brothers, who commanded the rebel army, had done well to catch the enemy so comprehensively off guard. Francis laughed. What would King Edward have to say, if he could see how his army had been caught in such a state of complete and utter disarray? This in stark contrast to, and in full view of, the rebels who were already drilled, armed and ready to attack, their weapons and armour glinting in the morning sun.

Francis had been impressed by the great number of Neville adherents who had enthusiastically answered the Earl of Warwick's call to arms. The Yorkshire men's ranks had been swollen further with the addition of many common people who had joined the rebellion, angry at both the King's decadence and the countrywide decay in law and order. Warwick's brother, George Neville the Archbishop of York, incensed at his dismissal as Lord Chancellor, had also assisted in the recruitment, the cleric spreading malcontent throughout his diocese and northern England. Francis could still not believe the King's naivety in not earlier suspecting the Earl's involvement in the rising, especially when one considered their deteriorating relationship. Amazingly, Edward, on hearing of the rebellion, had initially concluded that it was a minor affair and had chosen to go on a pilgrimage to Walsingham, rather than riding north to deal with it. The King had taken Richard and some of his Woodville relations with him. Edward had been completely misled and had even issued summonses requesting that both Warwick and the Duke of Clarence come to his assistance. Ironically, and unbeknown to the King at that point, the rebellion had been staged by both the Earl and Clarence. Edward's increasingly desperate appeals for help had amused the Earl, that is until news had finally reached the King of the two men's involvement. The King must not have been able to believe such treachery on the part of his brother and cousin, for even as recently as the second week of July he'd written to them both, asking that they support him and show him that they weren't, '*Of any such disposition towards us, as the rumour here runneth.*' Francis smiled at the irony, the King's final message had been intercepted at Coventry by the rebel's, yet in spite of this, it had still reached its intended recipient. For many of the King's intended allies were in fact his enemies!

Francis was amazed that the King, with his network of spies and informants, had not guessed earlier that the Earl and Clarence would come out in open rebellion against him, as rumours of their increasing disaffection had abounded. Francis had believed that it had been common knowledge throughout England, that the Pope, bribed with Neville gold, had finally been persuaded to issue a papal dispensation, enabling the marriage of the King's brother Clarence to Warwick's eldest daughter Isabel, to go ahead. This marriage had been strictly forbidden by the King who had, perhaps hypocritically, requested that his brothers both marry according to his wishes and not their own. Francis found it hard to believe that Edward's spies in Rome had not notified him of this development. Surely, Francis thought, the King can't have believed the Earl's lie, that he was visiting the port of Sandwich, a location extremely close to Edwards court, to 'personally supervise' the refit of his flagship the 'Trinity', when in fact his intention was to take ship to Calais, where the marriage ceremony was to be held. Nor had the Duke of Clarence been honest with his brother. He'd assured Edward that he was going to Canterbury, there to visit his mother the Duchess Cecily and to embark on a pilgrimage to the shrine of Thomas a Becket at the cathedral. For even as the King had made his last desperate appeal for their support, both Clarence and Warwick were already in Calais, where, on the 11th July, Archbishop Neville carried out the ceremony that not only joined Clarence and Isabel in marriage, but also tied together the rebel alliance. It was, Francis thought, at this juncture that many people could be forgiven for being confused as to the Earl's true intentions. From Calais both the Earl and Clarence had issued a manifesto in which they'd denounced the King's exclusion of 'Princess of the Blood Royal' from his Royal Council. They had named both the Woodville's court faction of Earl Rivers, Scales and Sir John and his brothers together with Herbert and the recently created Earl of Devon, Humphrey Stafford, as having, *'Caused our said sovereign Lord and his realm to fall into great poverty of misery, disturbing the ministration of the laws, only intending their own promotion and enriching.'* The manifesto had concluded by stating that their intention was merely to look to Edward for 'remedy' and 'reformation'.

Francis, however, felt that the intentions of both the Earl and his new son-in-law were not so straightforward. Although at that point, in truth, neither Francis nor his comrades knew for sure what their leaders ultimate aims were. Clarence was once again circulating rumours of Edward's alleged illegitimacy, maintaining that Edward was born of an English archer from Rouen called Blaybourne. This suggested that Clarence, as the second eldest surviving son of Richard of York, would himself make a play for the throne. Moreover, anyone with a limited knowledge of history could see that their manifesto was almost a carbon copy of those circulated prior to the deposition of Edward II; Richard II and Henry VI. In an effort to find out what was really intended, Francis had questioned, amongst others, his father-in-law, asking him what he thought the Earl's real aims were, be it 'reformation' or 'revolution'. Even Lord Fitzhugh wasn't quite sure what the rebellion's ultimate objective was and Francis was left wondering. Were they to rid the Kingdom of Edward and place his brother Clarence, a puppet of both the Earl and the French, on the throne? Or was their aim, as the manifesto maintained, merely to rid Edward of his 'cronies', the Woodville, Herbert and Stafford influences? Francis scratched his head, even he couldn't guess what game the Earl was playing. Surely the Earl was far too clever to place the arrogant and unpredictable Clarence on the throne. Yet if this was the case, why then would he marry his eldest daughter to the King's brother? Francis smiled, maybe the Earl was playing a clever yet dangerous game, not wholly ruling out the prospect of Clarence ascending to the throne, thus securing his son in laws not inconsiderable support, whilst hoping at the same time to persuade Edward, by force of arms, to 'toe the line' and renew their previous arrangement. That is, the Earl effectively ruling the Kingdom through the personage of his young cousin. It might be, Francis wondered, that the Earl had devised a plan that would cater for all eventualities. Should the King meet an untimely death during the campaign, the 'Kingmaker' had yet another Prince of York, his son-in-law Clarence, to place on the throne in his stead. But should the Edward survive, he may once again be forced to rule England on behalf of the Earl. Indeed one could even be forgiven for believing that, in certain circumstances, the Earl may have even countenanced a Lancastrain restoration! (With him being the power behind Henry's throne). For the Earl had somehow managed to secure the support of some of the more prominent Lancastrians, one of whom was none other than John De Vere the Earl of Oxford. Apparently Oxford had even crossed over to France with the Earl's retinue, as a guest at Clarence's wedding! Francis smiled at the irony of it. Did this mean that the Earl was even willing to resolve his differences with King Henry's French Queen, Margaret of Anjou?

At some point the northern army would have to meet up with its southern counterpart that was coming up from London and was commanded by the Earl, Clarence and Oxford. Francis smiled, he hoped that he would have the opportunity of seeing his young cousin, Thomas, whom he'd not seen nor heard from since that fateful day in January 1462, when both of their lives had taken off in seemingly opposite directions.

Since they'd left Yorkshire Francis had, on many occasions, tried to discuss his thoughts and theories with his comrades. He was however sorely disappointed, as all they seemed interested in was making war! Francis was amazed, they said that they were happy to die in the service of their Lord, yet all seemed unconcerned as to the real reasons why they were expected go into battle. Francis sighed even Francis's father-in-law, a man for whom he had the greatest of respect, failed to appreciate the complexities of the plan on which they were all embarked. As for his brothers-in-law, when he'd spoken to both Henry and Richard, Francis had been met with apathy, neither boy caring why or for whom they were fighting, just that they were at last able to prove their 'Mettle in an engagement.'

The rebels numbers had swelled to vast proportions as they'd marched southwards along the old Roman Roads, firstly Dere Street and latterly the Fosse Way. Surprisingly, in spite of their numbers, their commanders had taken great care to avoid any engagement with the smaller army that Edward, in haste, had recruited and positioned at Nottingham. Francis, when he considered the size of their army, had truly believed that they could never be bested on the field and, as such, he had failed to appreciate why the northerners, led by Sir William Conyers, had avoided a direct confrontation with the King's army. Sir William, known to the rebels as Robin Redesdale, or Robin 'mend all', was accompanied by his brother John, the Earl's cousin by marriage and the steward at Middleham castle. The Conyer's had, Francis argued, failed to capitalise on what had been the perfect opportunity to defeat Edward on the field of battle. Both brothers had maintained that it was not their intention to destroy the King nor to harm his person. The Earl merely wished, they said, 'To remove once and for all the Woodvile and Herbert influences from around Edward,' thus ensuring that the King once again 'listened to the Earl's counsel alone.' Francis, who had had the benefit of many discussions with Richard, felt that he knew Edward's character well and, as such, he believed that the Earl would never again be able to use the King in this way.

'The King is his own master now,' Francis had argued, only to be reminded that he was still little more than a child and 'knew nothing of such things.' Indeed both Richard and Henry Fitzhugh had continually teased their brother-in-law saying that Francis always, 'Looked for answers where there were none.' For once Francis, who was sick and tired of arguing his point on the subject, chose to, 'Put up and shut up.' In spite of this, Francis still ached for answers to his questions and as time went by and the situation became even more confused, he could only wonder what would transpire. Even now, as he stood waiting patiently for those orders that would take him into battle, he did not truly know what, or even who, he was going to be fighting for!

The Conyer brothers had been extremely successful in their strategy of isolating the King and through a series of gruelling forced marches, they'd managed to place their own army between that of Edward and the larger force that had been mustered on his behalf in the western marches. This Welsh army which was commanded by William Herbert, the newly created Earl of Pembroke, had intended to relieve Edward at Nottingham, instead it'd been caught here in Northamptonshire.

'We can now destroy all of our enemies in one engagement, without harming the King and thereby incurring the wrath of the common people,' Sir William Conyers had jovially exclaimed, at the hastily convened counsel of War that had been arranged, once their scouts had finally reported that the Welsh army was now within striking distance. In contrast to the Conyers who'd wanted to give 'immediate battle', Lord Fitzhugh had counselled caution, advising that they wait, 'For the Earl and Clarence' who were en route from the capital with more men, the sight of which would, he argued, put even 'Herbert and his Welshman to flight.' After a long and heated argument the Conyers had finally got their way.

Even Francis, as always the realist, was confident of a speedy victory. He smiled as he considered the ease with which their rebellion had so far achieved it's objectives. All this, he thought, in spite of the fact that in the beginning things had gone alarmingly wrong. Like all large scale disorder, Francis appreciated that it was practically impossible to successfully co-ordinate such a rising. The initial rebellion had begun much too early and had unfortunately coincided with a completely separate rebellion, that led by the mysterious Robin of Holderness, who had hoped to restore Henry Percy to the Earldom of Northumberland, an objective contrary to that of the Neville rising! The Earldom of Northumberland was presently held by Warwick's brother John and he was reputed to jealously guard the prized office that he had earned through his support for the King. John Neville held the earldom at the cost of the Lancastrian Percy family, a family who had historically held the post. As such, the pro Percy Holderness rebellion was ruthlessly suppressed on behalf of the King by Warwick's brother. It's followers scattered and it's leaders mercilessly executed by the Neville Earl of Northumberland. Warwick's brother had, however, given an indication as to where his true loyalties lay. For he'd allowed Conyers and his men, who were both weak and unsupported at that point, to escape. The Yorkshire rebels avoided an armed confrontation with Warwick's brother by retreating back through Wensleydale and over the Pennines into Lancashire. Here they were able to melt away into the surrounding countryside, uninjured and able to raise their rebellion at a more appropriate time. This they did and on the second occasion they were successful in co-ordinating the rising. Now, here in the Northamptonshire countryside, they were at last ready to do battle. Francis felt physically sick with nerves, brought on by the thought of the confrontation at hand. He wondered if he too were ready.

It was said that when the King had finally realised the precariousness of his position, he had sent his Woodville relatives into hiding, Scales to Norfolk and ironically both Earl Rivers and Sir John Woodville, to join William Herbert and his brother Richard in Wales. As a result, rather than being out of harms way, both men had found themselves co-opted into Herbert's army. Francis laughed, for it was conceivable that the rebel's could, in a single day, capture almost all of the King's 'cronies'.

One had to admire Warwick's patience, Francis thought. He smiled as he remembered the advice that Wenlock had given to the Earl at Reading. Ultimately in spite of his fiery temperament and his reputation for impetuousness, the Earl had waited fully two years before he'd finally played his hand, during which time, Edward, rather than ready himself for any rebellion, had only grown in complacency. Francis smiled again as in his minds eye he pictured the King at Nottingham. Edward waiting patiently for the Earl to join him, confident of his cousins support, when in fact it had been the Earl who had masterminded the rebellion against him! Francis couldn't help but laugh. Indeed on his return from France, the Earl had even had the audacity to convince the Pro Yorkist Londoners to loan him the not inconsiderable sum of £1000, with which he was to raise an army on the Kings behalf! It was said that the rank and file of the Earl's army still believed that they were marching north to relieve the King not to defeat him!

The sense of excitement that Francis had felt once the Conyer's had received word to raise the rebellion had not left Francis, who became keener still as he examined the royalist army that, arrayed beneath his position, had now been marshalled into some semblance of battle order. Today Francis was to have the honour of fighting in their armies van or front guard, alongside his father and brothers-in-law, and those other FitzHugh retainers who had accompanied them from Ravensworth. Lord FitzHugh had told his sons that he wanted them all to remain at his side throughout the battle. Slow as ever, the FitzHugh boys had taken this to be a compliment, an indication of their prowess. Francis, on the other hand, knew that the old man merely wanted to keep a watchful eye on his offspring. Francis, much to his chagrin, was to be accompanied once again by Miles Dobson. Warwick having appointed Dobson as Francis's 'Tutor in Arms', his orders being to 'safeguard' the 'Young Lord Lovel' upon the field. Remembering the incident en route to Reading, Francis wondered if Miles could be trusted to take his protective duties seriously!

The council of war convened between the rebel leaders, had, after lengthy debate, decided that the situation that their army found itself in was too advantageous to ignore. The confidence of the Conyers brothers had therefore prevailed over the caution of Fitzhugh, and the rebels had decided to engage Herbert's army without waiting for the arrival of the Earl's army. Lord FitzHugh had been greatly concerned. Francis was well aware of his father-in-law's dislike for both the newly created Earl of Pembroke, William Herbert, and his brother Sir Richard, but he knew that Lord Fitzhugh still had the greatest respect for both men's military abilities. William Herbert had earned his Earldom from a grateful King, in return for his suppression of Jasper Tudor's Lancastrian rebellion of the previous summer. Indeed during a particularly successful campaign, Herbert had even managed to take the great fortress of Harlech, which had been in the hands of the Lancastrians and had been a thorn in the King's side, since as long ago as the Battle of Towton in 1460. Unfortunately, Herbert's continued advancement had displeased the Earl of Warwick as, up until that point, many of Jasper Tudor's lands in Wales had been under Warwick's control. Thus, in contrast to the Conyers, Lord FitzHugh counselled prudence. Having scouted the field, Fitzhugh had said that he'd had an uneasy feeling about the position and formation of the Welsh army. He maintained that the situation in which they'd found it seemed 'to good to be true' and, as such, he'd 'sensed a trap,'

'For why else would one as capable as William Herbert place the bulk of his army in such an exposed position.' 'This without the support of archers,' he'd added, as with the use of cups cutlery and anything else to hand, he'd demonstrated the disposition of the Royalist army.

Fitzhughes scouts had discovered that the Earl of Devon, who was in command of the Royalist's archers, had for some reason become detached from the main body of the army. Worryingly, they had not managed to locate either Devon or his men. Francis's father-in-law, pointing out both the high ground to Herbert's rear and the scrubland on his left flank, had argued that the 'smallest body' of archers or mounted men at arms, secreted at either location until the opportune moment, could intercede and decisively change the course of the battle. Exasperated, Fitzhugh had argued that no-one of Herbert's ability,

175

without good reason, would be foolish enough to detach his archers from the main body of his army, thus leaving his men at arms both exposed and unprotected.

Sighing he'd added, 'It's almost as if he's trying to force us into a premature battle.'

Even Francis, with his limited knowledge of such things, could clearly see that for some unknown reason, Herbert had placed his men in a difficult position. The Welshmen, who were unsupported by archers had conceded the high ground and now found themselves in the valley bottom with a river at their backs!

Fitzhugh had asked that the Conyers brothers consider delaying the attack, at least until his scouts had located Devon's archers or better still until their own army was reinforced by that of Warwick and Clarence, whose arrival, he said, was imminent. The Brothers, who Lord FitzHugh said were, 'Too eager for glory' and who no doubt hoped to crush Herbert before the arrival of the Earl, had said that they should all accept their, 'Good fortune' in catching the royalists so unprepared. They argued that the strength of their position was too good to ignore and as such they must strike at once. Alarmingly the Conyers had maintained that the ambush which Fitzhugh feared, was extremely unlikely and in any event was 'unchivalrous' and would therefore incur the displeasure of God.

Ultimately Lord FitzHugh had been outvoted.

As he stood waiting patiently, Francis became increasingly more anxious and the frown upon his father-in law's brow became even more furrowed, as to the sound of a slow yet rhythmic drum beat, the Royalist Battle Captains marshalled their troops back across the small river. With a dry mouth Francis could only stand and stare, as Lord Fitzhugh blinking nervously, scanned the scrub and woodland to the enemies left, which, thick and tangled, failed to disclose any secrets that it might hold.

'They could at least have sent a small force of men at arms to clear the woods,' Lord Fitzhugh spoke out loud to no-one in particular. He went on, 'It'd only have delayed the advance by a couple of hours.'

Francis himself was undecided, he could see that even the few hours needed to check the brush, would allow the Welsh to deploy their troops into a much stronger position. However, although he was keen to fight, Francis could also see the advantages of firstly, finding out exactly what they were up against and secondly, awaiting the arrival of Warwick and his army. Francis turned to his 'tutor in arms', who was stood uncomfortably close to his young charge.

'Surely if we waited and were reinforced, our army would enjoy an unassailable superiority in numbers.'

Dobson laughed as he pointed out the topography of the land upon which they were arrayed.

'That may be so, but you tell me where you'd deploy such a force.'

Francis sighed as he considered his own naivety, he should have known better, for it was clear to him that their own army completely filled the confines of the hill on which they were assembled.

Smiling, as he no doubt congratulated himself, that for once he'd got the better of Francis in an argument, Dobson patted Francis on the back and in a loud voice added, 'Lovel, you've still much to learn, sometimes too many men will hinder an army, what use are troops who aren't in a position to engage the enemy'? Increasing Francis's growing sense disquiet, Dobson laughed ominously as he added, 'No doubt by the time my Lord of Warwick arrives, our forces will be sufficiently depleted to allow his men to engage the enemy.'

Shivering Francis became quite cold, yes up until that point he'd been nervous, wondering how he would perform in the coming action, but previously he'd not considered the fact that both he and his friends may never return from this battle. Clearly sensing Francis's discomfort, Dobson turned in his direction and, leaning towards him, hissed, 'You do know that if the King's men carry the day they'll spare only the commoners'. Francis wondered if it was the stench of Dobson's foul breath or the prospect of the executioner's reward for his treason, that made him shudder.

Surprisingly, Francis felt a great sense of relief when at last the order was given to advance. The dated armour that he wore had become increasingly heavy as the morning wore on and shifting his weight from one foot to the other, had long since failed to relieve the dull ache that Francis felt all along the length of his back and across his shoulders. Why couldn't the English fight on horseback like the French, he wondered, as he pictured in his minds eye, destriers bearing the weight of both rider and his arms, as the great war horses thundered down towards the opposing forces ranks. Francis smiled as he also recounted in his minds eye the French defeats at both Crecy and Agincourt. Cavalry slaughtered in a hail of English arrows. Yes, perhaps he'd rather bear the discomfort of his armour after all!

Francis tightened his grip on the battle-axe that he held in his favoured right hand, as together with his comrades, he began the slow march that would take them down the hill towards their enemies positions. He could see that the Herberts had, by then, been successful in pulling back the majority of their men across the ford and now appeared intent on defending the river crossing. Even now, Francis could see no archers and he nervously surveyed the brush to his right, expecting any minute to be subjected to a deadly hail of arrows. As the rebels closed upon the royalists, Francis lowered the visor of his dated bascinet helmet and fumbled with the gorget about his throat, keen to ensure that none of his bare flesh would be left exposed. Francis stumbled to keep up with the other members of his retinue and he jealously eyed his father and brothers-in-law, all of whom wore the latest in Italian designed armour. Francis tutted as he noticed that Lord Fitzhugh's eldest son, Henry, wore the visor of his Salade helmet up. Although this would afford Henry a better view of the fight and, as such, he would be able to react more quickly to any attacks upon his person, it would also leave his face exposed. And Francis had heard that arrows and crossbow bolts always had an uncanny habit of finding any gaps within a mans armour. In spite of the fact that he struggled to make out was going on through his thin eye slits, Francis still felt that he'd prefer this safer, yet slightly more restricted view of the proceedings.

Even if Francis's fear had got the better of him and had totally overwhelmed and incapacitated him, he could not have stopped. For the press of the men at his rear. Those who were, no doubt, keen to get to the front where the fighting was to take place, propelled him onwards and downwards towards their enemies. The grunts and curses of the men who bumped and barged and tumbled into each other as their speed increased down the steep slope, slowly began to give way to the battle cries of 'a Warwick' or 'for Clarence'. Francis even found himself bellowing out the name of his benefactor, making himself hoarse in the forlorn hope that his cries alone would somehow drive their enemies away from the river crossing, thus allowing him to return home to his wife, unscathed.

Thankfully the onslaught from an unseen host that Lord Fitzhugh had earlier gloomily predicted, failed to materialise and, consequently, only a few arrows ineffectually peppered the ranks of the rebel's vanguard. The northern army's archers, who the Conyers had cleverly placed on the wings of their army, this to give them a clean line of fire, replied in earnest and a hail of arrows darkened the sky as they whistled towards their intended target. These projectiles returned to earth within the massed ranks of the Welsh men at arms, who were stood both exposed and unprotected in the open ground that surrounded the river ford. For the first time in his life, Francis was able to witness first hand, the devastation that the longbow could wreak, this in spite of the recent advances in the design of plate armour. The enemies insults and war cries soon turned to screams of agony as the rebel's arrows, as Francis had earlier prophesied, seemed instinctively to find those few gaps that were evident within the men's armour. As he continued towards the Welshman, Francis saw many hundreds of them fall. Some made no sound at all as their life was ended in the swiftest of moments. Others clutched and grasped at that part of the shaft that protruded from their body, desperately tugging and pulling in vain at the arrows whose barbs merely tore deeper into their flesh and opened up those wounds that would, as a consequence, surely bleed more speedily and would therefore hasten their demise.

Horrified, Francis recalled in an instant the advice that he'd been given on many occasions, 'Snap the arrow shaft, it can be cut out later.' Those casualties amongst the Welsh, in their panic and terror, had clearly forgotten this good advice.

Heartened, Francis hoped that arrows would be sufficient to drive the Royalist army from the battlefield. He was again disappointed, for the Welshmen were obviously men of mettle and those who survived the hailstorm of arrows, stood their ground and waving their weapons, bade the rebels to come on to them. Francis was at once surprised by the ferocity of the hand to hand fighting, as the two forces at last clashed. He was unprepared for this kind of combat, used only to the luxury of time and space that he'd enjoyed when training and jousting in the lists. Despite being in the very front rank of the northern army, it was some moments before Francis could deliver his first blow as, pressed in on all sides, he had not sufficient room with which to raise his axe higher than his shoulder. Alarmed and angry, Francis was initially unable to return or parry the blows that were rained down upon him by the man in Herbert livery, who wielded his chained mace with skill. Francis jealously eyed their archers who had, by this time, discarded their bows and arrows, and free from the restrictions of plate armour, were able to skip in and out of the ranks of the more cumbersome men at arms. The archers ruthless as they knelt over stricken men, plunging their daggers through the eye slits of the knights' helmets or crushing and smashing their enemies' faces with the small rounded hammers that they carried especially for that purpose.

As another of his companions fell to the floor, thankfully, Francis felt the pressure on his right ease. Gripping his axe at both ends he raised it, just in time to parry the blow that had been aimed at his already battered helmet. Thankfully, as Francis had intended, the chain of the Welshman's weapon caught and tangled on the shaft of Francis's axe. Remembering his lessons well and summoning all the strength that he could muster, Francis pulled his axe shaft back in an effort to loosen the mace from the grip of his adversary. The Herbert man, no doubt fearful that he would lose his weapon, refused to let go and, consequently, Francis was able to pull him forwards and onto the floor. The unfortunate man immediately disappearing from view amongst the mass of sprawling bodies that had, until recently, been the orderly ranks of the opposing armies. Within minutes the faltering rebel vanguard, reinforced by their main 'battle', surged forward towards the crossing. Herbert's men, outnumbered and unsupported, immediately gave way. Francis felt no pity for the Welshmen, many of whom were crushed to death under the weight of the rebel advance or were dispatched by the archers who followed the men at arms. Francis surprised himself, for he had never before felt such hatred for his fellow man. Aggressive and angry, Francis ground his teeth until his head pounded, as he joyously allowed himself to be carried along towards the river crossing and their goal, as he went jabbing and striking with his axe at Herbert's men, who, forced backwards, were reluctantly giving ground to the Yorkshire men. Francis was deafened by the din of battle. Both men and horse alike, crying out in pain and anger. Although uninjured, Francis too screamed, whooping with delight as his adversaries fell at his feet. He had the smell of blood in his nostrils and rather than consider it repugnant, Francis delighted in it. He forgot to count how many of his opponents he managed to kill or maim, as he tirelessly and repeatedly brought down his axe, splitting and crushing both the helmets and the skulls of his enemy. In truth, despite all of the lessons that he'd had in the preceding years, Francis forgot all that he'd been taught, of how he should remain in the line to support and be supported by his companions. Heedless for his own safety, he pushed onwards deep into the royalist army, no longer feeling the weight of his armour or fearing his own mortality.

It was with a start that Francis was brought back to reality as he was yanked backwards by a strong hand that gripped his pauldron or shoulder armour. Above the noise of the battle he heard a voice that he instantly recognised as that of his 'tutor in arms', Miles Dobson.

'That's enough for now,' Miles laughed as he pulled Francis backwards and out of the fray. Their places in the fractured battle line were soon taken by others who were keen to get involved in fighting, that was now taking place on a number of small fronts.

'You'll tire yourself to death if you carry on like this,' Miles added, as he marched Francis down to the rivers side where the fighting was less intense. Both men greedily slaked their thirst in water that was now red with the blood of others. For the time being, at least, others could take their place in the battle line.

Francis, in an instant, felt exhausted and he went to his knees. His thoughts were for his relations.

'Do you know where my wife's father and brothers are'?

Sterner Miles answered him at once,

'No, as soon as we met the Welsh at the crossing everything became quite confused,' shaking his head he added ruefully, 'It was only with luck that I found you.'

Francis felt extremely proud as smiling Miles said, 'You were fighting like a lion, I saw you despatch at least three of the Welsh.'

Once he'd taken time to compose himself, Francis looked up and was alarmed to see that Herbert's men who'd somehow rallied, had retaken their side of the river bank and were themselves now advancing into the river.

Clearly Miles also saw this reversal, for he spoke with urgency, 'Come Francis, if we don't get back we'll find ourselves cut off.'

Realising that they may soon become trapped by the royalist advance, Francis was spurred into action. Rising to his feet, together with Miles he scampered up the riverbank, joining those others amongst the rebel army who were now in full retreat and were making, once again, for the summit of Blackbird Hill. Francis at last able to appreciate just how easily battles could be won or lost in the space of a few minutes. What had begun initially as a slight faltering in the rebel advance, this when their troops had reached the ford and had hesitated before advancing into the river, had soon become an orderly withdrawal. This withdrawal had in turn developed into a full scale retreat. Francis felt that unless something was done very quickly, it may easily become a rout.

Francis was amazed to see just how quickly panic spread throughout their army. Items of armour and weapons were discarded as, in their eagerness to escape, men fought with each other and clambered over the bodies of their fallen comrades. It was not until he reached the summit of Blackbird hill, that Francis at last turned to see what it was that they'd been running from! Thankfully, the Welsh had not pressed home their advantage and rather than pursue the fleeing rebels, they appeared to be regrouping around the ford.

With little difficulty Francis was able to find his father-in-law, for as Miles had earlier predicted, the rebel armies numbers had been significantly reduced by their unsuccessful attack. His first thoughts were for his brothers-in-law.

'Where are Richard and Henry'? he enquired with an urgency brought on by a sense of foreboding.

'Henry's dead and Richard's been carried to the baggage train, injured,' Lord Fitzhugh spoke without feeling, almost as if, Francis thought, his father-in law had managed to detach himself from the reality of the situation.

Before Francis had time to reply or show his distress at the receipt of such awful news, Miles whispered in Francis's ear.

'The time to grieve is later, if the men see your sadness they'll take it for weakness.' As if to explain the harshness of his words, he added, 'For presently there's quite enough disquiet in our ranks?'

Francis couldn't help but admire his father-in law, who in spite of his loss, for the sake of their men had managed to keep his composure.

Thankfully the royalist army, which had also been severely battered, had not been in a position to capitalise on their success and the panic that had spread like wildfire throughout the Rebel army soon passed. As a result the rebel battle captains were once again able to exercise control over their ranks and managed to regroup what was left of the northerners into some semblance of order.

Francis was once again overcome with fatigue and as such it was decided that he would remain with the rearguard for the remainder of the action. Francis was too tired to object to this and merely nodded his acknowledgement, as his father-in-law explained to the Conyer brothers that he could ill afford to lose any more of his kin. Prior to retiring to the rear, Francis was at least privy to the hastily convened council that had finally decided that perhaps a more prudent approach to the battle was now required. Consequently, the rebel leaders resolved to stand their ground and await reinforcement from the army which, commanded by Warwick and the Duke of Clarence, was said to be in the vicinity.

Once at the rear, Francis had no difficulty in finding his injured brother-in-law. He was relieved to find that Richard's injuries consisted only of a number of very minor flesh wounds. Francis wondered whether the cause of Richard Fitzhugh's pale and sickly pallor was the loss of blood, or shock and fear brought on by his first experience of warfare. Francis was disappointed to discover that it was the latter. Richard who, in contrast to his father, appeared to feel no shame. On seeing Francis, the boy gave full vent to his emotions and began sobbing loudly and uncontrollably. This much to the embarrassment of Francis and his tutor in arms.

'Control yourself,' Miles Dobson's firm command seemed to temporarily stem the flow of Richard's tears and the lad immediately began to recount his own part in the earlier engagement. Francis soon realised that, contrary to his physical appearance, Richard definitely wasn't soldier material. Francis was shocked to discover that Richard and those retainers under his personal command, had all stood by and watched as his brother Henry, fighting manfully and almost at the river crossing itself, had been overcome by the enemy. Henry had been felled and butchered by a number of Welsh men at arms whilst Richard, too scared to act, had watched on. Humiliatingly, many of Richard's injuries had been caused not during the fighting, but as he'd been dragged screaming hysterically from the field.

Try as he might Francis could neither sympathise with his brother-in-law, nor condone his actions, he was disgusted by Richard's cowardice. He turned and walked away from Richard, unable to bring himself to say anything, as both he and Miles left to take up their allotted positions within the rearguard. Neither turned to answer Richard as he shouted after them with increasing desperation.

'What would you have done?'

'We were outnumbered, where was our father when we needed him?'

'For pity's sake Francis, I tried my best.'

Both Francis and Miles stood silent for some time as, together with the remnants of the northern army, they grimly awaited Herbert's counter attack. The Welsh troops who had all formed up in battle order, appeared in good heart and Francis felt that Herbert's army was sure to press home its advantage, before the arrival of Warwick's men. To make matters worse, a large body of royalist archers, under the banner of Humphrey Stafford Earl of Devon, had joined the battlefield from the direction of Banbury. At this point Francis felt sure that an attack was imminent, as their two armies were now practically equal in strength and Devon's troops were fresh. Thankfully, Herbert prevaricated for too long. Perhaps the Welsh had been about to launch an attack, but now no-one would ever know, for any plans that the royalist army may have had were soon abandoned, as the Welshmen were forced to witness the reinforcement of their enemy. Cheers thundered out from the Yorkshire men's ranks as some 15,000 men, the majority of whom wore the Bear and Ragged staff livery of the Earl of Warwick, arrived upon the battlefield. These men were, for the most part, experienced professional soldiers from the Earl's garrison at Calais. Once incorporated into the northern army, it was Warwick's troops who led the second attack upon the river crossing.

Sadly, Francis was ordered to remain with the reserves in the rearguard, unable, for the time being, to rejoin the battle. Luckily, both he and Miles found an excellent vantage point from which to view the renewal of hostilities.

It was now the Bear and Ragged staff that was proudly held aloft by Warwick's men, as they slowly, yet determinedly, advanced down the hill towards the royalist army. The rebel's, suitably reinforced and refreshed, once again attempted to carry the day. The earth on which Francis stood seemed to reverberate to the sound of their battle cries and the clash of armour as the two armies renewed the engagement. Francis, no longer directly involved in the fighting, had the luxury of witnessing the whole of the battle from a position of relative safety. Initially, once again, all went well. The front ranks of the royalist army soon buckling under this fresh onslaught, but amazingly, despite the ferocity of Warwick's attack, it held firm. 'These Welsh are stubborn indeed,' Francis thought, as he saw how the gaps that appeared in the Royalist battle line, were soon filled with those men whom Herbert had wisely held in reserve. Luckily for the rebels, the Welsh had once again failed to deploy their archers to best effect. The Earl of Devon's archers remained towards the rear of the royalist army from where, without a clear line of sight, their arrows caused as much destruction within their own ranks as within that of their enemy. Francis, in spite of his hatred for the enemy, could not help but admire the exploits of two mounted Welsh knights, who repeatedly crossed the battle lines to rally and encourage their hard pressed troops, swinging both mace and pole axe. The men, who seemed oblivious to danger, were ideal targets for the rebel archers, but the arrows that were flighted in their direction glanced ineffectually off their armour, as the two men continued to hack down all those who stood in their way. 'These men are brave indeed,' Francis thought, as he once again became worried. The rebel armies advance was again losing its impetus, as it faltered and became 'bogged down' in the large meadow that surrounded the river crossing. Francis became increasingly nervous, as he witnessed large numbers of Warwick's men scrambling back up the slope, towards the summit of the hill on which he stood. The rear guard battle captains began to bark out orders to those troops who were held in reserve to, 'Hold their line and stand firm.' Unfortunately, the Captains words of encouragement did little to steady the men, as they were repeatedly forced to open up their lines, to allow through those men who had clearly had enough of the fight. Francis, looking to his right, saw that Miles too appeared nervous. Everyone seemed concerned and all anxiously eyed their companions, as they all no doubt thought, 'Who will be the first to run.'

Incredibly, once again thoughts of defeat soon turned to those of victory. This time it was Francis, who was delighted to see that the fortunes in battle could change so quickly. As all had seemed lost, a large body of mounted men at arms, all wearing the Duke of Clarence's livery, appeared on the high ground to the rear of the Welsh. These men immediately charged down the hill and into the rear of Herbert's army. Devons archers were no match for the heavily armoured knights and those who turned to fight were soon skittled aside, as the cavalry literally tore the Royalist army apart. Within seconds their army disintegrated as the King's troops began to flee the field in all directions. Devon and his archers were the first to make off, bolting to their right along the valley bottom. In doing so they left the main body of their army, that which was commanded by the Herbert brothers, exposed to the full impact of the mounted charge. The attack was, Francis thought, almost too successful, as a number of the enemy became sandwiched between the rebel forces and, having nowhere to run, were forced to continue the fight, long after all hope of a royalist victory was gone.

Francis, took no part nor pleasure in that which followed. He remained atop Blackbird Hill as, brave again, the rebel reserves charged down the hillside, clamouring to get involved in the slaughter. Others sought out their horses and, mounting them, rode further afield in their efforts to run down the fleeing Welsh.

It took less than an hour for those of the Royalist army, who had been left upon the battlefield, to become completely overwhelmed. In less than two, Francis found himself wandering over the battlefield, as both he and his companions sought out plunder from the dead. Francis did not baulk at this grim task, for his experience of the battle had shown him just how outdated and ineffectual his armour had really been. Now, having been battered repeatedly, much of it was beyond repair. Eventually, Francis was fortunate enough to find a worthy replacement and he was able to strip some fine, although a little blood stained, Italian armour from the lifeless body of youth who appeared to have been no older than himself. Francis smiled ruefully as he realised why the armour, in contrast to its owner, had come through the battle virtually unscathed. An arrow shaft protruded from the open visor of youths salade helmet. Francis reminded himself that when he next wore the armour, he would keep the helmets visor firmly shut!

The Neville armies victory at Edgecote field and the events that followed, were to have much more far reaching consequences than even Francis could have imagined. The victorious northern army, now under the command of Sir John Conyer's, his brother William having been killed in the second attack, retired northwards into Yorkshire, where it was disbanded. The Rebels, who'd all expected to fight a prolonged campaign, were apparently no longer needed by the Earl, who'd achieved all of his goals through just one engagement.

On hearing of the Herbert Brother's defeat and upon realising that reinforcements were not going to come to their aid, the small army that had remained with the King at Nottingham had soon melted away. Edward, together with both Richard and Hastings, had had no option but to ride south, hoping to meet up with any survivors from Edgecote. It was said that news of the defeat and of the execution of the Herbert's at Northampton on the day after the battle, had finally reached the King and his small band of followers, when they'd arrived at the village of Olney. Edward had had little time to brood on the downfall of his 'favourites', as he was soon joined there by Warwick's brother George. The Archbishop, who, in spite of the fact that he was meant to be a man of God, was said to have worn full armour, had 'politely requested' that the King, who was in no position to refuse, join his brother the Earl at Coventry. It was said that both Edward and Richard were now the 'guests' of Warwick and were to be brought north to Middleham. The King, a prisoner of the Earl, who once again intended to rule England in his name.

It was fair to say that Francis had felt extremely sorry for the brave Herbert brothers who, captured during the battle, had been executed without trial on the orders of the Earl. Francis wondered how the Earl was able to justify such a sentence, for both men had been beheaded for treason!

Francis's mood had however lightened somewhat when he'd finally discovered the real reason for the Herbert's defeat. For he'd been vanquished, not only by the northerners, but also by his own vanity! Francis's father-in-law need not, after all, have feared an ambush at the hands of Devon and his archers. For they hadn't even been on the battlefield at the start of the Battle, all having quit the field earlier, this because Devon had squabbled with William Herbert, over a woman! On the eve of the battle, the royalist commanders, unaware that the rebels were almost upon them, had decided to billet themselves at nearby Banbury. Devon, who'd arrived in the town first, had chosen for his accommodation, the best inn that the small town had to offer. By the time the Herbert's had arrived, he'd apparently already consumed much wine and had also managed to seduce the innkeepers daughter. Jealous, William Herbert had insisted that protocol dictated that as the senior commander, he was entitled to take his first choice of accommodation and, much to Devon's annoyance, Herbert chose 'his' inn. After a long argument, Devon had finally conceded defeat and had given up the accommodation to his senior officer. He had, however, left the town in a 'huff', taking his men with him. Unfortunately by the time Devon had finally returned to the field of battle it was too late. Unlike the Herbert Brother's who'd apparently fought bravely and whom Francis believed must have been the two Knights he'd seen at the river crossing, Francis felt that Devon had met a deserved end when, in August, he'd been caught by the 'common people' of Somerset and had been summarily executed. The King's other 'favourites' all met with similar fates. Lord Rivers and his brother having been captured on the banks of the river Severn, had been carried off to Coventry, where they were both executed on the orders of both Warwick and Clarence.

Francis, on his return to Yorkshire, had for the most part remained at Middleham, returning only briefly to Ravensworth to witness the internment of his brother-in-law Henry and to make what had been a vain attempt to persuade Anne to join him at Warwick's Castle.

During the Edgecote campaign, Francis had been disappointed that he'd been unable to meet up with his cousin Thomas, who'd remained throughout the proceedings, at Coventry with his master the Earl of Oxford. He hoped now that by remaining at Middleham, he would not miss out on another re acquaintance, for Richard was rumoured to be accompanying the King north, into an 'honourable captivity'. How, Francis wondered, would his friend feel about his, that is Francis' involvement in a rebellion that had all but deposed his brother?

Chapter 12
August 1969. Middleham Castle, North Yorkshire.

As with all of the other occupants of Middleham Castle, Francis eagerly awaited the return of the Earl of Warwick, who had been absent from his northern palace for quite sometime. The Earl was expected to arrive at Middleham that day and was said to be bringing with him the King, who'd been in the Earl's 'care' for the past month, this since being detained by the Earl's brother at Olney. Apparently, the Earl now felt that it was unsafe for the King to remain at Warwick Castle where he'd been taken after his capture, for Edward still had quite a following in both the midlands and the south of the country and consequently the Earl feared that the King's supporters may attempt to free him from his 'Honourable captivity.'

Francis had never before seen Middleham so busy! News of the Earl's imminent return had spread like wildfire and hundreds of people from all over the North were arriving on a daily basis, all eager no doubt, to see their King in captivity!

The Castle, which had remained relatively quiet since their armies triumphant return from Edgecote, once again burst into life. Francis too found himself newly invigorated, the lethargy that he'd begun to feel in the days following the homecoming, replaced with a sense of excitement and trepidation. For Francis truly believed that in the not too distant future all of his questions would finally be answered. Francis was also keen to be re acquainted with Richard. Unfortunately Francis had heard little of his friend, since Edward had recalled Richard from his tutelage at Middleham earlier that year. As Francis had earlier predicted, in stark contrast to his brother Clarence, Richard had stayed loyal to Edward throughout the 'troubles'. Now Francis worried, would Richard still consider him a friend? Especially when one considered that each had found themselves on opposing sides. At least Francis was able to comfort himself with the thought that he'd not actually borne arms against his friend. Francis smiled as he remembered his relief on hearing the news that both the King and Richard had surrendered. At the time he'd felt that all of his prayers had been answered, for he'd no longer had to face the prospect of being forced to chose between his loyalty to his family or to his friend.

What really worried Francis was that Richard may not appreciate why Francis had fought for the Rebels, especially when one considered that many of Richard's friends had lost their lives at Edgecote.

Frustratingly, Francis had failed to glean much information in respect of his friend's movements since the battle. It had been reported that Richard had been at his brother's side when Edward had been captured at Olney. Unfortunately, Francis had failed to discover what had happened to his friend since. Had Richard, as was the case with the other Yorkist nobles who'd accompanied the King, been sent away? Or had he, as the King's brother, been 'asked' to join Edward in captivity? Now, Francis prayed that his friend would be amongst the Earl's party, so at last he'd be able to let Richard know that their friendship meant a great deal to him.

That evening after supper Francis had chosen to avoid the crowds of Neville supporters who had all gathered together in the Great Hall to await the arrival of the Earl. Instead, Francis sought out the solitude afforded by the castles outermost battlements. And armed with a thick blanket and an extremely large flagon of wine, Francis was prepared for a very long wait! Francis who knew the Castle inside out had chosen his vantage point carefully, as from his position he would be able to observe any who approached the Castle from the east, this being the route from which he expected the Earl and his retinue to arrive. As he settled down Francis estimated that from the position of the sun which was still quite high in the sky, there was still some three hours of daylight left. Francis sighed, he hoped that the Earl would arrive sooner rather than later, for once darkness fell he'd be forced to rely upon any view afforded by the available artificial light and this was limited to the few torches that were positioned in and around the gatehouse and the inner keep. Francis smiled, at least his wait had been made easier by the balmy summers evening, Francis smiled again as he discarded his blanket, trusting that he wouldn't need it for quite some time, if that is he needed it at all!

Francis, who was the first to admit that he quite enjoyed keeping his own company, did wonder if at some point he'd be joined by Anne, as both she and her father had finally arrived at the Castle that very day. Since Edgecote Francis had been doubly disappointed by his wife, firstly by the fact that Anne, despite his repeated requests, had not joined him at Middleham sooner and secondly that when she had finally come it had been at the behest of her father and not her husband! Unfortunately, since her arrival, despite the excitement that he felt to be once again in her company, Francis had sulked. As a consequence it was now extremely unlikely that Anne, whom he'd left in the Great Hall with her many 'admirers', would join him, especially in such austere surroundings as these!

Sadly, after her elder brothers burial at Ravensworth, Anne had chosen to remain with her grieving parents. As if to add insult to injury, in Anne's stead Francis had been joined at Middleham by her brother Richard, who since Edgecote, annoyingly, seemed to follow Francis everywhere. Francis wondered if his brother-in-law hoped to bask in Francis's 'reflected glory'. For surprisingly, since his return Francis was now considered quite a celebrity, this as Miles Dobson had extolled 'his' pupil's prowess on the field of battle, to anyone who was willing to hear. Alternatively, Francis speculated that Richard was merely fearful that, if left alone, Francis would tell others of his abject cowardice at Edgecote.

Fortunately, after supper, for once Francis had been able to give his brother-in-law the slip. Francis chuckled as he pictured Richard in his minds eye, his brother-in-law anxiously searching for him amongst the crowds of people who'd all gathered at the Castle, to greet both the Earl and their King.

Frowning, Francis shivered and sighed as once again his thoughts turned to far more serious matters. Now, it appeared as if the Earl, in spite of the apparent success of his rebellion, had found himself in an extremely difficult position. Yes, on the face of it both the Earl and Clarence, had seemingly achieved the objectives that they'd set out in the manifestos that they'd circulated, in the weeks that had preceded the rising. Those being to, *'Save his grace (the King), from the deceivable and covetous rule and guiding of certain seditious persons'*, namely the Woodvilles and those others whom Edward had raised to the peerage. The Herbert Brothers were now dead, summarily executed in the immediate aftermath of Edgecote. Within days they had been joined by the unfortunate Earl of Devon, who captured by the 'common people' of Bridgewater had been 'Shortened by a head' and by both the Queens father and brother, who were hunted down and murdered. But now in spite of his success the Earl was in a quandary. Clarence had made it quite clear that he wanted the throne. Yet Edward was still alive and even the 'Kingmaker' baulked at killing a King! One could, Francis felt, be forgiven for assuming that Edward wouldn't have survived the rebellion, for he'd never in the past shied away from a fight and if he had stood and fought at Nottingham, he would in all probability have died on the field of battle. Instead, having allowed himself to be taken, Edward had apparently become a 'model prisoner', doing all that was asked of him. What then, Francis wondered, was the Earl to do? Surely in the current climate he couldn't possibly kill Edward. And if he did so who was to take Edward's place? Surely the Earl was far too clever to place the unpredictable Clarence on the throne and anyway, it was rumoured that he now had little time for his arrogant son-in-law. Francis smiled, in recent months having spent quite sometime in Clarence's company, the Earl had clearly experienced first hand a number of his son-in-law's less than agreeable qualities! Yes, if the Earl was to make Clarence King, he'd first have to ensure that he could control him and as such he still needed time to 'work' his legendary charm on his stubborn son-in-law. That said, potentially Clarence may in the future prove to be of use to the Earl, especially if his marriage to the Earl's daughter produced a male heir. Even Francis doubted that 'The Kingmaker' would be able to resist the prospect of his grandson one day becoming King of England.

But at present the Earl couldn't realistically consider killing Edward. The only recent precedent for such an act was the usurpation of the last Plantagenet King, Richard II by Henry of Bolingbroke, who became the first King of the house of Lancaster, Henry IV. Even after he'd been crowned King, fearful of incurring God's wrath, neither Henry nor any of his followers dared lay a hand on Richard, choosing instead to starve King Richard to death at Pontefract castle! Many said that the unhappy times experienced since by the House of Lancaster, were God's punishment for Richard's murder. Even now Bolingbroke's grandson, King Henry VI, spent much of his time in silent prayer, apparently seeking atonement for the sins of his forbear.

In an effort to discredit and disinherit the King, Clarence had circulated rumours of the King's illegitimacy, but it'd soon become apparent, that few amongst the common people believed this allegation. Surprisingly, in spite of the King's rumoured excesses and his unjustified patronage of the Queen's relations, Edward was still held in great regard by much of the population. The Earl of Warwick was an astute politician who could always accurately gauge public opinion and it was said that presently none, other than Clarence's own retainers, wished to see Clarence ascend to the throne. So, what was the Earl to do? In spite of the fact that he too was 'much loved by the common people,' he had failed to restore law and order. Moreover, he no longer had the support of the middle classes, the money in England, who were resentful that the Earl's pro French foreign policy had disrupted their trade with both Burgundy and the Low Countries.

Francis sighed, after only a month or so the Earl was already said to be exasperated with Government!

Francis sighed again, as always, at times of social unrest, the nobility of the land had not disappointed, rather then lend their support to the Earl's administration, they had seized upon this opportunity to settle old feuds. The Berkleys fought the Talbots, the Harringtons the

Stanleys and even Edward's friend and ally the Duke of Norfolk, rather than trying to secure Edward's release, was busying himself at Caister, wresting control of that Castle from the Paston family, its lawful owners.

The Earl had at least been able to summon a parliament that was due to be held at York in September. It seemed to Francis that, in moving the Government northwards, the Earl hoped to have more success and for the time being at least, he would be able to continue to rule England through Edward. Francis smiled, at least at York the Earl would be able to 'pack' parliament with his supporters, thereby ensuring that all of his recent policies and appointments would be ratified. Chuckling to himself, Francis wondered if the Earl would even go so far as to seek both money and approval for a war against the Burgundian's! Francis chuckled again, for war could always be relied upon to unite the population and such a conflict at this time would undoubtedly deflect any criticism away from the new regime. Francis smiled again, hopefully the answers to these questions would soon arrive at Middleham in the person of the Earl himself.

As the sun was slowly sinking behind the Pennines, Francis was at last joined by his wife. Anne slipped underneath the blanket that Francis had only recently placed loosely about himself, the sun's warmth lessening as the shadows had grown longer. Francis could never stay angry with Anne for long and he delighted in the warmth of her body next to his. He kissed her smooth skin and stroked her soft hair, enchanted once again by her beauty, framed as it was by the blood red sky. Momentarily Francis forgot his worries: of Richard; of the Civil War; of the complicated politics of that time; of the Earl's predicament. Almost immediately, both Francis and Anne, their bodies moulded together and their breathing in perfect harmony, fell into a contented sleep.

Francis awoke with a start as the Captain of the guard, mounted, clattered over the drawbridge below him and barked out an order for the gatekeeper to open the gates,

'For my Lord of Warwick is nearly upon us'.

With a smile, Francis lightly kissed his wife awake. His expression soon turned to a scowl, however, as he realised that they were not alone. Anne's brother Richard, obviously experiencing one of his few moments of lucidity, had found their hiding place and had even gone so far as to finish what was left of Francis's wine!

Biting his lip and choosing for the time being to ignore his brother-in-law, Francis shrugged his shoulders as he redirected his attention from his oafish relative towards those proceedings that were taking place below him. It was by now quite dark and, judging from the chill in the air, Francis guessed that it must be extremely late. Those amongst the Earl's retinue whom Francis was able to pick out in the flickering torch light, appeared both tired and dishevelled and all looked as if they'd been in the saddle for quite sometime. Rubbing his eyes Francis peered through the gloom in an effort to locate his friend Richard. He was disappointed and merely caught a brief glimpse of the Earl who seemed to be scowling at his immediate companion, from whose garb Francis guessed to be the Duke of Clarence. Once inside the courtyard the Earl hurriedly dismounted from his horse and handing his reigns to the stewards who'd rushed out to wait upon their Lord, he shouted impatiently, 'Take the horses and gather together those of substance in the Great chamber.' Almost as an afterthought, pointing towards a figure at the rear of the procession, whom Francis only barely recognised as being that of the King, The Earl shouted angrily, 'Take him to his chambers in the Princes Tower and make sure he's guarded at all times.' In spite of himself, Francis sighed as he noticed that Edward was cloaked in the plainest wool and leather, rude garments that pulled tightly about him hid his athletic frame.

To Francis's disgust both Richard and Anne seemed to delight in the King's captivity. Francis cast his mind back to those times when he'd previously seen Edward. To the Tournament, to Grafton Regis and the King's wedding day. Francis who couldn't believe how much changed Edward was, began to wonder how long the King, a proud man, could bare to be kept in such captivity.

The stewards were not the only ones to catch the sharpness of the Earl's tongue. As both Francis and the Fitzhughes rushed down from the battlements to get a closer look at the new arrivals, Sir John Conyers, half running and half falling down the external stone staircase of the keep, had come out to meet the Earl. Sir John, the victor at Edgecote, was no doubt expecting to be congratulated by the Earl, he was clearly disappointed and could hardly hide his dismay as the Earl glowered at him and hardly even noticing his presence brushed him aside, shouting,

'Where is my brother the Bishop? Bring him to my chambers for we have much to discuss.'

With that the Earl hurried into the keep and out of view.

Disappointed in the Earl, Francis sighed as he wondered if this was how Warwick always repaid his followers, especially those like Sir John Conyers, who had risked and given so much to the Earl's cause.

Sir John had risked his life and had lost his brother William at Edgecote, yet it now seemed as if he'd receive nothing for his loyalty!

Within the hour washed and changed, Francis joined those others of the northern nobility, who as directed to do so by the Earl, had all assembled in the great chamber that was situated within the Castle's inner keep. Francis, as a lesser member of that group, was seated towards the rear of the hall. His father-in-law, as the Lord of Ravensworth and the Earl's brother-in-law was seated amongst the front ranks and Francis noticed that the old man appeared to be in deep discussion with his immediate neighbours. Francis took time to look around the room, smiling as he noted how many members of the northern nobility were present, all of whom were showing their support for the Earl. Indeed it appeared to Francis as if there was a representative from each and every one of those great families who resided north of the River Trent.

The Earl who was seated at a lage table was clearly now in far better spirits than when he'd arrived, laughing and joking with both Clarence and with his two brothers, John Earl of Northumberland and George the Archbishop of York. Observing the King's brother Francis smiled, maybe Clarence had been right after all about his elder brothers illegitimacy! For there appeared to be no family resemblance between Edward and Clarence. Both men were fair but that was where any likeness ended, Clarence, like his younger brother Richard was both short and slender. Francis had never seen their father Richard Duke of York, who'd been killed by the Lancastrians at the battle of Wakefield almost a decade before, however many said that both Clarence and Richard resembled him closely. In contrast Edward was tall and of a much heavier build. Francis could easily see why so many had questioned Edward's legitimacy and continued to do so.

The Earl wasted no time in updating them with his immediate plans. As expected, all present were ordered to attend the York parliament that was to be convened on the 22nd of the following month. As Francis had earlier anticipated, they were instructed to ratify all of those appointments that the Earl had made in the King's name. But 'furthermore', and this was the greatest surprise for Francis, Parliament was 'to declare the King illegitimate' and, as next in line, Clarence was to ascend to the throne. All present were clearly both shocked and surprised by the Earl's unexpected revelation and an awkward silence descended over the Hall that had, up until that point, been alive with the chatter of many people. The silence, Francis felt, was testament to how the majority of those gathered felt about the prospect of Clarence becoming their King. Francis cringed as the Earl, who couldn't fail to notice the negativity that greeted his announcement, continued on regardless, adding that as his daughters husband, Clarence, who had spent little time in the north, was an 'adoptive Yorkshireman' on whom they could all rely upon to represent their interests at court.

'Rather than that southerner Edward who thinks little of us.' He added.

The Earl then went on to outline their response should the Yorkist nobles and the Woodvilles attempt to rescue the King. Francis heard little of what followed as he struggled to come to terms with what he'd heard. Surely it was pure folly for Warwick to depose Edward and support Clarence. Once again Francis studied Clarence, who sat to the right of Warwick and, smiling, seemed oblivious to the discord which he'd provoked. Clarence remained silent and this angered Francis, who felt that the least he could do was to thank them all for their efforts on his behalf. Francis's attention was only drawn back to the Earl when the Earl finally gave news of the whereabouts of Richard, whom was now scornfully referred to as 'Gloucester'. Upsettingly Richard was spoken of in terms of a foe rather than friend. Apparently, since the King's capture at Olney, Richard had been residing in the midlands with Lord Hastings. Not unsurprisingly, despite the Earl's efforts to bribe Hastings with the post of Chamberlain of South Wales, Hastings had remained loyal to the King. The Earl laughed as he pointed out that neither the Woodvilles nor the 'old Yorkist nobility' had been able to forget their differences and mobilise together on behalf of Edward. Apparently the Queen remained ensconced within the royal apartments at the tower of London. There, apparently grieving for the loss of her father and brother and swearing vengeance upon both Clarence and the Earl. Although according to the Earl, she was neither 'willing' nor 'able' to 'move against' them. Clapping his hands together the Earl smiled as he declared that at some point he would have to deal with the 'Woodville woman' as they could all 'expect no mercy from either her or what remained of her family' should their fortunes 'be reversed!'

Francis who initially had been disappointed that his friend had not accompanied the Earl northwards, on reflection, was delighted to discover that Richard, for the time being at least, was safe in the care of Lord Hastings, one who was after all, probably Edward's oldest and most loyal friend. Moreover, even though Francis hated the Hastings brothers with a passion, he had to admit that they enjoyed much support in the midlands and, as such, even the Earl and Clarence would be reticent to move against them at that time.

It was only as dawn was almost upon them, that Francis, exhausted, was at last finally able to retire to his bed. Unfortunately he enjoyed little sleep, his mind awash with all of the various possibilities. But ultimately Francis was forced to concede that at present both he and Richard remained on opposing sides. Francis's fortunes were tied to those of the Earl. Now it seemed that the Earl had committed himself to Clarence, whose objectives contrasted sharply with those of Richard who remained loyal to his brother the King. If the Earl should fall then so would the Fitzhughs and as a consequence Francis. Francis shuddered as he wondered if in this event his friendship with Richard, one who in truth could be quite ruthless, would save both he and Anne.

Thankfully, both Francis's humour and his confidence in the Earl were finally restored when some days later both he and his father-in-law were summoned to a very private meeting, held with the Earl and Sir John Conyers. Thankfully the meeting that was held within the Earl's inner chambers, was well away from prying eyes and was also conducted without Clarence's knowledge. Clarence having been 'encouraged' to enjoy what hunting the surrounding countryside had to offer. Francis sensed that the Earl was not at all sad to see his son-in-law gone for a few days and he felt that the Earl's high spirits were evidence of that fact. Francis still couldn't quite believe Clarence's arrogance, even now Clarence behaved as a King might and expected everyone else to treat him as such! Francis smiled, Clarence might have got away with this behavior at court in London, where people seemed to thrive on such nonsense, but here amongst the northern folk, Clarence's behaviour was in Francis's opinion both embarrassing and nonsensical. Especially when one compared him to his brother the real King, who in spite of his imprisonment continued to behave impeccably.

Thankfully the Earl seemed much rested and was wholly changed from the man who, only a few days earlier, had competed with Clarence in respect of bad humour and poor manners. Both the Earl and Sir John had obviously made up there differences and, upon the arrival of Francis and his father-in-law, were sharing a meal and a drink. On seeing the Fitzhughs, the Earl rose at once and clapped both Francis and his father-in-law on the back. Obviously noting the look of puzzlement on Francis's face, the Earl laughed,

'Don't worry Francis, I hear that Clarence wont be back for some days, my men have been told to take him almost to the head of Wensleydale, where the hunting they say is amongst the best in the country',

Francis guessed that it most probably wasn't, judging by the Earl and Conyer's raucous laughter.

The Earl began the meeting by humbly conceding, to those present, that he was no longer able to maintain the status quo and that at some point, he said, he would have to give up the King. This revelation was incredulous to Francis, who was equally dumfounded by the news that the Earl had never intended to go through with his plan to place Clarence on the throne. The Earl saying that he'd only made this anouncement to placate Clarence and ensure his continued support, 'For the time being at least.'

Francis was perplexed even further when the Earl, grinning, added 'Well I don't intend to make Clarence King at the moment anyway.'

The Earl went on, as both Francis and his father-in-law, nonplussed, remained silent. 'One can't expect the people to support a constitution with the Duke of Clarence at its head, not when there remains another who is far more suitable.'

Francis immediately wondered who the Earl was referring to. Was it Edward or Richard , or maybe even some other 'royal cousin'?

Warwick went on to say that even if he could control the country through Clarence, presently the policy that he favoured, that being an alliance with France against Burgundy, would only serve to alienate them both further and would be bound to invite further civil war.

'By which we could all be undone', the Earl conceded.

The Earl said that he had recently received word that two prominent Lancastrian's, Sir Humphrey Neville of Brancepeth and his brother Charles, both of whom had been in hiding since the battle of Hexham, had once again raised rebellion and were presently recruiting an army all along the Scottish border. The Earl grudgingly conceded that the Lancastrians had timed their rebellion well and with growing support from a disaffected country posed quite a serious threat to them all, especially when one considered the present disunity within the Yorkist ranks. The Earl added ruefully that none could expect any mercy from Henry's French Queen Margaret, who'd sworn revenge against both he and his followers.

The Earl sighed as he added, 'Without Royal assent we can't hope to raise the necessary troops to quell such a rebellion.' Shaking his head he added, 'And Edward has said that he'll only give his support if we release him forthwith.'

Francis wondered why the King, who'd previously both 'humbly' and 'meekly' complied with anything that was asked of him, had hardened his approach to them.

The Earl sighed again as he explained, 'He knows now that I'm no longer in a position to safely destroy him, nor is he able to deal with me in the present climate, thus we find that we are at a stalemate. Edward

197

knows that I cannot dispose of him but I am able to safely release him, for the time being at least, because he needs me to help him to quell the present rebellion.'

The Earl cautioned them, that even though they may receive the King's pardon they could never expect Edward's forgiveness, 'For he will never forget disloyalty on this scale and mark my words, maybe not this year or the next, but at some point in the future, he will come after us one by one and given the opportunity will utterly destroy our Houses.'

Forgetting himself and hoping that the rift between the Earl and Richard could somehow be healed, Francis interjected,

'But who then must we support if it's neither the King nor Clarence?'

The Earl smiled once again as he retorted,

'We, my friends will do as we have done in the past, we will support whosoever we feel can offer us the greatest advancement.'

It was at this point that the Earl finally disclosed his plan to those present

'I will explain to Clarence on his return, that it is with great regret and in response to the rising in the north, that we cannot hope at this time to continue with our plans to place him on the throne,'

Francis's mind swirled with all of the various possibilities as the Earl continued, 'Once the rebellion in the north has been dealt with, the King who has no time for his northern subjects will no doubt return to London. We will then have time to plan our next move before he can gather his resources for a strike against us. I still feel that an insurgence involving the common people is the answer. This time, hopefully, the King will be more proactive in his response, when he leaves London with what troops he can muster, both Clarence and I will remain behind, ostensibly to continue to gather further troops on his behalf. We will then follow the King northwards and catch him betwixt our two forces. This time gentleman we will force him to stand and fight and this time he will be killed.'

'And will Clarence then be King', Sir John replied with an air of resignation, that did little to disguise the disappointment which he obviously felt at such a prospect.

The Earl was measured in his reply,

'As in the past gentleman, we will support whosoever can advance our cause,'

Francis spoke at once,

'But Clarence is your son-in-law',

Warwick replied with a smile on his face,

'I still have one unmarried daughter Francis, Ann, do you not remember her? She can marry Richard of Gloucester or perhaps even King Henry's son, Edward of Lancaster.' The Earl smiled again before he added, 'Should I determine that it is politic for her to do so.' Becoming serious again the Earl said, 'This is where I need your assistance Francis, I've approached Richard of Gloucester on a number of occasions and have asked him to join us. At first I was optimistic that he would join me, especially when one considers all that he has lost at the expense of both Clarence and the Queens family.' The Earl added ruefully with a smile, 'After all, wasn't he one of my finest pupils.' Before Francis had time to ask how he could possibly help, sighing the Earl added, 'But Gloucesters headstrong and he adores his brother the King, almost as much as he dislikes Clarence whom he distrusts.'

Francis recalled the many discussions that both he and Richard had shared in relation to Clarence. Richard often complaining that Clarence's jealousy had ensured that those few titles that were bestowed upon him, were soon removed and given instead to Clarence, once he'd complained to the King.

Lord Fitzhugh voiced that which they were all thinking.

'And what of Gloucester's motto,'

The Earl scoffed,

'Loyalty in me Lieth,' Rubbing his chin the Earl added, 'At least Richard's been true to his word, in spite of everything he's remained faithful to Edward.' The Earl sighed as he said, 'I fear that Richard's lost to me, unless Francis,'

Warwick smiled again,

'You're able to convince Richard that his future lies with me and his northern kinsman. I want you to go to him and tell him of my proposals. If convinced of Edward's illegitimacy he will be forced to chose between Clarence as King or himself. Tell Richard that if he agrees to marry my daughter I'll make him the King of England.' Becoming sterner the Earl frowned as he added, 'But make it clear to him, that if he doesn't join me I will place either Clarence or Edward of Lancaster on the throne and then he can expect no mercy.'

It was at this point that Francis finally understood what he must do. Yes, he had many reasons to support each of those men who were present, be they his relatives, his tutor or his benefactor. But Francis now understood that these men were no different to anyone else and they were only interested in furthering their own interests. As such, there was nothing that these men could give Francis that could ever compete with the friendship that both he and Richard enjoyed, this relationship developing in their time together at Middleham. Francis smiled. When the time was right he was determined to throw in his lot with Richard, that's if his friend would have him. 'Loyalty would bind' Francis to his friend. Yes, for the time being at least Francis would do as the Earl had asked. Yes he would happily leave Middleham to attend upon Richard when called upon to do so. But if Richard chose to reject the Earl's offer, Francis would remain at his friend's side. At this point Francis's thoughts turned to his wife and he earnestly hoped that this was one journey that she would make with him.

Lord Fitzhugh gently shook Francis's shoulder and chided him once again for his 'day dreaming',

The old man smiled, 'Come Francis we're to return to Ravensworth. For the time being you can forget about politics and can concentrate on producing my first grandson!'

On the following day, together with the Fitzhughs, Francis made the short journey north to the their castle at Ravensworth, there to await the Earl's orders. When it was safe to do so, Francis was to travel south to visit Richard to tell him of the Earl's proposal.

Francis had no doubts that the Earl was an extremely clever man, but he felt that the Earl was much too sure of himself and presently was treading quite a fine line. And in Francis's opinion there was much that could go wrong for the Earl. Surprisingly, for the first time in months, Francis slept well and dreamt little. When he attempted to rationalise this, he decided that he must now be satisfied with that course which he had decided to take in the future, as friend and supporter to Richard. But he did still have his 'dark moments', especially when he considered his family, both new and old, and wondered who amongst them would chose to follow him!

Chapter 13
Winter 1469. Ravensworth. North Yorkshire.

The excitement that Francis had felt, since his return from Middleham in August at the prospect of joining his friend, Richard, had slowly dissipated. This with both each passing day and with the increasing animosity that was developing between the Earl and Richard. Acrimony due mainly to the formers aggrandizement under the patronage of his Brother the King, this advancement made invariably at the expense of the Earl. Any form of alliance between the young Duke and his former mentor now appeared fanciful at the very least and Francis felt, with increasing consternation, that it would now be some time before he would see his friend again.

One had to admit that since his release the King had been extremely clever in his manipulation of his subjects and Edward's astuteness contrasted sharply with the Earl's stagnation and increasing isolation in the North. The King was it was said now fully reconciled with Clarence and both brothers had even taken part in a public ceremony of reconciliation that had been held at Westminster during the Christmas festivities. Admittedly the Earl had also been present but both he and his allies had been told in no uncertain terms that their attendance was obligatory and immediately after the ceremony the Earl, who had nothing to celebrate, had retired Northwards.

Francis sighed, it was fair to say that things had not gone at all well for the Earl since his resounding victories of the previous Summer and his subsequent imprisonment of the King. From being in a position from where he could dictate policy and almost rule England as a King might, his role had diminished to that of a helpless onlooker, this as events shaped themselves independently of his influence.

In contrast to the Earl, Richard was now beginning to reap the benefits of his loyalty to his brother Edward. Whereas in the past he'd had cause to bemoan his treatment at the hands of the King, now rewards had been heaped on the 'poor younger brother', who despite his young age had even been created Constable of England, ironically this appointment being made at the expense of the Earl himself! It was Richard and not the Earl, who now filled the vacuum that had been created in Wales by the Earl's destruction of the Herberts. Since his release from Middleham Edward had made Richard his principal representative in Wales, giving his younger brother a number of positions which the Earl, keen to advance his own families influence in that region, had coveted for himself. Francis sighed again, any alliance between his friend and his patron now seemed extremely unlikely. Richard who had received much from the King in return for his loyalty, was now, without doubt, the King's favorite. Whereas in relation to the Earl, it seemed now that Edward was merely biding his time until he was in a position to strike at his former mentor and deal with the 'King maker,' 'once and for all.'

In spite of all of this Francis, desperate to be reacquainted with his friend, had implored the Earl, through his father in law, to even now allow him to visit Richard, as they had earlier planned. Unfortunately for Francis, the Earl was far to clever to continue to place any reliance upon any potential alliance with Richard. Consequently Francis's deputation's had received the same resolute reply each and every time that his father in law had returned to Ravensworth from Middleham,

'Stay where you are until the time is right, but fear not Francis, I will find you much to do in the coming months.'

Francis felt that this reply could have meant anything, especially when one considered the Earl's recent policies!

That Autumn the deterioration in the Earl's position had raised much consternation within the ranks of his followers. Casting his mind back Francis felt that things had begun to go wrong for the Earl when the Lancastrians had rebelled in the North. Ironically the rebellion had been organised by the Earl's Westmoreland relatives, who in contrast to the Earl had remained loyal to King Henry throughout the Civil Wars. It had all ended with the Earl being publicly disgraced, as the Offices that he'd recently bestowed upon himself, were stripped from him and given to the seventeen year old Richard, one who had until recently been in the Earl's tutelage! Shaking his head Francis smiled wryly, as he recalled how at the time, he'd even considered that the rebellion may even have been instigated by the Earl himself. The Earl conspiring with his Westmoreland relatives to create a diversion in the North, which requiring a military response, would have united the Country under his regime! Francis smiled again, this notion had been well and truly dashed as he had witnessed, first, how the Earl had been forced to release the King and secondly how, at the head of a Royalist army, the Earl had ruthlessly crushed the rising, showing no mercy towards his cousins, whom he'd brought before the King at York and had summarily executed.

Humiliatingly to be able to deal with the rebellion the Earl had had to rely on Edward to summon the necessary troops, this as the Earl's summonses had been ignored by many amongst the nobility and the gentry. In return for the King's help, the Earl had reluctantly released Edward from his captivity at Middleham. Apparently it had been quite a 'sight to behold' as the King was joined at York by those amongst the aristocracy who'd remained loyal to him. From York Edward had made a 'triumphal' progress Southwards to London, almost as if it had been he who had been the victor at Edgecote! Whilst the King received accolades wherever he went, the Earl was forced to remain in the North to deal with those Lancastrian rebels who remained at large.

Francis sighed, even now he still couldn't believe how fickle people were. After Edgecote all of those families north of the Trent and many from the Midlands and South had enthusiastically swarmed to the Earl's banner, now these people absented themselves from the Earl's court and whispered their dissent, all no doubt wondering if their trust in the Earl's judgment had been misplaced. Indeed it seemed to Francis that now, the Earl's future, despite what he'd said to both Francis and his father in Law at Middleham, once again rested squarely with that of the duplicitous Clarence. And worryingly still, at that point in time Clarence was once again one of the Brother's of York and was enjoying, not the Earl's, but the King's hospitality at his Palace of Westminster. Nor could the Earl now count upon any of the other Yorkist Lords to support him. Upon Edward's release they'd all enthusiastically flocked to his side. Indeed now, in spite of the Earl's ruthless suppression of the Lancastrian rebellion, it was muted in many circles, that the Earl may even be forced to throw in his lot with the Lancastrians. Francis smiled, even he doubted that the Earl and Margaret of Anjou would ever be able to forget their differences, for they were both said to hate each other with a vengeance. Francis smiled again, albeit, in these uncertain times one could no longer be quite sure of anything! Throughout that winter rumours had abounded that the French King Louis, still keen on an Anglo-French alliance against the Burgundians, had proposed a thirty year truce with the Lancastrians. This alliance having been negotiated with Queen Margaret who at that time was at the French court with her son Edward of Lancaster. Louis was no fool and the French King obviously realised that the only hope for a Lancastrian restoration and as a consequence of this England's support in a war against the Burgundian's, was to take advantage of the deteriorating relationship between the King and the Earl, who in spite of everything was still one of England's foremost magnates. Francis knew that Louis had already approached the Earl, sending agents to Middleham who had apparently proposed that the Earl, with French aid could assist in a Lancastrian restoration. Shaking his head Francis tutted, even when one considered the precariousness of the Earl's position, he still doubted that any agreement between the Earl and the Lancastrians was possible. It was common knowledge that the Earl hated Margaret, whom he blamed for the death of his own father at Wakefield and Margaret blamed the Earl above all others for her present predicament. Indeed it was common knowledge that Henry's French Queen had taken each and every opportunity to besmirch the Earl to any who would listen, bewailing that he had;

'Pierced her heart with wounds that could never be healed; they would bleed till the day of judgment, when she would appeal to the justice of God for vengeance against him. His pride and insolence had first broken the peace of England and stirred up those fatal Wars that had desolated the realm. Through him, she and her son had been attainted, proscribed and driven out to beg their bread in foreign lands, and not only had he injured her as a Queen, but he had dared to defame her reputation as a woman by divers false and malicious slanders, as if she had been false to her royal lord the King- which things she could never forgive'.

So Francis once again nonplused, could only sit and wait and guess at that which the future held for him and his kin. And sadly, here at Ravensworth he now had kin aplenty. No his wife Anne was not with child as he had hoped, Francis smiled, unless of course one believed in immaculate conception! No, instead he'd recently been joined by his own sisters, Joan and Frideswide, who upon the death of their grandmother, had made the trip Northward from Oxford shire to Ravensworth. Francis sighed, he had been saddened by his grandmothers death, for as a child he'd loved her with all his heart, but he hadn't been able to cry, for it now seemed to him as if his grandmother Alice had belonged to another lifetime, a lifetime that was long gone. Unfortunately for Francis, both of his Sisters had now entered this lifetime! And as the only surviving Lovel patriarch, Francis was duty bound to find husbands for them from amongst the northern gentry. Francis sighed again, for he felt that this was going to be quite an onerous task, especially when one considered the plainness of his siblings features, this exacerbated by both girls propensity to Gossip. Moreover both of Francis's sisters had seemingly inherited the Lovel's Lancastrian sympathies and as such they hated the Yorkist establishment, which they blamed for their fathers death. Consequently their first meeting with the Fitzhughs, rather than being the joyous occasion that perhaps naively Francis had hoped for, had been quite a bad tempered affair. As a result, in public the Lovel sisters treated their new family with a distant disdain, in private, however, they wore Francis down with their vehement attacks on anything remotely Yorkist, Neville or Fitzhugh!

Thankfully, here at Ravensworth Francis was surrounded by the beautiful Yorkshire dales. Muddled by his misgivings and agitated by his responsibilities, Francis took each and every opportunity to escape the confines of Ravensworth castle. And now after a number of weeks of such behavior, he no longer even needed to create an excuse to leave. Each morning immediately after breakfast, Francis would have his horse liveried. He would then ride up the valley side to this his favorite spot. The churchyard where he'd been married in much happier times. From here Francis would sit silently and enjoy his quiet contemplation's. Yet he could still observe those comings and goings from within the Castle below.

Upon returning to Ravensworth Francis had hoped that the respite in hostilities would enable him to spend some quality time with his young wife. To get to know Anne in ways that their enforced separation had in the past prevented. Yet now Francis saw little of Anne, who spent much of her time with her parents and surviving Brother, still, after all this time, grieving the loss of her eldest Brother. Recently Francis, who was usually quite unobtrusive and mild mannered, had exploded in rage at Anne's continued coldness towards him. Francis screaming that it was as if he, Francis, had plunged the dagger into her brothers chest. Unfortunately this outburst had achieved nothing, save that is to shatter the fragile peace once and for all. As Francis once again sat in his churchyard, he trembled both with the cold of the chilly December air and with the fear and anger that he felt as he recalled the look on Anne's face, as she too had returned his screams. His wife bemoaning the fact that it was her brother Henry who lay dead and not he her 'pathetic Husband.' That night Anne had left his bed and had not returned. Francis, as always, had been the one to aplogise, but try as he might he could not calm Anne, nor could he persuade her to return to his bed. Francis shivered again as he wondered if his wife had ever loved him and if so, whether she would ever do so again.

Francis unused to such extreme emotion felt tears well up in his eyes, he gritted his teeth and tightened the cloak around his body in a futile attempt to resist the increasing chill that accompanied the end of yet another day and with it his unavoidable return to the Castle. Francis sobbed, what had he done to deserve this life? Had he not done all that had been asked of him? As a husband, a brother and a liegeman. Had he not been loyal to his friends? Once again he screamed out, as he considered those who were cowards, liars and cheats. Those who always seemed to prosper, whilst good men suffered. At once Francis worried, for his screams reverberated and echoed throughout the darkening valley, to such an extent that Francis felt that they must have been heard by the Castle's occupants below, whose comings and goings Francis could still see in the growing gloom.

As it turned out Francis need not have worried. As always he was hardly noticed at all, as he rode back into the Castle's small courtyard and proceeded to unsaddle and wash down his horse. Francis grimaced, nowadays it was easier to see to his own horse, than it was to ask those few sullen servants, who seemed to share everyone else's disrespect for him. Moreover what few servants there were busy elsewhere, in the kitchens preparing the supper that Francis would once again take in isolation. Francis hugged his horse, as he cleaned from it the sweat and grime that had accumulated during that days riding. Still chilled, Francis was at least able to take some solace from the horses warmth. Surprisingly he was able to smile, as he cheered himself with the prospect of an evening alone, in front of a roaring fire, with food and wine aplenty. He smiled again, as he resolved that for once he would please himself and would try not to concern himself with the troubles of others.

Francis's evening did begin as he'd hoped, with a fine meal of roasted venison washed down with copious amounts of fine red wine. Unfortunately his solitude was rudely interrupted as his Sisters, as always unannounced and uninvited, burst into his apartments. Merry from drink, Francis politely turned to greet them, but before he could even utter one word of welcome, Joan let loose with an outburst that was both unexpected and in Francis's opinion unwarranted. Joan's diatribe was as ugly as her features and it took Francis some moments to fully understand what his sister was saying, her words coming thick and fast, in a southern dialect to which Francis was unused. Nor did it help that Francis's had finished off two bottles of un watered claret prior to the Sisters arrival! It was only after some moments that Francis slowly began to realise what it was that Joan was saying.

'We've both been here in this God forsaken place for almost six weeks now and we've yet to receive any meaningful introductions,' Joan whined.

'And you as the head of our family you're duty bound to find us suitable matches,' Friswelde completed her sisters sentence, a common habit that did little to endear the Lovel ladies to others.

Sighing Francis sank deeper into the armchair in which he was sat. He gazed into the fire and for the briefest of moments his Sisters voices paled into the background as Francis lost himself. After some minutes, save for the crackle of the fire, all fell silent as both Joan and Friswelde having aired their complaints, seemed to have run out of things to say.

Francis, calm, was measured in his reply, he smiled inwardly for this worm had finally turned.

'Do you both think that I have not tried my utmost to find you husbands since you joined me here in Yorkshire.' Laughing he went on, 'As children we loved each other, but as Adults? Pah, I would happily pay my last penny to see you both off my hands and in the house of another. But please help me. Tell me who would have you. I'm sorry to say that neither of you are as I recall from our childhood years. You're both as ugly in nature as you are in looks and with no lands to speak of and a minimal dowry, how do you expect me to find suitable husbands for you both?' Sighing Francis turned away from his sisters and gazing once again into the fire, he added, 'And God knows I have tried, I've used up every last favour due to me to arrange those few introductions that you've had.' Raising his voice, Francis turned on his Sisters who both stood silent, dumbstruck by their Brothers outburst, 'But have you helped? Even my wife has offered to help you make the best of yourselves, but you've scorned her help and turned her away. If presented with that which I now see before me, is it no surprise that the men who are introduced to you, determine that they will search for a wife elsewhere.'

Francis continued, whilst his sisters remained mute.

'Northern folk are amongst the most welcoming people in England, but even they will not suffer bad manners for long. I know you hate the Nevilles and anything that is remotely Yorkist. But these are the politics of our time, if you hadn't already noticed our parents are dead. King Henry is a captive and both his son and queen wander Europe, in the hope that they may find new supporters to replace those who have died serving them. Had it not been for both the Earl of Warwick's patronage and my friendship with the King's brother Richard, I'd have long since had my lands and titles attainted. Sisters I have chosen my allies well and I'm afraid that you must do the same. These are turbulent times and the key to success at each and every level in society is to find succor from those who at that time are in the ascendancy.'

Francis who'd already resolved to join his friend Richard at the earliest opportunity, lied for the sake of his Sisters, whose lives would become unbearable if they continued upon the course on which they were embarked.

Joan began to say something but stopped as she no doubt felt better of it and considered that arguing with this new masterful version of Francis was futile.

'Go now,'

Francis waved towards the door,

'And think hard of what I have said, otherwise I will have no option but to send you both back to Oxfordshire to remain as spinsters or even become Nuns.'

To Francis's amazement both Sisters bowed low in deference and bid their brother a 'pleasant and enjoyable evening' before retiring to their own chambers.

Francis sat for a while in silence, as he considered what had just happened. Yes, it was good to be reasonable and good natured. But at certain times one had to speak out. Francis felt guilty for his outburst, but his sisters had shamed him with their behavior and understandably he'd finally snapped. Surprisingly through this outburst, it appeared at last, that he'd gained their respect. Stiffened, Francis resolved to take this opportunity to settle his affairs once and for all. Strengthened further by a stiff measure of brandy, Francis marched to the solar where he knew that he'd find both his wife and her family.

Francis blinked as he entered the brightly lit room. All was quiet as Francis's presence was acknowledged by the rooms occupants, who judging by their expressions had not expected to see him at that time of night.

Surprised Anne immediately rose from the lap of her father on which she'd been sat. Lord Fitzhugh as was custom also rose to acknowledge his son in laws presence. Both Lady Fitzhugh and Anne's brother Richard, merely stared at Francis in puzzlement, which soon turned to alarm as Francis's words boomed and reverberated throughout the room.

'I've come for my wife,'

Francis's demand was stern, forthright and to the point.

As he spoke Francis looked towards Anne, who clearly shocked had turned to her father, expecting no doubt that he would deal with this outrage.

Francis smiled, his wife's confidence faltered as seconds melded into minutes and Lord Fitzhugh remained silent.

Francis had gambled well, even Lord Fitzhugh whose love for his daughter was legendary, knew better than to come between a man of noble birth and his wife.

Francis spoke again.

'Anne, you may not love me, you may not even like me, but you will no longer humiliate me'.

Francis then took a firm hold of his wife and led her silent from the room, turning only once to bid the remaining occupants 'a good evening'.

That night Francis slept well, this in spite of the fact that Anne's body lay stiff and cold next to his. If he could not expect Love from her, then the least he would demand was loyalty.

Over the following days Anne's attitude did not mellow, however she like Francis had been well versed in etiquette and knew that which was required of her. She grudgingly went about the onerous task of making Francis's sisters more appealing to the outside world in clothing, attitude and looks. She submitted to Francis's demands both inside and outside of the bed chamber with what Francis could only describe, as an air of resigned melancholy. Hardened, Francis was happier than he'd been for quite some time, this as he found that the life of a despot was far easier than that of a philanthropist.

Chapter 14
October 1470 Ravensworth.

Sat at this his favourite spot once again, it seemed to Francis that little had changed since he'd last been here. The Churchyard, the valley, the Castle and the village of Ravensworth, all seemingly unaltered by recent events, merely continued to go about their daily routines. The fields had been harvested and the countryside and its people had readied themselves for yet another winter, just as they had done for centuries past. Francis smiled, there was nothing in the Yorkshire landscape to indicate that which had happened in the past year. Invasion, exile, rebellion, England had experienced them all and all in the space of just a few months! And even now after everything that had happened, the question of the governance of the realm was still not truly decided. Indeed, Francis himself had only recently returned from exile, having spent the last few months at the Scottish court. This after both he and his father in law, as planned, had staged the sham rebellion, which had been designed to draw King Edward northwards and thereby enable the Earl of Warwick's invasion of England via the South Coast. And Francis had not been alone in being exiled! Initially both the Earl and Clarence had been forced to seek refuge at the French court, this after their spring rebellion had been crushed by Edward. Francis smiled again, but now it was Edward's turn to taste exile, for when the Earl and Clarence had returned to England with an army, it was the Edward, who this time had been abandoned by his men, save that is for Richard and the Hastings brothers. Francis smiled wryly, and Edward had very nearly been caught, had it not been for a dash across the Wash to the Port of Kings Lynn, where he'd apparently secured a passage to Burgundy, for the price of the cloak from his back!

Francis who as always tried to rationalise things, found it extremely difficult to see any logic in the recent events. Yes, he could understand why, in that Spring, the Earl had turned once again to Clarence. By early 1470, it had been clear that Richard would never abandon Edward and join the Earl. Moreover Francis could also see, that at that point the likelihood of the Earl having supported any form of Lancastrian restoration, was still extremely unlikely, especially when one considered that the feeble minded King Henry was still in captivity and his French Queen was herself a penniless exile in France. Thus the Earl, the 'Kingmaker' whose relationship with King Edward had at that point seemed irreconcilable, had had no alternative other than revive his plans to place the Duke of Clarence on the throne and thus attempt to rule the Kingdom through his son in law. Apparently in preparation for his accession, Clarence had even made efforts to temper his character and as a result was said to have earnt the 'love of the common people.' Francis who'd had the misfortune to meet Clarence on a number of occasions doubted this and put the Duke's newly found popularity down to the Earl's legendary propaganda! Anyway the plan had been simple. Clarence's retainers in Lincolnshire, under one of his retainers Sir Robert Welles, were to instigate a rebellion, ostensibly on behalf of the common people to resolve some local grievances. Edward who'd lost the Edgecote campaign because he'd prevaricated for far too long and had also relied upon others to deal with that insurrection, was expected to march Northwards, to personally deal with the rising. The Earl and Clarence would follow him, seemingly recruiting troops on behalf of Edward en route, but in reality intending to catch and crush the King, betwixt there own forces and that of the Lincolnshire rebels and those who were to join them from Yorkshire. In an effort to delay the King and allow the rebels to muster, Clarence had visited Edward in London. Despite their previous treachery, both he and Earl had managed to convince the King to issue them with commissions of array, these enabling them to recruit the additional troops on Edward's behalf. Francis chuckled, an army which they ultimately hoped to use against the King! All had seemed to be going well. The Welles family were much loved in Lincolnshire and when Clarence's spies spread rumours throughout the East of England, that the King, who was in no mood for mercy, was coming North 'to personally mete out his punishment' for their rebellion, many more men had joined the uprising. Hoping to cut off the rebels before they could enter the Midlands, Edward had arranged for own his army to muster astride the great north road at Grantham. The Earl and Clarence, on the other hand, had instructed all three of their armies to converge upon Leicester. Unfortunately this was where things had started to go wrong for the Rebels. Unbeknown to the Earl, from the outset Edward had suspected treachery and had ordered the arrest of Lord Welles, the father of Sir Robert. Fortunately under, interrogation Lord Welles had not revealed the true nature of the rebellion, merely pointing out that it arose out of a feud between one of Edward's retainers, Sir Thomas Burgh of Gainsborough, the master of his horse and the Welles family. Burgh, who, as a result of his relationship with the King, was said to have considered himself above the Law, having sacked the Welles' manor house after he'd accused the Welles of stealing his horses! For once quite astute, Edward had brought the old man north with him and at Grantham he'd forced him to write a letter to his son, telling Sir Robert that if his army failed to disperse, he (Lord Welles) would be executed without trial! Ironically the Lincolnshire rebels were almost at Leicester, when Sir Robert, upon receiving the letter, and in a desperate attempt to save his father, turned eastwards towards Grantham. Sir Robert had hoped that his army was large enough to defeat that of the King, without him having to wait at Leicester for the assistance of both the Earl and Clarence. Nor could Welles have expected any assistance from the north, for the Yorkshiremen under Sir John Conyers had been too late in mustering and as a result had failed to make the rendezvous as planned. As it was, both Lord Welles and his friend Sir Thomas Dymock, who'd been taken with him, were both summarily executed in front of the two armies of Edward and Sir Robert, as they faced each other in battle order, at Empingham, a small village on the outskirts of Stamford. Francis smiled as he considered the irony of it! What followed was not recorded in history as the battle of Empingham, nor even the Battle of Stamford, it was humiliatingly referred to as the 'Battle of Losecote field.' As Sir Robert had hoped, the Lincolnshire rebels had outnumbered the Royalists, albeit that the majority of their army was comprised of inexperienced and poorly armed peasants. Conversely Edward's army although outnumbered by some two to one, were well provisioned and contained within it many heavily armed Flemish mercenaries, together with a great deal of ordinance which the King had brought with him from the Tower of London. The battle, if in fact it could ever be called 'a battle', lasted for only a few minutes. Horrified by the execution that they'd all been forced to witness and fearing the King's wrath, one salvo from the Royalist artillery had been sufficient to disperse the Rebels, who massed together in the open and waiting for orders, had been decimated by this bombardment. As, to the sound of fanfares Edward's vanguard had slowly advanced towards what was left of Sir Robert's army through the smoke, the Rebel lines had disintegrated as the men scattered in all directions and ran for their lives, discarding what arms and armour they possessed as they went. Thus the debacle was satirically referred to as the 'Battle of Losecote field'. Upon interrogation the captured Rebel leaders had soon revealed the true nature of the rebellion and Edward's earlier suspicions had been realised when both Clarence and the Earl, who by that time had reached Leicester, were implicated in the plot. Edward had been in no mood for forgiveness and neither the Earl nor Clarence had expected to avail themselves of his mercy once again. Both men retreated Westwards with what troops they had left, choosing to ignore the King's demands that they disband their army and surrender to him forthwith. The Earl was no fool and he'd realised that with what men they had left and without reinforcements from Yorkshire, he had no hope of defeating Edward's army. Ultimately then, both the Earl and Clarence, together with their immediate families, had made for the South coast, where at Exeter the Earl had been able to salvage much of his navy and from there their small fleet had made its way to Calais. Surprisingly the Captain of Calais, Sir John Wenlock, who was a retainer of the Earl, had refused the rebels admission to the town. The Earl and Clerence's misery had been compounded when the Duchess Isabelle, heavily pregnant had gone into labour whilst onboard ship. The baby, stillborn, was buried at sea.

Ultimately, the Earl, who'd been forced to seek refuge in France, made landfall in Normandy. As it turned out, the Earl had Wenlock to thank for his life, for had the Rebels landed at Calais, they would have fallen into Edward's trap, for he'd arranged for a Burgundian army to be positioned in the Calais pale, ready to move against the Earl and Clarence, should they have come ashore as planned. Whilst at the French Court, as a result of what had happened, the Earl had been forced to concede that any plan to place Clarence on the throne of England, was doomed to failure. Moreover as a result of her recent still birth, the Earl had seriously doubted that his sickly daughter Isabelle would ever be able to produce a male heir. Francis chuckled to himself as he remembered how at the time, he'd been astounded to hear the news, that whilst in France, the Earl had abandoned Clarence and had made his peace with Queen Margaret! That said, when he'd weighed up those options left to the Earl, Francis was forced to concede that in reality the Earl had had no option other than to attempt a Lancastrian restoration. Henry's Queen, Margaret, despite her legendary hatred of Warwick, was also sensible enough to realise that the Earl, with French support was her only hope of ever seeing her son inherit the Crown. Francis chuckled again as he pictured in his minds eye the scene at King Louis's court. The Earl, 'the Kingmaker' and perhaps the greatest magnate in all of Christendom, forced to kneel before Queen Margaret for over twenty minutes before she even acknowledged his presence! And finally, only after many hours, Margaret had reluctantly forgiven him for the sins that he'd committed against both her and her family. To cement this new alliance the younger of the Earl's two daughters, Ann, whom Richard himself had hoped one day to marry, had been married to Henry's heir, Edward of Lancaster, at Tours cathedral, which was situated on the banks of the River Loire. It had then been Edward's turn to taste defeat. In August, as planned, Francis and his father in law had staged their sham rebellion and as expected, Edward, confident that the Earl's navy was blockaded in the French port of

Harfleur, had once again ridden north with an army to deal with it. Unfortunately for him, storms, had scattered the blockading English fleet and as a consequence the Earl, together with Clarence, who by that time had rejoined his father in law, after he'd been promised both a position of prominence at King Henry's court and the Crown itself should Prince Edward fail to produce any heirs, sailed unhindered to England, landing at the Port of Exeter where they'd both declared for King Henry VI. Francis smiled again as he considered how fickle some men could be! Apparently after he'd been abandoned by the Earl, Clarence had vowed to do everything in his power to prevent a Lancastrian restoration. Yet within weeks he was joining the Earl in a Lancastrian invasion of England! Francis smiled again, Clarence who'd clearly burnt all of his bridges with Edward and Richard, had obviously received word from England that he wasn't going to be pardoned so easily this time! Amazingly, within weeks, as during the Edgecote campaign, Edward had once again found himself both isolated and abandoned, this as one by one, the English nobles, sick and tired of Edward's patronage of the Woodvilles and of 'his favourites', had declared for Lancaster. Francis felt that perhaps Edward's greatest failure had been his demotion of the Earl's brother John, who'd supported the Yorkist's throughout the Wars and whom he'd earlier created the Earl of Northumbeland, as a reward for this loyalty. Foolishly, to counter the Neville families influence in the north, Edward had released the Lancastrian Henry Percy from tower of London and had reinstated him to his Earldom of Northumberland. Edward had tried to compensate John Neville by creating him the Marquis of Montagu and by betrothing Montagu's son George to his eldest daughter Elizabeth and giving the lad the Dukedom of Bedford. But it hadn't been enough and as Edward, confidant of victory, had mustered his army at Doncaster, he was to learn of Montagu's defection to the Lancastrian's. And as Montagu, with a sizeable army of his own, was almost upon him, Edward had had no option but to disband what remained of his own army and together with Richard and the Hastings brothers he'd taken flight, luckily, only just managing to evade capture and certain death, making his way to the the court of his Burgundian allies. Francis chuckled again, yes he was sad to see Richard driven out of England, but at least Edward's reversal had meant that he, Francis, was able to return to Ravensworth. Smiling Francis reflected on the fact that one could only put up with the Scots for so long and if he'd have been forced to stay north of the border for any longer, he felt that he'd have either gone mad or would have drank himself into an early grave! But even now Francis could see no end to the troubles. In sanctuary at

Westmister Edward's Queen had given birth to a son, King Edward's first male heir. As soon as the weather permitted, most probably in the Springtime, both Edward and Richard, with Burgundian aid, hoped to invade England. And who was to say that they'd fail! The Duke of Burgundy who feared a joint Anglo French invasion of Burgundy was said to have been wholeheartedly behind the scheme and England's middle classes, the money in the country, were all up in arms, as the Earl's Pro French Lancastrian regime alienated the rest of England's continental trading partners. Moreover, King Henry remained feebleminded, whilst Queen Margaret, fearful for the safety of her only child, steadfastly refused to allow Edward of Lancaster to come to England, until the throne was secure. Francis sighed, in his opinion there was still no solution possible, that is, whilst all of the various adherents still lived. Either the house of Lancaster or that of York would have to be exterminated forever, otherwise the Wars would continue. Francis could have been forgiven for rejoicing, for as one of the Earl's retainers he was, for the time being at least, in the winning camp and was in theory once again a Lancastrian. Francis smiled to himself, no, he wasn't rejoicing, but at the same time he was no longer either scared or confused, for at the very least he now knew where he stood. Richard had consistently proven himself to be a loyal Prince of the House of York and he would no doubt accompany Edward when he finally returned to England, and when he did Francis, despite his previous affinities, resolved to join him!

Chapter 15
April 1471 Barnet.

Anxious, Francis awoke early on Easter Sunday to discover that a thick and impenetrable mist had risen upon the Battlefield. The swirling fog enveloped and concealed both armies, which were now, Francis assumed, in all probability ranged against each other. Pulling his cloak tightly about himself Francis shivered, it seemed to him as if God, on this holiest of days Easter Sunday, had chosen to hide from view, the slaughter which Francis knew was now inevitable, this regardless of who the ultimate victors may be. At least, Francis mused, with both of the Neville Brothers and all of the Brothers of York in attendance on opposing sides, this Battle may, with luck, settle the matter once and for all.

As he contemplated his own situation, Francis, despite his previous experience of warfare felt sick with nervousness. For even if everything went to plan, his role that day would be less than straightforward! Fortunately for Francis, the Earl's spies had somehow managed to procure details of the proposed Yorkist's dispositions and as a result Francis had managed to secure a posting with the Earl of Oxford, who was to command the Lancastrian right flank. Hopefully this would ensure that Francis and his men would be deployed against William Lord Hasting's troops of the Yorkist left flank. Thus in the event that Francis was forced to fight, at least he would do so against a contingent of troops that were commanded by his old enemies the Hastings and not, as he'd earlier feared, men who were led by his friend Richard. For Richard had apparently been given the honour of commanding the Yorkist's right flank. Despite his nervousness, Francis was at least able to allow himself a smile, this as he pictured in his minds eye how the Duke of Clarence must have reacted to the news, that he'd been overlooked by Edward in favour of his younger brother! Francis smiled again, Edward was no fool and even though he may have pardoned Clarence yet again, this when Clarence had once again changed sides, he'd only done this because it had been politic for him to do so. In spite of everything Clarence surprisingly still enjoyed a great following and Edward had been in great need of the troops that Clarence had brought with him when he'd abandoned the Earl and the Lancastrians. That said it was clear that the King still didn't trust him and in Francis's opinion, after all that had happened in the past, would probably never trust him again! As it was Clarence was to fight with the King in the main Battle, where Edward could no doubt keep an eye on him. If everything went to plan, Richard's men on the Yorkist right, would face the Earl of Exeter's troops.

Francis sighed, over the past few weeks he'd thought long and hard about how he would try to free himself from his obligations to his family and to the Earl and join Richard . When in late March he'd received word that both Edward and Richard's invasion force had finally landed in England, somewhere on the Yorkshire coast, he'd thought about joining them there. But none were sure, where exactly the Brothers had landed, as their fleet had apparently been scattered by a storm. Moreover, the East Riding of Yorkshire was alive with Lancastrian spies and agents, all of whom were on the lookout for anyone who hoped to join up with the Yorkist invasion. When Edward and Richard had arrived in York on the 18th of that month, Francis had still prevaricated, but he had ultimately chosen to remain at Ravensworth, as by that time, Edward, who was both weak and unsupported, in an effort to gain admittance to the City, had declared that he'd returned to England not to reclaim his throne from King Henry, but to merely recover his dukedom of York. Indeed it was not until Edward's growing army had reached Nottingham on the 21st of March, that Edward had been confidant enough to declare that he had in fact returned to England to reclaim his throne. By that time the brothers of York were well within the Yorkist heartlands of the Midlands and had gathered together quite an impressive army, especiallyafter they'd successfully secured the support of the duplicitous Clarence, who, having gained nothing by King Henry's re-adept ion, had changed sides yet again!. Sadly, for Francis at Ravensworth, Nottingham was well out of his reach and as such he'd reluctantly mustered with the rest of his family at Middleham, this in answer to the Earl of Warwick's call to arms. From Middleham the Yorkshiremen had once again made the long march South, this time on behalf of the House of Lancaster, to relieve the Earl who was being besieged at Coventry by Edward. For once, it had been the Earl who'd been caught off guard! Initially the Earl had trusted that the Yorkist invasion would have been crushed before it'd gained any impetuous, as both Richard and Edward had landed at Ravensworth to the north of the Humber estuary, with pitifully few men. Unfortunately the Earl's men in the East Riding, who were reticent at the best of times to meet a King in battle, especially one with Edward's military pedigree, didn't need much of an excuse and when Edward had cleverly maintained that he'd only come only to reclaim his Dukedom, they'd happily backed off and allowed him to continue on unmolested. Furious, the Earl could only sit and wait for his own reinforcements to join him at Coventry. And it was there that he'd been confronted by both Edward and Richard, who by that time had been joined by Clarence and a sizable force of his retainers. Outnumbered and alarmed by Clarence's sudden and unexpected defection, the Earl had steadfastly refused to answer Edward's repeated challenges to ride out of the City and fight him, this even after the Yorkist's had drawn up their forces in full battle order within sight of the cities walls. Unfortunately Edward, who had no artillery, was too weak to attack the City and as the Earl's Yorkshiremen had approached from the north, it was he who was forced to retreat, this time, Southwards towards the Capital.

With the arrival of much needed reinforcements, the Earl had at last been stirred into action. Neither Francis nor his companions had had much time to rest from their long march, as the Earl's combined army, set forth in a race with Edward, for London. Both Edward and the Earl reasoning that control of the Capital was vital in their quest for victory. Unfortunately for the Lancastrians the Earl lost the race and in spite of leaving London and King Henry in the care of his brother the Archbishop and a number of other prominent Lancastrian nobles, the Earl failed to prevent Edward from taking both the City and the King without bloodshed. Apparently Archbishop George Neville, fearful for his own safety at the hands of the Londoners, who hated the Nevilles for the anti Burgundian policies that had all but commercially ruined the City, had thrown himself at King Edward's feet and sought his forgiveness. The Archbishop happily surrendering King Henry whom he'd earlier sworn to protect with his life! Nor had those Lancastrian nobles who'd been left in the City done much to oppose the Yorkists. As Edward's army had approached, in an effort to drum up support, they'd paraded King Henry throughout the streets, but this pitiful sight had merely angered the Londoners further, so, fearful of Yorkist retribution, all of the Lancastrian Nobles had fled the city, making for the South East and Exeter, where Queen Margaret and Prince Edward were due to land, both having at long last set sail from France with a French army.

But Queen Margaret and her French army had come much too late for the Earl and here at Barnet, he would now have to face Edward alone! Few other than the Earl himself were confident of Victory, for Edward was a capable commander and he'd yet to lose a Battle. Moreover, despite being outnumbered, the Yorkist army, with their Burgundian funded Flemish mercenaries and their battle hardened men at arms and archers, who'd all seen much service throughout the Civil Wars, were a formidable fighting force indeed!

Scratching his head, Francis, who'd been joined on the march Southwards by his friend Ned and a few his Lovel retainers from Oxfordshire, sighed as he wondered how he'd manage to extricate himself from the Lancastrian army and defect to Richard. Luckily as they assembled on the Battlefield, both Francis and his men found themselves arrayed alongside strangers, men of Essex, the Earl of Oxford's household troops.

Sadly, in the confusion that had accompanied the call to arms, Francis had not managed to locate his cousin Thomas, who as head of the Earl of Oxford's household, was said to have been given the honour of carrying Oxford's colours into battle that day. Francis sighed again as he considered his defection and wondered if he and his cousin were destined always, be on opposing sides.

Thankfully Francis's friends and family, the Fitzhughs together with Sir John Conyers and the rest of the Earl's Yorkshiremen, were to be positioned behind the Lancastrian centre, with the Earl himself, to be held in reserve. Indeed Francis had only managed to secure his place in the front ranks of the Lancastrian Right flank, after he'd forcefully maintained, that once again he wanted to be in the 'Thick of it.'

Luckily Miles Dobson, who'd been eager to accompany Francis into battle, had been dissuaded from joining the Lovel contingent, this after Francis had angered him by giving his Lovel colours to Ned to carry into battle. Francis shivered again, now at least everything was in place and he could only hope that during the battle, some opportunity would present itself, that would enable him to join the Yorkists, without having to turn against his friends and family. Francis turned to Ned and smiled. Ned his oldest friend smiled back and Francis was glad that they were together again and that their friendship had endured, this in spite of Francis's earlier revelations to Ned and their men about his allegiance to Richard and as a consequence of this, to the Yorkists. As it turned out, Francis needn't have worried about either Ned's nor his men's reaction, for when he'd told them all of his proposal, that given the opportunity he would join Richard, to a man, they'd all assured him that their loyalty was not to King Henry but was to their Lord, Lord Lovel and as such they would follow Francis, 'wherever' and 'whenever' he went.

As through the mist he heard the Yorkist Battle Captains continuing to bark out their orders, Francis smiled wryly. Throughout the night, as the Earl's artillery bombardment had continued unanswered, he'd hoped that in the morning he'd awake to discover that the Yorkists had decided to retire from the field. Francis's confidence in the Yorkist armies reticence to fight had however disappeared as dawn had broken and through the fog and swirling mists he'd heard the unmistakable sounds of an army preparing for battle. Biting his lip, Francis chided himself for his optimism, he should have known better, for Edward already outnumbered, was bound to have been keen to bring the Earl to battle, before he'd been reinforced even further by the Queen and her Frenchmen who were expected to land on the South coast at any time and also by Jasper Tudor and his Welshmen, who were reputed to have been coming out of the South of Wales.

At long last it was the Earl of Oxford himself who signaled the attack. The Earl with sword in hand, astride a great black destrier, ordering his bowman forward, to unleash a number of volleys through the swirling mist, that were all aimed in the general direction of the enemy. After each man had loosed off what Francis estimated to be at least four arrows, the archers happily stood to one side, as their arrows were followed into the thick fog by the men at arms, who, in spite of the waterlogged and uneven ground, doggedly made there way forward towards the Yorkist lines, which at that point, were still invisible to the Lancastrians. Looking to his left, Francis could see that those men who comprised the Lancastrian armies right flank, had all begun there slow march over the rough terrain, that separated them from their enemies. But try as he might Francis could see no further than some hundred feet or so and could only guess that Oxford's advance had been coordinated with that of the Lancastrian's centre and left. After their trumpeters had heralded the start of the assault, it was almost surreal, as an eerie silence, broken only by the odd curse or cry as men stumbled into each other or fell, descended upon the battlefield. For once in his life Francis was genuinely scared, it was something to face ones enemy on the field of Battle, but to do so knowing that he was out there somewhere, yet not being able to see him, was to Francis both alarming and disconcerting. Peering in to the thick and impenetrable mist, Francis too stumbled into his comrades, as he continued forwards, in what he thought must be the general direction of the Yorkist's left flank. With every step Francis became more and more disorientated, until that is he was immediately bought back to his senses, as he heard the sudden and unnerving 'whoosh' that signified that the Yorkist archers, in spite of the fog, knew where they were and had replied to the Lancastrian archers earlier volley's.

The Longbow, in spite of the advent of firearms was still a devastating weapon and at close range in the fog it decimated the front ranks of the Lancastrian army. Oxford's men neither heard nor saw the onslaught until it was too late and the arrows themselves were falling amongst them. Many had not even the time to cry out, as the arrows thudded home and grunting the stricken men fell quietly to the ground. Francis knew that these men, were as always, expendable and that their many casualties would soon be replaced by those from the rear, who were all keen to get up into their front lines, to exact their revenge upon the as yet unseen enemy. The distance between the two armies must have been slight, for those Lancastrian bowmen who'd accompanied the men at arms into battle, had no time to reply to their counterparts within Hasting's force, before the two armies clashed. In an instant Francis was deafened by the din of battle, the sound of sword and Mace upon armour and the cries of those who were struck down in the early exchanges. But to Francis's surprise, none of the enemy came out of the mist towards either he or his men. The first contact with the enemy, had it seemed, come somewhere to Francis's left, towards the centre of the Lancastrian right flank, although, try as he might Francis couldn't see the fighting through the mist. Unsure what to do Francis paused and sensing that this may just be his opportunity, he ordered his confused men onwards. At any moment Francis expected to engage with his counterparts within the Yorkist army, yet with every passing minute he became more and more excited, this as he slowly began to realise what must have happened. As both he and his men continued their advance, Francis smiled as he noticed that the noise of Battle to their left was diminishing. Laughing out loud, Francis finally realised what must have happened.

That morning in the fog and mist, both armies had failed to line up exactly opposite to each other and as a result it seemed that the furthermost reaches of each armies wing had overlapped the other. Francis and his men, on the extremity of Oxford's right flank, having faced nothing other than fresh air, had marched right past there as yet unseen opponents and from the sound of the battle behind them, it seemed as if they were now quite someway behind the Yorkist lines!

The old battle captain who wore the Earl of Oxford's livery of the rising star, who's own contingent of troops had accompanied the Lovel men into the attack, laughed too as he realised their mistake, a mistake which he clearly saw as an opportunity. Oxford's man, in contrast to Francis, who was planning to use this opportunity as a means to avoid the fighting and to join Richard, saw the miscalculation as their chance to outflank Hasting's men and as such he was soon barking out orders and mustering both his own men and Francis's retainers, for a charge towards the enemies rear.

Francis took Ned, who also at first, seemed intent on joining in the maneuver, firmly by the arm, with difficulty he made himself heard above the whooping and Battle cries of the De Vere retainers, as together with some of the more excitable of Francis's men, they wheeled to their left and dashed back into the mist.

'This fight's not for us,'

Francis shouted, as he took the Lovel banner from his friend, which he at once furled.

Ned nodded and followed, as Francis, waving towards those of his own men who hadn't gone with Oxford's battle captain to follow, made his way away from the sounds of the battle.

'We'll make for Barnet,'

Francis said, adding, 'If we can find King Edward's baggage train and if I can find any of my old friends their, we can make out intentions plain and can await the outcome of the Battle.'

With difficulty, in the mist, both Francis and his friend, together with a handful of their men, made there way away from the fighting, to Hadley Green, from where they took the St Albans Road to Barnet. Once on the cobbled roadway and with there armour loosened, they all made good time and soon left the noise of battle far behind, as they came across the small town that consisting of a church, houses and a number of Inns, was Barnet. As Francis had expected, the Yorkist baggage train was tethered in the village square, but disappointed, he did not see any familiar faces amongst the King's household troops who guarded it. Edward's men easily identifiable by the King's 'sun in splendor' device that was emblazoned upon their tunics. Francis sighed, not the white boar device of his friend Richard, the Duke of Gloucester, that he'd hoped to see. Wary both Francis and Ned agreed that it would be better to secret themselves amongst the headstones of the nearby churchyard and from there see how events shaped themselves.

Alarmed, both Francis and his men witnessed what appeared to be the total rout of the Edward and Richard's Yorkist army! They'd been in the churchyard for only a few minutes, when they began to notice that a steady stream of men, all wearing Hastings livery, had begun to arrive in the square. None lingered as they took both fresh horses and the London road, the men, as they went, bewailing the destruction of the King's army and advising those of Edward's baggage train who remained unscathed, to join them in their flight,

'For we are all undone!'

Francis's guessed that some 500 men at least had taken flight and as the slow and injured began to arrive, so did the Earl of Oxford's men. A large number of Oxford's troops had it seemed recovered their horses and mounted, they rode down the unfortunate Yorkists with ease. Even

Francis, who'd witnessed much savagery in his time, was appalled by the Lancastrian's butchery, for no quarter was given as they hacked and slashed, until the square itself was awash with blood. Both Francis and Ned retched at the slaughter that they both saw and smelt.

As Francis watched on aghast, it was Ned who spurred him into action.

'Francis it'd be pure folly to reveal our designs now, even if we could make our way to Richard. We must hope that the Earl's men have been merciful to your friend, or that he's fared better than Hasting's men and has escaped the field,' patting Francis on the back and sighing Ned added, 'Francis we've got to save ourselves, we must rejoin the Battle with Oxford's men.'

Francis too sighed, he hoped that Richard had taken flight but he doubted that he had, knowing his friends character the way that he did.

'He'll fight to the last to protect his brother the King and a Yorkist defeat will surely bring his death,'

Francis lamented.

Practical as always, Ned replied truthfully,

'Well if that proves to be the case I'm afraid your friend's beyond our help then.'

From their hiding place in the churchyard, both Francis and his companions tentatively made there way back to the square, where once again they were unfortunate enough to meet up with Oxford's battle captain who'd led the earlier charge that now appeared to have been so successful.

'Where did you lot get too,'

The old man growled in disapproval at their apparent cowardice,

'One minute you were there and the next you were gone', the Captain shook his head as he added, 'My men don't take kindly to faint hearts, especially when they're of noble blood,'

Quick thinking, Francis spoke with the confidence of one of 'Noble Birth.'

'We came for the baggage, but none followed us as all were committed to your attack and even lightly guarded it would have been too difficult a task for my men and I to have taken it.'

Francis leaned in towards the soldier,

'And a coward I am not, gather your men and follow me, we must all rejoin the battle to complete the rout.'

At the head of a body of mounted men at arms, Francis, with Ned at his side and his banner once again unfurled, rode back into the fray. By this time the Marquis of Montagu, who'd commanded the Lancastrian centre at the outset of the Battle, had been reinforced by his brother the

Earl of Warwick, who had by now committed all of their reserves. As such, by force of numbers alone, the Lancastrians seemed to be gradually gaining the upper hand and they were slowly yet surely forcing the hard pressed Yorkist centre and right back towards Hadley Church. The mist has all but cleared and on returning to the Battle Francis's could see that both battle lines had swung about by almost 90 degrees and now both armies were engaged in savage hand to hand combat all along the St Albans Road. Yet in spite of the destruction of Hasting's left flank, both Edward in the centre and Richard on his right fought on! From the position of the various contingents who still remained on the battlefield, it was clear to Francis that the Earl of Exeter who'd commanded the Lancastrian left had also been outflanked by his counterpart and he had fared no better than Hastings. Despite being reinforced early in the Battle, Exeter's men had been rolled up by Richard's men, who were now engaged with the Lancastrian's centre. Francis panicked, he knew that a sudden and unexpected charge from his mounted troops may have decided the matter in the Lancastrian's favour. Yet if he changed his allegiance again, both he and Ned would be cut down by Oxford's men who followed them, yet clearly still distrusted them.

Ned no doubt realising that they must fight and fight for the Lancastrians cast down the banner which he'd held and drawing his sword, he shouted encouragement to Francis as he spurred his horse onwards towards the Yorkist lines.

'Come Francis we must fight for our lives.'

As he drew close to the melee, to Francis's surprise, he saw a number of Montagu's archers who'd turned towards them, begin to fire upon their men. Men were dropping on either side of Francis, yet he smiled, for he slowly began to realise that the Marquis's men, in the confusion of the Battle, had obviously mistaken Oxford's livery of the rising star, for that of Edward's Sun in Splendor! Fearing that they were about to be outflanked by Francis's men, whom they'd mistakenly identified as King Edward's cavalry, the Lancastrian centre had turned upon its own men as they'd returned to the fray to support them!

Francis guessing that he could use this unprovoked attack to his advantage at once cried out,

'Treason there's Treason here,'

Ned no doubt reading Francis's mind joined him in this tirade, this as they now bore down upon the leather clad bowmen, running them down and then turning there attention towards Montagu's men at arms, who having come to their colleagues aid, now faced attacks from all directions. Even Oxford's Battle Captain joined in.

'That bastard Montagu's declared for York'.

The rumour, began by Francis, spread like wildfire throughout the exhausted Lancastrian troops, who all now clearly sensed defeat rather than victory. As a consequence the Earl of Warwick's battle lines slowly began to crumble and disintegrate, as men cried foul and discarding their weapons, quickly made off towards their rear in the direction of their horse lines.

Francis wondered if those men, whom he'd led in such treachery, would realise their error and if so what effect this still may have on the outcome of the Battle. He need not have worried however and he cared not, as he tore off his sur coat and joined Richard of Gloucester's men, as they engaged with those few Lancastrianss who'd chosen to stand their ground.

The Marquis of Montagu, together with those of his retainers who'd remained at his side, were mercilessly cut down. Upon witnessing the disintegration of his battle lines, the Earl of Warwick who by that time had used up all of his reserves, fled the field, making for the woods and his own baggage train. Ironically it was Oxford retainers, led into the fray by Francis himself, who had finally dispatched Montagu, in Francis's opinion, the only Neville of honour. A man who had wrested with his conscience, when he'd earlier abandoned King Edward out of his loyalty to his brothers. This 'honourable man' died under the blows of his allies, with cries of 'Treason' ringing in his ears, not a fitting end, Francis felt, for one so noble.

The other Neville Brothers had thought only their own safety. George having capitulated in London and the Earl of Warwick, upon witnessing the dramatic collapse of his army, having abandoned Montagu on the field, fleeing with his household men as his brother had pleaded for his help.

With the death of Montague, all of the Lancastrian leaders now either lay dead or wounded on the field, or were making off in full flight. With both their leaders and the fight gone from them, the Lancastrians began to cast aside their weapons and place themselves at the mercy of their adversaries. As always the common men were spared, yet those of Noble birth were killed where they stood,

'Lest they hope in the future to seek revenge for this day.'

Summary executions of those who'd survived the battle itself abounded and Francis could only look away as those who'd so recently been his comrades died, pleading for there lives as their captors decapitated them with the axe or cut their throats, as they kneeled before them. Francis quietly crossed himself in thanksgiving that his own life had been spared and that had it not been for his own quick thinking in discarding his own colours when he had, he too might have been kneeling in front of his captors. Luckily as the battle had petered out both Francis and Ned had been able to join a band of Ricardian retainers, many of whom Francis had recognised from there days together at Middleham.

After the Battle Francis was brought before King Edward, who pardoned him, as Richard, with tears in his eyes, clapped his arms around Francis and thanked both he and Ned for their charge, which he said, had turned out to be the catalyst, which in turn had ultimately led to the Lancastrian's defeat.

Grinning, Richard added that when he'd heard that Francis had mustered together with the Nevilles at Middleham, he'd 'feared' he said that he might next see his 'old friend', 'naked dead and spoiled upon the field.'

Exhausted the victorious Yorkist army remained at Barnet for all that remained of that day and the next. Unusually those makeshift courts that usually followed such an affair were not necessary, as those Lancastrian nobles who'd had not fled the Battle, for the most part, had either been killed or had been executed upon the field. This gave both Richard and Francis a little time at last, to catch up with the events that had occurred in each of there lives. Not unexpectedly this conversation lasted on and off for the period that their army remained at rest.

Whilst at Barnet news soon filtered in of the fate of both the Earl of Warwick and of the rest of those Lancastrian Nobles who'd fought in the Battle. The Earl of Oxford had made good his escape and was said, once again, to be making for the Scottish court and exile. The Duke of Essex, who was thought to have died at the height of Battle when felled by a Yorkist battle axe, had been found some hours later, gravely wounded on the battlefield. Exeter, a stalwart Lancastrian, who'd spent many years in exile at the Burgundian court, where he'd become friendly with the Countess, Edward's sister, was deemed much to poorly to execute and King Edward, now calmer had spared his life. If Exeter was to recover from his injuries, he was bound for the Tower and captivity.

The Earl of Warwick lay dead. Francis felt little sorrow for his past master, as he heard how the Earl, running from the battlefield, had been caught by the Yorkist men at arms, as he'd tried in vain to reach his horses. Ironically, the early Lancastrian successes in the Battle, had ensured that when he'd turned to run, the Earl had been much further away from his baggage and his horse lines than he had been at the outset of the Battle. Consequently, the Earl fully armoured and on foot, had soon been overtaken by his pursuers. In his ornate armour and surrounded by his household troops, the Earl had immediately been recognised and knocked to the floor and helpless he'd been killed when a lowly archer had stabbed him through the eye slit of his helmet. Both the Earl and his brother Montague's bodies had been recovered from the field and stripped naked, they'd been ingloriously displayed in open caskets, so that all could see that the 'Kingmaker' was finally dead.

Francis had felt no emotion has he'd gone with Richard to see what remained of their benefactor. Francis's sentiments were clearly shared by Richard who'd laughed as he'd said,

'You'll not rule England now my Neville cousin,'

Smiling as he pointed out the numerous defensive wounds upon the Earl's body which contrasted to those of the Earl's brother, the Marquis of Montagu, Richard added,

'And it won't be too difficult for people to see who indeed was the man of honour, for only one chose to fight to the last.'

In there time together after the Battle, it cheered Francis to discover that Richard too seemed to value their friendship and it was at Richard's side that Francis, with banners unfurled and in full armour, together with what remained of the Yorkist army, entered London in triumph on the 16th April, merely two days after the battle. Although the two friends still had much to discuss they did not remain in the City for long. As expected Henry's French Queen, together with her son Prince Edward, had landed with a French army at Weymouth, where she'd been joined by a large number of those Lancastrians who'd escaped from Barnet. Presently Margaret's army was marching westwards, towards the River Severn, which she hoped to cross into Wales where she would join up with Jasper Tudor and his Welshmen.

'Our victory at Barnet will have been pointless if Margaret's army joins with that of Tudor,'

The King had pointed out at the council of War that had been hastily convened once, after arriving in the capital, he'd led his Queen and there new born son from sanctuary at Westminster. A son named Edward who'd been born whilst the King was in exile, a boy in whom it was hoped the Yorkist dynasty would continue. King Edward was forthright in his plans.

'We must march for Bristol, if we manage to intercept Margaret and her son before they cross into Wales, we may once again be victorious and hopefully if it is God's will, this matter will be decided once and for all.'

Thus victual led, but no less tired from there recent trials and tribulations, the Yorkist army struck out Westwards from the capital, embarking upon a forced march that was designed to run Margaret and her Son's army down, before it could acquire those Welsh reinforcements that would give the Lancastrians an almost unassailable advantage in numbers.

Chapter 16
The 4th May 1471 Tewkesbury.

It had been touch and go as to whether the Yorkist army of Edward would be able to bring the remaining Lancastrians to battle, before they were able to cross the River Severn into Wales to join up with Jasper Tudor's Welshmen.

None were aware that their pursuit had been succesful, until that is the Yorkists had arrived at Tredlington, a small hamlet which was situated a few miles to the East of Tewkesbury. There Edward had received the news that they'd all long been waiting for. That the Lancastrian army, which had eluded them for the past two weeks, had at last been forced to turn and face them. According to Edward's spies, Queen Magaret's army, had been drawn up in battle order, upon a hill, betwixt the two main roads that entered Tewkesbury from the direction of Gloucester to the South and Cheltenham to the North.

For sometime it had appeared to everyone within the Yorkist army that the Lancastrians would be successful in crossing over into Wales. Their commander, the Duke of Somerset, had used a number of feints and ruses that had both confused and delayed his pursuers. Throughout the race to the River Severn, Somerset had sent detachments of troops out in various directions, in an effort to conceal his true intentions. At times it had appeared to the Yorkists as if the Lancastrian army had been making for London via the Southern Counties. On other occasions it'd looked like they'd been marching towards the Lancastrian heartland's of Cheshire and Westmoreland. Most recently, Somerset had cleverly hoodwinked them into believing that his army had in fact turned to face them at Sodbury. In this instance, Edward having been forced to deviate from his line of march, had arrived at that Town, to be faced not with an army, as he'd been led to believe, but by a small diversionary force, which on seeing the Yorkists had soon melted away into the surrounding countryside. Frustratingly, Edward had been forced to delay his advance for a number of hours, whilst his army had been marshaled into position, this whilst the main body of Somerset's army were some miles to the West, making for one of the few Severn crossings and thereafter for Wales and relative safety. Francis smiled one had to admire the 'bullish' Somerset, who for once seemed to be displaying some brains, rather than brawn, when it came to military matters. As it was Somerset's tactics had succeeded in delaying the advancing Yorkists and had as a result gained the Lancastrian Army precious hours, in their efforts to evade King Edward's army.

Unfortunately for the Lancastrians, it now seemed as if all of Somerset's efforts had come to naught, as the Lancastrian army exhausted, had been caught at Tewkesbury, tantalisingly and frustratingly within sight of their goal, the River Severn and beyond it Wales.

Francis smiled again, for Somerset hadn't been the only clever one. After Somerset's diversion at Sodbury, when it'd become clear to Edward that the Lancastrians were going to win the race and would reach the first of the Severn crossings at Gloucester, before the Yorkists could intercept them, he'd sent a body of horsemen forward, to 'persuade' the towns governor, Sir Richard Beauchamp, to hold the town and with it it's river crossing, against the Lancastrians. With Gloucester's gates closed to them and without either the time or the ordinance to reduce them, dispirited, Somerset's men had been forced to turn northwards and make for the next crossing which was located at Tewkesbury. Upon arriving at Tewkesbury, it had been clear to Somerset that he hadn't the time to get his army across the River, before Edward's men would be in a position to attack him. He had therefore, reluctantly turned to face his pursuers. At least, Francis mused, Somerset would be able to congratulate himself on choosing some excellent defensive positions, upon the high ground around Tewkesbury Abbey. It was here that the Lancastrian army had dug in and waited for the Yorkists to arrive.

Relieved that the chase was finally over, the King accompanied by a small group of followers, which included both of his brothers, together with Hastings and Francis, had ridden at once to a small hillock, which was situated to the South East of the Town of Tewkesbury. This location, which in elevation, was practically level with the ridge upon which the enemy was entrenched, afforded the Yorkist commanders the best position, from which they could observe their enemies dispositions.

'Somerset's chosen well.' As Edward spoke, Francis noticed that for one who was usually quite optimistic, the King was clearly troubled. Francis could clearly see why Edward appeared less than confidant, as he saw the ground over which their troops would have to advance, if they hoped to engage the enemy on the following day.

Edward sighed as he added wryly, 'And he's not just got the advantage of the high ground.' Edward's frown deepened as he pointed out the mass of hedges, brambles and thickets that littered the hillside, dense vegetation that was bound to slow down and break up any Yorkist attack.

'We'll have to make sure that they come to us then,' Richard smiled as he spoke with the confidence of one who'd only recently tasted victory.

'And how will you manage that then, only a fool would give up that ground.'

Clarence sneered at his younger brother.

Laughing, Richard chose to ignore Clarence and instead addressed his answer to Edward.

'We'll use the lessons that History's taught us. King Harold and his Saxons were no fools and they'd won many Battles. And at Hasting's they too had chosen their ground well. But Duke William still defeated them, he brought them down from the high ground and the protection of their shield wall.'

Edward smiled at his younger Brother.

'I knew your books would be good for something one day,' he said.

Encouraged Richard went on.

'A feint. We all know that Somerset's got a reputation for recklessness. Tomorrow we must exploit his impetuosity, we must think of some kind of ruse, something that'll bring him down the hill to us, so we can fight him on ground of our choosing'.

Clarence scoffed.

'Both Somerset and the Prince may be inexperienced, but they've got Wenlock with them and he's far to clever to give up such an advantageous position.'

Richard smiled. Francis could see that his friend was enjoying himself at Clarence's expense, almost condescending, Richard continued, this time he chose to address Clarence, 'Trust me Brother, I make it my place to know my enemy. Somerset is a Beaufort through and through, an arrogant and vain man, he's a Duke and as such he doesn't listen to the counsel of others, especially when it comes from an aging Knight such as Wenlock.'

Rubbing his chin Edward began to smile, clapping Richard on the back, Edward said, Brother, I do believe that you might just be right.' Laughing Edward continued, 'Remember Towton and Hexham, on both of these occasions this Duke's brother was quick to reject the advice of others, if Richard's right and this man is cut from the same cloth, we may just be able to persuade him to come down from his hill.' Smiling Edward winked at Richard as he added, 'that is of course if my younger Brother can tempt him.'

Serious again, Richard pointed towards the Lancastrian armies right flank where Somerset's banners fluttered in the warm evening breeze. 'See it's on their right where the hill is steepest, a feint directed towards

Someret's men will bring both the Duke and after him, the rest of his army down to us.'

Richard went on,

'By such an attack we cannot hope to prevail , but when we retreat, trust me they'll bring the whole of the Lancastrian army down upon us and we can then fight them on ground of our own choosing.'

Richard turned to Edward as he added,

'This Duke is eager to prove himself to the French Queen, trust me Edward he'll take the bait.'

With fondness, Francis remembered how his father had described to him the feint had been used with such devastating effect at the Battle of Hasting's, when their Norman ancestors, all but beaten, had finally defeated the Saxons. How the Normans had attacked and feigning retreat had drawn King Harold's army down the hill, from which they'd enjoyed a practically unassailable position. How those of the Saxons army who were less experienced, sensing absolute victory, had charged down from the hill and there, exposed and vulnerable upon open ground, they had been decimated by the Norman cavalry.

'And who'd lead such a foolhardy attack,' Clarence sneered.

Edward who was obviously irritated by Clarence's negativity silenced him with both a smile and with sarcasm replied,

'Don't you worry too much brother, for it won't be you,'

Much to Clarence's additional discomfort Edward continued,

'You'll stay with me where I can keep an eye on you,'

Edward who seemed to be enjoying himself at Clarence's expense had not finished there, for, with an obvious reference to Clarence's humiliation at Barnet, he added, 'It'll be sometime before I trust you with a command again.'

Not unsurprisingly Richard was eager to volunteer his services,

'Give me the command Edward,'

The King however was forthright in his reply,

'No I'll not risk you on such a risky a venture. Someone who is more expendable will lead the attack,'

Much to the relief of both Hasting's and Francis, upon whom the King's gaze had centered, Richard at once countered the King's argument.

'Somereset may be inexperienced, but he'll not be drawn down unless he believes that we're fully committed to the attack, that's why I, as the Duke of Gloucester and the King's brother must lead the assault.'

It was clear to all present that the present Lancastrian positions, were practically speaking, unassailable and that their only real hope of a victory was, as Richard had poointed out, to lure Somerset's men down from the hill and hope that they'd be followed by the rest of the Lancastrian army. With a troubled look once again on his face, sighing Edward finally acquiesced, 'But Richard you must promise me that you'll disengage at the earliest opportunity and that you'll not fight in the foremost ranks as you did at Barnet.'

With a twinkle in his eye Richard readily agreed to his Brother's conditions, he winked at Francis who could only wonder if, on the following day, his friend would obey his brother's wishes.

Frowning again Edward turned to Francis, 'And you Lord Lovel will have but one opportunity of proving your loyalty to me.' He went on, as Francis, fearful that he may miss anything of significance, edged his horse closer to that of the King.

'Do you see that wood to the East,'

Francis nodded and mumbled in agreement,

'I want you to take two hundred of my cavalry, if you need to clear the wood of any Lancastrians do so, but you must hold that ground. You must prevent Richard from being outflanked, otherwise he'll never get out of there alive.' Grinning Edward continued, 'And if Richard's feint succeeds and Somerset does come down from the hill, you can have some fun, for I'll expect both you and your men to trouble the Lancastrian army in the rear.'

The King laughed as he added,

'And hopefully, with God's will, you'll have as much success as you had at Barnet, when you led your charge on behalf of the Earl of Oxford, against Montagu.' Chuckling Edward who was now clearly much happier, crossed himself before he said, 'God bless him.'

Even Clarence and Hastings smiled as they all cast their minds back to Barnet.

Francis prickled with pride. The King had entrusted him with a most important role. One which would allow him to safeguard his friend and may also, God willing, enable him to have a direct influence upon the outcome of the Battle.

It had been decided then. Once again Richard would take command of the Yorkist's left flank. From that position, at first light on the following day, Richard's troops would advance towards the right flank of the Lancastrian army, which was entrenched in and around Tewkesbury Abbey. The King with Clarence by his side, would command the centre and in the early stages of the Battle his men were to hold their line. Lord Hastings, who was, metaphorically speaking, still licking his wounds from Barnet, would command the Right flank. Hasting's troops would be held in reserve. Francis smiled, he still hated the Hastings Brothers and it pleased him that they'd failed at Barnet. Here at Tewkesbury, the King clearly didn't want to expose Hasting's jittery and inexperienced troops to Somerset's charge, that's if it came of course! For at Barnet, under pressure, the Midlanders had been very quick to flee the field.

Excited Francis woke early on the following day. Despite the fact that it was some hours before dawn, the Yorkist camp was in a frenzy of activity, as once again the men prepared for battle. Ned was at hand to help Francis into his armour, once that is, he'd eaten all that he could manage of a hurried breakfast. It was still quite dark as Francis, armed and at the head of his command, a band of some 200 of the most experienced of the King's own household troops, left the King's camp. Francis's troop riding out towards their proposed position within the Wood, long before those others within the Yorkist army were going to be drawn up in Battle order.

On reaching his destination Francis was at least relieved to find that the dense woodland was both silent and empty. Francis smiled, the Lancastrian skirmishers who'd surveyed the location, had no doubt felt that the wood was too far away from their own lines to be of any use to either side during the Battle. Francis could only hope that the days events would prove them wrong.

Silently the men dismounted and fearful that, as their horses became increasingly more restless, they may give away their positions, they tethered their horses towards the rear of the wood, yet still within easy reach, should they need them at short notice. On foot, Francis carefully led his men through a mass of nettles, brambles and branches, until they reached a position on the eastern edge of the wood, from which they could just see the Lancastrian army assembling on the ridge line. Frustratingly for Francis, the small hillock, upon which they'd formulated their plans on the previous day, concealed much the Yorkist army, which he assumed, must have been forming up in the valley below them. Worried, Francis could see that if after his feint, Richard retreated back too far, he would be hidden from Francis's view. This would mean that Francis would be unable to to see how the Battle was progressing and may not know when to commit his own men to greatest effect.

'Go quickly to Gloucester,' Francis commanded his dispatch rider,

'Tell the Duke that when he advances he must keep to the right of the hillock and must retreat back no further than it, otherwise we'll not be able to see how he's faring.'

Sighing, Francis could only hope that his message would get through to Richard and that when Somerset's troops charged, Richard's men would be able to turn and hold him short of the hillock. Finally, yet nervously, both Francis and his men settled down and waited for the Battle to commence.

As dawn broke upon the field, to the sound of the nearby abbey bells that were calling the monks to morning mass, Richard's men at last appeared from behind the knoll. Slowly, the Yorkist van guard negotiated the mass of hedges and thickets that lay between themselves and the enemy. Richard's banner of the white boar rose and fell, as it was carried with difficulty over the rough terrain. Despite his distance from their army, Francis could easily make out his friend upon the Battlefield, as the young Duke, attired in the finest armour and wearing a sur coat that also carried a depiction of his white boar device, sword in hand, waved his men forwards. Francis wasn't at all surprised to see that, contrary to the King's instructions, Richard was amongst the very front ranks of his men. Francis smiled, for Richard was a fine example to his men and despite his heavy armour and with his helmet open, he hurried this way and that, shouting encouragement to his soldiers, who with difficulty, were slowly making their way uphill towards the Lancastrian entrenchment's.

Turning to study the dispositions of their enemies, Francis could see that, as expected, the Duke of Somerset commanded the Lancastrian van which was positioned on the enemies right flank, here the hill was at its steepest. Francis smiled, it was clear to him that the Lancastrian commander, given the opportunity, obviously hoped to exploit any advantages that presented themselves to him during the Battle, 'for the glory of Lancaster and King Harry,' to lead a charge down this part of the hill. Francis chuckled to himself, if he did so he'd play right into their hands!

The Earl of Warwick's old friend and Battle Captain, the 70 year old Lord Wenlock, an extremely competant and experienced soldier, who'd held Calais for both the Lancastrians and the Yorkists in his time, commanded the Lancastrian Centre. It appeared as if Wenlock had been entrusted with the safekeeping of Prince Edward, the heir to Lancaster. Francis smiled, he'd not expected to see the seventeen year old Prince on the Battlefield. Francis smiled again, as he pictured in his minds eye how Queen Margaret must have reacted when the Lancastrian commanders had told her, that for the sake of their troops morale, her beloved son would have to be present upon the Battlefield and could not join his mother, as she retired to the Abbey to watch the Battle from its tower. Grinning Francis noted that the Lancastrian rearguard, upon whom Somerset would have to rely upon on for reinforcements, was to be commanded by the Earl Devon, a man of 'doubtful courage'.

As he considered the advantageous position in which the Lancastrian army found itself, Francis sighed, he could only wonder, how Richard's brave yet audacious plan could have any hope of success. Fortunately, Francis didn't have long to ponder on this, for as Richard's men slowly came within range of the Lancastrian lines, Somerset's bowmen, taking one step forward, unleashed a volley of arrows and crossbow bolts, in the direction of the Yorkists, who were struggling up the hill towards them. Richard's archers tried in vain to reply, but due to the steep hill up which they fired, the majority of their arrows fell ineffectually short of the Lancastrian positions. Shouting insults towards Richard's men, the Lancastrian archers enthusiastically continued the fusillade, as they were joined by the few artillery pieces that had been bought forward, when the Lancastrians had realised that the Yorkists had chosen to direct their opening assault towards Somerset's flank. Few Lancastrians fell in these early exchanges. In contrast to their enemies, Richard's men faltered as they were exposed to an increasingly devastating onslaught. As the Yorkist advance stuttered and countless Yorkists were killed or wounded, Francis could only bite his lip and cross his fingers, hoping that Richard's ruse would work. Frustratingly Somerset's men, who were clearly enjoying themselves, remained entrenched on the ridge. Francis felt that he could almost cry as he saw how the Duke of Somerset, seemingly content to rely upon the advantage of the high ground, stubbornly held his position. The Lancastrian archers and artillery willingly engaging in an exchange with their Yorkist counterparts, which it was clear to all, only they could win. Despite the hailstorm of arrows and gunshot, once again Richard rallied his men together and led them from the front, had it not been for his example, Francis truly believed that the Yorkist vanguard would have broken and routed after just a few minutes. As anticipated and despite his friend's best efforts, Francis saw that the Yorkist attack petered out, long before Richard's men had got within, what Francis estimated, was a 100 paces of the enemy lines. Eventually, Richard's men at arms could take no more, without even being able to exchange a single blow with their enemies, they slowed and stopped and hesitating for only the briefest of moments, they were slowly driven back down the hill, upon which they'd sacrificed so many lives to climb. The retreat, initially an ordered maneuver, soon became a rout, as the men, under the relentless fire of their enemies, turned and half running and half tumbling, fell back towards their own lines. Desperate for any sign that Somerset had taken the bait, Francis scanned up and down the Lancastrian lines. Initially resolute, Somerset's men remained upon the high ground and Francis could only shake his head, as all seemed lost to them. However, as the Yorkist's retreat became increasingly less organised, no doubt sensing a speedy and absolute victory, Somerset's men slowly began to abandon their own positions. Initially, small pockets of men charged down the hill. Francis and his men cheered as these Lancastrians, isolated and in open ground, were easy pray for the revengeful Yorkist's, who turned to face them and cut them down with ease. Francis smiled, it was Richard's men who now hurled abuse at the Lancastrians. Francis felt that Somerset must have been becoming increasingly alarmed, for as his men continued to stream down the hillside, it was clear that he was quickly losing control of discipline. Ultimately, it seemed to Francis that Somerset had had no option but to order what remained of his vanguard forward. As the Lancastrian buglers sounded the advance, the whole of the Lancastran right flank appeared upon the ridge high above Richard's men and to the Battle cries of 'King Harry' they charged down the hill, in support of those who'd earlier broken ranks and clearly disregarding orders, had chased after the Yorkists, but were themselves now extremely hard pressed, engaged in hand to hand combat with Richard's men who had all rallied and turned to meet them. Francis almost pitied Somerset. He was certainly a better commander than they'd given him credit for, for it was clear to Francis that had his hand not been forced, he'd have remained in position upon the Hill and there would have slowly ground out a Lancastrian victory, that in those circumstances would, Francis felt, have been inevitable. That said, perhaps a more experienced general would have sacrificed those troops who'd gone forward without orders. But whatever his motivation, Somerset had ultimately fallen into their trap and it was clear that he'd ordered forward both his vanguard and the main battle of his army, which was commanded by Lord Wenlock and his young charge, Prince Edward.

Had all of the Lancastrian troops been so committed, Francis felt, then Somerset may still have carried the day. But as Somerset's vanguard moved forward, the greater number of the Prince and Wenlock's soldiers stubbornly remained upon the hill. Both Francis and his men cheered again, as Somerset's men were soon engulfed by the Yorkist army, as the King and Clarence led their own contingent forward into the fighting, which was now centered upon the northernmost slopes of the hillock. Somerset, deprived of the advantage of the high ground, desperately attempted to outflank Richard by committing the majority of his troops against the far left of the Yorkist line. Those of his men who remained in the more central positions, although thinly spread, fought on like lions! At this point all was not lost for the Lancastrians. Had Wenlock committed the main body of his troops in support of Somerset's maneuver, then the outcome of the Battle would certainly have been very different. As it was the majority of those within the Lancastrian centre, despite seeing Somerset's vulnerabilities, remained in their entrenchment's, watching silently as their comrades were slaughtered below them. Francis could clearly see those runners, which Somerset repeatedly dispatched back up the hill. Men who must have carried orders for Wenlock and the Prince to engage. But as time went by and Wenlock and his young charge remained in their position upon the ridge, it became clear to Francis, that both Somerset and his men were to be abandoned to their fate.

It was Francis who now found himself in a dilemma. If he committed his own men in support of Edward and Richard, he would be vulnerable to any attack that may still come from the main body of the Lancastrian army. However if the Prince and Wenlock stayed on the ridge, Francis could see that an intervention on his part, may just break the deadlock that was beginning to develop at the base of the hill, this as Somerset's men determinedly fought on to the death. Edward had by now committed many of his reserves and both he and the Duke of Somerset's armies were slogging it out upon the slopes of the hillside. Francis waited. Hoping that both Richard and Edward's men would prevail. Alarmingly, after some minutes of viscous hand to hand fighting, it appeared to Francis that Somerset may even have been gaining the upper hand, this as he was reinforced by a few small pockets of Wenlock's troops, who had heeded their commanders requests for help and had charged down the hill in support of their comrades. At least Francis's choice was taken from him and he could wait no longer, having earlier ensured that their horses had been brought forward, Francis ordered his men forward and out of the wood. A trot became a canter which in turn soon became a gallop, as Francis's mounted men at arms thundered down the hillside and into Somerset's exposed and unprotected right flank. The effect of Francis's cavalry charge was devastating and the whole of the Lancastrian right flank was rolled up, as the Lancastrian infantry, powerless against Francis's skilled horsemen, were easily skittled aside. In an instant Francis's bold maneuver nullified any Lancastrian gains as Somerset's men now faced a battle on two fronts! Yet still the brave Lancastrians stubbornly fought on. Eventually and only after some minutes of bitter hand to hand fighting, the breakthrough came in the centre. Without reserves or reinforcement, the thin Lancastrian battle line slowly broke and men who were injured and exhausted and who could fight no longer made off. These men were soon joined by those who'd fought on the flanks, as what was left of Somerset's vanguard retreated Westwards in the direction of the River. Francis showed no mercy to those who until recently had been his comrades. The Yorkists couldn't afford for these men to escape again, as they had done after Barnet, this time to join Tudor's Welshman and to fight against them again. Francis ordered his horseman to run their enemy down and they didn't disappoint him. Francis's men at arms ran down hundreds of the unfortunate Lancastrians, before they could reach the relative safety of the River, slaughtering them in the meadows that led to the Rivers edge. As Francis and his men went about their grim task, Richard rallied his troops and together with what was left of the King's men they were joined by Hasting's troops who'd been held in reserve. The Yorkist army then advanced towards those Lancastrians who'd remained entrenched upon the ridge. Men who had by now witnessed both the complete annihilation of Somerset's force and how the Yorkist's rewarded those who stood against them!

Once his own men had destroyed what had been left of Somerset's van and the fields that gently sloped down towards the River had been littered with Lancastrian dead, Francis men returned to the field. This, as the advancing Yorkist's engaged with what was left of the Lancastrian center and left. As it was the matter was decided upon in minutes, the Lancastrian's dispirited and disorganised, clearly no longer had the stomach for the fight and the Prince and Wenlock's line soon broke, as their men threw down their weapons and turning away from the Battle, made off in the direction of Tewkesbury and the Abbey. As Francis had earlier anticipated, even fewer of Devon's men chose to fight and his men made off to the East, eagerly pursued by Hasting's troops, who by this time had at last found their nerves!

Exhausted, Francis joined Richard on the ridge. It was here, at the location at which the Lancastrians, had some hours earlier confidently mustered for the Battle, that the King planted his standard.

'I thank God for this victory,' he shouted,

As Francis added precociously,

'And, your brother, Richard Duke of Gloucester.'

After the Battle the Yorkist army, exhausted from their exertions of the previous three weeks, rested in the many makeshift tents that were erected in and around the abbey and its confines. Many of the fleeing Lancastrians, including Somerset himself had sought sanctuary in the Abbey. Unfortunately for them the Abbey was deemed not to be lawful sanctuary and after much debate, on the understanding that the men would receive a fair trial, the Abbot had finally given them up to Edward's troops. Neither Wenlock, Devon nor Edward of Lancaster had survived the battle and all now lay dead upon the field. Ironically Wenlock himself having been murdered by the Duke of Somerset, who after witnessing the annihilation of his own brave men, had sought out Warwick's friend and finding him in the Towns market place, without waiting for an explanation for Wenlock's inactivity, had dashed the old man's head in with a battle axe. This act no doubt adding further to the consternation amongst those Lancastrian troops who'd remained upon the field. The unfortunate Earl of Devon had been summarily executed on the field by Hasting's men, who in seeking revenge for their humiliation at Barnet, had run the Earl down and despite his pleadings for mercy, had cut him to pieces with axe and sword. It was rumored that Prince Edward, easily identifiable by his fine armour and his sur coat that bore the arms of England, had actually been murdered by both Richard and Clarence. This as the teenager was said to have begged for mercy from his brother in law Clarence. Apparently it'd been Richard who'd drawn the knife across the Prince's throat, this as King Henry's only heir had knelt before his Yorkist cousins, promising them on the lives of his parents, that he would never again bear arms against them. When Francis had quizzed his friend later, Richard had neither admitted nor denied the allegation. He had however smiled, as he'd replied that, regardless of how the Prince had died, Prince Edward had been true to his word and he would now never again, 'Bear arms against the House of York.'

In the days that followed the victory the Duke of Somerset and those other predominant Lancastrians who'd been 'captured' with him, were beheaded in the Market Square. As King Edward had earlier promised to the Abott, all had received a fair trial, but their deaths had been inevitable from the outset, even before they'd been charged and had appeared before their judge, the 'Constable of England'. An office that was still held by the King's brother, Richard of Gloucester and he, in contrast to his Brother the King, had been in no mood for mercy!

Chapter 17
May 1471, London.

To a fanfare of bugles and pipes King Edward and what was left of his army entered his Capital in triumph. The brothers of York were at the head of a great procession that included much of England's aristocracy and their various retinues, those few nobles who still lived or remained uninjured that is! To Francis, who was amongst the few men who had the honour of riding at the head of the procession with both the King and his brothers, it was if the whole of Christendom had come out onto the streets of London to celebrate their countries deliverance from the Nevilles, the Lancastrians and their French allies. Francis smiled wryly as they all received the acclaim of the common people, for he understood the reality of the situation, that is, that the citizens of London could always be relied upon to grasp each and every opportunity to brighten their dreary lives and this was just one of those 'opportunities'. The majority of the Capital's population would therefore, as a matter of course, leave their homes and places of work to witness such a spectacle, to meet and to greet those armies who entered London in triumph from time to time. Francis himself had witnessed many such spectacles, although even he had to admit that this triumphant entrance of King Edward's army must have ranked amongst the best. This was indeed a display of Yorkist might. All of the Knights and men at arms wearing full armour as they negotiated the City's narrow streets astride their great war-horses. Francis's crest of the chained wolf hound, proudly displayed alongside those other devices of the prominent Yorkists. Those men who, for the time being at least, were in the ascendancy in what had seemed to Francis to have become a continual cycle of civil war and feuding. Francis smiled as he reflected upon the English's resilience and adaptability over the past few decades. For most people had by now, albeit the majority grudgingly, become accustomed to the conflict. On this occasion however, it struck Francis that things seemed strangely different. Rather than merely enjoying the sights and sounds, the crowd seemed to take great delight in the Yorkist success. Almost as if they were beginning to appreciate that the battles of Barnet and Tewksbury had been more than just mere victories and would instead, usher in a new era of peace and tranquility. For the battles had seen not only the death of the war's main adherents but also, potentially, the final demise of the House of Lancaster itself. Francis then, with a sense of optimism and with a grin that reached from ear to ear which must have made him look more than faintly ridiculous, rode throughout the crowd to receive the accolades of both young and old, poor and rich. Paupers stood shoulder to shoulder with merchants, who in turn were hugged and kissed by clergymen. Bishops, Knights, serfs and freemen all stood together and rejoiced, not only for the Yorkists but also, Francis felt, for the prospects for a long and lasting peace.

England had by 1471 experienced nearly two decades of civil war and this conflict had come upon the back of over a century of war against the French. Could it, at long last, now all be at an end? Francis smiled as he considered the prospect that there now no longer seemed to be anyone else alive to fight! Could the country at last settle down to enjoy a peaceful and prosperous future? God knows they deserved it. Francis sighed, as memories flooded back to him. He recalled his own experiences of war. As a child perched upon the chilly battlements of Minster Lovel, nervously awaiting the return of his father. As a soldier, at the head of his retainers with axe in hand as he sallied forth into battle. Francis smiled, all had different stories to tell and all, in one way or another, had been touched by the conflict. Be they those of the aristocracy and their retainers who had been directly involved in many of the engagements. Men who had seen at first hand those horrors that humankind was capable of. Or the common folk, those who hadn't actually fought in any of the actions but had been affected by them, men who had their own stories to tell. Merchants who'd lost markets for their wool when England had adopted the Earl of Warwick's pro French and anti Burgundian policies. Serfs and farmers whose lands, homes and families had been ravaged by marauding armies. Soldiers were violent men who demanded to be victual led and have even their basest of needs met. If this at last meant an end to the war, Francis could envisage none, save for those few, the staunchest of Lancastrian die-hards who still remained at large, that would not delight in its conclusion.

In contrast to his companions that day, Francis did not delude himself. These people were not actually celebrating a Yorkist victory, they were celebrating what they hoped was a final victory. Francis smiled wryly, what if things had turned out differently? What if it had been he and his friends who had lain dead on the fields of Barnet and Tewksbury? If that had been the case, then Francis had no doubt that it would have been the Earl of Warwick, his brother Montagu and Prince Edward who would all have been celebrating, whilst Richard and his brother Edward would have been the ones who lay cold and still. In that event the people would have toasted a Lancastrian victory, the men who had delivered them from the 'Evil brothers of York', those who in usurping King Henry's throne had started the war in the first place! Francis smiled, yes, he had to admit that the majority of Edward's policies were favoured by the common people, especially here in London, but ultimately that really didn't matter in the greater scheme of things. In Francis's honest opinion what these people longed for, more than anything else was a peaceful, strong and united government and much as he appreciated the crowds accolades, Francis had to admit that this was what they all now applauded. As he gazed towards Richard, who was riding in and out of the crowd waving to those who eager to get a better view of the proceedings, as Richard stooped down to shake hands with those who'd been fortunate enough to find a position closest to the procession, Francis laughed and decided that perhaps he wouldn't share his opinions with his friend, not on that day anyway!

Francis was not at all surprised when the crowds mood turned ugly, this as the litter which bore Margaret of Anjou turned into the street. In an instant cheers were replaced by boo's and insults as the French woman became the object of much derision. Francis who'd spent most of his adult life fighting Margaret and her followers had good cause to despise her. Nor could he have expected any mercy from this ruthless Frenchwoman had the tables been turned. That said, surprisingly, Francis felt strangely sorry for Henry's Queen. When one considered how things had turned out Margaret had, perhaps above all others, lost most. She had been forced to witness the destruction not only of her cause, but also that of her beloved son, Edward the Prince of Wales. In the days after the Battle of Tewkesbury, at the behest of King Edward, Margaret had been detained at Little Malvern Priory in Worcestershire. It was said that when she'd heard the news of her son's death, she'd collapsed into a stupor and had to be carried lifeless to Edward, who at the time was holding court at Coventry. Now Margaret silently sat upon a litter, her head bowed low. This Woman, renowned throughout all of Europe for both her strength of character and her resilience, clearly no longer had the will nor the strength to go on. Margaret had pinned all of her hopes and aspirations, not on her husband Henry, who was still a prisoner in the Tower, but on her son. With Edward's death she had nothing to continue living for. Thankfully, it seemed to Francis that Margaret was at least in a trance and, as such, she appeared immune to the crowds disdain for her. Not for the first time, Francis chided himself for his compassion, yet still he sighed. For this once fearsome woman, one whose great northern army had marched upon London only eleven years earlier and had such spread fear and panic amongst its citizens, was now little more than a shell. Francis sighed again as he wondered what the world now had in store for Margaret of Anjou. Saddened by the Queen's plight, Francis tried in vain to pacify the crowd who yelled abuse at Margaret and threw at her anything that they had to hand. Richard shouting to make himself heard over the commotion told Francis to,

'Let her be,' for,

'The people can't hurt her or get to her where she is, she's finished, as are those who chose to fight for her.'

When Francis continued to ride amongst the crowd in a futile attempt to quell them, impatient, Richard said,

'For goodness sake Francis, don't show her any pity for she'd have shown none to us given half a chance.'

Not unsurprisingly, Francis failed in his attempts to subdue the crowd and after a few minutes, fearing that he too might even be subjected to their hostility, he meekly returned to the cavalcade. Throughout their progress through the City, he did however allow himself the occasional sideways glance towards Margaret. He pitied her but also wondered if Richard was right to believe that Margaret would never again be in a position to do them harm, for her husband did still live.

It hadn't been easy for the victors. In the day's following Tewkesbury, news of the recent events that had circulated throughout the Kingdom had been both confusing and contradictory. Some had reported that the Lancastrians had been victorious and that King Edward had been killed, others said that both the Earl of Warwick and his brother Montagu still lived. They foretold that the Earl, at the head of a great army, would once again march upon the Capital. Consequently, there were rebellions in both Kent and Essex, these instigated by the Earl's cousin Richard, 'the bastard of Fauconberg', who seemed intent on spoiling the Yorkists triumphant return to their Capital. During the Barnet campaign, the Earl of Warwick had placed Fauconberg in command of his fleet and had instructed his cousin to prevent any reinforcement of the Yorkists by their Burgundian allies. Thus, the 'Bastard' had avoided both the battles of Barnet and Tewkesbury. When it had become obvious to Fauconberg that Burgundian aid for the Yorkists was purely financial, he had landed in Kent with men from the Earl's Calais garrison. The 'Bastard' had hoped to recruit an army, with which he could come to the aid of his cousin the Earl who, unbeknown to him, was at that point already dead. Worryingly, Fauconberg was soon joined by many men and he had marched on the capital at the head of what was by then quite a sizeable army. Moreover, in the immediate aftermath of Tewkesbury, King Edward short of gold with which to pay and victual his troops, had disbanded those of his army who had not already deserted or gone off in search of plunder. Thus, before he could return to the capital, the King had been forced, once again, to recruit a new army. Edward who had sent word of his victories to London, had asked that its citizens resist the rebels until he was able to return at the head of an army. Thankfully, both the Lord Mayor and the Aldermen, trusting Edward's word, had resisted Fauconberg's attempts to gain entry into the City. Many of the Bastard's men had been killed in the fighting that had ensued, this when the Earl of Essex had bravely and perhaps recklessly, led the men of the Tower's garrison out against him. Soundly defeated in the skirmish that had followed, Fauconberg had been forced to withdraw to the south of the river, a spot from where he'd ineffectually used his artillery against the Tower. Many amongst the rebel army had deserted, as did the prospect of any further plunder, as reports were received that King Edward was approaching at the head of an army that was reputed to number some 30,000 men! Francis smiled, apparently the only casualties of any note on the Yorkist side had been 50 head of Butcher Gould's oxen, cattle who were being grazed outside the Tower's walls. Beef that was being fattened for the Queen's table. Fauconberg's men had led away the unfortunate animals who'd become the very last casualties of the war, filling the bellies of those who'd been impudent enough to steal them! Ultimately it had been Richard and not his brother the King, who'd advanced on the Bastard's men and had finally received Fauconberg's submission on Blackheath. In truth the Earl's cousin had had no alternative but to seek terms, once all but his most loyal retainers had deserted him. Francis chuckled to himself, Fauconberg must have been bitterly disappointed when he'd finally come face to face with the meagre army with which both Richard and Francis had run him to ground!

As it was Richard, fresh from the executions that he'd overseen at Tewkesbury, had ruthlessly demanded Fauconberg's head. Fortunately for him, it appeared as if the Bastard had inherited all of that legendary 'Neville charm' and consequently Richard's hard line had been tempered by King Edward, who had pardoned the 'Bastard', as,

'Fauconberg has experience both on land and sea and I feel that he may well serve our purposes in the future.'

Surprisingly the normally intransigent Richard, had accepted Edward's decision without further argument. Later when Francis had suggested to his friend, who in recent months had become quite stubborn and dogmatic, that he would do well to pay more attention to the advice of others, especially one of Edward's experience and understanding, Richard had become furious, telling Francis to 'mind' what he said to him in the future, for he, 'Richard Duke of Gloucester, the Constable of England' listened to no man and it was 'the office of King' which he'd obeyed without question and not his Brother.

It seemed to Francis now that the wars were at an end, that none but the most hardened had the stomach to carry on with the butchery. Unfortunately, and surprisingly to Francis, who on many occasions had seen his friends 'kinder' side, Richard appeared to be one of those few and after their victories at Barnet and Tewkesbury, he'd resumed his role as Constable of England with relish, despatching with or without trial those Lancastrians who'd survived the fighting. Reluctantly, Richard had granted the King's pardon to Fauconberg, but judging from his friend's poor humour over the incident, Francis felt that it would not be long before the 'Bastard' would, like his cousin before him, suffer Richard's vengeance. On seeing Richard's expression as he'd issued the King's pardon to Fauconberg, sadly and for the briefest of moment, Francis had had a vision of a previous Constable with whom he'd had the misfortune to have dealings, the now very dead Earl of Worcester, John Tiptoft. Francis hadn't liked what he'd seen in Richard and could only hope that it'd been the Wars that had hardened his friend and that perhaps with a period of peace Richard would 'soften up' again. Thankfully during King Henry's re adeption, Tiptoft who'd been trying to escape England for his beloved Florence, had been captured by the Earl of Warwick. Francis couldn't help but smile, when he was a child his Grandmother had always said to him that everything came around 'full circle' in the end, and that everyone would get their 'just deserts', here was a perfect example of her precept. For John De Vere, the Earl of Oxford had finally got his revenge upon Tiptoft for the executions of both his father and his brother, although sadly, on this occasion Francis hadn't had the opportunity of witnessing Tiptoft's 'comeuppance' for himself. The Earl of Warwick, who himself had plenty of reasons for hating Tiptoft, had graciously given De Vere the 'honour' of executing Tiptoft. Those present at the 'Butcher's' execution had described it as quite a 'theatrical affair' and in a way one had to admire Tiptoft, who was said to have been defiant to the end and had died without complaint, his head, as per his last wishes, being cast off in three strokes, this in honour of the trinity! Now Francis could only pray that his friend wouldn't also earn a reputation as 'The Butcher of England'. He hoped that people would see Richard as he did, as an honest and forthright man, who was firm in his dealings with others. This firmness, Francis believed, brought on by necessity rather than desire, for in Francis's opinion, Richard was a man of his time, one who reacted to events, rather than being one who shaped them or who delighted in their horror.

Thankfully, Magaret was soon 'safely' deposited in the Tower and from there the cavalcade rode on to the Palace of Westminster, where the king was reunited with his Queen and his young heir, Edward of York. Gathering the infant boy up in his arms Edward turned to the crowd and holding the child aloft, declared,

'Your Kingdom's safe in Plantagenet hands, the true House of Royal blood. At long last both King Richard the second, bless his soul and my family have been avenged. Lancaster took that which they had no right to, and it is they now who must pay for their crime.'

Those gathered cheered as they'd never cheered before and deafened, Francis was forced to hide his head in his hands, to protect both his ears and to conceal the tears that were beginning to well up in his eyes. Feelings that were, Francis felt, understandable but were less than soldierly.

Much merriment and rejoicing followed, as one after another his subjects approached Edward and swore their allegiance to both the King and to the House of York. The brothers of York were showered with gifts of food and drink. Even Richard and Clarence were for the time being at least, able to put aside their differences and joining with their old enemies, Queen Elizabeth's Woodville relations, they toasted the King and wished him a 'long' and 'prosperous' reign. It was Francis who noticed that Richard, in contrast to the others., had been careful not to wish for peace, when Francis queried this, Richard replied,

'I'm my King's youngest brother and now he has his heir my only hope of continued advancement is that which can be gained through conflict.'

Francis disagreed with Richard. Times were changing and in his opinion, in this new England of theirs, there was as much to be gained through Politics as there was through War. Smiling Francis pointed out to Richard that he now had quite an opportunity. For the Earl of Warwick's death, without male issue, had created a political vacuum in the north, especially as King Edward still mistrusted the pro Lancastrian Earl of Northumberland. And Richard, in spite of his role in the Earl's destruction, was still 'much loved' by the 'northerners.' Richard could, Francis argued, if he was clever enough, carve himself out a 'northern palatinate,' whilst at the same time representing the King's interests in that area. Richard, who always seemed to have an answer for everything, had obviously thought long and hard about his future role within the present Government, he smiled,

'The Queen has enough politician's in her own family, she doesn't want any more on the scene to complicate thing's for her and her brood. The King took her side against that of his cousin and mentor the Earl of Warwick and look what happened to him! Do you truly believe that she'll not influence him in his future dealings with me. I'm the youngest son, I'll take what I'm given and be thankful for it, although in truth I fear that it won't be much. Francis I'm no fool, I can see that I'm only useful to my Brother as a soldier,' Richard as modest as ever smiled before he added, 'Although even I have to admit that I'm a damn good one at that, but if I'm to get anywhere in this world it's as a Soldier and not a Politician.'

Obviously noting the worried look on Francis's face Richard said,

'Don't worry Francis, I'll always find someone for us to fight. What about the Scottish and the French?'

Richard laughed and clapping Francis on the back added,

'For someone's got to reward them for their support for the House of Lancaster.'

It was extremely late when Francis at last managed to extricate himself from the banquet. Staggering back to his lodgings he dodged with difficulty the many people who still filled the City's streets. Despite the lateness of the hour and a mind befuddled by drink, Francis could still see that many people were out and about, stood around in groups, excitedly discussing recent events or celebrating the war's end.

Francis was billeted in an inn at Cheapside. Earlier he had declined Richard's kind offer of accommodation at Richard's London residence that, close to John of Gaunt's old palace at the Savoy, was ideally situated for access to the Palace of Westminster, the location of the festivities. It had been awkward for Francis to turn down his friend's offer and initially Richard had been quite insistent that Francis join him, for the two friend's had shared much over the past few weeks. Finally, Richard had taken 'no' for an answer, only once Francis had practically begged to be left alone and had lied that his wife Anne was due in the City at any time. He'd told Richard that he'd wanted to spend some time with his wife as they'd been parted for so long. In reality, Francis had not heard from Anne for quite sometime and all of his recent letters to Ravensworth had gone unanswered. At least now that the wars were over, if he was able to extricate himself from his comrades and the court, Francis would at last be able to travel north to Ravensworth, for a confrontation with his errant wife. And for once it was Francis who was in an extremely strong bargaining position. In his 'majority', a Lord in his own right and a member of the King's inner circle of friends, it was Francis who would now have the upper hand in any future dealings with his wife's family. Especially since it'd been Francis's father-in-law who had instigated the risings in the north that had led to Edward's deposition. The Fitzhughs were, and for sometime to come, would be, marginalised, this in spite of the fact that both Henry and his son Richard had recently received the King's pardon. In fact as one of the Duke of Gloucester's closest friends, it was Francis who would now be able to dictate to his father-in-law and on his return to Ravesworth, Francis, who was determined to continue where he'd left off, would make every effort to bring Henry's daughter to heel and he would, he hoped, at long last, bring her 'home' to Minster Lovel. Francis knew in his heart of hearts that he could not now win the love of his wife, but as divorce was practically unheard of amongst the ranks of the nobility, he would have to impose his will upon her. Francis who was not usually so cold hearted, could at least satisfy himself with the knowledge that he would not be the first husband to have had to do this.

Francis's plans for both an early escape northwards and for some much needed rest were soon frustrated however. Having retired late, Francis was just beginning to drift off into a deep sleep when he was woken, alarmed by repeated banging on his bedroom door. Struggling to work out if the noise was real or was part of a dream, Francis got out of bed and fumbled with the door to let in his visitor who, judging by how insistent the banging had become, seemed increasingly impatient to be admitted.

It was Richard. Francis rubbed his eyes. His head throbbed with fatigue and with a hangover that was even now beginning to set itself behind his eyes.

Francis swore.

'What the hell.....'

He was unable to complete his sentence as brushing him aside Richard strode into the room.

'There's no time to spare, there's work to be done at the Tower. I need you Francis you're the only one that I can trust to help me.'

Richard continued to explain himself as, perplexed, Francis continued to wipe the sleep from his eyes.

'We've got to be rid of Henry and it's got to be done tonight whilst the people are still very much on our side.'

Francis's thoughts turned at once to the old King. Many said that Henry, a man who was more interested in religion than in politics, now spent many of his waking hours engaged in acts of piety, praying alone at the shrine that he'd had installed within his lodgings at the Tower of London.

Forgetting himself Francis objected,

'No Richard, you can't have him killed. They say he's a Saint, no-one will ever forgive those who order his murder.'

Richard was terse in his answer.

'We're not having him killed by another'

Francis was shocked as Richard added grimly,

'It's us who are doing the killing, at the behest of my brother the King.'

Richard explained himself as Francis, mouth open, stood aghast.

'As the Captain of the tower Edward asked the Queen's brother to deal with the matter for him. But that coward merely threw himself at the King's feet and implored Edward not to ask such a thing of him. I'm afraid that when he's around his wife and her family Edward's weak, he wasn't able to order Rivers to carry out his orders'

Adding to Francis's discomfiture Richard smiled as he continued,

'Who alone do you think the King has turned to? Who alone can the King rely upon to carry out his wishes in this matter?'

Francis didn't need to ask Richard the answer to his question, for he already knew it. He sighed, and nodding towards his friend, he hurriedly began to pull on his clothes, as he did so thinking to himself, 'here we go again.' Sighing again, Francis wondered if he'd ever be free from his obligations towards his friend.

It was through dark and now strangely quiet streets that the pair slowly made their way to the Tower of London. Tired Francis tarried, for in truth he was reticent to become involved in such a crime. Francis could also sense that for once, even Richard seemed nervous.

For obvious reasons Richard was eager that they should not be seen in the immediate vicinity of the Tower, as they reached Tower Hill he quickened his pace and berated Francis for his 'dawdling'. On their arrival at the Tower, Lord Rivers met them at the guardhouse. This structure, which was situated in the middle of the moat, guarded the only access to the fortress via tower hill and the land ward side. Not surprisingly none of those present were interested in exchanging the normal pleasantries that were associated with such a meeting of gentlemen. With a few mumbling and unintelligible words, Rivers thrust the Tower's keys into Richard's outstretched hands and having done so retreated back towards his private lodgings, which fortunately for him were situated in the White Tower, well away from the Wakefield Tower, the location of Henry's private apartments and what was to be the scene of his murder. As Rivers hurried away from them, Francis could clearly hear him sobbing to himself, bemoaning the fact that he'd been party to such a crime. Left alone, both Francis and Richard nervously eyed each other, both worried that Rivers' ranting would alert others to their plan.

Francis didn't like the Queen's brother, one who had a reputation for cowardice, a trait which neither Francis nor Richard could abide. Although still young Rivers had advanced far. This due not to his abilities, but as a result of his blood relationship with his sister. Francis had often described Rivers as having 'rat like features' and as the Queen's brother scurried away, Francis felt only revulsion for him. In an instant Francis recalled much of that which had been said of Rivers in those whispers and rumours, which had circulated throughout the Court since their return from Tewkesbury. River's had received much in the way of praise on account of his so called exploits in driving Fauconberg and his men from the City. Francis, on the other hand, had heard it said that although the Tower's garrison had taken part in the engagement, their Captian hadn't. The men of the Tower having been commanded by the Earl of Essex who, despite his previous loyalty to the Lancastrians, had led the garrison against Fauconberg's men in an action that had ultimately saved the day. This all going on whilst the 'Captain of the Tower', Rivers had remained in hiding with his sister the Queen and her children. Unfortunately, none at court had dared to tell the King the truth and consequently it was Rivers who was rewarded and Essex who was not! Furthermore, try as he might, Francis could not think of any engagements in which Rivers had actually ever been involved! Francis shuddered, River's was one who was happy to share in the victories of others but was not willing to risk anything in contributing towards them.

Both Richard and Francis had different reasons for knowing the layout of the Tower's various rooms and lodgings. As such, they had no difficulty in making their way through dimly lit and deserted passages and both soon arrived at the Wakefield tower where the old King was 'detained',

'In honourable captivity.'

Despite the passage of time, Francis felt physically sick as he discovered that the fortress had changed little since his last visit to it.

Crossing over the small enclosed footbridge that led from the outer wall to the Wakefield Tower, Francis shivered. He'd taken this self same route all of those years ago, when both he and his father had visited John De Vere. This after both Aubrey and his father had been subjected to much torture in the days that had preceded their executions. As both Francis and Richard turned the corner at the end of the corridor, it soon became apparent that they needn't have disturbed Rivers after all, for Henry's lodgings were insecure, his door, slightly ajar. Surprisingly despite the lateness of the hour a light shone brightly within. Almost as if, Francis thought, that Henry was expecting them! Without knocking on the door or requesting to be admitted into the old King's presence, as was the custom, Richard burst into the chamber. If he'd hoped that by the manner of his entrance he'd have provoked a violent and aggressive response from it's occupant and that this would have somehow have justified his subsequent actions, Richard was soon disappointed. Henry of Lancaster knelt at the altar that he'd had built in the corner of the Tower. As Francis gazed around the room he could see that this shrine was the only item in the room that was personal to the old King. Apparently it had been the only thing that Henry had ever asked for and it had been added on Edward orders, this as the Yorkist King had been keen to lessen the impact of imprisonment upon his cousin. Otherwise the room was as it had been when Francis had seen it last. The chamber was rudely furnished and in addition to the altar, Henry's room contained only a small wooden bed with a straw mattress and a small desk that was situated beneath the heavily leaded window, which overlooked the 'water gate', the entrance to the Tower from the river. A small fire burned in the hearth and candles flickered and struggled to remain alight in the draughts that pervaded throughout the room. Francis knew that the prevailing wind came straight down the river from the direction of the sea and that night, blowing hard, it easily found each and every chink and crack in the rooms apertures.

Henry could not have failed to have heard them enter as their boots thumped and clattered on the bare wooden floor boards, sounds which echoed and reverberated throughout the emptiness of the chamber. Yet the old King remained quite still. Henry remained kneeling, his head bowed in silent prayer, as Richard followed closely by Francis strode into his room. They were almost upon him before at long last the old man slowly turned to face them. It was Henry who spoke first, he was calm.

'Who has my cousin sent to send me at from this world.'

Richard replied at once and Henry, who up until that point had seemed quiet composed, appeared for a brief moment to be taken aback as Richard replied with confidence.

'Only the brother of a King could carry out such a deed.'

After a few moments Henry, shocking Francis with his forthrightness, responded angrily to Richard.

'Even the brother of a King hasn't the right to take the life of one who has been anointed by God'.

The old man's voice, firm and unfaltering, contradicted both the slight and rudely clothed frame from whence it came and the earlier impressions that Francis had had of Henry.

Both Francis and Richard were taken aback.

At last Richard advanced again saying.

'You should thank us. Your son, if he was in fact your legitimate heir and not another Beaufort bastard, is dead. Your House is finished. Your grandfather usurped the throne from my forbears. We merely take back what is ours and now we choose to punish you for your family's misdeeds.'

He spat out his final words at Henry,

'Cousin, do not expect any pity from me.'

Henry replied with a self assurance, which surprised Francis, for all present knew that the old man would not survive the night,

'I forgive you for your petulance, as I forgive you for your actions. You're both clearly young and have little experience of life. I hope for your sakes that God can forgive you for this cold and brutal murder. A crime committed at his altar upon consecrated ground.'

A deeply religious man himself, Richard was silenced by the old man's words.

Perceptive, Henry pressed home his advantage.

'Yes, my grandfather usurped the throne from Richard Plantagenet,'
He smiled,
'Is it not ironic that another of that name has been sent to avenge this misdeed.'

He sighed.

'But you, Duke Richard, would do well to ponder upon the misfortune and misery that this throne has brought to my house. My grandfather, my father and my son have all died prematurely.'

Henry smiled again,

'And so it seems must I.'

'But be assured my young Cousin, to kill God's truly anointed is no small task and all I ask, for your own sake, is that you take time to consider your actions wisely.'

Francis was surprised by, but secretly approved of the old man's bravery. He can't hope to gain the upper hand physically so he's taking the moral high ground, Francis thought. He admired how a person apparently so weak could make this seemingly easy task so difficult, especially for Richard, who'd had much experience of death. On any other day Richard would have despatched his quarry without question, however, Henry's words seemed to strike him harder than any blow from an axe or sword. Richard took a step backwards and seemed for a moment nonplussed, he opened his mouth but was unable to reply.

Francis was once again surprised by the 'Saintly' Henry, who clearly resigned to his fate, even went so far as to forgive his killers!

'I know what you must do and I accept that I can no longer be allowed to live in this world. My time has come. Understand that I'm content to die and I'm am at peace in the knowledge that I go to a far better place than this. To my God, to be at his side in his Kingdom. I never wanted this burden of Kingship. Let those who covet the crown take it for it is a poisoned chalice. All I ever wanted was to serve God in whichever way that he saw fit. If by dying I will bring an end to these wars then I die happily, for my passing in this way will save countless lives.'

Henry sighed as he added.

'I just hope that God can forgive your actions as readily as I do.'

Francis knew his friend well and Richard had a profound faith in God. As Francis studied his friend he guessed that Richard, who was silent and appeared deep in thought, must have been seriously considering how his actions of that night might impinge upon this own future.

Francis, whose loyalty to his friend meant more to him than anyone or anything else, knew at once what he had to do, no matter how unpalatable this may be. All present understood what had to be done, all that remained was for it to be decided how it was to be done. Francis felt that as long as Henry died, regardless of how this came about, their mission would be completed and the wars would finally be at an end. If Richard could not risk the effect that this murder may or may not have on him and the future of his family, then Francis knew that he'd have to step forward and act on behalf of his friend.

None had time to think or act as Francis, side stepping the old man, seized the mace which Richard held limply at his side. In a single stroke Francis brought the heavy weapon crashing down upon Henry's skull that, bare and unprotected, exploded in a haze of blood, brain and bone. This action, which roused Richard from his thoughts, sent the old man crashing to the floor. Now far less eloquent, Henry of Lancaster gurgled and his eyes rolled back into his head as his body strove for life that, with every moment, was seeping from his body, this as his blood flowed freely from the open wound upon his skull. Francis gagged and vomited as Henry died. Francis had seen many people at the point of death, yet this passing seemed somehow different and it had a profound effect on Francis. The saintly Henry died without dignity, thrashing around in a pool of his own blood and brain matter as, fitting, his body continued shuddering and shaking long after life had left it. Yet once Henry was still and motionless it seemed as if a calm resonance once again descended upon his body. Horrified, Francis could see that Henry's bloody and lifeless corpse, had actually developed a smile upon its face.

Neither Richard nor Francis lingered long in the Tower. The deed was done. Others could tidy up the mess, as it is they who would have to present the late King's corpse to the populace and in doing, so it was they who would have to attempt to explain what had happened to him. Edward had said that he'd wanted it known that Henry had died of natural causes, of a 'melancholy' bought about when he'd heard the news of his son's death. As he hurried from the Tower, trying in vain to clean the blood from his clothing and hands, Francis worried, as he wondered how this could be achieved. In his minds eye he once again pictured the startling effect that the mace had had on Henry's thin skull.

Nothing more was said as the friends parted company outside Francis's accommodation. Francis knew that Richard would be ashamed of his inactivity, but as his friend embraced him even tighter than was customary, Francis could tell what effect his actions had had upon Richard by relieving him of his burden. That night Francis enjoyed little sleep, he rose early on the following morning bleary eyed and feeling a strange sense of doom. None in the City were surprised by the news that the old King had died. What did surprise many however, although none dared to say it, was the official account of the old King's death. That Henry's demise had been brought about by 'the displeasure that he'd felt on hearing of the fate of his son and heir'. As Henry's body was displayed for all to see, many people's suspicions as to the true nature of the unfortunate man's death were confirmed, for Henry's corpse bled upon the litter on which it was lain.

Francis could not bear to pay his respects to one he had murdered in cold blood. In the days that followed, he spent much of his time in silent prayer as he sought to atone for this sin. He found neither sleep by night nor peace by day and soon began to doubt that any amount of prayer would achieve absolution. He cried as he considered that he could never dare confess such a thing to any priest.

Henry of Lancaster was buried, without ceremony, at Chertsey. Many who'd criticised him in life came to worship him in death. They called upon the Church of Rome to canonise this saintly figure. Many miracles were reported at Henry's tomb, it was even said that to touch the late King's sarcophagus was an excellent cure for headaches! In contrast, Francis received no such relief. He constantly worried that the consequences of his actions would return later to haunt both he and his family. Often in his dreams, Francis was visited by Henry's expressionless corpse. On such occasions Francis would waken, shrieking and sweating from yet another fitful sleep, why did Henry appear to him in such a way. Had the old King not said to Francis that he'd forgiven his killer?

Chapter 18
February 1472. The Royal Palace of Sheen.

'These three brothers, the King and the two Dukes, are possessed of such surpassing talents, that if only they were able to live without dissension's, such a threefold cord could never be broken without the utmost difficulty'.

The Chief Justice's sentiments were shared by all present. Francis however smiled, for he knew the brothers of York intimately. Edward and his two brothers were both stubborn and obstinate in equal measure and as such Francis gauged, with some certainty, they would never truly be *'able to live'* together *without dissension's'*. The chief justice together with the rest of the King's council had gathered in the great hall at the Palace of Sheen. All were there to assist the brothers to come to some form of settlement that would be acceptable to all, so that, at long last they could rule the Kingdom as one united political force.

In the aftermath of the Earl of Warwick's failed insurrection and Clarence's admitted complicity in it, one could be forgiven for believing that Clarence, for the time being at least, would have lain low and kept out of the limelight. Surprisingly this was not case and Clarence continued on as he had done before, jealously complaining as various titles and offices were bestowed upon his younger brother, Richard. Rewards for the young Duke's unswerving loyalty and service to the crown, which contrasted sharply with Clarence's treachery. Richard, who richly deserved these benefices, had been stunned when the King, surprisingly sympathetic to Clarence's representations, had given them a semblance of reasonableness when he'd convened this meeting, to debate what should be done!

One had to admit that Richard had fared extremely well since he'd helped Edward to his victories at Tewkesbury and Barnet, having recently been granted the Office of the 'Great Chamberlain of England', a title that was previously held by Clarence. This Richard added to his recent promotions to both Constable and Admiral of England, together with all of the wealth and kudos that went with them. But Clarence had complained bitterly, pointing out that he too had fought for the King during the recent campaign, albeit it in a lesser role. Thus each of Richard's new appointments brought more 'jealous mutterings' from Clarence. Matters had, however, been brought to a head when both Francis and Richard had recently paid the Clarence's a visit. Well, to say 'the Clarence's' wouldn't be entirely true. Francis smiled as he remembered their coup, which had seen them storm Clarence's London residence in an attempt to seize Edward of Lancaster's widow, Ann, who had been hidden there. Ann Neville was the youngest daughter of the Earl of Warwick, and Richard had wanted her for his wife. Francis knew that Richard didn't really love Ann, for Richard didn't really know her, although they had spent some time together whilst children at Middleham. But what he did know was that Ann, along with Clarence's wife Isabel, was the heiress to possibly what was the greatest estate ever amassed. Assets of the Earl of Warwick which consisted of many lands and titles and included both his Countess's Beachamp inheritance along with his Neville inheritance. Unfortunately there were a number of slight problems for Richard. Firstly he had to locate the girl, then he had to 'acquire' her, then he had to marry her and finally he would then have to deal with those legitimate claims on the estate held by both Clarence's wife, Isabelle, the elder of the two sisters and also that of Warwick's widow, the Countess, who still lived.

But as always, Richard threw himself into the project with his usual 'never say die attitude, laughing as he'd explained to Francis,

'First I'll take the Lady and then I'll settle the division of the spoils.'

Until his own experience of marriage Francis had believed in love and previously would have objected to his friend's sentiments. Now, after all he'd been through, it seemed to Francis quite reasonable that the brother of a King should take such a wife and with her, a dowry that included many lands and titles. It also seemed quite appropriate to Francis that the bulk of the Earl's inheritance should come to Richard, for Richard had effectively been brought up by the late Earl and had, in his time at Middleham, come to look upon the Earl almost as a father. Until, that is, he'd finally and reluctantly been forced to choose between the Earl and his elder brother Edward. That said it was perhaps ironic that Richard, who above all others had been responsible for the Earl's destruction, would 'acquire' the Earl's legacy! Francis smiled as he wondered what the Earl would have made of it. The person who'd been responsible for his own undoing, inheriting his vast wealth! Lands and titles that the 'Kingmaker' had spent a lifetime amassing, be it by marriage, alliances or by conquest. Francis smiled again as he considered the paradox, riches that had been acquired for the benefit of the Earl's family, which would now go to those who'd brought about his death. Francis chuckled to himself as in his minds eye he pictured the Earl, frowning and pacing up and down the corridors of his private chambers at Middleham, as he was wont to do, ranting and raving about those things that displeased him.

As it was both Francis and Richard together with a number of their armed retainers had descended upon the Duke's London residence, where Ann Neville had been hidden by Clarence after he'd heard rumours that Richard would have her for his wife. Luckily, at the time Clarence had been away and Ann's captors had soon capitulated at the site of Richard Duke of Gloucester, sword in hand at the head of a band of ruffians! Ann, now a widow at only fifteen, had been as Francis had remembered her from their time together at Middleham. The Earl of Warwick's youngest daughter, pale and slight of figure, plain in her looks but of a calm countenance.

'Quite different from her sister,'

Francis thought, as he compared Ann to Isabelle, her older sister, who was now old before her time, her many disagreeable qualities worsening, if that were at all possible, through her marriage to Clarence.

Francis smiled, both the Duke and Duchess of Clarence seemed suitably matched, unlike both Richard and Anne, who were in Francis's opinion, poles apart. Ann the quiet and unassuming one and Richard, who it seemed, had always got something to say, who was both forthright and determined.

Ann, who had not seemed best pleased to see them, had not complained as they'd disguised her as a maid and hurried her away. Initially Richard had chosen to hide his fiancee in sanctuary at St Martins church. From there, when it was safe to do so, he had had both her and her mother the Duchess of Warwick conveyed to Middleham, where Francis's wife and his mother-in-law were waiting to make her ready for her wedding. The marriage was to take place as soon as a Papal dispensation arrived from Rome, this required as both Richard and Ann were first cousins. On hearing of the kidnapping, it was said that Clarence had been incensed and had demanded that the King punish his younger Brother. Richard shrugging off Clarence's protestations, had challenged Clarence to make him give up his bride to be, for everyone knew that at that time Clarence hadn't the means to oppose Richard. As it was Clarence, who was said to have become increasingly alarmed as it had dawned upon him that he may have to share the Earl's of Warwick's inheritance with Richard, was limited to making a number of hollow threats towards Richard, one of which, that particularly amused Richard, was that Richard 'may have the Lady but he wouldn't have her lands!'

Francis had never liked Clarence and what irked him even more was the fact that this present crisis had further delayed his return home. Francis had, without success, tried to convince Richard that he should be the one to convey Ann to Middleham, but his friend would have none of it, arguing that at that time he'd needed all of his friends with him, for when the inevitable showdown with his brother finally came. Much to Francis's consternation, grinning Richard had added,

'And if you leave Court who will be my scapegoat should the King side with my brother over the kidnapping of the Lady Ann.'

Francis, yet again, would have to wait to see his own wife Anne, who had still had the audacity to refuse to visit Francis in either London or his suggested compromise at Minster Lovel.

Francis's lip curled as he studied Clarence who was sat on the King's left. Francis hated the man, whose physical features, which had once been considered attractive, had become increasingly unpleasant as had his character, as Clarence had grown both older and bitter. This to the extent that Francis now wondered if Clarence's expression was set in a permanent scowl.

Francis smiled as Clarence's frown deepened, this as Richard, who had risen from his seat on the King's right, launched into an eloquent and reasoned argument as he attempted to justify his right to have a 'wife of' his 'own choosing'.

'The fact remains that both of my brothers took wives of their own choosing. My brother the King in defiance of his Royal Council and my brother the Duke in contravention of the express orders of the King!'

Richard argued, adding,

'Am I to be judged by different standards to those employed in the question of my brother's marriages?'

Francis couldn't help but smile as grinning Richard said,

'And how can I help it if the person for whom I have such feelings happens to be the heir to such a fortune. I say so be it, for who am I to challenge that which fate has in store for me.'

Shrugging and turning away from the audience, Richard addressed the King, who by that time was also smiling.

'And if some portion of these lands and titles become mine by right of such a marriage, then so be it.'

As Richard returned to his seat many in the hall muttered in agreement. Clarence who was clearly incensed by Richard's arguments, rose from his seat, shouting.

'He may have the lady but he'll only have the lands over my dead body.'

Francis smiled, he'd heard this comment countless times over the previous few weeks, couldn't Clarence think of anything more original to say?

Unfortunately for Clarence his outburst failed to have its desired effect upon Edward, who up until that point had listened patiently to all of those representations made. The King who wasn't known for his patience at the best of times, had clearly lost what little he had, as Clarence sat down the King rose up out of his seat and assuming his full height he brought his staff crashing down to the floor, crying,

'I'll have no more of this.'

The King's voice echoed and reverberated throughout the hall and none dared to move, least of all interrupt him.

Having gathered his composure Edward continued,

'I am the King. It is I who will decide who Richard marries and it is I who will decide who will have a share of the Earl of Warwick's fortune. Must I remind you all that the Earl's countess still lives and in Law, the Earl's Beauchamp inheritance, that which came to him through his mariage to her, belongs to her. And if I chose to ask parliament to attaint the Earl for his treason against me, then in that event all of his Neville lands and titles will revert to the Crown, me. Brother's you'd both do well to leave this matter to me, for you'll have me and me alone to thank should either of you get anything out of this.'

Turning to Clarence Edward said,

'Brother I know that you would be King in my place. Anyone else would have had your head by now. Do not presume to tell me what I can or cannot do, I will deal with this matter as I see fit, you Sir should be satisfied that you are still able to draw breath.'

Turning to Richard Edward said,

'Yes I agree Richard, it would be hypocritical of me to impose a marriage of my own choosing upon you, especially after you've risked so much for me, you have my blessing to choose whichever wife you wish.'

Smiling Edward added 'But please take it from someone who knows, make your choice with care, for as well as riches wives can bring much trouble and marriages, once made, cannot be undone.'

The room erupted to the sound of male laughter, this as all present no doubt considered their own marital situation. Francis smiled and with a less than complimentary image of Queen Elizabeth in his minds eye, he wondered if in saying what he did, Edward too, was reflecting upon his own marriage.

Adjourned, it was only after a number of hours that the meeting was reconvened and then both Edward and his council preceded to carve up those lands and titles that had previously been held by the Earl of Warwick and his allies. The king, despite its illegality, 'requested' that those present, who were to sit at Westminster in the forthcoming parliament, were to ratify his judgements and were to make them law. In a society that was ruled by men, the legitimate claims of the Earl's widow were therefore overlooked. Surprisingly Clarence, who after the King's outburst had clearly expected to gain little from his ruling, was granted much, this predominantly at the expense of Richard. Clarence was given Richard's post of chamberlain of England and was also formally created both the Earl of Warwick and of Salisbury. Ultimately however, Richard was not too disappointed, for he accepted, with gratitude, the Earl of Warwick's northern lands, which included both his castles at Middleham and at Sheriff Hutton.

It was Francis who was disappointed, for he remembered that it'd been he who had suggested to Richard that he might try to create a Northern Palatinate for himself. But after the meetings conclusion, as Richard's close circle of followers all stood around discussing its outcome, it was clear to Francis that Richard now credited another with the idea. Francis had just been introduced to Richard's new lawyer friend, William Catesby. Smiling Richard nodded towards Catesby as he explained to Francis,

'The titles and lands that Clarence now has are piecemeal and are scattered throughout the country,'

Patting Catesby on the back Richard added,

'I, on the other hand, have all that I came for and more, those Neville lands in the north will enable me to create my own Duchy, far away from London and the interference of the Queen and my brothers. The King must allow me to rule these lands independently and as I see fit, for I'm the only one who can keep both the northerners in check and the Scots out of the Kingdom.'

Catesby, smiling, spoke with the confidence and smoothness of one associated with his profession.

'Perhaps now the Duke of Gloucester will recognise that on occasions one can gain more from diplomacy than one can from a headlong confrontation.'

Francis bit his lip, as laughing Richard replied,

'Yes all right, you win this time Catesby.'

Richard excused himself.

'I'm not a man of words but of actions, but even I can now see that it would do me no harm at all to have men of learning amongst my friends and retainers.'

Francis was beginning to dislike Catesby, but even he had to admit that the lawyer had got a way with words, with eloquence Catesby replied to Richard on all of their behalfs,

'My Lord, you do yourself a great disservice. Today you spoke with a confidence and a manner that would not be out of place in the highest court in the land. sire, we're all happy to serve you.'

Perplexed Francis queried,

'I thought you were Hastings man.'

He said, referring to the Lord who'd financed Catesby's education and who had introduced him into the Order of Templars. Surely it was Hastings who Catesby should serve and it was his interests that the young lawyer was meant to support in Parliament where he sat as the member for the midlands.

Catesby said nothing to either ingratiate himself with Francis or to change Francis's opinion of his profession.

'I have much to thank Lord Hastings for. Without the benefit of his patronage I would not be where I am today.'

The lawyer smiled as he added.

'That said, I feel that I am now ready to move up in the World.'

Turning to Richard Catesby said,

'And it seems as if my Lord of Gloucester has much more to offer me than Hastings.'

Chuckling, Richard patted Catesby on the back as he replied,.

'And Lord Hastings doesn't need to know whose employing you now.'

Once Catesby had left them, Francis, worried, turned to Richard and taking him by the arm led him to one of the quieter corners of the hall.

Whispering, he advised caution.

'Believe me Richard, these Templars are not to be trusted,'

Richard shrugged off Francis's concerns.

'Don't worry Francis, I pay well and besides that, I know what Catesby and his cronies have been up to, what I know about William Catesby is enough to hang him twice over. No, now he's my man he'll be my eyes both at Court and at Hasting's residence.'

Still concerned, Francis implored Richard,

'Please don't trust these people Richard, they'll sell us down the river as soon as anyone else.'

Richard smiled.

'But do you not see how useful they can be to us in the meantime? They say that Hastings shares a bed with the King, to know what he is thinking is to know what Edward thinks. If I am to spend much of my time in the north I need as many spies as possible at court. Both the Queen, her relatives and my brother Clarence would delight in my downfall. I need to know when they hope to move against me, for I'm sure that they will, then I can be the one who strikes first. Presently I am in the King's favour, but how long this will last I cannot say.'

Richard's suspicions both upset and scared Francis whose own future was now inextricably linked to that of his friend.

Richard seemed to sense his friends disquiet.

'Don't worry Francis, when we've established our northern empire even the King himself won't have the power to move against us,'

He smiled as he added.

'Remember the last time that Edward went north with an army, he lost his kingdom.'

Francis felt reassured as he recalled how he and his father-in-law, at the behest of the Earl of Warwick, had raised rebellion in Yorkshire, thereby drawing the King, a southerner, northwards where he was soon exposed and abandoned by his troops and was forced to seek refuge abroad. Northerners had a fearsome reputation and were renowned for there loyalty. Francis, who'd been brought up in the Cotswolds but had, since his father's death spent much time in the north, knew these people well and he knew that in choosing the men of the North, Richard had chosen his future allies well. Francis sighed. It seemed to him that for as long as he could remember, death and danger had been his all too constant companions. Even now, despite the fact that the Wars were over, when one considered all of those various affinities who sought power and influence, Francis found it extremely difficult to imagine a world without these companions.

Chapter 19
Late February 1478. London.

To be fair, life for Francis had been quite uneventful in the years that had followed their victory at Tewkesbury. In contrast to Francis's, things had been extremely busy for Richard, this as he'd set about creating his palatinate in the north of England. That said, throughout the intervening years, away from both the hustle and bustle of the Capital and from the intrigue at the King's court, Richard had lived in relative peace and as a consequence he'd prospered. This, in spite of the odd Scottish raid across the border, which Richard, as the King's representative in the Northern marches, was expected to deal with. In stark contrast to Richard's rise in stature, the nature and rapidity of the Duke of Clarence's fall from grace, had left even Francis both breathless and perplexed. In Clarence's downfall, England had witnessed the undoing of one of the country's greatest and most powerful magnates. And what an inglorious end! In certain circumstances one could be forgiven for finding the whole incident quite amusing. Clarence drowned in a butt of his favorite tipple, Malmsey wine! Amusing, that is, as long as one hadn't been present to witness the execution first hand. Francis smiled, it had been Clarence's preferred means of execution and ultimately it had been the only concession that King Edward had granted to his brother. Francis chuckled to himself as relived the event in his minds eye. How Clarence, right up until the very last minute, had expected to be pardoned, trusting that Edward would, 'Come to his senses' and would rescind the death warrant and as he had done so on countless occasions in the past, would forgive his errant brother for his sins. Francis smiled as he wondered if in choosing the means of his death, Clarence had been expecting clemency all of the time! Or had he felt that to drown in a barrel of one's favorite wine, whilst not being the most noble or honourable of deaths, would at least have been relatively painless.

As with most things in life, the reality of the situation had been anything but that which had been envisaged. Francis shuddered as he recalled how the King's brother, previously so arrogant and aloof, had been dragged kicking and screaming from his bed. How Clarence, stubbornly refusing to walk, had been carried to his death. How he'd been plunged face forwards into the butt of wine, this without either ceremony or prayer. Nor had the death been quick. Francis knew this because it had been he who had forced the oak lid down onto the barrel and it had been he who'd held it in place. All this whilst Clarence's flailing limbs, with increasing desperation, had vainly attempted to dislodge it.

Francis smiled, it seemed to him as if, right up until the night of his death Clarence had not taken the matter at all seriously. With good reason Clarence had doubted the King's resolve in finally calling him to account for his misdemeanors. Clarence could, Francis felt, have easily been forgiven for his belief in his brother's compassion. For Edward had pardoned him on countless occasions in the past and for far more serious allegations than these. But this time there had been a number of subtle differences; Firstly, the charges had been lain against Clarence by both the Queen and her Woodville relations and although these allegations paled into insignificance when compared to Clarence's past 'indiscretions', the relationship between the accusers and the King, had ensured that Edward had been forced to take them extremely seriously; Secondly, Parliament had supported Clarence's impeachment for treason. But then again why wouldn't they have? It was after all, 'packed' with Woodville retainers all of whom could be expected to 'tow their parties line'; And finally and perhaps most importantly, Richard had decided at long last that Clarence was becoming far too dangerous to be allowed to go on living. On this occasion Clarence had fatally underestimated the combined effect that both the Queen and Richard had upon the King. It was, Francis felt, quite ironic that one who'd made war against his King, one who'd openly questioned Edward's legitimacy, one who was perhaps the greatest magnate of the realm and who was third in line to the throne, would finally be utterly destroyed by dubious charges brought against him by the Woodvilles, A family of lowly birth, albeit with the support of his younger Brother!

Shaking his head Francis wondered, at what point had Clarence finally began to realise that his time had come?

Was it when he was arrested for treason and placed in the Tower pending trial?

Was it after Parliament, having impeached him, had asked that the King sign a warrant for his execution?

Was it when he was dragged partly clothed from his bed in the dead of night?

Was it when he was manhandled without ceremony to the scene of his execution?

Or was it when he'd been plunged face downwards, kicking and screaming into a barrel of what had up until that point been his favorite beverage?

Francis smiled again they'd never truly know the answer to this question, for now Clarence lay dead!

Although Francis felt no pity for Clarence, for in truth he'd always hated him, he had at least begun to understand him. Francis knew that throughout Clarence's adult life, due in part to deficiencies in Clarence's own character, as well as the way in which King Edward had spoilt him and had repeatedly forgiven him, that Clarence had come not only to anticipate leniency from his brother, but to expect it. Francis laughed out loud, as he pictured in his mind's eye the look on Clarence's face as they'd roughly taken hold of him, an expression that had told them in no uncertain terms that he, the Duke of Clarence, a Prince of York and the King's brother, would have his revenge upon them for 'this outrage'.

'Once' that is, 'Edward has come to his senses'.

Sadly for Clarence, on this occasion the King had not come to his senses and as a consequence of this Clarence now lay dead, mourned by none, for his wife Isabel had pre deceased him, having died in childbirth some two years earlier. Clarence had left an infant son, another Edward, who would, Francis presumed, now became yet another Earl of Warwick. But this child, who was rumoured to be a 'simpleton', neither knew nor cared for a father whom he'd only seen infrequently. And now Francis, who had to admit that when it came to children he was quite tenderhearted, feared for the child. This because of Clarence's allegations in respect of King Edward's illegitimacy, as a result of which, the child now faced a dangerous and uncertain future, Francis sighed, that is of course if the boy had any future at all!

As he was wont to do, Francis once again tried to rationalise those events that had led to Clarence's startling and unexpected decline. One had to admit that Clarence had faced many such crisis's in the past and had not only survived them, but seemed to have flourished in spite of them. But this time however things had been quite different. Francis believed that on this occasion there had been a number of issues, which taken in isolation may not have had such a dramatic effect, but together had ensured that Clarence's downfall was practically inevitable. Yes on this occasion the Queen and her relatives had sought Clarence's death, but when Richard, who was in London on one of his increasingly rare visits, had not only failed to act on Clarence's behalf, but had also actively sought Clarence's execution, it had, Francis felt, been the last nail in Clarence's coffin.

Many argued that Clarence had died because Richard, when he'd had the opportunity to do so, had failed to intervene on his brother's behalf. Francis knew that this was only partially true, for Richard had gone further than mere inaction and behind the scenes it had been he who had actively plotted the Duke's downfall. In private, Richard had wholeheartedly supported Clarence's impeachment. Indeed when Richard had heard that the charges had been lain upon his Brother, he'd immediately traveled to London to ensure that this time they'd stick and that this time Clarence would not, once again,

'Wriggle free.'

Surprisingly Richard, who'd seen little of the Lovel's in recent years, had asked both Francis and his wife to accompany him to the Capital. A journey that was made ostensibly to attend the marriage of Edward's youngest son Richard Duke of York, to Anne Mowbray, heiress to the Dukedom of Norfolk.

Richard had surprised Francis when he'd ridden the short distance from Middleham to Ravensworth to meet up with his 'old friend', apparently to discuss the arrangements for the trip. Initially, Francis had been quite bemused, for Richard had been promising to visit them for quite sometime, yet previously, for one reason or another, he'd canceled at the last minute. Francis smiled as he recalled that Richard's real motive for their visit to London had only finally become clear to him, after his friend had had the opportunity of speaking to him in private. This as the two friends had ridden up into the north pennines, supposedly to enjoy a day's hunting. Whilst he'd been at Ravensworth Richard had left Sir John Conyers, who was now the head of Richard's household at Middleham, with the unenviable task of making the necessary arrangements for the transfer of the Duke of Gloucester's court, from Yorkshire to London. As they'd both been saddling up their horses and had been anticipating a great days hunting, Francis had remarked that Conyers, who also enjoyed his sport, would have loved to have joined him, laughing Richard had replied, 'Privileges of rank, and anyway I need Sir John to organise the men.' This had confused Francis, who hadn't understood why in peacetime Richard felt the need to go to London had the head of his own private army!

Once they were well away from Ravensworth Castle, all had at last, become clear to Francis. Confiding in his friend, Richard had told Francis the real reason for their proposed trip to Edward's court. This was not, as Francis had been led to believe, to attend the celebrations that were to accompany the betrothal of the King's younger son, but was to enable them both to preside over the 'judicial murder of the Duke of Clarence.' At the time Francis had silently chided himself, for he should have known that something was afoot, when some days earlier Richard had sent word that he was going to visit them at

Ravensworth and at the time had asked that Francis, should in 'all haste, Gather together as many armed retainers as possible for the journey southwards.'

As he'd finally disclosed his plans to Francis, no doubt expecting Francis's unquestioning support, Richard had said, 'We'll need as many men as possible. For my brother must be found guilty of these crimes.' Francis, who in a way was quite upset that Richard, whom he'd not seen for quite some time, had seemingly taken his support for granted, could only stand and stare at his friend, aghast at this unexpected turn of events. As if they hadn't enough already to seek forgiveness for, now it seemed that Richard intended to commit the crime of fratricide! Failing to notice Francis's misgivings, Richard had continued,

'My Brother still has many supporters, we must go to London with sufficient troops to ensure that none will dare to move against us in any attempt to save him.'

Francis, who'd been both surprised and confused by Richard's resolve had asked why at that point in time Richard had decided to 'move' against Clarence.

Laughing Richard had exclaimed,

'Francis you've been in that backwater Ravensworth for far too long my friend.'

Becoming serious Richard had explained to Francis that the King's health was failing and that he had it on 'good authority' that in the event of Edward's death Clarence would resurrect his claim to the throne, 'to the detriment of them all.'

Francis had to admit that at that point, having not spent any meaningful time with Richard for quite a number of years, he'd noticed quite a change in his friend, who it seemed had now become quite 'the statesman.'

Much to Francis's amazement this 'new Richard' had even been willing to openly criticise Edward's government.

Sighing Richard had said that it appeared to him as if 'Edward's ambitions,' were limited to 'the number of whores and mistresses that he can bed, or the volume of the food and drink that he can consume at one sitting.'

Not waiting for any reply from Francis, Richard had described how the King, due to 'his excesses', had grown old before his time.

Richard had shocked Francis when he'd told him that he'd been told that Edward's physicians had warned the King that, unless he changed his ways, he would die prematurely.

Frowning Richard had pointed out, much to Francis's increasing sense of foreboding, that Edward's sons were still children and that in his opinion, in the event of the King's untimely death, Clarence, one who'd often questioned the King's legitimacy, would never allow 'the infant son of a bastard to inherit the throne?' Richard had explained to Francis that, 'after much thought' he'd determined that given the opportunity Clarence would seize the throne. And in that event, Richard had asked, 'Where Francis will that leave me? For we all know that Clarence despises me and would have me dead.'

Francis, who knew Clarence only too well, could not disagree with Richard who went on to explain his rationale to Francis, saying, that in the event of the King's death, with the help of his allies amongst 'the old aristocracy', he believed that he had the measure of the Queen and her Woodville relations. But Clarence', 'on the other hand', was an altogether different proposition. Clarence being a prince of the royal blood, a capable commander and a leader of men.'

Sighing and scratching his head, Richard had added,

'And for some reason unbeknown to me, the people still seem to love him'.

Francis had appreciated the logic of Richard's arguments. Yes, if Edward died prematurely there were those in positions of power who, rather than see the country suffer under the rule of minor, as they had done when Henry VI had come to the throne, would have readily supported Clarence's candidature for the throne.

Although initially skeptical, Francis had soon found himself convinced by his friends arguments. As he'd listened to his friend, it had soon become apparent to Francis, that when it came to matters at court Richard was extremely well informed. This in spite of the fact that he'd been away from London for quite some time and, at Middleham, was at least three day's ride from the Capital. Francis had not been at all surprised to discover that Richard had had an extensive network of spies and agents, through which he was able to follow those events both at court and in each and every household of note. And word had had it that in the months that had preceded his death, Clarence had become even more intolerable than usual. Apparently, Clarence had been paranoid that there were those at court who were plotting against him and fearing both the Queen and her Woodville relatives, Clarence had, once again, begun scheming against the King. Most people would have mourned the death of a wife, Clarence on the other hand, had seen the death of his wife Isabel as an opportunity. Before Isabel was even cold in the ground, Clarence had made preliminary arrangements to marry Mary, the heiress of Burgundy. Richard had pointed out to

Francis, that once in possession of the Netherlands and all of its wealth, Clarence was bound to have laid claim to the English throne. Evidently, even after all of this time, Clarence had still alluded to the agreement that he'd had with both the Earl of Warwick and the French during Henry's re adept ion. That is, should Henry's line fail, as it had done with the death of Henry's son Edward of Lancaster at Tewksbury, then upon the death of Henry the crown would revert to Clarence and his heirs.

Richard had explained to Francis that it was only after much deliberation and only after hearing of Edward's failing health, that he'd finally decided to act against Clarence. Once however, he'd decided upon his course of action, it seemed to Francis that Richard had wasted no time in communicating this fact to the Woodville faction, this despite the fact that up until that point one couldn't really have described the Queen and her relatives as Richard's allies! Unfortunately for Clarence, as soon as they'd discovered that Clarence no longer had the support of his younger brother, the Woodville's had wasted no time in leveling those charges that had ultimately brought about Clarence's destruction.

En route to London Francis had spent a great deal of time in the company of Richard and his new circle of friends. But it was not until they'd all arrived in London, that Francis had finally fully appreciated the level of intrigue that now seemed commonplace at Edward's court. And it was at Edward's court, exposed to the scheming of the various parties, that Francis finally began to appreciate why Richard had had to change and by how much! Francis did appreciate, that what had clearly been a gradual process, had to him seemed quite startling, for, although they'd both resided in Yorkshire, the two friends hadn't really seen much of each other in recent years. Richard having split his time between his fortresses at Middleham and Sherrif Hutton, whilst Francis for the most part had stayed at Ravensworth, only managing the odd trip to his manor house in Oxfordshire. Thus regrettably, the two men's paths had crossed only infrequently. In truth, although Francis, who'd always valued their friendship, had missed Richard, he'd not minded this at all, for he'd always appreciated that Richard was going to have been extremely busy, as he'd set about creating his 'northern fiefdom'. This in contrast to Francis who as a soldier was redundant now that the Wars were over, and who, as a consequence of this had enjoyed a more sedentary existence. Francis smiled, for as he'd got to know this 'new Richard' he couldn't help but admire him. Where in the past, Richard had mostly concerned himself with the here and now, with age and responsibility Richard's priorities had clearly changed quite significantly. Back in his friends company again, it'd soon become clear to Francis, that Richard was now thinking of both his own and his families future. This 'new Richard' clearly hoped to pass on a significant inheritance to his own heirs and fortunately to this end, both Richard and his wife Ann had been blessed with a son, yet another Edward, Edward of Middleham, a child whom they both adored. Yes, Richard, as befitted one of his rank and position in society, had had many mistresses and with them a number of illegitimate children. But publicly the Gloucester's had striven to portray an image of domestic contentment, a God fearing couple who were extremely family oriented. In contrast to his friend, Francis had not been quite so fortunate and presently had no-one to pass his legacy on to. After Tewkesbury Francis had hoped to move back to Minster Lovel where he'd longed to bring up his own family. But stubbornly, his Anne had refused to leave her own family in Yorkshire and as a consequence of this Francis had been obliged to assuage himself with only a small number of all to infrequent trips to Oxfordshire. Trips that at least enabled Francis, once in a while, to catch up with Ned who now managed both Francis's manor house at Minster Lovel and his Oxfordshire estates. And over the past few years, lonely, Francis had grown to love these trips, during which both he and Ned would spend hours reminiscing, as they'd embarked upon long rides in the Oxfordshire countryside, or had enjoyed hunting trips in the Wychwood forest, or fishing excursions on the Windrush. Much as they had done when they were much younger.

Yes, in the intervening years Francis had missed Richard, but he understood that his friend had been far too busy to carry on with there previous acquaintance. When they had met, invariably by chance rather than by design and usually on those few occasions when Francis just happened to be at Middleham on business, Francis had been delighted to discover that none of the warmth had gone from there relationship. Within a very short space of time both he and Richard would once again be 'as brothers'. Francis would often smile as he recalled these chance encounters, how Richard would clap his friend on the back and hurriedly ask him about his family. Francis knowing only too well that Richard was far too busy to concern himself with the Lovel's and if he was being completely honest with himself, Francis would have to admit, that his friend never really seemed to be listening to, nor did he appear at all interested in Francis's replies. Francis hadn't resented Richard for these hurried meetings, for he understood that his friend was bound to be distracted. As the Duke of Gloucester Richard was sure to have had matters of great importance on his mind and Francis appreciated that Richard had enquired after Francis and his family out of politeness. Consequently, Francis had been careful never to trouble his friend with his own problems and he would therefore merely smile and nod in agreement each and every time that Richard asked after the Lovel's and had assured him that.

'This summer.'

'We will take that hunting trip to Wensleydale.'

Both men had known that Richard neither had the time nor the inclination for such a trip and thus, when Richard, having suggested that together with their families they'd both go to London, had visited Francis, Francis had known in his heart of hearts, that something momentous must have been at hand. Francis smiled, as it turned out he'd been correct in his assumption and when he'd been asked by Richard to assist in Clarence's 'execution', Francis hadn't hesitated and in truth had been glad that after so long his friend had thought to seek his help. As such, he'd happily accompanied Richard to London. A soldier 'through and through,' Francis appreciated that in a world full of intrigue, up until that point, Richard hadn't had much use for him and instead had chosen to surround himself with Politicians, the Catesby's of this world. Yes Francis, disappointed in his own situation, had enviously eyed Richard and his new circle of retainers and yes, in truth, he'd felt excluded from his friends busy existence. Francis smiled as he considered how Richard, one who in the past had been extremely straightforward, as was the way with most soldiers, now appeared to have an extremely complex character. Francis could see that Richard had become 'quite the statesman,' a man of his time, who it seemed could now easily adapt and respond to the ever changing political climate.

But if he was being completely honest with himself, Francis had to admit that on occasions it had hurt him, to be excluded from Richard's new life. Especially in those instances when he felt that he could have been of assistance to his friend. Francis sighed, he still couldn't quite believe that when Richard had accompanied the King on his recent 'invasion' of France, what could potentially have been the most momentous undertaking of their age, Richard had not asked Francis to join him, instead ordering Francis to remain in Yorkshire, 'To safeguard the northern frontier against any incursions made by the Scot's.'

It had saddened Francis further when, upon the expeditions return, he'd been summoned to Middleham, where Richard had recounted to him, with disgust, how the King, one who up until that point Francis had always admired, had effectively been bought off by the French King Louis. Louis securing a truce with England in return for a yearly pension for Edward and a series of advantageous betrothals for his unmarried daughters. Richard had bitterly complained that by this one act, in his opinion the Edward had nullified each and every one of his previous nine victories.

Richard had condemned his brother for allowing 'the greatest English army ever amassed on French soil.' An extremely well armed and provisioned force who'd been promised much plunder and who'd all been 'spoiling for a fight,' to stand idly by whilst Edward and Clarence had enjoyed the hospitality of their 'enemies'. Apparently, the King 'in all of his finery' had met the French King Louis at Picquigny, not as expected across a field of battle but instead across a 'table laden with food and fine wine.' Since returning to England from France, Richard had done little to hide his disgust for Edward's capitulation. At least, Francis thought, Richard had had no part in it, his friend having stormed out of the peace conference, arguing that he'd rather spend his time in the company of Soldiers. Francis was astounded that the King, who in the past had been so astute, had appeared oblivious to the contempt in which he was held by the French. The French King adding insult to injury, when apparently fearing assassination, he'd attended their first meeting in disguise and thereafter had insisted that the negotiations be conducted via a purpose built screen! Enraged Richard had asked Francis 'who do these Europeans think we are,' unfortunately Francis knew only too well the answer to Richard's question, for whilst in the Earl of Warwick's tutelage he'd had the misfortune to meet Ambassadors from each and every one of the European powers and he could say with a degree of certainty that they all saw the English as a savage and uncultured race. Richard had done nothing to hide his disdain for both the French and the Burgundian's when he'd said, 'They might be happy to deal in Assassinations but we prefer to deal with people face to face.' Remaining silent Francis had chosen not to remind his friend of how they'd dealt with King Henry. Shaking his head Richard had said that both of his Brother's had disgraced their families name and had insulted all of those who'd gone before them, by allowing themselves to bought off with French gold instead of claiming that which was rightfully theirs, the crown of France.

Ultimately the English army had returned home empty handed and England's population, who'd contributed much to the expedition, by way of manpower and taxation, had had nothing to show for the venture. Francis had done nothing to cheer Richard as he'd pointed out that, 'at least' with the 'French money', 'Edward would at last be financially secure.'

Choosing to ignore Francis's point of view, Richard had gone onto describe how the French King had at least had the decency to divulge Clarence's plans to Edward, that is how Clarence had hoped to marry the late Duke of Burgundy's daughter and once in a position of power in the Netherlands and with Burgundian support, how he planned to seize Edward's throne. Although Francis, who knew only to well Louis's penchant for trouble making, appreciated that the French King's motives in giving out this information had been less than honourable.

When later, Richard had disclosed his own plans for Clarence to Francis, he'd chuckled, as he'd described how Clarence, having been confronted by Edward had denied the accusations, but on his return to England, having become increasingly paranoid, had eventually absented himself from Edward's court altogether. This apparently on the pretext that there were those there who would poison him, as they'd poisoned his wife the Duchess.

Richard had laughed as he'd explained that, 'The King had just about had enough of Clarence, but rather than lay low and hope that it would all blow over, true to form my Brother continued to meddle and upon his own authority, yet without a shred of evidence, and clearly hoping to ingratiate himself with the King, Clarence had arrested, charged and executed a number of people, ironically, on the grounds that they'd sought to bring about Edward's death through the black arts. Petitioned by the families of those whom Clarence had accused, Edward had been forced, once again, to censure Clarence for acting above the Law. But rather than apologise for his misdemeanors, Clarence had had the audacity to appeal over the head of the King to the council, asserting to them that both he and his retainers were innocent. Furious, Edward finally ordered Clarence's arrest when the Queens agents implicated him in a minor rebellion that had begun in Clarence's Cambridgeshire estates.'

Francis smiled to himself, for even after all that, the King had still prevaricated about what to do with his Brother! After they'd all attended Richard of York's betrothal ceremony at Westminster, the King had summoned them all to his presence, where he'd asked for their advice about what to do with his brother. It'd been clear to Francis that in spite of everything, when it came to the question of Clarence Edward had still been in quite a turmoil.

Having had the opportunity of seeing Edward once again at close hand, Francis had been shocked by the change in him. Edward was not the man whom Francis remembered, the handsome young King who, less than a decade before, had swept all before him as he'd re-conquered his Kingdom. Unfortunately, when he'd earlier described Edward to Francis, Richard hadn't exaggerated and upon meeting the King again Francis had gasped, as he'd been introduced to a man who was 'old before his time.' Once tall, this Edward had stooped before them in a most unseemly manner. Previously attractive Edward had appeared quite bloated, almost ugly, his tanned and weather-beaten complexion replaced by a pale and insipid pallor, which much to Francis's surprise and despite Edward's age, was covered in acne! To Francis, who'd remembered the King as being extremely powerful, Edward had appeared quite frail and almost infirm! Large rolls of fat that had lain beneath both the King's waist and his chin, had replaced the muscle that had been there before. As Edward had told them that the matter of his brother's alleged treason was due to be heard before Parliament on the following day, Francis had silently chided himself for staring at Edward, for he still hadn't quite believed the change in the King. Surprisingly Edward, who in the past had been extremely forthright, had told them that he'd been waiting to hear Richard's opinion on the matter, before he'd finally give his assent to the proposed charges. Francis smiled, it was clear to him that Edward still wanted to pardon Clarence and in waiting for Richard, he'd obviously hoped that Richard would convince him to do so. But if that had been what the King had expected he must have been sorely disappointed with Richard's response.

As the King had addressed them, Francis had been taken aback that one who'd always been so self-assured could now appear so unconvincing. As he'd spoken Edward's hands had shaken and he'd stammered, 'I know, er I'm sure, yes I can trust you all to give me good counsel in this matter. We've fought together and I know you to be er... men of honour, er... both chivalrous and brave. If you my er ... friends would have me do this then I know it must be done.' Pausing for quite sometime and deep in thought Edward had appeared quite troubled. Eventually, almost as if he'd been thinking out loud to himself, he'd continued and, looking at each of the men in turn, he'd said, 'For none of you have anything to gain by my brother's death... have you?'

Sadly for Edward and perhaps more importantly for Clarence none had spoken on Clarence's behalf.

As always William Hastings counseled caution, as Hastings had spoken, Francis who hadn't seen him for some time had smiled as he'd noticed that as with Edward, neither time, nor peace or prosperity, had been kind to the King's right hand man. Hastings, as with Edward, albeit to a lesser extent, had exhibited a wider girth, graying hair and many more chins than he'd previously had. Hastings who'd also clearly mellowed with age, had smiled towards Francis as he'd said,

'As you all know my estates in the midland's border those of Clarences, yet for quite sometime I have lived peacefully with the Duke as my neighbor. That said, it is with increasing sadness that I've been forced to witness Clarence's repeated and unwarranted treachery towards his brother the King. It is clear to me that the Duke of Clarence is dissatisfied with his exalted position amongst the aristocracy and I feel that he will only continue to plot against Edward's Government'.

Smiling Hastings had continued, 'Yet, despite Clarence's insolence I truly believe that we have nothing to fear from him, yes he will in all probability continue stirring up the odd insurrection to keep us on our toes, but in my honest opinion he'll never again take to the field against us, for Clarence values his life.' Laughing, Lord Hastings had concluded that with, 'the death of his ally the Earl of Warwick the Duke of Clarence lost both his father in law and his backbone.'

Edward too had laughed but Richard who'd not seen the funny side of it, without waiting for an invitation and much to the surprise of everyone present, had launched into a tirade that had left none in any doubt that he felt quite differently to Hasting's.

Sighing Richard had began. 'Come now surely we can all speak freely.' He had then turned towards Hastings. 'William, I know that you love my brother the King above all others and I truly respect you for this. As such I forgive you for your opinion, your obvious sympathy and compassion for Clarence has it seems clouded your judgment.' Pausing Richard had turned to address the King before he'd continued, 'Sire forgive me for saying this but to me, someone who had been away from court for sometime you are much changed. As your brother and your most loyal supporter, I fear both for your well being and for the continuation of your dynasty in the event of your death.'

Francis, shocked by his friends frankness, had gasped as he'd expected once again to witness the King's legendary fury, for Richard had predicted his untimely death! Surprisingly, rather than erupt in rage, Edward, slowly massaging one of his chins had nodded at Richard to continue,

Encouraged, Richard had explained himself, 'Edward, in the past it has been you who has successfully thwarted our brother's attempts to seize your throne. I ask you to consider this. If you die whilst your sons are still in their minority, do you think that our brother will allow them to succeed you? If your answer to this question is yes, then by all means forgive him yet again, but if it is no, then you know what you must do.' Smiling Richard had added, 'But if you do so know that I will support you in this.'

It was at that point that George Duke of Clarence's fate had been sealed. And as Richard had exclaimed after the meeting,

'The rest will be recorded in our history.'

As once again Francis pictured in his minds eye the somewhat comical scene of the Duke of Clarence, drowned to death in a butt of malmsey wine, he smiled and wondered how would the historians record Clarence death!

Chapter 20
July 1482, Hexham.

Thankfully by 1482, King Edward was relatively secure upon his throne. It was therefore perhaps ironic, that with his middle age plagued by ill health, Edward was less able to enjoy the fruits of his endeavors. All were extremely concerned for the King and were worried that in the event of his untimely death, the Kingdom would be left to his child, Prince Edward. Francis had to admit that the young Prince was both a cultured and capable youth who, from an early age, had been groomed for Kingship. But he was however, still a minor and, as a result, many feared for the Yorkist government should the Prince succeed to the throne whilst still in his minority. Indeed, one didn't have to travel too far back in history to witness the devastation that could be wrought by the accession of a child to the throne! As a consequence of Edward's continued ill health and of his physicians prognosis, in an effort to strengthen the Yorkist dynasty abroad, both the King and his council had decided to deal once and for all with the troublesome issue of Scotland. Historically, Scotland, a staunch ally of the French, had always been hostile in her dealings with England. Indeed throughout the Civil War, and since, both the French and the Scottish courts had become renowned as havens for Lancastrian dissidents and for those 'naer do wells' who'd opposed the Yorkists. Moreover in recent years it seemed to the English that the Scottish King James, who was weak and ineffectual, had become nothing more than a puppet of both the King of France and of the Scottish barons. And lately, the Scots seemed to be taking each and every opportunity to cause trouble for Edward's government. Hence, now that a treaty of sorts had been negotiated with the French, a decision had been taken to invade Scotland, with the intention of deposing James and replacing him on the throne with his brother, the Duke of Albany. In contrast to his brother James, it was hoped that Albany would become a puppet of the English King! To this end, Edward had resolved to personally lead the expedition into Scotland. Unfortunately, for much of the Summer the King had been incapacitated and as the campaigning season was nearing its end his health had deteriorated further. In fact Edward had only managed to get as far north as Nottingham, where he'd finally been forced to take to his bed. As both the money and the men had been raised for the proposed invasion, it was decided, in Edward's absence, that Richard would lead the expedition. Thankfully, on this occasion Richard had asked Francis to accompany him. Excited, Richard had told Francis that he saw the

279

invasion of Scotland as being a golden opportunity to dispel those rumours that had circulated throughout Europe since the truce had been agreed with the French. That is, that the English had 'gone soft.' When he'd invited Francis to join him, Richard had laughed as he'd enthusiastically exclaimed that there was, 'Much sport to be had with our neighbors in the north.' Francis who'd had a number of grave misgivings in respect of the undertaking, had been surprised to discover that Richard, who as a 'northerner' knew Scotland well, had not appeared to share these concerns with him.

Both Francis and Richard had met Albany, the 'English pretender to the throne of Scotland,' on a number of occasions and Francis could say, with certainty, that Albany shared all of those qualities that had made his brother such an unsatisfactory monarch. When Francis added this fact to the prospect that Albany seemed willing to utterly destroy his own brother, he shuddered at the prospect of their expedition being successful. Richard had attempted to reassure Francis, by arguing that at least Albany would be 'their puppet' and that, as a sign of good faith Albany had 'at least undertaken' to 'marry one of Edward's daughters, Cecily.' Richard's assurances had done little to comfort Francis who'd already heard rumours that Albany was betrothed to a French Princess and had been so for some time! Moreover, Francis saw the Duke of Albany as only part of their problem. For they were also going to be accompanied on their expedition by the 'duplicitous' Thomas Lord Stanley and by the 'cowardly' Henry Percy Earl of Northumberland. Francis trusted neither of these men, both of whom had little love for Richard. Indeed Richard had already crossed swords with Lord Stanley, this when Stanley and his 'Cheshiremen' had supported Warwick and Clarence's rebellion. That is, until it had appeared to Stanley that the insurrection would fail, at which point, true to form, he had once again affirmed his allegiance to Edward and to the house of York! Northumberland also hated Richard whom he blamed for both his families attainder for treason and for his consequent imprisonment within the Tower of London. As a result, Francis, who was often apt to worry about such things, had hardly slept at all since he'd learnt of the King's illness and of the revised plans for the campaign against the Scots.

As he once again contemplated these misgivings, Francis smiled weakly, at least he'd been able to use his concerns to his advantage. Richard, sensing Francis's disquiet, had taken each and every opportunity to reassure his friend and assuage his fears. Thus, when Francis had asked Richard for permission to leave the army and to visit 'friends' in Hexham, surprisingly, his friend had readily agreed. But only on the understanding that Francis was gone for only one day and that he would rejoin their army at Alnwick Castle, the Earl of Northumberland's ancestral home and the Percy family's seat.

With relief to both horses and riders alike, both Ned and Francis reigned in their mounts in a wooded glade that situated next to a small river, afforded them brief respite from the hot bright sunshine. In spite of that summer's drought, the sound made by the river, as it negotiated its rocky bed and cascaded down a number of small waterfalls was, at this secluded spot, almost deafening. On any other day one would have been overwhelmed by the beauty of this location, set deep in the Northumberland countryside. The high sided river banks, home to a variety of flora and fauna. The bubbling water, that clear and fresh glistened in the sunlight as it reflected the various shapes and colours of its surroundings. Those high grassy moors that swept down from the nearby hills to the valley bottom, vast swathes of green that were speckled with the yellow flashes of cowslips and buttercups. Francis smiled, even the man made structure, the rudely constructed 'rustic' timber bridge over which they'd just traversed the river gorge, seemed to fit in perfectly with this rural idyll of peace and tranquility. However, as Francis took time to examine their surroundings he began to frown and soon became oblivious to the loveliness of this location. Aghast, now that he was here at Hexham, Francis was at last able to appreciate the incompetence of the Lancastrian commander, the Duke of Somerset, who, on the evening of the 9th May 1464, had chosen this site to set up his camp and in doing so had brought about the destruction of King Henry's army and with it the premature deaths of both Ned and Francis's fathers. Yes, Francis mused, it may be an excellent place to enjoy the Northumberland countryside, but as a defensive position for an army in hostile country, one that was anticipating battle at any time, it's selection was nothing more than an unmitigated disaster.

Ever since he'd been made aware of how his father was thought to have died at the battle of Hexham, Francis had wanted to visit the site. He hoped that in doing so, and in the absence of either a funeral or body, he would somehow finally get closure and would at last be able to grieve for the man whom he'd perhaps loved above all others. Francis turned to his friend and smiled, it was perhaps befitting that he was accompanied by Ned, whose own father had in all probability also died near to this spot. Ned smiled back and Francis felt that he too must be pleased to be here at last.

Fortunately for them, Richard, who'd obviously had much on his mind, had accepted Francis's explanation and had not questioned him any further about 'these friends' whom Francis was prepared to leave their army to visit. Francis hated to deceive Richard, but even now after eighteen years, the brothers of York could never know that Francis's father had been present at the battle. At the time, King Edward had appeared satisfied with the explanation given that the eighth Baron Lovel had 'died peacefully of natural causes' at his manor house at Minster Lovel. This in the year that had preceded the Lancastrian's disastrous campaign of 1464. By this deception the Lovel family had successfully evaded the Baron's attainder for treason and, as a consequence, the loss of both their lands and titles. This a fate that befell many of those other families whose lieges were proven to have fought against the Yorkists in the Lancastrian defeats of 1464 at Hedgeley Moor and after that here at Hexham.

Francis smiled again, Richard presently commanded an army that had been mackled together with contingents from a number of various counties and even nations! Preoccupied and distracted by the numerous logistical problems encountered by such a large body of men on the march, Richard had finally given in to Francis's pleas and had released him. But Francis had been relieved of his command for one day only and only on the understanding that both he and Ned would rejoin the army at Alnwick. Francis shuddered, for he had no desire to visit Alnwick and renew his acquaintance with the Earl of Northumberland, Henry Percy. The Percys, a family who had been Lancastrian in there sympathies throughout the war, were now, presumably, allies of the Yorkist government in London. Unfortunately, in recent years the Earl's Northumbrian power base had been an obstacle to Richard's expansion northwards and as a result the two men's retainers had often clashed. Francis chuckled to himself, for Richard's Yorkshiremen invariably came out on top in any encounters that they had with Northumberland and his men, whom Richard had often described as having, 'No stomach for a fight.' Richard had told Francis that the Scottish campaign would 'at least' give him the opportunity to test both Northumberland's mettle and his loyalty towards their regime. Not surprisingly, Richard had chosen not to reply when Francis had asked him what was to be done, should Northumberland fail the test. Try as he might Francis couldn't share his friends confidence in Northumberland but, in spite of everything, Francis did hope, for Richard's sake, that the campaign would be a success and that after it, hopefully, both Richard and Northumberland would at least be able to peaceably coexist. But Francis was still extremely concerned, yes,

Northumberland was renowned for being 'faint hearted', but Francis also felt that Richard was seriously underestimating the Percy families power and Francis believed, that, should he be so minded, Northumberland had the potential, one day, to cause them all great harm. Anyone who knew anything about History, knew that the Percies had been at the forefront of the nations governance for generations. Francis smiled as he considered how, even after it'd appeared to everyone that the Percy families influence in England had at long last been eclipsed, their title had been responsible for a one of the greatest crises of Edward's reign! The present Earl of Northumberland's predecessor had lost both his title and his life fighting for the Lancastrians against the Yorkists at the Battle of Hedgeley Moor in 1464. His heir, the present Earl, held as a prisoner of the Yorkists in the Tower, had had to wait six years to be restored to his Earldom. In the meantime the title had been given by Edward to the Earl of Warwick's brother, John Neville, this as a reward for his continued loyalty and for his services to the House of York. Francis sighed, it had been John Neville who'd commanded the victorious Yorkist army here at Hexham. Neville had given the King no reason to deprive him of this title, when in 1470 Edward had restored it to the Percy family. By way of compensation, John Neville had been created Marquis of Montagu, but the snub had been too much to for the Marquis to bear. What had been King Edward's means of counterbalancing Neville power in the North had backfired on him, this as Montagu, angered at the King's slight, had joined his brother, the Earl of Warwick's, rebellion. A rebellion that had so nearly been successful. Francis sighed again, for he understood all to well the power that the Percy family still wielded in the North, he hoped that somehow the present Earl of Northumberland, who was much maligned for both his cowardice and his duplicity, could develop into a trusted ally of Richard and the House of York and would not, as Francis feared, continue as their enemy, as had all of the previous Earl's of Northumberland, be they Percy or Neville!

Thus, both Francis and Ned had come to this quiet spot, the scene of the battle that had ended the Lancastrian's campaign of 1464 and with it, the lives of both of their father's. Excited, Francis leapt from his horse, which, un-tethered, remained in a small glade by the river. In contrast to his mount, Francis strode about 'the battlefield', that is, of course, if one could describe such a 'death trap' as a battlefield!

Shouting to make himself heard over the sound of the river and as ever sensible, Ned advised caution.

'Hadn't you better tie that up,'

He said, pointing to Francis's horse that seemed happy enough, grazing in the shade.

Ignored Ned continued,

'One horse won't carry the both of us to Alnwick if we're to be there by the morning.'

Francis merely waved away his friend's cautionary advice, 'And where do you think he'd go,' he replied, as spinning around he pointed out the precipitous river bank that was at their backs and steep hillside that faced them.

Although Ned didn't reply to him, Francis knew that his friend must have agreed with his observations, for he too dismounted and joined Francis, leaving his small yet compact Welsh cob, untethered. Free at last, Ned's mount sidled up to Francis's black destrier, who unconcerned by the additional company, continued with his meal of lush green grass.

'How could he have chosen such a site.' Francis cried as he walked the length and breadth of the meadow, vainly trying to find some feature that may have supported Somerset's choice of such an indefensible position.

'He'd be well hidden,'

Ned replied, as he too attempted to justify the Lancastrian commander's decision.

Francis forgave Ned his lack of knowledge in respect of military matters.

He sighed as he replied. 'Yes, I know that the majority of his troops would have been concealed, but from this position his pickets could neither have seen nor could they have warned of any approach made by the enemies forces.'

Ned appeared nonplused, sighing again Francis added, 'Somerset couldn't have kept his troops in battle order all day and night, on the off chance that the Yorkists would come at him. At some point he'd have had to stand them down for they must've been marching for much of that day. In such a dangerous location he needed to be warned of any enemy activity at the earliest opportunity.' Francis pointed both to the valley bottom and to the high hills that surrounded them. 'Look around you, lookouts here in the meadow would be useless as they'd only be able to see the enemy when they were almost upon them. On the other hand, if he'd placed his pickets upon the surrounding hills, they'd have been much too far away to warn the main body of any attack.'

Smiling wryly, Francis added sarcastically, 'In fact judging by his poor choice of site I wouldn't be surprised if Somerset hadn't bothered posting lookouts at all!'

In the preceding years Francis had taken each and every opportunity to quiz those men who'd been present at the battle. As such, he'd slowly managed to piece together those events that had led to the disastrous Lancastrian defeat at Hexham, which had effectively ended their campaign of 1464. On the morning of the Battle, the Yorkist army, in receipt of excellent intelligence, had found the Lancastrian army sleeping in the valley bottom, which was known as the 'linnells' and could be found on the Bywell road out of Hexham. The few pickets that Somerset had in fact posted in the surrounding hills, were isolated and unsupported. None made it back to the Lancastrian camp to warn of the enemies approach. Indeed those who had remained at their post and had not fled into the surrounding countryside, were cut down where they stood. As a result, the Yorkists, armed and in full battle order, swept down the hillside and trapped the bulk of Somerset's army in the small meadow in which Francis and Ned now stood. Somerset's men had barely time to clothe themselves, never mind organise any kind of defense, before the Yorkist's were upon them. Confident of a swift victory and delighted that he'd caught the rebels off guard, the Yorkist commander, John Neville had even dispensed with the usual artillery barrage that preceded such an action and had ordered his men into an immediate attack. With the deep ravine, which was known locally as the 'Devil's water' at their backs, Somerset's men had had no means of retreat. Many who attempted to surrender were mercilessly slaughtered where they stood. Those who chose to stand and fight were soon overcome as, outnumbered and unprepared, they were unable to form any kind of battle line and were forced to engage the Yorkists without either support or armour in a number of small pockets of resistance that had developed, all along the valley bottom.

With difficulty, both Ned and Francis climbed up the hillside down which the Yorkist Army had charged to such great effect. Francis wanted to see for himself the sight that would have greeted John Neville as he'd drawn up his forces upon the high ground that overlooked Somerset's camp. Francis sighed, the ridge itself was the highest point for many miles and even without the burden of plate armour, the incline down which the Yorkists had charged, took a great deal of energy to climb. The view afforded to Francis from the hilltop was no less comforting than it had been from down in the valley floor. The loop of the river, inside which Somerset had chosen to camp, had ensured that the bulk of his army faced a very steep slope and had a deep ravine at their backs. Admittedly, the Yorkists could only have attacked from one direction, but that way was directly down the steep hillside. Francis could see that even without the element of surprise, the Yorkists attackers would have had an insurmountable advantage over their Lancastrian counterparts.

Ned could obviously guess what Francis was thinking, as scowling, Francis studied the topography.

Charitably, Ned tried to excuse Somerset's error.

'He must've chosen the site at short notice at the end of a long day's march. I heard that he was let down by his pickets who ran away as soon as they sighted the enemy,'

Francis remained silent as Ned continued,

'I heard it said that even King Henry, who'd spent the night at Bywell castle, wasn't even willing to forewarn his army. He made off when he'd heard that the enemy were close by.'

Ned's tone became increasingly bitter as he added, 'They didn't stand a chance.'

As the two friends rested on the heather and turf that marked the apex of the hill, sighing, Francis could only agree with his friend.

'Our fathers deserved better than this, to be betrayed by both cowardice and incompetence.'

After some minutes both rose and, in silence, retraced their steps to the valley bottom.

Francis, proud and normally unemotional, hoped that his friend would not notice the tears that were beginning to well up in his eyes as he suggested.

'Let's try and find the burial plots. Our fathers may not have a marked grave, but at least we can pay our respects to them.'

Despite the passage of time, some eighteen years since the battle, both Francis and Ned easily found the sites where those who had been killed during the encounter now lay. All about the meadow there were large humps and hillocks which, unnatural to the surroundings, were obviously of man's making. These grassy mounds signified the great burial pits into which the bodies of those slain had been thrown, once that is, they'd been stripped of their possessions and those men of rank had been identified. Thankfully no one had been able to identify Francis's father and Francis could only assume that, taken by surprise, the Baron had fought without the armour that would have identified him to his enemies. Sniffing Francis reminded himself that he should at least be 'thankful for such small mercies.' For recognition would have proven his father's presence at the battle and thus his complicity in the rebellion. Wiping a tear from his eye Francis tried to picture his father's last minutes. He knew that his father would have chosen to stand and fight, for he'd been a brave man, and anyway, by the time of the battle of Hexham, he'd already been pardoned once by Edward and as such he couldn't have expected clemency again. Francis smiled, his father had been a proud and stubborn man and Francis knew that it'd all but destroyed his father to seek the King's forgiveness in the first place. No, Francis knew that his father would never have surrendered. To lose both his pride and his dignity again? No and anyway, it must have been clear to the Lancastrians from the outset, that the Yorkists, delighted that they'd caught their enemies in such a trap, were in no mood to take any prisoners. Francis knew, from talking to those who'd been present at the battle, that the majority of those who'd thrown their weapons aside and had attempted to surrender had been slaughtered where they stood.

Francis knelt at one of the largest of the hillocks, which was situated in the very centre of the valley floor. Unashamedly, he cried for his father. For a moment he was inconsolable as Ned tried in vain to comfort him.

'Francis, they're in a better place than us,' he said.

'Our father's lost their lives,' Francis replied.

'And I lost my childhood' he added somewhat selfishly,

'And for what' Francis added bitterly, 'for a cause that was doomed.'

Ned interjected.

'Yes, but they must have been destined to fail. No-one can change fate. If they hadn't died here they'd have probably been killed at Barnet or at Tewkesbury, that's if they'd escaped execution. At least here it would have been quick.'

Ned even allowed himself a brief smile as he added,

'And I can think of worse places than this to spend eternity.'

Ned clapped Francis on the back, in an obvious attempt to cheer him he added. 'It may be a poor choice of battlefield but it makes a perfect burial ground.'

Unfortunately, Ned's words did little to cheer or placate Francis. As he knelt at what he believed to be his father's grave, he began to consider the implications of his father's untimely death. What if his father had lived? What if the Lancastrians and not the Yorkists had been victorious? What then would have become of Francis? Ironically, it seemed to Francis that it was his father's passing, and not his fathers love and support, that had had the greatest impact upon Francis's life. His childhood at Middleham under Warwick's tutelage, his friendship with Richard, his marriage and attachment to the Fitzhughs. His alienation from the Lancastrian cause, and his corruption and brutalisation through both the horrors of civil war and the intrigues at Court. All this the result of his father's death at Hexham. 'How ironic,' Francis thought. 'All of this because of the incompetence of one man, the Duke of Somerset, who, on that summers evening some eighteen years ago, had chosen such a poor site to set up his camp!'

Ned once again clapped his friend on the back. Continuing in his attempts to cheer Francis he said, 'Francis, at least we can say that our fathers fought and died with honour. What about those who deserted the field? Our fathers' legacy to us is one of virtue, one of paying the ultimate sacrifice for both the cause they believed in and for their comrades.'

Francis was unconvinced.

'But were they right to fight and die for that cause. Who's to say that they were fighting for the right side? Is God not on both sides? Who's right and who's wrong, I can't say Ned, can you?'

Ned merely shrugged his shoulders before he too sighed. As Francis listened to his friend he became quite surprised and was taken aback by Ned's insight.

'Francis you're lucky, as a member of the aristocracy you may choose who you support. Us mere commoners have that choice made for us.'

Laughing Ned continued as Francis remained silent.

'Surely History always decrees that it is the victorious who were right and the defeated who were wrong.'

Ned sighed, 'There will always be wars, for men will always strive for power over others.'

He smiled as he added, 'It is those who have the choice who must try to predict the outcome of these contests. When you commit to a cause you gamble with both our lives and the lives of our families.' Ned sighed again as he added, 'That's the way of the world, It'll never change.' Smiling Ned turned towards Francis as he added, 'Judging by Richard of Gloucester's successes, it seems as if you've chosen well Francis and I for one am thankful of that.'

Francis, angered by his friend's somewhat simplistic view of the world that depicted them all as meaningless pawns in a game that was greater than them all, replied at once.

'Right then,' he said brusquely.

'I have my own mind. There's nothing to stop me getting on my horse and riding back to Minster Lovel right now. What's to prevent me from living out what's left of my life in the pursuit of personal pleasure. What of loyalty to my Lord, to my friends or to my family?

For where does that get me? I was the ninth Baron Lovel before and, despite many victories and much personal risk in the service of Richard and the house of York, am I not still the ninth Baron Lovel? I have helped restore the Plantagenets, but what have they done for me?'

Ned, openmouthed, did not reply as Francis added, 'Ned, trust me, you don't know the half of it.'

As Francis spoke, in an instant vivid pictures and scenes flashed through his mind. Of Tiptoft, of the Oxfords and the Herberts, of Clarence and King Henry. Francis sighed and almost felt as if he was going to cry again. 'If only Ned knew what I have been party to,' Francis thought as he considered the relatively sheltered upbringing and adolescence that both he and Ned had enjoyed in Oxfordshire.

Almost as if he too was recalling their childhood and life in Oxfordshire, a smile flickered upon Ned's face before he became sterner, saying, 'You won't leave Francis, you can't. Your rewards will come. There are men about the King and his brother who do not possess your qualities. Your sense of honour. Your notion of what is right and wrong. Ultimately, these men will fail' Ned smiled again, 'You've inherited these qualities from your father. He chose and he died. He tried to play the political game when he made his peace with Edward but he couldn't maintain that charade for long and when called upon, he came out once again for Lancaster.' Ned smiled reassuringly as he clapped Francis on the back before he added, 'You, Francis, have chosen your allegiances, I know you and in spite of everything you will not waiver.' Ned sighed, 'I'm afraid, Francis, that you couldn't live the easy life even if you tried. I'd think it was great if we could both hop onto our horses and ride back to Minster Lovel.' He sighed again, 'But no, I know that that can never happen, you are Richard of Gloucester's man for life, as I am yours. This, I'm afraid, is the only life that we know and we must live it as best as we can.'

Francis agreed, both he and Ned, men of their time, were straightforward in this respect. But Francis did fear for the future. Clearly Ned hadn't noticed yet but Francis had and he could see that times were changing. In Francis's opinion the 'noblesse' and 'chivalry' that had characterised the early medieval period had gone. The recent Civil Wars had witnessed little in the way of chivalry and compassion. In fact the conflict had become renowned throughout Europe for its ruthlessness, treachery and double dealing. Many of the old aristocracy were dead and Francis could see that they'd been replaced by a new class, men of money or of learning. This new breed of men were no longer empowered by their noble blood, but by the money that they had in their pockets or by the letters they had after their name, nor were they restricted by etiquette or a number of 'age old rules' that they felt did not apply to them . Francis had often complained that these men, 'Sought to turn the world upon it's head,' to introduce a society based not on birthright but on wealth. That said, and despite everything, Francis was still confident that in the long run these men would not succeed, for in his opinion, 'Money breeds greed yet blood is given by God.'

Ned, who no doubt agreed with Francis, echoed Francis's thoughts as he concluded, 'We are what we are. We're born to it. We, my friend, will continue to serve because that is God's will and that is what we do best.'

Surprisingly, Francis was not depressed by Ned's observations. He knew and accepted that this was how life was. Francis believed that ultimately everything would come full circle and people would eventually get 'their just desserts.' For Cowards, cheats and liars never prospered. Francis smiled as he cast his mind back to a number of examples that supported his reasoning. Even here, at Hexham, those men who'd deserted their comrades and had fled the field had not fared at all well after the battle. At Hexham Lords Hungerford and Roos had commanded the Lancastrian right flank, there they were fortunate, in so much as the river at the rear of their position, was navigable. When they'd seen the Yorkists attack, both Hungerford and Roos had fled the field and in doing so had taken with them almost a third of the Lancastrian army! Francis sighed, yet another mistake made by the Duke of Somerset, giving such a command to the very men who'd done the self same thing at the earlier Lancastrian defeat at Hedgeley Moor. Francis smiled. Neither Hungerford nor Roos had prospered by their treachery and both had been taken by the Yorkists, hiding like outlaws in the woods that surrounded the battlefield. Both men were executed without trial at Newcastle. Francis chuckled to himself as he considered that these mens cowardice had merely prolonged their lives by two miserable days.

Both Ned and Francis ate like Lord's that evening. Brown trout caught by Ned, who'd spent many years honing his skills on the Windrush. Francis had planned to spend the night camped in the meadow, hoping to rise early and make the short journey north to Alnwick, to rendezvous as planned with Richard and the English army. However, as the sun disappeared and darkness descended upon them, Francis began to feel an increasing sense of disquiet. As such he suggested to Ned that they leave that night. Ned, who was in the process of making himself quite comfortable, seemed surprised by

Francis's unease and asked Francis why he wanted to leave at such a time. Francis dithered, he couldn't really describe how or why he had these feelings. He did say that he felt perturbed to be in a spot that had been the scene of such slaughter, resting so close to the graves of those men who'd been killed in such awful circumstances.

The meadow, which in daylight had appeared quite beautiful, took on a whole new appearance as dusk slowly gave way to darkness and with the arrival of the night the valley assumed a much more sinister guise. As the days heat had left the earth, the meadow become enveloped in a low and swirling mist. The woods, by daytime cool green glades, now appeared to them as a dark impenetrable mass, full of twisted and knarled trees that creaked and groaned as they swayed in the freshening wind. The river, previously so clear and sparkling, now appeared almost ethereal, its cold waters reflecting the ghostly images of the half moon and the clouds that were now racing across the dark yet moonlit sky. Francis shuddered. He now appreciated that no site, no matter how beautiful, could ever hope to recover from those horrors that this valley had witnessed. Francis now bitterly regretted his decision to come to this place. He believed that the souls of those men who lay about them could never hope to rest in peace. Betrayed and abandoned and mercilessly slaughtered by a ruthless enemy.

As the wind gusted and their fire spluttered, Francis shuddered again. These men would curse this spot for all of eternity and who could blame them? Now Ned too was nervously eyeing the surrounding woods and hills, this as Francis stamped out what remained of their fire and hurriedly packed up their few belongings. Thankfully, within a relatively short space of time both Francis and Ned were able to renegotiate the bridge over which they'd earlier entered the valley and without a backward glance they bade a last farewell to their fathers and to the battlefield of Hexham.

Unexpectedly, Alnwick Castle, the home of the present Earl of Northumberland, was a very welcome site to Francis. Upon leaving Hexham, both he and Ned had ridden in silence initially through the wild Northumbrian countryside and once back in civilisation, through the narrow streets of the small town of Alnwick. Here in the 'cold north', Alnwick's rickety houses and makeshift buildings of wattle and daub appeared to Francis to be incapable of providing much in the way of shelter or warmth to their occupants. Yet the commoners 'rude dwellings' contrasted sharply with the Percies Castle. Francis gasped as he first laid eyes on the magnificent building. A fortress that had been built both for defense and for splendor. The Percy family's stronghold, situated close to England's border with Scotland, was indeed a site to behold. It's thick walls towered above the surrounding town and, despite the lateness of the hour, its numerous fires and torches lit up the surrounding countryside like a great beacon. No one had ever breached the fortresses defenses and Francis knew that in its long history, the Castle had only ever been taken once, this after a long siege had forced it's defenders, through starvation and disease, to surrender. As Alnwick Castle's walls had never been reduced by attackers, over many years they had been fortified and added to, these improvements had now made the fortress virtually impregnable. Indeed, it was due almost entirely to Alnwick and to the other Northumberland fortresses that the Scots, even in times of superiority, had never been able to mount a successful invasion into England. The Northumbrian Castles prevented both the resupply and the reinforcement of any Scottish army in England and as a result the Scots were forced to satiate their desire for conquest with a number of minor skirmishes and small raids carried out across the border. Francis smiled wryly, in the past these castles had also been quite a 'thorn in the side' of the Yorkists, as on a number of occasions they'd offered shelter to the Lancastrians in defeat and in doing so had in Francis's opinion, ensured that the Civil wars had continued, long after they should have been concluded. Thankfully, until recently the Scots had had no such stronghold on their side of the border. Thus, any incursions into Scotland by the English, could be supported and victual led almost to the very gates of Edinburgh itself! Unfortunately, in 1482 there was a 'thorn in the side' of Richard's expedition. This presented itself as the walled town of Berwick that was situated on the mouth of the River Tweed, the natural border between the two countries. As an English garrison town, it had for many years been foremost in that country's defence. Unfortunately, in 1455, in return for aid, it had been surrendered to the Scots by the Lancastrians. Thus, garrisoned with a large number of experienced Scottish soldiers, it now stood against their proposed invasion Indeed one of the primary aims of their present campaign, was to retake Berwick and to restore it into English hands.

Expected and recognised, Francis was admitted into the Castle via the main gate. Tired, Ned was fortunate enough to be able to retire to bed, whereas Francis on the other hand, was summoned to the great hall, where Richard and his commanders were apparently making the final preparations for the invasion that would begin in earnest on the following day. On entering the hall, Francis deferentially acknowledged those present. William Catesby and Richard Ratcliffe who were both now men of Richard's inner circle of confidants, upon recognising

Francis acknowledged his presence by politely nodding in his direction. Less courteous were those of higher birth, Lord Stanley, the Earl of Northumberland and the Scot, Alexander Duke of Albany, all merely looked briefly in Francis's direction, before shrugging, they rudely turned away.

It was clear to Francis that the majority of those present had obviously been drinking for sometime. And as always, the alcohol consumed served to reveal the true nature of men's characters. And Francis knew that the Bastard of Fauconberg, who was present as he was to command the English navy, had a penchant for boasting. Francis smiled as he recalled how in 1471, Fauconberg had escaped execution by the skin of his teeth. Francis had to admit that King Edward, whatever faults he may have had, was always adept at maximising an individuals potential, and after the 'Bastard's' failed rebellion, he'd obviously recognised Fauconberg's abilities and surprisingly, given the two men's histories, had, contrary to Richard's advice, spared him and had recruited him into his own army. Fauconberg, clearly having had more than enough to drink and true to form, was clearly trying to ingratiate himself with both Catesby and Radcliffe with whom he was conversing, or perhaps a more accurate description would have been, who he was talking at! Francis smiled again, as he noticed that both men appeared extremely impressed with that which Warwicks cousin had to say for himself. As he caught snippets of their conversation, Francis chuckled to himself as he heard Fauconberg recount, in the greatest of detail, the various battles in which he'd apparently been involved. Battles in which Francis, who had actually been present at them, knew that Fauconberg had not been involved in the slightest!

Richard who was in conversation with the Earl of Northumberland, the Duke of Albany and Lord Stanley seemed relieved to see Francis and immediately called him over.

'Lords can I take this opportunity to introduce to you my friend Francis Lovel. Trust me you'll not find a better man to have at your side.'

Once again, none present seemed even remotely interested, either in Francis or in what Richard had to say about him.

'Of too high birth to take any notice of a mere Baron from Oxfordshire,' Francis thought.

As Francis sat himself down he sensed that Richard too was displeased.

As he poured himself a glass of Brandy and was rebuffed yet again by those present when he offered to serve them, Francis began to reflect upon the cause of his friends poor humour. Francis knew that Richard, who had little time for those who considered themselves above others, had always said that one should judge a man by his actions and not by the nature of his birth. Clearly, much to Richard's angst, those present did not share in Richard's sentiments, for they rudely continued with their conversation, almost as if Francis was not even there! Francis wasn't at all surprised for it was obvious to him, that all present, save that is for Richard, were totally inebriated. The Duke of Albany, brother to the Scottish King James and presently the pretender to his throne, slurred his words and dribbled as he spoke of how he and he alone as a 'True Scot', would wrest the Kingdom of Scotland from his 'weakling brother.'

'Who' Albany said, was under the 'control' of his 'scheming courtiers' the majority of whom were of 'foreign birth'.

Francis smiled at the irony of Albany's words, for he knew that Albany wasn't even a true Scot, having spent much of his own life abroad at the French court. Francis chuckled, for one who spoke of patriotism and who showed disdain for others of foreign birth, Albany sounded remarkably like a Frenchman, having an accent that would be better suited to Paris than to Edinburgh! In his time Francis had met with many Scots, especially during those months in the summer of 1470, when having instigated the rebellion on behalf of the Earl of Warwick, both he and his father in law had retired to Scotland. In Francis's opinion Scotland was a Kingdom of two halves. The 'lowland' Scot's who came from the environs of Edinburgh, were effectively Englishmen. These 'lowlanders' had only the faintest of accents and these they often tried to disguise, almost as if they felt that to be Scottish was to be somehow uncouth or uncultured. The 'lowlanders' contrasted sharply with those whom Francis considered to be the true Scots. The 'highlanders', men from the north and for whom Francis had the utmost respect. Rugged and aggressive men who spoke an altogether different language and dialect to their counterparts in the South. Francis didn't mind admitting to anyone that he hoped that during their forthcoming campaign, he'd meet few, if any, of these so called 'barbarians'. For Francis knew that the highlanders, wielding their Claymore's, great swords that could all but cleave a man in two, were true killing machines. Francis smiled wryly, he knew that their 'highland charge', a rather simple tactic that had been adopted by the highlanders, which consisted of running at ones opponent whilst screaming and waving ones sword about, would spread blind panic throughout the ranks of the highlanders enemies and had in the past caused many armies, to break and run, long before they were able to come to blows with this 'horde'.

Clearly irritated Richard interrupted Albany, 'You would do well not to talk of strength in Government, for there are many in Scotland who favour your brother's regime for it affords them the opportunity to flaunt his laws and make there own wars without fear of punishment.'

Richard continued as Albany, dribbling and befuddled, seemed to have difficulty in understanding Richard's train of thought.

'Yes your brother is controlled by his favorites, but they aren't at all interested in Scotland, they merely seek their own personal gratification. When we get to Scotland you'll find that the rank and file of your nobility would rather that their King was diverted so.'

Albany at last seemed to grasp what was being said.

'Ah, I see. Let the fools think that with me they're getting an equally weak King, one who will allow them, to er,.....enable them to carry on with their petty feuds. But when I've got the throne,' at this point Albany cackled in a most unseemly manner, 'they'll have a shock...........for I'll rule them with an iron fist.'

As Albany said this, no doubt for added effect, he brought his fist down onto the table with a bang. Clearly unimpressed by either the man or his gesture, Richard merely shrugged his shoulders and sighed. Choosing to ignore Albany's outburst, Richard continued to caution him,

'Fools they may be, but if you hope to rule them one day, it might be wise for you to keep your opinion of your subjects to yourself. For one day you may have need of these 'fools', for it is they who will have to follow you into battle and lay down there lives for you.'

Francis, who was embarrassed on behalf of Albany, attempted to change the subject by introducing himself to the Earl of Northumberland.

Northumberland, who was also extremely drunk, offered Francis a limp an ineffectual hand as he too boasted that he would 'take much plunder from the Scots.' As Northumberland continued Francis found it increasingly more difficult to hide his disdain for both the Earl and Albany. Northumberland was clearly a poor judge of character, for failing to notice Francis's disapproval he clapped Francis on the back saying that 'with the help of such men,' 'his friend' Albany would soon be crowned 'The King of the Scots.' Francis smiled as he noticed that Richard too appeared to be eying Northumberland with a level of suspicion. It seemed to Francis that Richard too had little regard for the Earl. Indeed all knew that Northumberland, who's land in the North lay closer to the Scottish court than to the English, given the option, would make peace in an instant with whoever was in power in Scotland.

It was almost too much for Francis to bear as he was forced to listen to the rhetoric of both Albany and the Earl of Northumberland. Excusing himself, Francis left the room on the pretext of visiting the latrines. He was soon joined there by Richard, who away from their 'comrades' and despite the smell, seemed to be in much better humour. Francis had been correct in his earlier assumption that Richard was equally unimpressed with his commanders.

Richard laughed as, having checked that there were no other persons present in the latrines, he whispered to Francis, 'Have you ever heard the like,'

Chuckling Richard continued, 'Pah, I bet they've never been close to a proper battle.'

As Richard obviously contemplated the task that lay ahead them he sighed before he added, 'And my Brother wants me to conquer Scotland with these people.' Francis smiled too as Richard, with a twinkle in his eye, said that which both of the friends were no doubt thinking. 'They say Edward's too ill to join us. I'd wager that he's too embarrassed to be associated with these fops. I for one wouldn't trust any of them.'

Becoming serious Richard said, 'Francis we must be extremely careful, for they'll all stab us in the back given half the chance.' Richard sighed as he added, 'I fear that this whole enterprise may be a complete and utter waste of men money and of my time.'

Richard appeared perplexed as he questioned, 'Why would Edward want to replace one fool with another?'

Francis knew that now in the company of his friend he could speak freely. He agreed with Richard as he replied grimly, 'I really don't know how this expedition is going to turn out, for I can't see how either Albany, Northumberland, or even Lord Stanley, can be off much use to us when we finally meet the Scots.'

Richard laughed as he added sarcastically, 'Well at least we have Fauconberg to help us. According to him he's single handedly won every battle that's ever taken place on English soil, even those at which he wasn't even present!'

Sighing and with an obvious sense of resignation, Richard added,

'As always I'll do my Brother's bidding. I'll take Berwick, I'll even put Albany on the throne for him, but I'll go no further than Edinburgh. I'm not risking my men on the likes of Albany and his cronies.' He sighed again as he added, 'My men tell me that Albanys in the French King's pocket, mark my words Francis, once he's secure on the Scottish throne he'll be no ally of England.'

In spite of his opinion of the Scot this revelation surprised Francis who said, 'But is he not betrothed to your niece Cecily, surely that will tie him to Edward.'

Richard smiled, 'Sometimes your much too naive Francis. My spies at the French court tell me that our friend Albany has already secretly married a French Princess.'

Richard added grimly.

'It appears to me as if our ally Albany likes to keep all of his options open, I don't trust him nor do I trust his friends.'

Clearly referring to both Northumberland and Lord Stanley as well, Richard added,

'Due to their rank I must give them each a command but I will appoint both you and Ratcliffe to serve under them. Francis I need you both to keep an eye on them to make sure that they don't do anything that may be ruinous to our army.'

Richard sighed once again as he added, 'I just hope to God Francis that we never have to rely on such men to save us, for I fear that they'd sooner lay down their arms before they'd lay down their lives.' As Francis listened to his friend he shivered. Francis's grandmother Alice would have said that someone must have 'stepped upon his grave.'

Upon returning to the Hall Francis who really was exhausted made his excuses, not that anyone appeared in the least bit interested in him anyway! Thankfully Francis was able to retire to his bed, in doing so he left Richard with the thankless task of continuing to entertain there comrades who, despite the early start that was planned for the following morning, seemed intent on taking this opportunity to drink the Castle's cellars dry.

As Francis had earlier gloomily predicted, it was in fact late into the morning of the following day before the English Army, which had assembled outside the Castle walls, was joined by three of its commanders. It then began what Francis could only describe as a 'slow' and 'laborious' march northwards towards its first goal the Town of Berwick.

Both Francis and Ned assumed there positions within the armies van guard. Unfortunately they were soon joined by the Earl of Northumberland who, Francis quipped, appeared 'resplendant' in his ornately fashioned armour that had obviously seen little use. The main battle was commanded by Richard, who was accompanied by Albany and the rearguard by Stanley who was to be 'shadowed' by Richard Ratcliffe. Fauconberg had left Alnwick earlier that day to join the English fleet at Ravenspur. The 'Bastard' was to command the squadron of ships, which Edward had provided to support the invasion.

Fauconberg's orders were to blockade the mouth of the River Tweed, thereby preventing Berwick from being either reinforced or resupplied from the sea.

For Francis who'd witnessed first hand the frenetic pace at which the Yorkist army had run the Lancastrians to ground in the days preceding Tewksbury, in comparison, the march to Berwick was almost 'leisurely'. Francis who in the past had experienced much hardship in the field, was forced to bite his lip and remain silent, as Northumberland, who was clearly not used to 'campaigning', complained bitterly to any who cared to listen, that they traveled, 'over rough roads' at 'far too great a pace.' Frustratingly it was not until the afternoon of the third day of their campaign that Richard's troops found themselves camped outside the walled town of Berwick upon Tweed, at a place that was known locally as 'Hoten field'. Not surprisingly due to the slow pace of their advance, the English army had by that time lost any element of surprise that they might have had. As such when they finally arrived at Berwick they discovered that the Scottish garrison, which had been reinforced, was expecting them. Thankfully Richard's scouts had performed admirably and as a direct result of their intelligence, which suggested that Berwick was, practically speaking, virtually impregnable from the South, Richard had chosen, not as one might have expected, to approach Berwick from the direction of the English border, but had instead descended upon it from the North. The English army, adding to the Earl of Northumberland's discomfiture, had detoured many miles inland. There they had finally been able to ford the River Tweed upstream at a narrower, shallower and undefended point. This maneuver had enabled Richard's troops to approach Berwick from the North, thereby avoiding the estuary to the South of the Town that was far too deep and wide to ford and was protected by a single heavily fortified bridge. Francis smiled, in the years that they had lain idle Richard had lost none of his abilities as a master tactician, namely his aptitude and his adaptability. Francis knew that many commanders, heedless of the potential losses, would have attempted to force the bridge from the South. Francis smiled again, rather than facing the problem head on, Richard had merely circumnavigated it! Despite losing the advantage of surprise, which in truth they'd lost anyway, in one stroke Richard had gained the upper hand and had succeeded in cutting Berwick off from the remainder of Scotland and in doing he'd not lost one soldier! Francis who'd seen the effect that a prolonged siege could have upon a Castle's defenders pitied the Berwick garrison. Ironically the Scottish King, by reinforcing the town, had merely increased the number of mouths that the garrison commander now had to feed. Moreover upon their arrival Francis had noticed that there were no ships at anchor in the estuary, nor was there now any prospect of any arriving in the near future. For the sails of Fauconberg's squadron were evident upon the horizon and Francis knew that he'd had express orders to engage any ship that attempted to force his blockade and reinforce the besieged town. Francis smiled, those Scots who now found themselves trapped within the town were in for a really hard time.

Berwick's walls bristled with cannon and Francis was surprised that the Scottish gunners had resisted the temptation to open fire upon either the English army or upon its navy. Francis could only think that either the garrisons artillery were short of ordinance or they were anticipating a long and drawn out siege and as such were preserving what ammunition they had. In contrast to the Scots, Francis hoped that somehow they'd be able to bring the proceedings to a speedy conclusion. The townsfolk of Berwick were still predominantly English and as such Francis seriously doubted that they would accept those privations that would undoubtedly be imposed upon them by the garrison commander as a result any siege. Francis knew that any English rebellion from within Berwick was bound to help their cause, especially if it could somehow be coordinated with an attack from the outside. As he surveyed Berwick's defenses Francis began to frown, for it was evident to him that their army would have great difficulty in reducing the heavily fortified town by force of arms even with the help of Berwick's English townsfolk. Thankfully, in contrast to their Southern counterparts, Berwick's northern walls didn't benefit from the added protection of a deep and wide river estuary. That said these walls were still extremely high and thick and they were protected by a wide moat, as a result Francis doubted that they'd be able to reduce them by either artillery action or by 'undermining' them. Francis was forced to concede that at that point in time, any attempt to storm the walls would result in the loss of many men and was therefore unwarranted and could almost be considered as suicidal! Francis felt that their only option open was to sit tight and hope that the besieged garrison would eventually be forced to surrender. If Richard chose this option and Francis who knew his friend well, believed he would, Richard would be forced to split his army. Leaving a number of men to continue the siege, whilst the others struck out for the Scottish Capital. Francis, a man of action, hoped and prayed that he would be amongst those who were chosen to continue on the march northwards into Scotland in search of King James' army. Those amongst Richard's army who were less fortunate would have to remain at Berwick and be subjected to the tedium of siege warfare.

As the sun set upon their first day in Scotland, Francis together with the other English commanders, assembled in Richard's tent for a 'council of war. Richard was very much a 'Soldiers Soldier' and rather than seek out more sumptuous accommodation in the nearby villages and towns, Richard's quarters, easily identifiable by his white boar pennant, were situated in the very centre of their armies encampment. Francis had left Ned with the job of erecting their accommodation and preparing their evening meal. Fortunately food was still in plentiful supply as from the outset the expedition had been well supplied and victual led. Francis did however wonder how long it would be before their men were forced to either scavenge or to rely upon the generosity of their Scottish brethren!

As Francis entered Richard's tent he shuddered and the hairs on the back of his neck stood on end as he was forced once again to listen to the highly irritating Franco-Scottish nasal whine of the Duke of Albany.

'Give me just two hundred men at arms and archers and I'll scale the walls on the North side and will bring the garrison to it's knees.'

Richard who was clearly losing patience with Albany, was curt in his reply.

'I'm not prepared to throw away the lives of my men on such a desperate attempt, we must all be patient for we won't be able to take this town by force of arms alone.' Rubbing the single gold ring that he wore upon the index finger of his left hand, as he was often want to do when he was concentrating, Richard fell silent and was clearly deep in thought. A hush descended upon the tent as none dared to speak. Francis, as always, was extremely impressed with the respect that his friend clearly commanded from others who were much older than he, deference which clearly belied Richard's age, for he was still only in his twenties! After a few moments, both calm and measured Richard continued, 'We must reduce Berwick not by direct action but through deprivation brought about by a properly coordinated siege of the town and blockade of its harbour.' Richard smiled before he added, 'In this case starvation will be our greatest ally.' Richard clearly saw the disappointment upon Albany's face, for he added, 'Trust me Albany I don't like to fight in this way, but if we hope to succeed in this expedition we must take this town, yet in doing so I don't want to deplete our army, for we'll need every able bodied man that we have when we meet your brothers army.' Richard was quite clear in his orders, 'And nor should anyone make any attempt to either undermine or reduce the towns walls, the King wants the town and it's castle intact.'

Albany bemoaned, 'But what of the men. There's little sport to be had in these parts at the best of times. How are we going to keep them occupied for the weeks or the months that it'll take to take the Town in this way.'

Not unsurprisingly Richard had clearly considered all of the various options and he was able to answer Albany immediately.

'I intend to divide our army, both you and I will take the larger proportion and will march upon Edinburgh, if we either defeat your Brother in Battle or we are able to take the capital, the Scots may be forced to come to terms even before Berwick falls.'

Francis was extremely disappointed to discover that he would be amongst those left behind. For Richard, winking at Francis added, 'I will leave both Northumberland and Lord Lovel at Berwick with a force of five hundred, together with Fauconberg's squadron this should be sufficient to maintain the siege.'

Seeing that the Earl of Northumberland was as unhappy as he at being left behind did little to cheer Francis, who took time to consider his role. Ordered not to attack but to sit and wait for the Town to surrender!

As both Northumberland's protestations together with his request to accompany Richard northwards fell upon deaf ears, Francis felt that for him to object would be futile and would not only irritate his friend but may also serve to undermine him in front of the others. Francis therefore merely sighed as Richard chided Northumberland, asking him,

'And who would you have me leave behind in your stead.'

Northumberland glanced towards Lord Stanley but said nothing. Francis smiled, Nothumberland for all of his bluster was clearly not that self-assured that he dare confront Lord Stanley who was a wily old statesman, for Stanley was renowned for being both a clever and a dangerous character. Francis smiled again. He knew that even if he had been challenged, Stanley was bound to have come up with a reasoned and compelling argument as to why he and not Northumberland should accompany Richard Northwards, that is of course if Stanley wanted to go with Richard's men.

It was clear that for some reason or other Richard hadn't considered leaving Lord Stanley at Berwick, for he completely ignored Stanley and turned instead towards to Albany before he continued. 'The Duke of Albany must accompany me into Scotland, for the Scottish people must have the opportunity of seeing there future King in the field.' Smiling Richard patted the scowling Northumberland on the back as he added, 'It's a crying shame but the Scots will have to wait to meet you my cousin in the field.' By now Richard, much to Northumberland's increasing discomfort, was clearly enjoying himself. Once again Richard clapped Northumberland on the back as he joked, 'Despite his excellent pedigree when it comes to the art of War.'

For Francis the bitter pill of being left behind was at least made more palatable, as unexpectedly and no doubt as a means to placate him, both he and Ratcliffe were knighted by Richard, in the name of his brother the King.

As he knelt before his friend Francis smiled at the irony of it. He'd suffered much and had faced great danger in the service of the house of York. Yet here he was, at Hoten field by Berwick, only now created a Knight of the King. And why? Because the King's brother hoped to assuage his disappointment at being asked to remain there and baby-sit the errant Earl of Northumberland, whom Richard could not trust to do his bidding.

As Francis rose a knight Richard took him to one side and whispered.

'As soon as my backs turned I'm sure that he'll try and take the Town by force. You're to make sure he stays put and follows my orders.'

Worried, Francis wondered how he, a mere Knight and a Baron could hope to countermand the directions of an Earl, who was now effectively his commander in chief! As Francis began to grumble Richard merely waved aside his protestations. It was Francis's turn to sulk as he wondered how he'd be able to manage Northumberland. Francis sighed for Richard, as he was apt to do on occasions, had now made his problem Francis's problem!

Initially the siege of Berwick went extremely well. As predicted, within days of sighting the English army, the townsfolk had risen up against the Scottish garrison. Rioting and looting, the towns populace had succeeded in driving the Scots from the town's walls and into the castle itself. Not surprisingly Northumberland saw this development as a great personal victory! In contrast, Francis, who was far more realistic about such matters, saw the event for what it was. Berwick's Castle was positioned close to the Rivers edge and in it, the Scottish Garrison still had control of both the River and its crossing. Strategically speaking therefore, in taking the town the English had derived no actual benefit. Ironically the English had now gained more mouths to feed, whilst for the time being at least, the Scots were far better placed to defend that which they held.

News had it that Richard had also met with initial, yet superficial success. As planned together with Albany and the majority of the

English army he'd marched on Edinburgh and save for those Scots who'd remained ensconced within the City's Castle, Richard had taken the majority of Edinburgh without bloodshed. Unfortunately he too was now at a stalemate. Richard's army didn't have sufficient resources to take the Castle, yet its garrison stubbornly refused either to come to terms, or to ride out and meet them in battle. King James had also failed to engage Richard's army and with his army he'd retreated northwards. It was even rumoured that James was being held prisoner by the Scottish barons who didn't want to see him fall into English hands. Francis knew that Richard was far to clever to follow the Scots into the barren and inaccessible highlands where entire armies could find themselves swallowed up in the bleak and inhospitable environment. The English who were already well within hostile territory, could not risk stretching their lines of supply and communication any further. At present all Richard could do was to sit and wait and hope that the Scott's pride would get the better of them and angry that much of their country was now partially occupied by the English, they would come to battle.

Despite Richard's difficulties Francis felt that his friend had had a far easier time of it than he had, as he'd found it increasingly more difficult to keep both Northumberland and Fauconberg in check. Rumour had it that the English Admiral, keener on lining his own pockets rather than in furthering their cause, had taken bribes from the Scots to allow some of their supply ships access to Berwick. When challenged Fauconberg had come up with some 'cock and bull' story about how his blockade had been temporarily raised when his squadron had been scattered due to a squall at sea. Fauconberg had sent word to Francis that 'regrettably' upon reestablishing the blockade he'd 'discovered' that a number of Scottish merchantmen had slipped through into Berwick's harbour unnoticed. Francis didn't believe Fauconberg's explanation. On shore the weather had been fine and throughout that period the masts of the English ships had always been evident upon the horizon. Adding to Francis's suspicions, Fauconberg had repeatedly refused to come ashore to account for his actions. Consequently Francis, who was never the best of seamen, had been forced to take to ship to confront him. Francis had soon discovered that Fauconberg, despite his families fall from grace, had lost none of the charm and eloquence for which the Nevilles were famous. Thus for the time being at least, Francis was obliged to accept the 'Bastards' explanation. However upon finally leaving the ship, Francis had promised his old adversary that Richard, upon his return, was 'bound' to 'initiate an enquiry into the matter.'

On reaching dry land again Francis had smiled, 'Little does he know.' He thought.

'Once Fauconberg is no longer of any use, this just might be the excuse that Richard needs to have his head.'

Francis smiled again. If Fauconberg knew just how hard Richard had sought his execution in the aftermath of Tewkwsbury he'd perhaps not be quite so confident as he had been. But then again, Francis mused, it was clear that Fauconberg was a Neville through and through and as such he possessed all of that charm and confidence in his own abilities, that had made his cousin the Earl of Warwick 'so much loved by the common people.' As such, Francis supposed, Fauconberg could be forgiven for believing that these qualities would once again save him.

'For his sake.' Francis thought. 'I hope that he has better luck than those others of his family who've gone before him.'

Francis had always believed that a man was only as good as his word, as such he had no time for those who habitually told untruths. Francis was annoyed not only by Fauconberg's lies and deceit, but also by the fact that Fauconberg had thought so little of Francis's intellect, that he'd expected Francis to believe him without question when he'd come up with his 'cock and bull' story! Despite his anger Francis, who at the best of times wasn't renowned for his impetuosity, had chosen to bite his tongue and bide his time until Richard returned. As he'd left Fauconberg's flagship Francis had icily bid Fauconberg good-bye and had returned to the English encampment at Hoton. Never a good sailor Francis hated both the movement of the ship and the cramped conditions that the sailors were forced to endure.

Pleased that once again he was on solid ground and that he had yet another good reason to dislike his Neville kinsman, Francis had immediately reported the content of his conversation with Fauconberg to Northumberland.

In contrast to Francis's anger at Fauconberg's alleged treachery Northumberland seemed quite delighted that the Scottish Garrison had been resupplied! Unfortunately the reasoning behind Northumberland's perverse good humour had soon become apparent to Francis. Sadly Northumberland now had the excuse that he'd been waiting for. Upon hearing of Northumberland's 'revised' plans Francis had winced and had even wondered if Northumberland, keen to attack the Scots, had also been party to the provisioning of Berwick! Upon hearing that the Scottish garrison had been re provisioned the English commander happily exclaimed, 'Well that decides the matter. We must now make the necessary preparations and attack at once.'

Francis's protestations fell upon deaf ears as Northumberland excitedly described how, 'His army' would storm the redoubt that was situated within the Castle's north wall and by doing so, 'Would secure the fortress,' for the English.

Francis knew that the Castle's defenders were in too strong a position and that presently the English had neither the men nor the resources necessary to secure such a victory. He cautioned restraint.

'Let me get word to Richard.'

He said, 'By fast rider, his orders will be with us in a matter of days.'

From the way in which Northumberland was slowly shaking his head from side to side, it was clear to Francis that the decision to attack the Scottish garrison had already been made. Francis was forced to resign himself to the fact that he would now have to be party to such folly. Sighing Francis could only wonder if the cause of his nervousness was the prospect of attempting to storm Berwick's walls or the fact that he'd failed to carry out Richard's orders in preventing such an impetuous act.

At the conclusion of the meeting Francis immediately sent Ned to Edinburgh to inform Richard of Northumberland's plans. He didn't want to lose any more friends than he needed to, in what he felt was sure to be both an unsuccessful and futile action. Ned had said that Francis ought to wash his hands of the matter and ride with him, but Francis had declined his offer, arguing that someone with at least a modicum of military experience was needed to be present to lead the attack.

At dawn on the following day, as the English army was mustering in the fields opposite Berwick's northern redoubt, alone, Francis rode forward and scoured the stronghold in the vain hope that some chink in it's defenses might at last be revealed to him. He was disappointed. Downhearted, Francis returned to their camp just in time to hear the Earl of Northumberland, who was resplendent in his unblemished plate armour, try in vain to rouse their men with a speech that spoke of honour and chivalry. Thankfully, the Earl's words were soon drowned out by the sounds of the English artillery, which opened fire on the redoubt with the few guns and the limited ordinance that they had to hand. Unfortunately, as Richard had earlier predicted, the English cannon balls had little or no effect on the thick walls of the redoubt, the greater number of them ineffectually bouncing off the walls into the wide moat that surrounded the redoubt on three sides. Every now and again the odd shot did meet with limited success, managing to chip away some slithers of stone from the Castle's walls. These rare and infrequent successes were met both with ironic cheers from the English infantry and by boos of derision from the Scottish defenders, who anticipating an imminent attack had began to muster in force upon the battlements. Francis shuddered as all of his predictions came true. Northumberland, by insisting upon this pointless artillery barrage had merely alerted the garrison to their plans. To add insult to injury the Scottish gunners replied in earnest, laying down an altogether more successful barrage that wrought havoc amongst the ranks of the unprotected English infantry, as they stood out in the open waiting for orders to attack. Upon being forced to witness the debacle and knowing that it was only going to get much worse, Francis rode to the rear in a final attempt to implore Northumberland to reconsider. Disgusted Francis soon discovered that Northumberland, thinking only of his own personal glory, was both oblivious to and was disinterested in his armies hardships. Once again disregarding Francis's advice and ignorant to the potential losses that the English army would suffer, Northumberland insisted that the attack must still take place.

Upon returning to their front line Francis had no alternative but to order their men to advance. As the English men at arms and archers moved forward, more of the garrisons defenders, buoyed by the success of their artillery, took up their positions upon the ramparts. Through a hailstorm of arrows and shot the English, led by Francis, charged across the field which separated them from the moat and beyond it their goal, the redoubt. Those who were fortunate enough to make it across the meadow launched themselves into the wide but shallow waters that surrounded the stronghold. The English soldiers carried little in the way of arms as many of them were weighed down by the ladders, with which they hoped to scale the walls. Walls that had stubbornly remained intact, despite the best efforts of the English artillery. Francis despite being involved in many previous engagements had no experience of such an action, that is for an army to attempt to storm an almost impregnable position. He was horrified to see how many of his men fell, as the defenders immune to attack and cosseted by the redoubts walls fired down upon the English with impunity. One couldn't fault the spirit of the English men at arms, who in the face of such extreme hardship continued on doggedly. Francis smiled. His men were even able to cheer, on those rare occasions when their own archers managed to pick off one of the Scots from the walls above them. As the men stumbled forward through the mud and silt towards the base of the redoubt's wall, the stench that emanated from the foul and stagnant waters of the moat was almost unbearable. As a pitifully few number of Englishmen managed to reach their initial goal, the base of the redoubts walls, the defenders efforts intensified and soon rocks and even burning oil were thrown down upon them through those gaps in the wall that were designed for such murderous attacks. As he too reached the base of the wall Francis backed himself into a slight enclave, to rest and to try and take stock of their situation. Of the three hundred or so men at arms and archers who had begun the attack, Francis estimated that at least half of their number were already either dead or wounded. From his position Francis could see that Northumberland and his entourage, who not unsurprisingly hadn't joined in the attack, were trying desperately to rally those troops who had already had enough and were dejectedly making there way back towards the English camp. Angered Francis desperately wanted to call a halt to the proceedings but he knew that to do so at this point would be deemed desertion. Etiquette dictated that Northumberland, as the highest ranking officer within the English army, would himself have to call upon their heralds to sound the retreat. Presently however Northumberland seemed oblivious to their situation and both he and his household men, rather than concentrating upon the enemy, were preoccupied with the task of driving their dispirited men back towards the moat and into the unanswered and unwavering fire of the enemy. Francis knew that it was only he, amongst the English commanders, who actually appreciated the precariousness of their position. If the Scots seized the initiative they could easily ride out of the Castle and drive the English from both the meadow and their now undefended camp.

Rested, Francis together with the few men who were in his immediate vicinity planted their ladder at the base of the wall, with difficulty they swung it upwards. Disbelieving, Francis groaned and his men swore at the incompetence of their leadership. The ladder was a full four feet short or the top of the wall, it was of no use to them.

'Right that's it.'

Francis said as he discarded what arms and armour he had to make his retreat that much easier.

Shouting loudly, to make himself heard over the furor, Francis screamed at his men to retreat. The Englishmen needed no further encouragement and those who were still able to, hastily made there way back across the moat and over the meadow that was now strewn with their own dead, all making for the relative safety of their camp.

Not unexpectedly Northumberland was furious and he threatened both Francis and his men with immediate execution for their cowardice. That was until Francis pointed out to Northumberland that they'd failed, not through the want of trying, but as a result of his ineptitude, incompetence that had cost them the lives of at least fifty percent of their army. Now, Francis said, the English army, which had been left at Berwick, one that had always been small, was in real danger of being overwhelmed by the Scottish defenders. Even Northumberland winced when Francis said that they could only guess what Richard reaction would be when he heard news of the defeat.

Fortunately for the English, when it came to matters military, the Scots were almost as incompetent as Northumberland. As such Berwick's defenders chose not press home their advantage by attacking the English camp, but remained within the Castle, whilst the English regrouped and awaited reinforcements. Francis fearing that the Scots may attack at any time had ordered the men to perform double guard duties and had also ensured that each man lit two fires in the evening, this in the hope that the defenders would assume that, despite the defeat, the English army at Berwick remained intact. By way of compensation for the survivors, Francis was at least able to relax the rationing that had been in force for the duration of the siege, for now they had far fewer mouths to feed!

It was with mixed feelings of excitement, which were tempered with trepidation that Francis received the news that Richard and his army were at long last returning to Berwick.

Ned had ridden south to Berwick in advance of the English army. Shocked at how their force had become so seriously depleted, Ned was at least able to tell Francis that Richard too had met with little success and that his own expedition had also come to naught.

As it transpired, the duplicitous Duke of Albany had been in secret correspondence with his brother King James all along and James had managed to buy Albany off with the promise of Land and titles. Consequently, the coward that he was, Albany had made off in the dead of night and had joined the Scottish army. Moreover many from amongst the Scottish nobility had unexpectedly supported King James. These men choosing to blame James's 'Evil' and 'Selfish' councilors for the misgovernment. As a result James' advisors were forced to pay the ultimate price for their mismanagement of Scottish affairs, all being hanged from the bridge at Cawdor. The Scots keen to expel the hated English from their homeland had flocked to James's banner and as Richard no longer possessed an alternative to James kingship, he chose not to fight but to retire to Berwick and hoped that by taking the town he'd at least be able to salvage something from the expedition.

'Goodness know', Francis thought, what Richard would think when he saw what was left of the force he'd left behind.

Initially, as Francis had anticipated Richard was furious with him. Thankfully once Richard had vented his anger, which in reality was directed more towards Northumberland and Fauconberg than towards anyone else, Richard accepted that Francis had had no option but to comply with Northumberland's orders. Francis had pointed out that had he completely washed his hands of the whole matter, as he'd been advised to do so by Ned, then they would have found themselves in an altogether worse predicament.

Richard at once held a board of enquiry into the matter, this resulted in the Earl of Northumberland being sent home to Alnwick in disgrace. Fauconberg fared much worse and once again found himself clapped in irons and branded a traitor. Warwick's cousin was immediately dispatched to Middleham, where he was at long last dealt with as such. Fauconberg had outlived his usefulness to the Yorkists and as a result Richard had finally got the head, which he'd so earnestly sought in the aftermath of Tewkesbury. With the death of Fauconberg the Yorkshire branch of the Neville family were finally consigned to history. Happily the English lost no further men in the Scottish campaign, as Berwick's garrison, upon seeing the reinforced English army and upon being threatened by Richard's heralds that if they failed to surrender they would be 'butchered to the last men,' soon came to terms. They were allowed to march unscathed from Berwick and return to Edinburgh, to the King who'd failed to come to their assistance. It was said that King James saw Berwick as a small price to pay for getting the English off his back and both Richard and Edward were relieved that they'd at least got something from a campaign that so easily could have gone disastrously wrong. All, save that is for the Earl of Northumberland and the 'Bastard' of fauconberg, returned home, both with their reputations intact and with a useful insight into the weaknesses and characters of those men who'd accompanied them on their expedition into Scotland.

Chapter 21
April 1483, Ravensworth.

Since returning from Scotland, Francis had led a somewhat peaceful, if solitary, existence, dividing his time between Yorkshire and his beloved Minster Lovel. Anne, his wife, increasingly distant, singularly refused to accompany him on his trips to Oxfordshire, even here, at her family home in Yorkshire, she refused to spend time with her husband. That said, Francis had long since given up hope of restoring himself to Anne's good grace and, as a consequence, willingly to her bed. As his father had done so before him, and as he'd promised himself that he would never do, Francis was now obliged to satiate his desires for the opposite sex with those village woman who, unlike his wife, seemed to appreciate his attentions. Francis, in his vanity, had often wondered if these woman were attracted by his looks or by his money! In all honesty it mattered not to Francis, who smiled, as he considered how in recent months he'd even managed to acquire quite a reputation for himself amongst the woman folk of Wensleydale. Even if this was only as one who would pay only too well for their services! Resigned to this life, Francis was only really saddened by the thought that it was now highly unlikely that he would ever be able to produce a legitimate heir to carry on after him. A son, who would share in the inheritance that Francis had fought so long and hard to amass. A fortune that would now, in all likelihood, be shared out amongst his sisters and their families. Francis sighed, he could not hope to remarry whilst his wife still lived and presently Anne was as strong as she was stubborn. Francis smiled as he considered that Anne, probably out of spite alone, would no doubt do her damnedest to outlive her husband! In recent years Francis had often wondered how their marriage had come to this? Their early relationship, that had promised so much, now seemed but a distant dream. Other people in another lifetime. Children who, despite being thrown together by circumstances beyond their control, had willingly given themselves to each other. Francis had often tried to rationalise where it had all gone wrong and when their relationship had started to break down. Yes, it had been a gradual thing, but things had really started to deteriorate with the death of Anne's eldest brother Henry at Edgecote. This was a death for whom Anne, without cause, had deemed Francis responsible. In reality it had been Anne's younger brother Richard who, through his cowardice, was really to blame for his brother's demise. Unfortunately, in an effort to protect his wife, Francis had never told her the truth of what had happened and now, ironically, and much to Francis's chagrin, Richard Fitzhugh remained his sister's favourite, whilst Francis, who was blameless in the matter, had become increasingly alienated.

As with Francis, his friend Richard had also remained for the most part in the north. Thankfully, the Scottish campaign had rekindled their friendship and now they met regularly, invariably at Middleham. There they would hunt in the surrounding moors and heathland and on their return they would both sit and talk for hours, just as they had done at Middleham all those years ago! They talked of that which had passed and also that which their futures may yet still have in store for them. On these occasions, Richard would share with Francis his many fears and misgivings. How his brother the King, through his legendary excesses, was becoming increasingly more unfit. How, as a consequence, Richard feared for Edward's well-being. How the Queen continued to promote and marry off her many Woodville relations into the upper echelons of society. How the King's eldest son and heir, Edward Prince of Wales, a resident at Ludlow Castle in the tutelage of the Queens brother Lord Rivers, was rumoured to have fallen under the influence of that family. Richard had confided in Francis that he no longer felt safe in London, where he said the Woodvilles had 'spies everywhere.' Francis had tried to reassure his friend, pointing out that since they'd returned 'triumphant' from Scotland, Richard had established himself as one of the nations foremost magnates. Indeed, Richard now presided over what could only be described as his own northern palatinate. Moreover, in the past year alone, the King had conferred upon Richard many titles, these honours in addition to those privileges which Edward had already bestowed upon his last surviving brother. The wardenship of the west marches, the castle and City of Carlisle and all of the crown lands of Cumberland. Francis had tried to reassure Richard by pointing out that the King was his greatest ally and was, above all else, a friend and a comrade who had much to thank him for. Francis argued that Edward would never move against Richard, for he loved him, this in spite of what his Queen's opinion may have been. Unfortunately, Richard, as always both stubborn and fatalistic, never really listened to Francis's arguments. Richard alarmed Francis, as with the news of his brother's ailing health, he became increasingly more upset, disturbed, and on occasions even quite paranoid! Richard had often asked Francis what would become of him and his own family in the event of the King's death. Concerned for his friends mental well being, Francis had always tried to make light of Richard's concerns by laughing them off. Yes, he said, Edward might be obese and unfit, much given over to the pleasures of the flesh, but relatively speaking the King was, even by the standards of the age, still a young man. Francis had pointed out that Edward, who'd been quite a warrior and an athlete in his time, at only forty must have had many more years of life in front of him!

It was, therefore, with both surprise and alarm that Francis received the news that both he and Richard had dreaded. That of the untimely death of the King. In the second week of April, Francis, sleeping alone at Ravensworth, was woken in the early hours by one of Richard's servants who'd been admitted to his chambers to deliver the news that the King, who was still not yet forty one, had died in London after a short and unexpected illness.

The servant, who'd rushed to Ravensworth from Middleham where Richard was currently residing, had added with dismay.

'My Lord of Gloucester has asked that you come at once. He says that the Queen and her relations have poisoned the King and are now daily plotting his demise.'

Francis, who'd witnessed first hand Richard's increasing insecurity, took little persuading and within hours he was at his friends side.

Richard's features were both pale and drawn. It was obvious to Francis that his friend had slept little since he'd heard news of his brother's death. As Francis entered Richard's chambers, Richard, who appeared deep in thought, hardly even acknowledged his presence. Francis smiled wryly as he noticed that Richard was nervously fiddling with his signet ring, as he was apt to do when under pressure.

'I'm so sorry to hear of your loss,'

Francis wasn't able to express his condolences further as Richard interrupted him.

'My brother's in a better place than I and, much as I loved him, I don't fear for him as I fear for those of us who are left behind.' Richard sighed deeply as he added, 'Edward was the only thing that stood between me and the Queen and her relations.'

At once he became sterner.

'Francis, that Woodville woman won't rest until we're all undone. Elizabeth and her brood detest us. She's always sworn to have her revenge upon those who refused to acknowledge the legitimacy of her marriage to the King. She won't be satisfied until she's destroyed all of us.' Richard sighed again and as he turned towards him Francis could see that his friend was wearing a deep frown upon his forehead.

Richard was clearly concerned. 'Did you know that the Queen even tried to prevent me from being told of my brother's death. I only found out that Edward had died from Lord Hastings, who, fearing that the

Woodvilles would attempt to seize power before I could act, sent his personal messenger to me.' Without giving Francis the opportunity to reply, Richard continued. 'Apparently Elizabeth has already sent to Ludlow for my nephew the Prince of Wales. Hastings has told me that the Queen hopes to crown the Prince before I'm able to claim the Regency that was promised to me by my brother and that office, I fear, is the only thing that can prevent our ruination.'

Now, even Francis was concerned. Why would the Queen delay in telling Richard of his own brother's death? Unless of course she was plotting to exclude him from the government, or even worse!

Calmer, Richard went on, 'I've thought long and hard about this. Francis, there is only one way to prevent the Woodvilles from destroying us all. We must intercept the Prince before he's able to reach London. I'm sure that given time I'll be able to convince Edward that he has nothing to fear yet much to gain from my Regency. He's too young and impressionable to be allowed to rule alone, but with the benefit of my experience, given time, he could become a great King.' Francis, who was still trying to take it all in, massaged his brow and remained silent as Richard continued excitedly. 'Francis, we have only the slightest of opportunities. My agents tell me that the Prince is due to leave Ludlow in the next few days. If we're able to intercept him en route to the capital, I can accompany him into London. Hopefully, I'll then have time to convince the Prince that his future security is dependent upon my being able to govern on his behalf. Until, that is, he is mature enough to succeed to the throne.' Sterner, Richard added, 'Hopefully I can make him understand that I mean him no harm. If I can do this then my nephew may accept me as his Regent and I can thereby maintain the status quo.' Richard sighed as he added. 'On the other hand if I do nothing and the Prince reaches the capital and his mother, then neither Hastings nor myself can hope to dissuade him from assuming the throne and in doing so becoming a puppet of the Woodvilles.'

Francis's mind was in a whirl as he began to appreciate the precariousness of their position. Richard, on the other hand, had obviously thought long and hard about his next move. He spoke with confidence as he added. 'My brother decreed that in the event of his death, whilst his son was still in his minority, I alone should be Protector of the realm. The Queen will resist this.' He smiled at Francis as he added, 'We must endeavor to secure the Prince's person. For it is only by doing so that we may prevent the Queen and her relations from seizing power.'

'But what of the council.'

Francis asked, referring to those other magnates through whose counsel the King had previously ruled.

Richard, who'd obviously been extremely busy in the short period that had elapsed since he'd heard of his brother's death, did little to cheer Francis as he warned.

'Many of the old nobility are weak and they are divided. They fear the Queen and will never act on their own.' Richard smiled as he added, 'Catesby, whose been with his master these past few weeks, assures me that Lord Hastings is with us. It's no secret that the Queen hates him and blames him for the excesses that, she maintains, led to Edward's untimely death. We can also rely on my cousin the Duke of Buckingham, he is on the move as we speak. He's agreed to meet me at York. I've already called out our own men and they're to muster either here at Middleham or at York. From there we will all march upon the capital. If we leave at first light and travel with speed we should be able to intercept the Prince and his party once they join the Great North Road somewhere in the Midlands.'

Francis prickled with pride. What other Duke was so highly regarded by his subjects that, at such short notice, he could call them out, to follow him to the capital and into a situation that could easily develop into civil war? Especially when one considered that, for the most part, these men had had a belly full of war and could easily be forgiven for ignoring Richard's call to arms.

As Francis had predicted, Richard of Gloucester was much loved by the northerners, who turned out in force to join him on his march upon London. Francis estimated that, together with the five hundred men that Henry Stafford, Duke of Buckingham had brought with him, their small army numbered some three thousand men-at-arms and archers, with an additional two hundred horse. Quite a host to have been assembled at such short notice! All of the old names and faces were there, men who'd lived and fought together for many years. In fact, out of all of the battle captains, it was only the young Duke of Buckingham who had no experience in the ways of war. That said, what Buckingham lacked in experience he made up for in the magnetism of his personality. Buckingham was of the old nobility, of the house of Stafford, a direct descendant of Thomas Woodstock, who had himself been the Duke of Gloucester and was the youngest son of Edward III. Born to lead, Buckingham was the epitome of all that was aristocratic. A proud man who carried himself as a Prince of the blood royal. Unusually for one so young, Buckingham at once commanded the men's respect. Richard had seen little of his Royal cousin since

Buckingham had been married off, whilst still a minor, into the Queens family. That said, Richard was clearly extremely impressed by his new ally. Taking Francis to one side, Richard had told Francis how relieved he was that both Buckingham and Hastings were on his side. Richard had said that now there were few in the Kingdom who could stand in their way. This had puzzled Francis who understood that their intention had been merely to safely escort the Prince to his capital and in doing so, Richard had hoped to appraise his nephew of their good intentions towards both him and his regime.

It soon became apparent to Francis that Buckingham despised both the Queen and her family. Whilst still a small child and very much against his will, Buckingham had been forcibly married to the Queen's cousin Catherine Woodville who was much older than he. As a result of this unhappy union, Buckingham bore an intense hatred for anything Woodville, those who had, he said, used his family's power and influence for their own ends. It was Buckingham who, above all others, was most vociferous in his condemnation of the Queen and her family.

'They'll not settle until they've destroyed all of the old nobility.'

He said, as once again they'd concluded their days march late and were settling down for the night after yet another hurried evening meal. Richard's scouts had reported that the Prince, who was ahead of them on the road, was accompanied by his uncle and tutor, Earl Rivers, and was traveling lightly with few men. As such, Richard pointed out that it would be extremely difficult for their own army to catch them before they reached the capital. Consequently, Richard had ordered that they were all to march from daybreak until nightfall, this being the only means by which they could hope to intercept the Prince's party. Surprisingly, few of their men had grumbled at the prospect of either a forced march or at sleeping out in the open, for tents would take too long to erect and take down each day. This was further evidence, if one needed it, of both the Yorkshire men's robustness and the respect that they all had for Richard.

Francis couldn't help but notice the hatred that was evident upon Buckingham's face as he continued, 'It's even said that the Woodville woman poisoned our King because she was jealous of both his mistresses and of his love for Hastings and my Lord of Gloucester.' As Buckingham said this, he nodded in deference towards Richard, who was leaning close to the fire in an effort to escape the chill of the evening. In spite of the intense pressure that he was clearly under, Richard, the archetypal soldier, seemed to be thoroughly enjoying himself, smiling as he gnawed on a piece of lamb bone and nodding in agreement towards Buckingham. Francis also smiled, they might be in for another cold and uncomfortable night, but at least they were all well fed, he thought. Richard, finishing his meal, tossed what remained of the young sheep onto the fire. The poor mite who only hours earlier had been skipping and jumping in the field in which they were all bivouacked, had been caught, butchered, cooked and devoured, all in the space of two hours! Francis smiled again, what had until recently been a relatively large flock of ewes and their new born lambs, was now seriously depleted in numbers, reduced by an entire army of hungry men. Francis chuckled to himself, the landowner would have a shock on the morning when he discovered that an army of Yorkshire men had all dined that evening at his expense! Well, he could afford it, Francis thought, for now it seemed that the middle classes of the Midlands had far more in the way of wealth than their northern counterparts.

Buckingham, who was drinking heavily, became increasingly agitated and vociferous.

'It's even said that she had the Duke of Clarence killed after she'd put a spell on the King, turning him against his brother and forcing him to sign Clarence's death warrant against his will.'

Cheekily, Richard agreed with Buckingham. Francis smiled, for only they and a few others, men who could be trusted not to talk, really knew the truth behind Clarence's execution. It was probably better, Francis felt, that those assembled added this misdemeanor to those crimes attributed to the Woodvilles, rather than to Richard who needed their support.

Not for the first time on the march the conversation lasted long into the night. This as no-one relished the prospect of their makeshift accommodation and all were keen to hear more revelations from Richard and Buckingham, both of whom seemed intent upon blackening the Queen's reputation even further.

By the evening of the 28th April, Richard's army had reached the town of Northampton which, situated astride the great north road, was still some miles short of Stony Stratford, where both Rivers and the Prince were said to be. Surprisingly, upon their arrival at Northampton, Richard commanded their men to halt. He then ordered them to dig up ordnance and arms that King Edward had had buried there some decades before. The arms had apparently been secreted by Edward in the event that they should ever be needed in a war against the Scots. After a number of years in the ground the arms were, in Francis's opinion, of little use. Not unsurprisingly, the steel was rusted and the leather was rotted. Francis found it difficult to understand how Richard could ever deem these arms of any use to them at present. Even after

Richard had ordered that the armaments be displayed in open wagons, with those carrying the Woodville insignia being the most prominent, Francis couldn't guess what their true purpose was. That was until Richard at last confided in him. Richard said that upon their arrival in London they would use the weapons to discredit the Queen and her relations. They would accuse the Woodvilles of stockpiling the arms in the expectation of a civil war. When Francis began to protest at this untruth, Richard merely brushed aside his concerns and laughing said that all was 'fair in war.' He added wryly, that, 'The end justified the means.'

'And anyway.'

Richard added.

'I've a far more important task for you.'

Francis looked at his friend quizzically.

'What would you have me do?'

He asked.

Serious, Richard said.

'I need you to bring the Prince to me. I have had word that he's at Stony Stratford with a small contingent of Welsh men-at-arms. We've marched flat out for these past few days and I must concede that in the present circumstances we have little hope of catching the Prince before he reaches the capital. If he reaches London before us the Queen will do her best to ensure that he's crowned forthwith. Francis, take two hundred of our horse and ride to Stony Stratford. You must persuade the Prince to turn back and join me here at Northampton. He must come, and Francis, you must see to it that he respects his uncle's wishes.'

Richard smiled, as he added. 'If I have control of the Prince the Queen will be forced to acquiesce and accept me as the Regent, just as my brother wished.'

'But what if he refuses to come.'

Francis said, wondering why the Prince would give himself up to one whom he'd no doubt been warned to be extremely wary of.

Richard, who was beginning to worry Francis, smiled.

'Francis, come now, you're a soldier. You must attend upon my nephew regaled in full armour. You will be at the head of two hundred horse.' Richard chuckled as he added, 'I think in such circumstances, any request that you make for Prince Edward to do his duty by his uncle, cannot be refused.'

Francis was perplexed, only he could speak to Richard with such candor. 'I thought that you merely hoped to gain an audience with the Prince before he reached London and came under the influence of the

Queen. Why don't you ride with me and we can both speak with Edward at Stony Stratford.'

Adding to Francis's increasing sense of foreboding, Richard disclosed his true intentions.

'Francis, have you not been listening to what my cousin Buckingham has had to say about these Woodvilles. Surely he must be believed, for he's been at court whilst we've remained in the north. Prince Edward has spent all of his life amongst the Woodvilles. Do you honestly believe that a brief audience with me will correct all of those years of bias and Woodville indoctrination? No, I'm now sure that unless I'm created Regent as my brother intended, I am undone. So Francis my friend, the Prince must come, he will come.'

With these words ringing in his ears, Francis, fully armoured and at the head of two hundred mounted men-at-arms, in the growing dusk of a calm spring evening, clattered down the Great North Road. In a relatively short space of time both Francis and his men, unhindered by any foot soldiers, were able to negotiate the few miles that lay between Richard at Northampton and Prince Edward and his followers at Stony Stratford.

With the good grace and the manners that one would expect of one of such high birth, Edward Prince of Wales immediately, and without question, admitted Francis into his presence. If the Prince distrusted his uncle's motives he gave nothing away as he asked after Richard, his 'late father's' 'dearest' and 'most loyal subject.'

Physically the Prince was certainly his father's son, for he was both tall and fair. Although of a lighter frame than his father had been, Edward possessed all of the beauty and grace for which the late King was renowned in his earlier years. In demeanor however, Francis at once noticed that the Prince was not quite as straightforward nor as plain speaking as his father had been. Francis smiled, Edward had obviously been schooled well in both politics and diplomacy, for before the Prince spoke he took time to give a measured and thoughtful response. Francis soon noticed that the Prince, who belied his young age, said nothing that wasn't first carefully considered. Indeed, if Prince Edward had nothing of note to say he would happily remain quiet, a custom that Francis, one who was used to 'plain speaking', found quite disconcerting. Francis, who had never been much of a diplomat, would try to fill these embarrassing silences with all kinds of polite drivel and then he would silently chide himself for speaking such foolishness in the presence of the Prince and his uncle, Lord Rivers. Francis smiled, in his opinion, one day Edward would make a good

King. Francis chuckled to himself as he considered that the young Prince's manner contrasted sharply with that which had been adopted by his father before him. The late King Edward, in all of the time that Francis had known him, had never minced his words and would always speak his mind, regardless of the consequences. Francis smiled again, this was probably why King Edward would invariably get himself into difficulties in those negotiations that he'd personally undertaken.

On arriving at Stony Stratford, Francis had been pleased to see that the Woodvilles had accepted Lord Hasting's advice, when he'd earlier counseled them that the Prince, for fear of inflaming the populace, should march upon the capital with only a small force of Welshmen. Thus, when the Prince received Richard's invitation, which was delivered by both Francis and his two hundred mounted men-at-arms, he was in no position to resist his uncle by force. Francis could not tell if Richard's request alarmed the Prince, who remained quite calm as he listened politely to Francis. Once Francis had finished the Prince turned to Lord Rivers, who was sitting at his side. After some whispering between themselves the Prince replied.

'Unfortunately I must decline my uncle's kind offer. We've already been on the road for a number of days and my mother, the Queen, says that it is of the utmost importance that I join her as soon as possible. She has commanded that I be at her side in London before the week is out. Please tell my uncle Richard that I hope to meet with him in the near future, to personally thank him for the loyalty and the support that he has given without question, to both my father and hopefully to me.'

The Prince must have noticed the grimace upon Francis's face as he replied, for he added, with only the merest hint of distress. 'You must appreciate, Lord Lovel, that if I go to him now my journey will be delayed by at least another two days.'

For the briefest of moments the Prince glanced away from Francis. Having composed himself again he smiled sweetly, before he added.

'Surely Uncle Richard would not wish to come between a mother and her son, especially at such a time as this.'

Francis winced and hoped that his expression would not give away his uneasiness. For Richard had been quite clear in his instructions and Francis knew that he must now insist. If the Prince refused to come, Francis was under orders to arrest him and forcibly bring him before Richard at Northampton. As he stood there before his future King, Francis could only imagine what would become of him in the event that Richard's plan failed, as, once crowned, the Prince would be in a position to exact a terrible revenge upon those who'd wronged him.

Francis tried to be positive, thankfully as he'd ridden to Stony Stratford he'd at least had some time to consider how he would proceed, should the Prince be reticent to accompany him.

'Sire I must insist. Your uncle, the Duke of Gloucester, fears for your safety in these troubled times. I see that you have only a small force of men-at-arms with you and this road is renowned for being the haunt of many ruffians and villains. Those who, in spite of your noble birth, would think nothing of robbing both you and your men. That is why I stand before you armed as I am and why you must come with me now and submit yourself into the protection of your uncle.'

Smiling Francis added, 'I understand that your father wished it so.'

Francis wondered if, like him, the Prince had also anticipated this conversation, for having listened to Francis Edward appeared unmoved and immediately offered a compromise.

'After so many days traveling I'm tired. Let Lord Rivers go with you now. He has spent too long in the company of children and is desperate for meaningful debate. Both he and Richard can supper together and can talk long into the night, for there is much to be decided. Let Rivers pay my respects to my uncle on my behalf. I'm safe here and I will wait with my bodyguard until my uncle is able to bring up the remainder of his men and then, in safety, we will all enter the capital together.'

Francis now found himself in a real dilemma. Surely, if the Prince did as he wished, they could still achieve all that they'd sought without having to resort to violence. They could secure the Prince's person but would still remain in his good grace. But on the other hand, it was possible that Edward, fearing foul play, as soon as Francis's back was turned, would take the first opportunity to make a run for the capital.

Sighing at last Francis acquiesced to the Prince's request.

'Only on the understanding that I leave half of my force with you to ensure your continued safety.'

The Prince could not object. He too sighed and Francis smiled triumphantly, for with Francis's men to keep him company Edward would now have to stay put at Stony Stratford.

The Prince did ensure however that he had the last word. 'My Lord Lovel, you worry me, my advisors tell me that I inherit a peaceful and prosperous kingdom, yet you tell me that I have subjects who wish me ill. I pray to God that you are wrong and that this isn't so.'

Francis winced again, as he wondered to whom the Prince referred?

On the short journey back to Northampton, Francis didn't speak with Lord Rivers who, with his head bowed and deep in thought, behaved more as a prisoner than a guest. Even Francis, who was perhaps as close to Richard as any other man, could not guess how his friend would react to the news that Prince Edward had refused to join him at Northampton. Moreover, Francis could only guess what Richard had in store for Rivers and the other pro Woodville retainers who'd accompanied the Prince. Did Richard have a plan that was known only to him? Or was he merely reacting to events as they occurred? One could only guess. Was Rivers a friend or was he an enemy? Was he a guest or was he a prisoner?

Thankfully, once his party had arrived at Richard's camp Francis's mind was put at ease. Richard had at last ordered that the tents be erected and that the men rest for a couple of days. On hearing the news that the young Prince had chosen to remain at Stony Stratford, Francis saw only the briefest wave of anger appear upon Richard's face. Looking at Rivers, Francis couldn't tell if the older man had noticed it too. If Richard was in fact angry, he cleverly concealed it as, much to Francis's surprise, he warmly welcomed the Queen's brother with open arms.

'My dear Rivers, it's been quite sometime since we last spoke. We have a great deal to discuss. Please do me the honour of dining with me this evening. The Duke of Buckingham is here and I have lately heard news from Hastings in London.'

Almost as an afterthought Richard added.

'And how is my young nephew. The Prince, who has had much to take in during recent weeks, has traveled far. I understand that he is settled at Stony Stratford and I look forward to seeing him there tomorrow or the day after. Perhaps it's better that we have time alone to talk, for there is much to decide and my nephew cannot yet be fully versed in the niceties of government.'

Richard smiled at Francis as he added.

'I thank God that I am able to serve my brother's son, as I served his father before him.'

That evening the men enjoyed an extremely pleasurable meal in Richard's tent and all retired at a very late hour, not a little drunk! During the evening all had professed both their loyalty and their continued support for Prince Edward and the Yorkist regime. Francis was not the only one who was relieved that the atmosphere was one of friendship. To him it appeared as if a great weight had been lifted from all of their shoulders. Rivers, who with good reason had no doubt expected trouble, appeared overjoyed as Richard spoke of how he would be the Prince's champion, as he'd been Edward's before. They all discussed how they would meet the challenges posed by King Edward's untimely death. How they would deal both with England's lawlessness and the French, who, hoping to take advantage of the political instability within England, were already rumoured to be moving towards an all out war. Apparently the French King, upon hearing the news of Edward's death, had put his navy to sea and presently his ships were harrying English merchantmen in the channel. Rivers was at least able to reassure them that the Queen had given the command of the fleet to her kinsman Sir Edward Woodville and that he too had put to sea in an effort to bring the French to battle. Richard laughed.

'I heard that he'd taken to sea to avoid me. It gladdens me to learn that your family's motives are far more patriotic than I could ever have imagined.'

All of those others present joined Richard in his merriment, clapping each other on the back and toasting each others future. Friends at last, Francis wondered, as hr noticed that Richard now appeared to be intent on forging an alliance with the Woodvilles, who'd have believed it!

Not for the first time, Francis was however soon brought back down to earth with a thud. He woke on the following day to discover that Richard's mood had darkened considerably. One couldn't excuse Richard's poor humour on the grounds of a hangover alone, for it went much further than mere headaches and nausea. Lord Rivers, suspecting nothing, arrived at Richard's tent early, having been invited on the previous evening to breakfast with his new found friends. It didn't take Rivers very long to realise that a great deal had changed in the few hours that had elapsed since he'd left his companions in such good spirits.

Neither Richard nor Buckingham took the hand that Rivers offered in friendship. Clearly alarmed, Woodville was soon flanked by armed guards, each of whom took hold of his arms as he began to protest and question the reasons for such a reversal in Richard's attitude towards him.

Francis was forced to concede that Richard played his part well, for he seemed genuinely distraught, as he bewailed both Rivers and the Woodville's treachery. This having apparently been reported to him during the night by one of Catesby's spies who'd traveled up from London.

Richard, appeared genuinely affronted as he addressed Rivers, who by that time had stopped struggling and, non plussed, stood meekly before them. 'And at what point were you going to tell me that your sister, my brother's Queen, had approached the council with a view to crowning the Prince in all haste, thereby excluding me from the Protector ship?'

Rivers seemed confused.

'Surely, my Lord, you would like to see the Prince crowned, for an early coronation would show the rest of the world, especially France, that all of England are squarely behind our new King. At York you insisted that your men swore fealty to their new King. Surely if we are together in this and we all have your nephew's interests at heart, then we have no need of a protector ship. The Prince, in spite of his tender age, can govern his Kingdom through the council, of which you would still be the principal member.'

Richard was clearly well rehearsed and to Francis, who knew his friend well, it was obvious that both he and Buckingham had already decided the Queens brothers fate. Rivers looked around the room, desperately searching for a friendly face, for someone in whom he could trust to argue his case. His eyes rested upon Francis, the one person who'd earlier personally guaranteed his safety to the Prince. Francis could offer nothing and, embarrassed, he looked away as Richard continued his tirade.

'Do not dare to question my loyalty towards my brother's son. The late King made it known to all that in the event of his death, whilst his son was still a minor, I would become the protector and the defender of this realm. A regent who would rule England until the Prince comes of age.'

Trembling with anger Richard screamed at the Rivers, 'By opposing my brother's will you commit treason and for this I'll have your head.'

All present knew that it was pointless for Rivers to complain further, even though they were all aware that in common law Rivers actions could never be deemed treasonous. One couldn't commit treason against a King who was already dead! But clearly both Richard and Buckingham had made up their minds and presumably they were supported in this by Lord Hastings. Thus, none present said anything in defence of either the Queen or her family. Richard and Buckingham both glowered as their retainers cried 'treason' and Rivers, head bowed and shoulders slumped, was led away. Afterwards, concerned and in an effort to understand why Richard's policy towards the Woodvilles had seemingly taken yet another turn, Francis had sought out his friend.

Richard smiled.

'Francis I thought that you of all people would have guessed that I always intended to deal with them so. Ratcliffes at Pontefract gathering troops and Lord Rivers will join him there,' Richard laughed as he added, 'Although I doubt that Rivers will enjoy making Ratcliffe's acquaintance.'

Richard chuckled, 'I couldn't tell you of my plans before, you're far too honest for your own good, one would only have to look at your face for you to have given the game away. That's why I sent you. Francis, your reputation precedes you wherever you go. If the Prince had feared that I intended to seize him, he'd have made all out for London and the Queen. As it is, I have him. Rivers will soon be joined by those others who'd have happily seen me deprived of the regency.' Francis, open mouthed, could only gape as, laughing, Richard added, 'I've posted pickets all along the road to Stoney Stratford. The Prince will hear of our coup only when we pay him a visit. When all of his household men are sent away, my young nephew will no doubt wish that he'd been more accommodating when I requested the pleasure of his company.'

Francis didn't now know whether to admire or to fear his friend. If he, Francis, who'd been Richard's friend for many years, couldn't read Richard's thoughts, then who could?

As planned, Prince Edward had no inkling as to what was afoot when his uncle Richard, together with Buckingham and Francis, visited him later that morning. Edward did however appear to Francis to be mildly alarmed when Richard failed either to kneel before him or to offer him fealty. The King's chamberlain Sir Thomas Vaughan and Prince Edward's half brother, Lord Richard Grey, were waved aside by Buckingham as they attempted to protest at this insult. For the second time that day, Richard cried treason and as he did so a large number of armed men, who'd been waiting outside the chamber, rushed in and carried off both Vaughan and Grey, who were obviously so shocked by Richard's propensity for violence that neither had the time, nor the inclination, to protest further.

Surprisingly, Prince Edward who throughout the incident had remained quite composed turned towards Richard and demanded.

'On whose authority do you arrest my servants?'

Once again Richard repeated his accusations of Woodville treason.

The Prince replied.

'These men were chosen to serve me by my father and can therefore be only faithful and good, they have my interests at heart and I can believe no ill of them unless it is proven to the contrary. I have full confidence in all of the peers of this realm and in my mother the Queen, I have seen no evil in them.'

Rudely, Buckingham did not wait to be addressed as he replied on Richard's behalf. 'Young Sir, you would do well to remember that it is men and not women who govern Kingdoms.' He smiled as he added,

'If you still cherish any confidence in your mother you had better relinquish it, for we will not be ruled by your mother's loathsome race.'

Shouting Richard joined in his cousins tirade,

'Proof, you demand proof from one whom your father would have as your Regent. Are you Plantagenet or Woodville? It was I above all others who helped your father win his throne. I have given my all in the service of this family. I've lost my father, brothers who were all dear to me, as well as countless friends as a consequence of my loyalty to your father. Yet you, a pimply youth who's not yet fourteen dares to demand proof from me. Is your uncle's word not good enough? Am I right to assume that you have been brainwashed by your mothers family? Do you believe their lies above my own honesty?'

It was fair to say that even Francis was quite shocked, he couldn't recall ever seeing his friend so angry. Richard was red with rage as he screamed, 'I am a Prince of the blood royal. Don't you ever dare to question me again.'

Prince Edward trembled and Francis wondered whether it was through anger or fear.

He too was now far less polite, nor was he measured in his words. 'Why do you speak to your King in such terms?'

Richard, who was clearly in no mood to be talked down to, replied.

'I don't address a King. I see before me a mere child, one who would be a King.'

Scoffing Richard added, 'And presently I see no crown upon your head.'

It seemed to Francis that the Prince, who up until that point had managed to maintain a semblance of composure, could now no longer control himself. Deprived of both his close friends and of the only family that he'd ever known, Edward burst into floods of uncontrollable tears. Buckingham sniggered and smirked. Richard, whose anger had clearly not dissipated, ignored his young nephew's distress. Turning his back on the Prince, Richard strode about the room, biting his lip and wringing his hands together as he chuntered to himself about how he'd been right about the Woodvilles all along and of how the Queen and her family had even managed turned his own brother's children against him.

Francis knew what it was to be young and alone amongst strangers. What it was like to lose a father at such a tender age. Forgetting himself he immediately went over to the Prince and putting his arms around the lad he tried to console him. Richard on the other hand angrily shouted to his guards to secure the Prince's person.

Angered, Francis waved the men away as he undertook to personally take charge of Edward and to convey him to his chambers.

Still sobbing, the Prince at least seemed a little calmed by the compassion that Francis had shown towards him.

He wiped his eyes with the silk kerchief that Francis had given him.

'My Lord Lovel, what is to become of me.'

Francis immediately and honestly sought to reassure the youth.

'Don't worry, presently your uncle's not himself. He fears for his safety for he's heard that your mother the Queen is plotting his downfall. You have nothing to fear from him for all he desires is the continuance of the Yorkist dynasty. Trust me, I've been friends with your uncle for many years. You will, I promise, find him to be your most loyal and fervent supporter.'

Edward seemed genuinely surprised by Francis's assurances.

'But my counselor's have all warned me that the Duke of Gloucester would see me dead and would have my crown for himself. Surely they have no cause to lie about such things. Does my uncle's recent behavior not support this theory?'

Francis laughed.

'Richard doesn't want your throne, he's busy enough in the north. You're mistaken. It is your mother and her relations who hope to rule England through you. The only people who can stand in their way are those Princes of the Royal blood. Both the Dukes of Gloucester and Buckingham fear for their own personal safety in a government dominated by your mother's family. Once they understand that they've nothing to fear from you, trust me they will become your most loyal subjects.'

As Francis left the young man alone in his chambers he wondered if the Prince believed him and would at least take time to consider what the intentions of both his mother and his uncle were. Francis smiled, when the young Prince became King he'd need to be a skilled negotiator indeed, if he was to bring together these two opposing factions under his rule. Francis knew that this couldn't be done whilst Edward was still a minor. As Regent Richard would have a number of years in which to prove to Edward that his intentions were entirely honourable. That said, Francis was worried. By publicly berating the Prince and by arresting his household men, Richard had created a rift between himself and the Prince. When one considered that the Prince had already such a poor opinion of his Uncle, Francis wondered if this could ever be healed. Francis sighed, now only time would tell.

Chapter 22
May 4th 1483. Hornsey Meadows, London.

Once Richard had successfully secured the person of the Prince of Wales both he and his army were able to adopt an altogether more leisurely march upon the capital. As the Northerners approached London they received numerous reports from Catesby's men about how the situation in the capital was changing on a daily, and almost on an hourly, basis! Even Francis, who normally had a fair understanding of such matters, was finding it difficult to keep up to date and abreast of the current state of affairs. The Queen, on hearing the news that Richard had arrested her brothers and had seized the Prince, had attempted to turn both Hastings and the council against Richard. When this had failed, together with her daughters and her other son, Richard Duke of York, Elizabeth had sought, and received, the sanctuary of the church and was presently ensconced within Westminster Abbey. Not unsurprisingly therefore, the capital was in a state of turmoil, with both the Woodville factions and that of the old aristocracy ranged against each, neither trusting the other to do as they promised. The Queen maintained that Richard, with the help of both Hastings and Buckingham, wanted the Crown for himself, yet Richard was adamant that he remained loyal to the Prince and was merely claiming the Protector ship. An office which, he pointed out, had been promised to him in his brother's will. Richard argued that in these dangerous times, when a renewal of the War with France was highly likely, the country needed both a strong and resilient leader. Francis could only agree, for one didn't have to go too far back in history to find the perfect example of just how disastrous a King in his minority could be in such circumstances. It had, of course, only been a matter of decades since the minority of King Henry VI had resulted in the ruination of England's continental ambitions and a bloody civil war which had lasted for some twenty years.

It was then with a sense of trepidation that Francis wondered what reception they would receive when they finally entered the capital. Surprisingly, Richard, who often worried about such things, seemed unconcerned as to what reaction they would receive from the Londoners. Francis continued to worry, for it seemed to him that Richard had changed greatly since he'd renewed his acquaintance with his cousin the Duke of Buckingham. Since Buckingham had joined them at York, both he and Richard had become firm friends and Buckingham's hatred for anything Woodville was, in Francis's opinion, beginning to affect Richard's judgment. Francis, who during the journey southwards had spent quite some time with Buckingham, was probably better placed than most to judge the young man. Unfortunately, Francis had discovered that the Duke of Buckingham's true character differed greatly from his outward persona. It was apparent to Francis that Buckingham was very much used to getting his own way. If things went against him Buckingham could, and would, be quite spiteful and was apt to sulk for hours until matters were reversed. It was, then, with growing concern, that Francis noticed that Richard, who was normally an excellent judge of a man's character, seemed blinded by Buckingham's charm, almost as King Edward had been influenced by the Earl of Warwick in the early years of his reign. Presently, Richard could see no wrong in his new friend and he had, on more than one occasion, stood up for his cousin, even after it was clear to all that Buckingham was plainly in the wrong! Worryingly, it now seemed to Francis that Richard, through Buckingham's flattery and with Lord Hasting's perceived support, was becoming overconfident. To Francis, Richard now appeared to be impervious to any thoughts of opposition to his plans. Unusually, Richard no longer seemed to treat his potential enemies with any respect but viewed them with disdain and, as such, Francis feared that he was seriously underestimating his opponents. For the Woodvilles still enjoyed much support in the south. In fact Francis had heard that many of the Londoners, those who still remembered Margaret of Anjou's march upon the capital in 1460, were extremely suspicious of the motives of both Richard and his army of northerners. Although Richard was less paranoid than he had been in the months that had preceded the King's death, Francis was becoming increasingly alarmed, for in a matter of a few weeks Richard appeared to have gone from one extreme to another and, as such, he now seemed almost blasé to any potential opposition to his will.

As it turned out Francis need not have worried about their entry into London, for their passage into the City met with no opposition. As custom dictated, the Mayor and Alderman, together with five hundred of the most prominent citizens, all arrayed in violet, met their future King's 'entourage' outside the City walls. From here the Prince, Richard and a number of their closest supporters were escorted into the capital. Not for the first time it appeared to Francis that the capital's populace had taken to the streets to welcome their new sovereign. Francis grimaced, for the Londoners, who were all cheering wildly, contrasted sharply with the northerners who were quite sombre, dressed as they were in black, to signify their mourning for the late King's passing.

In spite of his subjects gaiety, the Prince, who was chaperoned by a number of Richard's men, remained tight lipped as the Mayor greeted him and led them all in a cheer of 'God save King Edward.'

Francis winced, for none of Richard's northerners joined in and Richard, who was riding slightly ahead of the Prince, immediately raised a hand to quieten the reception party.

It was Richard and not the Prince who replied to the Mayor.

'Where is my brother's wife?'

He asked, much to Francis's surprise, for Francis had been with Richard when he'd received word from Catesby that Elizabeth and her children had sought sanctuary in Westminster Abbey.

Richard continued.

'I was under the impression that the Queen was desperate to see her son. Why then is she not here to greet him and to join us on our entry into the City?'

The Mayor, who was no longer smiling, bowed slightly as he replied. Almost as if he was addressing the King himself, Francis thought.

'Have you not heard sire. I'm sorry to say that the Queen has sought sanctuary in the Abbey. She has taken her daughters and the Duke of York with her. She says that you wish both her and her sons ill.'

Rubbing his brow, Richard feigned surprise.

'It's a grave business indeed, if I've come between a mother and her son. If she's innocent why should the Queen have cause to fear me? Does her behavior not prove beyond doubt that my evidence against both her and her family is flawless?'

Choosing to address all of those others who were present, Richard announced, 'Let it be known that I have it on good authority that my late brother's wife is plotting to deprive me of the protector ship. Elizabeth Woodville hopes to rule this Kingdom of ours through her son, who would be a puppet of both her and her family. To this end she has conspired against Lord Hastings, the Duke of Buckingham and myself and is intent on fomenting yet another civil war.'

Theatrically, at this point, Richard gestured towards a number of his men who immediately pulled back the covers from those wagons that had preceded their group. The weapons that Francis had earlier seen being loaded on the wagons were, as he remembered, much rotted and despoiled and, as such, any person well versed in war could see that they were useless. However, the Woodville's devices upon them were plain for all to see. Melodramatically, Richard picked up one of the swords and raising it aloft said.

'This is what the Queen had in store for me and her northern subjects. She would have this country plunged once again into a bloody civil war and would happily see me dead. All I ask is that my brother's last wishes are honoured and that I am afforded the opportunity to serve my nephew the Prince, in the manner that the late King intended.'

The Prince, who was sitting quietly on his pony as Richard spoke, shifted uncomfortably in his saddle and moved forward as if to speak. Francis, who was at his side, nudged him into silence, whispering.

'Sire, now is not the time. This matter will be decided upon not by the mayor and his aldermen but by your council.'

One could tell by the murmuring of the crowd that many of the Londoners were unconvinced by Richard's 'evidence'. Clearly sensing this negativity, in one swift movement Richard dismounted and knelt before the Prince, swearing fealty to his 'future King' and encouraging all of those others present to do so.

With this their procession slowly made its way through the City to the sound of many bells and much cheering. For fear of panicking the population, the majority of Richard's northern army remained camped outside the City walls. But everyone knew that they were close at hand should their assistance be required.

Despite the conflicting rumours that circulated as to the motives of the various parties, many citizens had come out of their homes and places of work to greet the youth who was to be their King. Relieved that Richard had at last personally sworn his allegiance to the Prince, those present in Edward's entourage waved and acknowledged the crowds cheers, as Richard clapped his young nephew on the back and pointed out to his young charge the many landmarks that they passed on their progression through the Capital. Once inside the City gates they'd been met by a number of members of the King's council who, in the light of recent events, were all keen to see that the Prince was both well and was in safe hands. Lord Hastings, who was accompanied by Catesby, immediately took Richard to one side, saying that it was 'regrettable' that the Queen had chosen to seek sanctuary.

Richard smiled as he replied.

'Don't worry Hastings, it just proves that we were right all along to question her motives, for why, if she has nothing to hide, has she felt it necessary to seek refuge from the church.'

Hastings nodded as, smiling, he reassured Richard saying,

'I have instructed Archbishop Bourchier to speak with the Queen on our behalf. Elizabeth trusts him and I'm sure that he can convince her that for the good of the country she must leave sanctuary. For how can her son be crowned King whilst his mother and his siblings seek the sanctuary of the Church?'

In reply, Richard, who clearly needed no reassurance, scoffed,

'I don't give a jot for my brother's Queen. In fact it wouldn't bother me if I never had sight of that wicked woman again.' He smiled as he added, 'I must however have the children.'

Hastings too smiled.

'Yes they're your brother's children and they are after all the future of your house.'

Francis was pleased to see that Richard nodded in agreement before he turned once more to receive the crowds accolade.

'He's clearly still not himself.'

Francis thought as he saw that, once again, in his quieter moments, Richard was nervously playing with his signet ring.

Unusually, the procession did not make it's way towards Westminster Abbey to give thanks for their safe journey. Instead their entourage made for the Tower, where the Prince was, for the time being, to reside. 'For safety' Richard said, as a result of the political instability that prevailed in the country. If any felt it strange or unusual that they'd departed from tradition, none said so. For how could they enter the Abbey whilst the Prince's family were also present there, seeking refuge from his uncle and his Protector!

When he'd been told of the plans, Prince Edward had complained that the Tower was far too austere and had, he said, been the scene of much misery and bloodshed. Edward had politely requested that he be allowed to reside with his uncle at Richard's London residence, Crosby Place. Richard's house, which was situated on Bishop's gate, was now reputed to be the finest in all of London. Far more luxurious than the Royal apartments in the Tower. Richard had refused his nephews request, stating that for the time being at least, the Tower was to be the seat of Government and, as such, it was necessary for the Prince to be present there at all times. And 'in any case,' he'd added, 'As protector' he alone was 'responsible' for the Prince's 'safety and well being' and in 'such uncertain times' I can 'better protect' my 'brother's son' in such a 'fortress.'

The Prince had also requested that his household men and servants be returned to him. Richard had denied this request stating that he could trust no-one other than those northerners who'd accompanied him to the Capital and had been, 'consistent in their loyalty to the Yorkist regime.' As a concession, Richard did allow his nephew access to his father's old physician who was a family friend, Doctor Argentine, adding that he was doing this as the 'happiness and well being' of the Prince were 'uppermost in his thoughts.' Francis, who'd met the late King's doctor on a number of occasions, could vouch for the physician whom he remembered as a kindly old fellow. Argentine, who was a native of Strasbourg, was fluent in many languages, including English. As one who was extremely well educated, it was felt that the Doctor would prove to be excellent company for the Prince.

Thus, upon their arrival at the Tower, the Prince retired to the rooms that had been made ready for him in Wakefield Tower. Prince Edward, tired and disheveled, was a sorry sight indeed as both Francis and Richard took their leave of him. Francis sighed, the Prince's first night in his capital should have been a joyous occasion, an excuse for much feasting and merriment. Instead, the young man cut a lonely figure as he sat in silence at his desk, bent over his prayer book, whispering a silent prayer. Francis shuddered as he'd remembered what had happened to King Henry as he'd sat in silent prayer at that very spot.

Francis, who'd developed quite a rapport with the Prince on the final leg of their journey to the Capital, had offered to stay awhile with Edward. Richard had shrugged off Francis's concerns saying that the lives of Princes and Kings were, by there very nature, lonely and that his nephew would benefit from a period of 'quiet reflection,' he added that in any case they'd got business of their own at Crosby Place, with Catesby, Buckingham and the rest of their small circle of 'friends'.

Chapter 23
Friday June 13th 1483. The Tower of London.

Francis felt that he had good reason to dislike London and in particular the Tower of London. Although even he was forced to concede that as a member of the Council and as one of Richard's most trusted supporters, he was duty bound to attend it's meetings there. Francis hated visiting the Tower and, as a consequence, when required to do so he would invariably leave at the very first opportunity which presented itself to him. Thankfully, at least the council would always meet in the chapel which, situated next to Tower Green, was some distance away from the scenes of both King Henry's and the Duke of Clarence's passing. At least, and after much personal wrangling, Francis had finally managed to appreciate that these two men's deaths hadn't been murders, but had in fact been necessary executions. Now, regardless of the manner in which they'd both been carried out, Francis believed that the killings had been carried out in the interests of the country and had ultimately prevented many more deaths.

Presently, the Royal council busied itself both with the normal day to day mechanics of government and also with those arrangements that were being made for the Prince's forthcoming coronation, this event being planned for the 22nd June, a date that was fast approaching! Francis worried constantly. Yes, he hoped to see Edward's son crowned, but after the coronation he could only wonder what would become of them all. The Queen remained in sanctuary. The Prince remained in the Tower and took no meaningful part in government, merely signing that documentation which was placed in front of him by Richard's officers. Despite Richard's earlier predictions, the Prince, as with his mother, still despised Richard and when mother and son once again found themselves in positions of power, one could only imagine what their revenge would be! Indeed, Francis had even begun to wonder if, given the circumstances, Richard would now be able or even willing to allow his nephew to ascend to the throne! That said, nowadays even Francis, who was possibly Richard's oldest friend, could no longer guess what Richard's true intentions were!

Since assuming the Protector ship, Richard had divided the government into the official council, which met daily at the Tower, and into a far less formal group which was comprised of Richard's most loyal and trusted supporters. This clique, if one could call it that, met at Crosby Place, Richard's London residence. It was here and to this gathering that Richard could speak freely of his fears for a country that was seemingly about to be ruled once again by a minor. 'A child King who was dominated by an ambitious and ruthless mother.' It seemed to Francis that it was at Crosby house and not at the Tower, that all of the meaningful decisions in respect of the governance of the realm were made. This long before they were ratified by those other members of the nobility who made up England's 'official' council. Thankfully, for the time being at least, the official council seemed either unwilling or unable to oppose Richard's wishes. In fact, when Francis took time to consider it's business, it was clear that Richard's council was at that time the real decision making body in the kingdom! Cleverly, Richard had ensured that William Catesby attended the Crosby House meetings as the representative of William Lord Hastings. It was by this means that Lord Hastings, one of England's principal councilors, was kept away from the meetings, yet at the same time was fed that information, which Richard deemed necessary. Since Richard's arrival in London relations between both he and Hastings, who up until that point had been chief amongst Richard's supporters, had begun to deteriorate. It was said that as time went by and the Prince remained ensconced within the Tower, Hastings was becoming increasingly more suspicious of Richard's true motives. Richard, on the other hand, had been alarmed to discover that Hastings, who had taken Jane Shaw, King Edward's old mistress, to his bed, was now rumoured to have made approaches to the Woodville faction, through Shaw, who was also the mistress of the Queen's son, the Marquis of Dorset. Initially, Francis had disbelieved these allegations, but unfortunately all of their fears had seemingly been realised when Hastings disloyalty had been confirmed by his servant Catesby.

Catesby was the one in whom Hastings had mistakenly placed his trust. It was perhaps ironic, Francis felt, that William Catesby, who had much to thank his master for, had ultimately betrayed him. For Catesby had been educated at the behest of William Lord Hastings, who'd treated his namesake as he would his own son. Now it seemed that Hasting's reward for this patronage was Catesby's disloyalty! Unbeknown to Hastings, Catesby was now Richard's man and any maneuvering by Hastings behind Richard's back, was reported without delay, both to Richard and to his alternative council.

Francis's mind was still a whirl, what with all the chopping and changing of the past few weeks. He couldn't recall specifically when or by whom, but it had been decided that Lord Hastings had now become a liability to them! Even Francis, who had good cause to hate the Hastings family, could not think ill of a man who'd dedicated his life to the service of the house of York. Francis suspected that Buckingham must have had a part to play in the matter. Unfortunately, even Francis was no longer privy to all of the conversations that Richard held with Buckingham. Indeed it was fair to say that Francis was as shocked as all of the other members of their group when, for the first time, Richard had declared to them that Hastings was a traitor who would have to be 'dealt with.' Francis had tried in vain to defend Hastings, only to be told, in no uncertain terms, that Hastings was in league with the Woodvilles and, as such, he'd been the 'author of his own downfall.' Eventually, and after much heated debate, it was decided that Hastings would be confronted at the next council meeting and that the matter would 'there and then be finalised.' Francis had counseled restraint, arguing that Catesby's allegations were, at that point, uncorroborated. Surprisingly, Richard had ignored Francis's protestations and had merely expressed his disappointment that Francis could not accept the word of their 'friend' Catesby.

'Who has nothing to gain from his master's destruction.'

Unfortunately it was Francis alone who'd argued that in coming out against one who'd been one of Edward's most trusted councilors, they would incur the wrath of all of the 'old Yorkists'. Men whose support they needed in any future conflict with the Woodvilles.

Richard had ignored Francis's reasoning as, smiling, he'd said,

'My brother's old household men won't have the means to oppose us when Ratcliffe joins us in London with more men from the north.'

Richard, clearly irked by Francis's advice, had thrown him a copy of a summons that had recently been dispatched northwards, he'd urged Francis to read it.

The letter had been written with an extravagance, that until recently, Francis hadn't associated with Richard, who was usually so forthright and straightforward in his dealings with people. The summons was addressed to the people of York and in it Richard commanded his northern subjects to arm themselves and come to London.

'To aid and assist us against the Queen, her blood adherents and affinity, which have intended and daily doeth intend, to murder and utterly destroy us and our cousin, the Duke of Buckingham, and all the old royal blood of this realm, and....by their damnable ways........the final destruction and disherision of you and all other inheritors and men of honour, as well of the north parties as other countries, that belongen us.....'

Francis had shuddered as he'd read Richard's words. Did Richard and Buckingham intend to remove from power all of those who opposed their will? But what did they hope to gain from such a radical policy, to destroy all of those who might stand in their way? Was it, as both Richard and Buckingham maintained, a 'necessary evil' to ensure their own safety and to secure their political futures within the new regime? Francis had shuddered again as he'd considered the possibility that Lord Hastings had been right to suspect Richard's motives and Richard, aided and encouraged by Buckingham, may go even further and might even claim the throne for himself! Francis, who since he'd returned to London had given the matter much thought, was not one to let matters lie and on one of those rare occasions when both he and Richard had found themselves alone together, he'd challenged Richard. Richard, who at the time had appeared quite aggrieved by Francis's accusations, had assured Francis that he merely wished to isolate the Prince from his enemies, until 'Prince Edward', through 'maturity' and 'good counsel', was better able to make up his own mind about both his kingdom and his subjects. Francis had initially been satisfied by his friend's explanation, however in truth he was still unsure as to what Richard's true intentions were. Francis honestly believed that Richard had never intended to seize the crown for himself. But now Francis worried that circumstances, beyond their control, may be forcing Richard towards that goal. Indeed, one could argue that by seizing the throne, or by preventing Prince Edward from being crowned for the foreseeable future, Richard was only trying to ensure his own safety and that of his family!

That morning Francis had been one of the first to arrive at the Tower. Once there he'd waited nervously in the chapel for the other members of the council to arrive. Buckingham, John Howard, John De La Pole and Catesby, men of Richard's 'alternative government', all of whom were aware that Richard was going to confront Hastings that day, had all arrived punctually. They all chatted amicably with those members of the council who were not yet privy to their plans. All amongst Richard's inner circle behaved as if it was just another routine meeting of the Royal council and none gave away anything that would alert the others to the fact that Richard was going to 'deal' with Hastings. Francis knew that a not inconsiderable number of armed guards, under the command of Howard's son Thomas, had been secreted in a small room adjacent to the council chamber. On hearing Richard call 'treason' they were to rush into the chapel and had orders to arrest Hastings together with Bishop Morton and Archbishop Rotherham, both of whom were also said to be in collusion with the Queen and her followers.

As time dragged on Francis began to feel increasingly more uncomfortable. When William Hastings came up to Francis and asked him how he was, Francis feigned illness and sought leave to retire from

Hasting's company, fearing that his nervousness would somehow give away Richard's plans. Francis could still not believe that Hastings, a man who'd devoted most of his life to the late King, would ever plot against Richard. As Francis made his excuses he could only hope that Richard, who was late for the meeting, had somehow reconsidered.

If William Hastings had any inkling of what was afoot he did nothing to reveal it as he bade Francis well, and, 'Hoped that' he would 'Soon be feeling better.'

Unusually, the Duke of Gloucester, who was normally extremely punctual for such meetings arrived late. Richard excused himself, stating that he'd overslept, a fact that was clearly untrue when one examined his pale pallor and the black bags under his eyes, evidence, Francis felt that his friend had enjoyed little sleep.

Francis was cheered, and hoped that his friend had indeed reconsidered his decision, as Richard greeted Hastings jovially, hugging the old man and kissing him on both cheeks as he asked how his late brother's 'greatest friend' was. Richard then turned to Bishop Morton and, smiling, said.

'Bishop, I hear that you have some very good strawberries in your garden in Holborn. I require you, let us have a mess of them.'

The Bishop, who also clearly suspected nothing, immediately despatched a servant to his home with instructions to bring back 'as many as he could carry.'

With that, Richard excused himself, stating that he had business elsewhere but would return forthwith. In Richard's absence the council discussed how the preparations for the forthcoming coronation were progressing. It was decided that the date set, the 22nd June, despite being just over a week away, was still both realistic and achievable.

Unfortunately, Richard's humour was much changed when, after approximately one hour, he returned to the chamber. Richard's complexion was pale and Francis noted that his friend who was biting his lip was once again nervously fiddling with his signet ring.

Without addressing anyone in particular, Richard stormed into the centre of the room and, much to the alarm of those present, he interrupted the hushed proceedings by repeatedly screaming the word 'treason'. Even Francis, who'd been expecting some kind of outburst, was alarmed and seriously wondered if Richard had taken leave of his senses. Those others present stared incredulously at the 'Protector of the realm' who appeared to be quite deranged. As arranged, Thomas Howard, together with a dozen or so armed guards, rushed into the chamber. Both Bishop Morton and Archbishop Rotherham were bustled out of the chamber as Thomas, together with two of the larger members of his retinue, directed their attentions towards Lord Hastings, who could only stand by, mute and open mouthed. Surprisingly, Lord Stanley, one who normally chose to avoid confrontation, was most vociferous in his objections. Immediately, and with little thought for his own safety, Stanley placed himself between Howard's armed guards and their quarry. Thomas Howard, a large man, had no difficulty in dealing with Stanley and with a gauntleteered hand he struck Stanley full in the face with such force that the old man fell to the floor, blood pouring from his shattered lips. As Stanley swore that one day he'd have his revenge upon Howard, Howard's guards took hold of Hastings and began to drag him from the chapel. Francis had hoped that Richard's men would have dealt with Lord Hastings with the respect and decency that his position deserved. Francis had understood that the old man, properly arrested, was to have been led away to the Wakefield tower pending trial. William Hastings did not object, indeed it was almost as if Hastings had resigned himself to what was happening, almost, Francis felt, as if he'd been expecting it all along! Whilst others objected, Hastings remained silent as, shoulders slumped, he was half carried out of the chamber and out onto the Tower Green. It was as if everything was happening in an instant, yet at the same time in slow motion. Francis was horrified to see, that once on the lawn, Hastings tunic collar was ripped away and the old man was thrust onto his knees before a pile of timber that had been left in the centre of the green and had been intended to be used for the repairs that were being carried out to the chapel roof. As if from nowhere, an executioner, sporting a white apron and carrying a large axe, appeared before Hastings. This had not been part of the plan! Surely, Francis felt, Lord Hastings at the very least deserved a fair trial, an opportunity in a court of law to refute those charges that had been leveled against him. Disbelieving, Francis immediately confronted Richard who, shaking uncontrollably, was still pacing about the floor of the chapel screaming 'treason', almost as if he were in a state of delirium. It was only once Francis had taken his friend by the shoulders and had shaken him, that Richard seemed to calm a little and Francis was at last able to make himself understood. He begged his friend saying, 'Richard, please tell me that this isn't your doing, surely you can't be party to this madness.' Richard didn't reply as he waved Francis away and turned his back on both Francis and the window that overlooked the Tower Green. Francis could not control himself as he shouted, 'Richard, you cannot order the summary execution of a Lord of this realm. Hastings is a principal member of the Royal council.' Unmoved, Richard stood with his back to Francis as, sighing, Francis whispered, 'He's your brother's oldest and most trusted friend.'

After some moments, Richard turned back towards the window and, staring past Francis, almost as if he wasn't even there, he gazed out onto the green where, what was a most bizarre scene was now unfolding before their very eyes. Lord Hastings, head bowed and held by Howard's men, was still kneeling before his executioner.

For once Francis was determined that he wouldn't be put off quite so easily, he spoke again with a raised voice, 'Richard, you cannot do this. Think of the precedence that it will set. The only thing that keeps our society together is everyone's trust in the King's justice and their belief that all are entitled to a fair trial. By doing this you're going against everything that we stand for, everything that we've fought so hard to preserve. If we, the ruling classes, behave like the common people, then I fear that it won't be long before the lower classes will begin to question our right to hold such power over them.' Francis implored Richard, 'Please Richard, I'm begging you to reconsider.'

Richard's lip quivered as he replied angrily to Francis.

'Francis, you try me and you push our friendship to the limit. Who are you to question my actions? I am the Lord Protector of this realm. I've been entrusted with the powers of the Crown and I will use them as I see fit. I will not allow myself to be constrained by either custom or tradition. The King governs through a divine right bestowed upon him by God himself, no-one may question that right. If I decide Hasting's guilt, then in the eyes of God he is guilty and he will suffer accordingly.'

With that Richard marched past Francis and out onto Tower lawn to personally take a hand in the proceedings. Francis did not know if his friend heard him as hurrying after Richard he shouted.

'But Richard you aren't a King.'

At double pace, Francis followed in Richard's wake as the 'Lord Protector' made his way towards the crowd that had gathered in the centre of the lawn. A large number of people surrounded the wood pile upon which, Francis surmised, the execution of Hastings would now take place. Francis sighed, all stood silent and none were willing to speak up for Hastings, who was still held fast as both Richard and the Duke of Buckingham stood over him. Smiling, Buckingham seemed to delight in the proceedings, as he read out the indictment that had clearly been prepared earlier. To Francis the indictment seemed remarkably similar to that summons which Richard had earlier sent to York requesting reinforcements, this time however it named both Lord Hastings and the Queen. Hastings had, it alleged, been conspiring with the Queen and her adherents in plotting the downfall of both Richard and his cousin Buckingham. Bizarrely, it also included an accusation that Hastings had set Prince Edward a bad example by sleeping with his mistress Jane Shaw! When Buckingham had finished, it was Richard who turned to the executioner and said, 'You've heard the indictment, it is the solemn wish of your Protector that you dispatch this traitor with all haste,' As he spoke Richard looked down in the direction of Hastings who, head bowed, had remained silent and motionless throughout. Smiling triumphantly Richard added, 'May God have mercy upon him for he'll receive none from me.'

At last Hastings began to struggle. Despite his age he was still an extremely fit man and, as such, he was able to shrug off his captors grip. Raising his arms towards Richard and Buckingham and shouting to make himself heard over the furor of the crowd who, stirred up by Buckingham, now bayed for his blood, Hastings addressed his tormentors.

'I know that when it comes to the subject of my alleged treason your minds are made up. I'll not waste what time I have left on arguments, which I know will have no effect. I do, however, implore you to grant my final requests. Please tell my wife that I love her and that I'm sorry for any hurt that I've caused her in the past by my indiscretions. I also ask that priests are instructed to pray for my soul and that my castle at Kirby Muxloe is completed, so it can be a lasting memorial to my time on earth. Finally, will you allow me to confess my sins before I'm sent from this world into the next?'

Richard, who was a godly man, acceded to Hasting's request and incredibly the proceedings were halted for some minutes whilst Bishop Morton was brought forward to hear the condemned man's final confession.

Francis smiled, but then immediately chided himself, as he considered that, in the few minutes made available to him, Hastings could not possibly have confessed all of his sins, for Francis knew the man and if Hastings had been entirely truthful in respect of his past indiscretions they'd have been there well into the following week!

His confession over, Hastings once again knelt before the large log that had been chosen by the executioner as a makeshift block. Francis turned away and was well on his way back to the Tower's gatehouse, when he heard the thud of the axe as it came into contact firstly with Hasting's head and secondly with the block beneath it. Sounds that were quickly followed by the cheers of Richard's men who'd witnessed the spectacle.

Francis sighed as he considered that this time even he felt that Richard had gone too far. Francis shuddered, he could only wonder now where it would all end?

Chapter 24
16th June 1483. Crosby Place London.

Since the news of Lord Hasting's execution had been publicised throughout London, the capital had become awash with both rumour and speculation. Since his outburst at the Tower Francis had become even more marginalised and he now found himself all but excluded from Richard's 'ever decreasing' circle of 'trusted supporters.' Now, when it came to Richard's plans, Francis was as much 'in the dark' as everyone else and, as such, he was becoming increasingly concerned by his friend's erratic behavior. It was fair to say that in the last day or so, on more than one occasion, Francis had seriously considered his own future with Richard and had even been prepared to abandon his old friend and return home to either Yorkshire or to Minster Lovel. There he could wait and see what would become of it all! However, when he took time to reflect upon his present circumstances, Francis was forced to concede that his service to Richard had been the only thing that had given his life any meaning and without Richard he had nothing! Francis therefore determined to confront Richard once again, to find out once and for all what his friends intentions were, in respect of both the Prince and the Crown.

It had become apparent to Francis that both he and Richard had reached a crossroads in their lives. Unfortunately, since King Edward's untimely death, events had overtaken them and they had both been propelled forward at a blistering pace, guided not by reason but by circumstances. Francis truly believed that they would both now benefit from taking time to assess their present situation. To pause and to reflect, to consider their actions, policies and plans and to determine that path which was most appropriate to their future well being. To make reasoned decisions and resolutions that Francis believed, without being too melodramatic about it, would shape and influence both the rest of their lives and indeed the life of the country! In the past Francis might have expected to enjoy a few days hunting and feasting in Wensleydale with Richard, to discuss such matters. But here in London, due both to the frenetic pace at which things were happening and to Richard's extremely busy schedule, Francis would have to satisfy himself with a hurried audience with the 'Protector', held at Richard's London residence, prior to one of the many meetings of Richard's council.

Unfortunately, as it turned out, Francis had precious little time to prepare for the meeting, which had only finally been confirmed that morning, when one of Richard's household men, a person with whom Francis was unfamiliar, had called upon him at his lodgings. Richard's messenger, dressed plainly in black and armoured, had worn nothing in the way of livery and upon seeing him, Francis had feared that the rumours, which he'd heard in recent days, were in fact true. That is that Richard's northerners would now only venture out onto the Capital's streets fully armoured and with extreme caution and when they did so, they would not wear anything that may identify them as the 'Protector's' retainers, which would thereby bring the wrath of the common people down upon them! Apparently, since hearing the news of Lord Hasting's summary execution, many of the Londoners, who were now said to be bordering on outright rebellion, were seeking to avenge Hasting's death upon anyone or anything that could be deemed 'Ricardian'. Francis was at least cheered by the fact that the meeting with Richard was to be held not at the Tower, but at Crosby place. Here Francis hoped that both he and Richard could meet in private, confident that they would neither be overheard nor interrupted.

Upon his arrival at Crosby place Francis was disappointed, but not surprised, to be joined in the large dining room of Richard's London residence, which now served as the makeshift council chamber, by both Richard and the Duke of Buckingham. To add to Francis's chagrin it was Buckingham and not Richard who spoke first.

'Francis, I hope that you don't object to my presence, as both Richard and I have decided that if you're here to discuss matters of future policy, it would be extremely unfair to exclude me.'

As if to rub salt into Francis's wounds Buckingham added, 'Both Richard and I have always been extremely open and honest in our dealings with each other.' Turning to Richard, and much to Francis's increasing outrage, Buckingham added, 'It'd be a shame to lose that trust after we've both come so far together... and in such a short space of a time.'

Francis could hardly control the anger that welled up in him, fury, which brought him almost to the point of tears. 'The arrogance of aristocracy' Francis thought, as he replied as honestly and as forthrightly as he could, choosing to direct his reply not to Buckingham but to Richard.

'Richard I feel that I must talk to you, for I fear that you're in danger of becoming something... someone so different to the man whom you've striven all of your life to be. If this means that I must come between you and your cousin Buckingham, then so be it.' Buckingham scowled as Francis, without waiting for a reply continued, 'If by saying that which I must, I destroy our friendship forever, then so be it. But don't think that I've come to this decision lightly, Richard be assured, our friendship is and always will be the most precious thing in my life.' Turning his back on Buckingham Francis added, 'If your cousin is so insecure and so unsure of himself and his position within your affinity, that he cannot allow your oldest and dearest friend to speak to you in private and you allow him to dictate to you in such a way, then I fear that you're already lost to me. If that is so then we must surely go our separate ways. But for the sake of our friendship, let us talk and let us do so in private.' As Richard nodded Francis noticed the faintest of smiles appear upon his friend's face. Encouraged, Francis continued, 'Surely your cousin wouldn't dare question your honesty and integrity by insisting that he be present at such a meeting of old friends?'

For a brief moment Francis felt that he almost saw a twinkle in Richard's eye, a flicker of his former self. Frowning again, Richard turned to Buckingham and waving his arm towards the door at the end of the chamber Richard said, with a finality that did not encourage further debate, 'Go cousin, we will speak later.'

For a moment Buckingham stood his ground and appeared as if he were about to protest until, that is, Richard, turning his back on his cousin, took Francis in his arms and, hugging him, kissed him on each cheek. Looking over Richard's shoulder, Francis smiled as Buckingham, who, as would a scalded child, sighed and finally skulked from the room.

As they sat at the bench that was closest to the fire, the focal point of the room and its only source of heat, both friends remained strangely silent, almost as if each was wondering where to start. At long last Francis broke the silence, 'Richard, please tell me, what are your plans now? When we left Yorkshire I felt confident that we were coming to London merely to protect your interests and to maintain your inheritance. Surely we succeeded in this when you secured the Prince, the Protector ship and the support of the Yorkist nobility. Now that we've marginalised both the Queen and her followers, is your future not secure?' Francis sighed heavily, before he added, 'Forgive me for saying this Richard, but in executing Hastings and in keeping the Prince locked up in the Tower, I fear that you've gone too far, much further than we ever envisaged' Francis sighed again as he said, 'And where will it all end?'

Richard who was staring into the fire remained silent, as Francis continued, 'Tell me honestly Richard, do you want the crown for yourself?'

Even if he'd wanted to, Richard didn't have time to reply before Francis blurted out all that which had been troubling him, 'Don't we have a duty to secure Edward's dynasty and thereby the right of his sons to succeed him peaceably? Are the very number and the nature of all of our victories not testament to the fact that Edward was, in the eyes of God, the rightful King? Surely if you disinherit your nephew you'll be going against both the will of God and that for which we've all fought so hard to achieve. Richard, if you seize the throne now I truly believe that you'll bring both the wrath of God and that of the people down upon our heads.'

Richard took some time to answer, but when he did so, it was clear to Francis that those decisions, which had obviously been forced upon Richard had brought him great sadness. Richard began by reaffirming that he'd originally come to London to, 'secure' both his 'own rights as Protector' and his 'position as the Duke of Gloucester,' for 'the Queen and her family would have sought to destroy me once they'd placed Prince Edward on the throne.'

Sighing, Richard slowly shook his head as he continued, 'I know now that this outcome is highly unlikely. I've spoken to my nephew the Prince on more occasions than I care to remember and it's clear to me that he hates me now more than ever. Francis, I'm afraid that the Prince has been thoroughly brainwashed by the Woodvilles, he truly believes that I've only ever coveted the throne for myself.' Exasperated, Richard laughed ironically, as he added, 'He even says that I only ever supported his father because I hoped one day to be King in my own right. He said that I'd killed the heirs of Lancaster and my brother Clarence, to lessen the number of people between myself and the Crown!' Shaking his head Richard sighed heavily as he said, 'He must think that I'm some kind of ogre, he even says that the only thing that presently keeps him alive, is the fact that his younger brother, his heir, is safe with his mother in sanctuary.' As Richard continued, Francis became increasingly alarmed by the look of concern on his friends face. 'Francis, believe me when I say this, if my brother's son ascends to the throne then we're all undone, for my nephew is neither our ally nor is he my brother's legitimate heir.'

Francis, who himself had been present at King Edward's marriage all those years ago, spluttered as he interrupted.

'What do you mean your brother's legitimate heir? How can you cast doubt upon the Prince's legitimacy?'

Serious, Richard continued, 'Francis what if I were to tell you that I'd become privy to evidence, that casts doubt... no that proves beyond doubt that my brother's sons are illegitimate and, as such, they have no rights of inheritance.'

Francis wondered how his friend could countenance such an allegation.

'But Richard, you know that your brother's marriage to the Queen was lawful, it's sanctity cannot be questioned.' Francis laughed as he added, 'I even witnessed it with my own eyes, don't you remember?'

Smiling, Richard replied, 'Yes, of course I remember and I do believe you did witness my brother's marriage to Elizabeth Woodville, but I ask you. Why do you think he attempted to conceal it for so long?'

Francis also smiled, he could easily answer this, 'Edward tried to hide it from the Earl of Warwick. He owed his throne to the 'Kingmaker' and he couldn't risk angering the Earl, who at that time was in the process of negotiating a marriage alliance between the King and a French princess,'

Slowly, shaking his head, Richard replied, 'Yes Francis, but by that time Edward was secure on his throne, he had no need to fear the Kingmaker. Was this not proven when Warwick ultimately failed to depose him? No Francis, the marriage you saw was invalid because my brother was already betrothed to another. Edward kept this second marriage to Elizabeth Woodville secret because he knew that it would be annulled when the people discovered it.' Richard laughed as he added, 'Francis you know how my brother was. What you saw was a sham, cooked up by my brother and designed to get Elizabeth Woodville into his bed.' Richard sighed as he said, 'Unfortunately, once Edward had taken the Woodville woman into his bed he allowed himself to be beguiled by her.'

Perplexed, Francis remained silent as Richard added. 'No, by the time he married Elizabeth Woodville Edward was already betrothed to one Lady Eleanor Butler, the daughter of the Earl of Wiltshire. The match had been arranged by my father and the ceremony had been conducted by Richard Stillington. This union predated and therefore invalidated Edward's marriage to Elizabeth Woodville, it therefore illegitimises all of their offspring.'

Francis protested, 'But how was your brother able to keep this earlier betrothal a secret for so long? And why, when the King's marriage to Elizabeth Woodville became public knowledge, did it not all come out?'

Smiling knowingly, Richard replied, 'As you know my father died young and my mother Cecily, who's always been so saintly and trusting, kept the matter secret. She believed Edward when he told her that if his secret came out, our House would be undone. My mother told me that when the Lady Eleanor died in 1468, it no longer seemed to matter that much. Everyone in the country had by that time accepted Elizabeth Woodville as my brother's Queen and anyway, few people still lived who were privy to the earlier marriage.

Richard interrupted Francis before he was able to reply, 'Marrying Edward to Lady Eleanor was the best thing that Bishop Stillington ever did in his miserable life.' Laughing, Richard added, 'Surely Francis, you must have wondered how such an incompetent could have become both a Bishop and even Edward's chancellor for a while? Whilst Stillington remained silent he enjoyed the patronage of the King, who promoted him way beyond his competency. It was only when Stillington stupidly demanded more and more that Edward drew a line and refused to be blackmailed further.' Richard looked at Francis quizzically as he asked, 'Do you not recall Stillington being arrested and stripped of all of his offices just two years after the Battle of Tewkesbury?'

Richard smiled as he said, 'It was no coincidence that Edward removed Stillington from power just as soon as he was secure on his throne. Didn't you wonder why the Pope had summoned Stillington to Rome? Francis, Stillington was questioned for weeks by a papal legate about matters which were never made public knowledge.' Richard smiled again, 'Fortunately, by that time both Henry of Lancaster and his son were already dead, for I'm sure that if Rome could have used this information to depose Edward then they would have, for at that time England was allied to both the Burgundians and the Dutch who themselves were opposed to Rome and her allies the French. As it was the Pope remained silent, for a price of course.'

Sighing Richard added, 'I always wondered why my brother was bought off so easily by the French, now I know.'

Francis's mind was now definitely in a whirl! He could never have foreseen the revelation that Richard had made.

Eager to know how Richard had come across this information, Francis asked, 'Who told you about this and how did they become privy to such information'?

Richard's reply didn't surprise Francis in the least, for he'd felt all along that Buckingham must have had some part to play in it.

My cousin the Duke of Buckingham appraised me of the facts after he'd joined us on our march southwards. I couldn't discuss it with anyone before I secured London, for if it had come out at that point Civil War would have been inevitable.'

Richard no doubt saw the skepticism in Francis's face, 'I know what your thinking Francis and yes my cousin is both an arrogant and an ambitious man.'

Francis smiled as he listened to Richard and slowly began to appreciate that Richard had understood Buckingham's true motives all along.

Richard said, 'I know that by removing Edward's offspring from the line of succession Buckingham's own claim to the throne, through his grandfather Thomas of Woodstock is strengthened. But presently I still need his support. I knew that I would have to go against the Woodville faction and possibly even the Yorkist Lords and without Buckingham's help I wouldn't have had the resources to do so. I hoped that Hastings would join me and I met him on the ninth and told him all that I knew.' Richard sighed, 'The old fool accused me of lying to him to secure the throne for myself. Not surprising really, for it transpired that even then he was negotiating with the Queen and intended to come out against me.'

Richard sighed again as he added, 'Try as I might I couldn't convince Hastings that I spoke the truth. I told him that as soon as I'd arrived in London I'd confronted my mother and she too had confirmed to me that Buckingham's revelations were true. I also showed Hastings a number of letters that Stillington had sent to my mother, proof positive that my brother was already betrothed when he'd met Elizabeth Woodville. Unfortunately Hastings refused to believe that Edward's marriage to the Queen was illegal.' Richard tutted as he said, 'In fact when I took time to consider his reaction to my news, it was apparent to me that Hastings must also have been party to the deceit, he was after all my brother's oldest and dearest friend.'

Richard sighed again, 'Thus I reluctantly found it necessary to destroy Hastings, before both he and the Queen moved against me'.

In reply to Richard, Francis questioned Buckingham's motives in revealing this information when he did. Despite his skepticism for his cousin, Richard defended Buckingham arguing that Buckingham could not have dared reveal such information whilst King Edward still lived. Richard added that it was only after the King had died and the Queen had purposely delayed in telling them of Edward's death, that Buckingham had finally realised that she wished to destroy both he and Richard and, as such, he'd hurried northwards with the news.

Smiling, Richard said that it was 'just a happy coincidence' that by removing Edward's sons from the Yorkist line of descent Buckingham himself moved much closer to the throne.

Richard spoke with sincerity.

'Francis, can you not see that if I allow Edward's sons to succeed him and this information gets out then it will utterly destroy our House forever.'

Francis, who could only agree with Richard's assessment, asked, 'But what of Clarence's son, is he not therefore next in line to succeed.'

Richard, who'd clearly considered this possibility, had obviously discounted it. He was quite forthright and seemed to Francis almost practiced in his reply, 'Firstly the Act of Attainder against the Duke of Clarence disbars his issue from the line of succession.'

Francis shrugged, he knew that Acts of Attainder could and were regularly reversed by Parliament. How could an innocent child be held responsible for his father's treason?

Clearing sensing Francis's cynicism Richard continued, 'Francis, surely you've met my nephew at Middleham, he's a fool.' Richard scoffed as he added, 'He has all of Clarence's arrogance, yet none of his intellect.'

Francis could not disagree with Richard for he had met with the young Earl of Warwick on many occasions and Richard's assessment of his nephew, although concise, was extremely accurate.

Any questions in respect of the hapless Earl of Warwick's immediate future were immediately answered as Richard said, 'I've sent to Middleham for the Earl of Warwick and he will join his cousin in the Tower, whilst I consider what's to be done with all of my brother's children. If the people agree with me that they have no rights to the throne then that is where they shall remain. If however they become the focal point for more disaffection, I may be forced to become more ruthless in my dealings with them.'

Francis shivered, he could only guess what Richard meant by this.

Perversely, Francis was actually quite relieved, for he now understood why over these past weeks Richard had been acting so unusually. That said, Francis still remained extremely concerned about their futures and, keen to know what Richard's immediate plans were, he asked, 'But what of your cousin Buckingham, if he himself has ambitions for the throne is he not a greater threat to you than the Queen.'

Nodding Richard agreed, 'Yes and we will have to keep a very close eye on him. But I can only deal with my opponents one at a time and presently I still need Buckingham's support to deal with the Queen and her followers.'

Richard grinned as he added, 'but if I'm correct in my assessment of Buckingham's true motives, it'll only be a matter of time before he makes his move against me and when he does we'll be ready for him.'

Richard smiled again as he added, 'You never know, my cousin might even be satisfied with even more titles and land, especially when one considers that after my own son Edward, he is my heir.'

At that point a servant entered the room, apologising profusely for the interruption he bowed low, saying, 'Lord, please excuse me but both the Archbishop Bourchier and Bishop Russell have arrived to see you'. The servant hesitated before he added, 'and the Duke of Buckingham is also impatient to be re admitted.'

Francis nodded towards his friend. They'd cleared the air and for that Francis was grateful.

As Francis assured Richard of his own continuing support, Richard smiled and clapping Francis on the back said, 'Good, I always knew I could place my trust in you.'

It was a very different Richard who coldly greeted both the aging prelates and the Duke of Buckingham as they were all finally admitted into the chamber.

The Protector turned first to Archbishop Bourchier, an elderly and kindly man who had served the House of York well throughout his long life. Francis thought that it must have upset Richard, to have had to speak so harshly to one who'd been unquestioning in his support of their cause. But Francis knew that at such dangerous times, Richard as the Protector of the realm, could not afford to let anyone see any sign of weakness, for the time being at least Richard would have to play the role of tyrant.

'And what of the Queen and the Duke of York, Bourchier. I hope that you've better news for me than that which you gave me last week. Will Elizabeth give up her son?'

Sneering, Richard added, 'Have you told her what the consequences will be for her other relatives, if she opposes me in this?'

Archbishop Bourchier, clearly fearing Richard's wrath, could only stutter out his reply.

'I er.... er have er.... good erm I think.....'

Thankfully, Bishop Russell came to the Archbishop's assistance, speaking on the old mans behalf he replied, 'Sire, the Queen assures us that she will give up her son, but only on the understanding that you release those other relatives of hers who are held captive and that you take an oath on a holy relic not to harm either her, her children, her relations or her supporters.'

Richard smiled, 'Make it so. Go to the Queen now and assure her that I have made such an oath in your presence, but tell her that the Duke of York must be with his brother in the Tower by nightfall.'

Richard turned to address Buckingham who, not unsurprisingly given Richard's earlier revelations, seemed delighted by the news, 'Take an armed guard. If the Queen does not fulfill her side of the bargain, enter the Sanctuary and take the Prince by force if necessary.'

As the other members of the Royal council were arriving, both Buckingham and the clerics left for Westminster.

That afternoon's meeting dragged on for sometime and Francis, who invariably found such events extremely tiresome, found it almost unbearable. Especially when one considered that the subject matter discussed, that is Prince Edward's forthcoming coronation and the associated festivities, could not now, ever take place! Richard the 'Protector' of his nephews realm, played his part impeccably, leading the discussions in respect of Edward's forthcoming coronation and even going so far as to raise the question of the Prince's future marriage. Richard spoke as if the transition from his protector ship into the reign of King Edward V was progressing quite smoothly. He even brought up the subject of a potential alliance with Burgundy which may, Richard argued, help facilitate another war with France where, 'The Prince could prove himself to his subjects on the field of battle, just as his father had done so before him.'

Francis understood why until then he'd been kept in the dark. Why even when he was amongst friends, Richard had not dared to disclose his knowledge of Edward's earlier marriage. Information that could never have found its way into the public domain until Richard had all of the 'Princes of York' under his control. For if the common people refused to believe these revelations and these children had still been at large, they would without doubt have become the focal point for disaffection and rebellion.

After the meeting had at long last drawn to a close and only Francis and Richard remained, Buckingham returned alone. Richard grinned as Buckingham triumphantly announced that Richard of York was, 'In our hands' and was at that very moment, 'Being conveyed to the Tower.'

Turning to Francis Richard said, 'Send word to Ratcliffe at Pontefract, he's to execute Rivers, Grey, Vaughan and Haute without delay.'

Surprised that Richard would renege on his promise to the Queen, Francis inquired, 'On what grounds.'

Richard, who was quite matter of fact in his reply, said, 'For Treason of course.'

'But what of your oath,' Francis asked.

Richard smiled again as he replied truthfully, 'I made no oath.'

As Richard strode out of the room he added, 'We must all act without delay as there is much to be done.'

Buckingham smiled smugly at Francis who smiled back, not in friendship but in the knowledge that, unbeknown to himself,

Buckingham was in an extremely precarious position, yet he had no knowledge of just how vulnerable he really was!

'Just let him show his hand sooner rather than later,' Francis thought, 'And when he does we'll cut it off.'

Chapter 25
June 26th 1483. Baynard's Castle London.

Francis adored Baynard's Castle. The residence of Lady Cecily the Duchess of York, Richard's mother, was situated in the very heart of London. Francis had often wondered what it was that made Baynard's Castle so appealing to him. Was it the grand design of the building itself? Was it the homes stylish yet simplistic decoration, so different from the opulent houses of the majority of the aristocracy? In truth it wasn't really any of these things that made the Duchess's home such a wonderful place for Francis to visit. It was the qualities of Cecily herself that ensured that whenever he visited the house, Francis felt both safe and loved. Thus, despite the fact that Richard's house at Crosby Place and Francis's lodgings were in closer proximity to the Tower and Westminster, recently the two friends had spent much of their time here at Baynard's Castle, where they could both enjoy the Duchess's warmth and hospitality.

Today had seemed like any other day at Baynard's Castle. Both Richard and Francis had risen late, having spent much of the previous evening in discussions with Catesby. In contrast the Duchess, as was her custom, had been up for sometime. Indeed, by the time Francis and Richard had come down stairs, Cecily had already spent many hours at prayer in her private chapel. As soon as the two friends had entered the small solar, as always, Richard's mother had greeted them with the offer of breakfast. A ritual that, as always, was accompanied by a kiss on their foreheads and a stroke of their cheeks.

Smiling, Francis couldn't help but admire Richard's mother who, despite her age still loved life. Francis was astounded by this gentle lady's fortitude, for Cecily could easily have been forgiven for loathing a life that had brought her more than her fair share of heartache and pain. Cecily was a Neville by birth, from the Westmoreland branch of that family. She'd been married at an early age to Richard, Duke of York. Known as 'The Rose of Raby', Cecily was said to have loved her husband dearly and she had given him many children. Sadly, most of her offspring had preceded her to the grave. Of the four sons who had survived infancy, three were now dead, two, George and Edmund, 'passing' unnaturally and before their time. Even Cecily's husband had died before his time, the Duke executed in the aftermath of the Battle of Wakefield and his head wearing a paper crown, adorning the gates of Micklegate bar in York. Sadly, Cecily's youngest son Edmund, who was reputed to have been her favourite, and who was said to have taken after his mother when it came to her 'gentleness of spirit', had also joined his father on Micklegate Bar. Cecily was said to have been devastated by the news of the death of her husband, but her grief had been compounded and her suffering had been made immeasurably worse when she heard the news of the murder of Edmund, stabbed to death on Wakefield Bridge by the vengeful Lord Clifford, this as Edmund had pleaded to be spared. Edmund, who'd been Cecily's second son, was said to have been the antithesis of his elder brother Edward. Edward was a warrior and an athlete whereas Edmund was a gentle boy who was more suited to the pursuit of learning than of warfare. Given the circumstances, Cecily could easily have been forgiven for turning away from a God who'd taken so much from her. Instead, and in spite of her misfortune, Cecily had embraced religion. Almost as if she believed that the answers to the complexities, the intolerance and the harshness of the society in which she lived, lay somewhere within its teachings.

As Richard's mother fussed over them Francis smiled, for it was clear to him that Cecily still loved a world that in reality had all but destroyed her family.

Upon the death of her husband, defying custom, Cecily had steadfastly refused to take another husband, this despite numerous offers of marriage. At Baynard's Castle she lived an almost saintly existence, her day's filled with hours of quiet contemplation and prayer. Cecily, who always saw the best in people, had long since forgiven those who'd wrought such devastation in her life. She spoke often of those whom she'd lost, saying that she was sure that she would meet them all again in a 'far better place than this world into which we've all been born.'

It was fair to say that Francis, who before he'd been sent to Middleham had been brought up by his grandmother, had not received much in the way of maternal love. Consequently he adored Cecily, almost as if she were his own mother and he found it impossible to comprehend how anyone could fail to be charmed by this wonderful woman, who in Francis's opinion, was an example to them all.

Much as he loved Richard, it appeared to Francis as if his friend had inherited much of his father's pragmatism and sense of duty, but had received none of his mother's compassion and empathy for others. Francis couldn't help but smile when he saw Richard in his mother's company, for even Richard, who was always so hard and stone faced, was 'softened' by her, Consequently, Francis would always encourage his friend to spend as much time as possible at Baynard's Castle. Yet Richard, who loved his mother dearly, always said that she was, 'A bad influence on him.' Richard would often complain that, 'On more than one occasion' his 'mother' had persuaded him to be overly lenient towards those whom he'd chosen to punish. That said Cecily knew her place and in contrast to many of her contemporaries she chose not to adopt an active role in politics. As such, she did not attract the public derision that was associated from time to time with more forceful women, such as Elizabeth Woodville, Margaret of Anjou and Margaret Beaufort, all of whom, on occasions, had angered their male counterparts by meddling in a world that was dominated by men.

Thus as she greeted them warmly Cecily showed no interest in those matters that had kept them from their beds until the early hours. Francis smiled as Richard's mother asked them what they wanted for breakfast and chided Richard, telling him that the lack of a proper nights rest would make him ill. Francis hugged his adoptive mother and as he breathed in the essence of rose petals and lavender, her favourite fragrance, which accompanied her wherever she went, he delighted in both the softness and warmth of her small frame. In return Cecily stroked Francis's head and turning to Richard she censured him saying.

'Why can't you be like Francis and show your mother such affection.'

Richard laughed as he replied.

'Mother, you'd not have me any other way. Besides which, if you like him so much why don't you adopt him, for I don't want him and I've heard it said that neither does his wife.'

Francis pulled away from Richard's mother and walking over to the window he gazed out over the city's streets that were still very much awash with rumour and speculation. Richard could be cruel at times and bringing up the subject of Francis's loveless marriage at that time, when Francis had been feeling quite happy and content was, in Francis's opinion, both thoughtless and insensitive.

Richard, who had little time for such emotion, joined Francis by the window. Looking out towards the gathering crowd Richard clapped his friend on the back and impervious to the hurt that his comment had caused he said, 'What do you think this day has in store for us my friend.'

Richard frowned as he added, 'Francis can you gauge the mood of the crowd? Who do you think they would have as there King?'

At least Francis felt that he now knew the answer to Richard's question, for they'd all spent each and every waking moment of these past few days discussing it!

Four days earlier Richard had finally publicised his revelations in relation to the invalidity of Edward's marriage to Elizabeth Woodville and the consequential illegitimacy of their children. Ratcliffe had by that time assembled a northern army and as its arrival in the capital was anticipated at any time, Richard had decided that he'd at last been in a position to release the information so that he could test the reaction of the commoners to it. None had stood in Richard's way, for the Queen remained in sanctuary and those relatives of hers who were still alive had chosen to flee, taking with them, much to Richard's fury, both the late King's treasure and the majority of his fleet!

Richard had cleverly chosen the 'great orator' Ralph Shaw to deliver the news via a sermon, which Shaw had delivered at St. Paul's cross. It was fair to say that Shaw's revelations had initially 'stunned' his audience! Francis who'd been present had been alarmed as Shaw's speech had been greeted both with both boos and with cries of 'usurper' and 'tyrant'. Richard had however chosen his man well and Shaw was a skilled public speaker, who'd clearly taken some time over his speech. Slowly and cleverly Shaw had introduced the 'compelling evidence', which had established the illegitimacy of Edward's sons and as a result had excluded them from the line of succession. Ingeniously, Shaw had also included numerous references, which had alluded to the perceived threat from both France and Brittany who were said to have been plotting an invasion of England. Both nations, Shaw said, intended to finance and equip an expedition that was to be led by the present Lancastrian pretender to the throne, Henry Tudor, Earl of Richmond. 'A Welshman descended from John of Gaunt through the illegitimate Beaufort line.' Shaw had pointed out that England had benefited from many years of peace especially throughout the latter half of King Edward's reign and, as such, any future civil unrest or invasion would spell an end to that prosperity. Thus a nation of men whose commercial and personal interests benefited from both political stability and a strong government, had been slowly convinced by Shaw, that in the light of these revelations, Richard Duke of Gloucester was the, 'Only suitable candidate for the throne of England.'

Since Shaw's speech had been delivered Richard had of course repeatedly refused the offer of the Crown for he'd told Francis that he, 'Didn't want to appear too eager to accept', and as a consequence, 'Shed doubt upon his honourable intentions.'

Again on the 24th of that month at the Guildhall in London, Buckingham had asserted that the Crown should be offered to Richard. On this occasion however Buckingham had gone too far! Neither Francis nor Richard had been present at Buckingham's speech but they were both soon made aware of its content and Richard had been furious. In addition to the question of the validity of King Edward's marriage, Buckingham had had the audacity to go so far as to question the legitimacy of King Edward himself! Richard had seen this as the gravest insult that could ever have been leveled against his mother. In truth the rumour had been nothing new and had been used on many occasions in the past by both the French and the Lancastrians in an effort to discredit King Edward. The rumour maintained that Edward had been conceived whilst his father was away campaigning in France. The late King sired by a lowly archer from Rouen called Blaylock, with whom the Duchess Cecily had embarked upon an affair.

In spite of Buckingham's intentions, this slur against the virtue of his mother had been too much for Richard to bear and it had led to a great quarrel between the cousins. Buckingham, realising no doubt that this time he had gone too far, with Catesby in tow no doubt for moral support, had called upon them on the previous evening. Francis had known of course that it was too much to expect the egotistical Buckingham to apologise unreservedly for his comments and he'd been right. Instead of apologising to both Richard and his mother, Buckingham had argued that, as he'd only ever made the allegations for the benefit of Richard he'd, 'Got nothing to apologise for!' Buckingham had even had the audacity to say that his actions couldn't have upset Richard's mother, who'd already heard the rumours many times before and had, 'never chosen to refute them!' Fueled by both alcohol and anger Richard had exploded at Buckingham saying, 'To date I have only said that which is true and beyond reproach. You cousin have not. My mother is an honorable woman who can never be harmed by the truth, she knows that Edward's marriage was unlawful and she is appreciates the consequences that this has upon her grand children. But by questioning my mothers virtue, by besmirching her character you have gone too far. You Sir, will apologise to the Duchess and then you will rescind that which you've said on your knees before the Council.'

In a strange way Francis had admired Buckingham's courage, for even in the face of Richard's onslaught, true to his nature Buckingham had stubbornly and steadfastly refused to make such an apology. For something that he'd merely 'Repeated' for the benefit of 'Richard' and 'Not for his own ends.'

Ultimately, Richard had sent Buckingham away telling him that if he wasn't prepared to apologise there was nothing more for them to say to each other. With that Buckingham had left their company and had thereby been excluded from any further debate. Catesby on the other hand had remained and they'd all talked long into the night in respect of how and when Richard would finally accept the Crown.

Once the friends had breakfasted they remained at Barnard Castle.

That morning Catesby was to bring the Mayor of London, together with the Alderman and those nobles who were currently resident in London, to Richard's mother's house. Here the Crown would again be offered to Richard, but on this occasion Richard had decided that he would finally accept it. From Baynard's Castle Richard was to go immediately to Westminster to take his place, as the Sovereign, upon the King's bench.

As arranged just before midday a 'great multitude of commoners' assembled in the narrow streets outside the Duchess's home. The crowd were soon rewarded for their patience as a procession, which included the mayor and all of the aldermen of London, who were dressed in the robes and finery of their various offices arrived outside Baynard's Castle. Surprisingly the cavalcade was led by the Duke of Buckingham, who was himself resplendent in his noble's garb. Francis scowled at Buckingham as, gazing out of the solar's window, he tried to compose himself for what was to follow.

Still scowling Francis turned to Richard and pointing to Buckingham, who was by now standing in the street below them, said, 'He's only come here to try and ingratiate himself with you.'

Richard smiling, shocked even Francis with his reply, 'We'll see how gracious he is when I'm finally in a position to call him to account for his actions. I don't forget and I will not forgive one who casts such a slur on my mother's good name'. Richard continued, 'He comes from a den of thieves and vagabonds, his family have always supported the House of Lancaster over my own,' Richard sneered as he added, 'Such people can never be trusted,' Sighing, Richard said, 'And to think that presently I'm beholden to such people.'

At that juncture Francis chose not to remind Richard that his own family had been devout Lancastrians and, unbeknown to Richard, his father had died fighting for that cause.'

Thankfully their conversation was interrupted, as breathless Ned came running into the room. Bowing, Ned addressed Richard who was standing next to Francis at the window. 'Sire both the mayor and your cousin the Duke of Buckingham have requested the pleasure of your company.'

Smiling once again Richard turned to Francis who prickled with pride, for he knew that which would follow. Richard said, 'What do you say Francis shall we let them in.'

Eagerly and in both a proud and forthright manner, Francis replied to his friend, 'Yes, let them in and take that which is yours by right.'

Once admitted the Mayor once again implored Richard, 'for the sake of the country' to take the Crown. The Duke of Buckingham did nothing to ingratiate himself with Richard as he added, that if Richard did not accept the Crown then it would be offered, not to Edward's children but 'elsewhere'. Francis wondered if Buckingham was referring either to the Lancastrian, Henry Tudor or to himself!

Francis felt that after all the two'ing and fro'ing of the recent days Richard could for once be forgiven for taking time to enjoy himself, even if it was before such a distinguished gathering. Francis smiled as Richard, feigning surprise, appeared for some time somewhat reluctant, until sighing he thanked those present for their confidence in him and finally accepted the Crown.

'King Richard the III' was carried aloft on a litter through streets of cheering people to Westminster where, in the company of many Lords and Prelates, he formally accepted the Crown of England.

Giving his 'oath' Richard said that he would do his 'utmost to protect the interests of both his subjects and their nation' and he would administer 'justice' with both a 'fair' and 'even hand'.

Excited, Francis eagerly joined Richard's subjects as they cheered, 'God save King Richard'!

Chapter 26
6th July 1483. Westminster Hall London.

Even by the standards of the time, the coronation of King Richard III was a particularly lavish affair. That said Francis wasn't at all surprised by this, for in spite of the fact that Richard's investiture was a hurried affair, those arrangements that had already been made for Edward Prince of Wales had easily been adapted to suit Richard's needs.

In contrast to that of the Lancastrian Kings, the Yorkist court of Edward IV had enjoyed a reputation throughout the civilised world for its extravagance. Richard clearly hoped to continue with that precedent, which had been set by his brother before him, and the ceremony that saw the crowning of both Richard and his Queen, Ann, certainly maintained this standard. Francis had hoped that the fact that the event was so well attended, with almost all of the countries nobility being present, was indicative of the fact that the majority of England's aristocracy supported Richard's coup. Unfortunately, the realist in Francis was forced to concede that the truth of the matter was that many people had made their travel arrangements months before and had initially intended to attend the coronation of Edward. It just so happened that Richard would now be crowned in his nephews stead! Moreover, if one was being completely honest, it mattered not to the attendees whether or not they approved of Richard, for who in their right mind would purposely miss such a fabulous event! Needless to say however, a significant number of people were still conspicuous by their absence, namely Elizabeth Woodville and her offspring together with all of those Lancastrian diehards who presently shared their pretender Henry Tudor the Earl of Richmond's, exile in Brittany. But today even Francis, who was liable to worry about such matters, tried to forget those men whom Richard, once crowned, would eventually have to deal with if, that is, he were to keep his crown.

Once he'd finally accepted the offer of the crown Richard had sent for his wife Ann who'd remained at Middleham for these past few months. Once joined by his future Queen at Baynard's Castle, both Richard and Ann had been borne to their royal apartments at the Tower along the Thames. The couple were carried upon barges, which were richly adorned with fine silks and exquisite furnishings. Francis had been encouraged to see that many of the 'Londoners', who'd clearly forgotten their earlier misgivings when it came to the subject of Richard and his 'northerners'', came out in force to greet their future King and Queen. As the royal barges slowly made their way up the Thames towards the Tower, Francis had been delighted to see that the shoreline swarmed with a multitude of citizens, all of whom were desperate to get a glimpse of the royal couple. Indeed, in an effort to get a closer look many had even taken to the water itself and, as a consequence, the river had been teeming with numerous boats of every conceivable shape and size. As the royal barge had docked at the Tower, Francis, once again recalling his previous experiences of it, had shuddered as he'd looked up at the great fortress's battlements. He'd sighed as his gaze was drawn to the numerous small windows of those rooms that faced onto the river and he wondered if Prince Edward and his younger brother Richard, and perhaps even their cousin Edward Earl of Warwick, were also witnessing their uncle's arrival at the Tower. Francis couldn't help but pity the boys who'd seemingly lost everything and now faced an uncertain, if not dangerous, future in a Kingdom that was to be ruled by their uncle.

Once at the Tower Richard had wasted no time in removing the three Princes from the 'public gaze' and within days of his taking up residence there the boys had been spirited away, withdrawn from their royal apartments into rooms that were situated within the deepest recesses of the Tower, a place where only a small number of Richard's most trusted retainers were permitted to have access. Francis, who in spite of everything couldn't help but feel pity for the children, had visited them in their 'new accommodation' on a number of occasions and he'd been disgusted to see the conditions in which the Princes were kept, which were, in his opinion, no better than those found in a prison!

It was from the Tower that Richard and his Queen, this time on foot, were led in a 'grand progress' throughout the streets of London to Westminster Abbey, where the coronation was to take place. If any had wondered what had become of the Prince's none showed it, for once again the capitals streets were lined with a multitude of people, all of whom cheered enthusiastically and wished their future King and Queen well, all crying 'God save King Richard'. As he too happily received the accolade of the crowds, Francis could only wonder what their old mentor the Earl of Warwick would have made of it all! For Warwick had striven throughout his life to have one of his daughters crowned Queen. Francis couldn't help but smile at the irony of it all. Warwick's failed rebellions, his daughters 'arranged' marriages and his efforts to place their husbands, who were both clearly unsuitable to rule, on the throne. All had ultimately resulted in failure. Yet now, in spite of all that had gone before, it seemed as if Warwick's ambitions had finally materialised, for his daughter Ann, as a consequence of her marriage to the man who was perhaps above all others responsible for Warwick's defeat and death, was at last going to be crowned Queen of England!

As he admired the royal couple, Francis smiled again. Ann, who'd never been known for her beauty, was radiant, her slight yet 'boyish' figure enhanced by a dress that was fashioned from a cloth of pure gold, which had been specially commissioned for the coronation. Richard, as handsome as always, was resplendent in a robe of deepest purple, the colour of Kings.

Once they'd all arrived at Westminster Abbey, where the ceremony was to take place, Francis smiled as he again considered the various ironies. The future King and Queen were led into the Abbey by the 'cowardly' Earl of Northumberland who carried 'Curtana', the sword of mercy. Ann's train was borne by the Lady Margaret Beaufort who, although she was now married to Lord Stanley, was the mother of the present Lancastrian pretender, Henry Tudor Earl of Richmond. And finally the Duke of Buckingham, who Richard had forgiven for the day, bore the future King's train. Francis was pleased to see that at least some men of honour were involved in the ceremony, John Howard who'd always been one of Richard's staunchest supporters and who'd been created both the Duke of Norfolk and the Earl Marshall of England, was given the honour of presenting the future King and Queen to the shrine of Saint Edward. Thomas Howard, his son, who'd played such a pivotal role in the arrest and execution of Lord Hastings, as a reward for his services had been created the Earl of Surrey and it was he who carried the sword of state.

The service, which was conducted by Archbishop Bourchier, lasted for quite sometime.

Eventually, after both custom and tradition had been satisfied, Richard Plantagenet Duke of Gloucester, was proclaimed King Richard the third of England. As the crown was placed upon Richard's head all present cheered and threw their hats into the air as, not for the first time that day, they all shouted 'God save King Richard'.

At long last the attendees were able to leave the Abbey for the great hall at Westminster, where they were all able to enjoy the great feast that had been prepared to celebrate the occasion and which Francis, to everyone's amusement, joked was 'fit for a King.'

Both Richard and his Queen sat at the head table together with those members of the 'higher aristocracy', who'd attended the coronation. As Richard's chief butler, Francis was given the honour of serving the new King and, as always, he undertook his duties seriously and with an eagerness that, reminiscing, took him back to his time as a henchman at Middleham. Unfortunately, Francis's enthusiasm, together with his lack of recent experience, meant that on more than one occasion his patrons received more than they'd requested, delivered elsewhere than expected! As Richard was once again wiping up the wine that had been spilt he laughed saying that Francis must never consider buying a hostelry when, 'He ultimately retires from public life.'

Francis couldn't help but smile broadly when Richard referred to this 'public life', for he too had been promoted and was no longer a mere Baron but was now a Viscount and a Knight of the Garter, who was to be both 'the King's chamberlain and his butler.' Francis laughed as he considered the fact that he was now probably one of the most powerful magnates in the Country!

Indeed, Richard had rewarded all of those subjects who'd supported him in his 'coup d'etat'. The old soldier Sir John Conyers had also been created a Knight of the Garter, William Catesby was to be the speaker at the next parliament and even the errant Duke of Buckingham had been provided for, having been given greater powers and titles in Wales. Although Francis knew that in promoting his cousin in such a way Richard had sought to marginalise him, sending him from London the seat of Government and into Wales to fulfill his obligations to these new appointments.

For Francis, who'd always delighted in 'chivalry' and 'noblesse', the highlight of the day was when the King's champion Sir Robert Dymocke, in full armour, rode into the hall on Richard's horse, the beautiful, 'White Surrey.' Throwing his gauntlet onto the floor, Dymocke challenged any who disputed Richard's title to pick it up and to fight him. Francis smiled as all present were silent and no one dared move, never mind take Dymocke, who was renowned as a great warrior, up on his challenge. Two of Sir Robert's forbears had also previously been King's champions, Sir Thomas Dymocke laying down a similar challenge at coronation of Henry IV and Sir Philip Dymock at that of Henry VI. Francis sighed as he remembered what had become of these two Kings and he hoped that Richard's choice of Dymocke as his champion would not bring him similar bad luck.

As Richard's champion laid down his challenge Francis looked directly at Buckingham, who in return smiled at him as he continued to flirt with the serving girl who was sitting on his lap. Francis clenched his fists and gritted his teeth before he too was able to bring himself to smile back, yes they all appreciated the fact that Buckingham despised his Woodville wife, but to behave in this way as he did at the King's table and in front of all of those people who were of noble birth was, Francis felt, an insult to them all. Perhaps, Francis wondered, if Buckingham had been paying more attention to the proceedings, he may have even thought to have picked up Dymocke's gauntlet. For Francis was now quite sure that at some point in the not too distant future, Buckingham hoped to have Richard's crown for himself.

Throughout that afternoon and into the evening Francis took the opportunity to study each of the guests in turn. In spite of the merriment and the alcohol induced jubilation of all of those who were present, he still felt extremely uneasy. Yes, presently Richard did appear to have the support of the majority of the aristocracy. But over the past few decades during the civil wars, the ranks of the old nobility had become seriously depleted, to such an extent that now, in real terms, their support counted for little. Moreover, who in their right mind could trust that coward Northumberland or even, when it came to it, the duplicitous Lord Stanley! As he turned to their friends the Howards, Francis could at least smile. Richard had made a shrewd move when he'd promoted both father and son to the peerage, for both men were strong, honourable and trustworthy and would, Francis felt, support Richard to the end. Richard had, Francis felt also been extremely clever in providing the Howards with estates in East Anglia. This area had historically been Lancastrian in its sympathies, albeit that the Lancastrian Earl of Oxford, who also enjoyed much support in that area, was safely under lock and key in Hammes Castle near Calais. Frowning, Francis sighed as he struggled to find any others amongst those who were present who could be relied upon to stand beside them in difficult times. Yes, there were the old stalwarts John Conyers and the Scropes who, together with the host of men that Ratcliffe had brought with him from Yorkshire, would without doubt follow Richard anywhere. But here in the south? Francis sighed again, he knew that Hasting's execution had alienated many of those southerners who'd previously supported Edward's government. Moreover, many amongst the southern gentry and middle classes now eyed both Richard and his northerners with increasing suspicion.

Indeed, it was rumoured that Henry Tudor, in exile on the continent, was being joined by a growing band of disgruntled exiles, many of whom had previously been diehard Yorkist's! As Francis turned to Richard it seemed to him that his friend was presently oblivious to the difficulties that they would potentially face in the future.

Smiling, Francis once again refilled Richard's glass and laughing he joined his friend at the table. At least today of all days they should try to enjoy themselves, for in a short space of time they'd all come a very long way and after all Richard was now King of England! There would be plenty of time in the coming weeks, months and even years for them to worry about how Richard would hold onto his throne!

Chapter 27
July 1483. Minster Lovel, Oxfordshire.

Within two weeks of his coronation Richard had left the capital and had embarked upon a royal progress that was planned to take him on a tour of his entire Kingdom. This as regrettably, in spite of all of their best efforts, it was evident that many within England still harbored suspicions and mistrusted both their new King and his 'northern retainers'. Unbelievably, Richard was even rumoured to have murdered the Princes in the Tower, it was said that he'd committed such a heinous crime in an effort to remove all potential opposition to his 'tyrannical regime'.

Richard, who was both a God fearing and an honourable man, had been devastated when he'd heard of these allegations, which he said had been 'invented' by those who only sought 'their own aggrandizement.' Unfortunately the slander, which seemed to have been publicized by both Lancastrians and Yorkists alike, was spreading like wildfire throughout England, especially within the southern shires. What made the matter even more upsetting, was that those who chose to promulgate such allegations, for the time being at least, remained anonymous. They were too afraid to come out in open rebellion against Richard who, like Francis, preferred to deal with people face to face. In an effort to assuage any speculation as to their well being, Francis had advised Richard to produce the Princes from their captivity within the Tower. Unfortunately Richard, as stubborn as always, had refused to do this arguing that to 'pander' to his subjects 'whims' would be to show weakness at a time when the Kingdom needed both a strong and powerful ruler. Ultimately, Richard had decided instead to take a tour of the Kingdom. He hoped that by, 'taking the King to his people,' he would be able to reassure his subjects of his good intentions. Initially, both Francis and Catesby had been quite skeptical, arguing that, for the time being at least, Richard would be better placed in London to deal with any potential insurrection, made either by or on behalf of either the Princes or the Lancastrian heir apparent Henry Tudor. Richard, who as always trusted his own instincts when it came to matters of such importance, had eventually convinced them that he could only hope to win the hearts of the people by making himself available to them, 'So that they can judge for themselves' that he 'wasn't the ogre that so many would have them believe' and that 'he had only England's best interests at heart.' Ultimately, Francis had been forced to concede that as it was by then well into July and the campaigning season was all but over, any invasion or rebellion that year now seemed highly unlikely. Especially when one considered that Richard's sudden and decisive seizure of power had left many of his potential enemies both weak and divided. It would be a brave man indeed Richard argued, who would dare raise rebellion at such a time and in such a climate.

At least, Francis felt, they would now have what was left of 1483 and the spring of 1484 to try to convince England that Richard was the rightful King and that it was his Government that had the most to offer to all classes of society, be they the common people, the middle classes, the gentry or the aristocracy and be they northerners, Midlanders or southerners. Francis could only hope that in the time that was available to them they'd be able to assure the English people of the validity of Richard's claim to the throne and of the fact that without Richard as its King, England had much to fear, both from civil unrest at home and from French ambitions on the continent.

Having left London, Richard's court had made slow yet deliberate progress along the Thames Valley through Oxfordshire towards Gloucester and the Welsh marches. As expected, Francis had been given the honour of entertaining the King and his courtiers at Minster Lovel. Keen to impress, Francis had left the Royal party and had returned to his Manor at Minster Lovel some days in advance of the court. Ostensibly to ensure that all was made ready for the Richard's arrival.

It had been some time since Francis had visited his family home and, as always, Francis was delighted to discover that this idyllic location, which was situated within the delightful Cotswold countryside, was little changed from when he'd seen it last. Indeed, if one took time to consider it, both the Hall, the village and the surrounding woodlands had changed little in many generations. Save of course for those characters who'd inhabited them throughout the years. Ancestors who were now long dead, those who'd been replaced on Earth by others whose task it now was to replenish the population and to continue the cycle of Life and Death. It had in fact been Francis's grandfather William, the seventh Baron Lovel, who'd perhaps been responsible for most of the changes within Minster Lovel in recent years. On his return from the French Wars William had rebuilt both the Hall and the Church, as the original structures, both dated and decaying, had been built some centuries earlier by their Norman ancestors. Francis's forbears had accompanied William on his invasion and conquest of England and had initially been known by the surname D'ivry, a name which evolved over time into the more 'English' sounding Lovel, this as the family sought to integrate itself into a

'Saxon nation' which, at that time, had detested anything Norman or French.

Surprisingly, Francis's wife Anne, without the need for either coercion or persuasion, had accompanied Francis to Minster. Moreover, it was fair to say that since her arrival in London just in time for Richard's coronation, Francis had noticed a considerable change in his wife's demeanor towards him. Unexpectedly, since rejoining him, Anne had even played the part of the 'dutiful wife', remaining at his side both by day and even more suprisingly by night! Suspicious as always, Francis had initially questioned his wife's motives, but ultimately he'd decided to stay silent, determined that he shouldn't 'look a gift horse in the mouth'. And in looks, what a gift horse Anne still was! Many said that she was the most beautiful lady at Richard's court and Francis couldn't disagree with them, although he did wish from time to time that Anne would smile, for when she did her whole face lit up. That said, with good reason Francis still harboured a deep distrust and suspicion as to his wife's true motives, although he appreciated that to question her in this respect would achieve nothing and would probably drive her away again. Francis had, therefore, chosen not to confront Anne and had decided instead to enjoy the attention that he was receiving from her. Even Richard had been pleased to see the Lovels back together as husband and wife. As always never afraid to voice his opinions, Richard had joked that in his opinion Anne's renewed interest in her husband had more to do with a 'rise' in his fortunes than in respect of any other items of 'Francis's anatomy', that as a consequence of Anne's 'rediscovered love' might from 'time to time' have 'risen again'! Richard's Ann, who'd been present during the conversation, had appeared quite shocked by her husbands vulgarity and had scalded him. This moralising, as always, had amused Francis, for it was well known and was indeed accepted, that even as a committed Christian, Richard had a large number of mistresses and as a result had sired a string of illegitimate children. The hypocrisy of 'noble society' was something that never failed to amaze Francis, who felt that if one chose to marry one should make every effort to remain monogamous. Richard on the other hand had often poked fun at Francis for his 'prudishness' and had also critisised him for his own hypocrisy, pointing out that to his knowledge Francis had often 'satiated his desires elsewhere than with his wife.'

Francis's entourage entered the courtyard at Minster Lovel Hall via the South East gate, the very route that had been adopted by Francis's father all those years earlier when he'd returned, defeated, from Towton. As he rode into the courtyard Francis could still clearly picture, in his minds eye, the sorry state of those survivors who'd returned home with his father. Men who were exhausted, defeated, dejected and who were, above all else, thoroughly demoralised. This in stark contrast to those brave soldiers whom Francis had earlier waved good-bye to, as they'd left Minster Lovel in answer King Henry's summons, all no doubt confident that they would return home victorious. Today however, this Lord Lovel who returned to his family's ancestral home, wasn't merely a Baron but was a Viscount! And in contrast to his father before him, Francis returned to his manor house, not in defeat, but in triumph. Countless people from both the village and its environs, some from as far away as Burford, had visited the Hall to witness the return of both the Lord and his lady, of whom they'd heard lots, but over the past few years had seen little. Each side of that portion of river bank that was adjacent to the manor house's southern wall swarmed with servants, retainers, commoners and with those of the local gentry who'd been invited to call upon the Viscount who was expected to be in residence for some weeks. As they entered the courtyard Francis's small party were greeted by all of the household servants whom Ned, as master of the house, had lined up to attention, almost as if they themselves had been a company of soldiers. Once dismounted, addressing 'his people' Francis thanked them all for their, 'warm welcome'. Continuing he said, 'I bring you greetings from your King who is to honour us with a visit in the coming days.' Smiling, Francis declared, 'I bring you the best of news. King Richard has decreed that Wychwood Forest which, much to your detriment, was previously deemed to be a Royal hunting ground, is once again to be opened up to you all as common land.' As if to emphasise the enormity of his announcement Francis paused for a few moments, in his minds eye he'd practiced this speech many times before over the past few days, shouting to make himself heard over the crowds excited chitter chatter, Francis pointed out that, 'Once again you'll all be free to hunt and forage in the Forest,' winking Francis added, 'Without having to worry about the attentions of both the Sheriff of Oxford and his men.'

Thankfully, this news achieved that which both Richard and Francis had hoped it would. Many of those present whose livelihood had always depended on the Forest, whooped and cheered in delight. For the news meant that those vast tracks of Forest, which had recently been denied to them on pain of death or imprisonment, were now no longer inaccessible. Francis knew that this reversal in Royal Policy would bring much in the way of prosperity to Richard's Oxfordshire subjects and would, he hoped, bring him many new friends and supporters in an area that had traditionally been Lancastrian in its sympathies.

The crowds cheers were almost deafening and as Francis at last took his leave from them and entered his manor house, Anne, who always seemed to delight in such shows of strength and authority, kissed and hugged Francis. Still unaccustomed to such familiarity Francis initially pulled away. Physically he was little changed from the man who, until recently, Anne had scorned, in fact judging by the increase in his girth and his receding hairline it could be argued that Anne would now have some justification in losing interest in him. Francis sighed for it was depressingly obvious to him that presently his wife's attentions had everything to do with his recent advancement. After all he was now one of the most powerful and influential men in England and, as a consequence, it seemed that Anne now loved him again! Francis's indifference to his wife was, however, momentary and as always he could do little to resist her attentions that until recently had been so cruelly withheld. Anne appearing not to notice her husband's coolness, gave herself wholeheartedly into an embrace that promised much and only ended when, uninvited, Ned entered the room. On seeing his friend, Francis, conscious that Ned would disapprove, stole himself from Anne. For Ned above all others had witnessed first hand both the neglect and the hostility that Anne had previously shown towards Francis. Indeed it was he who'd spent much of his own time consoling Francis for his loveless marriage. Anne scowled at Ned who returned the compliment as, unconvincingly, he apologised for 'disturbing' them.

Prior to his return to Minster Lovel Francis had spent much time worrying over Richard's proposed visit. From his experience at Court Francis knew that it was no mean feat to cater for the King and his vast array of courtiers. A host that would often number into the hundreds and included some of the nations most powerful and influential Lords and Ladies. Pleasingly, it soon became apparent to Francis that he need not have worried after all. Ned, as reliable and dependable as ever, had planned meticulously for each and every eventuality. Francis smiled as both he and his friend pored over the various itineraries. Ned had it all covered! Timetables, lodgings, menus for the numerous feasts that they were to host, he'd thought of everything. Even down to the private hunting and fishing trips that he'd organised for the benefit of Francis and Richard, both of whom loved their sport. Whilst the two friends were deep in conversation Anne remained with them, scowling and sulking she stood arms crossed, next to the Solar's large window. As his wife's 'tutting' and 'sighing' got louder and louder, Francis was once again forced to acknowledge her presence. Smiling at her Francis reassured Anne, telling her that both he and Ned would 'soon be finished.' Turning once more to his friend and looking forward to the hunting trips that he'd arranged, Francis was forced once again to concede that it was Ned and not Anne who knew that which gave him the most pleasure in life.

Francis smiled, Ned was far cleverer than many people gave him credit for. 'He may struggle with his words and figures,' Francis thought. 'But practically speaking he's much more astute than most.' Francis smiled again as he noticed that without even being briefed as to the purpose of the King's progress throughout England, Ned clearly understood Richard's true motives. As he was going through the planned schedules, Ned said that he hoped that, 'Their King' would soon earn both the 'respect' and the 'admiration' of the 'people of Oxfordshire.' In Francis's opinion many of Ned's abilities were wasted in his current role. Francis sighed as he considered that had Ned been of noble birth, he would no doubt have risen to a very high office indeed!

Thankfully, Ned's predictions proved to be correct and despite their preconceptions the people of Oxfordshire soon came to love their new King. Richard's timetable was both exhausting and unrelenting. On the very day of his arrival at Minster Lovel both he and his Queen were the guests of honour at a banquet that had begun early and, unusually for such an occasion, had continued long into the night. In the first week of his stay Richard must have personally visited each and every religious house and order, almshouse and hospital within the vicinity of Minster Lovel and Burford. No-one was left out for fear of alienating any portion of society and all had received the benefices and the patronage of a King who was keen to ingratiate himself with his people. In private both Francis and Richard scorned the hypocrisy of these people. Publicly they were quite content to receive the King's money, yet privately many of them still critisised Richard. The Dominican monks gratefully accepted the King's patronage, yet their master, the Pope in Rome, was said at that time to have been considering Richard's excommunication for, 'usurping the throne of England from his nephew.' In public however, Richard remained the dutiful and virtuous monarch. Francis marveled at how his friend seemed to revel in his new position. Richard rose early and retired late but was never heard to complain about the burdens of Kingship. Indeed, Richard said on countless occasions that he was honoured to have been given this opportunity to serve both his people and God. Francis had joked one evening that it was almost as if Richard was 'born to be King.' On hearing him Richard had at once become deadly serious and had replied angrily that he was indeed 'born to be King.' Richard maintained that it was he 'Richard Plantagenet' who was his father's rightful heir. Francis mused that it had now been quite some time since Richard had referred to himself as his brother Edward's heir and he wondered if even Richard now believed that Edward had after all been illegitimate! Francis smiled, for he doubted that Richard would ever admit this to his cousin the Duke of Buckingham who remained in Richard's bad books. Francis never dared to voice his own opinion on the matter, however one had only to look at the early portraits of King Edward to see that he bore little resemblance to either his siblings or to his father. Since Richard's accession many people had tried to pin him down in respect of that which specifically gave him the right to the throne. Was it the fact that Edward was a bastard? Or was it that Edward's marriage to Elizabeth Woodville had been invalid, by reason of his earlier betrothal to Lady Eleanour Butler? Richard always refused to be drawn on the matter in either public or in private. On occasions, when pressed, he would merely say that he loved both his parents and all of his brother's equally and would never 'stain their reputation', nor would he describe his father as a 'cuckold' or his mother as a 'harlot'.

Pleasingly, the Duke of Buckingham was not due to join them at Minster Lovel until the third and final week of Richard's stay and thankfully Buckingham only planned to stay for a couple of days, until the Court resumed it's progress through Oxfordshire and on into Gloucestershire. Since Richard had began his progress Buckingham had remained in the Capital, ostensibly to guage if any opposition to Richard's rule surfaced once the King had left the Capital. All of Richard's close circle of friends had warned him to be extremely wary of his cousin and not to leave him in London, but to insist that Buckingham accompany them throughout the period of the progress, whereby they could all keep a watchful eye on him. For worryingly in the days that had followed the coronation, in private Buckingham had suggested to them on numerous occasions that they would all do well to, 'rid themselves' of Edward's sons, 'once and for all.' Buckingham had argued that whilst they still lived the princes would always be a focal point for any potential rebellions. He'd asserted that with both of the princes dead, the Yorkist rank and file would have no option but to 'fall in line' with the new government. Both Richard and Francis had been appalled by Buckingham's proposal and Richard had rejected the plan out of hand, berating his cousin for considering that he would ever countenance such a heinous crime. An act, which Richard said would, 'bring down the wrath of both God and the people upon them all.' But Richard, who by that time had hated being in Buckingham's company, had refused to bring him with them and reluctantly Francis had finally been forced to acquiesce and agree to leave him in London and anyway, Richard said, 'even Buckingham would never dare' to disobey his orders when it came to a matter of such great importance. Francis, on the other hand, continued to worry that Buckingham might ignore Richard's orders and do some harm to Edward's son's, for he was an arrogant and a selfish man who may have just had the audacity to press on with his plans, in spite of Richard's opposition. And Francis was certain that Buckingham, who clearly had designs upon the throne, planned to remove each and every obstacle between himself and that ultimate prize. Throughout Richard's stay at Minster Lovel Francis had repeatedly voiced these concerns to Richard who'd laughed them off saying that, 'even the Duke of Buckingham would never dare to oppose my will in such a matter.' Richard had tried to assuage Francis's fears, pointing out that in no time at all Buckingham was to join them and that after the Court had reached Gloucester he was to leave them, to take up residence in his Castle at Brecon, from where he was to administer his newly acquired estates in Wales. Not unsurprisingly, Richard's assurances had done little to calm Francis's fears.

The Duke of Buckingham's entourage, when it finally arrived at Minster Lovel, was no less impressive than that of the King's. It had, however, been quite apparent to everyone at Court that the people of Oxfordshire had no love for Buckingham and the reception that he received, in stark contrast to that of both Francis and Richard, was somewhat muted to say the least! Buckingham, who was well known in these parts was generally disliked. As a consequence he was often greeted with indifference from those subjects, who having no choice in the matter, were from time to time duty bound to receive him into their homes. Nor was the lack of interest in his arrival lost on Buckingham. Upon reaching Minster Lovel Hall he'd immediately dismounted from his horse and, dispensing with the usual etiquette, had retired to his chambers feigning fatigue, without paying his respects to either his host Francis or to Richard. In doing this Buckingham had insulted both Francis and the King. It was not until well after dinner that Buckingham finally 'graced' them with his presence. Even then he was both cool and indifferent and neither the fine wine nor the good food did anything to cheer Buckingham, who was even more ill-mannered than usual. Worried, Francis felt sick and hoped that Buckingham's poor humour and impoliteness were merely due to his haughty and arrogant demeanor, rather than to some other reason that at some point he would have to share with them all. Unfortunately, the cause of Buckingham's unpleasantness when he finally discovered it, did nothing to assuage Francis's growing sense of alarm.

'What have you done you fool.' Richard's words were screamed and echoed throughout the Hall, that up until that point had been unusually quiet. Richard's reaction visibly rocked Buckingham backwards and even he appeared genuinely shocked by the effect that the news, which he'd whispered into Richard's ear, had had upon Richard. Even then the violence of Richard's verbal response gave no warning as to what was to happen next. In a fury Richard rose from his seat and with both hands grasped a shocked Buckingham around the throat, squeezing his windpipe so tightly that Buckingham's usually ruddy complexion turned into a pale shade of blue. It was only after some time and as Buckingham's eyes appeared almost as if they were about to exit their sockets, that Francis dared to intervene. Taking hold of Richard's arm Francis gestured towards his friend to let go. Surprisingly, Richard, who was white with anger and was shaking in an uncontrollable rage, let go of Buckingham who, unsupported, immediately fell to the floor clutching at his throat and gasping for air. Deprived, for the time being at least, of the opportunity to physically assault Buckingham, Richard resumed his verbal tirade and deafeningly sent his cousin from his presence, shouting after Buckingham, as he scurried from the chamber, that he wished, 'never to see him again.'

After some minutes and only after he'd guessed that Richard was slightly calmer, Francis was able to ask him the reason for his outburst, although in truth, much as he hoped that he was wrong, he'd all but guessed its true cause. Richard, quieter and more controlled, dismissed everyone from the chamber, save that is for Catesby, Ratcliffe and Francis himself. Once they were all alone Richard whispered to them, almost as if he dare not let anyone else hear what he had to say. Richard's words panicked Francis who, until recently, for one who was usually so pessimistic, had been quite optimistic about all of their futures, 'We're all undone.'

Ratcliffe, well known for his forthrightness turned to Francis who'd remained closest to Richard and said, 'What did he say?'

In an effort to quieten the Yorkshireman Francis put his finger to his lips as he urged Richard to continue.

Louder this time Richard repeated the words, 'I said we're all undone.'

Now it was Catesby's turn to look quizzically at his companions. On any other day Francis would have laughed. Two of the greatest and most powerful men in England and neither had any idea what was happening. Something that Richard was in all probability quite right in surmising, would destroy all that they'd achieved.

Francis, who in truth knew in his heart of hearts what Buckingham had done, tried to make it easier for Richard saying, 'He's killed them hasn't he?'

Momentarily Francis was heartened as Richard scoffed, 'That fop could no more kill anyone than the Pope could marry.'

Regrettably however Richard added, 'But yes Francis, you're right to assume that my brother Edward's children are dead.' Richard sighed deeply as he continued, 'Murdered on the orders of Buckingham who told my nephews gaolers that it was I who'd ordered their executions.'

Burying his head in his hands Richard tutted as he said incredulously, 'And the fools must have believed him, for who would carry out such an act without my assent?'

Yes, Francis knew that no-one would ever believe that Richard wasn't in some way responsible for the deaths. In the eyes of the public either Richard had ordered his nephews' murder or on the other hand, if he denied any involvement and was believed, he would be the King who was unable to control his over mighty subjects! Resigned, Richard sighed yet again and continued, 'In truth I am responsible for their deaths. For did you not all warn me not to leave Buckingham behind in London. I was stupid enough to think that he'd never dare to disobey me.'

Head bowed, Richard seized and tore at his own hair, almost as if he were strangling Buckingham again. Eventually Richard again broke the stunned silence, 'For the life of me I can't see any way out of this. To kill children, to kill my brother's children, the people will never forgive me for this,' sighing yet again Richard concluded, 'This is the end for us.'

In truth there was nothing more to say and clearly no-one could think of anything that would be of any help to them. Dejected, Richard retired to his bed adding as he left, 'Let me sleep on it. I promise we'll talk again in the morning.'

Ratcliffe, as always the practical one, immediately sent for his valet, who in turn was dispatched in 'all secrecy' to Sir Robert Brackenbury, The Constable of the Tower. His purpose, 'to ascertain with all haste the facts surrounding the rumoured death of the princes.'

Ratcliffe's valet was one whose trust and loyalty were beyond reproach, but even he was given a powerful incentive to keep this secret, as Ratcliffe added, 'If any of this gets out I'll have your head.'

The valet, bowing and nodding nervously, left the room.

The small group of friends met again in the solar on the following morning. It was obvious from their disheveled state that few, if any of them, had slept. Richard looked particularly tired and drained, 'old' as Francis had never before seen him. Time had clearly done little to raise his spirits as all he seemed able to repeat over and over again, was that this one 'act' would destroy them all! Not surprisingly Buckingham was nowhere to be found. Apparently on being sent from the King's presence he'd immediately left Minster Lovel for his Castle at Brecon.

It was early afternoon by the time that Ratcliffe's valet returned from London. It was as they'd all feared. The princes were dead, murdered on the orders of Buckingham who'd assured Brackenbury that he was acting on the King's orders. Buckingham had even produced documentation to support this claim. These warrants, which were clearly forgeries had been designed to convince the princes' jailers of Richard's assent. It appeared that it had been Brackenbury, as the Constable of the Tower, who'd initially been ordered by Buckingham to carry out the murders. Initially, Brackenbury had refused to become involved in the scheme but, after much persuasion, he'd eventually agreed to a turn a blind eye, allowing others direct access to the princes' apartments. Two paid ruffians, Miles Forest and James Dighton, had been recruited by Buckingham and under the direction of Sir James Tyrell they'd entered the boys' rooms as they both slept. Both Edward and his younger brother Richard had been smothered to death with their own bedclothes. In secret the bodies had been buried at base of the staircase that had led to their apartments.

All present wept unashamedly as they heard the graphic details of the children's murder.

The one saving grace, if anything at all could be salvaged from this fiasco, was that few presently knew of the murders. Brackenbury, fearful for his life, could be trusted to remain quiet and Tyrell and his cohorts could easily be bought off with a combination of favours and threats. Thankfully, over the previous weeks the Princess had been withdrawn into the inner apartments of the Tower where few had seen them. This being a conscious decision by Richard to keep them out of the limelight in the hope that one day they would be altogether forgotten. Even the boys' personal physician, Doctor Argentine, had been dismissed and had returned home to his native Italy. Once those present had heard the full horrors of Buckingham's crime, Richard, deep in thought, took time to consider their options. Standing at the large Solar window he gazed blankly out towards the river and the forest beyond, clearly contemplating what to do next. Francis, Catesby and Ratcliffe, could do nothing other than to wait for Richard to speak, for none seemed able to think of anything that could be done to rescue the situation.

Eventually Richard turned to his friends and spoke, 'I can't do anything to undo what's been done. We've got to face it, my brother's children have been murdered. I neither ordered nor was party to this crime. Yet there are none, save of course for the people in this room and those who were responsible, who know the real truth of the matter. And who will believe the truth? Either here in England or abroad? Sadly the reality of the situation is that I, above all others, had most to gain from their deaths.' Richard sighed, 'Buckingham acted alone and without orders, but by leaving him in London I did give him the opportunity to carry out the murders.'

Irate, Francis could keep quiet no longer, 'Given half the chance he'll also have your throne.'

The words were blurted out in a rush with little thought.

Richard looked as his friend quizzically.

'What did you say?'

Francis quantified his allegation, 'With you gone who would stand between Buckingham and the throne? Does he not as the principal member of the House of Stafford, have a claim through Thomas Woodstock and through John of Gaunt? Trust me Richard, now it'll only be a matter of time before Buckingham comes out against you. By killing the princes, in one act Buckingham will have turned the country against you and has also removed two people who could be argued to have had a greater claim to the thrown than he'.

After listening to Francis, Richard immediately turned to Ratcliffe.

'Arrest him, bring Buckingham to me here, he'll answer to me for what he's done, I'll get the truth from him.'

Catesby replied, 'Richard, Buckingham left last night for his castle in Brecon.'

Ratcliffe added, 'Buckingham's castle is well fortified and he has many retainers, presently we've insufficient troops to take his castle by force'.

Francis added, 'I'll send to the Howards for more men, when they arrive we can move against Buckingham.'

Deep in thought Richard took quite some time to consider his next move, when he spoke at long last it was clear that he'd changed his mind, 'No, if Buckinghams gone we must be patient. If I deal with him now everyone will find out what's become of the princes, we must wait, I'll have my day with Buckingham but presently I think that he'll be of more use to us at large. We must act as if nothing's changed. He'll expect me to come after him and he's no doubt already making the necessary arrangements to defend himself. No, if we do nothing he'll be forced to make his move and then we can react to that.' Smiling, Richard added, 'And when he does attack me he's bound to be joined by all of those others who oppose us and we'll be able to deal with all of our enemies in one fell swoop.' Rubbing his chin Richard smiled again, 'With his tenuous claim to the throne Buckingham can't hope to raise the necessary support in his own right, he'll be forced to come out in favour of the princes' and as such, for the time being at least, he'll have to keep their deaths a secret, that'll give us time to plan and when his rebellion comes we'll be ready for it.'

Francis did feel confident that they'd be able to deal with any challenge made by or on behalf of Buckingham, however he was still extremely concerned as to what would become of them once Richard's cousin had been dealt with, for nothing would have changed. They'd all still be held responsible for the princes' murder, whatever the truth was! Francis sighed, the only thing that did encourage him was the knowledge that at least God knew the truth of the matter!

Chapter 28
October 1483, Grantham.

As planned, they had all waited patiently for some months before the Duke of Buckingham finally made his move. As both September and, with it, the campaigning season had drawn to an end, Francis had begun to seriously doubt that anything would happen that year. Richard, on the other hand, since hearing the news of the Prince's murders and despite his earlier optimism that there would be no rebellion until at least the following spring, had believed that regardless of the worsening weather, Buckingham would still make his challenge before the year's end. Ultimately, it had been Richard and not Francis who'd been correct in his assessment. Amazingly, in spite of the seriousness of the situation which they now faced, Richard, who always seemed to enjoy it when it turned out that he was right, had taken each and every the opportunity to remind Francis of that fact! Francis on the other hand had maintained that it was of no consequence to him who'd prophesied the event, what had mattered was that they now faced a rebellion which, if it spread, had the potential to bring the whole country out against them. That said, in one of their lighter moments together, Francis had felt that it had been his duty to point out to Richard that in coming to his conclusions about Buckingham, he'd had benefit of a 'vast network of spies and agents,' all of whom had kept him extremely well informed in relation to Buckingham's plans. Francis on the other hand, had been forced to rely on his experience and instincts alone. But even now, Francis still couldn't quite believe Buckingham's naivety and lack of far sight in planning such insurrection for a month when the unreliable English weather was bound to interfere with his plans

When they had first received news of Buckingham's rebellion they'd been here at Grantham. Thankfully, having been located in the very centre of England and positioned astride the Great North Road, they'd been ideally placed to face Buckingham's challenge. Richard's intelligence had indicated that Buckingham's strategy required that both he and his allies organise and co-ordinate a series of risings that were to take place throughout England, from Kent in the east, Dorset, Devon and Cornwall in the west and through into south Wales.

Anticipating that the rebellion would take place in the first weeks of October, Richard had planned his response well. Francis had been extremely impressed, for his friend had even managed to make these arrangements without pre warning those whom he suspected of being involved and who, he hoped, would soon reveal themselves to him. The

Duke of Norfolk and his son the Earl of Surrey had both been sent into East Anglia and the South East, ostensibly on a tour of their newly acquired Mowbray inheritance. In reality they were to recruit troops to deal with any attempt on the part of the rebels to march upon the capital from that direction. Francis and Richard were to remain in the Midlands to await developments, as Grantham was an ideal location from which they could easily march westwards to thwart any effort made by Buckingham to enter England from Wales. Alternatively, they could move southwards down the Great North Road towards the channel ports, to oppose any landing made by or on behalf of Henry Tudor.

Long before they'd received news of the insurrection, Richard had had the far sight to compile numerous Commissions of Array. These documents, which commanded Richard's subjects to come to his aid in times of rebellion, were despatched by fast rider as soon as news of Buckingham's rebellion had been received by Richard at Grantham. Ironically, many were addressed to those of dubious loyalty, in spite of the fact that these men were expected to join Buckingham's revolt. 'Good evidence' Richard said of these men's 'treason', when the rebels were finally brought to book for their actions. As always, fearful of defeat, Francis had at least been gladdened by his friend's confidence that the rebellion would soon be dealt with and a positive outcome achieved.

Apparently, once he'd left Minster Lovel for his Castle at Brecon, Buckingham had wasted no time in 'testing the waters,' to see how any claim made by himself for the throne would be received. Not surprisingly, he'd been disappointed by the lack of enthusiasm for his candidature and it had soon became apparent to him that no-one within the aristocracy were willing to support his claim. It was fair to say that Francis had been astounded by Buckingham's impudence! For when he'd finally been forced to concede that in the present climate he would be unable to claim the throne in his own right, Buckingham had had the audacity to make it known that he hoped to restore Prince Edward to the throne! This despite the fact he already knew that the boy had been murdered, on his orders! What annoyed Francis most of all was the fact that both he and Richard had been forced to bite their tongues and remain silent on the issue. For it was clearly in no-ones interests to reveal the truth of the matter. Unfortunately, by supporting the Prince, Buckingham had received a great deal of support from amongst the old Yorkist nobility and from the surviving Woodvilles, all of whom had remained loyal to King Edward's lineage. Since Richard had ascended to the throne, these men, who in the past had supported the Yorkist regime, had come to resent Richard's government and his increasing reliance upon his 'northerners'. Unfortunately, by October 1483 many of the old stalwarts of Edward's government had been removed from office, to be replaced by a number of Yorkshiremen, all of whom had had to be rewarded for supporting Richard's coup.

As always, Francis never failed to be amazed by the dishonourable behaviour of those of high birth who should have known better. And even then Buckingham was still playing a duplicitous game! Rumour had it that, unbeknown to his Yorkist allies, he'd even made approaches, through Bishop Morton, to Henry Tudor in Brittany. Sadly, in one of his rare misjudgements, after Hasting's execution, Richard had spared Morton who'd been imprisoned in Buckingham's castle at Brecon and now it seemed that the wily old Bishop had come back to bite them! Clearly influenced by Morton, Buckingham had made it known that if it were 'discovered' that any 'ill had befallen the princes,' he would support Tudor's claim to the throne! Apparently, he'd secured Woodville support for his plan on the understanding that Tudor, if he became King, would marry Edward's eldest daughter Elizabeth of York, thereby uniting once and for all the Houses of York and Lancaster. Francis could only guess what Buckingham hoped to gain by such an alliance. It was clear to Francis that at some point Buckingham would have to reveal the fate of the princes, whose deaths he would no doubt blame on Richard. If he was clever enough to do this at the very last minute, his 'Yorkist' followers would, by that time, be so heavily committed to the rebellion that they'd have had no choice but to support the Tudor, Woodville and Stafford alliance.

At least it appeared, for the time being, that Buckingham had relinquished his own ambitions to the throne. Richard had not been surprised by this and he'd laughed as he'd pointed out that when only a handful of people had initially agreed to support him, even the 'thick skinned' Buckingham must have realised just how 'universally hated' he was. Francis, on the other hand, couldn't believe that Buckingham had given up all hope of ever being King, he still felt that given half a chance, Buckingham would resume his claim to the crown. Indeed, in Francis's opinion, Buckingham must have been delighted by the prospect of the only two people who now stood between him and that throne, meeting on the field of battle. If anything happened to either Richard or Tudor it could only further Buckingham's claim. After Richard's reaction to his killing of the princes, Buckingham must have known that he had no future in an England ruled by Richard. Yet if he was able to bring about Richard's downfall and could place all of the blame for the Princes' murders wholly and squarely on Richard's shoulders, he'd once again be safe and in a position of power. In those circumstances, Francis believed that it'd only been a matter of time before Buckingham would begin to plot against his new allies. If on the other hand Tudor was defeated, Buckingham could rally together all of the remaining Anti-Ricardians, who could then take to the field against a weakened Richard.

As Francis had earlier predicted, the weather in early October was atrocious. Thankfully, Richard's spies were able to report that Tudor's small invasion fleet was forced to remain at anchor off the Brittany coast, unable to risk a crossing of the channel for fear of being scattered by one of a number of storms and squalls. As a result of the inclement weather, poor communication between the rebels and a consequent lack of co-ordination, the rebels in Kent had risen prematurely, a full ten days before the rest of the country. Norfolk and his son were therefore easily able to secure all of the Thames crossings, thereby cutting the 'eastern rebels' off from the capital, which had been their ultimate goal. Deprived of both supplies and reinforcements the Kentishmen chose not to face Norfolk and his son, and all but a few 'hard-liners' had returned to their homes without giving battle. Presently, Norfolk was in the process of rounding up the ringleaders, many of whom were executed or, in some cases and in Francis's opinion 'over generously', a number were pardoned, on the understanding that they swore allegiance to King Richard.

Storms in the west country had swollen both the Avon and the Severn. Consequently, both river valleys were severely flooded. With all of the crossings into England impassable, Buckingham's small army was unable to join up with that of his allies in England. Francis felt no pity for Buckingham and couldn't help but laugh when he'd heard the news that when he'd left his castle at Brecon, even his own servants, expecting him to be defeated, had sacked his castle and stole what had remained of his personal possessions.

Ultimately, by the third week of October it was clear that Buckingham had failed to secure much in the way of support. As Francis had earlier feared, both weak and unsupported, Buckingham had declared for Tudor, but in doing so he'd announced that he'd had it on 'good authority' that the princes had been murdered in the Tower of London on the orders of 'their uncle, Richard.'

Both Richard and Francis, together with Ratcliffe and the small army that they'd mustered at Grantham, intended to march to Leicester, where they hoped to meet up with Lord Stanley and his Chesire retainers. From there Richard planned to advance into Worcestershire and the Welsh borders, to deal with Buckingham and those few troops that he still commanded.

Francis was sad to be leaving Grantham, for here in the East Midlands he'd felt secure and the local people loved them. Richard had always enjoyed a great deal of support in the east, a swathe of land that stretched all of the way from the Lincolnshire border with Norfolk and up into the East riding of Yorkshire. Moreover, the Angel Inn where they'd stayed for these past few weeks was extremely comfortable. Initially a hostelry, the 'Angel' had earlier been acquired by King Edward who'd restored and updated the building and had then given it as a present to his mother, the Duchess Cecily. Presently, it was amongst Richard's favourite residences and it had been sumptuously bedecked for the benefit of both the King and his guests.

As Francis stiffly mounted his horse he smiled as he considered that he was getting far too old for campaigning. He sighed as he reflected on the prospect that this may only be the first in a long line of challenges to Richard's rule, for a disgruntled nation were only now hearing the news that Richard had allegedly murdered his nephews. Francis could only hope that, if victorious, in one fell swoop they'd be able to rid themselves of all of the pretenders to the crown. Maybe in the absence of any other claimants to the throne, Richard could then attempt to convince his subjects that he was not only innocent of the princes' murders but also that he was perhaps the best and possibly the only option left for England. Francis sighed again, what was most upsetting to him was the fact that since Richard's coronation they'd already achieved so much in the little time that they'd had. Now it was a distinct possibility that all of their efforts may come to nought!

As planned, after his coronation Richard had progressed throughout the realm and, as expected, he'd thereby gained many new allies. By the autumn of 1483 Richard's only legitimate son, Edward of Middleham, had been universally accepted as his heir and had even been invested as the Prince of Wales during a splendid ceremony that had taken place in York Minster. Shaking his head Francis grunted, and all for it to be undone by one man, Buckingham a jealous, selfish and an arrogant man!

Once rumours of the princes' murders had begun to circulate throughout England, both Richard and his friends had been undecided about how to respond to them. Francis, who'd always believed that the 'truth will out,' had argued that they should tell the people what had really happened. Nevertheless, he was forced to concede that Richard was probably right when he'd pointed out that by that time they'd probably lost any opportunity that they'd had to reveal the truth. Richard had reasoned that the, 'people will ask why, if we are guiltless, did we not reveal the truth when we discovered it and why, at that time, did we not punish the perpetrator, the Duke of Buckingham?' Furthermore, he argued, since they'd all become aware of the murders they'd exacerbated the problem when they'd all set about threatening or bribing those who knew of the murders to remain silent. Now they could not escape from the fact that once it had become known that the princes had been murdered, they would all be blamed! After much debate Richard had ultimately decided that the best course of action was to continue to deny the allegations. Overruled, Francis could do nothing as Richard issued a series of proclamations maintaining that Edward's sons still lived. Unfortunately it now appeared as if few, if any, of his subjects believed him. The situation was soon made much worse when, in answer to a 'request' from a number of Royal councillor's, they were unable to produce the princes for all to see. Richard did parade Clarence's son, Edward Earl of Warwick, through the streets of York. At the time he'd pointed out that if he were guilty of killing Edward's son's, then why would he leave his other brother's son alive. Unfortunately, this had done nothing to assuage public suspicion and within weeks it'd become almost universally accepted that the Princes were in fact dead and that it was Richard who was guilty of the crime. Indeed, this loss of general support for the King had been evidenced by the poor response that they'd received to the commissions of array that Francis had circulated on Richard's behalf. This was doubly upsetting for Francis, for it'd been the first time that his friend had entrusted him with such an important task. As he sat motionless on his horse and looked towards the pitifully few numbers of troops that had joined them, Francis was extremely disappointed, for he truly felt that it was he who'd let his friend down. Richard, on the other hand, was quite philosophical about the lack of support and he smiled resignedly as, clapping Francis on the back, he said that he'd expected no more from, 'these people.' Francis smiled back, keen to reassure his friend he'd replied that he was sure that the public would once again learn to love Richard as they'd done so before. Francis added that he still truly believed that they'd be able to, 'Win back the hearts of the people.' In reply, Richard merely shrugged his shoulders and sighing said, 'I'm afraid Francis, what will be will be.'

Since they'd received the news of the princes' murders Francis had become increasingly concerned for Richard, who now slept little and seemed to be becoming quite morose and fatalistic. Usually one who was extremely religious, Richard had lost all interest in the church, withdrawing his patronage from a large number of religious houses and orders. He had even gone so far as to cancel his plans for a new religious order which he'd been setting up in his beloved Middleham, a project which he'd previously been extremely excited about. Wrongly now, every time something went against them, Richard would say that it was God's punishment for their misdemeanours. Francis would always try to reassure his friend, pointing out that they were guiltless of the princes' murders and surely God above all others must know of their innocence. In reply, Richard would always say that although they may not have carried out the act itself, by association they were as guilty as the perpetrators themselves.

It was during their march westwards, once they'd been joined at Leicester by Lord Stanley, that they finally received word that the Duke of Buckingham, unable to cross into England and devoid of any reinforcements, had been abandoned by his men and had gone into hiding. With this news Richard, intent on thwarting any potential invasion by the Lanacstrian pretender Henry Tudor, ordered their army to turn southwards. Francis still seriously doubted that Tudor would dare to put to sea, for the weather was still appalling and it was obvious that he now had little in the way of useful support in England. Worryingly however, Lord Stanley, who was married to Tudor's mother Margaret Beaufort, was unable to disguise his displeasure as they'd received word of Buckingham's capitulation. Upon being challenged by Francis the old man maintained that he was merely disappointed that he would not now .hve the opportunity of serving his 'new King in the field'. Unconvinced, Francis openly questioned Stanley's loyalty, only to be quieted by Richard who took him to one side and advised him to drop the matter saying, 'Careful Francis we don't want to alienate what little support we do have.' Francis understood how Richard felt, especially when one considered that he'd been present with his elder brother at both Olney and at Newark when Edward had been deserted by his men. That said, Francis found it extremely difficult to countenance a potential traitor in their midst. Especially when one considered that their enemy Tudor was his son-in - law! Recalling how treachery had been the cause of numerous defeats in the past Francis pointed out to Richard that any potential defectors in their ranks were far more dangerous than those who plainly opposed them. In reply Richard asked Francis to trust his judgement in this matter, adding grimly, 'Don't worry Francis for I'm sure Lord Stanley's day will come.'

At Salisbury, the royal army, who'd marched many miles since they'd left Grantham, rested and awaited any news of Tudor's invasion. It was here that the hapless Duke of Buckingham was brought to them in chains. Having gone into hiding in Shropshire it was of no surprise to anyone that, when his money had run out, Buckingham had been betrayed by his companions. As was his right as a peer of the realm, Buckingham demanded that he be granted a personal audience with the King. Francis, considering Richard's fragile state of mind and fearing that Buckingham, using his legendary charm and charisma, would once again manage to talk himself out of trouble, argued against such a proposal saying, 'Surely this time there's nothing that can be said to exonerate him.'

Richard took some time to consider Buckingham's request but, thankfully, he eventually refused the audience. Richard was not prepared to forgive his cousin and when he finally replied to Buckingham Richard let him know what he thought of him describing him as, 'The most untrue creature living,' there never being 'a falser traitor purveyed.'

It was decided that Francis would represent the King in this matter and, as such, it was he and not Richard who'd visited Buckingham in his cell in Salisbury Castle. Francis didn't usually take delight in the misfortune of others, but when it came to the Duke of Buckingham even he made an exception. As he entered the dark and airless dungeon in which Buckingham was held he couldn't help but grin. Unusually for a nobleman, Buckingham was restrained by chains and even if he'd wished to rise to greet his visitor he wouldn't have been able to. Throughout Francis's visit, Buckingham was forced to remain in the corner of his cell, both dishevelled and soiled. It seemed to Francis that the pitiable conditions in which Buckingham was kept were testament to the universal loathing in which he was held. Obviously disappointed that Richard had refused his request for an audience, Buckingham took the briefest of moments to study Francis before his nose went up in the air and shrugging he said scornfully, 'I hoped to speak with the master and not his servant.'

In the present circumstances Francis couldn't resist a jibe and smiling he replied truthfully, 'You underestimate the influence that I have upon the King,' Laughing, Francis added, 'And judging by your present circumstances it seems that you, my Lord, have none.'

In reply Buckingham hissed out the words that revealed his hatred for Francis, 'You Lovel are a nothing. Trust me one day you too will fall from grace,' sighing he added, 'I just regret that it now seems that I may not be here to see it.'

Francis didn't pity Buckingham, he loathed him. Angered by Buckingham's retort he sneered as he replied, 'Don't even dare to compare my circumstances to yours. I am and will always remain the King's most loyal servant, I've lived all of my life in his service and I will die serving him. You on the other hand are in Richard's own words a loathsome creature, you're everything that I despise in humankind. Don't dare to judge me by your own lowly standards. You had much to thank Richard for,' Francis sighed before he added, 'Yet in spite of everything you turned against him. Richard not only afforded you the privileges that your rank deserved but he also loved you as his cousin.' Francis sighed again as he added, 'He was mistaken to have ever trusted you. I now know why King Edward kept you isolated and away from his court. I only regret that Richard didn't follow his brother's example.'

In spite of the piteous conditions in which he was being held Buckingham laughed haughtily as he replied, 'Yes but I'll go to my grave knowing that at least I've brought you all down with me.' Clearly seeing the concern on Francis's face, Buckingham smiled as he added, 'Yes it is true isn't it?' Francis was dumfounded and found it quite strange that a condemned man who was soon to die and who was held in chains and was sitting in his own filth, could appear so triumphant. Buckingham, obviously sensing Francis's disquiet, was on a roll, he sniggered as he added, 'The whole nation's awash with rumours that Richard's murdered his nephews. I ask you Lovel how do you think you'll all be able to get out of that one?' Nonplussed, Francis stuttered, for once he could think of no meaningful reply. Even he was disappointed with his response when the words finally came to him, 'Well, er we've kept it a secret until now, what makes you think that we can't continue doing so?' Buckingham sneered as he replied, 'Are you really that naive?'

Francis could not reply and thankfully it was Buckingham who again broke the silence. Surprisingly his words, which now seemed almost conciliatory, were both calm and measured, 'Now only I can help Richard. If I chose to tell the truth I could tell the people that the murders were arranged and carried out by myself and without the knowledge of the King.' Buckingham could clearly see the doubt in Francis's face as he assured Francis that, 'The people will believe me,' before he added resignedly with a sigh, 'For I now know that they hate me even more than Richard.'

Having composed himself Francis looked upon Stafford with disdain as he asked, 'And why would you do this for us?'

Buckingham, who'd obviously spent sometime considering the matter, was quick to reply. Francis noticed the increasing desperation in his voice which had become quite high pitched and nasal, 'It's his last throw of the die', Francis thought.

'I'm not ready to die, tell Richard that he can send me into exile, anywhere he wants, I promise you that I'll never trouble you again.'

Buckingham had obviously convinced himself that his scheme would work. It was clear to Francis that in Richard's absence he now hoped to convince him.

'Can't you see that this is Richard's only hope if he wants to keep his crown.'

Francis laughed again, 'Do you really think that Richard will go for that. Yes I do believe that you would willingly go into exile. And I'd be willing to bet that you'd make for Brittany and your new ally Tudor. From there you'd rescind all of those promises that you'd made to Richard and you'd return to England with Tudor at your side. To serve him, until of course it no longer suited your aims.'

Buckingham appeared genuinely shaken by Francis's response to his offer. Turning away from Francis it was clear that he no longer wished to continue the conversation, he spoke with renewed arrogance and a confidence that belied his present circumstances, yet which Francis would always associate with Henry Stafford Duke of Buckingham, 'I don't want your opinion Lovel, you're merely a messenger. I demand that you put my offer to Richard, it is he and not you who will decide my fate.'

Laughing as he left the cell Francis repeated once again, 'My Lord of Buckingham, I say again, I fear that you underestimate my influence with the King.'

In reality Richard needed no persuading to ignore Buckingham's offer. Cruelly, Francis chose not to visit Buckingham to tell him of Richard's response to his proposal. Instead Francis decided to let him stew. Not knowing if he was going to be reprieved was in Francis's opinion a fitting way for Buckingham to live out his last few days on earth.

Ultimately it was probably only as his executioner came for him and he was led out to the scaffold some days later that Buckingham must have finally realised that Richard wasn't at all interested in his proposition. Surprisingly, Buckingham took his death well. Richard had at least allowed him a wash, some clean clothes and the dignity, a right afforded to those of his rank, to be beheaded. Apparently these concessions, granted at the last minute, had only been given on the understanding that Buckingham made no speech. As it turned out, probably for the first time in his life but certainly for the last time, Buckingham kneeled meekly before the block and wept as the presiding priest prayed for his soul. Finally, Buckingham gave some coins to executioner before he offered his exposed neck to the block. Francis felt that it was perhaps ironic that one who'd caused so much distress in his short life did not suffer, as unusually Buckingham's head was cast off in a single blow. Francis could not tell whether or not Buckingham's decapitated head displayed either an expression of surprise or horror, for in spite of his rank Francis couldn't get anywhere near to the scaffold, for the rows and rows of cheering spectators, all of whom were jostling to get a closer look at Buckingham's corpse.

Chapter 29
Nottingham Castle. March 1485.

Once Francis had been summoned to Nottingham 'with all urgency,' he'd wasted no time in hurrying to be at his friend's side. Ratcliffe's messenger, who'd called upon Francis at Minster Lovel, had reported to him that the, 'Queen was gravely ill' and according to the Royal physicians, 'Wasn't long for this world.'

Francis's own wife Anne, whose coldness towards Francis had over the past year returned with a vengeance, had refused to join Francis on his journey northwards. Francis had, however, been unconcerned by his wife's reluctance to accompany him, for he knew that without her he could travel much quicker and what was more, her company at present gave him no pleasure at all.

As Francis had journeyed to Nottingham he'd wondered what further misfortunes could visit themselves upon Richard, who'd endured much in the way of bad-luck throughout the past year. In contrast to Francis, who had often questioned why they'd seemingly been subjected to one disaster after another, Richard had slowly become resigned to the adversity that now seemed to plague both his professional and his personal life. On those occasions when he'd been in Richard's company, Francis had tried everything to restore his friend's faith in life. Sadly he'd failed as one catastrophe followed on from another. In February 1484 the King's only legitimate son, his heir Edward of Middleham had died. Francis had been with both the King and Queen at Nottingham when they'd heard the news of their son's death. It was fair to say that both had been, 'mad with grief', although Richard had said at the time that he hadn't been at all surprised that such a tragedy had been visited upon them adding, much to Francis's consternation, that as he'd been responsible for the, 'taking of others children' it was only fair that he should suffer the same fate! As always when Richard was in such a state of mind, Francis had attempted to reassure his friend that he'd nothing to be repentant for. Francis had repeated once again and for the umpteenth time, that it had been Buckingham alone who'd been responsible for the murder of the princes and that Richard was guiltless of the crime. Unfortunately there was nothing that either Francis or anyone else could say to convince Richard otherwise. Ironically, when one considered how sickly Richard's son had been throughout his short life, it wasn't at all surprising to Francis that the child had succumbed to the sweating sickness, which had been prevalent throughout England in the winter of

1484. Francis sighed as he remembered how many people, dismissing Richard's grief, had cruelly blamed him for the epidemic that was, they said, God's vengeance upon a nation that had been responsible for the deaths of its princes.'

Distraught, it'd been some weeks before Richard had been able to consider the question of his succession. Sadly, at that time the Queen was of an age and of such a delicate disposition that any more children seemed highly unlikely. Initially Richard had sited his brother Clarence's son, Edward Earl of Warwick as his heir. Thankfully he'd soon rescinded this. Richard had earlier disbarred Warwick from the succession by reason of his father's attainder for treason. Moreover, according to the Royal physicians, the boy was affected by some kind of mental debilitation, similar to that which King Henry VI had suffered from in his later years. Francis, who if the truth be known quite liked the boy, hadn't been disappointed to see Warwick excluded. He felt that had Richard nominated Warwick, then surely those who wanted to see an end to Richard's rule, who would have pointed out that as the legitimate child of Richard's elder brother, Warwick was entitled to be King at that time and in Richard's stead! Thus Richard had had no option but to nominate as his heir his sisters son, John de la Pole Earl of Lincoln. Francis knew De La Pole well and he felt that although Richard's nephew was a fine young man, who since they'd come to power had ably governed the north on their behalf, his nomination was bound to cause them difficulties. Francis was concerned, for in addition to all of their other problems, now it seemed as if Richard no longer had a viable line of succession. De La Pole's claim to the throne, which came via his mother, Richard's sister, was in truth no more plausible than that of the Lancastrian pretender Henry Tudor. A title that they'd all spent the last two years rebutting! Indeed, whilst Richard's son had lived they'd all made much of the fact that Tudor's title came via his mother Margaret Beaufort, who in turn originated from John of Gaunt's illicit liaison with Katherine Swynford. Now Richard had been forced to nominate a successor whose own claim to the throne also came through his mother! Admittedly, there was no Salic Law in existence in England and, as such, succession via the female line was not disbarred in common law. However in reality they all knew that the 'conservative' English aristocracy didn't look kindly on such lineage.

Worryingly, with each new disaster Richard seemed to care less and less about their futures. As Francis made his way to Nottingham he could only wonder how his friend would react if Queen Ann did in fact die. Francis was doubly concerned, for news of the Queen's terminal illness could not have come at a worse time. Recently, rumours had been circulating throughout England that Richard, deprived of a legitimate heir, had planned to poison his 'barren' wife so that he would be free to marry his brother's daughter, Elizabeth of York. It was said that by doing this Richard hoped to thwart Tudor's plans to take Elizabeth as his wife. Moreover, Elizabeth was young, strong and beautiful and through her, it was said, Richard hoped to sire many sons. Unfortunately these tales had gained more than a semblance of authenticity when, during the Christmas festivities at Westminster, both Elizabeth and her uncle Richard had flirted unashamedly with each other. Francis felt that one couldn't really blame the girl, for she was still very young and had only recently been brought out of sanctuary by her mother. Richard, on the other hand, should have known better. What had really saddened Francis was the fact that by that time the Queen was clearly ailing. Francis had witnessed the effects of consumption on many occasions before and when he'd last seen the Queen, he'd been forced to concede that Ann had exhibited all of the classic symptoms. That is, the coughing and vomiting of blood combined with an alarming loss in body weight. Unfortunately for Richard, these symptoms were also indicative of poisoning! Humiliatingly, Richard had eventually been forced to swear an oath upon holy relics that he was neither poisoning his wife nor had he any intention of marrying his niece. Francis had been dismayed that his once proud friend had been subjected to such an indignity! Francis knew that as the Duke of Gloucester Richard would never have allowed himself to be so humbled. Indeed, Francis found it quite ironic that as a King, Richard seemingly wielded far less power than he had done previously as a Duke! Adding to Francis's consternation, Richard, who seemed to care less and less for life, had appeared unmoved by this ignominy, although since his humiliation he'd spent much of his time alone. For reasons that should have been obvious to all, after Christmas Richard had left his wife's bed. Unfortunately, with gossip and conjecture being what they were, in leaving his wife's side Richard had added even more fuel to the fire. Rather than be quashed, these stories had continued to circulate and presently many in both England and abroad still believed that Richard intended to kill his wife and marry his niece.

On numerous occasions Francis had attempted to shake his friend from this depression, but Richard, who was in Francis's opinion a shadow of the man that he'd once been, would always merely shrug his shoulders and reply that the 'responsibility of Kingship' had worn him down and he no longer had either the strength nor the will to fight on.

Try as he might Francis could not convince his friend that he was neither responsible for his nephews' murders or for the state of the Kingdom and, as such, he shouldn't expect to incur the wrath of either God or the people - he should fight back. That said, at times even Francis found it hard to believe why, since Buckingham had ordered the princes' murders, they'd all been subjected to such bad luck. As he cast his mind back to Richard's route to the throne, Francis felt that they must be being punished for something.

Eventually, and reluctantly, for the sake of his own sanity, Francis had given up trying to reason with Richard and had retired from court to Minster Lovel. Francis had prayed that time alone might restore Richard's fortunes and, as a consequence, his faith.

Now as he reached Nottingham Castle Francis could only imagine how his friend was feeling and how he would react in the event that the Queen did in fact die. In spite of everything, Francis knew that his friend cherished his wife. Francis sighed, yes Richard had left Ann's bed but only because his insomnia and, when he was finally able to sleep, his recurring nightmares were interfering with her rest. Sleep that her physicians said was vital for her continued well being.

Nottingham Castle, perched upon a great hill, overlooked the River Trent which was still seen by many as being the divide between the north and south of England. The fortress dominated both the surrounding countryside and the growing city of Nottingham, with its famous markets. In happier times Nottingham Castle had been Richard's pride and joy and was amongst his favourite residences. The fortress, that had originally been established by marauding Danes who'd chosen the location to over winter, was well sited and was, in Francis's opinion, now quite a feat of modern engineering. The cliffs on the south side of the fortress and the curtains of newly built outer walls to the north had made the Castle virtually impregnable.

In recent months Richard had spent much of his time at Nottingham, preferring its central location, which Ratcliffe had pointed out was perfect when it came to launching a counter attack, if and when news of Henry Tudor's invasion finally came.

Upon his arrival at the Castle Francis eventually found his friend within the royal apartments that were situated within the keep which was in the very heart of the Castle grounds. Francis was saddened to find his friend in such a state that Richard hardly even acknowledged Francis's presence. As Francis strode into the room Richard remained quite still, slumped in a chair, his eyes red and swollen and his complexion both pale and sickly. Francis wondered if the cause of his friends malady was either grief or a lack of sleep, after some moments of silence he finally determined that its cause was probably a combination of the two!

Richard Ratcliffe, who'd been unswerving in his loyalty to Richard and had remained at his side throughout these trying times, was with the King. It was he alone who, as if to make up for Richard's melancholy, enthusiastically greeted Francis. Clapping Francis on the back with a hand that was as large as a frying pan, the Yorkshireman, who was clearly excited to see Francis back again with them, gathered him up one of those great bear hugs for which he was famous. In return, winded and gazing in Richard's direction, Francis could only offer a weak smile. Francis had always liked Ratclife, for this blunt Yorkshireman could always be trusted to speak his mind and with him, 'you always got what you saw.' However, therein lay yet another problem for Richard. As the King's sole counsel during these past months, Ratcliffe had advised some extremely rash responses and ill thought out solutions to a variety of issues that had required a great deal more in the way of sensitivity and guile. Ill considered knee jerk reactions that had done nothing to endear Richard to his subjects at a time when he'd been desperate for public support. It had been Ratcliffe who amongst other things had recommended that Richard agree to swear an oath to his people promising not to harm Elizabeth Woodville and his nieces should they come out of sanctuary. It was Ratcliffe who'd convinced Richard that he must order all members of the aristocracy to kneel before his son and swear an oath of fealty to the Prince. These actions, together with Richard's public humiliation, had done nothing to ingratiate the King with England's deeply suspicious and resentful population. In Francis's opinion, in following Ratcliffe's advice Richard had merely undermined further his increasingly precarious position.

Sadly, in spite of everything that Richard had done for his country, no-one had shown any sympathy for his predicament. Many people in both England and on the continent pointed out that Richard was merely reaping his just desserts for his past crimes, namely the murders of Clarence, Edward of Lancaster, the saintly King Henry and King Edward's sons, which they said were all now coming back to haunt him. Unfortunately, as time went by and one disaster followed another, it was becoming increasingly difficult to refute these claims. Francis had tried to, time after time arguing that one made there own luck and that the recent reversals in their fortunes had resulted not from bad luck or from any kind of divine retribution, but from both Richard's depression and his resultant loss of confidence. Indeed, before he'd finally left the court Francis had worked hard to try and maintain some semblance of order. He alone had brought pressure to bear on the Duke of Brittany who, at that time, had harbored Henry Tudor. It'd been Francis's strategy of threatening to isolate Brittany that had culminated in the near arrest of Tudor. Unfortunately however, the scheme had ultimately backfired on them when Tudor, warned of his imminent arrest, had fled to France where he'd sought and received the support of the child King of France, Charles VIII. And sadly, the French had good reason to hate Richard who, during Edward's invasion of France in 1475, had been the only person of note who'd denounced Edward's treaty with the French King. At Tours, the French parliament had recently publicly denounced Richard as both as a tyrant and murderer and it'd been reported that King Charles, who wanted to stir up as much trouble as possible for Richard, had offered Tudor significant military and financial aid for his proposed invasion of England.

In an effort to distract his friend from his troubles and to instill in him a renewed sense of purpose, Francis had brokered a resumption of the war with Scotland. Unfortunately, the campaign had been all but abandoned in the wake of the Prince of Wales death and the action had been limited to the reinforcement of the English garrison at Dunbar Castle. With his only legitimate child dead and his sickly Queen unlikely to produce another heir, Richard had all to soon succumbed once again into a deep depression. Reluctantly, yet for the sake of his own sanity, Francis had been forced to leave his friend. All that'd been left to Francis was to assure Richard that should he require his help in the future, then all he had to do was call.

Silent and expressionless Richard hardly acknowledged Francis who knelt before his friend and gently kissed his hand. Unfortunately it soon became clear to Francis that Ann was dead and that it'd been Ratcliffe and not Richard who'd summoned him to the King's side. Ratcliffe said that he'd hoped that as Richard's 'oldest and dearest friend,' Francis would somehow be able to bring the King back to his senses. In whispers, not that Richard seemed remotely interested in anything that they had to say, Francis assured Ratcliffe that he would do everything in his power to restore Richard but, given the circumstances, even he seriously doubted that his presence would make any difference to Richard's depression.

Returning to Richard, Francis once again took hold of his friend's hands as he offered his heart felt condolences for the Queen's death, adding that 'Ann' had been as a 'sister' to him.

In an effort to release Richard from his personal despair, Francis spoke of happier times. Of their various victories, the hunting trips and of their childhood together at Middleham. Times when they'd not been burdened with, 'all of the worries of the world.' Eventually, Francis felt that he'd seen the faintest flicker of a smile pass over Richard's lips. Encouraged, and sensing a breakthrough, Francis continued, 'Richard, all I ask is that you consider how your father and all of those others who've gone before us, would feel if they saw you now. Yes, you're on your own, but surely that brings its own responsibility, for now you're the last of the Plantagenets?' Richard appeared unmoved as, sighing, Francis added, 'Your families fought for many years to retain and then to recover the Crown. What would they say if they could see how you seem willing to give it all up without even a struggle.' Tutting, Francis added scornfully, 'And to give it up to whom? A Lancastrian, an upstart, a nothing, who comes from an obscure branch of that family, which in itself was borne of a bastard!' Pulling his hand away from Francis, Richard glowered at Francis. Undeterred, Francis continued, 'Too many of the old families are gone, the Mowbrays, the Bohuns, the Mortimers, the Beauchamps, where are they now? They're consigned to history where one day they'll all be forgotten. But your family, the Plantagenets, have outlived them all. Richard, you stand idly by whilst your dynasty dies out. I ask you, if Tudor comes to power, what will become of this nation of ours.' It was fair to say that Francis had always been extremely passionate about the issues that were facing the old order in the latter years of the fifteenth century. Some argued that what they were experiencing was the inevitable death of feudalism. Francis on the other hand believed that after the recent Civil Wars, the war with France and the various pestilence's that they'd all suffered, the aristocracy just needed a period of time to recover and then it could re-impose its will once again on the middle classes.

For the third time, Francis took hold of Richard by the hands as he added, 'Tudor can only ever hope to win your crown with the help of mercenaries who've been paid for by the French and the middle classes. If he succeeds he'll be duty bound to pay them back. Richard, do you want your legacy to be a society that is governed not by chivalry and honour but by the money that men have in their pockets? We all know that Tudor has few if any supporters from amongst the aristocracy. In his efforts to gain allies within England Tudor will be forced to grant concessions to the gentry and those of the lower classes. If he succeeds to your throne and he's forced to repay these people who don't need any more in the way of riches, all that he'll be able to offer them is political power and we'll end up with a country that's ruled not by the King but by a nominal monarch who governs through and with the assent of a Parliament of commoners!' As he said this Francis himself was almost crying, for it seemed as if he was prophesying the demise of the feudal order the only society that they knew. Surprisingly neither Richard nor Ratcliffe objected to Francis's outburst and both remained silent and allowed Francis to continue. Francis needed no further encouragement for by that time he was on quite a roll. As Francis concluded his argument even Ratclife, who on his own admission was quite slow when it came to politics, understood where he was leading them. Francis merely said that which they were were all obviously thinking. 'A King who's reliant on his people will be governed by them. He won't rule through the divine right of Kings, but through some form of concensus. Trust me Richard, if Tudor prevails the result will be the destruction of society as we know it and with it all that's left of the old order.'

With that Francis left his friends to consider his arguments, promising that,

'We'll talk again tomorrow.'

Sadly, once he'd left both Richard and Ratcliffe, Francis visited his Queen for the very last time. Pale and silent, Ann, whom Francis remembered as being so full of life, lay dead upon her bed. Upon entering the Queen's bedchamber Francis slowly knelt by Ann's side and gently kissed her cold forehead. Francis wept as once again that evening he remembered their childhood at Middleham, in altogether happier times. Occasions when Francis's kisses had been long and lingering and had been enthusiastically reciprocated by Ann. Then, as always the naive one, Francis had even fancied that Ann may one day have been his wife! But no, Ann, who'd been the daughter of 'Warwick the Kingmaker', had always been destined for far greater things. She was of too high a birth and, in truth, it had not taken Francis long to realise that she was not for the likes of him. It'd been Ann's destiny to be a Queen. And ultimately she'd become Richard's Queen. But what had it brought her? She'd spent a lifetime seeing those whom she loved being taken from her one after the other, firstly her father, then her first husband and her elder sister and last of all her one and only child. And finally, she herself had died a slow and lingering death whilst she'd witnessed all that Richard had fought for slowly begin to crumble away. Sobbing, Francis was truly heartbroken to see Ann lying dead at such a tender age, yet another victim of the burden of being born into the ruling class.

Surprisingly, on the following morning both Richard's appearance and his mood were greatly changed. For the first time in months it was clear to Francis that the King had been meticulous in his grooming, his hair was freshly cut and washed and his face clean shaven. Richard enlivened the air with the aroma of both lavender and rose water. Francis smiled as he noticed that the King's new clothes, clean and pressed, were of the height of fashion and were cut from the finest silk and velvet. Unusually, for one who'd always been quite modest, Richard wore a diadem of gold and jewels and Francis smiled again, for it seemed as if his friend intended to remind them all that he was still very much their King.

As Richard had entered the solar, Francis, not quite believing what he was seeing, turned away blinking. When Francis looked back again he knew that he wasn't dreaming, for Richard was still standing in the doorway smiling. Neither Francis nor Ratcliffe could believe that such a change could come about a person in such a short space of time, both could only stand and stare at their friend. Catesby, who'd arrived at Nottingham in the early hours of that morning, glanced suspiciously over towards Francis and Ratcliffe. Francis smiled in return, pleased that he'd obviously misled Catesby when, that morning, he'd described Richard as both inconsolable and defeatist.

Richard, who was clearly enjoying the effect that the change in him was having upon his friends, laughed as he succinctly answered all of their queries, 'Today my friends is the first day of the rest of our lives.' Turning to Francis Richard added, 'Francis, yesterday you spoke sense to me. It does me no good to worry about our present predicament. This won't bring back either my wife or my son. And anyway the burden that I carry is far greater than I as a man shall ever be. The crown that I wear was bequeathed to me by my forbears, many of whom, including my own dear father, paid for it with their lives. How could I have been so selfish, to think that I'd be able to wallow in my own self pity, whilst their legacy to me is lost forever? If I no longer have the will to fight for myself then I must do it for my family.' Smiling confidently Richard added, 'I will endeavor to maintain and preserve the house of York and I promise that I will do this to my dying breath.'

All clapped and Richard smiled once again as his friends surrounded him and welcomed him back.

Their King continued, 'Once we've buried my wife we must all ready ourselves. With his new French allies Tudor must be assembling an invasion fleet and I'm sure that he'll come for us this summer. I intend to be ready for both Tudor and for all of those who would dare to join him, for I'm determined to end this matter once and for all.' Gob smacked, no-one was able to reply as laughing Richard continued, 'My friends, Henry Tudor will rue the day that he ever had the audacity to challenge for my Crown.'

All were delighted in Richard's renewed outlook. However, as his friend turned to gaze out of the solar's window Francis sighed, he'd known Richard for a long time and it seemed to him that there was still a faint air of melancholy about his friend. Always the realist, Francis began to wonder if Richard was actually as hopeful about their future as he would have them all believe.

Chapter 30
August 1485 Nottingham.

Once again, in response to a summons that was accompanied by bad news, Francis, in all haste, 'and with as many men as possible' had joined the King's army at Nottingham. As expected, Henry Tudor's invasion force had finally made landfall and Richard was in the process of organising his response to this significant challenge to his Crown.

For the entirety of that summer Francis had been away from court, stationed at Plymouth on the south coast and entrusted with organising the coastal defences, should Tudor's fleet make landfall there. Unfortunately, it now appeared as if Francis had done his job too well, for Tudor had chosen to avoid making a landing in England and, in spite of the challenges associated with a longer crossing made in treacherous seas, he'd chosen to make for south Wales, where he'd ultimately come ashore, unscathed, at Milford Haven on the Pembrokeshire coast. Tudor had been born in Pembroke Castle and as a Welshman, who's uncle Jasper was the attainted Earl of that region, he'd clearly expected to secure more in the way of support and reinforcements than he would have received had he made for the southern shires of England. And word had it that he was in desperate need of reinforcements, for Richard's agents in Wales had described Tudor's army as 'woefully small'. Unfortunately, they'd also reported that Tudor's expedition, as they'd all earlier feared, had been joined by the Earl of Oxford. Oxford, who'd fought for the Lancastrians at Barnet, in addition to being a brave and experienced commander who enjoyed a great deal of support in his ancestral homelands in Essex, had been all too aware of those problems that Queen Margaret and her son Edward of Lancaster had experienced when they'd landed on the south coast in the lead up to the Battle of Tewkesbury. At Exeter, despite earlier assurances to the contrary, Margaret's army had failed to recruit sufficient additional troops from within the southern counties and, outnumbered, she had been forced to try and outrun the Yorkist army of King Edward, making for the relative safety of Wales and Jasper Tudor, rather than for London as they'd intended. In directing his small fleet towards south Wales, it was clear to Francis that Tudor, listening to Oxford's advice, had learnt from Margaret's earlier mistake.

Francis had been doubly disappointed to receive news of the landing in south Wales. Firstly, he would be forced once again to don his armour and face yet another challenge to Richard's authority, albeit they had predicted this invasion for the past two years. And secondly, and perhaps more importantly, it now appeared that they'd be unable to deal with the invasion in its infancy as they'd planned, to drive Tudor and his French allies back into the sea, before they were able to recruit any reinforcements. By landing in Wales, where for the time being at least Richard couldn't get at him, Tudor and Oxford had cleverly bought themselves precious time in which to enlist additional troops to bolster their small invasion force. From the intelligence that they'd received from Richard's spies at the French court, Richard had gambled on the invasion taking place in late July, with a landing being made somewhere along the south coast of England, that location being the closest point to the fleets proposed departure point, the French port of Harfleur. As a result, Francis had spent all of that summer preparing for such an eventuality. By mid July he'd been able to report to the King that he was in a position to engage Tudor within days of his landing, wherever and whenever the Lancastrians came ashore anywhere along the south coast of England, be it as far as Dover in the east or Falmouth in the west. Francis, having recruited a large number of highly experienced men-at-arms, had also confidently predicted that his men would be more than a match for the few mercenaries and the small number of exiled nobles that comprised Tudor's expeditionary force.

It was fair to say that Francis had been extremely surprised to hear that Tudor had chosen to risk the longer and more hazardous crossing to south Wales, a route which would have brought him around the perilous coast of Cornwall and into the waters of the Irish sea off Milford Haven, a port which was situated on the southern tip of Cardigan bay. Grudgingly, Francis had to admit that it appeared to him as if Tudor's gamble had paid off. For having landed safely in south Wales, Tudor was now ideally placed to attract a significant number of new recruits. Especially from amongst the fiercely independent Welsh, who were said to have seen Tudor as some kind of modern day Owen Glendower! Sadly, during his crossing Tudor had encountered unusually calm conditions and his small squadron of ships had completed their voyage without either incident or injury, ultimately landing safely and unopposed at the port of Milford Haven. That said, Richard had not been entirely negligent in his preparations, for although they'd planned for a landing somewhere along the south coast of England, Richard had made a number of arrangements in the unlikely event that the Lancastrians did make for Wales. Unfortunately, to date Richard's representatives in south Wales, Sir Walter Herbert and Rhys ap Thomas, who'd both been ordered to resist any landing by Tudor and his men in south Wales, had failed to engage the invaders. Herbert had reported that after two of his captains, together with a large number of his troops had defected to the Lancastrians, he'd felt that he had insufficient men to launch a successful attack against the beachhead that Tudor had established around Milford Haven. Herbert had argued that as he hadn't wanted to bolster the enemies confidence or to encourage any further desertions by giving them, 'any easy victories', he'd chosen instead to pull his troops back towards the English border.

Of more concern to them was the news that Rhys Ap Thomas, who was perhaps the greatest landowner in all of south Wales, had allegedly been involved in secret negotiations with the Lancastrians. This after Tudor was said to have promised him the lieutenancy of Wales, should his forces be allowed to proceed through Ap Thomas's lands unmolested. In an attempt to ensure the Welshman's loyalty, Richard had ordered the arrest of his son. Unfortunately, the move had backfired on them when the Ap Thomas family, having been tipped off by a Lancastrian sympathiser, had all gone into hiding.

Sadly, as a result of both Herbert's inaction and Ap Thomas's treachery, there was now no-one in Wales either willing or able to resist Tudor, whose men had enjoyed both a leisurely and an uneventful march, as they'd advanced up the coast of Wales towards Aberystwyth and then, turning inland, had made for the English border at Shrewsbury, via both Machynlleth and Welshpool. As a result, many men who'd previously prevaricated had, by that point in time, found the courage to join Tudor. By the time the Lancastrian army had crossed the Severn at Welshpool and had entered into England, what had originally been quite a small army had all but doubled in size. Worse still, the town of Shrewsbury, which had earlier professed its loyalty to Richard, had opened its gates to the Lancastrians without even a struggle! At Shrewsbury, Tudor had been joined by a large number of prominent Englishmen together with their retinues. One of whom, Sir Gilbert Talbot, uncle to the Earl of Shrewsbury, whose family had traditionally supported the house of Lancaster, had brought with him some five hundred troops!

Within weeks of its landing Tudor's army had, therefore, grown alarmingly and had numbered not in the hundreds as they had done when they'd landed at Milford Haven, but in the thousands, to such an extent that in Francis's opinion Tudor now posed a serious threat to Richard's government. Indeed, at that point in time all that had stood between Tudor and the King at Nottingham were the Stanley brothers, who at that time were resident within their Cheshire and Shropshire estates. Regrettably, Richard had good reason to distrust both Thomas Lord Stanley and his brother William and Francis seriously doubted that the brothers, in spite of the large number of men that they had at their disposal, could be relied upon to engage Tudor on their behalf. Henry Tudor's mother Margaret Beaufort, who was proven to have been involved in Buckingham's rebellion of 1483 and had been under house arrest ever since, was still married to Lord Stanley. Moreover, Francis knew that Lord Stanley had always disliked Richard, indeed the two men had even come to blows on a number of occasions throughout both Richard and Edward's reign. It was said that Stanley had never forgotten how he'd been both 'insulted' and 'assaulted' by Richard's men, when he'd attempted to intervene in the arrest of Lord Hastings at the Tower. Moreover, since Richard had ascended to the throne Stanley had lost many of his northern offices, benefices which Richard had stripped from Stanley and given to his own supporters. Equally, Richard had never forgiven Stanley for his treachery when he'd supported Warwick and Clarence's rebellion of 1470. And Francis, who'd been present during the Scottish campaign of 1482, had witnessed first hand their mutual dislike and distrust of each other. No-one had therefore been the least bit surprised when, having landed in Wales, Tudor had made not for London, but for Cheshire and his father-in-law.

As the prospects for an invasion that year had become increasingly more likely, ominously, Lord Stanley, without good reason, had absented himself from Richard's court. Suspicious, Richard had sent Stanley's son George Lord Strange to the Tower. The youth was, Richard said, a 'hostage to ensure both his father's loyalty and the old man's early return to London.' In spite of his son's incarceration, Stanley had repeatedly ignored the King's summons. By August, Lord Stanley, who was fast running out of excuses, had maintained that he was unable to join them at Nottingham as he was suffering from the sweating sickness. Richard was no fool and in spite of the fact that the disease was prevalent throughout the northern shires that summer, he refused to believe that the old man was ill. It appeared as if Stanley's treachery had finally been confirmed when his son was captured whilst trying to escape from the Tower. Interrogated, Lord Strange maintained that it'd been his uncle Sir William Stanley and not his father who'd been involved in secret negotiations with Tudor. Apparently, Sir William intended to support Tudor's claim to the throne in return for a title, which had been denied him by Richard. What had complicated matters further was the fact that despite 'pressure' to do so, Lord Strange had resolutely refused to implicate his father in the plot and although they'd all guessed that the wily old man was involved, presently nothing could be proven against him. Unfortunately, on the advice of Ratcliffe, Richard had immediately declared Sir William to be a traitor. In Francis's opinion this was unfortunate, as he believed that it'd only serve to drive the Stanleys deeper into the arms of the Lancastrians. At least to date Richard hadn't made a similar announcement in respect of Lord Stanley.

Upon Francis's arrival in Nottingham it was clear to him that Richard still wasn't taking the matter at all seriously! Laughing, Richard pointed out that the, 'Old snake Stanley', couldn't even be trusted to side with his own family if it weren't in his interests to do so! On Francis's advice, Richard sent yet another summons to Lord Stanley suggesting that it may be in the interests of his son's, 'continued good health,' that he either engage Tudor 'forthwith' or alternatively join them in Nottingham.

Worryingly, Richard's 'call to arms', which had been sent out as soon as they'd received news of Tudor's landfall had, for the first time ever, included threats of attainder and forfeiture for any who failed to join his army. Richard had argued that the threat had been necessary as he no longer felt that he could rely on the majority of his citizens' loyalty. Unfortunately, Francis knew from bitter experience that those who had to be threatened and coerced into joining them, could never be relied upon on the battlefield.

As it turned out, be it through either fear or loyalty to their King, many had joined them at Nottingham in answer to Richard's commissions of Array. Francis, who since his arrival at Nottingham had been responsible for many of these summonses, now guessed that their army numbered somewhere in the region of ten thousand men! He believed that, despite the series of recent setbacks, they were still in an extremely favourable position to deal with the threat posed by Tudor, whose army was said to number only five thousand.

It was clear to Francis that Richard was furious that Tudor's army had been allowed to advance such a distance unmolested. In fact it was fair to say that in all of the years that he'd known him Francis had never seen his friend so angry. 'At least' Richard said , when he'd calmed down a little, 'the present crisis' would achieve that which Buckingham's rebellion hadn't, in that it was bound to reveal all of those people who thought to oppose him. Richard promised them all that this time however, the 'traitors' need not expect any 'leniency' from him.

Once Tudor had entered into England, it was unclear what his next move would be. Ratcliffe said that the Lancastrians were bound to march upon the capital, just as many such rebellious armies had done so in the past. Both Richard and Francis disagreed with him, for they reasoned that once in England, Tudor couldn't have expected to receive much more in the way of support. They felt that, as a result, Tudor would attempt to bring them to battle before Richard was able to reinforce his army with his Yorkshiremen who, at that point in time, were in the process of mobilising on his behalf. This procedure was turning out to be infuriatingly slow due to the fact that it was still harvest time and the men were reticent to leave their fields. Less bold than his companions, Francis recommended a staged withdrawal from Nottingham to Middleham, this giving them sufficient time to assemble an army which consisted of those whom they could trust implicitly. Indeed, due to the extraordinary speed in which the crisis had developed, other than those troops who'd arrived from the midlands and the east, only those from further afield who'd had access to horses had been able to join them at Nottingham! In Francis's opinion they now faced quite a dilemma. Although larger than that of Tudor's army, one couldn't with certainty guarantee the loyalty of their troops. Yet any retreat northwards, whether staged or otherwise, was bound to be interpreted as a sign of weakness. Richard pointed out that such a maneuver, in addition to undermining the morale of their troops, would also give his subjects even more reason to defect to Tudor. Indeed, Richard said that he didn't have to remind them just how quickly an army could desert its leaders, once their confidence in absolute victory was doubted. Thus, on the 17th August, with those troops that they had at their disposal, Richard's army made the short march from Nottingham to Leicester, where they hoped to meet with the both the Duke of Norfolk and his son and with any Yorkshiremen who'd been able to mobilise on their behalf in time for the battle. From Leicester, Richard hoped to intercept Tudor's army somewhere to the west of Leicester, as it was reported that the Lancastrians were marching southwards down Watling Street, in the direction of the Staffordshire town of Tamworth.

On what was a bright summer's morning, those Lords who'd remained loyal to the King proudly unfurled their banners and to the sound of a great fanfare Richard's army marched out of Nottingham Castle and across the bridge that took them over the River Trent and out of the City. Once clear of Nottingham, their army soon joined the Fosse Way, the Old Roman Road that was to take them all of the way to Leicester.

At some point, presumably, they hoped to be joined by both the Earl of Northumberland and the Stanleys. Francis smiled wryly, for he believed that none of these men could they be counted on in a fight! What were they to make of these two nobles! Northumberland the arrogant coward who, in Francis's opinion, should never be allowed to join their army, as in all probability he'd be more of a hindrance than a help. And the duplicitous Stanleys. There was still no news of Lord Stanley and Francis could only wonder where the old man was. He seriously doubted that Stanley was incapacitated by the sweating sickness and could only hope that he hadn't already joined Tudor. Francis sighed, militarily the Stanleys themselves may have been inept, but their Cheshiremen were renowned for their fortitude. Francis shuddered, in the event of the Stanley brothers' defection to the Lancastrians, their men would be a sad loss to Richard's army. Sighing, Francis knew that only time would tell if the Stanleys and their men were either going to join them at Leicester, or if they would choose instead to side with Lord Stanley's son-in-law, Tudor.

At Leicester, the King, together with his closest friends, were billeted at the White Boar Inn. As a surprise for his friend, Francis had even arranged for Richard's bed to be brought up from Nottingham. Hopefully, the King, who nowadays did not sleep at all well, would at least be rested before the battle took place. It was at the White Boar, whilst they'd all been enjoying their evening meal, that Richard's agents brought them the news that they'd all been fearing. Tudor had indeed met with the Stanleys at Atherstone. The only saving grace had been that, true to form, the brothers had still prevaricated and refused to openly commit their troops to Tudor. No doubt in an effort to lighten the mood, Ratcliffe had laughed as Richard's spies had described how Tudor had even apparently gone on his knees before his father-in-law, as he'd implored the Stanleys to join him, so that he may be 'better placed' to array his smaller army against that of Richard. In reply, Sir William had apparently told Tudor to concern himself with 'organising his own men, as he would his own!' Smiling, Richard pointed out that Tudor now had the 'honour' of joining a long list of people who all had cause to 'complain about the Stanley's duplicity.' A list which, he added scornfully, included both Lancastrians and Yorkists in equal numbers! 'We should at least be grateful' Richard said, 'That Tudor has much more need of the Stanleys than we.' Indeed, Richard even went so far as to say that he no longer cared if the Stanleys were going to join him, just so long as they remained uncommitted. Francis, on the other hand, pointed out that before they were able to give battle, 'surely' they'd be foolish not to get some form of commitment from the Stanleys. Their agents had reported that the brothers commanded a size able army of at least three thousand men-at-arms and archers, many of whom were mounted. Francis asked Richard how, without any idea as to how the Stanleys would act, they'd be able to plan effectively for the battle. Smiling again, Richard pointed out that they still had Stanley's son, Lord Strange, in custody. Richard said that he'd send word to Lord Stanley that he, 'Wouldn't hesitate to dispatch Strange, should the Stanleys dare to join Tudor.' Richard also added that if things went their way on the day of the battle, and judging by the strength of their numbers there was no reason to suggest that they wouldn't, regardless of whatever promises they may or may not have made to Tudor, the 'faithless' Stanleys could always be trusted, 'Not to join a losing side.'

On the following morning, the 21st August 1485, Richard, at the head of an army that numbered in the region of some twelve thousand men, marched westwards out of the City of Leicester in the direction of Tamworth. A great number of Richard's subjects lined the city's streets, all eager to get a glimpse of the King at the head of his army, as it slowly negotiated Leicester's cramped and narrow streets. Crossing over the River Soar, and finally free from the constraints of the City, Richard's army picked up speed as it headed out into the gently rolling countryside of rural Leicestershire. Confident of victory, many of their men sang lustily as they marched.

As always, Richard relied heavily on intelligence and during the preceding days his scouts had been extremely busy as they'd reconnoitered the land that lay between Richard's army at Leicester and that of Tudor's at Atherstone. It had been reported to Richard that the land consisted mainly of flat open farmland and heath land with nothing much in the way of high ground of any significance. In fact, the only rising of any note was a prominence known locally as Ambion Hill, which was situated just a few miles west of the village of Sutton Cheney, some fifteen miles or so to the west of Leicester.

At that time, Tudor's forces were said to have still been in the vicinity of the town of Atherstone, which was situated astride Watling Street, the Roman Road that connected London with Shrewsbury. In their present location, the Lancastrian army was considerably closer to Ambion Hill than Richard was at Leicester. Although not key to the battle's outcome, Richard felt that the army, which was able to gain control of Ambion Hill would have a distinct advantage. In an effort, therefore, to secure this high ground, Richard sent forward a contingent of armed horsemen under the command of Sir Robert Brackenbury. These experienced soldiers, who were all men of the garrison of the Tower of London were under strict orders to take the hill, 'at all costs', before the Lancastrians themselves recognised its importance and made their own efforts to secure it.

In contrast to Brackenbury and his cavalry, the bulk of the Yorkist army was able to travel towards Ambion Hill at a much more sedentary pace. That said, despite the lack of urgency, their progress was no leisurely affair and in the heat of a summers day it reminded Francis much of that march that had taken them to Tewkesbury and to victory some fourteen years earlier. 'On that occasion we were victorious just as we will be tomorrow,' Francis predicted during one of the rare and all too short breaks which were taken ostensibly to water their horses. Grimly, Richard had reminded Francis that at Tewksbury it was they who'd been outnumbered without the benefit of the high ground, the self same position in which they hoped to place Tudor on the following day! Francis, unable to recover from his gaffe, chose to ignore Richard's observation. Ratcliffe, on the other hand, laughed at Richard for his superstition, stroking his battle axe he said that it was through such weapons and a determination to win that they would prevail and nothing else. Catesby, who was normally much more careful with his words, added without thinking, 'It helps if one has God on his side.' Francis, who knew more than anyone else just how Richard had suffered since his nephews' deaths, immediately turned towards Richard, whose head was bowed as if in prayer. Both Catesby and Ratcliffe on the other hand seemed perplexed by Richard's silence. Thankfully, after a few moments, sighing Richard replied, 'God's will be done.' Richard's actions had done nothing to instill any confidence in his circle of friends, until that is, Ratcliffe, shrugging his shoulders and stroking his axe again, said, 'And his vengeance will be mine.'

They all laughed and agreed that they were delighted that Ratcliffe had remained loyal and would be with them and not against them on the following day!

It was early evening by the time that the main body of the Yorkist army reached the eastern slopes of Ambion Hill. Thankfully, despite the fact that Tudor's men had advanced towards the hill, Brackenbury had been successful in securing both the summit and its environs for the Yorkists. As they approached the village of Sutton Cheney the Yorkist commanders cantered off, in advance of the army, to join Brackenbury upon the hill. During what remained of the daylight hours, Richard hoped to survey the ground over which they were to fight on the following day, if, as expected, Tudor brought his own troops forward and attacked at first light. To its western side, Ambion Hill was far steeper than Francis had expected it to be. From the small plateau on its summit they could clearly see the Lancastrian camp that lay on the outskirts of a village, which Brackenbury identified to them as Stoke Golding. Indeed, Tudor's army was alarmingly close to those positions that their own army was going to adopt in and around the village of Sutton Cheney. Brackenbury clearly appreciated their concerns as, smiling reassuringly, he said, 'They've been there for some hours and save for a very minor skirmish with some of Oxford's cavalry we've had no contact with them.'

In spite of Oxford's Lancastrian sympathies, Francis had a great deal of respect for him, both militarily and as a man. Even if one disagreed with Oxford's allegiances, one couldn't criticise him for his faithfulness and loyalty to the House of Lancaster, which had continued throughout the Civil Wars and beyond. Francis smiled, for it was this loyalty which had kept Oxford alive when he'd finally been captured by the Yorkists in 1473. The Yorkist brothers had always admired such traits and, as such, they'd spared Oxford the fate that had befallen many of his kind. It'd been no surprise to Francis however when he'd heard that Oxford, having escaped from Hammes castle, had wasted no time in joining Tudor's growing band of dissidents at the French court.

Oxford must, Francis felt, have recognised the strategic importance of Ambion Hill. He was, therefore, extremely surprised to find that the Lancastrian's efforts to secure the hill had been limited to a minor skirmish involving only a few of Oxford's retainers. Francis smiled, this was great news, for in Francis's opinion it was evidence of the fact that there were those amongst the Lancastrian hierarchy who, having not shared Oxford's interpretation of the situation, had clearly overruled him. Consequently, the Lancastrians had failed to make any concerted effort to seize the high ground from Brackenbury's small force of horsemen and, as a result, they'd placed their army at a distinct disadvantage.

Laughing, Richard clapped Brackenbury on the back as he exclaimed, 'It's first blood to us I see,' as he pointed to a pile of corpses all of whom bore the blue boar device of the Earl of Oxford. Studying the bodies Francis noted with some relief that none included that of his cousin Thomas, whom he'd heard was still with Oxford and was even reputed to have been promoted to the head of his household.

Francis's spirits were raised even further as he began to survey their surroundings. As foretold, Ambion Hill was the only high ground of any note in the locality. As such, Francis judged that any army arrayed upon its summit would have a clear advantage over their adversaries, who would be forced to form up in the shallow valley below it. The woodland and dense vegetation that lay all along the eastern reaches of the hill meant that a defending army's left flank would be protected from any flanking attack which came from that direction. Any attempt to take the hill would, therefore, have to come from either the west or via the hill's steepest gradient to the north. Francis smiled, for in addition to his failing to secure Ambion Hill, when it came to choosing his camp Tudor had also shown both his ineptitude and his inexperience. From their present location, before they'd be able to engage Richard's army, the Lancastrians would have to march directly past the woodland on Ambion Hill and would then be forced to wheel their troops around to the right to face the Yorkists on the summit of the hill. Remembering both Towton and Tewkesbury, Francis felt that a body of archers and spear men, secreted in the woods, would find themselves in an excellent position from which to strike at Tudor's troops before they came into contact with the main body of Richard's army. These men could either harry or attack the enemy's exposed right flank whilst it was still in marching order. Smiling, Francis also clapped Brackenbury on the back as he congratulated him on a 'fine day's work.' In Francis's opinion, any army drawn up upon the summit of Ambion Hill would find itself in an almost unassailable position. What did worry Francis, however, was the fact that the hilltop itself was quite small and narrow. As a result it was clear to him that it wouldn't be possible to deploy all of the men in Norfolk's vanguard within their army's front ranks. Consequently, they would lose their advantage of numbers. Richard also shared Francis's misgivings, but he pointed out that the benefits of the higher ground, 'far outweighed' those problems posed by the 'limited space' upon the summit of Ambion Hill. Smiling, Richard winked at Francis as he added, 'And anyway it'll mean that all of those men within our front ranks with be made up of my most loyal and experienced troops.' Turning to both Norfolk and his son and indicating the northern slope of Ambion Hill, Richard smiled as he said, 'And who'd be able to withstand any attack made down that hill by my East Anglians.'

Francis too appreciated that Norfolk's men would be key to the battle's outcome. One could only guess what would become of their army if the East Anglian's failed. On a number of occasions Francis had seen how fear and hysteria could spread like wildfire throughout an army. Especially one which contained within it those who were less than wholehearted in their commitment. Francis knew that once the initial furor of battle had receded, men's basic instinct for self preservation took over and if pressed many, given half the chance, would turn and run. If Norfolk's charge failed to bring them a speedy victory Francis worried that the rest of their army may not have the stomach for a longer drawn out affair.

Once they'd taken time to study the field, Richard secured their positions by posting pickets all along the hill's summit. He then convened a council of war that was to be held in his tent. This meeting was to include only the most senior amongst the Yorkist commanders. Unusually, the individual battle captains were not invited. Richard said that this was because he was concerned that there were those in their army who may betray their plans to Tudor. Francis wasn't at all surprised by Richard's precautions, for alarmingly, since their arrival at Sutton Cheney desertions from their army were becoming increasingly widespread. To such an extent that Richard had even been forced to issue orders that any found deserting their posts would be summarily executed on the spot!

His mind wandering, Francis took time to examine all of his present companions in turn, this in an effort to gauge those whose loyalty Richard could count upon. Without question Ratcliffe, Brackenbury and even the un soldierly Catesby could be trusted upon to serve Richard to the end. Both John Howard Duke of Norfolk, and his son Thomas, Earl of Suffolk, had much to thank Richard for. Both men having been promoted from relative obscurity to high office in the short time that Richard had been on the throne. As such, in Francis's opinion both could be relied upon to repay this patronage and remain loyal. John De la Pole, the Earl of Lincoln, had been nominated as Richard's sole heir and without question his future therefore lay with the King. The commitment of Henry Percy, Earl of Northumberland, was however unclear. Northumberland, who'd not contributed anything to the discussion, although this in itself didn't surprise Francis when one considered his ineptitude when it came to matters militarily, remained skulking towards the rear of the tent. As Francis looked in his direction Northumberland glared back at him and then, as if in shame, averted his eyes. It was fair to say that Francis had been extremely surprised that Northumberland had bothered to join them at all. Since the debacle that had been the siege of Berwick, the Earl had remained largely on his estates in Northumberland and had rarely visited the court. Northumberland could never have honestly expected to have been given command of the royalist van, yet when that honour was given, as expected, to Norfolk, he'd had the audacity to object to the appointment! Chastened by Richard, and true to form, he'd then proceeded to behave as a spoilt youth, complaining that as a member of one of England's 'oldest families' he alone deserved the command. The wicked side of Francis's nature hoped that Richard would call his bluff, for it was obvious to him that Northumberland had neither the skill nor the inclination to accept such a commission. As he was wont to do, Northumberland was merely causing trouble. Ultimately, and unfortunately in Francis's opinion, Richard, who understood both the niceties and the etiquette of feudal society, ended up by compromising and giving Northumberland the command of the army's rearguard, giving him orders to, 'Come up and support our line as soon as you are requested to do so.' Richard clearly appreciated the concerns of the other Yorkist commanders who would, it seemed, have to rely on Northumberland to cover their backs and to reinforce them when required to do so, for he added with a grin, 'Hopefully you'll not be needed, as I'm hoping that Norfolk's vanguard on its own will be sufficient to scatter Tudor's army.' Francis could only hope that Richard would be proven right. Sadly in his opinion, if they were forced to rely on Northumberland, they would all be in serious trouble! All of those present, save that is for the Earl, clearly understood the King's quip and as he winked at them they all laughed. Northumberland on the other hand, despite his commission, continued to sulk and contributed nothing further to the debate.

As Francis had earlier predicted, Richard directed Brackenbury's cavalry, together with a body of archers, to take up positions within the woods on the eastern slopes of Ambion Hill. Their orders were to do everything in their power to disrupt the Lancastrian advance towards the hill and to prevent Tudor's army from drawing up good order so that they'd be even more vulnerable to Norfolk's attack when it came. Richard said that he'd place the few artillery pieces that Brackenbury had brought with him from the Tower, amongst Norfolk's vanguard. Together with the archers the artillery were to subject the Lancastrian army to a massive barrage as it wheeled around to face the Yorkists on the hill. If this action was unsuccessful in scattering the Lancastrians, Norfolk was to lead his infantry directly down the hill in a frontal attack.

It was agreed that Richard and the rest of his knights would remain on top of Ambion Hill towards their army's right flank. From that position they would be able to monitor the progress of the battle. Unusually, Richard asked that they all keep their horses close by, so that they would be able to react to events at a moments notice. As Catesby sighed heavily they all laughed, for it was common knowledge that he was no horseman. Thankfully, for the duration of the battle, Northumberland was to remain in the rear guard and was to monitor their left flank. Only to come forward in the unlikely event that both Norfolk's 'vanguard' and Richard's 'battle' failed to defeat the Lancastrians. Relieved, Francis knew that the woodland and dense vegetation on the southern slopes of the hill meant that any attack from that direction was highly unlikely.

That evening both Francis and Richard remained up until very late. Richard, who had difficulty sleeping at the best of times, said that he couldn't even consider retiring to his bed in his present state of mind. Francis was both surprised and anxious to see that, once alone, his friend was far less self- assured than he'd ever seen him before on the eve of a battle. Francis worried that if discovered, Richard's lack of self-confidence would spread amongst the ranks of those on whom they depended for victory. Eventually, and only after being pressed by Francis, Richard retired late, but he enjoyed only a fitful nights sleep. Francis, who remained at his friends side throughout the night, was woken often as Richard called out in his sleep. When Francis asked him what was wrong, Richard remained silent and, despite being pressed, refused to tell him what troubled him. Francis, keen that others didn't witness Richard's disquiet, roused himself and kept guard at the entrance to his friend's quarters to ensure that none, other than Richard's personal servants, were admitted.

Both camps rose early on the 22nd August 1485. Through the early morning mist Francis could clearly see that their adversaries were readying themselves for battle. Francis had never forgotten the sounds, which he'd always associated with those final preparations for battle. The clang of hammer on metal as minor adjustments were made to the armour of the Knights and men-at-arms. The screeching sounds that the grinding stones made as the soldiers sharpened their weapons. The great war-horses who snorted and neighed in objection to those great burdens that were placed upon them.

Pale, Richard looked awful as once armoured, he left his tent to address their troops before the battle. Worryingly, he appeared visibly shaken as, well drilled and in good order, the Lancastrian army marched out of its camp and slowly began to wheel to its left to face Richard's men who were drawing up in battle formation upon the summit of Ambion Hill. Francis sighed and wondered if his friend had somehow hoped that Tudor's men, outnumbered and outmaneuvered, may have melted away into the night, just as so many other armies had done in the past. Francis, however, had known that this would never have been possible for despite the fact that the odds were stacked against him, after years of planning and preparations, this was Tudors one and only chance of victory.

As each of the Lancastrian standards came into line, Richard grimly pronounced the names of those traitors who stood against him, 'Henry Tudor, Earl of Richmond, a man descended from a line of bastards who would have my crown. John De Vere, Earl of Oxford.' Richard sighed before he added, 'Whom my brother and I mistakenly saw fit to pardon. Jasper Tudor, Earl of Pembroke, the pretender's uncle who has spent his whole life fighting me.' Richard spat as he saw the banners of both Rhys Ap Thomas and Sir Walter Herbert, 'Men who owe me much and to whom I foolishly entrusted the security of Wales.' Richard sighed again as he added, 'And finally Sir Gilbert Talbot, one who was born into a family of great soldiers.'

To their north they could all clearly see Stanley's Chesiremen who were also drawn up in battle order, at a point that was equidistant between the Lancastrian and Yorkist armies. Ominously, the Stanleys were ideally placed to intervene on behalf of either army.

'And what of the Stanleys,' Richard said, 'Can I trust them to remain neutral,' sneering, he added, 'Or will they literally stab me in the back!'

Francis wasn't sure if Richard was talking directly to him or was just thinking out loud. He settled on the latter and chose not to reply. In truth, there was nothing that Francis could do or say to assuage Richard's fears. For even he had no idea who the Stanleys would chose to fight for, that's if, of course, they fought at all! That morning they'd discovered that the night before Tudor had again met with the Stanleys who this time, although they still hadn't committed themselves to joining him, had agreed to deploy on his left flank. Upon hearing this news, enraged, Richard had ordered that Lord Strange be brought forward and beheaded in front of all three armies. Both Francis and Catesby had advised caution as it was still unclear as to what action the Stanleys would take. They implored Richard not to do anything that would provoke the brothers. Thankfully, once they'd managed to calm him down, Richard had listened to them and for the time being at least, Strange remained towards the rear under close supervision, no doubt in constant expectation of death! As Stanley's men drew up in battle order, some distance from both the Yorkists and the Lancastrians, it was clear that even at this late hour they were still not willing to wholly commit to Tudor. Observing the Cheshiremen's preparations Francis guessed that the Stanleys commanded somewhere in the region of 3000 men, most of whom, resplendent in their red coats, were mounted. Earlier, Richard had sent a messenger to Lord Stanley whom he ordered, 'To join his King without delay or suffer for his son and heir to lose his head.'

The reply, when it came back, was typically uncommitted, but worryingly Stanley had impertinently retorted that Richard should do what he thought best, for he, 'Had other sons.'

Angered, Richard made it clear that in the event that the Stanleys deployed on behalf of the Lancastrians, Lord Strange must be, 'Executed without delay.'

As the Lancastrian army slowly advanced along the rough track that led from Stoke Golding in the direction of Ambion Hill, Richard clapped Francis on the back and, laughing, pointed out the inherent weaknesses in Henry's right flank. Smiling, Richard said that, as expected, due to the thickets and brambles on the hillside, Tudor had obviously felt that he'd be able to concentrate what troops he had towards his left. Richard didn't have to remind Francis that it was these men, within the Lancastrian's right flank, who would pass closest to Brackenbury's troops who lay in wait for them in the dense woodland of the southern slopes of the hill. Smiling, Francis was relieved to see that, with the battle imminent, Richard at last seemed much more like his old self.

Earlier that morning a number of the Yorkist commanders had made there peace with God during a short mass which had been held in their honour at the nearby church of St James at Sutton Cheney. Those who weren't of a religious disposition, which included Francis in their number, had remained in camp to ensure that their own army was made ready for battle. Ratcliffe, together with both Norfolk and his son, had gone throughout the ranks of their army giving the battle captains their final orders and encouraging those men who appeared either anxious or dispirited.

As the early morning mist dispersed and the sun, rising in a cloudless sky, had warmed their backs, Richard's army waited patiently for Tudor's men to complete the maneuver that would finally bring the two armies face to face. Francis smiled as he noted that the Lancastrians whose weapons and armour glinted in the bright sunlight, would be practically blinded by it, as they wheeled around to face both the Yorkists and the rising sun.

As Tudor's men passed Brackenbury's, revealing themselves Brackenbury's archers let loose with a volley of arrows. With the benefit of both surprise and their elevated position, the majority of these arrows easily found their mark and brought down many men from within the Lancastrians already weakened right flank. What had begun as an ordered advance faltered. When struck by yet another volley of arrows and confronted by Brackenbury's cavalry, who came at them from out of the trees at a canter, the entire Lancastrian army fell back in disorder in the direction of their camp at Stoke Golding.

The main bulk of the Yorkist army, which remained unscathed upon Ambion Hill, cheered but neither Richard nor Francis shared in their delight.

Yes, Tudor had suffered a number of casualties, but from their position atop Ambion Hill Norfolk's men were in no position to capitalise on Brackenbury's success. Any hope that they might have had that the Lancastrians would attempt an attack directly up the slopes of Ambion Hill were now gone. Indeed, Richard pointed out to them that if Tudor chose to retreat from the field, he had Watling Street to his rear, a road, which would take his army all the way to London!

Alarmed, and determined to bring Tudor to battle that day, Richard sent word to Norfolk to lead his vanguard, together with what ordnance he could muster, down from Ambion hill. Thus, as the Lancastrian army slowly regrouped astride the road that led to Stoke Golding, Norfolk's men, supported on their right flank by the main army which was under Richard's command, drew up before them in battle order. Not unsurprisingly, Northumberland seemed to be having difficulty in marshaling his own men forward. And as a consequence, and for the time being at least, the Yorkist rearguard remained stationary and inactive upon Ambion Hill. Worryingly, as the Yorkists had come down from Albion Hill, thereby relinquishing the advantage of the high ground, Stanley's army had tracked it until they too halted at a point to their right that was once again equidistant between the two armies. Now, despite their earlier reversal, defensively speaking, Tudor's men found themselves in an excellent position. A marsh protected their weakened right flank and the Stanleys' army to their left were ideally placed to intervene should Richard decide to attack from that direction. Consequently, Richard decided that it was better to remain as faithful as possible to their earlier plans. That is, an artillery barrage followed by a frontal assault by Norfolk's van. Richard smiled as he pointed out the various weaknesses in the Lancastian's army which, he said, had been brought about by the Stanleys continuing failure to deploy on Tudor's behalf. Indeed, the entirety of the Lancastrian left was held by Sir John Savage's men who, unsupported, were spread extremely thinly upon the wide open plain. Smiling, Richard told his companions to ready themselves, for, 'If neither our artillery nor Norfolk succeed we will strike,' laughing, he added, 'Even if Norfolk doesn't suceed in his own right, if he's able to tie down Oxford's men in the centre, we'll be able to mop up the rest of Tudor's army with a flanking attack.'

Fearing that as a result of their earlier successes Richard had become overconfident, Francis counseled caution. 'But what of the Stanleys,' he exclaimed, 'Such an attack would pass directly by their men and if they chose to intervene it would spell disaster for us.'

Richard laughed again as he replied disdainfully, 'I don't think for one moment that the Stanleys would have the nerve to commit if it appeared as if Tudor was losing the battle and let's face it,' he added, with more than a hint of sarcasm, 'Tudor's generalship to date can't have inspired much confidence in them.'

As both armies came into line and faced each other, those in the front ranks began to hurl abuse and insults at their counterparts in the opposing army. These insults were soon replaced by projectiles as Norfolk finally gave orders that the artillery barrage should commence. Unfortunately, it soon became clear to Francis that Richard's confidence in the abilities of his gunners had been misplaced. The artillery men, who were inexperienced when it came to the operation of the continental artillery pieces, which Richard had only recently acquired from their Burgundian allies, failed to account for both the increased power of the new guns and the distance that lay between the two armies. As a consequence, their shot, rather than decimate the enemy, fell ineffectively towards its rear. Thankfully, in contrast to the artillery, Norfolk's archers, who'd had much more experience with their weapons, displayed great skill as they unleashed a deadly hail of arrows that fell upon Oxford's men and, as a consequence, caused much death and suffering. It was clear to Francis that Oxford had appreciated that without the assistance of the Stanleys he had insufficient troops to maintain a traditional battle line. Instead, he'd chosen to Marshall what troops he had into a tight phalanx formation with which he hoped to thwart any Yorkist attack. Unfortunately for the Lancastrians, this disposition ensured that the Yorkist archers were presented with an excellent target. Norfolk's men didn't waste this opportunity and they wrought devastation amongst their enemies, whose armour was ineffective against the long bow at such a short range. In reply, Oxford brought his own archers forward and although seriously outnumbered, they slowly began to harry Norfolk's men, who remained stationary awaiting the order to attack. From their vantage point within their army's right flank, both Richard and Francis could see that many East Anglians fell as wave after wave of arrows fell amongst their battle lines. Although the Yorkist archers returned this fire in earnest, both armies held fast and it soon became obvious that the exchanges would remain inconclusive.

Richard turned to Francis and with difficulty to make himself heard above the din of battle he shouted.

'Remember Tewksbury.'

Francis needed no other reminder as he cast his mind back fourteen years and pictured, in his minds eye, how the main body of Prince Edward's army, which had been harried by unrelenting archery fire, when exposed to a frontal attack, had broken. This in turn had caused panic and had provoked mass desertions, so that within a matter of minutes the entire Lancastrian army had been routed.

Richard immediately gave the order to attack and as his buglers sounded the advance. Needing no further encouragement, Norfolk unleashed his men-at-arms upon Oxford's men. No doubt pleased at last to be in a position to retaliate against their adversaries, the heavily armoured men-at-arms clambered off in the direction of the Lancastrians, slowly gathering speed as they went. As the East Anglians clashed with their counterparts in Oxford's van, their momentum drove them far into the enemy's lines. Unfortunately, Oxford had organised his men's dispositions with great skill. Francis sighed as he saw that his unusual phalanx formation, which was many men thick, buckled but did not give way to Norfolk's onslaught. Francis sighed again, for it was clear that any traditional battle line would have easily been breached by such a concentrated attack. As it was, the Lancastrians stood firm, guaranteeing that Norfolk's men would not enjoy the 'easy victory' that they'd all hoped for. The struggle continued for some time as Norfolk's men repeatedly threw themselves against Oxford's troops who, huddled together around their various standards, stubbornly refused to give any further ground. Alarmingly, it soon became apparent that the Lancastrian phalanx itself was beginning to advance, slowly pushing the Yorkists back from whence they'd come. In comparison to his advance towards the Lancastrian lines, Norfolk's withdrawal wasn't at all ordered. Within minutes it seemed to Francis as if the retreat, which quickly gathered a momentum all of its own, was capable of causing the whole of their vanguard to rout. Oxford's men, released from the restrictions that their tightly packed formation had placed upon them, surged forward and engulfed the East Anglians. Norfolk and his household men were soon swallowed up in the attack and Francis was saddened to see Norfolk's standard crash to the floor. Unfortunately, no-one picked it up, this signifying that Norfolk too had fallen on the field. Thankfully, and in spite of the suspected death of his father, Suffolk bravely rallied his men and was at least able to lead them in a counterattack that halted the Lancastrian advance. A stalemate soon ensued as both armies, now much more evenly matched and in the absence of further orders and drawn up in traditional battle lines, faced one another as they grimly traded blows.

Worried, Francis turned to Richard who appeared to be studying the proceedings intently. Earlier, when it'd appeared as if Norfolk's men may have given way completely, Richard had asked that his horse White Surrey be brought forward. He ordered that should their front line collapse altogether, in an effort to restore order, he would be forced to mount a charge. Turning to his friends and smiling, Richard explained that, 'This impasse can only serve to assist us to prevail. Suffolk will suck in more and more of Tudor's reserves as Oxford attempts to shore up his own front line,' Richard laughed as he added,

'The Lancastrians haven't got sufficient men to fight such a battle of attrition,' pointing towards the Stanley's men, who'd remained quite still, he added gleefully, 'The Stanleys will never commit their men to Tudor in such circumstances.'

Francis, on the other hand, pointed out that if they were able to bring up Northumberland's men and attack the Lancastrian's left flank, which although it hadn't yet engaged was still weak, they would be able to roll up the whole of Tudor's army.

Confidant, Richard smiled at Francis's impetuousness saying, 'For the time being we must be patient. At this stage of the battle I don't want to commit all of our reserves. Let Tudor make the next move and we can react to that.'

They didn't have to wait long for Tudor to show his hand. All of the Yorkist commanders watched in amazement as Tudor, with what was little more than his own personal bodyguard, perhaps fifty mounted men-at-arms, broke away from the main body of his army and made his way behind Savage's men on the Lancastrian left and out into the open countryside.

Initially, Francis's heart leapt, for it appeared to him as if Tudor was quitting the field. His optimism soon changed to alarm however, as the Tudor and his horsemen veered in a north westerly direction, towards the Stanleys.

Francis turned to Richard, who at first seemed non plussed by Tudor's bold move. Judging by the Stanley's inaction to date, none could tell how they would react to what was clearly going to be a last desperate personal plea for them to intervene on Tudor's behalf. The battle was going well for them but Francis knew that any intervention at that point by the Stanleys on behalf of the Lancastrians could easily prove decisive. Richard could never have expected Suffolk, who was hard pressed in the centre, to resist an attack from Stanley's Chesiremen. In that event, Richard would be forced into committing what remained of the main body of his army. This would leave Northumberland who, despite numerous requests to do so, had still not brought his troops forward, as the Yorkist's only remaining reserves. This was the very situation that Richard had always sought to avoid!

All now looked to their King who, without conferring with his fellow commanders, immediately made his decision.

Steering White Surrey around to face their Knights and mounted men-at-arms, Richard shouted, 'We can take him whilst he's in the open.' Confidant, Richard pointed out that, 'With just one final charge the day can be ours.' Yes, Francis knew that if they were able to catch Tudor out in the open and were able to kill him, they'd bring the battle to an immediate and successful conclusion. But to risk everything on such a bold maneuver!

Dismayed, Francis frantically looked about them. With fewer than two hundred cavalry, Richard hoped to secure victory. Surely a charge by so few a number could never hope to succeed. Clearly sensing his men's reticence, Richard pointed out that Tudor had, 'far less men than they and if they were to catch him in the open he'd have no chance of surviving such an attack. Shouting to make himself heard over the tumult Richard added, 'With Tudor dead the Stanleys will never dare to intervene against us.'

Discounting any further debate and taking his lance from his squire, Richard pulled down the visor of his helmet and spurred White Surrey into a gallop in the direction of Tudor and his body guard. None had time to argue with Richard and they all had no option but to follow him into battle. Not trusting that the Stanleys remain inactive, Francis reiterated Richard's orders that should the Stanleys deploy against them, then Lord Strange must die.

Catesby, who was a politician and had never been much of a soldier, had up until that point looked extremely ill at ease on his horse, which he was having great difficulty in controlling. As Catesby tried to follow Richard, spooked by the din and its riders heavy handedness, the startled animal reared up and finally managed to rid itself of the unfortunate Catesby. Francis, remembering how long it'd taken Catesby to get onto the horse in the first place, felt that to do so now and in time to join the charge would have been a near impossibility. As he too galloped off after Richard, he shouted after himself for his friend to remain where he was, to rally those of their right wing and centre in the event that Oxford attempted a counter attack. Francis smiled as he saw that Catesby was clearly extremely relieved not to have had to take part in the charge. For the first time that day Catesby smiled as he waved off his friends who, gathering in their mounts spurred them onwards after both Richard and White Surrey.

Exhilarated, Francis kicked his own horse from a canter and into a gallop. As he gathered speed he could only imagine what a spectacle their charge must have presented. Two hundred heavily armoured horsemen, lances lowered, bearing down upon Tudor and his unfortunate bodyguard! Within seconds the Yorkist knights were upon Tudor and his men. Surprised by both the ferocity and the speed of Richard's retort, the Lancastrians had failed by quite a distance to reach the relative safety of Stanley's men and, as Richard had planned, had been caught out in the open. As Tudor's bodyguard closed ranks to protect their leader, some of their mounted archers were at least able to loose off a number of arrows in the direction of their attackers. Excited and keen to come to blows with the enemy, whom he'd spent much of the morning watching, Francis was extremely disappointed as an arrow struck his own mount in the chest. Dead, the horse crumpled beneath Francis and threw him sideways and downwards and onto the hard packed and uneven ground of the heath. Miraculously, although winded, uninjured Francis picked himself up as his companions thundered by. Those amongst Tudor's bodyguard who turned to meet the Yorkists were dispatched with ease and, in an instant, skewered on the lance tips of Richard's Knights. Neither shield nor armour could withstand the charge which was directed towards the stationary Lancastrians, who were powerless against such an attack. With pride Francis saw how Richard, who was amongst the first of his men to fall upon their enemies, cleanly ran through Tudor's standard bearer. The man fell stone dead at his masters feet as Tudor's red dragon fell to the floor. For a brief moment it appeared to Francis as if Richard's charge had succeeded in killing Tudor. Unfortunately, and not for the first time that day, Francis's optimism was both unfounded and short lived. After its initial impact, deprived of either momentum or additional reinforcements the attack faltered and soon developed into a melee, as men on each side began to hack at each other with both axe and sword. Sadly within minutes Tudor's dragon was once again raised aloft. Francis, who was some distance from the skirmish, could no longer see how Richard was faring. From the few brief glimpses that he got of White Surrey, it appeared to Francis as if Richard, still mounted, was deep within his enemies ranks. Incredibly, Richard's white boar standard flew only a feet away from that of his adversaries! It was at that point in time that Francis heard the battle cry which he'd spent the whole day fearing. 'A Stanley, A Stanley.' Turning to his right, Francis saw what he could only describe as a red hoard descending upon them, as the Stanleys finally committed their men to the battle. Standing in the face of many thousands of men, Francis wasn't able to deliver a single blow as he was knocked to the ground and knew no more.

It was early evening before Francis regained consciousness, disturbed by those who'd been given the macabre task of stripping the soldiers corpses of anything of value. As these scavengers approached him, Francis tried to remain motionless, hoping to give them the impression that he too was dead. It was obvious from the men's red tunics that they were Stanley's retainers. This, together with Francis's last memories of the battle, led Francis to believe that they had been defeated. Moreover, knowing his friends the way that he did and having witnessed the last stages of the battle, Francis seriously doubted that any of them, including Richard, had managed to escape. As he lay there, Francis hoped that somehow Richard had been saved and even now, together with Ratcliffe and Brackenbury, he was en-route to Yorkshire. To take refuge and regroup before he could once again lead his Yorkshiremen south to reclaim his crown. His eyes closed tightly, Francis dared not breathe as he felt his enemies breath upon his face. The Lancastrian bending over Francis began to loosen his breastplate. Francis remained quite still as the man chortled and congratulated himself on his good fortune in coming across one of rank, who no longer had any need for his finely crafted armour. Stupidly, Francis remembered just how excited both he and Richard had been when, years earlier, they'd taken delivery of the armour that had been many months in the making. He recalled how overwhelmed he'd been to discover that upon ordering his own suit of armour, Richard had purchased an almost identical suit for Francis, which only differed from Francis's in that it was designed especially to cater for Richard's deformity, a curvature of his spine, which Richard had always been careful to hide from those other than his closest friends and retainers. Francis smiled inwardly as he pictured in his minds eye both the bravery and ferocity that Richard had always displayed on the Battlefield, one would never have imagined that Richard had possessed such a dissibility, which in others would have been so debilitating.

Not for the first time in his life Francis quietly chided himself for daydreaming. Taking stock of his situation he realised that it was only a matter of time before the Lancastrian realised that he was still alive and either dispatched him or took him prisoner. Through half opened eyes Francis could see that this man was the only person in his immediate vicinity. As the Lancastrian continued to loosen the buckles that secured Francis's breastplate and was momentarily off guard, in an instant Francis took hold of the hilt of the dagger that was protruding from the man's scabbard and unsheathing the blade he plunged it upwards and into the mans stomach, twisting it as the blade slipped underneath his enemies ribcage. Grunting, the Lancastrian exhaled and Francis smiled as he wondered if this was through either pain or surprise. Luckily, Francis was able to roll over on top of his quarry. He held the man for those few minutes that it took him to die. A hand placed over the Lancastrian's mouth to prevent any further sound that may have given Francis away. Francis quietly congratulated himself not only for killing the man but also on his luck at having been approached by one of Stanley's men, for he was able to pull on the man's tunic, which heavily bloodstained, was still no redder than it had been before!

Once clear of the field, Francis managed to acquire one of the many horses who, relieved of their burdens and out of the din of battle, now quietly grazed in the meadows that surrounded the battlefield. Judging by the number of corpses scattered about him, Francis guessed that the fighting must have been quite intense. Unfortunately, many of the dead displayed Yorkist insignia, which confirmed Francis's worst fears. He immediately determined to make for the north. He judged that if he made good time he could be at either Middleham or Ravensworth within a few days, both were places where he was bound to hear of any news of Richard.

Francis had never been afraid of his own company, however, to be alone and hunted in what was now a hostile environment was a frightening prospect for one who no longer knew whom he could trust. Thus, Francis was greatly relieved to see some friendly faces when just days after the battle he happened across the Stafford brothers whilst he was traveling on the road northwards. Unfortunately, the brothers were going in the opposite direction to Francis. After Francis had spoken to his friends at length, he knew that he had some difficult decisions to make.

Thomas and his brother Humphrey, although related to the late Duke of Buckingham, shared none of their cousin's character. In fact both knights shared Francis's philosophy when it came to honour and loyalty. Both brothers had fought for Richard at Bosworth and both had been fortunate enough to escape, only leaving the field when all had appeared lost. The Staffords confirmed Francis's fears that not only had the battle been lost but that King Richard had been killed. White Surrey had been felled as Stanley's knights had sandwiched Richard's men between themselves and what had remained of Tudor's bodyguard. Unhorsed, Richard had refused all offers of help and a horse that may have carried him to safety. Instead, he'd fought on bravely until, overwhelmed by sheer force of numbers, he'd been hacked to the ground and butchered. Francis was devastated to finally hear the news of his friend's death. And worse still, few others had survived the battle as almost all of Richard's close circle of friends and retainers had been killed during the fateful charge and in its aftermath. Both Ratcliffe and Brackenbury had died at the King's side. Gervase Clifton and Lord Ferrers on the other hand had been killed by the volley of arrows which had unhorsed Francis and had ultimately saved his own life.

'But what of Catesby?'

Francis inquired, as he pictured in his minds eye Catesby vainly attempting to control his errant mount.

Unfortunately, the Staffords were all too well informed. Thomas replied, 'He was taken prisoner after the battle together with Suffolk, Lincoln and Northumberland.' Humphrey added, 'It's said that Tudor, wherever possible, hopes to pardon the nobles, as he's desperate for the support of the aristocracy.'

Compounding Francis's distress, Humphrey continued, 'Unfortunately Catesby was of no use to Tudor and anyway we all know how during his time in Parliament he'd made many enemies.'

Thomas went on to describe how Catesby had been put to death at Leicester on the day after the battle. Francis was at least thankful that his friend had not suffered both the pain and shame of a traitors death. As a man of honour and one who'd fought for his King, he'd at least been beheaded. Francis smiled as the brothers recounted how the wily politician had even tried to save himself. Once it had become apparent to him that Richard had been killed and defeated, and disregarding Francis's orders, Catesby, trusting that the Stanleys would return the compliment, had interceded on behalf of Lord Strange and had prevented his execution. Unfortunately, at Leicester Catesby had joined the long list of those who'd been betrayed by that family and he'd apparently been led out to his death cursing them.

When Francis told the Staffords that he hoped to make for Richard's strongholds in North Yorkshire the brother's had advised caution, adding that this too had been their intention until they'd discovered that for the time being at least, Yorkshire was far too dangerous for them. They said that Tudor had dispatched Sir Richard Willoughby, together with a large contingent of troops, northwards with orders to secure both Richard's castles and the Earl of Warwick, who'd been moved by Richard from the Tower of London to his castle at Sheriff Hutton.

After some deliberation Francis took the Stafford's advice and joining them on their journey southwards, he turned around. The brothers had friends in Essex and they argued that this area was probably the safest in the Kingdom, as the Lancastrians would no doubt assume that those Yorkists who'd escaped the battle, would make there way northwards. Francis was content, for the time being at least, to join the Staffords who intended to seek sanctuary in Colchester. Distraught at the death of his friend Richard, Francis couldn't quite believe the irony of it all. For their proposed route to Colchester would take them directly by Castle Heddingham, the home of both the Earl of Oxford and presumably Francis's cousin Thomas, a place where it had all started all of those years ago.

As they traveled, the three men all vowed to each other that they would avenge Richard's death and right up until their 'dying breaths' they would endeavor to recover the crown for Richard's heir, for it was rumored that John De La Pole had survived the battle and was presently a prisoner of Tudor's, ensconced within the Tower of London.

Chapter 31
May 1486 Broughton Tower Cumbria.

Relieved at what had been yet another narrow escape, Francis was at last able to enjoy the hospitality of his friends, the Broughton brothers, from within the relative safety of their Cumbrian stronghold, Broughton Tower. It was fair to say that Francis's mind was still very much in a whirl! Attempting to take stock of his present situation, he tried to understand how his scheme to topple Tudor's fledgling dynasty, a plan that had initially shown much promise, had come to naught. It was incredible, Francis mused, how fickle men were. How, in a few days, a large and well victual led army, which had been intent upon the destruction of the King, had melted away into nothingness. Perhaps most upsetting was the fact that, at that point in time, Tudor, who'd been poorly prepared, had been extremely vulnerable. In fact, as it turned out, the new King had seriously underestimated Francis's challenge to his throne. Instead of recruiting an army to deal with the rebellion, Tudor had embarked upon a previously planned progression throughout England. The new King's itinerary even including a tour of Yorkshire, the centre point of Francis's uprising and an area that was renowned for its Pro- Ricardian sympathies! Furthermore, throughout this 'progress' Tudor had been accompanied by only a small company of men, which in real terms had amounted to no more than a personal bodyguard!

Unfortunately, yet again, events had conspired against Francis and his comrades and ultimately they'd failed. Francis sighed, in his opinion they'd squandered what had been a golden opportunity to topple Tudor's fledgling regime. As he sat alone gazing out onto the barren Cumbrian fells, Francis groaned inwardly, as he remembered how his army had come to desert him. 'War weary' from the outset, as at Bosworth, many of their troops had been weak in their resolve. As such, they'd allowed themselves to be seduced by yet another promise of a pardon from the King, which had been delivered in the form of Tudor's henchmen, Sir Richard Edgecombe and Sir William Tyler. Francis despised these men. 'Cronies', 'nothings' who'd approached the Yorkist camp, at Tudor's behest, under the protection of a flag of truce and, under the auspices of such, they'd displayed such incredible arrogance towards the Yorkist commanders. Unfortunately, fearful of retribution should they fail yet again to defeat Tudor, their soldiers had listened. Francis had tried in vain to persuade his men to stay and fight, but ultimately he'd been frustrated by both their lack of fortitude and foresight. Francis sighed again, in the early days of the rising the King, who'd been at Doncaster with his small retinue, had been in no position to oppose them. At that point in time the Yorkist army, camped upon Bramham Moor, had been less than a days march away from the King. Shaking his head Francis could have wept, for he was sure that any attack by them at that point in time would have brought about certain victory and with it either the King's destruction, or at the very least his flight and return into a forced exile.

Presently, Francis now seriously doubted that they would ever have another opportunity to defeat the King. Perversely, Francis did at least allow himself a wry smile, for he'd heard that Tudor had been seriously disturbed by the whole incident. Indeed, as a result of Francis's rebellion, despite his famed frugality, Tudor had increased the number of fighting men within his retinue, in effect creating what now amounted to his own standing army. Experienced soldiers, these men were to be known as 'The Beefeaters', in recognition of the fact that Tudor was going to make sure that they were always well fed and were well looked after! Francis sighed again, how would he ever be able to raise another army who'd be willing to take on, amongst others, what now amounted to a professional fighting force!

Whatever faults he may have had, Francis could never be accused of being naive. He'd always appreciated that the common soldiers within any army were always liable to worry and panic at the slightest of rumours. In any campaign this was to be expected. Stories would be told and retold by men who were all too easily bored and became impatient as they waited for battle. Sadly, as it turned out, on this occasion many of the rumour mongers who'd been responsible for 'spooking' their men, had actually been veterans of the civil wars! Experienced soldiers who, in Francis's opinion, should have known better! These men, pointing to Tudor's victory at Bosworth, had argued that the Lancastrians must have had God on their side. How else could they explain such an unexpected yet resounding success? Ultimately, these rumours had circulated throughout the entirety of the Yorkist camp. In Francis's opinion they'd been nothing more than baseless conjecture, believed by men of limited intellect. Those who feared not only for their safety in this world, but also for their salvation in the next! Francis, keen to nip these stories in the bud, had given orders that any who spread such tales were to be whipped or, at the very least, placed in the stocks. Many had been punished in this way but, frustratingly, the stories had continued to circulate. As they'd done so, they'd taken on a life of their own, embellished and exaggerated with each and every telling. They told of miracles that had taken place within the Lancastrian camp in the hours before the battle of Bosworth. Of soldiers who'd been struck down with dysentery or with the sweating sickness who'd risen up from their beds and, calling for their weapons, had followed the Earl of Oxford into battle! They'd even described how dozens of Richard's men had been struck down by bolts of lightening! This despite the fact that there had been no storm on the day of the battle!

Francis sighed yet again, his men had deserted in their hundreds and ultimately he'd been defeated not by another army, but by rumours, the offer of a pardon and even by the Pope, who'd threatened to excommunicate anyone who fought against his latest ally, Henry VII!

But as he sat there all alone, Francis still felt that they still should've won. Shaking his head Francis still couldn't quite believe all that had happened. Indeed, for once in his life even the Duke of Northumberland had been of some use. Northumberland, who'd clearly been keen to ingratiate himself with his new King, had been quick to mobilise his own retainers. As a result, within a couple of days of the Yorkists arriving at Bramham Moor, he'd been able to reinforce Tudor's meagre force at Doncaster. Sadly, none in the Yorkist camp, save that is for Francis himself, were personally acquainted with the Earl and as such they had all failed to appreciate the fact that they'd got nothing to fear from this 'arrogant' and 'incompetent' 'coward'. That said, both Lord Stanley and the Earl of Oxford were also rumoured to have been en route to reinforce the King with contingents of men from Chesire and East Anglia.

Sadly, no-one had believed Francis when he'd pointed out that Oxford was the only one who could be truly trusted to fight for Tudor and at that point in time even his support was no longer guaranteed. Especially when one took into account his widely publicised dispute with the new King over patronage and retinues. Indeed, when it came to Oxford, Tudor, who had a great deal to thank Oxford for, had promised much but had delivered nothing. The gravest of insults when one considered the facts that, firstly, it'd been Oxford's efforts above all others that had effectively secured Tudor's victory at Bosworth and secondly, that those who'd actually fought against the Tudor had, after the battle, received much more than Oxford in the way of rewards!

Francis had argued until he was blue in the face that, regardless of what potential support Tudor may or may not have expected, the fact remained that they'd caught him off guard and, as such, he was extremely vulnerable to attack. Francis smiled, apparently on initially hearing the news of Francis's rebellion the King had been in quite a quandary. Should he issue his nobles with the commissions of array that would enable them to recruit men on his behalf? Or was he to wait and see what support Francis received. Reticent to resurrect those armies that'd been so destructive throughout the civil wars, Tudor had ultimately chosen the latter course of action, only finally issuing the commissions of array once it'd become clear to him that he was in fact facing quite a significant threat. As a result, Francis had reasoned that it would have been quite some time before the King could have expected any additional reinforcements. That is, if they'd come at all!

Chuckling to himself, Francis smiled again, he'd heard it said that Lord Stanley had been up to his old tricks again. Apparently upon receiving the King's summons, the old dog had once again taken to his bed, this time complaining that he was suffering from the 'dropsy'! In his stead Stanley had promised to send his son Lord Strange, Francis laughed again, everyone knew just how expendable Strange was!

What had also exasperated Francis about his men's capitulation was the fact that their own army had not been entirely friendless. They too had expected reinforcements, as at the outbreak of the rebellion Francis had sent the Stafford brothers into the Midlands to recruit troops on their behalf. In areas that had been both 'Clarence's' and 'Warwick the Kingmaker's' heartland's in Warwickshire, they'd expected a great deal in the way of support. Indeed, even if the Staffords and their army hadn't been in a position to join them in time, at the very least, Francis had pointed out, they'd have served as a distraction to any of Tudor's supporters who were coming to the King's aid from either South Wales or from the West Country.

Ultimately however, abandoned by the majority of his troops, even Francis had finally been forced to concede defeat and for the sake of those men who'd remained loyal to him he'd disbanded what was left of their army. This once, having taken into account all of the available intelligence, it'd become obvious to him he that they were no longer in a position to prevail. Ultimately, what had been an excellent opportunity to succeed had in the end been frittered away into nothing. Indeed, one could argue that the whole affair had even served to strengthen Tudor's position on the throne!

Scratching his head Francis still couldn't quite believe how stupid they'd all been. Regardless of all of the various excuses that he now came up with, be they 'the stories that the soldiers spread', 'the pardons that the King had promised' or 'all of the promises of help in the world', Francis himself had to accept some of the responsibility for their defeat. It was on his advice that they'd delayed attacking Tudor at Doncaster and once he'd been reinforced by Northumberland, it was the King who'd been in a position to take the offensive against them. In fact much as he hated to admit it, cautious as ever, Francis had been the one who'd suggested that they delay the attack for a for a day or so, to enable the Staffords time to join them. Unfortunately, as it turned out these reinforcements had failed to materialise. The Staffords sending word that they were having difficulty paying what few men they'd gathered together, never mind recruiting any more! That said, with the benefit of hindsight Francis knew that the Stafford's failure hadn't really made that much difference to them. By the time they'd received the news that no reinforcements were coming, many of Francis's own men had already deserted him. In what had been a startling reversal of fortune, and within the space of only a few days, the Yorkists had found that it was they and not the Tudor, who'd been both outnumbered and outmaneuvered. Ultimately, Francis had had no other option but to dismiss what had remained of their troops.

It still hurt him to think of it. As he'd bade farewell to his men Francis had told them to 'remain in a constant state of readiness' for one day he would call upon them again. But even Francis had known in his heart of hearts that it was all but over and that any opportunity that they'd had to defeat Tudor was gone.

Once again, Francis had been forced to flee. This time, however, he'd made his way via both Middleham and Wensleydale, to the Broughton brothers' lands in the Cumbrian fells. A place where, for the time being at least, he would be safe.

Desperate to salvage anything from the whole debacle and before he'd left Bramham Moor, Francis had however conceived a plan to assassinate the King at York. He sighed again, for even in this he felt that he'd been badly let down by others. After their army had finally been disbanded the Scropes and Francis's brother-in-law, Richard Fitzhugh, had been summoned to York to receive the King's pardon. Francis had handpicked a number of would be assassins who were to join Fitzhugh at York, disguised as his personal retainers. Once admitted into the King's presence, these men were to set upon Tudor and his bodyguards. Unfortunately, but not unsurprisingly, at the very last minute Fitzhugh had panicked and had sent Francis's men away. Francis later discovered that the Scropes, who'd always been confident that the plan would succeed, had been dissuaded from going through with it by Fitzhugh. True to form, and not for the first time, Francis's brother-in-law had lost his nerve and having gone to his knees before his co-conspirators, he'd pleaded with them to abandon the plan, which he said was bound to fail and would result in all of their executions for treason. As always, the Scropes had remained firm, but without their promised support, even they had reluctantly been forced into capitulating and accepting the King's pardon.

Whilst at Broughton Tower, Francis had also been saddened by the news from London that Humphrey Stafford, who'd been taken by the King's men from sanctuary at Culham, had met a traitor's death at Tyburn. Conversely, and perhaps perversely, Humphrey's brother, whom it was said had betrayed him, had received both the King's pardon and all of his elder brother's various lands and titles!

Depressed, Francis once again found himself a fugitive with no realistic prospect of any help in the foreseeable future. But even he had to admit that he was lucky to be alive and, with a price on his head, at Broughton Tower he was at least in a relatively safe place where he'd be able to rest and recuperate and take stock of the situation.

Goodness knows, much had happened in the short period of time that had elapsed since Bosworth!

Immediately after the battle, together with the Staffords, Francis had made what had turned out to be an extremely hazardous journey to Colchester. There, having narrowly avoided capture on a number of occasions, they'd all sought and received the sanctuary of the church at St Johns Abbey. It had soon become common knowledge that they were there and at the time it'd surprised Francis that Henry, who like King Edward before him had had no qualms in flaunting the laws of sanctuary when it suited him to do so, had chosen to leave them be. This in spite of the fact that within weeks of their arriving at the Abbey, it'd become a recognised centre for disaffection to Tudor's regime. Indeed, in the early days they'd been joined by a large number of Yorkist and Ricardian diehards who, like Francis and the Staffords, had all refused to come to terms with the new King.

Francis smiled as he remembered how delighted he'd been when Ned had finally found him there. As a squire, Ned's life had been spared at Bosworth and after the battle he'd spent a number of days scouring both the battlefield and the surrounding countryside in an effort to find Francis. Eventually, having been forced into the realisation that Francis must have been killed during the fateful charge, Ned had made his way back to Minster Lovel. It was there that he'd heard of Francis's escape to Colchester. Without delay Ned had travelled to St Johns to be at Francis's side. Although delighted to see his friend again, Francis had been upset, although not surprised, to discover that his wife Anne had joined her brother Richard in seeking terms from Tudor. Moreover, according to Ned, she'd been unmoved when she'd heard that Francis, having survived the battle, was both safe and well. Ned, who neither trusted nor liked Francis's wife, had shrugged as he'd imparted this news to Francis. Even Francis had taken the news remarkably well, although he had to admit to himself that he'd half been expecting it anyway for, as with her brother, Anne could never be trusted to support a lost cause!

Francis had ultimately discovered the real reason for Tudor's inactivity when it came to both him and his fellow dissenters at Colchester, when he'd unexpectedly received a visit from his cousin Thomas. Keen to hear his story Francis discovered that Thomas, who'd still been in the Earl of Oxford's employ, had accompanied his master throughout both his captivity at Hammes Castle and his subsequent exile at the French Court. Indeed, by the time that he'd visited Francis at Colchester, Thomas, or 'Saxon' as Francis still preferred to call him, had risen through the ranks and, as Oxford's most trusted retainer, he'd finally been appointed as the head of his household. Quite a lucrative position when one considered that after Bosworth, Oxford was once again one of the foremost aristocrats in the country. Both Francis and 'Saxon', despite being on opposing sides throughout the civil wars, were still kin and at Colchester, having not seen each other for many years, they'd had much to catch up on. In fact, the cousins had talked for many hours, Francis marveling at 'Saxon's' story which was not at all dissimilar to his own! How 'Saxon' had shared in his master's misfortunes throughout the Yorkist restoration. How he'd momentarily savored victory when both King Edward and Richard had been driven into exile and how he'd once again seen his hopes dashed at Barnet, where the tables had been turned and it was Oxford's benefactor King Henry who'd lost his crown. As they'd spoken of the wars, both Francis and his cousin had cast their mind back to that foggy day in 1470. Each had agreed that it had been a close run thing.

'Decided on by divine intervention,' Francis had quipped as, smiling, he remembered how of all things it'd been fog that had had the greatest influence on the battle's outcome. How Oxford's contingent, which had included 'Saxon', having swept Hasting's men from the field had left the battle to plunder the Yorkist baggage train. How upon their return to the field, having been mistaken in the mist for Edward's troops, they'd been fired upon by their own men! With the resultant accusations of treachery culminating in the Lancastrian's rout and defeat.

As it turned out 'Saxon' had also fought for Tudor at Bosworth, where he'd been amongst those men who'd stood firm and had stoically borne the brunt of Norfolk's charge. As he'd described the battle to Francis it'd been 'Saxon's' turn to smile as he added that both he and Oxford had been lucky to escape with their lives. Indeed, 'Saxon' had even conceded to Francis that their men had been extremely close to defeat as their phalanx had been battered and worn down by Nofolk's determined attacks. As he'd finished his account of the battle, 'Saxon' had smiled again as he'd described how defeat had been turned into victory as their men had counterattacked and first Norfolk had been slain and then King Richard. Francis had immediately and vociferously disagreed with his cousin, pointing out that Richard's defeat had been brought about not by Oxford's counterattack, albeit that by standing firm Oxford's men had prevented Tudor's early defeat, but by the treachery of the Stanleys and the inactivity of the 'cowardly' Northumberland. Sighing, Francis had added that many of their men, Richard included, had by that time lost their faith that God was on their side. 'Saxon' had shocked Francis as he'd laughed at him pointing out that in his opinion, 'God' wasn't at all 'interested in the petty jealousies and wranglings of England's nobility.' 'Jealous and ambitious men' who'd stop at nothing in their 'quest for power and tittles? No,' Saxon had added with an air of resignation, 'I'm afraid many of us who've been involved in these wars will have much to answer for when we finally meet our maker.' Francis, who'd been about to object, had been silenced as Saxon had added wryly, 'I'm afraid that loyalty and honour to our lords will be deemed a poor excuse for that which we've all done.'

Even now, Francis shuddered as he remembered his cousin's words and pictured in his minds eye just some of the horrors that he'd both witnessed and been party to!

Both Lovells had, however, brightened as Saxon had told Francis that as a reward for his efforts at Bosworth and at the behest of the new King, he'd been promoted by Oxford. On hearing this Francis had smiled ruefully as he'd contrasted his cousin's experiences with those of his own.

Eventually, and after both men had finally caught up with those events that had brought them back together, Saxon had finally revealed the true purpose of his visit. As Francis's kinsman, he'd been asked by the King to visit him. Saxon had been authorised to offer the King's pardon to both Francis and to all of his companions at St Johns. Indeed, Saxon had hoped to persuade all of those Yorkists who'd remained at Colchester to surrender directly to him. Despite the fact that it had been sometime since he'd seen Saxon, Francis, who truly believed that 'blood was thicker than water,' had trusted his cousin's word implicitly. He'd neither suspected subterfuge on Tudor's part nor doubted his cousin's sincerity. Thomas had even assured them they were to have both an armed escort and a warrant entitling them all to a safe passage to the King's palace at Sheen. Once there they were to have received 'pardons' from 'their new King', in return for oaths of loyalty. Apparently, Tudor had been so confident of their submission that he'd even gone so far as to arrange for their lodgings whilst in the capital. Initially, Francis had felt quite insulted by Tudor's offer and had rejected it out of hand. However, when one considered the behavior of the other Yorkist lords in acquiescing so easily, one could, he felt, have forgiven the King for his optimism in expecting those at Colchester to have submitted to him. For in truth, by that time, countless so called 'die hard Yorkists' and 'Ricardians' had already submitted! Despite the fact that they were his sworn enemies, Francis could never blame Lancastrians for their loyalty to their King, but he resented those Yorkists who'd come to terms with Tudor after only one battle! Cowards who'd capitulated once it appeared that they'd nothing more to gain from the Plantagenets. In Francis's opinion, those who'd accepted Tudor's terms had insulted both Richard's memory and that of the men who'd gone before them. That said, Francis had to admit that his cousin had timed his visit well for, by that time, only a few had remained in sanctuary. As the weeks had passed by uneventfully, bored, many of their number had defected to Tudor. Each day Francis would waken to discover that yet another of their number had slipped away in the dead of night to make their peace with the King. Most distressing to Francis had been the news that the Earl of Lincoln, Richard's nominated heir, had even come to terms with Tudor. This before Richard had even been cold in his grave! Lincoln's submission had been followed by that of many more so called 'Ricardian stalwarts.' Those who Francis would have expected to have fought for the Plantagenets to their dying breath! What had rankled Francis more than anything else was the fact that with Richard now dead and of no further use to them, these men, who were only interested in their own self aggrandizement, had abandoned the cause without a struggle! Sadly, it had been during his cousin's visit that Francis had come to the realisation that Tudor's policy of reconciliation seemed to have been paying off for him.

Since his victory at Bosworth Tudor had rewarded a number of the aristocracy but, short on money, he'd also cleverly left others believing that they too would receive honours at some point in the future. No doubt at the insistence of Tudor's mother, Lord Stanley had been created the Earl of Derby and even Buckingham's son, possibly as a reward for his father's failed rebellion of 1483, had been restored to his lands and titles.

Francis shuddered as he recalled the daily despair of that period of time at St Johns. How both he and the Staffords had been close to giving up and had in fact taken some time to consider Saxon's proposals. At that time, in addition to those few men who'd remained at Colchester, Yorkist opposition to Tudor had been limited to the far reaches of the Kingdom. Areas in which the new King's Government still exercised little or no control. Men like Sir James Harrington in Lancashire and the Broughtons here in the Cumbrian fells and Sir Henry Bodruggan in Cornwall. Those who'd chosen to continue the struggle and who were, for the time being at least, able to do so without fear of interference from London. Unfortunately, with the exception of Harrington and the Broughtons, the remaining Yorkist dissidents had been 'battle hardened soldiers,' men who possessed none of those niceties that one might have expected from men of high birth. Those whose actions in despoiling the land and estates of their neighbors in the name of the 'Plantagenets', had done nothing to endear their cause to others. In reality these men's actions had only served to alienate further a nation which, after years of civil war, had been in the process of welcoming in an era of peace and it hoped prosperity that came off the back of Richard's defeat.

A further blow to their cause had come in early 1486 when the King had finally given in to popular demand and had married Edward's eldest daughter, Elizabeth of York. This had been seen by many as a coupling of both the houses of Lancaster and York. As a result of the marriage, many pointed out that any children born to the couple would be considered to be of the true royal line! That is, of course, if one 'conveniently' discounted Elizabeth's illegitimacy as a result of her own parents invalid marriage. Francis had been disappointed but not at all surprised to see just how quickly the English, no doubt keen to see an end to the civil wars, had conveniently forgotten this fact. Indeed, it'd saddened both Francis and the Stafford brothers that the majority of the population, those who'd enthusiastically supported Richard when he'd ascended to the throne, were all now happy to believe Tudor's propagandist description of Richard and now regarded him as a hideously deformed tyrant, a murderer and a despot.

Francis still couldn't quite believe the gullibility of the people. To believe that Richard had killed his nephews and after them his wife in order to marry his niece, the illegitimate daughter of his brother!

Francis had at least been pleased to see his cousin again and Saxon had changed little in the years that had passed since both Francis and his father had deposited him into the 'care' of the De Vere's at Castle

Hedingham. Yes, Saxon was now a man but his pale complexion, the reason for his nickname and the cause of so many jokes in his youth, had meant that he'd appeared a great deal younger than his years belied. Sadly, this was in stark contrast to Francis whose dark looks and swarthy complexion had been passed down to him by his Norman forbears. Characteristics which in his youth had made him handsome but in middle age had ensured that he was both wrinkled and furrowed and showed each and every year of his age! Even so, once again Francis had delighted in teasing his cousin. Arguing, with a touch of irony, that age had treated Thomas well but had dealt with Francis poorly. Francis had laughed as he'd pointed out that 'Saxon' had 'obviously enjoyed a much easier life' and had 'clearly' had 'far less to worry about in life than he!'

Francis had spent an extremely enjoyable day in the company of his cousin but ultimately both he and the Staffords had politely refused the pardon which had been offered to them. Francis smiled as he remembered how he'd amused Saxon when he'd even gone so far as to invite him to join them! In reply, and pointing towards the small band of men who'd still remained in the church Saxon had laughed adding that considering his present circumstances, it was clear to him that Francis needed each and every man. In reply, Francis had quipped that in the 'unlikely' event that their numbers were to increase, could he then. 'count upon' both Saxon and his master Oxford, to join them? Smiling, Saxon had merely shrugged his shoulders and said 'Who can tell.'

In Yorkshire when Francis had recounted this conversation to his comrades, he'd been surprised to discover that there were those who'd spent some time with Oxford at court, who said that they wouldn't have been at all surprised if at some point he should defect to their cause! Apparently it'd become common knowledge within court circles that Oxford was become increasingly disenchanted with the King whom, he said, had failed to reward him for his efforts on the latter's behalf. Indeed since Bosworth both Oxford and the King had even been involved in a much publicised dispute over the size of Oxford's retinue, which was said to have outnumbered even that of the King's!

Francis smiled, it seemed to him that one of the themes of Tudor's reign was going to be his attempts to 'limit' his 'over powerful magnates and their private armies'. This didn't surprise Francis at all, especially when one considered that at Bosworth the intervention of such a private army had proved so conclusive to the battle's outcome! As he'd strengthened his hold on the Kingdom, Tudor, keen to curtail the power of the aristocracy had also gone so far as to outlaw the wearing of livery. In Francis's opinion this was only the thin end of the wedge, as Tudor went about destroying a way of life that had endured for centuries and upon which, much of the nobility still relied upon for their livelihood.

Thus, whilst in Yorkshire, Francis had resolved that should he ever again be in a position of strength, he would add Oxford to his list of potential dissenters.

Surprisingly, once it had become common knowledge that both Francis and his friends the Staffords had refused to submit to the King, Colchester had once again became a focal point for dissent. Indeed the tide of desertions soon turned into a steady stream of recruits as the Yorkists were joined by many men who, for a variety of reasons, had become disenchanted with the new government. Francis had to admit that the Stafford brothers had chosen their sanctuary well! For, in spite of its close proximity to Castle Hedingham, Colchester was ideally situated to attract a significant number of recruits. Previously, East Anglia had been an area which had been controlled by one of Richard's greatest allies the late Duke of Norfolk. As a result, many of Norfolk's men had joined them. In addition, they'd also received offers of support from those amongst both the lesser nobility and the gentry. Perhaps most surprising of all had been those promises of financial aid from a number of London merchants who, despite Tudor's 'championing of capitalism,' were, it seemed, willing to finance a Yorkist insurrection. These men, who normally avoided such conflicts, had been concerned that the new King's pro French foreign policy, Tudor had had to repay King Charles for supporting his invasion, would disrupt their trade with the Low Countries. Francis smiled as he considered just how 'principled' people became, when it came to their own livelihoods!

Within months of refusing the King's pardon, Francis, having gathered together sufficient resources and promises of support, felt that at last they had a realistic prospect of success. Unfortunately, Oxford and a number of others from amongst the aristocracy whom they'd approached, had refused to join their rebellion. Reluctantly, Francis had been forced to lead the army himself. Sending the Staffords into the Midlands, Francis had made for Yorkshire where he'd assembled his army on Bramham moor. Unfortunately, in spite of Francis's reputation, their army had lacked a figurehead and this, Francis was forced to concede, had also been a significant factor in their defeat. If successful they hadn't really got a viable alternative to the King. Many of Francis's men had even had the audacity to complain that Francis had 'duped' them into supporting the rebellion on the pretext that there were those within the nobility who would declare for them once the campaign had begun.

But here at Broughton Tower, after everything that had happened, Francis was not one to give up, not that he was in a position to do so even if he'd have wanted to! For significantly, after Bramham Moor, he'd been the rebel leader who hadn't been offered the King's pardon! That said, Francis had always had a 'never say die' attitude to life and there were still many Yorkshireman, whom he'd been forced to send home, who'd all said that they were willing to try again. And it was clear to Francis that although there were still significant numbers of Englishmen who were still willing to support a Yorkist restoration, presently they had no-one in particular to follow. Without a natural leader, someone who could assume the throne in Tudor's absence, what alternative could Francis now offer to the country? De La Pole, Richard's heir apparent, remained at Henry's court and, despite assurances to the contrary, he'd failed to act on their behalf. Lincoln was even purported to have said that in his opinion the crown was a 'poisoned chalice', the possession of which, or the desire to obtain it, having been the 'undoing' of many of his forbears. Presently therefore, the only realistic Plantagenet pretender was Edward Earl of Warwick, the son of the late George Duke of Clarence, Richard's elder brother. In fact, if one chose to ignore Clarence's attainder for treason, Edward was presently the rightful heir to the throne! As Francis pictured Warwick in his minds eye he sighed. The young boy was presently confined in the Tower of London having been imprisoned by a succession of Kings since his father's execution in 1478. Francis sighed again. He'd met the boy on a number of previous occasions and it was clear to him that Warwick suffered from some form of mental debilitation. When one considered the charm and intellect of both the boy's father and grandfather it was clear to Francis that, sadly, the present Earl of Warwick was not 'cut from the same cloth.' To put it plainly, the lad was a simpleton! It appeared as if Warwick, who'd been born out of a union of first cousins, suffered from that scourge of the aristocracy, a feebleness of mind brought on by interbreeding. Even Richard had suffered as a result of this affliction that was all too common amongst the 'ruling classes', he being disfigured by a curvature of his spine, whilst his only legitimate child Edward of Middleham, having been a weakling since birth. Indeed, as a result of this the boy had succumbed to a fever at a very young age. Francis sighed again, realistically even he couldn't put such a child as Warwick on the throne of England. One didn't have to look back too far in history to see the effect that such a feeble minded sovereign could have on his kingdom!

God knows his mind was in a whirl. Scratching his head, Francis sipped his brandy and pulled his cloak tighter about his shoulders and moved closer to the fire. Hopefully the alcohol may just slow his mind down a little bit, so he could at least enjoy a moment of clarity! Bramham Moor, Colchester, Bosworth, what was he to make of it all! A cold chill spread throughout his body as Francis considered that perhaps, after everything that they'd been through, this was finally the end! For, in truth, what prospect did they now have of a Yorkist restoration? In fact what Plantagenet did they actually have to restore?

Thomas Broughton, as always, was the perfect host, even in adversity. As he entered the solar he immediately offered Francis a refill.

Clearly noticing Francis's disquiet. Thomas smiled reassuringly as he said, 'Don't worry my friend you're safe here.'

Gazing out of the window he added, 'My men will forewarn us if anyone tries to come for you.' Laughing, Thomas added, 'In spite of the extraordinary price that Tudor's placed upon your head.'

Francis interjected, 'But what of Urswick,' he said, referring to the King's Cumbrian ally whose lands bordered that of the Broughtons.

As he refilled Francis's glass, smiling, Thomas replied, 'Don't worry my friend, Urswick's always been hated in these parts and anyway you'll never ever find a Cumbrian who's willing to betray another, whatever the price.'

As he savored the brandy, Francis remembered that Henry VI had actually been betrayed and captured there or thereabouts. He thought it politic however not to challenge his host.

Frowning Thomas asked, 'What troubles you Francis?'

Despite his friends sincerity, Francis couldn't respond to the question without both sarcasm and bitterness, 'And what Sir Thomas, do you think might be disturbing me today?'

Giving his friend no time in which to reply Francis continued, 'I've been defeated and as a consequence I've lost my best friend, my wife and even my titles. There's no prospect of a Plantagenet restoration.' He turned to his friend and asked him, 'Pray tell me what is there for me now?'

Thomas was a tall man and he seemed to tower over Francis who was seated by the fire in a comfortable yet deep chair. As he looked up at Thomas, who in spite of Francis's retort was still smiling, for once Francis felt extremely vulnerable. Both acid and brandy rose from Francis's stomach and he wondered if this reflux was caused by either fear or anger. No longer able to control his emotions Francis broke down. Embarrassed by this show of emotion, through tears Francis stuttered.

'What'll become of us all.'

Ever the optimist, Thomas replied, 'Who can tell what tomorrow will bring. But I'm sure that it'll all be fine.'

Angered by his friend's hopefulness, Francis bitterly exclaimed, 'Perhaps once you've experienced half of what I've had to endure, I may take account of your opinion.'

Wincing, Thomas was clearly stung by Francis's outburst. He did, however, remain the perfect host, apologising profusely for any offence that he may have caused as, backing away from Francis, he retreated from the chamber. Left alone, Francis quietly castigated himself for upsetting yet another friend and as he sat in silence he again began to cry, this time unashamedly.

On the following morning, despite having enjoyed no rest and having consumed much more than his fare share of brandy during the preceding evening, Francis rose early. As he entered the solar, rubbing his eyes, Francis was greeted by Thomas, who was cheerfully breakfasting with two strangers. From the state of their attire Francis felt that these guests must have ridden some distance to be there. One of the men, whose wrinkly face brightened as Francis entered the room seemed vaguely familiar. Francis didn't recognise the elderly gentleman's companion, who paid little attention to Francis, as he continued to hungrily devour his breakfast of cold meat and bread. Scratching his head, Francis tried to remember where he knew the old man from. Thankfully he was reminded as Thomas introduced the two men as, 'Sir Richard Harleston' and 'Thomas Fitzgerald, brother to the Earl of Kildare the lieutenant of the Irish pale.' Francis smiled and chided himself for not recognising Harleston sooner. Richard Harleston, a native of Lincolnshire, had been King Edward's governor in Jersey and had been archetypal in expelling the French from that island. Initially a loyal supporter of Edward, Harleston had been a retainer of the Duke of Clarence and had remained loyal to Clarence throughout his 'difficulties'. Soon after Clarence's execution, Harleston had fled from Edward's court, returning to his beloved Channel Islands. There he'd escaped censure by Edward who'd appreciated Harleston's loyalty to his brother. After Edward's death, Harleston had refused to come to terms with Richard whom, together with the Woodvilles, he'd blamed for Clarence's murder. Therefore, although Harleston hated anything remotely Lancastrian, he'd not been present at the battle of Bosworth.

In contrast to Francis, Harleston immediately recognised Francis. Without a moments hesitation he took Francis by the hand saying, 'Well at last we meet again friend.'

Francis had never before considered himself to be Harleston's friend, for he knew the truth behind Clarence's death. Before Francis had time to reply or to apologise, their host interrupted, 'What did I say yesterday Francis?'

Smiling, Thomas reminded Francis as he repeated his words, 'Who knows what tomorrow may bring.'

Francis was puzzled. Yes, he still considered Harleston to be a Yorkist and yes the Irish had always traditionally supported the House of York, but how could these men be of any use to them now?

It was almost as if Harleston was able to read Francis's thoughts as, smiling, he said. 'It seems Francis as if we've been thrown together by circumstances beyond our control.'

Continuing to smile, he added with obvious sincerity, 'I'm sure that you'll make a fine ally.'

Francis was intrigued, what did the old man mean? Perplexed, Francis asked Harleston, 'Ally in what? Yes I'd have appreciated your assistance some weeks ago but now I'm afraid you're too late,' Sighing, he added quietly, 'Thomas has probably told you what happened at Bramham Moor'.

Still smiling broadly Thomas replied on Harleston's behalf, 'Francis just listen to what Richard and Lord Fitzgerald have to say.' He paused, before becoming serious, he added, 'It changes everything.'

Francis couldn't help but remain cynical. How could these two men be of any use to them? And anyway where had they both been when Francis and his men had needed them most?

The answer to Francis's questions came in the form of an inordinately long story that was both complex, yet intriguing. Throughout its telling Francis constantly interrupted both men as he sought clarification, that what they were saying was in fact true. Harleston and Fitzgerald were both obviously experienced in recounting the tale. Patiently they answered all of Francis's questions, however obvious or simple they seemed. And as the story unfolded, Francis was able to slowly piece together the events from his own perspective at both King Edward and Richard's court. As the two men spoke Francis remembered how towards the end of his life, the Duke of Clarence had become increasingly paranoid. Apparently Clarence, believing that Edward was illegitimate and that he was the rightful King, had prophesied his own murder at the hands of his brother's allies. Moreover, fearing for the life of his child and only heir Clarence had allegedly sent his infant son abroad and into the care of the Irish, replacing him with a changeling! As the story slowly unfolded, in spite of how incredulous it all seemed, Francis, against his better judgment slowly began to believe it! As he listened in awe, Francis castigated himself for finding such a tale plausible and he could only wonder if it was just merely wishful thinking on his part. But even if he played 'Devils advocate' and attempted to renounce the story as an untruth, Francis would soon find himself once again believing the tale! Harleston the voice of reason, whilst Fitzgerald's Irish brogue sounded almost musical as he 'passionately', 'Told his tale.'

Harleston began the story and Fitzgerald, who was clearly an excellent orator, finished it. Indeed ultimately it was some hours before they all emerged from the solar, but when they did, Francis felt both refreshed and invigorated, his mind clear, instilled with a renewed confidence, for now it seemed that they'd got both their figurehead and sufficient financial and military aid to go with it! Francis smiled, for once again it appeared as if he'd soon be in a position to defeat Tudor and supplant him with a Plantagenet.

'The Earl of Warwick who is imprisoned in the Tower, is a changeling. The real Earl is in Ireland. He was taken there as a baby by Harleston on the orders of the Duke of Clarence who, predicting his own murder, understood just how important his son would become to the future of England'.

As Francis recounted the tale to Ned, his friend laughed as he pointed out that Francis's story was preposterous. 'Have you been drinking again?' Ned asked before adding with a serious note, 'Come Francis surely these are the arguments of desperate men. Who'll ever believe you?'

Francis understood his friends dubiousness but, undaunted, he went on to tell Ned the story in its entirety, just as it'd been recounted to him.

When Francis had finished, Ned was still not convinced. Francis could appreciate this, for Ned hadn't spent the time at court that he had. Francis did, however, manage to placate his friend somewhat when he told him that he too would only truly be convinced once he'd been given the opportunity to meet and to question the boy.

Excitedly Francis did, however, point out that Richard's sister Margaret, the dowager Duchess of Burgundy, had already met the lad and even she was said to have been convinced as to his authenticity. Francis added that it'd been this above all else that had finally convinced him, for how could the boys own aunt be wrong! Indeed, Francis pointed out, Clarence had always been Margaret's favorite brother and she'd always shown a great deal of interest in both him and his family. In fact she'd known them all intimately. Apparently, upon questioning the child, she was said to have been convinced that his story was true. Since meeting the child Margaret had convinced her son-in-law, the Holy Roman Emperor Maximillian, that the boy was the rightful heir to the throne of England. As such, Maximillian had agreed to fund an invasion force so that her nephew could return to England to claim his throne. Apparently, the Emperor was even involved in negotiations with Martin Schwartz, for it was hoped that the German mercenary, who was famous throughout the world for his military prowess, and who had never lost a battle, could be persuaded to lead the expedition.

Francis smiled as he told Ned to ready himself, 'For they're expecting us in Dublin, we're going to meet the future King, Edward V!'

Chapter 32
June 1487. Foulney Island Cumbria.

Thankfully, the conditions that greeted the Yorkist invasion force, when it finally made landfall at Foulney Island on the northern shore of Morecombe Bay, were for that area of Cumbria, unusually benign. As always the poor sailor, Francis had been doubly pleased. Firstly, during their short voyage, as a result of fine weather, he not suffered too badly from sea sickness and secondly, the men, superstitious as always, had seen the excellent conditions as an extremely good omen. Especially when one considered that those who were well acquainted with that location had earlier pointed out the areas reputation for appalling weather, whatever the season.

Francis, who'd been somewhat perplexed when the plan to invade England via another 'island' had first been suggested, was amused when he finally saw for himself that Foulney 'Island' wasn't actually an island at all! It was, in fact, a small spit of land that projected out into Morecombe Bay from its northernmost shore.

Foulney Island had a fearsome reputation and was reputed to be the 'windiest place' in all of the British Isles and what's more, it'd been described by those who knew it as a 'barren wilderness'. As a result, there had been a great deal of discussion once it had been suggested that the Island may be a suitable place for their small invasion force to come ashore. Ultimately, and after much debate, in the absence of any other viable alternative, the Yorkist command had finally decided to risk a landing on the 'island'.

For all of those potential problems raised by an invasion of England centred upon Cumbria, that location did afford them a number of distinct advantages. By coming ashore at such a remote and inaccessible spot, Francis and his comrades hoped to catch the King unprepared, just as he himself had done so in 1485 when he'd landed in South Wales. Indeed, in making for Morecombe Bay they'd all gambled on the fact that neither Henry nor his generals would ever have predicted that their invasion force would make landfall so far to the north and in an area that was extremely dangerous, especially when one considered both the prevailing weather conditions and the geography of the land. Treacherous currents and frequent offshore storms and squalls could easily scatter and destroy a small fleet. Moreover, once ashore their army wouldn't be entirely free of risk. The shifting sands of Morecombe Bay were riddled with perilous quicksands and were washed with tides that could quickly, and with little warning, turn and outrun even the fastest horse! In addition to this, both Lancashire and Cumbria were extremely sparsely populated with little in the way of cultivated farmland. As such, foraging for the needs of a large body of men would be extremely difficult. Thus, in choosing Foulney Island they'd all hoped that the King and his allies, who were expecting their invasion that summer, would never have dreamt that it would be centered upon the northern edge of Morecombe Bay and, as such, the Yorkist command had gambled that Henry and his men wouldn't have taken any serious steps in the area to prepare for it.

Shaking his head, Francis couldn't quite believe their good fortune. Yes, although in many ways the area was clearly unsuitable, perhaps perversely this location was at the same time 'ideal' for their purposes. Firstly it was far to the north of Tudor's traditional power base, his ancestral lands in South Wales, and secondly, should they succeed in getting their men ashore unscathed, a relatively short march would bring them over the Pennines to the head of Wensleydale, an area that was still extremely sympathetic to their cause. Thus, after much wrangling, it had finally been decided that the northern shore of Morecombe Bay was perhaps the best location at which to attempt a landing and create a beachhead. From there it was hoped that they'd be able to advance far into England before Tudor and his allies were able to mobilize against them, thereby giving their army precious time to recruit much needed additional troops.

As their fleet entered the small yet deep natural harbour that was located towards the land ward side of Foulney island, it passed close by a castle that was sited upon another island which bore its name. Piel Island was another spit of land that projected out into Morecombe bay. However, in contrast to its immediate neighbor Foulney, Piel Island did deserve its name, when twice daily the rising tide would cut it off from the mainland. Thankfully Piel Castle, which was well sited to oppose any landing upon Foulney Island, remained eerily silent as their small fleet slipped by it on waters that were both clear and calm. Blinking in the bright sunlight Francis smiled as he noticed that, for the first time in many days, John De La Pole's brow was no longer furrowed and creased, in what had been an almost permanent frown. Francis knew that the cause of his friend's extreme anxiousness had been both the danger and the complexity of the gargantuan quest upon which they were all embarked. Indeed, for once John appeared quite relaxed and, like Francis, was clearly extremely relieved at their good fortune in entering the bay unmolested, on one of those rare occasions when weather conditions were benign. Francis smiled again, he'd long since forgiven John for his reticence in supporting them in their 'earlier schemes'. Indeed, having spent some time with John in the preceding weeks, Francis now appreciated the fact that John was an extremely practical man who was, like Francis, very much a realist. After Bosworth, with Richard dead and his army defeated, Francis could appreciate now why in 1485 John had felt that his earlier nomination as Richard's heir apparent, in real terms, had meant nothing! For they all knew that in medieval England political power was solely reliant upon an individual's strength of arms, this at the expense of man's rights, be they either lawful or hereditary. Thus, after Bosworth, if John had dared to challenge Tudor's claim to the throne, he could have easily been forgiven for not expecting much in the way of support. Moreover, in England at that time there'd been a number of men who were far more powerful and influential than John. Men who would undoubtedly have challenged any claim made by him or by others on his behalf. For, at that point in time, in real terms John had been extremely weak both politically and militarily. Yes, in addition to being Richard's heir, he was an aristocrat and a man of breeding, who also held a plausible claim to the throne through his mother, Richard's sister. But at that time, in political terms he was a 'lightweight', a relative 'unknown' and sadly a person of no real substance. Moreover, arguably there had also been those alive who'd had even stronger hereditary claims to the throne than he, the young Earl of Warwick and the late Duke of Buckingham's son, to name but two. And in addition to them, there were others still who had much more in the way of political muscle. Men who themselves were said to covet the crown. Those of noble blood who, despite having lesser hereditary claims to the throne, enjoyed much more in the way of wealth and power than their younger and far less experienced counterparts.

Francis's smile developed into a very wide grin, for now things were very different indeed! 1487 had been a year of great change. King Henry's policy of conciliation was coming to an end, as by the second year of his reign, the King, who'd successfully dealt with a number of challenges to his authority, was endeavoring to become far less reliant upon the old nobility.

Having strengthened his grip on the throne, Henry had sought to secure his tenure on it by tying the destiny of his own family to that of the Yorkists, by marrying King Edward's eldest daughter, Elizabeth of York. Although, interestingly, to date he'd refused to have her crowned as his Queen! Once married Henry had wasted no time in siring a son and heir. Francis scoffed as he remembered how, as part of yet another Tudor 'publicity exercise,' Henry had even had the audacity to name

445

the child Arthur. The King no doubt trying to evoke memories of that mythical King who was said to have united the country against various invaders during the dark ages, which had followed the Roman Empires withdrawal from England. Francis smiled again, now he truly believed that in trying to establish a monarchy that was independent of the aristocracy so early on in his reign, Henry was trying to run before he could walk. As a result, by 1487 it'd become clear to many amongst the old nobility that their influence at court and in government was diminishing. Moreover, it seemed as if Henry was also intent on targetting those who were said to have any claim to the throne themselves. John De La Pole, as a potential pretender to the throne, and in spite of the King's earlier pardon, had slowly begun to realise that his 'days at court' and, not wishing to be melodramatic about it, even 'his days on earth' were numbered! Rumour had it that Henry hoped to round up all of those whose claim to the throne rivaled his own and by inventing 'trumped up' charges, one by one, Tudor hoped to isolate and destroy all potential opposition to his rule. Consequently, John had begun to correspond with both Francis and a number of other Yorkist exiles and he had finally joined them in Ireland, once it'd become clear to him that the King was intent upon his eventual destruction. Surprisingly, John had enlisted only on the understanding that he was there to assist them in securing the restoration of his house. From the outset he'd stipulated, in the strongest of terms, that he did not want the crown for himself and was merely satisfied with any rewards that were offered to him by the new King. Francis smiled again as he remembered how this 'revelation' had come as a great relief to him, as from the outset he'd always worried that they'd be unable to satiate the ambitions of both John De La Pole and the young Earl of Warwick.

Despite his age and relative inexperience, as with many of his genre, John was extremely learned in military matters. Moreover, potentially he commanded significant support amongst both the English gentry and the aristocracy. John's defection to them had therefore been a massive coup and at the time Francis had pointed out to his coconspirators that it spoke volumes for their prospects of success.

Since he'd joined their army, both John and Francis had become the firmest of friends. Francis had met John previously at Richard's court, but this had only been on a few occasions and the two men had never really spoken about any matters of importance. Recently however, Francis had discovered that they both had much in common. Even now, as they arrived at Foulney Island, it was almost as if his new friend was able to read his mind. Studying the unoccupied castle, John echoed Francis's thoughts as he exclaimed, 'With only a small number of men and sufficient ordnance our enemies could have easily prevented us from coming ashore at this place.' Francis agreed, as he added that he hoped that this would be the first of a number of miscalculations made by the King and his allies, errors of judgment that would 'hopefully' see them, 'successful in their present enterprise.'

Thankfully, upon their arrival in English waters, their ships had been greeted not by cannon balls, but by the squeals and squawks of the numerous gulls and other seabirds, who'd circled excitedly overhead. Francis smiled again, it seemed as if Tudor wasn't the only one who'd got it wrong. Many of these stupid birds, who'd joined them far out in the Irish sea, had only accompanied them on the last leg of their voyage, after they'd all wrongly assumed that they were following fishing vessels and not an invasion fleet! That said, Francis's smile soon turned to a frown as he considered that, given the limited size and the small number of their boats, perhaps the birds could be forgiven for their mistake after all! John too must have shared Francis's misgivings for he said, 'Don't worry Francis, I'm sure that as soon as news spreads of our landing many more will join us.'

Despite his renowned 'pessimism', Francis could only agree with his friend as, in his minds eye, he recounted all of the numerous messages of support that he'd received from England. Offers of both financial and military assistance from those who'd given him 'their word' that they would join the Yorkist army at the 'earliest opportunity'. Francis was also able to comfort himself with the thought that many who'd gone before them had succeeded with far less than they had at present. Francis smiled again as he remembered how in 1470 both Edward and Richard had landed at Ravenspur with only a handful of men, yet within weeks they'd both succeeded in wresting control of the country from the Lancastrians. That said, the 'realist' in Francis was forced to concede that he'd always hoped to arrive in England with a much larger force and, worse still, at present the majority of their army consisted of poorly equipped and inexperienced Irish kerls, soldiers, if one could call them that, who'd been provided by their Irish ally, Gerald Fitzgerald the Earl of Kildare. Unfortunately, fearing an English invasion of Ireland, Kildare had only sent them men from the poorer contingents of his own army. The Earl choosing to retain his best troops for his defence of Ireland. Francis had tried in vain to convince Kildare that if their invasion of England was successful, his position in Ireland would be secure. Sadly, as it turned out Kildare had been unmoved by Francis's protestations and ultimately his only concession had been to send his brother Thomas, who was to command the Irish contingent. Francis smiled ruefully, for he knew that Thomas had always intended to join them anyway! Thomas Fitzgerald, Harleston's companion at Broughton Tower, had always been passionate in his support for their scheme. Indeed it was he to whom the Duke of Clarence had entrusted the safekeeping of his son, when he'd sent the young Earl of Warwick to Ireland in 1478. It was fair to say that since that date Thomas had effectively become the child's surrogate father, responsible not only for Warwick's physical well being but also for his education.

That said, even Francis was forced to concede that their Irish allies, quite the 'cheery bunch', were a welcome addition to their army. Despite their penchant for any form of intoxicating liquor and their resultant bawdiness and aggression, the Irishmen were, Francis felt, an asset to a camp that was often in need of lightening. Even Francis, one who'd often avoid merrymaking and dancing, was known to have performed the odd Irish jig, but only after he'd availed himself of his Irish comrades hospitality, which invariably came in the form of their whiskey! And it had always amused 'the devil' in Francis to see how this 'tomfoolery' would irritate their German allies and their commander the dour and surly Martin Schwartz.

Unfortunately, as it turned out, within their army the experienced and better equipped German mercenaries and English men-at-arms were very much in the minority.

From the outset Francis had always hoped that in both numbers and supplies their invasion force would have been all but self sufficient. In recent weeks however, it'd become painfully obvious to him that this wasn't going to be the case and their success would now depend, primarily, on the number of men that they could successfully recruit to their army, once they'd arrived upon English soil. Thus by the time that they'd finally left Ireland, Francis had estimated that they would have to be joined by a significant number of additional troops if they were to have any realistic chance of success. It was fair to say that Francis had worried about this constantly. Both he and John, when pressed to do so, had repeatedly assured their men that there were many from within England who'd promised to help them. Those who'd said that they would declare for the Yorkists and King Edward V, at the very first opportunity. If this help didn't materialise, what would their men's reaction be? As Francis scanned the barren shoreline for any signs of life, he shuddered. If they were able to convince all of the 'old Yorkists' to rise up on their behalf they'd have a good chance of defeating King Henry. But without the help of the Scropes, the Conyers and the Fitzhughs of this world, they would be facing a monumental task indeed!

At least, Francis reasoned, by arriving safely at Foulney Island they'd cleared the first hurdle! Francis smiled again, he'd never been the greatest of seamen and he'd been extremely relieved to find that their passage across the Irish Sea, a body of water with a fearsome reputation, had passed without incident. Once again, turning his back on Piel Castle, Francis took a moment to examine the small ship which had been his home for the past few days. As he did so, Francis breathed a sigh of relief. The cramped conditions aboard had not been conducive to good health and, as such, the boat was not really a place to be ill. Moreover, it would've been extremely unfortunate if the men had seen one of their leaders, a man whom they'd trusted with their life, to be both vulnerable to and weakened by seasickness.

Finally, and laboriously, the ships that had for the final leg of the journey been almost becalmed, drifted towards the shingle beach and weighed anchor close to the shoreline. The scene was almost ethereal. For once Francis felt much calmer as the sun warmed his face and, transfixed, he gazed down into the clear waters which sparkled in the bright sunlight. The sea's swell rose and fell as, lapping against the side of the boat, it ebbed backwards and forwards, wafting the vast swaths of dark seaweed that licked the pebbly shore. Its backdrop, the ghostly presence of the dark castle, strangely yet unexpectedly silent.

Their sailors had timed the landing to perfection and the rising sea level had granted their ships access to the small harbour that was situated to the land ward side of Foulney Island.

Francis was finally woken from his daydream with a start as the ships Captain, who was clearly impatient and all too aware of their present vulnerability, barked out his orders. Their longboats were to be lowered immediately to ensure that both the men and their provisions were brought ashore both quickly and efficiently. This before either the boats were cut off by the retreating tide, or they were attacked in what was effectively hostile country. John clapped Francis on the back and exclaimed in words that, once again, echoed Francis's sentiments.

'Francis, I do believe that Tudor's underestimated us.'

John laughed as he pointed towards the shore line that remained strangely silent. Despite the fine weather the bay was almost deserted, save that is for a few fishermen who were clearly not at all interested in their arrival! These men merely going about what must have been their normal routine of mending nets and pots, acting almost as if that day were no different from any other. Almost as if the invasion of England was a common occurrence that neither commanded nor deserved their interest!

John continued, 'I thought at the very least he'd have garrisoned the Castle, or would have posted pickets along the shoreline.' He smiled as he added, 'With little expense on his part, Henry could have caused a great deal of disruption to our plans.'

Francis could only agree with his companion although he, above all others, knew just how difficult it was to second guess where any invasion may or may not make landfall along the hundreds of miles of coastline that was mainland England! Francis sighed as he remembered how in 1485 he'd badly let Richard down. Wrongly assuming that Henry would attempt a landing on the south coast, when in fact Tudor and his men had come ashore many miles to the west in Pembrokeshire. Francis sighed again, albeit with the benefit of hindsight, it now seemed obvious to him that the Lancastrians would have always made for South Wales, Tudor's ancestral home.

But now the boot was squarely on the other foot and Francis grinned. He reasoned that anyone with a modicum of tactical awareness should, and would, have considered that a rebel landing here on the northern edge of Morecombe Bay, despite the obvious difficulties, would have been extremely likely. Especially when one considered that it was practically opposite their departure point Dublin Bay, it was an area in which the Broughton brothers had a number of significant connections and finally, and perhaps most important of all, it was a relatively short distance from there to Wensleydale and to Middleham.

It was fair to say that Francis was surprised yet pleased at their good fortune in finding the shoreline undefended. At the very least, one might have expected Henry to have posted lookouts at intervals along the coast. Men who, even if they weren't in a position to directly intervene in the landing, could at the very least have monitored and reported upon it.

Unless, of course, it was they who'd underestimated Tudor! Had the King cleverly disguised his spies as common fishermen! Francis chuckled to himself. No, it appeared to him that, for the time being at least, their landing would go both unreported and unopposed. Francis smiled again as he said to no-one in particular, 'First blood to us.'

Francis knew that from now on time would be their greatest ally. The longer it took for Tudor and his allies to mobilize against them, the greater the opportunity they'd have to recruit more men to their army.

Mindful that it was both he and John who'd 'repeatedly assured' their more dubious companions that making landfall at this location could be undertaken with 'little or no risk,' it was probably quite an understatement to say that Francis was 'greatly relieved.' That said, not wanting to gain himself a reputation for being a 'told you so' type,

Francis was careful not to share his thoughts with anyone else. As it turned out, both Francis and John smiled knowingly at each other as they quietly enjoyed this, their first victory, albeit it had been a bloodless one. Francis could only hope to God that it would be the first of many such successes.

That said, always the 'realist', Francis shivered as he considered that it may have been the case that Tudor, one who was usually so careful when it came to matters of finance, had in fact not miscalculated at all! Had the King decided that the dangers posed by their 'tiny' invasion force were so 'inconsequential', as not to be worthy of any expense on his part? As they stood by and watched their small army, if one were able to call it that, marshaled ashore by the seamen, John was grinning, almost as if they'd already wrested the crown from Tudor and his allies! Irked by his friends confidence which, in spite of their present good fortune, Francis felt was extremely premature, and frightened by the enormous task that lay in front of them, Francis remained silent as, smiling weakly, he tried to banish such thoughts from his mind. 'Realism' or 'borderline pessimism' was not what they needed at the present time!

Much had happened in the months that had followed the debacle that was now euphemistically referred to by King Henry and his cronies as the 'battle of Bramham Moor'. The depression, brought about in Francis by what he'd understood at the time to have been both a lasting and final defeat, had surprisingly and unexpectedly been replaced with an optimism. An optimism rekindled once Francis had been made aware of the possibility that the 'true' Earl of Warwick was at large in Ireland and, as a consequence, the boy who was imprisoned within the Tower of London was merely a stooge. On receiving the news Francis had made his way directly to Ireland, keen as he was to meet this lad, whom both Harleston and Thomas Fitzgerald had assured him was the late Duke of Clarence's son. A revelation which effectively made the boy 'the lawful Plantagenet heir of England.' Ned, as always, had advised caution. He'd asked Francis to wait, to take time to consider his response rather than throwing himself wholeheartedly into the scheme. A scheme that, 'if found to be false,' would make both him and all of those other 'learned' and 'respected' men who'd accepted the tale, appear to be 'extremely foolish' and not a 'little desperate.' Francis, who in Harleston and Fitzgerald's story had seen, 'just the slightest glimmer of light at the end of his own personal tunnel of depression,' not for the first time in his life, chose to ignore the advice of another. Arguing firstly that 'as a man with a price on his head' he had nothing, 'to keep him in England' and secondly, and perhaps more importantly, that he was desperate to discover if in fact 'the lad' in Ireland was the true Earl of Warwick, or if he was, a mere impostor.

Francis chuckled to himself since he too had heard the story which had been publicised throughout Europe, Tudor had done all in his power to prove that the lad in Ireland was a fraud. He'd even gone so far as to name the 'impostor' as one 'Lambert Simnall', a strange and unusual name. Tudor and his cronies maintained that Simnall was the son of a carpenter from the university town of Oxford. According to them the lad had been coached and instructed in his deceit by a priest who went by the name of Richard Simons. Tudor even maintained that he'd been successful in arresting Simons. Ironically, when it came to the lads true guardian the Lancastrians had not been far off the mark. When he'd arrived in Ireland, Francis had discovered that at the behest of Thomas Fitzgerald it was in fact Richard Simons brother, William, who'd been the young Prince's chaperone. Unfortunately for Tudor, in contrast to his brother Richard, William Simons was both fit and well and was at large in County Kildare with his young charge. Tudor, who'd effectively 'kidnapped' William's brother, had wasted no time in placing Richard Simons before an ecclesiastical court that had been convened at Canterbury in the February of that year. Not surprisingly, according to Francis's spies at court, Richard Simons had been convicted after he'd allegedly confessed to his part in the plot and had publicly denounced the Prince in Ireland as a 'fake'. Interestingly however, once convicted Richard had been 'spirited away' and to date no-one knew of his present whereabouts. This had surprised everyone, for surely one who'd been found guilty of treason would in normal circumstances have been subjected to the full might of both lay and canon law That is they'd have been excommunicated by the church and then publicly hung drawn and quartered. As it turned out, rather than suffering execution, Richard Simons had mysteriously disappeared! Francis smiled, Tudor must have been extremely fearful of what Richard Simons may have said given the chance, for he'd clearly gone to extraordinary lengths to keep both the trial and the subsequent punishment quiet. Francis smiled again, in his opinion this was yet further proof, if one needed it, that the story was true.

Tudor had even gone so far as to parade his 'Earl of Warwick', throughout the streets of London. The King's squires vociferously declaring that their prisoner was the Duke of Clarence's 'one and only son.' Unfortunately for the King, it'd soon became clear that he'd seriously underestimated both the mood and the intellect of the Londoners. Those who perhaps above all others had always adored the pomp and extravagance of the Yorkist court and had also profited from many years of a stable Yorkist government. These people, who were now beginning to feel the pinch of Tudor austerity, must have hankered after those halcyon days of both Edward and Richard's reigns, for they'd heckled and booed the small procession. Many from amongst the onlookers had even gone so far as to proclaim that Tudor was in no position to preach or dictate to them, nor indeed had he the right to question the pedigree and background of either the lad in Ireland or his prisoner in London. For as many had pointed out, Tudor himself 'had been in exile,' when the late Duke of Clarence had 'seen fit to send his child abroad and to replace him with a changeling.' The King was, they said, therefore, in no position to comment on the matter! As a result, the 'publicity stunt,' which many had seen as a 'desperate' attempt to disprove the story, had backfired and ultimately more, and not less, Englishman had believed that the boy in Ireland was in fact the real Earl of Warwick!

Thus Francis, keen himself to meet and to question the boy, had accompanied both Harleston and Fitzgerald when they'd returned to Ireland, to County Kildare and to the Fitzgerald's Castle at Maynooth. Here Francis had been both delighted and privileged to be introduced to, 'Edward Plantagenet Earl of Warwick,' who many said was 'The rightful King of England.'

Physically the young lad was, in Francis's opinion, unmistakably a Yorkist prince. Edward was of an extremely handsome countenance with the chiseled features, golden locks and smile that reminded Francis both of the boy's father and of his grandfathers. Indeed, in Francis's opinion, on looks alone the boy could easily have passed for a prince of the royal blood. Francis had truly believed that when the people of England were finally given the opportunity to see Edward, many would be convinced of his provenance.

Once Francis had had the opportunity of speaking with the prince at length, he'd been doubly convinced that the boy was the genuine article and was indeed the 'true' Earl of Warwick. Despite having spent most of his life in Ireland, the young Edward had inherited all of that charm and strength of character for which his forbears were famous. When he'd first been granted an audience with the prince, a meeting which had taken place in the great hall at Maynooth Castle, listening to the boy, Francis had seemingly been spirited back to a time when the Nevilles and Plantagenets had ruled supreme. It was almost as if Francis himself had been a child again, serving his master, 'The Earl of Warwick', at his table in the great hall at Middleham Castle. If the prince had had this effect on Francis, one who was renowned for a realism that verged on pessimism, what effect would he have on a population who were already beginning to tire of the dour King Henry and his miserly policies?

As one would expect of a person of his pedigree, Edward Earl of Warwick was well versed in etiquette, manners and in learning. That said, Francis was the first to admit that anyone could be coached in such matters. But throughout his life Francis had met many people who were said to be of the 'royal blood' and perhaps above all others he knew that no matter how well an individual was trained, no-one could ever hope to replicate those qualities exhibited by men who were truly 'born to rule.' When asked to describe this quality Francis always found it extremely difficult to define and could never quite express what it was. But there was an 'air of difference,' he said, 'about royalty,' a 'something' that although 'indescribable,' set them apart from others. When pressed for an answer Francis could only refer to it as, 'The divine right of Kings.' In Francis's opinion the 'Irish' Prince Edward exuded this quality.

Once in Ireland, Francis had been both surprised and concerned to find that neither Harleston, Simons nor either of the Fitzgerald brothers seemed to have any plans or proposals in relation to the prince's immediate future. In fact it was they who'd sought out and now looked towards Francis, a man 'experienced' in such matters, to advise them on how best they should proceed. Francis had bewailed the fact that they'd not approached him sooner, telling them that he wished, 'with all his heart' that they had come forward when during the Bramham Moor campaign he'd had sufficient troops to prevail but had lacked a suitable 'figurehead'. Upon finally meeting the prince and becoming convinced of his authenticity, Francis had thrown his arms up in the air in frustration as he'd exclaimed that he now had his 'figurehead', but sadly he no longer had the requisite troops with which to reclaim the English throne!

Many amongst their number had been keen to strike at once and had urged for an immediate invasion of England. They'd argued that once upon the English mainland they'd be able to count not only on the support of those in England who'd risen up on their behalf in Francis's rebellion, but also on those who hadn't participated in that insurgence, but who had now apparently pledged their support for Clarence's son. Francis had, however, disagreed with his new friends, urging them to ignore those precedents which had been set by both King Edward's invasion of England in 1470 and that of Henry Tudor in 1485. Francis, who'd been directly involved in both campaigns, did concede that both men had landed with few men of their own, counting instead on their ability to raise sufficient troops once they'd safely come ashore. And yes, both Edward and Henry had eventually prevailed. But on each occasion, he said, it'd been an 'extremely close run thing.' In 1470 Edward having initially been so weak that he'd had to rely on deception to keep his hopes alive, assuring the people of York that he'd returned not to recover the throne, but his ducal rights. Francis had to remind his comrades that even after Edward had recruited sufficient troops to seriously challenge Warwick and the Lancastrians, his army had still been outnumbered on the two occasions that he'd taken to the field. The battles of Barnet and Tewkesbury could therefore, Francis said, have easily gone either way, as could that of Bosworth! Moreover, Francis had also pointed out that at that point in their lives both Henry Tudor and Edward had had nothing more to lose and both had faced a stark choice, a life in perpetual exile or a 'do or die' attempt to take the throne. Conversely, Francis maintained, their Prince Edward was still a youngster who was in good health and had time on his side. He was safe in Ireland where the Yorkists still controlled the Irish pale through the person of the Earl of Kildare. Francis had laughed as he'd pointed out that even after he'd secured the throne of England, it had been Tudor who'd humiliatingly been forced into making peace overtures towards Kildare and not, as one would have expected, the other way around! Francis had also pointed out to those who'd been keen on the idea of an immediate invasion, that although Tudor's popularity in England was said to be waning, this as people began to appreciate just how much his miserly domestic policies and his proposed alliance with the French would adversely affect them, Tudor was still very much the 'new King' who was the antithesis of both Edward and after him Richard. As a result, when it came to the question of the success of his Government, there were many who were still undecided. Francis had argued that it was only a matter of time before the population of England began to tire of the new regime and then, once they'd had the opportunity of recruiting a 'great army', they'd strike.

Although at that time there had been some cause for optimism, Francis had pointed out to his new comrades that, regrettably, any proposal to invade England with what resources they had at that time was really out of the question. This because they couldn't realistically expect any meaningful support in England from those who'd only recently rebelled themselves and had only just received the King's pardon! These men were, Francis said, sick and tired of war and moreover any additional misdemeanors on their part would mean certain execution and attainder should their campaign result in defeat. Francis had also been forced to admit that many of these men were still angry with the Yorkist leadership, rankled both at the way in which they'd felt let down after repeated assurances of support during the Bramham Moor campaign had come to naught and also after they'd been abandoned to their fate when many of their leaders had chosen to take flight. In contrast to the Fitzgerald brother's, Irishmen, who were apt to let there emotions run away with them, and to the deeply religious Harleston, who felt that with 'God on their side' they could 'prevail with few men,' Francis had based his judgments on sound common sense. 'Yes', he was as 'passionate' as anyone in his 'desire' to see Tudor deposed and replaced by one of their own, but 'surely they must all be able to see that it was in their interests to 'proceed with extreme caution.' This was, after all, 'going to be their last realistic opportunity to topple the fledgling Tudor dynasty.' Francis had gone on to explain that in his opinion they had a number of options open to them. Firstly, for the time being at least, they could stay put in Ireland and wait and see if Tudor was able to summon up enough courage and troops to invade Ireland and confront them on 'ground of their own choosing.' Alternatively, they could invade England, but only once sufficient troops had been raised, an army whose size alone would ensure a realistic prospect of success, regardless of the support which they may or may not receive once they were safely on English soil.

As the weeks and then months had gone by, it'd become obvious to them that Tudor, as cautious and as fearful of defeat as ever, was stubbornly refusing to be drawn into Ireland. This despite the fact that the Fitzgeralds regularly taunted him with proclamations challenging both his authority over them and his right to the throne of England. The new King remained in England whilst his spies no doubt kept him informed of events across the Irish Sea in Dublin. Thus, ultimately the Yorkists were forced to concede that Tudor had neither the desire nor the wherewithal to invade Ireland and it was they who would have to 'take the fight to him.'

Luckily, within a relatively short space of time the Yorkists had been successful in raising a number of troops. Unfortunately however, when it came time to make their move, the army was still much smaller than Francis had hoped and, worryingly, it was comprised of many men who were both inexperienced and ill equipped. Thus, as their fleet had left Dublin Bay, Francis had seriously doubted that it would be large enough for their purposes and even he was forced to concede that the success of their enterprise now depended largely upon how many men could be persuaded to join them once they'd finally landed on English soil.

Once he'd arrived in Ireland and had satisfied himself of the authenticity of the Earl of Warwick, Francis's first task, after he'd convinced his comrades to 'stay their hand,' had therefore been to secure sufficient monetary and military support for their purposes. Francis had immediately written to Richard's sister Mary the dowager Duchess of Burgundy, asking for her support either in a proposed invasion of England or in the defence of Ireland should Tudor choose to invade. Thankfully, despite having left England for Burgundy many years before, Mary still took a keen interest in English politics. A fiercely proud woman, the Duchess had repeatedly and vociferously represented her family's interests on the European stage. The Duke of Clarence was said to have been Mary's personal favorite amongst all of her other siblings and the prospect that his only son was at large and was not, as she'd previously been led to believe, a feeble minded captive in the Tower of London, had apparently, 'brought joy to Mary's heart.'

In an effort to maximize any potential Burgundian support, Francis had decided to take the Prince with him to Burgundy to make a personal plea to the lad's aunt. This would give Mary the opportunity of meeting with her nephew again as, up to that point, she'd been reluctant to make the hazardous journey to Ireland herself. Apparently, when as a young woman Mary had traveled to Burgundy to marry the late Duke, she'd had a terrible voyage and had very nearly been shipwrecked in a great storm. As a result, she was said to fear the dangers of sea travel more than anything else. Even though she was desperate to see her nephew again, the Duchess could not be persuaded to make the voyage to Ireland. This in spite of the fact that in his many letters to her, Francis had extolled to her the virtues of travel in 'modern' ships that were now far more safe and comfortable than they had been previously. Thus, Francis had decided to take Prince Edward back to the Burgundian court to meet with his aunt, their potential benefactor, once again. Thankfully, as Francis had earlier predicted, the journey to Burgundy had been relatively uneventful. The resultant benefits secured, however, were extraordinary and surpassed anything that they'd previously hoped for! As anticipated, Mary had been overjoyed to meet with her nephew again. The Duchess, who was said to have cried when she'd first laid eyes on the Prince, had become convinced of his authenticity. Francis had expected some support from the Burundians, but happily the assistance which they'd subsequently received far outweighed that which had been anticipated. It would have been nice to have imagined that this had been due solely to Mary's philanthropy. But in reality this was not the case and, as with many things in life, self interest played its part. Not that Francis was complaining, of course, for any help, wherever it came from, was greatly appreciated.

The Duchess's son-in-law Maximillian, the Holy Roman Emperor, had recently come to terms with the French after many years of war. Throughout his wars with the French, Maximillian, who had no standing army of his own, had been heavily reliant upon German and Flemish mercenaries. Necessary in times of war, these soldiers of fortune were problematical in times of peace. When redundant, the unoccupied and unpaid mercenaries caused chaos and mayhem wherever they went, lawlessness being the only means by which they could earn a living. Thus, Francis's proposals assisted both Mary and Maximillian in solving, what was to them, a significant problem. By providing Francis and the Prince with troops, the Duchess and her son-in-law, in one fell swoop, were able to rid themselves of a significant number of their most violent and ruthless citizens!

Consequently, once he'd arrived in Burgundy, Francis had been given the dubious honour of being introduced to the 'charismatic', 'intelligent', 'illustrious' and unfortunately the 'arrogant', 'selfish' and 'stubborn' German mercenaries commander, Martin Schwartz! Schwartz was renowned throughout the Western world as 'the greatest soldier who had ever lived.' Of humble birth, the German had apparently declined the opportunity of a life in the priesthood and had chosen instead to ply his trade throughout Europe as a soldier of fortune. Schwartz had fought in many of the conflicts that had plagued western society in the latter half of the fifteenth century and it had not been long before Schwartz's remarkable military abilities had been recognised. As a result, despite his lowly birth, Schwartz had received a number of lucrative commissions and by 1487 he was seen throughout Europe as an expert in the art of warfare. Schwartz's pedigree spoke for itself and the record of the German's victories, many of which had been secured in the face of almost insurmountable odds, were extremely impressive indeed. Upon meeting Schwartz, when it came to 'matters military' Francis had not been disappointed and the German was everything that he'd been described as and more! That said, Francis was frankly astounded to see how a commoner was able to defy convention. Despite his lowly birth, Schwartz expected to be treated almost as if he himself were the King! On their first meeting, Francis had been shocked to see how Schwartz refused to show due deference to his betters and had treated the Emperor Maximillian and the Duchess Mary almost as if they were his peers! As a result, Francis, who placed great store in etiquette and manners, especially when it came to respecting those of noble birth, had immediately taken a dislike to the

German. Although it had soon become clear to Francis that Schwartz was unconcerned when it came to other people's opinion of him. Having said that, Francis knew that when it came to the German he would have to control his feelings and would have to find a way to work with Schwartz, because militarily he was a genius! Once he'd had the opportunity of speaking at length with Schwartz, Francis soon began to realise that with such an 'icon' on their side, even with fewer men than they'd hoped for, they were far better placed to succeed in their venture.

Thankfully, when Francis and the Prince finally returned to Ireland, they did so at the head of an army of some three thousand German and Flemish mercenaries! Indeed, once back in Dublin they'd both been delighted to receive the congratulations of their comrades, all of whom had assumed that it was Francis's negotiations alone that had secured such a windfall. Both Francis and the Prince had been raised aloft by the most enthusiastic amongst their Irish allies, who had then carried them all the way from the harbour side to Dublin Castle. Schwartz, who knew only too well the real reason for the Emperor's generosity, had surprised Francis when upon seeing this he'd remained silent, merely winking at Francis and smiling.

That night as they'd all discussed their plans for the forthcoming campaign, Francis had once again voiced his concerns that in spite of the Burgundian's support, they would still require far more troops with which to mount a successful invasion of England. 'One had to,' he argued, 'learn the lessons from Tudor's coup' of 1485. For Henry's invasion had very nearly failed for want of support amongst the population at large. Tudor had landed in Wales with an Army that consisted of mainly foreigners and mercenaries, a body of men that were not too dissimilar to their own! In Tudor's case the success of his invasion had been reliant upon that support which he'd secured once he'd landed. Tudor's expectations of additional assistance had, of course, been reasonable, especially when one considered the general ill feeling and discontent felt by many towards Richard's government, which by 1485 had pervaded throughout the realm. Moreover, in the months that had preceded his invasion Tudor had mounted an extremely successful 'propaganda' campaign, accusing Richard of being some kind of 'monster', 'guilty' of the most 'heinous' crimes against his 'foe's', 'friend's' and even against his 'own family'. In 1485 Tudor had also counted upon the support of his father-in-law Thomas Lord Stanley and Stanley's brother William. A powerful family, the Stanleys had been in a position to put a large number of experienced and well armed cavalry and infantry into the field. As it had turned out however, even Tudor had very nearly failed to secure that support and it had only been at the eleventh hour, when all had seemed lost to him, that the Stanleys had made their crucial intervention on his behalf! In Dublin, Francis had pointed out to his comrades that he was determined that they wouldn't repeat Tudor's error of judgment. If Tudor, despite his purposely slow progress through Wales and the borders, areas that were his ancestral homelands and were historically very pro Lancastrian, had failed to secure the support that he'd so desperately needed, then what hope would there be for the Yorkists in 1487! For they would be landing in what was now a hostile country, amongst people who were sick and tired of civil war and who, thanks to Tudor propaganda, still remembered the 'tyrant' Richard who was said to have 'cruelly slain' his own nephews! The rebel leaders had to appreciate, Francis said, that many of the old Yorkist Lords were now either dead, attainted or exiled, deprived of both their money and their men. Moreover, many other potential supporters had been amongst those who'd recently been pardoned by Tudor. As a result, these men were bound to be fearful of risking all again so soon after the disappointment and defeats at Bosworth and at Bramham Moor.

Therefore, in spite of their good fortune in securing additional Burgundian support, once Francis and the Prince were back in Ireland, the rebels had soon found themselves in quite a difficult position. On the face of it they hadn't sufficient troops with which to mount a successful invasion of England and in all honesty they couldn't have expected vast numbers of men to flock to their banner once they'd landed. However, as the days and weeks passed they soon began to realise that staying put in Ireland was no longer a viable alternative either. As a result, Francis had been forced to rethink their position. Schwartz's mercenaries had only been paid for a short campaign and no-one within the rebel command had the resources to pay them once Maximillian and Mary's money ran out! Indeed, within days of arriving in Ireland, with money in their pockets many of the mercenaries had already deserted them! Moreover, poor discipline amongst the continental soldiers had meant that the Irish, who'd initially greeted them with such enthusiasm, were soon quite keen to see the back of Schwartz's men.

Both Francis and his comrades had therefore been forced to conclude that they would have to invade England as soon as possible and certainly before that summer's campaigning season was over. The only concessions made to those who'd still advised caution had been twofold. Firstly, they would delay the invasion long enough to enable

Francis to write to any potential allies in England asking for their support and secondly, they would crown their King in Ireland.

Consequently, Francis had dispatched numerous letters to individuals, to cities and to towns, requesting their assistance at some point in the 'not too distant future.' Unfortunately, these letters had had to be purposely vague, as Francis could not afford to give away any dates nor reveal any pattern that may, if the letters had been intercepted by Tudor's spies, indicate when or where the invasion would take place.

It had been Schwartz, who was not only an accomplished soldier but was also an extremely astute politician, who'd recommended that it would be in all of their interests to crown Prince Edward in Dublin, rather than to wait until they could do so in Westminster. The German had argued that they would gain much more support once they arrived in England, if they did so with a King at the head of their army rather than a 'mere Prince.' The rest of the Yorkist leadership had all seen the sense in this argument so, on ascension day, the 24th May 1487, Edward Plantagenet Earl of Warwick was crowned King Edward VI at Christchurch Cathedral in Dublin. The Irish, who were famous for celebrating any event, did not let them down and they ensured that the coronation, despite it having been hastily convened, was quite a spectacle, especially as it was the first time that the Irish had had the honour of crowning a King of England. The young Prince was borne on a fine litter, from Maynooth Castle, which was located to the west of Dublin, to the capital of Ireland and his crown. The Irish had all whooped and hollered as the newly crowned King had been carried out of the Cathedral upon the shoulders of Lord Darcy. From Christchurch Cathedral they'd gone to Dublin Castle to enjoy a sumptuous banquet that was held in honour of the new King. The Irish, famous for both their hospitality and their ingenuity, had guaranteed that the coronation was a success and that for a few hours at least, they were all able to forget their worries and concerns about what lay in front of them. Francis, who had the utmost admiration for his new found Irish friends, remembered with fondness how they'd stepped in at the eleventh hour to save the day. When they'd all arrived at the Cathedral they'd soon realised that they had no crown for the young Prince! Thomas Fitzgerald had come to their rescue by depriving the statue of the Virgin Mary of her coronet, this serving admirably as a substitute crown for the young King. Smiling, Thomas had handed the coronet to the Archbishop of Dublin who'd conducted the service, adding as he did so that in the not too distant future he hoped that he would be on hand to replace it with the 'real crown of England in the not too distant future.'

As expected there had been no shortage of Irishmen who were happy to join their expedition. All were keen to vent their warlike dispositions upon the English gentry and, for the foreseeable future at least, to be fed and watered at 'these foreigners' expense. Unfortunately many of the Irish although eager, had little in the way of modern arms and armour. Prior to embarkation the Yorkists leaders had inspected their armies Irish division, which had paraded in the grounds of Maynooth Castle. Sadly, barely clothed and carrying spears and other makeshift weapons, the Irish had been a pitiful sight indeed. Francis feared that these men, in spite of their enthusiasm, would be of little use to them against King Henry's seasoned troops. Francis had sighed for he'd known only too well that at that point in time it was far too late to change their course. They were all now embarked on a journey that could not and would not be interrupted for anyone or anything.

Thankfully, prior to their departure Francis had received a number of replies to his letters, especially from those Ricardian stalwarts in Yorkshire, all of whom had promised their army both shelter and support. Francis could only hope and pray that in the fullness of time, these assurances would prove to be genuine.

It was some hours before the main bulk of the Yorkist army was brought safely ashore. As the sun was slowly sinking on the western horizon, to be consumed by the vast expanse of water that was the Irish sea, the rebels finally turned their backs on the beach and marched the few miles inland that would bring them to Swarthmoor. Swarthmoor was a large plateau of heathland which afforded fine views of both the bay and the surrounding countryside. Earlier it had been identified by the Broughtons as a suitable camp site for their first night on English soil, as it was, they said, a location that could easily be defended.

Throughout the short march to Swarthmoor, Francis was at least heartened to see a significant number of familiar faces who had joined their army once they'd come ashore. According to these new recruits, Tudor was still languishing in the midlands at Kenilworth. More concerned, it was said, that he'd been criticised by many amongst the aristocracy for failing to fund that years 'garter' celebrations in Westminster, than by their invasion!. Thus, Francis estimated they would now have a number of days and even weeks to recruit more men, for he truly believed that there was no-one in England who would be willing to take to the field against them without the King himself being present. That night, for the first time in many weeks, Francis slept soundly. He woke to the sound of bird song and to the beauty of a fine

English summer's morning. The excellent weather continued and the rebels made good time as they struck deeper into the English interior, on lanes and byways that had seen little or no rain over the preceding weeks. Many towns and villages welcomed the Yorkists both with 'open arms' and with much needed reinforcements and provisions. As a result of this generosity, even though their army grew substantially, the rebels weren't forced to scavenge for sustenance, this in turn lessened the negative impact that their army had upon the surrounding countryside.

A route via Sedbergh and over the Pennines soon brought the Yorkist army via Hawes down into Francis's beloved Wensleydale. A short march along this beautiful valley brought them firstly to Castle Bolton and to the indomitable Scropes and then on to Middleham, what had been the capital of Richard's northern lands. Thankfully, the Yorkist army was able to enter Middleham and its great Castle unopposed, for Henry's small garrison, hearing of Schwartz's fearsome reputation, had chosen flight rather than fight. Yorkist intelligence suggested that Tudor remained in the midlands recruiting more troops, whilst he'd sent a small force of cavalry northwards. These men, who ironically were under the command of Lord Strange, one who'd have been dead had Catesby carried out Richard's orders at Bosworth, were apparently under strict orders not to engage the Yorkist army but to harry them in an attempt to prevent the rebels from securing any more reinforcements. According to Francis's spies, it was only after they'd landed that Tudor had finally begun to appreciate the seriousness of their challenge. Belatedly, and with increasing desperation, he'd issued a number of commissions of array, demanding that his subjects and their retainers join him either at Kenilworth or at Nottingham. The Earl of Northumberland, who'd been pardoned after Bosworth and had subsequently been restored to his earldom, had been ordered to bring his own retainers south in an effort to trap the Yorkists between his army and that of the King's. Whilst at Middleham, many amongst the rebel leadership had become alarmed to hear that Northumberland, obeying the Kings summons, was marching towards them at the head of a significant number of troops. At a hastily convened conference of war, Francis, who'd witnessed first hand Northumberland's failings, attempted to allay his friends fears by giving them a short yet accurate insight into his ignominious military career to date. Both John and Francis knew Northumberland personally and both said that they would stake 'their lives' on the fact that he'd never dare to meet them in the field. They argued that Northumberland, as he'd done so on many such occasions, would prevaricate and postulate until the matter had finally been resolved, this without having had the benefit of his involvement! Schwartz, who'd no experience of either Northumberland or of English military etiquette, disagreed with them. The German wrongly assumed, as was the case in Europe, that those placed in positions of command were chosen to lead because they possessed more than a 'modicum of tactical awareness.' Overruled, Schwartz grimly added that he hoped that both John and Francis were correct in their assumptions that Northumberland would never move against them. 'Because' he said, 'if we choose to march southwards without first dealing with the army at our rear and the Earl of Northumberland choses to strike against us,' we would be 'dangerously exposed' and would, he retorted, be forced 'to stake our lives on it after all!' As with the German, neither Harleston nor Fitzgerald knew Northumberland personally and both were obviously concerned as they recounted all of his families famous victories. Francis vehemently reassured his friends that they had nothing to fear from Northumberland as he 'knew with certainty' that the present Earl possessed none of those qualities which had made his forbears so infamous. Indeed, when Fitzgerald suggested that Northumberalnd may at some point in the future even be persuaded to join them and may prove himself to be a 'useful ally,' Francis could no longer contain himself. Much to the Irishman's angst he scoffed at Fitzgerald's point of view, laughing as he recalled his experiences of Northumberland at Berwick, saying 'Trust me, I've fought with Northumberland and he'd prove to be a much more dangerous ally than he ever could an enemy.'

Unfortunately, the City of York also clearly knew nothing of Northumberland's reputation. Hearing that Northumberland and his army were approaching from the north, the City burghers refused the rebels leave to enter the City and prepared instead for a siege, 'until the Earl of Northumberland should arrive and deliver us from these rebels.' The opposition of York was, however, not the setback that it had first seemed and Francis remained unconcerned. Presently they had plenty of supplies and as they'd been on the march for sometime and had made extremely good time, as such, any diversion via York, a big and welcoming city, was a distraction that he believed their men could easily do without. Indeed, their army soon had a far better distraction than that which York could provide them with. Lord Strange and his cavalry, obviously expecting the Yorkists to attempt to force an entry into York, had been surprised by the rebels, whose army had swept down upon them as they were, perhaps ironically, camped upon Bramham Moor. After a brief skirmish, Strange's cavalry were soon put to flight. In addition to losing many of his men and horses, Strange also lost his baggage to the Yorkists whose morale received a massive boost by this small yet significant victory. Even Francis, who'd become concerned in recent days when what had been a steady stream of recruits to their army had all but dried up, was cheered. He felt honoured to witness first hand the proficiency of Schwartz and his mercenaries. During the battle it was almost as if the Germans were on the parade ground. Well drilled, the continental troops went about their task with a steely professionalism. In less than a few hours they had crushed the English and put them to flight. Having had the opportunity of seeing Schwartz's men in action Francis was now convinced that each of the German and Flemish mercenaries were worth three or even four of their counterparts in Tudor's army. Schwartz had truly impressed Francis who could only marvel at the German's instinct and insight. A leadership style that was strong yet fluid, so different to the rigidity of those tactics employed by the English commanders. In the English theatre of war, battle plans were devised and decided upon well in advance of any engagement, consequently, during the battle itself, individual commanders had neither the ability, nor in most cases the inclination, to change or adapt them as the battle itself fluctuated. To date, Francis's only experience of any alterations to pre defined plans during an engagement itself had been Richard's decision at Bosworth to abandon his position atop Ambion Hill and later to embark upon his fateful charge. At Bramham Moor, Francis discovered that Schwartz was, as the Emperor Maximillian had first described him, 'a professional amongst amateurs.' Moreover, Schwartz had always ensured that his men were both well trained and equipped with all of the latest technologies. At Bramham Moor, for the first ever time, Francis was able to witness first hand the destruction wrought by the continental soldiers firearms. Portable side arms that were carried by the men and were used in close combat. But most important of all were Schwartz's abilities as a leader. Throughout the encounter, the German had remained calm. He was able to alter his plans as situations changed and evolved. Schwartz achieved this firstly by ensuring that he was personally involved in the battle itself, so that he himself could appreciate how the battle was progressing. And secondly, he made sure that any decisions he made were based upon the very latest information and that any orders given by him were obeyed immediately by his troops and without question. He did this by employing riders and runners to great effect. These men would bring him information from all parts of the battlefield, enabling Schwartz to appreciate and to understand the true nature of the engagement. These runners and riders were then dispatched with new orders, thus ensuring that all of the armies various contingents reacted almost as one. As a result of Schwartz's tactics and superior fire power, at Bramham Moor the English did not know what had hit then! Even when the English, at various locations, seemed to be gaining the upper hand, Schwartz and his captains were soon able to react, bringing up reserves to plug the gaps and to relieve the pressure upon their own men.

Buoyed by their victory and with their bellies filled on the contents of Strange's baggage train, the rebels turned their backs upon York and made instead for Nottingham. Francis felt that they had probably recruited as many men as they were going to and, at that point, he hoped to bring Tudor to battle on ground of their own choosing. This would, he guessed, be somewhere in the vicinity of Nottingham and the Trent Valley. As it turned out, Northumberland didn't disappoint Francis. Upon his eventual arrival in York, this not surprisingly coinciding with the rebels leaving Yorkshire, Northumberland tarried for sometime, only leaving the City when ordered to do so by Tudor, who'd angrily summoned him southwards. Even after he'd finally taken the road, within days Northumberland and his men were back in York. This because the City was, at that time, being threatened by the Scropes who'd been sent back with a small force by Schwartz to serve as a diversionary tactic for Northumberland's army, which had still concerned the German. Schwartz had laughed and patted Francis on the back when he'd been challenged in respect of this 'over cautious approach.' The German justifying his actions by maintaining that 'surely' 'no-one' could really be as 'cowardly' and as 'incompetent' as 'the Duke of Northumberland' was reputed to be.

The victory over Lord Strange's cavalry was well reported and as a result even more men came out to join the Yorkist army. Indeed, by the time the rebels had reached Doncaster, their army, which had numbered some 10,000, was easily within striking distance of Tudor whose own army was marching towards Nottingham. Francis became increasingly excited as the day's passed and the two armies closed upon each other. He felt that he was at last within sight of his final goal. To bring about the destruction of the man who'd killed his friend and had then sullied Richard's reputation with his lies and his propaganda. Delighted, daily the Yorkist's heard reports of numerous desertions from within Tudor's camp. Now it was Tudor who was forced to resort to whippings and to the stocks in an effort to prevent rumour and dissension spreading throughout his army. Any men who were suspected of spying were hung without trial! That said, Tudor had succeeded in assembling an army which reputedly numbered in the region of some 30,000. But Francis steeled himself to remain calm and reminded himself that this number included the numerous camp 'followers' and 'hangers on', those who accompanied an army but were never directly involved in any of the actual fighting. 'And anyway' Francis said to himself, even if they were all fighting men, the skirmish at Bramham Moor had proven that their Germans were more than a match for their English counterparts.

From Doncaster, the rebel army proceeded southwards via the great north road. Fortunately, conditions remained fine and this enabled them to make excellent progress. By the time that Tudor and his army had reached Nottingham, the Yorkists found themselves in the vicinity of the north Nottinghamshire town of Tuxford. The rebels had been making for Newark, a town where the Great North road met the Fosse Way. Francis knew this area well as his family used to own the manor house at Stoke Bardolph, an estate that lay beside the River Trent, equidistant between both Newark and Nottingham. These lands having come into the possession of the Lovel family via Francis's mother upon his parents marriage.

Unfortunately, Francis had not visited the area for sometime and he was both surprised and disappointed to be informed that the bridge which spanned the River Trent at Kelham on the outskirts of Newark, was down and had been for sometime. Apparently, the old timber bridge had been swept away in flooding during the previous winter. The Bishop of Lincoln, who was responsible for the bridges upkeep, had tried to save himself the cost of rebuilding it by offering relief from purgatory to anyone who would complete the bridges repair. To date no-one had taken the Bishop up on his 'kind' offer and the river, therefore, remained impassable at that location. Unfortunately, the only other bridge over the Trent in that area was at Nottingham and this was now under Tudor's control. Thankfully, Ned, who'd visited the area in recent years to resolve a dispute between commoners on Francis's estate, knew a number of local people. As such he was able to secure the services of some fine scouts who knew where an army could ford the river safely.

According to the Yorkist fore riders, Tudor's army, expecting the Yorkists to make for Nottingham, was arrayed in battle order to the north of Nottingham, on a plateau known as 'Red Hill'. None amongst the Yorkist leadership wanted to advance upon the King and meet him on ground of his own choosing. Thus it was decided to select a site that was more suitable to their own needs in the vicinity of Newark. Ideally, the walled town of Newark with its castle would have been appropriate. However, the Yorkist scouts who'd forded the river at Newark had been met with hostility by its townsfolk. The residents of Newark clearly did not want the battle to be fought within their own streets. And anyway, even if the rebels had, in the time available to them, been able to force the towns fortifications, there had been a recent outbreak of the sweating sickness within Newark and, as such, many of their own men were reticent to enter the town. Ultimately, it was decided that Schwartz together with Francis, Ned, John and the local scouts would cross the Trent to survey any potenial battle sites. Sadly, the land that they presently held to the north of the river was both flat and featureless and would afford their army no advantages. On the other hand, the ground situated on the south bank rose sharply and as a result would, they reasoned, offer their army more opportunities for both defence and attack. Within the day their small party had settled upon the site at which the 'last battle of the Wars of Roses' would hopefully be fought. The high ground that was situated to the south west of Newark and was adjacent to the small hamlet of East Stoke, was known as 'Burham Furlong'. As Francis and his friends stood on the 'furlong', the highest point of the proposed battle field, they could clearly see below them the Fosse Way, as it bisected the Nottinghamshire countryside from the east to the west, the direction from which Tudor and his army would presumably come. Although slightly narrow, all present agreed that Burham Furlong would be large enough to enable them to deploy all of their available troops. This pleased Francis who was keen not to repeat the mistake that Richard had made at Bosworth when he'd been unable to deploy his entire army atop Ambien Hill. Moreover, any troops arrayed on the furlong would be visible to an approaching army for many miles, this would hopefully dissuade any who were less than committed to Tudor's cause, from taking part in the battle. What did concern Francis, however, was that at this location the Yorkist army, with the River Trent immediately to their rear, would have no direct line of retreat. Indeed, a loop in the river meant that any rout would certainly result in a bottleneck, as men attempted to escape from the battlefield. Francis could clearly hear his father chiding him, 'for not giving his troops a clear and obvious line of retreat.' Schwartz, as he was apt to do when he disagreed with another's point of view, merely laughed and shrugged off Francis's concerns, the German arguing that his men neither 'gave nor expected any quarter' and would, 'as was their custom,' either 'prevail or die' upon the battlefield. Francis, who in the preceding weeks had come to admire the mercenaries, did however protest, arguing that the Irish and English who made up the vast majority of their army may 'not display such a level of bravery and professionalism.' Once again Schwartz discounted Francis's concerns, maintaining that the lesser experienced amongst their ranks would follow the lead of their European counterparts and that he would personally 'ensure that the poorly armoured Irish' would be spread throughout their ranks and would, therefore, be protected by his own men. This, he said, would prevent both their panic and any possible rout. Francis however, remained deeply concerned and was only finally silenced when the German, who was clearly beginning to tire of listening to Francis's concerns, asked him pointedly, 'So my Lord Lovel, in the event that we are not victorious, 'you clearly want to live on?'

Francis felt insulted by Schwartz's assertion that he was only concerned for his own safety. Admittedly to date he had managed to survive a number of battles that had gone against them. But on this occasion he considered that this battle was going to be his 'last', be it a victory or a defeat. As such, Francis vociferously denied the German's insinuation that he hoped to survive any defeat. In reply, Francis said that he was concerned only for those amongst them who, in contrast to himself, 'may consider a life after the 'Plantagenets.' Unfortunately, ultimately Francis was unable to put forward an alternative site that offered those advantages afforded by East Stoke. It was, therefore, decided that in spite of the potential bottleneck to their rear, their army would cross the river that afternoon and would assemble on the furlong in 'battle order,' there to await the arrival of Tudor and his troops, who were said to be on their way from Nottingham.

As the sun, that was low in the sky, was setting at their backs, the Yorkists slipped into the shallow waters of the River Trent at Fiskerton and, using the ford that had been at that location since pre history, they slowly made there way across the river to its southern bank. The cool water was a great relief to both man and beast, for all had been on the road for sometime. As Francis entered the water he closed his eyes. Childhood memories of the River Windrush came flooding back. Of paddling and fishing, happier times when he'd neither cares nor worries. As he reached the opposite bank Francis turned to his friend Ned, who was at his side. He smiled and said, 'well here goes.' Francis reached up and, in an attempt to pull himself out of the river, he took hold of the vegetation at the river's side. Unfortunately for Francis, and much to the hilarity of his comrades, the plants gave way and Francis tumbled backwards and was briefly consumed by the shallow, yet murky, water of the Trent. Spluttering and with difficulty, Francis managed to regain both his footing and his composure, the laughter of his comrades still ringing in his ears. For they'd all seen one of their leaders 'defeated by some nettles.'

That evening in the little church of East Stoke, which could be found directly below the escarpment upon which their men were bivouacked, the rebel leaders held their final council of war. According to their spies, Tudor and his army had left Nottingham. Apparently, having realised that the Yorkists were not going to advance upon him there, Tudor had himself secured scouts with which he'd negotiated the coarse scrub and marshland to the east of Nottingham that separated the city from the Fosse Way, the road that would bring him to East Stoke. The Yorkist spies laughed as they recounted to the council how they'd managed to spread both fear and panic throughout Tudor's camp. How each and every time that Tudor had left the main body of his army, they would spread the rumour that he'd taken flight. To the hilarity of all present they described how, upon his return, Tudor had further alienated his own troops by hanging those whom he suspected of being spies from the branches of an ash tree that stood by the side of Nottingham bridge. Unfortunately, in spite of a significant number of desertions, Tudor's army still numbered in the region of 30,000. This outnumbered the Yorkists by some three to one and, although no one mentioned it, Francis knew that all present would know that no army had ever been victorious on English soil in the face of such overwhelming odds. Schwartz, however, pointed out that his men had defeated many armies that were superior in numbers to them. The German commander also reminded them that 'England's greatest moment' had come in 1415 at Agincourt, when a poorly equipped and starving English army, that had been outnumbered by some ten to one, had annihilated a vastly superior French army under the command of the French Dauphin. Schwartz asked those present to consider how the English had prevailed on this occasion. Francis, who knew much history, said that the victory was due in part to the English archers who, using their longbows, had decimated the French cavalry as it had charged at them. The German agreed, arguing that at that time the English longbow was far more superior in power, accuracy and speed of fire to its French counterpart, the crossbow. At this point, Schwartz, who always seemed to enjoy dramatising such things, drew out one of his side arms and brought it crashing down upon the table. He asked his comrades if any were willing to 'go up against this' with a 'bow and arrow.' Needless to say, no-one took the German up on his challenge! Francis, who'd witnessed first hand what destruction could be wrought by the longbow, did, however, worry and he wondered how effective these firearms would prove to be against Tudor's army, which didn't possess any of this 'new technology'. John, who agreed with Schwartz, pointed out that at Agincourt the English had picked their ground well.

King Henry and his battle captains choosing to deploy in a field which was extremely narrow at their end, yet was far wider where the French army had been drawn up. This had ensured that the English could deploy all of their few troops in the battle line, yet the French could not. Moreover, as the charging French closed in on the English lines they were increasingly pressed in on either side by thick woods that were on their flanks. Consequently, as the French had borne down upon the English battle line, their men had neither room to fight nor to escape as, trapped, they became easy prey for the English archers who picked them off with ease. Schwartz smiled as he pointed out to them that one could even argue that superior numbers could sometimes be the 'downfall' of an army.

As all of the rebel leaders in turn contributed to the debate, their confidence grew. Schwartz on the other hand remained silent, merely nodding as his smile broadened. When the English present had finished their deliberations and all prickled with national pride the German spoke, once again he drew on the parallels between their present situation and that of the English at Agincourt.

'Friends, tomorrow we have much in our favour. We have firearms which the English do not possess. We are outnumbered but we have possession of the high ground. The Furlong is large enough to allow us to deploy all of our men from the outset. The steep sides of the Furlong will protect our army's flanks. Yes, Tudor's army outnumbers ours but if we remain upon the furlong Tudor won't be able to use all of his troops against us at any one time?'

The German went on, as those present considered what he was saying.

'We must hold the high ground for as long as possible. We must try to draw our enemies up the hill.' Schwartz shook his head as he added, 'Please remember this, if we give up the hill before victory is assured, Tudor will be able to deploy all of his reserves and will reap the benefit of his superior numbers.'

Francis was the only one amongst the rebel leadership to raise any concerns. For protection, Schwartz hoped to arrange their men up in a wedge shaped phalanx. Once Tudor's army was committed to the battle he hoped to drive this phalanx deep into it, thereby causing a Lancastrian rout. Francis queried what target such a formation would offer to the Lancastrian bowmen. Schwartz, who never liked to have his opinions questioned, haughtily dismissed Francis's concerns, arguing that his men's firearms and their own archers would easily deal with the archers in the enemies vanguard. 'And anyway' he added, Tudor's men will be firing up a steep incline and, as such, most of their arrows 'are bound to fall short.' Francis sighed, he knew that the German would never change his plans at that stage, but he also knew that he was one of only a few people present who'd actually seen the longbow in action. Picturing in his minds eye the target that their phalanx formation would present to Henry's bowmen, Francis closed his eyes and shuddered. He could only hope that events would prove him, and not the German, wrong.

As expected, Schwartz advised that the poorly armoured Irish be spread throughout the army. These men, supported by their better armed and more experienced European and English counterparts, would he said be less likely to 'panic' and 'run'. Unfortunately, the German, who due to his nature and his poor command of the English language was apt to be quite abrupt, appeared less than complimentary when he described both the Irishmen's equipment and their nature. Unfortunately, Thomas Fitzgerald was offended by what he considered to be Schwartz's slight towards his fellow countrymen. When the German refused to apologise for his alleged insinuations, Fitzgerald even went so far as to threaten to withdraw all of his men from the battlefield. All present knew that without the Irish, in spite of the fact that they were poorly armoured, they would stand little or no chance. With difficulty, both Francis and John, capably assisted by Harleston, talked both Thomas and Schwartz around. Finally, and begrudgingly, each man took the other's hand. Unfortunately, concessions had had to be made and to ensure Irish participation in the battle the Yorkist leadership were forced to give Fitzgerald the 'honour' of commanding his men who were to be positioned within their armies left flank. Once Thomas had haughtily left the meeting, all remaining, voiced their concerns that, as a result of this compromise, the left flank of their army would be seriously weakened. Schwartz, no doubt concerned that it was he who'd created the crisis in the first place, tried to placate them by arguing that the situation was nowhere near as grim as they imagined. The German said that he could easily deal with any issues that arose as a result of the Irish's weaknesses, by holding a number of his best troops in reserve, ostensibly to protect King Edward but in reality to be available to plug the gaps in the line that would appear should the Irish begin to falter. Unfortunately, no-one appeared convinced that this would solve the problem. Until, that is, Schwartz pointed out that the Lancastrian army, marching from Nottingham, must approach the battlefield from a southwesterly direction, that is from the rebels right flank. As such, Schwartz argued, if they were able to harry Tudor's men as soon as they came close, they could ensure that the attack, when it finally came, would be centred upon the Yorkist centre and right flank. Here, both Schwartz and their finest troops would be positioned.

Thus, when in the early hours the meeting finally broke up, the majority of the Yorkist commanders went to their beds reassured that their battle plans would ensure the greatest chance of success.

Neither Francis nor Ned were able to retire to their beds, not that Francis would have slept anyway! For both men had an appointment to keep in the Lancastrian camp. Without either bodyguard or armour, and with the knowledge of just a small circle of Yorkist commanders, both Francis and Ned silently mounted their horses and rode the few miles that separated their army from that of the Lancastrian vanguard which, under the command of the Earl of Oxford, was also camped on the southern bank of the River Trent, close to the small Nottinghamshire village of Radcliffe. Oxford's pickets were obviously expecting both Francis and Ned who, having been searched, were admitted without delay to the Earl's tent. It had been some years since Francis had met Oxford and he'd wondered if the Earl would remember him. Surprisingly, Oxford smiled as he took Francis's hand and reminded him of their previous meeting in 'happier times.' The irony, and cynicism, of the statement was not lost on Francis who immediately offered his apologies for the manner in which John's father and brother had been dealt with. Oxford interrupted him saying that at the time both he and Francis had been children and as such neither had played any part in his familles downfall. Shaking his head, Oxford added that his father and elder brothers fate had been sealed, not by Francis's father, but by his elder brother Aubrey's, 'loose tongue and naivety.'

Relieved, Francis introduced Ned and then turned to his cousin Saxon whom he hugged and clapped on the back.

Oxford interrupted Francis as laughing he said, 'Well now Lovel, how can one of the King's most loyal subjects possibly be of any assistance to one of his most treasonable.'

Francis, who didn't know quite how to take this comment, took his time to answer, hoping that Oxford's flippancy was due to his sense of humour and not to his politics.

After a moment of uncomfortable silence Francis spoke again, 'Sire, my cousin Thomas has hinted that you may be willing to assist us in our venture, that is, to restore the crown to one of the old aristocracy.'

Francis waited for a response, but Oxford, staring at him, remained both motionless and silent. Finally Francis continued, desperate to fill yet another awkward silence that he felt was becoming quite oppressive.

'Er, My Lord, I respect your Lancastrian credentials and none have done more for your cause than you. But surely you cannot in all honesty associate yourself with Tudor's regime. The Lancastrian line died out with King Henry and his son. Tudor is born of a female of the illegitimate Beaufort line all of whom, through Act of Parliament, are specifically disbarred from the line of succession.'

Francis smiled as he added, 'Be assured I can personally vouch for the Prince,' Francis immediately corrected himself, 'Er King Edward's credentials.' He added, 'The boy is the one true son of the late Duke of Clarence.'

Worryingly, Oxford seemed unimpressed as he finally answered, 'Lovel, you make your point well but I do not have to tell you that I've no interest in the niceties of the line of succession. I, more than anyone, know just how destructive a bad King can be. Regardless of what my personal opinion is of the present King, what England needs now above everything else is a strong and stable government, I still believe that Tudor can give us this and as the chief est amongst his supporters, in his Kingdom my own family cannot fail to flourish. I ask you Lovel what can your boy, even if he is who he says he is, give to me in addition to that which I have already?'

His mind clear, Francis at once saw his chance, smiling he replied, 'From what I hear therein lies the problem.'

Silent and seemingly perplexed Oxford raised an eyebrow as Francis continued, 'What has this King done for you. Has he not raised taxes, has he not attempted to curtail the power and authority of the old aristocracy, indeed is he not said to be in the process of restoring the late Duke of Norfolk's son to his estates in East Anglia, surely the South East is not going to be big enough for the two of you.'

Francis had obviously touched a nerve, as he spoke Oxford clearly winced.

Francis pushed home the advantage.

'King Edward and his councilors give you their word. They have sworn that in the event that you join us, you will retain all of your power in East Anglia and can rule there unopposed. Indeed, in the event that Norfolk's son joins us, there are plans to establish him not in the east but in the Welsh marches.' Francis smiled again as he added, 'Once of course Henry's uncle Jasper has been dealt with.'

Francis continued, 'Under King Edward you will be a Prince in the East and your lands will stretch from the capital as far as the East coast.'

Oxford was clearly irked by what Francis had said and it was obvious that Francis had found his Achilles heel. That is that Oxford felt that he had gone unrewarded for his service to Tudor and in attempting to reduce the power of the old aristocracy, the King was directly challenging Oxford's power and authority over his own lands in East Anglia.

Yet another awkward silence followed as Oxford took some time to consider what had been said.

Sadly his answer, when it finally came, was non committal and Francis worried that in visiting Oxford he'd wasted his time. Why had Saxon been so positive when he'd hinted that Oxford was willing to join them? Had his cousin been merely trying to please Francis? Or had he been telling the truth all the time and was Oxford hedging his bets, just as Stanley had done so at Bosworth. Not willing to commit to them until he'd had the opportunity of seeing how the battle was going!

As he listened to Oxford's reply Francis sighed for it was clear to him that he'd have to wait until the following day to discover the answer to his questions. 'Lovel. I've always admired your loyalty to the Yorkists. But presently I can do no more that to wish you good luck, for I fear that we shall meet as enemies upon the battlefield. Please don't expect anything from me.'

As Francis turned on his heels and made as if to leave the tent Oxford shouted after him, 'Lovel don't despair. For I'm presently in two minds, let us see how the battle turns out. Sadly, Tudor's given me the command of his vanguard and I have been forced to accept this commission. As such, should I chose to join you it will be extremely difficult for me to disengage my men once the battle has begun. That said, if things go your way, which well they might when you consider both your position atop the furlong and your mercenaries, it may well be the case that at some point, I will declare not for King Henry but for King Edward.'

Oxford paused, he was clearly enjoying the moment for, rubbing his chin, he added with a smile, 'We shall see.'

Perplexed, both Francis and Ned were escorted from Oxford's tent by Saxon. Shaking his cousin by the hand Francis could only wish him the best of fortune, adding that he hoped that they would not be unfortunate enough to meet each other on the field of battle. Leaving Oxford's camp Ned and Francis reached their own camp just before dawn was breaking. There they found their men readying themselves for the battle that would now come that day.

Chapter 33
June 16th 1487. Stoke Field.

To the sound of pipe and drum the Yorkist army finally began its advance towards Tudor's troops who were drawn up in battle order at the base of Burham Furlong, the hill on which the rebels had gathered. Sadly, Tudor's army seemed, to Francis, both limitless and invincible.

As the various denominations within the Yorkist's ranks gathered speed the orderliness of the advance slowly gave way to a headlong dash towards the mass of armed men that was the Earl of Oxford's vanguard. The sounds of the 'cosmopolitan' Yorkist army's continental pipes and drums were soon replaced by the battle cries of the various components of the Yorkist host and the screams of those on both sides of the engagement who were unfortunate enough to have been cut down whilst the battle was still in its infancy.

Francis, who'd experienced many misgivings since the beginning of their present campaign, seemed in an instant to lose all of his nerves as the recklessness of his comrades impacted on his own consciousness.

The Yorkists struck Oxford's battle line with such ferocity that the opposition at once reeled backwards. Francis himself, deafened by the din and pressed in from each side, was not even able to exchange any blows with his first victim, a longbow man who bore the blue boar device of Oxford. The unfortunate man lost his footing on the uneven ground and on the incline that favoured the Yorkist attack and, as a consequence, fell to his death, trodden beneath the weight of Francis and the advancing Yorkist infantry.

Unfortunately, it was now eminently clear to Francis that Oxford had chosen not to join their rebellion nor had he given any indication that he may do so at some point during the battle itself. As a result, both Francis and his fellow commanders had reluctantly conceded that without Oxford's assistance, and as a result of the difficulties that their men had experienced in protecting themselves against the English archers, they would have to take their destiny into their own hands. Consequently, in an effort to force the issue, they had finally decided to sacrifice the advantage of the high ground and engage the enemy. Success was now solely dependant on the outcome of this daring yet dangerous assault.

Despite putting some 10,000 men into the field, the Yorkist army was outnumbered by Tudor's army by some three to one. Moreover, the entirety of the left flank of the Yorkist army was comprised of ill equipped and inexperienced Gaelic Irish tribesman. The better equipped and more experienced English men-at-arms and German and Flemish mercenaries, being positioned in the centre and on the right flank.

Francis had hoped that intrigue would obviate the need for arms. He had trusted that both his personal visit to Oxford's camp on the eve of battle and the persuasiveness of his cousin Thomas Lovel, would secure Oxford's support for their cause. This now seemed little more than a fruitless fancy and Oxford had seemingly given his reply when his archers had inflicted the Yorkist army to a withering fire that had wrought devastation within its ranks, especially amongst the poorly armoured Irish. Despite the fact that the Yorkist army had many of its own archers and its continental mercenaries possessed the very latest firearms, the Yorkists had comprehensively lost these early exchanges. Thus, despite the fact that they'd chosen the battle site well and had initially planned to remain atop the hill on which they'd been drawn up, the Yorkist commanders, concerned that their men would buckle under this onslaught, had had no alternative but to disregard Schwartz's advice and order the attack forthwith. Unfortunately, although no-one said so, all knew that this manoeuvre would not only relinquish the advantage of the high ground, but would also bring their men down into the Trent flood plain and the meadows that surrounded the old Roman Road, the Fosse Way. This was flat and open land, where Tudor would be able to deploy the entirety of his larger army to the greatest effect. Francis knew that unless they were able to secure a speedy victory their men would soon become prey to Tudor's men, who would now be in a position to capitalise on their numerical superiority.

Prior to the commencement of the battle, as planned, the Yorkists had amassed together on the summit of Burham Furlong. The Furlong had seemed to be ideal for their purposes. It's plateau was just large enough to enable them to deploy all of their available troops in a single wedge shaped phalanx, moreover its steep sides offered their army protection in the event that the Tudor attempted to outflank them either to the east or to the west. This phalanx formation, very much continental in design, was deigned to have been the only disposition that would offer both shelter and support to each contingent of their army in the forthcoming battle. Unfortunately, Schwartz, the main exponent of the plan, had had limited experience of the English longbow in the field. On the previous evening, during their final council of war, the German had haughtily dismissed the longbow as both 'outmoded' and 'inferior', when compared to his own men's firearms and crossbows. Francis had, however, remained unconvinced by Schwartz, who bragged that on the following day the English archers would be no match for his own men. In contrast to Schwartz,

Francis, who'd witnessed first hand just how destructive the longbow could be, had argued against the phalanx idea. He believed that such a formation would present the English archers with a perfect target. Sadly, as Francis had gloomily predicted, Schwartz's weapons, despite their technological superiority, had been no match for the longbow. Neither their crossbows nor the side arms had either the range or the rate of fire that was achieved by the English archers. Indeed, as if to add insult to injury, during the early exchanges the firearms had probably caused more injuries amongst their own troops than with their enemies as, with the gunpowder still wet from when they'd forded the River on the previous afternoon, they misfired and exploded into the faces of those who'd attempted to discharge them. As the Yorkist cross bowmen and the German gunners had fumbled with their own weapons, Oxford's archers had stepped forward and fired a number of volleys. Their arrows, sent high into the sky, had arked above the Yorkist phalanx and turning back towards the earth had rained down upon their men. Indeed, it'd seemed to Francis as if each and every arrow had found an easy target amongst the mass of men who had stood in open ground upon the apex of the hill.

Neither Francis nor his friend John, had previously had much experience in the marshalling of an entire army, especially one of these proportions. As they'd witnessed first hand the devastation that was wrought within their ranks during these early exchanges, they'd been dumfounded and had been stunned into inactivity. Dismayed, all Francis had been able to do was to watch in silence, as all of his earlier anxieties had materialised and their men had been exposed to a maelstrom, which had all but decimated their army. Even now, in the din of battle, Francis was easily able to picture in his minds eye how they'd all stood transfixed, observing the progress of the steel tipped projectiles, as they'd whistled through the still and quiet air. This exchange, the precursor to the commencement of hostilities, had also heralded a strange silence. This silence had separated the noise generated by those insults and abuse which were exchanged between the opposing sides before the battle began and the bedlam that had followed it, that is once the arrows had finally found there mark. Still ringing in Francis's ears were the sickening screams of the stricken men who, clutching at the bloodied shafts of willow that protruded from their bodies, had collapsed onto the turf to endure the inevitability of a slow and lingering death. The crossbow men within the Yorkist army had returned fire and a number of their bolts had reached those in the very front ranks of Oxford's battle line. Unfortunately, their volley had had only a limited effect and Oxford's slow yet deliberate advance towards the base of Burham Furlong, had merely been checked momentarily. It was perhaps macabre, but Francis never failed to be amazed to see how even that expensive and intricately worked plate armour, which was worn by the better equipped amongst the troops, was no defence against the tempered steel of the bowmen's bolts and the archer's arrows. Despite the armour, the missiles slid effortlessly through both breastplates and helmet to find their mark. Disappointingly, the enemies advance had soon recommenced as those smitten were replaced by men from the rear of Oxford's vanguard who, keen to be involved in the battle at the earliest juncture, had earlier obviously failed to secure a place within the forefront of their army. As Oxford's men had neared the base of the furlong, his archers had continued their ferocious and tortuous rate of fire. Eventually, both Francis and his colleagues, knowing that their men could stand no more and conceding that their archers were no match for their counterparts in Tudor's army, had reluctantly ordered the advance.

The Yorkist army, angered and wounded by Oxford's archers, had taken no time at all to cover the short distance that had remained between the two battle lines. As the Yorkists reached Oxford's men, the speed and ferocity of their advance stunned the enemy, whose battle lines immediately buckled and gave way. Within seconds Francis had sufficient room to wield his mace.

Seizing the initiative both Francis and his men continued their advance, crushing and smashing at their enemies, as the 'madness' that was battle took control of their psyche. Despite their previous military experience, Oxford's retainers appeared to be no match for the rebels, whose momentum carried them far into their enemies lines. The Scots-Irish gallow-glasses, with their fearful war cries, whooped with delight, as they wielded their double headed axes with remarkable dexterity. The continental mercenaries, well armed and well drilled, went about their task with a steely professionalism, using bill and pike and even, to the horror of the English, their firearms, weapons rarely seen in this theatre of war. Happily, as the two armies had closed upon each other, and had then combined and fought at close quarter, these weapons had come into their own. Even Francis, who'd had previous experience of the guns, was both amazed and horrified as he saw how a loud explosion and cloud of smoke, was immediately followed by one of their enemies head's disappearing in a red mist, or a hole, so large that one could place a man's hand in it, appearing in either a breast plate or a limb! One unfortunate Lancastrian, who'd foolishly chosen to stand firm against an armed mercenary, had had his leg blown clean off!

Both Francis and his companions delighted not only in the success of these new fangled inventions, but also in the fear and panic that these weapons generated amongst the enemy. This, in all honesty far outweighing their practical usefulness as, once fired, frustratingly the gunners seemed to take an age to reload their weapons.

Even the poorly equipped Irish tribesmen met with success as they were at long last able to exact their revenge upon Oxford's archers. Now, within the ranks of Tudor's army and no longer exposed to their arrows, they skipped here and there amongst the armoured English, jabbing and stabbing with their daggers and darts. Able now, in close contact and within the confines of the battle itself, to use their own shorter bows which, in contrast to the longbows of their English counterparts, were still of use to them. Francis, despite being in the press of his enemies, could clearly see that the Yorkist left and right flanks had, like the centre which was commanded by John and himself, made significant inroads into Oxford's van guard. The banners of the Yorkist leaders fluttered proudly above the carnage that had once been the ordered lines of the front ranks of Tudor's army. Francis prickled with pride as he saw his own device, that of the chained wolfhound, raised aloft by his friend Ned who, like his father before him, had accompanied his master into battle. Maybe, just maybe, this would be the battle that would finally bring an end to this conflict. 'Goodness knows,' Francis felt that he, like so many of his friends and even his enemies, those who'd fought on both sides during this long civil war, was now so weary of this struggle that all would be glad to see it come to an end. It had, in truth, brought nothing but misery and loss to their countries populace. Now it seemed as if it'd come down to this one last battle, the battle of Stoke Field, their final opportunity to wrest control of the Crown from the usurper, to replace Tudor with the young King Edward.

Smiling, Francis wondered how Tudor now felt as, from his vantage point, he saw his battle lines melting away under the ferocity of the Yorkist's attack. From the 'furlong', Francis had earlier seen how Tudor had afforded himself both a safe and excellent view of the forthcoming battle by retiring to the tower of the nearby church at Hawton. Francis and his companions had scorned the 'welshman' for his cowardice. They had earlier observed the progress of his standard, the red dragon, as it'd hastily retreated to that location once, that is, Tudor had addressed his anxious troops prior to the commencement of the battle. Francis wondered what Tudor was now thinking as he, just like King Richard before him at Bosworth, was forced to witness, first hand, the destruction of his vanguard. Did Tudor now worry, just as Richard had done so before him, if he could now count upon the loyalty of both the main 'battle' and the 'rearguard' of his army. Those of limited experience who'd been forced to stand by, watching and waiting for orders, as the cream of their army, Oxford's vanguard, had been slaughtered in front of their very eyes! Francis shuddered as he recalled how King Richard had vainly, and with increasing desperation, repeatedly requested assurances from his commanders of their continuing support. Francis smiled, for here at 'Stoke Field' it appeared as if the boot was now securely on the other foot. At Bosworth it'd been the Yorkist's most loyal and experienced commander, John Howard, Duke of Norfolk, who'd failed to carry the day. Now it appeared as if Tudor's most capable commander, Oxford, whose men were wilting under the ferocity of their attackers onslaught, who may fail! Was he to face a fate similar to that of the hapless late Duke of Norfolk? Francis smiled again, for without Oxford, Tudor would be forced to rely upon the middle ranks of his army for victory and these consisted predominantly of inexperienced and uncommitted feudal levies and retainers. Men whose allegiance rested solely with their own lord's and not with the King. Stanley's Cheshire men and Percy's Northumbrian's who, to Francis's surprise, had earlier appeared upon the battlefield. Francis smiled laconically as he considered the irony of it all. It now seemed to him as if Tudor's fate rested solely with those whose treachery had earlier undone King Richard at Bosworth! Yes, in Hawton Tower, surrounded by his personal body guards, the Beefeaters, Tudor may for the time being be safe. But there, in contrast to Richard at Bosworth, he was in no position to exert any direct influence over the battle itself. Francis smiled again, Tudor would be forced to stand idly by and observe events as they unfolded before him, hoping, no doubt, that this time, in contrast to Richard's at Bosworth, his army would stand firm.

Francis paused briefly as he recalled, with surprising clarity, his own experiences of the Battle of Bosworth. The exhilaration of that final fateful cavalry charge, an assault ordered by Richard that had so nearly brought them victory. Ultimately, and unfortunately however, it had been the intervention of the Stanleys, that had ensured that this manoeuvre, an action that had initially had such a promising and such a startling effect, had come to nought and had petered out. The Stanley's Cheshire men slaughtering Richard and his Knights, Richard dying as a King should, *'fighting manfully within the press of his enemies'*. Indeed, had Francis's own horse not been killed, the stricken horse throwing Francis clear, then he to, like his friend, would now no doubt be mouldering in a roughly hewn grave within Greyfriars, Leicester.

Francis sighed as he considered again, for the umpteenth time, that which might have been, had the King's mount, 'White Surrey', been struck by an arrow. Maybe in those circumstances it would have been Richard here now and not Francis, God knows, Francis would readily have sacrificed his own life for that of his friend.

Indeed, had Richard survived that battle then he would, Francis felt, almost certainly have secured more support for their present cause than had their present figurehead, the child King Edward VI. Yes, Edward was a Plantagenet, a Prince of the Royal blood, the son of Richard's elder brother the late George Duke of Clarence, but could he, a mere lad, ever be successful as a King? Moreover, there were many in England who clearly still believed Tudor's propaganda that would have them believe that the boy was an impostor, a commoner, one who'd been passed off as Edward, by Francis and his co-conspirators!

Francis was at once brought to his senses, as he encountered a particularly obstinate opponent. Trading blows with his adversary, a knight whose insignia of the white bear was not immediately identifiable to him, Francis was first to yield, as his enemies poleaxe connected with Francis's right shoulder. The blow crushed both the plate armour and the bone and muscle that lay beneath it and Francis felt a searing pain spread throughout his frame as his now useless right hand dropped the mace, his favoured and his only weapon. Pessimism soon replaced optimism as Francis raised his left arm to deflect yet another blow that was aimed directly towards his exposed face and was clearly designed to bring about his immediate death. Strangely, all now appeared to Francis as if in slow motion and the din of the battle receded as, once again, Francis heard the voice of his long dead father, chiding him 'for going into a battle with his visor raised,' his father dismissing Francis's argument that an open faced helmet was both 'less claustrophobic and afforded its wearer a better all round view.' Thankfully, the angle of Francis's arm and the fact that he'd sunk to one knee and was now well below his assailant, ensured that Francis was able to use his forearm to deflect the blow downwards and in contrast to his assailants earlier attack, it caused minimal injury.

It was Ned who, like his father before him, saved his master's life. Dropping Francis's banner, Ned drew his sword and, standing firm and resolute above his friend, he was able to fend off Francis's attacker. After trading a number of token blows with his new opponent, the Knight, no doubt feeling that Ned was more than a match for him, trudged off to find easier pickings from amongst the Yorkist army that seemingly, having lost both its impetus and its cohesion, had alarmingly begun to disintegrate.

Fatigue now enveloped Francis who, with Ned's help, reluctantly retired to the rear. With increasing alarm Francis noticed that unlike many of the other battles in which he'd taken part, where there had always been a ready supply of eager comrades to take his place in the battle line, here at Stoke field none seemed either able or willing to replace him. Indeed, as both pain and exhaustion cleared from Francis's mind the last vestiges of the rage of battle, he noticed that on all sides, their army was being forced back up the hill from whence they'd come. Francis could no longer hear the jubilant battle cries of his comrades, for these had been replaced by the cries of both the dying and the demoralised.

As Francis made his way back towards the top of Burham furlong, he hoped that once back on high ground and in a position to survey the whole of the battlefield, he'd at least be able to ascertain what troops they still held in reserve. Their charge had so very nearly won the day. If they were able to reassemble and reinforce the phalanx and this time concentrate their attack on the main body of Tudor's army, they still might just carry the day.

Sadly, once on the top of the furlong it took Francis no time at all to see that all appeared lost. Only those English and Continental troops who'd been positioned towards the very centre of the phalanx still fought on. It'd clearly been a close run thing for the standards of both John and Schwartz had been carried to the very base of the furlong and were almost upon the Fosse Way itself! Francis wept as he realised just how close they'd come to victory. Now he felt only anguish. Those troops from within the middle ranks of Tudor's army, men whose nervousness had no doubt dissapated as soon as they'd seen the Yorkist attack falter and fail, were all now pouring into the fray shouting, 'A Stanley. A Stanley'. It was clear to Francis that John and Schwartz meant to die upon the field. In spite of the hopelessness of their position both men's retainers gathered around their standards and stubbornly, yet bravely, fought on. Looking northwards, Francis could see that all of his worst fears had materialised. The Irish, under Thomas Fitzgerald, had been routed by the cavalry of Lord Scales, who'd obviously charged from his position on the right wing of Tudor's army. Francis could now see what had happened. When they'd attacked Oxford's vanguard, the Yorkist army had lost all of its shape and cohesion. The phalanx formation, key to their success and designed to protect the men throughout the battle, had disintegrated as they'd all charged down the hill. As a result of this those on its outer edges, especially the Irish on the left, had been exposed to the enemy's cavalry, which Tudor had cleverly positioned upon the wings of his army. Subjected to repeated attacks from mounted men-at-arms, the flanks of the rebel army had been decimated. Those who'd survived the resultant carnage were now in headlong retreat, their exposed and unprotected backs easy targets for the spears and swords of their mounted adversaries, as they scurried back up the Hill. Francis could hardly bare to look as his friends the Irish, poorly armoured, were slaughtered by Scale's cavalry who were clearly in no mood for mercy. Countless numbers of men from Fitzgerald's Irish contingent were cut to pieces by the experienced horsemen who rode them down with ease.

Alarmed, Francis again remembered those misgivings that he'd had before the battle. That morning prior, to the commencement of the battle, Oxford had cleverly manoeuvred his own men into a position whereby they'd effectively cut off the Yorkists line of retreat and had also exposed the Irish on the Yorkist's left flank. At the time it had seemed strange to Francis that Tudor's army, having encountered the Yorkist's on Burham Furlong, had all but ignored it as they'd continued their march along the Fosse Way towards Newark. Schwartz, who'd gambled on the fact that the enemy would direct there attack towards the Yorkist centre and right, had said that in his opinion the enemy had completed this manoeuvre to spread fear amongst the Yorkists by showing them the entirety of their army. Francis, on the other hand, had hoped that in marching past them, in some way Oxford had been trying to avoid commanding the vanguard, thereby freeing himself to join the Yorkists at some point in the battle! Francis shuddered, for he could now see that Oxford had been far more subtle than this. By marching past their army Oxford had effectively cut off any potential line of retreat that the Yorkists may have had northwards in the direction of Newark and he had also ensured that the Irish would have to withstand the full force of Tudor's army. Defeat was bad enough to stomach, but now, as Francis had feared all along, the only option left open to those men who chose to flee the field was to retreat back over the river, which would have to be forded at one of its deepest points. Francis wept as he wondered. Had Oxford been playing with them all along? Had Oxford ever truly intended to join them? Now it seemed to Francis as if Oxford had not only remained loyal to Tudor, but had also been intent upon their complete and utter destruction! Francis could only wonder if the Earl had been supported in his deception by Francis's cousin Saxon! What had Oxford said when they'd met? He could neither say whether or not he'd join the Yorkists. Francis wished above everything else that some day he'd have the opportunity to repay his cousin and Oxford for their deception. As Francis stood on the furlong and witnessed first hand the disintegration of their army, he knew that this would never now come to pass.

As Francis had always feared, the westerly loop of the river that was at their backs had created a bottleneck into which the surviving Yorkist troops were now pouring. These men now faced an unenviable decision, to face Scale's cavalry or to risk their lives in the swirling waters of the River Trent. Francis, who'd always been an exponent of the theory that troops in battle who are afforded an obvious and easy line of retreat are less likely to panic and flee, was once again reluctantly proven right .

Those amongst their army who chose not to die upon the battlefield converged on Burham Furlong. Not waiting to rally, rest or regroup, these men immediately made off in the direction of the River Trent that, situated to their rear, was accessed via a steep ravine. Not for the first time in his life, Francis's instinct for survival took over. He knew that his only hope now was to make for the river. Francis felt that if he were able to reach it and manage to get across safely to the other bank, for the time being at least Scale's cavalry would be unlikely to follow. For presently, these men had targets aplenty on the battlefield side of the river amongst those men who were reticent to risk the river crossing.

The narrow ravine that led down to the river was the scene of much slaughter. Both Francis and Ned stumbled and fell as, casting off what remained of their armour, they negotiated its steep sides which were awash with the blood of their comrades. In all of his life Francis had seen nothing quite like this! Scale's cavalry, whom they'd worsted at Bramham Moor, now seemed hell bent on revenge and as if possessed by the Devil himself they were heedless to any cries for mercy. No quarter was given.

Francis felt no shame as he cast aside his helmet and discarded those items of clothing and armour that identified him as a man of rank. Their cause was now lost and, regardless of what he'd said before, he had to think of himself and he wasn't quite ready to die here in ignominy.

The wounded man, propped up against one of the beech trees at the base of the ravine, didn't complain as Francis, unable to control his speedy descent, collided with him, sending both he and the man reeling. With surprise, on rising to his feet, Francis gazed upon a familiar face. 'Richard'............,

'Are you injured,'

Francis immediately regretted his stupid words for it was obvious that his brother-in-law wasn't just injured but was dying!

Richard weakly raised an arm. The young mans lips moved as if he was trying to speak, but Francis heard no words as those familiar eyes glazed over and rolled back within his head. Richard's arm fell limply to his side as Francis's brother-in-law died.

Surprisingly, Francis, who in the past had hated Anne's brother for his cowardice, felt sorry for Richard whose young life had been cut short, as had so many others of his generation. As Francis turned to see Scale's men pouring into the ravine behind them, he briefly considered the irony of it all. History would now remember Richard Fitzhugh as a brave man who'd died on the field of battle in the service of the Plantagenets!

Neds words stirred Francis into action and his friend echoed Francis's thoughts as he said, 'Come Francis, we must make it to the river if we're to have any hope of escape.'

Francis dared not look back again as, injured, he stumbled across the marsh that led to the water's edge. Was he scared of seeing his pursuers who, at any point, could catch and despatch him? Or was he scared to see what had become of both their brave army and the Yorkist cause? It was with this thought that the realisation finally dawned upon Francis. His life, a life spent serving Richard and the Plantagenets, had, like that cause, come to nought!

Both Francis and Ned threw themselves into the river which had, by that time, become a heaving mass of men and horses. Arms grappled Francis as men who could not keep themselves above water tried desperately to cling on to those who could. Francis wasn't a good swimmer at the best of times and with the weight of his sodden clothing and without the assistance of his now useless right arm, like many others Francis soon succumbed to the murky waters of the River Trent. As Francis gave up struggling and slowly slipped below the surface of the river, he surprised himself with a half smile. At least here he would be away from the horrors of defeat.

Epilogue
September 1708. Minster Lovel Oxfordshire.

Not for the first time that week Robert Parker awoke with quite a start. He'd had yet another dream. Lathered in sweat he lay there stunned, he could still remember the dream vividly! As with all of those other dreams that Robert had experienced since discovering the remains in the vault, it had been startlingly lifelike, almost as if he, Robert, had been there himself!

Robert sighed, if only the manuscript that he'd discovered in the vault hadn't crumbled into dust just as he'd lifted it out of the strongbox, which had obviously protected it for a number of years. Robert sighed again, 'clumsy as always,' he wished now, above everything else, that he'd been more careful with the papers. Robert, who'd always been fascinated by history, could have cried! Had the skeleton been that of Francis Viscount Lovel? Had the manuscript been Francis's version of the history of his times? Of Richard III's reign and the Wars of the Roses? Sadly, they would never know the answers to these questions. If the remains had been those of Lovel, it appeared now as if the only thing that he'd left for future generations, had disintegrated in Robert's own hands!

As he got out of bed Robert scratched his head, he'd never really been much of a dreamer, yet since discovering the vault and its contents he'd experienced these graphic dreams, which one could also describe as nightmares, on a nightly basis.

Surprisingly for a gamekeeper, and a pretty good one at that, Robert did have an excellent knowledge of and a thirst for history. Of course, he'd Reverend James to thank for that! And since discovering the vault, Robert had been desperate to discover more about this elusive Viscount Lovel, a man who'd been both the master of Minster Lovel and a prominent supporter of King Richard III. Robert was intrigued to discover if, in fact, the dreams that he was having corresponded with the history of that time. To this end, thankfully, Robert had been allowed to accompany the Reverend James as he'd taken the remains to Oxford, to be examined by a number of eminent Physicians and Antiquarians, who'd been recommended to Sir Thomas by a friend of his in London. At Oxford, they'd taken the opportunity to visit the Bodleian Library, where they'd researched the life of both Francis Lovel and a number of his contemporaries. That said, nothing that Robert had already known, nor anything that he'd discovered at Oxford, in respect of Francis Lovel's life, could explain the vividness of the dreams and, as a consequence of them, a version of the history that was so different to that which had been recorded. At the Bodleian Library Robert had had the opportunity of reading both Polydore Vergil's 'Historica Anglica', a book which had been commissioned by King Henry VII, and Sir Francis Bacon's history of the Reign of Henry VII. Both books portrayed Richard III and his followers as monsters, men who'd stop at nothing in their quest for power. That said, no-one seemed to know what had become of Francis Lovel. Bacon's history described how, after the death of Richard III at Bosworth, Francis had fomented two rebellions and after he'd been defeated by King Henry's army at the battle of East Stoke in 1487, *'There went a report that he (Francis) fled, and swam over the Trent on horseback but could not recover the other side...and so was drowned'*. Intriguingly, Bacon's history also ascribed anther end to Francis! *'But another report leaves him not there, but that he lived long after in a cave or vault'*.

Robert discovered that other reports placed Francis at the Scottish court of King James IV, where in 1488, a year after the battle of East Stoke' he was allegedly granted *'free passage'* throughout Scotland, and at Flanders where he was said to have subsequently died! Bacon who'd written his history in 1622, over eighty years earlier, could never have known about the vault and its contents. Did Bacon's account verify the story that Francis had in fact escaped from the battlefield and that subsequently he'd had spent the remainder of his life in hiding in the vault? Unfortunately, frustratingly, and after much research, when it came to Francis Lovel neither Robert nor the Reverend James were any the wiser!

Try as he might, Robert could not come up with any logical explanation for his dreams other than that, maybe, somehow, whilst in the vault he must have connected in some spiritual way with the dead man or with his writings.

Running his hands through his hair Robert sighed. Perhaps he'd never know what was behind it all. That said, his anxiousness must have been nothing when compared to the anguish that Francis must have felt if he had in fact been forced into hiding. Having to lay low whilst Tudor set about establishing his own dynasty. Having had to remain silent as the King commissioned his own history of the times. As an attainted traitor with a price on his head, there was nothing that Francis could have done to refute Tudor bias and propaganda. This must, Robert thought, have spurred Francis on to write his own version of the history. No doubt in the hope that one day it would be read and the 'wrongs' of Tudor's history would be righted. Now, sadly, it seemed as if that would never come to pass. Robert sighed again, in his opinion, the bones of this mysterious man, if they were in fact Francis Lovel, would never be able to rest in peace wherever Sir Thomas chose to lay them once, of course, the 'learned gentlemen of Oxford had finished with them'.

Every time Robert thought about it, it would almost make him cry. Francis had devoted practically all of his life to the service of King Richard III. Even now, here in the eighteenth century such loyalty to another was frankly astonishing! Yet where had it ultimately got him? A dank cellar for a home and a lonely death. Faithful service, which had gone both unrecorded and unremembered. If Robert's dreams were to be believed, Francis had been constant in his service to the Plantagenet's, yet ultimately it had got him nowhere! That said, in his short life Francis Lovel had enjoyed far greater wealth, power and influence than he could ever have expected had he remained a mere baron. And he did have his place in history, albeit that that history was in all probability inaccurate and in it he was 'infamous' rather than 'famous'. Robert smiled, for his research at the Bodleian Library had shown that no-one, either victorious or defeated, had really flourished after the Battle of Stoke. Henry Percy, the Earl of Northumberland, had only survived for a further two years, having been murdered by a mob of 'Ricardian' Yorkshireman at Thirsk, this in revenge for the Earl's betrayal of Richard at Bosworth. George Stanley, Lord Strange did after all predecease his father Lord Stanley, having been poisoned at a banquet in London in 1503, none knew who by. Sir William Stanley was executed in 1495 for treason, ironically for having been implicated in the Perkin Warbeck rebellion, whereby William and his co-conspirators had attempted to pass off a commoner as Richard Duke of York, the younger of the two Princes' in the Tower! At least the Earl of Oxford had died of old age at Heddingham Castle but in spite of his service to the Crown, as with all of those others of his kind, the 'old aristocracy', throughout Henry's reign, he became increasingly marginalised and isolated. Henry Tudor, King Henry VII of England died at Richmond Palace of tuberculosis in April 1509, a 'miserly misery' he'd been predeceased by his beloved son Arthur who had died of the sweating sickness at the age of 16 in 1502.

Robert smiled, and what would have become of Francis had he possessed all of those disagreeable qualities that had made his peers so different to him? Had he abandoned Richard and supported Henry VI, or his benefactor Warwick the Kingmaker, then he'd no doubt have lost his life at Barnet or at Tewkesbury. And had he abandoned the Plantagenets and accepted Tudors promise of a pardon, time had shown that there was no future for any of the 'old aristocracy' at Tudor's court.

As Francis had gloomily predicted, Henry, and after him his son King Henry VIII, had both set about destroying all of the 'old nobility' of England. In doing so they secured the Tudor dynasty but they were also responsible for the destruction of feudalism in England and as a consequence of this the loss of royal authority. As Francis had prophesied the Tudors were to be the first monarchs of England to have ruled, not through 'divine intervention' granted by God, but by the consent of the people. Robert smiled for their ancestor Charles I had paid for this concept with his head! Robert smiled again, perhaps it was better after all that Francis and his comrades had lost at Stoke. For times had been changing and there was clearly no future for him or his kind in this 'modern world'. And yes, the recorded history of that time may be inaccurate. But at least the name of Francis Lovel, whatever crimes both he and Richard were accused of, is after all is said and done a byword for 'loyalty'. Perhaps that's what Francis had always wanted after all. It is certainly the least he could have expected!

The End.

Lightning Source UK Ltd.
Milton Keynes UK
UKOW041928240613

212752UK00004B/589/P

9 781909 740082